1,000,000 Books

are available to read at

---

www.ForgottenBooks.com

Read online
Download PDF
Purchase in print

ISBN 978-1-5281-8773-2
PIBN 10925558

1 MONTH OF
FREE
READING

at

www.ForgottenBooks.com

By purchasing this book you are eligible for one month membership to ForgottenBooks.com, giving you unlimited access to our entire collection of over 1,000,000 titles via our web site and mobile apps.

To claim your free month visit:

www.forgottenbooks.com/free925558

English
Français
Deutsche
Italiano
Español
Português

www.forgottenbooks.com

Mythology Photography **Fiction**
Fishing Christianity **Art** Cooking
Essays Buddhism Freemasonry
Medicine **Biology** Music **Ancient**
Egypt Evolution Carpentry Physics
Dance Geology **Mathematics** Fitness
Shakespeare **Folklore** Yoga Marketing
Confidence Immortality Biographies
Poetry **Psychology** Witchcraft
Electronics Chemistry History **Law**
Accounting **Philosophy** Anthropology
Alchemy Drama Quantum Mechanics
Atheism Sexual Health **Ancient History**
Entrepreneurship Languages Sport
Paleontology Needlework Islam
Metaphysics Investment Archaeology
Parenting Statistics Criminology
Motivational

REPORTS OF CASES

ARGUED AND DETERMINED

IN THE

SUPREME COURT OF TENNESSEE

EASTERN DIVISION,

SEPTEMBER TERM, 1913

MIDDLE DIVISION,

DECEMBER TERM, 1913

WESTERN DIVISION,

APRIL TERM, 1914.

FRANK M. THOMPSON,

ATTORNEY-GENERAL AND REPORTER.

VOL. II.

E. W. STEPHENS PUBLISHING CO.
COLUMBIA, MISSOURI
1914

JUDGES OF THE SUPREME COURT OF TENNESSEE.

COURT OF CIVIL APPEALS OF TENNESSEE.

CLERKS OF THE SUPREME COURT
OF TENNESSEE.

S. E. CLEAGE   .   .   .   .   KNOXVILLE
JOE J. ROACH   .   .   .   .   .   NASHVILLE
T. B. CARROLL   .   .   .   .   JACKSON

C H A N C E L L O R S
OF TENNESSEE.

HAL H. HAYNES	1st Division	Bristol
H. G. KYLE	2nd Division	Rogersville
T. M. McCONNELL	3rd Division	Chattanooga
*A. H. ROBERTS	4th Division	Livingston
W. S. BEARDEN	5th Division	Shelbyville
J. W. STOUT	6th Division	Cumberland City
JOHN ALLISON	7th Division	Nashville
J. W. ROSS	8th Division	Savannah
C. P. McKINNEY	9th Division	Ripley
F. H. HEISKELL	10th Division Part I	Memphis
FRANCIS FENTRESS	10th Division Part II	Memphis
WILL D. WRIGHT	11th Division	Knoxville
V. C. ALLEN	12th Division	Dayton

*Holds Circuit Court of Fentress County.

[129 Tenn.

CIRCUIT JUDGES
OF TENNESSEE

DANA HARMON	1st Circuit	Greeneville
G. Mc. HENDERSON	2nd Circuit	Rutledge
V. A. HUFFAKER	3rd Circuit	Knoxville
S. C. BROWN	4th Circuit	Harriman
C. E. SNODGRASS	5th Circuit	Crossville
NATHAN L. BACHMAN	6th Circuit	Chattanooga
EWIN L. DAVIS	7th Circuit	Tullahoma
JNO. E. RICHARDSON	8th Circuit	Murfreesboro
W. L. COOK	9th Circuit	Charlotte
THOMAS E. MATTHEWS	10th Circuit	Nashville
M. H. MEEKS	2nd Circuit Court	Nashville
W. BRUCE TURNER	11th Circuit	Columbia
*N. R. BARHAM	12th Circuit	Lexington
THOS. E. HARWOOD	13th Circuit	Trenton
JOS. E. JONES	14th Circuit	Dresden
J. P. YOUNG	15th Circuit 1st Div.	Memphis
WALTER MALONE	15th Circuit 2d Div.	Memphis
ALFRED B. PITTMAN	15th Circuit 3d Div.	Memphis
H. W. LAUGHLIN	15th Circuit 4th Div.	Memphis
S. J. EVERETT	16th Circuit	Jackson
**DOUGLAS WIKLE	Circuit of Williamson Co., Franklin	

CRIMINAL JUDGES
OF TENNESSEE

A. B. NEIL, for Davidson County . . . . . . Nashville
JESSE EDGINGTON, for Shelby County, Div. I. Memphis
JAMES W. PALMER, for Shelby County Div. II. Memphis
T. A. R. NELSON, for Knox County . . . . . Knoxville
J. M. GARDENHIRE, for 5th Circuit . . . . . . Carthage
S. D. McREYNOLDS, for 6th Circuit . . Chattanooga
C. W. TYLER, for Montgomery County . . Clarksville

*Holds Criminal Court of Madison County.
**Holds Chancery Court of Williamson County.

ATTORNEYS-GENERAL
OF TENNESSEE

D. A. VINES	1st Circuit	Johnson City
W. H. BUTTRAM	2d Circuit	Huntsville
R. A. MYNATT	3rd Circuit	Knoxville
T. W. PEACE	4th Circuit	Madisonville
W. R. OFFICER	5th Circuit	Livingston
M. N. WHITAKER	6th Circuit	Chattanooga
W. W. FAIRBANKS	7th Circuit	McMinnville
W. S. FAULKNER	8th Circuit	Lebanon
JOHN B. BOWMAN	9th Circuit	Waverly
A. B. ANDERSON	10th Circuit	Nashville
HORACE FRIERSON, JR.	11th Circuit	Columbia
B. J. HOWARD	12th Circuit	Jackson
T. C. RYE	13th Circuit	Paris
D. J. CALDWELL	14th Circuit	Union City
Z. N. ESTES, JR.	15th Circuit	Memphis
JNO. A. TIPTON	16th Circuit	Covington

JNO. L. NEELEY, for Williamson County, Franklin

ASSISTANTS TO ATTORNEY-GENERAL AND REPORTER
OF TENNESSEE.

WILLIAM H. SWIGGART, JR.	.	Union City, Tenn.
NEAL L. THOMPSON	. . .	Chattanooga, Tenn.

ASSISTANTS TO ATTORNEYS-GENERAL
OF TENNESSEE.

M. G. LYLE, for Montgomery County . . . Clarksville
J WASHINGTON MOORE, for Davidson County, Nashville
T. POPE SHEPHERD, for Hamilton County, Chattanooga
W. R. HARRISON, for Shelby County . . . Memphis
HARRY T. HOLMAN, for Shelby County . . . Memphis

JOHN B. HOLLOWAY	2d Circuit	Morristown
J. R. MITCHELL	5th Circuit	Crossville
LAWSON M. MYERS	7th Circuit	Pikeville

CASES REPORTED.

Arbuckle v. Arbuckle et al. 485
Assurance Co., Commercial Union, Gulf Compress Co. v...... 586
Atlas Hardwood Lumber Co. v. Georgia Life Insurance Co.... 477
Automobile Co., McDonald, v. Bicknell 493

B

Baker Watkins Supply Co. v. Fowlkes 663
Bank, Wilson County, Dies et al. v. 89
Barnhill et al., City Lumber Co. v. 676
Birmingham & N. W. Ry. Co. et al., Williams v. 680
Barrett, State ex rel., Strong v. 472
Bicknell, McDonald Automobile Co. v. 493
Black, Carey Roofing & Manufacturing Co. v. 30
Board of Trust of Vanderbilt University et al., State, ex rel.
    College of Bishops of M. E. Church, South, v. 279
Bond v. State 75
Bond v. Ungerecht et al. 631

C

Calhoun v. McCrory Piano & Realty Co. 651
Cannon et al., Thomas et al. v. 182
Carey Roofing & Manufacturing Co. v. Black 30
Carter et al. v. State, ex rel., Woollen 182
Carter et al., Webb et al. v. 182
Carter, Union Railway Company v. 459
Central Railroad Co., Tennessee, King v. 44
City Lumber Co. v. Barnhill et al. 676
College of Bishops of M. E. Church, South, et al., State ex rel.,
    v. Board of Trust of Vanderbilt University et al. 279
Commercial Union Assurance Co., Gulf Compress Co. v. 586
Compress Co. v. Insurance Co. 586
Concordia Fire Insurance Co., Harowitz v. .... 691·
Crofford et al., Matthews v. 541
Cumberland Telephone & Telegraph Co. v. Peacher Mill Co. 374

D

Denny et al., Mitchell et al. v. 366
Dies et al. v. Wilson County Bank 89
Drug Co., Hessig-Ellis v. Stone et al. 608
Dunlap Lumber Co. v. Nashville, C. & St. L. Ry. Co. 163

E

Express Co., Southern, Palmer v. 116

F

Fidelity & Guaranty Co., Hunter et al. v. 572
Fire & Marine Insurance Co., St. Paul, v. Kirkpatrick et al.. 55
Fowlkes, Baker Watkins Supply Co. v. ....:...... 663
Franklin et al., Western Union Telegraph Co. v. 656

G

Georgia Life Insurance Co., Atlas Hardwood Lumber Co. v. 477
Goodman et al. v. Wilson 464
Grant et ux. v. Louisville & Nashville Railway Company, et al., 398
Graves et al., Keelin v. 103
Greene, State v. 619
Griffin & Son v. Parker 466
Griffin, Southern Railway Co. v. 558
Gulf Compress Co. v. Commercial Union Assurance Co. 586
Gulf Compress Co. v. Insurance Co. of Pennsylvania 586
Gulf Compress Co. v. Stuyvesant Insurance Co. 586

H

Hardee v. Wilson et al. 511
Harowitz v. Concordia Fire Insurance Co. 691
Hessig-Ellis Drug Co. v. Stone et al. 608
Hopkins, Menihan Co. v. 24
Hull, State, ex rel., v. Rimmer 383
Hunter et al. v. Fidelity & Guaranty Co. 572

I

Illinois Central Railroad Co. et al. May v. 521
Insurance Co., Concordia Fire, Harowitz v. 691
Insurance Co. et al., St. Paul Fire & Marine, v. Kirkpatrick
et al. 55
Insurance Co., Georgia Life, Atlas Hardwood Lumber Co. v. .. 477
Insurance Co. of Pennsylvania, Gulf Compress Co. v. 586
Insurance Co., Stuyvesant, Gulf Compress v. 586
Investment Co. et al., James Land & v. Vernon et al. 637

James' Land & Investment Co. et al. v. Vernon et al. 637

K

Keelin v. Graves et al. 103
King et al. v. Patterson et al. 1
King v. Tennessee Central Railroad Co. 44
Kirkpatrick et al., St. Paul Fire & Marine Insurance Co. et al. v. 55

L

Lee et al. v. Villines et al. 625
Lemma et al., Walker v. 444
Louisville & Nashville Railway Company, et al., Grant et ux, v., 398
Lumber Co., Atlas Hardwood, v. Georgia Life Insurance Co. .. 477
Lumber Co., City, v. Barnhill et al. 676
Lumber Co., Dunlap, v. Nashville, C. & St. L. Ry. Co. 163

Mc

McCrory Piano & Realty Co., Calhoun v. 651
McDonald Automobile Co. v. Bicknell 493
McKee et al., McMillan et al. v. 39
McMillan et al. v. McKee et al. 39
McTeer, State v. 535

M

Matthews v. Crofford 541
Mayor and City Council of Nashville et al., Ward Seminary for Young Ladies v. 412
May v. Illinois Central Railroad Co. et al. 521
M. E. Church, South, State ex rel. College of Bishops of, et al. v. Board of Trust of Vanderbilt University et al. 279
Menihan Co. v. Hopkins 24
Mill Co., Peacher, Cumberland Telephone & Telegraph Co. v., 374
Missio v. Williams 504
Mitchell et al. v. Denny et al. 366

N

Nashville, C. & St. L. Ry. Co., Dunlap Lumber Co. v. 163

P

Palmer v. Southern Express Co. 116
Parker, Griffin & Son v. 466

Parrish v. State 273
Patterson et al., King et al. v. 1
Peacher Mill Co., Cumberland Telephone & Telegraph Co. v. .. 374
Portis, State, ex rel., Woolen State Comptroller v. 455
Putnam County v. Smith County 394

R

Ragghianti, State v. 560
Railway Co., Birmingham & N. W. Ry. Co. et al., Williams v., 680
Railway Co., Louisville & Nashville, et al. Grant et ux. v. 398
Railway Co., Nashville, C. & St. L., Dunlap Lumber Co. v. 163
Railway Co., Southern, v. Griffin 558
Railroad Co., Tennessee Central, King v. 44
Railway Co., Union, State et al. 705
Railway Co., Union, v. Carter 459
Realty Co., McCrory Piano &, Calhoun v. 651
Rimmer, State ex rel. Hull v. 383
Roofing & Manufacturing Co., Carey v. Black 30

S

St. Paul Fire & Marine Insurance Co. et al. v. Kirkpatrick et al., 55
Scheibler v. Steinburg 614
Seminary for Young Ladies, Ward, v. Mayor and City Council
    of Nashville et al. 412
Smith County, Putnam County v. 394
Southern Express Co., Palmer v. 116
Southern Railway Co. v. Griffin 558
State, Bond v. 75
State, Parrish v. 273
State, Suggs v. 498
State v. Greene 619
State v. Ragghianti 560
State v. McTeer 535
State et al. v. Union Ry. Co. 705
State, ex rel. Barrett, Strong v. 472
State, ex rel. Carter et al. v. Woollen 182
State, ex rel. College of Bishops of M. E. Church, South, et al.
    v. Board of Trust of Vanderbilt University et al. 279
State ex rel. Hull v. Rimmer 383
State, ex rel. Portis, Woolen, State Comptroller v. 455
Steinburg, Scheibler v. 614
Stone et al., Hessig-Ellis Drug Co. v. 608
Strong v. State, ex rel. Barrett 472
Stuyvesant Insurance Co., Gulf Compress Co. v. 586
Suggs v. State 498
Supply Co., Baker Watkins, v. Fowlkes 663

T

Telegraph Co., Western Union, v. Franklin et al. 656
Telephone & Telegraph Co., Cumberland, Peacher Mill Co. v. .. 374
Tennessee Central Railroad Co., King v. 44
Thomas et al. v. Cannon et al. 182

U

Ungerecht et al., Bond v. 631
Union Railway Co., State et al. v. 705
Union Railway Co. v. Carter 459
United States Fidelity & Guaranty Co., Hunter et al. v. 572

V

Vanderbilt University et al., Board of Trust of, State, ex rel.
  College of Bishops of M. E. Church, South, et al. v. 279
Vernon et al., James' Land & Investment Co. et al. v. 637
Villines et al., Lee et al. v. 625

W

Walker v. Lemma et al. 444
Ward Seminary for Young Ladies v. Mayor and City Council of
  Nashville et al. 412
Webb et al. v. Carter et al. 182
Western Union Telegraph Co. v. Franklin et al. 656
Williams, Missio v. 504
Williams v. Birmingham & N. W. Ry. Co. et al. 680
Wilson County Bank, Dies et al. v. 89
Wilson et al., Hardee v. 511
Wilson, Goodman et al. v. 464
Woollen, State ex rel. Carter et al. v. 182
Woolen, State Comptroller, v. State ex rel. Portis, Sheriff 455

CASES CITED.

A

Acklen v. Thompson, 122 Tenn., 43 153
Adcock v. Adcock, 104 Tenn., 154 370
Allen, Trustee, v. Gilliland, 74 Tenn., 534 21
Allen v. Thomason, 11 Humph., 536 112
Alley v. Lanier, 41 Tenn., 541 689
Anthony v. Smith, 28 Tenn., 508 496
Avans v. Everett, 71 Tenn., 77 370

B

Bank v. Motherwell, etc., Iron Co., 95 Tenn., 172 ......513, 514, 515
Bank v. Vandyck, 51 Tenn., 617 496
Beeler v. Nance, 126 Tenn., 592 371
Beeler v. Nance, 126 Tenn., 589 109
Blackburn v. Clarke, 85 Tenn., 506 14
Box Co. v. Gregory, 119 Tenn., 537 454
Box Co. v. Moore, 114 Tenn., 596 .... 633, 634, 636
Branch v. Bass, 37 Tenn., 366 407
Brewer v. State, 86 Tenn., 732 215
Brick Co. v. Surety Co., 126 Tenn., 402 .... 482, 483
Bridges v. Cooper, 98 Tenn., 382 13
Briscoe v. Vaughn, 103 Tenn., 314 373
Brown v. Hamlett, 76 Tenn., 735 688
Brown v. State, 65 Tenn., 424 .... 388, 389
Brown v. Sullivan County, 126 Tenn., 689 154
Bruce v. Beall, 99 Tenn., 303 377
Bryan v. Larecor, 112 Tenn., 511 612
Byrns v. Woodward, 78 Tenn., 444 496
Burnett v. Turner, 87 Tenn., 124 612
Bussey v. Grant, 29 Tenn., 238 102

C

Cagill v. Wooldridge, 67 Tenn., 580 519
Cain v. Jennings, 3 Tenn. Ch., 131 110
Camp v. Ristine, 101 Tenn., 534 378
Cannon v. Mathes, 8 Heisk., 504 154
Carson v. Lumber Co., 108 Tenn., 681 633

Carrigan v. Rowell, 96 Tenn., 185 109
Case Co. v. Joyce, 89 Tenn., 337 370
Cayard v. Robertson, 123 Tenn., 382 .... 481, 482
Cemetery Co. v. Creath, 127 Tenn., 686 434
Children of Israel v. Peres, 2 Cold., 620 29
Childress v. Lewis, 61 Tenn., 12 674
Clarke v. Blackburn, 85 Tenn., 506 14
Cloud v. Hamilton, 11 Tenn., 82 13
Coile v. Hudgins, 109 Tenn., 217 109
Coke & Coal Co. v. Steel Co., 123 Tenn., 428 153
Collier v. Strudy, 99 Tenn., 241 ....:... 510
Collins v. Railroad, 56 Tenn., 851 462
Cox v. Keathley, 99 Tenn., 523 372
Crabtree v. Bank, 108 Tenn., 483 673
Craig Miles v. Hays, 75 Tenn., 720 13
Cumberland Lodge v. Nashville, 127 Tenn., 248 436
Cumberland Lodge Case 442

D

Darnell v. State, 123 Tenn., 663 .... 153, 159
Davidson Benedict Co. v. Severson, 109 Tenn., 572 .... 461, 462
Davidson v. Phillips, 17 Tenn., 93, 95, 96 553
Davis v. Williams, 85 Tenn., 646 .... 628, 630
Dillingham v. Insurance Co., 120 Tenn., 302 514
Dixie Fire Insurance Co. et al. v. American Confectionery Co.,
    124 Tenn., 247 68
Dixon v. State, 117 Tenn., 79 153

E

Elliott & Co. v. Jordan, 66 Tenn., 376 674
Emmett v. Emmett, 14 Lea, 369 109
Ex parte Chadwell, 62 Tenn., 98 326

F

Farquhar v. Loney, 24 Tenn., 502 674
Farris v. Sipes, 99 Tenn., 298 109
Faust v. Echols, 44 Tenn., 398 674
Finley v. Casualty Co., 113 Tenn., 592 .... 481, 482
First National Bank v. Fidelity & Guaranty Co., 110 Tenn., 10.. 579
Fitts v. State, 102 Tenn., 141 387
Fogg v. Rogers, 42 Tenn., 290 496
Foster v. Hall & Eaton, 4 Humph., 345 .... 111, 112
Foster v. Hall, 4 Humph., 346 111
France v. State, 85 Tenn., 478 621
Fulghum v. Cotton, 74 Tenn., 596 .... 13, 14

Furnace Co. v. Railroad Co., 113 Tenn., 731 208
Furnace Co. v. Railroad, 113 Tenn., 728 350

G

Gaines v. Horrigan, 72 Tenn., 610 186
Gas Co. v. Williamson, 56 Tenn., 314 616
Gilreath v. Gilliland, 95 Tenn., 383 329
Gilley v. Harrell, 118 Tenn., 115 153
Gilliam v. McCormack, 85 Tenn., 610 .... 19, 20
Glass v. Stovall, 29 Tenn., 453 674
Gold v. Fite, 61 Tenn., 248 688
Governor v. Allen, 27 Tenn., 176 430
Graham v. Stull, 92 Tenn., 673 110
Graves v. Keaton, 43 Tenn., 9 674
Green v. Allen, 24 Tenn., 170 327
Grier v. Canada, 119 Tenn., 17 109
Guthrie v. Railroad, 11 Lea, 372 34
Gwynne v. Estes, 82 Tenn., 673 20

H

Haley v. M. & O. Railroad, 66 Tenn., 239 414
Hall v. Fulgham, 86 Tenn., 451 .... 13, 373
Harris v. Hamby, 114 Tenn., 361 154
Hascall v. Hafford, 107 Tenn., 355 109
Hawkins v. Pearce, 11 Humph., 44 109
Heck v. McEwen, 80 Tenn., 97 326
Hicks v. Pepper, 1 Baxt., 42 109
Hickerson v. Insurance Companies, 96 Tenn., 193.......... 64, 593
Hickerson & Co. v. Insurance Co. 697
Hill v. State, 73 Tenn., 725 391
Hines v. State, 126 Tenn., 1 41
Hollins v. Johnson, 40 Tenn., 346 674
Hunt v. Glenn, 79 Tenn., 16 489

I

Insurance Co. v. Diggs, 67 Tenn., 563, 569 556
Insurance Co. v. Dobbins, 114 Tenn., 239 581

J

Jackson v. Coffman, 110 Tenn., 272 .... 15, 16
Jackson v. Manufacturing Co., 124 Tenn., 421 154
Jackson v. Manufacturing Co., 124 Tenn., 424 216
Johnson v. Johnson, 92 Tenn., 567 361
Jones v. State, 37 Tenn., 347 .... 86, 87

K

Kay v. Smith, 57 Tenn., 42 689
Kellar v. Baird, 5 Heisk., 46 111
Kellar v. Baird, 5 Heisk., 39 112
Kelly v. State, 123 Tenn., 516 149
Kenny v. State, 123 Tenn., 516 153
Kirk v. State, 126 Tenn., 7 .... 154, 159
Klepper v. Powell, 6 Heisk., 503 111
Knox v. State, 68 Tenn., 202 475
Knox County v. Fox, 107 Tenn., 724 458
Knoxville v. Gass, 119 Tenn., 438 .... 153, 156

L

Lane v. Jones, 42 Tenn., 318 674
Lane v. Marshall, 48 Tenn., 30 ....12, 13, 14, 15, 16, 17
Layne Ex. v. Pardee and wife, 2 Swan, 232 112
Ledgerwood v. Pitts, 122 Tenn., 570 153
Lisenbee v. Holt, 1 Sneed, 50 109
Lover v. Bessenger, 68 Tenn., 393 95
Luttrell v. Railroad, 199 Tenn., 507 .... 612, 684
Lyle v. Longley, 65 Tenn., 288 12

Mc

McClurg v. McSpadden, 101 Tenn., 434 13
McMillan v. Hannah, 106 Tenn., 689 .... 396, 397

M

Malone v. Williams, 118 Tenn., 445 326
Malone v. Williams, 118 Tenn., 438 153
Malone v. Williams, 118 Tenn., 390 153
Mallory v. Oil Works, 86 Tenn., 598 327
Manufacturing Co. v. Buchanan, 118 Tenn., 238 496
Manufacturing Co. v. Falls, 90 Tenn., 469 .... 156, 158
Martin v. McNight, 1 Tenn., 380 525
Mason v. Smith, 11 Lea, 67 102
Massadillo v. Railway Co., 89 Tenn., 661 407
Maxey v. Powers, 117 Tenn., 103 688
Mayfield v. State, 101 Tenn., 673 387
Mayor, etc., of Nashville v. Ward, 84 Tenn., 27..............
                    416, 422, 428, 429, 430, 431
M. E. Church, South, v. Hinton, 92 Tenn., 188....432, 435, 436, 442
Meek v. Thompson, 99 Tenn., 732 20
Memphis & Little Rock R. R. Co. v. State of Tennessee, 77
    Tenn., 218 725

Memphis Street Railway v. State, 110 Tenn., 608 612
Meredith v. Dibrell, 127 Tenn., 387 94
Methodist Episcopal Church, South, v. Hinton, 92 Tenn.,
    188 .... 420, 421
Metzner v. State, 128 Tenn., 45 621
Moore v. Burchfield, 48 Tenn., 203 408
Murphy v. State, 47 Tenn., 516 886
Muse v. Lexington, 110 Tenn., 655 208

N

Nashville & Chattanooga R. Co. v. Smith, 53 Tenn., 174...... 408
Nashville v. Ward 439, 441
Nelson v. Haywood County, 91 Tenn., 608 .... 188, 215
North German Insurance Co. v. Morton-Scott-Robertson Co.,
    108 Tenn., 384 593

O

Owen v. State, 37 Tenn., 493 .... 86, 87

P

Parker v. Swan, 20 Tenn., 81 674
Parks v. Hays, 92 Tenn., 161 552
Parr v. Fumbanks, 79 Tenn., 394 .... 20, 21
Patton v. Railroad Co., 89 Tenn., 372 50
Pearce v. State, 1 Sneed, 66 112
Pearne v. Coal Co., 90 Tenn., 619 43
Peek v. State, 21 Tenn., 78 276
Pharis v. Lamberts, 33 Tenn., 228 616
Polk v. Plummer, 21 Tenn., 500 430
Porter v. Lee, 88 Tenn., 783 628
Post v. Railroad, 103 Tenn., 202 177
Prater v. Prater, 87 Tenn., 78 110
Price v. Clapp, 119 Tenn., 430 .... 277, 510

Q

Queener v. Morrow, 41 Tenn., 123 276

R

Ragon v. Howard, 97 Tenn., 341 689
Railroad v. Byrne, 119 Tenn., 278 .... 153, 159
Railroad v. Cheatham, 118 Tenn., 160 403
Railroad v. Daughtry, 88 Tenn., 721 462
Railroad v. Fidelity & Guaranty Co., 125 Tenn., 690......... 581
Railroad v. Griffin, 92 Tenn., 694 408

Railroad v. Harris, 99 Tenn., 684 442
Railroad v. Hayes, 117 Tenn., 680 453
Railroad v. Hunt, 15 Lea, 261 175
Railraad v. Jones, 56 Tenn., 27 407
Railroad v. Lindamood, 111 Tenn., 463 454
Railroad v. Memphis, 126 Tenn., 267 154
Railroad v. Pugh, 95 Tenn., 421 .... 51, 53
Railroad v. Roberts, 113 Tenn., 488 .... 407, 408
Railroad v. Roddy, 85 Tenn., 400 .... 408, 409
Railroad v. Rush, 83 Tenn., 150 50
Railroad v. Shewalter, 128 Tenn., 363 462
Railroad v. Stacker, 86 Tenn., 343 408
Railroad v. Staub, 7 Lea, 397 .... 26, 27
Railroad v. Todd, 58 Tenn., 556 16
Ransom v. Rutherford County, 123 Tenn., 1 153
Remington v. Fidelity & Deposit Co., 27 Wash., 429 580
Rhinehart v. State, 121 Tenn., 420 153
Rhodes v. Rhodes, 88 Tenn., 637 327
Rhodes v. State, 41 Tenn., 352 389
Rice v. O'Keefe, 53 Tenn., 638 12
Richardson v. Young, 122 Tenn., 524 149
Richardson v. Young, 122 Tenn., 565 216
Roane County v. Anderson County, 89 Tenn., 259 396
Royal Ins. Co. v. Vanderbilt Ins. Co., 102 Tenn., 264........... 581

S

Samuelson v. State, 116 Tenn., 470 159
Schultz v. Blackford, 77 Tenn., 431 13
Scott v. Marley, 124 Tenn., 388 154
Scott v. Marley, 124 Tenn., 390 350
Sharp v. Fly, 68 Tenn., 4 95
Sherfey v. Bartley, 36 Tenn., 58 ....:...... 508, 509
Shields v. Land Co., 94 Tenn., 123 208
Sivley v. Nixon Mining & Drill Co., 128 Tenn., 675........... 33
Sloan v. McCracken, 75 Tenn., 626 616
Smith v. Story, 1 Humph., 345 111
Southwestern Presbyterian University v. Presbyterian Synods
    of Tennessee (Nashville term, March, 1905) 357
Sparks v. Sparks, 114 Tenn., 666 112
Spillman v. Walt, 59 Tenn., 574 556
Starkey v. Hammer, 60 Tenn., 445 489
State, ex rel., v. Algood, 87 Tenn., 163 188
State, ex rel., v. Baseball Club, 127 Tenn., 292 186
State, ex rel., v. Baseball Club, 127 Tenn., 296 189
State, ex rel., v. Baseball Club, 127 Tenn., 309 215
State, ex rel., Dobson v. Washington & Tusculum College (Mss.,
    Knoxville, September term, 1912) 349

State, ex rel. Duncan v. Martin Female College (Nashville term,
    February, 1888) 359
State, ex rel., v. Folk, 124 Tenn., 119 153
State, ex rel., v. Powers, 124 Tenn., 553 154
State, ex rel., v. Schlitz Brewing Co., 104 Tenn., 715.......... 158
State, ex rel., v. Taylor, 119 Tenn., 229 153
State v. Algood, 87 Tenn., 163 215
Steger v. Arctic Refrigerator Co., 89 Tenn., 453 689
State v. Brown, 103 Tenn., 546 350
State v. Fisk University, 87 Tenn., 241 .... 420, 436
State v. Fleming, 26 Tenn., 152 622
State v. Fleming, 26 Tenn., 154 617
State v. Kelly, 123 Tenn., 567 137
State v. McCann, 72 Tenn., 11 204
State v. McConnell, 71 Tenn., 333 215
State v. Misseo, 105 Tenn., 218 88
State v. Railroad, 124 Tenn., 1 433
State v. Railroad, 124 Tenn., 16 417
State v. Staten, 46 Tenn., 250 475
State v. Swiggart, 118 Tenn., 556 216
State of Tennessee, ex rel., v. J. J. Persica et al., 130 Tenn., —.. 571
Stole v. Gardner, 81 Tenn., 135 674
St. Paul Fire & Marine Insurance Co. v. Kirkpatrick, 129
    Tenn., 55 ....592, 594
Stratton v. Brigham, 2 Sneed, 420 111
Swepson v. Davis, 109 Tenn., 107 .... 616, 618

T

Tarbox v. Hertenstein, 4 Baxt., 78 26
Telegraph Co. v. Frith, 105 Tenn., 167 407
Telegraph Co. v. McCaul, 115 Tenn., 99 661
Telegraph Co. v. Nashville, 118 Tenn., 1 215
Telegraph Co. v. Nashville, 118 Tenn., 8 .... 186, 188
Terrell v. State, 86 Tenn.. 523 326
Thompson v. French, 18 Tenn., 453 525
Topp v. White, 59 Tenn., 165 648
Traction Co. v. Brown, 115 Tenn., 323 37
Traction Co. v. Carroll, 113 Tenn., 514 37
Trice v. State, 2 Head, 591 86
Tyree v. Magness, 33 Tenn., 276 674

U

University of the South v. Skidmore, 87 Tenn., 156 ...... 420, 433

V

Vanderbilt University v. Cheney, 116 Tenn., 259..420, 432, 436, 442
Vaughn v. Ballentine, 1 Tenn. Cas., 596 109

W

Walton v. State, 35 Tenn., 687 617
Weakley v. Page, 102 Tenn., 179 569
Weidner v. Friedman, 126 Tenn., 677 569
Weil v. Newbern, 126 Tenn., 223 154
White v. Fulghum, 87 Tenn., 282 19
White v. Fulghum, 87 Tenn., 289 21
White v. White, 3 Head, 402 112
Whitley v. Steakly, 3 Baxt., 393 110
Whitmore v. Roscoe, 112 Tenn., 623 20
Wilkins v. Railroad, 110 Tenn., 422 710
Wilson v. Schaefer, 107 Tenn., 300 329
Williams v. Saunders, 5 Cold., 60 112
Williams v. State, 74 Tenn., 553 .... 202, 215
Winfrey v. Drake, 72 Tenn., 293 648
Wright v. State, 23 Tenn., 196 388
Wyatt v. State, 32 Tenn., 394 388

Y

Young v. Cowden, 98 Tenn., 577 407

OTHER CASES CITED.

A

Academy v. Bohler, 80 Ga., 162 431
Adams Express Co. v. Kentucky, 214 U. S., 219 143
Adams Express Co. v. Kentucky, 206 U. S., 129 143
Adams v. Yazoo, etc., R. Co., 77 Miss., 194 433
Allen v. Kelly, 17 R. I., 731 552
Allen v. McKean, 1 Sumn., 276 345
Alston v. Newcomer, 42 Miss., 186 111
Alton Mfg. Co. v. Garrett Biblical Institute, 243 Ill., 298 655
Ark. Cattle Co. v. Mann, 130 U. S., 73 .... 407, 408
Arkerson v. Dennison, 117 Mass., 407 453
Arnold v. Yanders, 56 Ohio St., 417 143
American Bonding Co. v. Pueblo Investment Co., 150 Fed., 17.. 549
American Bonding Co. v. Spokane Building & Loan Soc., 130
   Fed., 737 579
Anderson v. Miami Lumber Co., 59 Or., 149 636
Attorney-General v. Pierce, 2 Atk., 87 332
Austin Mfg. Co. v. Johnson, 89 Fed., 677 455

B

Babcock v. Goodrich, 47 Cal., 488 159
Baker v. Stone, 58 S. W., 761 678
Ballard v. Titus, 157 Cal., 673 43
Bank v. Motherwell, etc., Iron Co., 95 Tenn., 172-181......
                                           511, 514, 515, 516
Bannatyne v. McIwer, 1 K. B, 103 653
Bear v. Whisler, 7 Watts (Pa.), 149 554
Bell v. State, 37 Tenn., 507 540
Belt Railway Co. of Chicago v. U. S., 168 Fed., 542........... 725
Bernhard v. Insurance Company, 79 Conn., 388 65
Berryman v. Board of Trustees, 222 U. S., 334, 350 442
Bierce v. Hutchins, 205 U. S., 340 496
Blair v. Nelson, 8 Baxt., 1-5 565
Blomquist v. Chicago, etc., R. Co., 113 Minn., 426 452
Blum v. Weston, 102 Cal., 362 43
Blunt v. Little, 3 Mason, 102 407
Bogard v. Ill. Cent. R. R. Co., 116 Ky. 429................... 530

Booth v. Clark, 17 How., 322 514
Bowman v. Chicago & Northwestern R. Co., 125 U. S., 465....
                                 134, 135, 137, 138
Bowman v. Rector, 59 S. W., 389 95
Boyd v. Gore, 143 Wis., 531 550
Brady v. Chicago Great Western Railway Co., 114 Fed., 100.... 725
Bretzfelder v. Merchants' Insurance Co., 123 N. C., 164........ 65
Brow v. Boston, etc., R. Co., 157 Mass., 399 468
Burch v. Sou. Pacific Co., 32 Nev., 75 37
Burdict v. Mo. Pac. R. Co., 123 Mo., 221 407

C

Cage v. Lawrence, 57 S. W., 192 678
Campbellville Lumber Co. v. Hubbert, 112 Fed., 718 688
Castner v. Davis, 154 Fed., 938 329
Cheatham County v. Dickson County (Ch. App.), 39 S. W., 734. 397
Christmas v. Mitchell, 38 N. C., 535 85
Clark v. Fry, 8 Ohio St., 358 468
Clark v. Manchester, 51 N. H., 594 26
Coffin v. German Fire Insurance Co., 142 Mo. App., 295........ 66
Coleman v. People, 55 N. Y., 81 276
Coleman's Ex'r v. Meade, 13 Bush (Ky.), 358 645
Com. v. Skaggs, 152 Ky., 268 501
Com. v. Snelling, 15 Pick. (Mass.), 321 526
Connecticut Fire Insurance Co. v. Cohen, 97 Md., 294 65
Continental Insurance Co. v. Garrett, 125 Fed., 590 68
Continental Life Ins. Co. v. Barker, 50 Conn., 567........... 96
Converse v. Hamilton, 224 U. S., 243 .... 513, 518
Cotton v. Atlas Nat. Bank, 145 Mass., 49 101
County of Boone v. Railroad, 139 U. S., 684 396
Cox v. Railroad Co., 2 Leg. Rep., 168 51
Crane Co. v. Construction Co., 73 Fed., 984 380
Crean v. McMahon, 106 Md., 507 552
Creigh's Adm'r v. Boggs, 19 W. Va., 240 645
Crowley v. Railroad, 108 Tenn., 74 .... 532, 534
Cummings v. Wichita R., etc., Co., 68 Kan., 218 37
Crescent City Live Stock, etc., Co. v. Butchers' Union Slaughter
    House, 120 U. S., 141 616

D

Dailey v. Houston, 58 Mo., 361 510
Daly v. State, 13 Let., 228 433
Dartmouth College Case, 4 Wheat., 563 345
Dartmouth College Case, 4 Wheat., 574 332
Davidson's Appeal, 170 Pa., 96 84
Dean v. St. Paul Union Depot Co., 41 Minn., 360.............. 725

Dennard v. State, 2 Ga., 137 500
Detroit Home v. Detroit, 76 Mich., 521 437
De Wolf v. Pratt, 42 Ill., 198 645
Dibert v. D'Arcy, 248 Mo., 617 101
Dillingham v. Insurance Co., 120 Tenn., 302 .... 514, 515
Doe v. Alexander, 2 M. & S., 525 554
Doe v. Masters, 2 B. & C., 490 554
Doherty v. Schipper, 250 Ill., 128 26
Donahue v. Buck, 197 Mass., 550 452
Doran v. O'Neal (Ch. App.), 37 S. W., 563 109
Doyle v. Dixon, 97 Mass., 218 407
Dunleavy v. Sullivan, 200 Mass., 29 453

E

Easton v. Bank, 127 U. S., 532 101
Edgewood Distilling Co. v. Shannon, 60 Ark., 133 495
Eichman v. Buchheit, 128 Wis., 385 470
Empire Spring Co. v. Edgar, 99 U. S., 645 ....508, 509
Engstead v. County, 10 N. D., 54 431
Eubanks v. State, 50 Tenn., 488 540
Everett v. Insurance Co. (Tex. Civ. App.), 36 S. W., 125........ 605

F

Farris v. Hughes, 89 Va., 930 645
Ferguson v. State, 178 Ind., 568 540
Fisher v. Denver Nat. Bank, 22 Colo., 373 97
Floody v. Great Northern Railway Co., 102 Minn., 81 725
Florida East Coast R. Co. v. Welsh, 53 Fla., 145............. 525
Foley v. Crow, 37 Md., 51 645
Fortenberry v. State, 47 Tex. Cr. R., 84 501
Fowler v. Osgood, 141 Fed., 20 518
Frammell v. Little, 16 Ind., 251 509
Frick v. Insurance Co., 218 Pa., 409 605

G

Garby v. Harris, 7 Exch., 591 159
Gardner v. Webster, 64 N. H., 522 43
Garrett v. Scouten, 3 Denio (N. Y.), 334 554
George v. B. of E., 33 Ga., 344 159
Gerke v. Purcell, 25 Ohio St., 229 431
Gila Valley, etc., R. Co. v. Lyon, 203 U. S., 465 379
Gilman v. Hudson River Boot & Shoe Mfg. Co., 84 Wis., 60.... 518
Globe, etc., Insurance Co. v. Johnson (Ky.), 127 S. W., 765.... 66
Goddard v. Enzler, 222 Ill., 471 380
Goddard v. Enzler, 222 Ill., 462 379

Godeau v. Blood, 52 Vt., 251 509
Grady v. Home Fire & Marine Ins. Co., 4 L. R. A., 555 703
Graham v German American Ins. Co., 15 L. R. A., 1060 703
Grand Rapids Fire Ins. Co. v. Finn, 50 L. R. A., 555 703
Graves v. Scott, 104 Va., 372 618
Gulf, etc., R. Co. v. Chenault, 31 Tex. Civ. App., 558 405
Gulf, T. & W. R. v. Lowrie, 144 S. W., 367 525
Guffy v. Hukill, 34 W. Va., 49 552

H

Haakensen v. Burgess, etc., Co., 76 N. H., 443 451
Haggart v. Morgan, 5 N. Y., 422 111
Hamann v. Milwaukee Bridge Co., 127 Wis., 550 381
Hanaw v. Bailey, 83 Mich., 24 549
Hardaway v. Lilly, (Ch. App. 1898), 48 S. W., 712 .... 153, 154
Haskell v. Cope, etc., Co., 4 L. R. A., 226-229 451
Hawk v. State, 84 Ala., 466 500
Hayden v. Sewing Machine Co., 54 N. Y., 221 407
Hennington v. Georgia, 163 U. S., 299 .... 141, 149
Hitch Lumber Co. v. Brown, 160 N. C., 281 636
Holmes v. Seely, 19 Wend. (N. Y.), 507 42
Horner v. U. S., 147 U. S., 449 540
Hopson v. Boyd, 6 B. Mon. (Ky.), 296 84
Howarth v. Angle, 162 N. Y., 179-182 513
Howarth v. Lombard, 175 Mass., 570 513
Hughes v. Jones, 116 N. Y., 67 .... 84, 85
Hunt v. N. Y., N. H. & Hartford Ry. Co., 212 Mass., 102 725
Hutchinson v. Sandt, 4 Rawle (Pa.), 234 84

I

Illinois Central R. R. Co. v. King, 69 Miss., 852 468
In re Mallon, 16 Idaho, 737 474
In re Waddell-Entz Co, 67 Conn., 324 .... 99, 101
International Trust Co. v. Union Cattle Co., 3 Wyo., 808 .... 99, 101
Iowa Insurance Co. v. Lewis, 187 U. S., 335 69

J

Jackson v. Crysler, 1 Johns. Cas. (N. Y.), 125 554
James v. Allen Co., 44 Ohio St., 226 26
Jerrils v. German American Ins. Co., 82 Kan., 320 65

K

Keefe v. Armour, 258 Ill., 28 380
Keepers v. Yocum, 84 Kan., 554 645
Kennedy v. Spring, 160 Mass., 203 450

Kent v. Quicksilver Mining Co., 78 N. Y., 179 342
Kentucky, etc., School v. Louisville, 100 Ky., 486 431
Kentucky, etc., School v. Louisville, 100 Ky., 470 436
Killea v. Faxon, 125 Mass., 485 450
Kimball v. Costa, 72 Vt., 289 496
Kimmer v. Weber, 151 N. Y., 417 450
Koenigsberger v. Richman Silver Mine Co., 158 U. S., 53 407

L

Lacas v. Detroit, etc., R. Co., 92 Mich., 412 381
Lambert v. Missisquoi Pulp Co., 72 Vt., 278 452
Lang v. Merwin, 99 Me., 486 540
Lee v. Leighton Co., 113 Minn., 373 452
Le Forest v. Tolman, 117 Mass., 109 508
Leisy v. Hardin, 135 U. S., 100 133
Lester v. Insurance Co., 55 Ga., 475 69
Lewis v. Hughes, 12 Colo., 208 552
Lindvall v. Woods, 41 Minn., 212 .... 451, 452
Little v. Heaton, 2 Lord Raymond, 750 554
Loiseau v. State, 114 Ala., 34 540
London, etc., Bank v. Parriott, 125 Cal., 472.............. 97
Loomis v. Terry, 17 Wend. (N. Y.), 496 508
Lotz v. Hanlon, 217 Pa., 339 470
Louisville v. Cumberland Tel. Co., 224 U. S., 649 396
Lyles v. Western Union Telegraph Co., 84 S. C., 1 661

Mc

McAdow v. Black, 4 Mont., 475 655
McCready v. Hartford Insurance Co., 61 App. Div., 584, 585.... 605
McCourt v. Johns, 33 Ore., 561 645
McHenry v. State, 16 L. R. A. (N. S.), 1063 566
McPherson v. Acme Lumber Co., 70 Miss., 649 497

M

Maitland v. Gilbert Paper Co., 97 Wis., 476 381
Marsh v. Jones, 21 Vt., 378 509
Marshall v. Oakes, 51 Me., 308 510
Matthews v. Associated Press, 136 N. Y., 333 342
Mechanics' Insurance Co. v. C. A. Hoover Distilling Co., 182
    Fed., 590 606
Merchants' Ice Co. v. Bargholt, 129 Ky., 60 37
Mercer v. Atlantic Coast Line R. Co., 154 N. C., 399......... 34
Met. Bo. Wks. v. Steed, L. R., 82, B. Div., 445 159
Meyer v. State, 112 Ga., 20 540
Miller v. State, 158 Ala., 73 501

Minnesota Rate Cases, 230 U. S., 352 .... 138, 140
Mobile v. Stonewall Ins. Co., 53 Ala., 581 433
Monitor Drill Co. v. Mercer, 163 Fed., 943 496
Moore v. Townsend, 76 Minn., 64 405
Morgan's Adm'r v. Brast, 34 W. Va., 332 645
Morris v. Lone Star Chapter, 68 Tex., 698 431
Muller v. Stoecker Cigar Co., 89 Neb., 438 540
Mundorff v. Wickersham, 63 Pa., 87 655
Mutual Reserve Fire Insurance Co. v. Tuchfeld, 159 Fed., 833.. 69

N

National Park Bank v. Koehler, 137 App. Div., 785 98
Neininger v. State, 50 Ohio St., 394 500
Nelson v. Cushing, 2 Cush. (Mass.), 527.................. 332, 336
New Haven v. Sheffield Scientific School, 59 Conn., 163 436
Niagara Fire Insurance Co. v. Bishop, 154 Ill., 9 66
Nobles County v. Hamline University, 46 Minn., 316...... 431, 436
Northern Pacific R. R. Co. v. Herbert, 116 U. S., 642 407
Noyes v. Wood, 102 Cal., 389 .... 451, 452
N. W. University v. People, 80 Ill., 333 437

O

Oklahoma v. Kansas Nat. Gas Co., 221 U. S., 255.............. 142
Olmstead v. Bach, 78 Md., 132 27
Olsen v. Nixon, 61 N. J. Law, 671 452
Osborne v. Wise, L. R., 2 Ch. Div., 968 41

P

Parsons Business College v. Kalamazoo, 166 Mich., 305 438
Peninsular Savings Bank v. Hoise, 112 Mich., 351............ 98
People's Bank v. Williams (Ch. App.), 36 S. W., 983.......... 111
People v. Creamer, 30 App. Div., 624 475
People, ex rel., v. Jenkins, 153 App. Div., 512.................. 540
People v. Hawkins, 157 N. Y., 1 143
People v. Molineux, 168 N. Y., 264 276
Pettyplace v. Groton, etc., Co., 103 Mich., 155 496
Pierce v. Finerty, 76 N. H., 38 635
Pierce v. Tennessee, etc., Co., 173 U. S., 1 26
Phillips Academy v. Andover, 175 Mass., 118 437
Phillips v. State, 100 Ark., 515 501
Pointer v. Klamath, etc., Co., 28 Ann. Cas., 1077 378
Popplewell v. Pierce, 10 Cush. (Mass.), 509 508
Powhatan Coal & Coke Co. v. Ritz, 60 W. Va., 395 566

R

Railroad v. Brewing Co., 223 U. S., 82 138
Railroad v. Cook Brewing Co., 223 U. S., 82.................. 133
Railroad v. Hefley, 158 U. S., 98 .... 117, 141
Railroad v. Herrick, 13 Bush (Ky.), 122 159
Railroad v. Jacobson, 179 U. S., 287 176
Railroad v. Larabee Flour Mills Co., 211 U. S., 614..........177, 179
Railroad v. Ohio, etc., 173 U. S., 285 .... 141, 149
Railroad v. Searles, 85 Miss., 520 174
Railroad v. State, 28 Okl., 94 ·............................. 189
Relfe v. Rundle, 103 U. S., 222 513
Rhodes v. Iowa, 170 U. S., 412 134
Rhodes v. Iowa, 170 U. S., 425 142
Richards v. Hayes, 17 App. Div., 422 453
Richmond & Danville R. Co. v. Payne, 86 Va., 481 529
Rider v. White, 65 N. Y., 54 509
Ripley v. Greenleaf, 2 Vt., 129 .... 97, 101
Risewick v. Davis, 19 Md., 82 111
Ritchey v. Welch, 149 Ind., 214 42
Roberts v. Gordon, 86 Ga., 386 501
Rollins v. Atlantic City R. Co., 73 N. J. Law, 64 525
Ross v. Walker, 139 Pa., 42 450
Rowan v. Carleton, 100 Miss., 177 636
Russell v. Jackson, 2 Pick. (Mass.), 574 42
Rutherford v. Green, 2 Wheat., 196 159

S

Sanderson v. White, 18 Pick. (Mass.), 328 345
Sever v. Minneapolis, etc., R. Co. (Iowa), 137 N. W., 937...... 381
Shaw v. Vincent, 64 N. C., 690 645
Shawnee Fire Insurance Co. v. Pontfield, 110 Md., 353........ 65
Skelton v. Fenton Electric Light, etc., Co., 100 Mich., 87 404
Smith v. Causey, 22 Ala., 568 508
Smith, Exec., v. Wilkinson et al., 45 Tenn. (5 Cold.), 157...... 531
Southern Car & Foundry Co. v. Adams, 131 Ala., 147.......... 618
Southern Railroad Co. v. Puckett, 121 Ga. 322 525
Sowles v. Narcross Bros. Co., 195 Fed., 889 452
Spillman v. Walt, 59 Tenn., 574 .... 548, 556
Spring Garden Insurance Co. v. Amusement Syndicate Co.,
    178 Fed., 519 65
Standard Sewing Machine Co. v. Royal Insurance Co., 201 Pa.,
    645 605
Standard Steam Laundry Co. v. Dole, 22 Utah, 311 496
Stanton v. Hart, 27 Mich., 539 618
State, ex rel., v. Ellington, 117 N. C., 158 221
State v. Charles, 207 Mo., 40 502

State v. Cobb, 44 Mo. App., 375 501
State v. Everitt, 164 N. C., 399 475
State v. Heman, 70 Mo., 441 159
State v. Hyde, 234 Mo., 200 381
State v. Johnston, 214 Mo., 656 436
State v. Lewis, 69 W. Va., 472 530
State v. Murmann, 124 Mo., 502 502
State v. Sanders, 153 N. C., 627 475
State v. Stewart, 74 Iowa, 336 500
State v. Toledo, 23 Ohio Cir. Ct. R., 327................... 333, 336
State v. Whitson, 8 Blackf. (Ind.), 178 500
State v. Wilson, 14 La. Ann., 450 501
Steffen v. McNaughton, 142 Wis., 49 470
Stewart v. Sonneborn, 98 U. S., 187 616
St. Louis Dressed Beef & P. Co. v. Maryland Casualty Co., 201
 U. S., 173 482
Stork v. Charles Stolper Cooperage Co., 127 Wis., 318 34

T

Teagan Transp. Co. v. Detroit, 139 Mich., 1 433
Territory v. Jones, 14 N. M., 579 540
Texas, etc., C. R. v. Watson, 190 U. S., 291 379
Thornton v. Findlay, 97 Ark., 432 495
Title Guaranty & Surety Co. v. Bank of Fulton, 89 Ark., 471.... 580
Transportation Line v. Hope, 95 U. S., 297 ....:..... 379
Tunnell Hill, etc., Co. v. Cooper, 50 Colo., 390 ....407, 408

U

Ughbanks v. Armstrong, 208 U. S., 481 476
Union Bank v. Laird, 15 U. S., 390 688
Union Depot & Railway Co. v. Londoner, 50 Colo., 22 725
United States v. Ballin, 144 U. S., 1 219
United States Fidelity & Guaranty Co. v. Citizens Bank (Ky.),
 143 S. W., 997 579
U. S. Coal & Oil Co. v. Harrison, 71 W. Va., 217 635

V

Van Blarcom v. Hopkins, 63 N. J. Eq., 466 645
Vindicator Consol. Gold Min. Co. v. Firstbrook, 36 Colo., 498.. 37
Vrooman v. Lawyer, 13 Johns. (N. Y.), 339 509

W

Warfield v. State, 116 Md., 599 530
Washington & Va. R. Co. v. Bouknight, 113 Va., 696 530

Watkins v. Cope, 84 N. J. Law, 143 531
Weakly v. Bell, 9 Watts (Pa.), 273 98
Weaver v. Toney, 107 Ky., 419 ....567, 568
Weber v. Weitling, 18 N. J. Eq., 441 111
Webster City v. Wright County, 144 Iowa, 502 436
Welton v. Missouri, 91 U. S., 281 134
Western Assurance Co. v. Decker, 98 Fed., 381 65
Western Assurance Co. v. Hall, 120 Ala., 547 66
Western Union Telegraph Co. v. Barefoot, 97 Tex., 159........ 661
Western Union Telegraph Co. v. Cobb, 95 Tex., 333 660
Western Union Telegraph Co. v. Mitchell, 91 Tex., 454 661
Western Union Telegraph Co. v. Redinger, 66 S. W., 485 660
Wey v. Salt Lake City, 35 Utah, 504 436
Whitney v. Brown, 75 Kan., 678, 468 .... 542, 552
Wilkinson v. Parrot, 32 Cal., 102 509
Wilson v. Campbell, 75 Kan., 159 552
Winkler Brokerage Co. v. Fidelity & Deposit Co., 119 La.; 735.. 583
Wolf v. McGavock, 23 Wis., 516 111
Woods v. Lindvall, 48 Fed., 62 452

Yauger v. Skinner, 14 N. J. Eq., 389 84

Z

Zimmerman Mfg. Co. v. Daffin, 159 Ala., 380 634

CASES CITED AND DISTINGUISHED.

A

Adams Express Co. v. Kentucky, 214 U. S., 219 143
Allen v. Gilliland, 74 Tenn., 534 21
Anderson v. Talbot, 48 Tenn., 410 674

B

Barnes v. Thompson, 32 Tenn., 314 687
Blackburn Bldg. Soc. v. Cunliffe, 22 Ch. D., 6172 653
Bogard v. Ill. Cent. R. R. Co., 116 Ky., 429 525

C

Carson v Carson, 115 Tenn., 50 354
Carson v. Lumber Co., 108 Tenn., 681 635
Cemetery Co. v. Creath, 127 Tenn., 686 434
Choctaw Coal, etc., Co. v. Williams, Echols, etc., Co., 75 Ark.,
    365 518
Choctaw Coal, etc., Co. v. Williams, Echols, etc., Co., 75 Ark.,
    365 519
Collier v. Union Railway Co., 113 Tenn., 96 707
Continental Life Ins. Co. v. Barker, 50 Conn., 567 96
Cotton v. Atlas Nat. Bank, 145 Mass., 49 101
Cunningham v. Sharp, 30 Tenn., 116 648

D

Dartmouth College Case, 4 Wheat., 563 352
Davis v. Lumber Co., 126 Tenn., 584 405
Dodge v. Williams, 46 Wis., 100 440

E

Ex parte Williams, 114 Ala., 29 501

2 Thompson]   (xxix)

G

Galloway v. Bradshaw, 37 Tenn., 70 648
Gilliam et al. v. McCormack et al., 85 Tenn., 610 19
Green v. Rutherford, 1 Ves. Sen., 471 345

H

Hardaway v. Lilly (Ch. App. 1898), 48 S. W., 712 154
Halliburton v. Jackson, 79 Tenn., 471 673
Hickerson & Co. v. Insurance Co., 96 Tenn., 198 ....695, 698
Hicks v. Pepper, 60 Tenn., 44 370
Hunt v. Glenn, 79 Tenn., 16 488

I

Illinois, etc., R. Co. v. Smith, 208 Ill., 608 380

J

Jackson v. Preston, 21 L. R. A. (N. S.), 165 417
Jones v. State, 37 Tenn., 347 86

L

Lee v. Security Bank & Trust Co., 124 Tenn., 582 555
Leisy v. Hardin, 135 U. S., 100 133
Luttrell v. Railroad, 119 Tenn., 492 684

M

Martin v. Light Co., 131 Iowa, 724 380
Miller v. State, 158 Ala., 73 502
Minnesota Rate Cases, 230 U. S., 352 ....138, 140
Mynatt v. Mynatt, 53 Tenn., 311 531

N

National Park Bank v. Koehler, 137 App. Div., 785 98
Newman v. Maclin, 6 Tenn., 241 646
Newsum v. Hoffman, 124 Tenn., 369 519

O

Oklahoma v. Kansas Nat. Gas. Co., 221 U. S., 255 142
Olmstead v. Bach, 78 Md., 132 27
Owen v. State, 37 Tenn., 493 86

P

Patton v. Railroad Co., 89 Tenn., 372 50
Phillips v. Bury, 2 Term. R., 352 345
Phillips v. Bury, 2 Term. R., 346 350

R

Railroad v. Brewing Co., 223 U. S., 82 133
Railroad v. Searles, 85 Miss., 520 174
Reversion Fund, etc., v. Maison Cosway, Ann. Cases, 1913,
    1106 654
Rhodes v. Iowa, 170 U. S., 412 134
Runk v. St. John, 29 Barb. (N. Y.), 585 518

S

Samuelson v. State, 116 Tenn., 470 159
Shacklett v. Polk, 51 Tenn., 104 677
Starkey v. Hammer, 60 Tenn., 445 488
State, ex rel., v. Algood, 87 Tenn., 163 188
State ex rel. Wellford v. Union Railway Co., 113 Tenn., 96.... 707
State v. Fisk University, 87 Tenn., 233 418
State v. McCann, 72 Tenn., 11 204
State v. Yardley, 95 Tenn., 546 350

T

Tilton v. Reecher, 59 N. Y., 176 527
Title Guaranty Co. v. Nicholls, 224 U. S., 346 579
Trice v. State, 39 Tenn., 591 86

U

United States v. Terminal R. R. Association of St. Louis, 224
    U. S., 383 722

W

Welton v. Missouri, 91 U. S., 281 134
White v. Fulghum, 87 Tenn., 282 19
Williams v. State, 74 Tenn., 553 187
Wood v. Mason, 42 Tenn., 251 647

CASES CITED AND DISAPPROVED.

Furnace Co. v. Railroad Co., 113 Tenn., 731 208
Muse v. Lexington, 110 Tenn., 655 208
Shields v. Land Co., 94 Tenn., 123 208

(xxxii)   [129 Tenn.

CASES

ARGUED AND DETERMINED

IN THE

SUPREME COURT OF TENNESSEE

FOR THE

MIDDLE DIVISION.

NASHVILLE, DECEMBER TERM, 1913.

(Continued from Vol. 128.)

KING *et al. v.* PATTERSON *et al.*

(Nashville. December Term, 1913.)

1. **ATTACHMENT. Necessary parties. Attachment of mortgaged property,**

A creditor attaching the property of a nonresident debtor under Shannon's Code, sec. 5211, must, where the legal title is in a mortgagee, make the mortgagee a party defendant; for otherwise the mortgagee may assert his rights and cut off the attachment by foreclosure, and the property, if sold under the attachment, will not bring a fair price. (*Post, pp.* 11-17.)

Code cited and construed: Secs. 5211, 5218 (S.)

Cases cited and approved: Lane v. Marshall, 48 Tenn., 30; Rice .v O'Keefe, 53 Tenn., 638; Lyle v. Longley, 65 Tenn., 288; Fulghum v. Cotton, 74 Tenn., 596; Cloud v. Hamilton, 11 Tenn., 82; Craig Miles v. Hays, 75 Tenn., 720; Schultz v. Blackford, 77 Tenn., 431; Hall v. Fulgham, 86 Tenn., 451; Bridges v. Cooper, 98 Tenn., 382; McClung v. McSpadden, 101 Tenn., 434; Blackburn v. Clarke, 85 Tenn., 506; Jackson v. Coffman, 110 Tenn., 272; Railroad v. Todd, 58 Tenn., 556.

2. **ATTACHMENT. Proceeding. Amendment.**

Where numerous creditors of a nonresident debtor were striving for priority by attachments on his property, complainants, who did not join as a party the mortgagee of land which they attached, are not entitled to permission to amend their bill so as

---

King v. Patterson.

---

to correct the defect; defendants having already acquired valid attachment liens thereon, having made the mortgagee a party. (*Post, pp.* 17, 18.)

3. **ATTACHMENT. Motion to quash. Nonjoinder of parties. Waiver.**

Defendants and complainants filed separate bills for attachments on the property of a nonresident debtor. After consolidation of the suits, defendants moved to quash complainants' attachments, and excepted to the report of the master fixing priority. *Held* that, as defendants were not parties until the consolidation of the suits, their right to object to the failure of complainants to join the mortgagee of the debtor's property, who was the holder of the legal title, as a party defendant had not been waived, and might be raised by the objections made. (*Post, p.* 18.)

4. **ATTACHMENT. Actions. Defenses. Mode of raising.**

Where numerous attachment suits were consolidated, motions to quash complainants' attachments and exceptions to the report of the master fixing the priorities of the parties are the proper methods of raising the question whether complainants' attachments were void for failure to join the holder of the legal title of the property attached. (*Post, p.* 18.)

5. **MARSHALING ASSETS AND SECURITIES. Right to marshaling.**

Where numerous creditors who had no liens upon the property of their debtor all sought to acquire liens by attachments, some of which were not duly perfected for want of necesary parties, there can be no marshaling of assets between the successful and unsuccessful creditors; for the doctrine of marshaling arises only where one creditor has a lien upon two funds or two parcels of land, and another having a lien upon only one of them, in which case the first creditor will, in equity, be required to seek satisfaction first out of that fund or property upon which the second creditor has no lien. (*Post, pp.* 19-21.)

Cases cited and distinguished: Gilliam et al. v. McCormack et al., 85 Tenn., 610 White v. Fulghum, 87 Tenn., 282; Allen v. Gilliland, 74 Tenn., 534.

King v. Patterson.

Cases cited and approved: Meek v. Thompson, 99 Tenn., 732;
Whitmore v. Roscoe, 112 Tenn., 623-636; Gwynne v. Estes, 82
Tenn., 673; Parr v. Fumbanks, 79 Tenn., 394.

6. EQUITY. Pleading. Multifariousness.

Under Shannon's Code, sec. 6137, providing that the uniting in
one bill of several matters of equity, distinct and unconnected,
against one defendant is not multifariousness, the joining in
one bill of attachment suits by numerous unsecured creditors
does not render the bill multifarious. (*Post, pp.* 22, 23.)

7. EQUITY. Pleading. Multifariousness.

Where a bill by numerous attaching creditors also sought equitable relief, defendants must, under the direct provisions of
Shannon's Code, sec. 6135, raise the objection of multifariousness by motion to dismiss or demurrer, or it will be waived.
(*Post, p.* 23.)

Code cited and construed: Sec. 6137 (S.).

FROM GILES.

Appeal from Chancery Court, Giles County.—JOHN
F. MORRISON, Special Chancellor.

E. E. ESLICK, R. H. MCLAURIN, and STEWART WILKES,
for plaintiffs.

CHILDERS & WOODWARD, for defendants.

MR. JUSTICE BUCHANAN delivered the opinion of the
Court.

This was a bill filed August 24, 1911, by J. H. King
and others against J. H. Patterson, a nonresident debtor, and divers of his creditors. Complainants were
also creditors of Patterson, and, as such, had, prior
to the filing of the present bill, filed attachment bills
against Patterson as a nonresident debtor, seeking to
subject his property to the payment of their debts. The

defendants in the main, as creditors of Patterson, had also filed attachment bills seeking to fix liens upon his property, and decrees subjecting the property to payment of their respective debts.

Under this bill, and after divers proceedings had been had in the cause, which need not be set out in detail, an order of consolidation was entered on November 15, 1911, on motion of complainants in each of the attachment bills which had been filed by creditors of Patterson, this motion being joined in by those creditors who were complainants and those who are defendants to the present bill; and, along with the divers attachment bills, there was also consolidated a bill filed by the Northwestern Mutual Life Insurance Company against Patterson and wife, seeking the foreclosure of a mortgage on certain of the lands of Patterson. This order of consolidation recited, in substance, that judgments and decrees had been taken for debts sought to be collected by attachments under said various bills, "and, liens having been fixed by said decrees upon the real estate attached in said various causes, and it appearing that a sale in each case is both impracticable and will entail a large and useless expense, and that one sale would be in the interest of all parties, it is therefore ordered, adjudged, and decreed by the court that said causes be consolidated for hearing, and, under such consolidation, there may be had a decree for sale, and such other orders, references, accounts, and decrees as the rights and equities of said various parties may entitle. It is not intended hereby to adjudge any rights or equities as between any of the parties complainant to said cause, but only to consolidate the same for hearing as aforesaid.''

After the order for consolidation, but of the same date, a decree was entered which recited as its caption the styles and caption of the present case and of each of the attachment cases, including those brought by complainants as well as those brought by defendant, and also including the foreclosure suit brought by the Northwestern Mutual Life Insurance Company; and this decree also contained copies of each of the decrees which had been taken in each of the attachment cases against the absconding debtor, and also a copy of the decree which had been rendered against him under the foreclosure bill filed by the Northwestern Mutual Life Insurance Company; and, after making all of these recitals, the decree in the consolidated causes adjudged that all of the land which had been levied on in the divers attachment suits, as recited in the decrees copied, should be sold by a special commissioner named. The lands to be sold were described, and those first described were those covered by the mortgage of the Northwestern Mutual Life Insurance Company, which consisted of three tracts, one containing 275 acres, on containing 123 $\frac{24}{100}$ acres, and one containing 212 $\frac{24}{100}$ acres, in all aggregating 610 $\frac{48}{100}$ acres. Divers other tracts were described which had been levied on in the attachment suits. The manner of making the sale and terms thereof were prescribed, etc. This decree also recited that the attachments sued out by complainants, naming them, purported to have been issued and levied upon the lands or equity therein of the debtor under the Northwestern Mutual Life Insurance Company's mortgage, but that said company was not made a party to any of said attachment bills, and that therefore all questions with regard to the validity of said attachments and the rights and liens acquired thereunder are reserved for future action by the court.

By virtue of the foregoing decree, the lands therein described were sold by special commissioner thereby appointed on December 16, 1911, and the sale was reported to the court on February 15, 1912, and the sale was confirmed, and a decree was entered divesting and vesting title as to each tract sold.

On April 9, 1912, there was an order as to payment of costs, and on the same day each of the defendant attaching creditors made a motion to quash and vacate the attachment sued out by each of the complainant attaching creditors. Each of these motions was based on two grounds: (1) That, as to the lands which had been mortgaged to the Northwestern Mutual Life Insurance Company, each levy purported to be on the equitable interest of Patterson, the debtor; but the owner of the legal title was not made a party to the bill or proceeding, and was in no way before the court in each of those attachments. (2) That each of the attachment bills of complainants "attempt on behalf of separate, distinct, and disconnected general creditors to impound and administer in one attachment cause the estate of an absconding debtor." Wherefore each motion insisted that each of said attachment proceedings was void and of no effect.

On the same day the foregoing motions were made in this cause, to wit: On July 9, 1912, the clerk and master made a report fixing the priority of the lien of each attachment which had been levied in the respective attachment suits, according to the date at which each levy was made; and to this report each of the creditors who made a motion as aforesaid filed also an exception to the report, and in each exception two grounds were relied on, each of which was identical with those relied on, in each of the motions. The motions and exceptions were passed on by a decree of date July 10, 1912, and the court sustained the first ground of each of said motions and each of said exceptions, and decreed that each of the attachments sued out by the complainants in this suit were void, in so far as the lands were concerned which had been mortgaged to the Northwestern Mutual Life Insurance Company, because that company, as the holder of the legal title, had not been made a party defendant or brought before the court; to which action of the court complainants in this cause severally excepted.

The court overruled the second ground of each of the motions and exceptions, and to this action of the court the defendants to this cause severally excepted.

Thereupon complainants in this cause moved the court to refer this case to the master to report from the record what properties, real and personal, had been levied on by complainants in each of the causes con-

solidated herewith, and that decree be had in this cause
marshaling the securities and liens in this cause an
the causes consolidated. But the court overruled this
motion, and to its action complainants excepted.

Thereupon complainants moved the court for leave
to make the Northwestern Mutual Life Insurance Company of Milwaukee a party defendant to this cause,
and also to make said company a party defendant to
the several attachment bills which had been filed by
complainants. But the court overruled this motion,
and to its action complainants excepted.

The decree then recites that the cause came on for
hearing on the whole record, and the bill was sustained
for the purpose of consummating one sale and determining in one suit the priorities of the attaching creditors. But, so far as the bill sought a marshaling of
assets and securities, the court was of opinion that
complainants were not entitled to the equity of marshaling, for that the valid attachment liens attached
as of the date of the respective levies on the land sold
or any part of it, and therefore, in so far as the bill
was one for marshaling of assets and securities, it was
dismissed; to which action the complainants excepted.

The complainants in this consolidated cause appealed from so much of the foregoing decree as they
had excepted to, and the defendants did the like, and
each appeal was duly perfected; and the cause is before us on assignments of error by the respective parties. The assignments for the complainants raise these
questions:

King v. Patterson.

(1) Was the chancellor in error in holding that the complainants' attachments were void because the holder of the legal title to the Northwestern Mutual Life Insurance Company lands was not made a party defendant to the bills under which those attachments were respectively sued out?

(2) Was the chancellor in error in dismissing the bill in so far as it sought a marshaling of assets and securities?

(3) Was the chancellor in error in refusing to overrule the motion of complainants for leave to make the holder of the legal title, to wit, the Northwestern Mutual Life Insurance Company, a party defendant to this cause, and to each of the attachment bills filed by complainants?

(4) Was the chancellor in error in taxing costs against complainants?

The assignments of error made by the defendants to this cause present these questions:

(1) Was the chancellor in error in refusing to hold that each of the attachment bills of the complainants herein was void and of no effect, because each was an attempt on behalf of separate and disconnected general creditors to impound and administer in one attachment cause the estate of an absconding debtor?

(2) Was the chancellor in error in adjudging the costs of the consolidated cause against J. H. Patterson, the absconding debtor, and directing such costs to be paid out of his estate before appropriation of same

to payment of the claims of defendants to this suit
as attaching creditors?

We will now proceed to dispose of the first question
made by the assignment of errors on behalf of complainants, involving as it does, the validity of their
attachments. It is to be noted in the outset that none
of these attaching creditors by their bills set up against
the equitable estate of the absconding debtor in the
lands, to which the insurance company held the legal
title, any legal or equitable lien whatever. These attaching creditors were mere creditors at large of the
debtor, seeking by their several attachments to secure
a lien on the equitable estate of the debtor in the land,
and their several attachment bills do not rest on a
service of process personally made upon the debtor,
but they rest upon the several averments of those bills
that he had become a nonresident of this State as a
ground for attachment set out under section 5211 of
Shannon's Code. See, also, section 5218 of Shannon's
Code, which provides that any person may also sue
out an attachment in the chancery court upon debts
or demands of a purely equitable nature, except causes
of action founded on torts, without first having recovered a judgment at law, whenever the amount in
controversy is sufficient to give the court jurisdiction.

It is to be further noted that, in each of the complainants' attachment suits, no personal service of process
was ever had upon the holder of the equitable estate, the
service on him being wholly constructive or by publication, as authorized by our statute; and in each of

these suits the holder of the legal title to the lands, that holder being the insurance company, was not made a party defendant to the bill, or served personally or constructively with process bringing it before the court as the holder of the legal title.

In each of the complainants' several attachment suits, a decree *pro confesso* in the usual form was taken against the nonresident debtor, and following this was a decree final in favor of each creditor and against the debtor for the amounts respectively set out in the bill, and declaring a lien on the property attached; and each of these decrees reserved the matter of the sale of the property attached, the decrees reciting, as a reason for this, that it appeared to the court that various attachments had been levied on the property, and a sale thereof could be more economically made under a bill consolidating the several attachment suits. Thus stood the attachment suits of the creditors who compose the parties complainant in this consolidated cause, and, while standing thus, divers creditors who are made defendants to this suit acquired liens on the insurance company lands by the levy of attachments under bills, in each of which the holder of the legal title to the land levied on, to-wit, the insurance company, was made a party defendant, and duly brought before the court.

There was between the attaching creditors, who are complainants in this cause, and creditors of the same kind, who are defendants hereto, a race of diligence and skill, and the goal was the acquisition of a valid lien on an equitable estate of a nonresident debtor. The complainant creditors failed to make the holder of the legal title a party defendant to their attachment bills. The defendant creditors did not overlook that important step. Was the failure by the complainants vital? Our cases answer the question, and, of these *Lane* v. *Marshall*, 48 Tenn. (1 Heisk.), 30, is the leading one. In that case King sold a tract of land to Johnson, and the sale was evidenced by a title bond which Johnson held as his assurance of title, when he should pay the balance of the purchase price of the land. Therefore the legal title to the land was in King, and the equitable title in Johnson, subject to King's lien for the balance of the purchase money. So stood the rights of the parties when, on February 6, 1865, an attachment bill was filed and the land levied on as the property of Johnson when he was a prisoner of war and beyond the limits of this State. The question for decision was the validity of the title acquired by a purchaser at a sale under a decree rendered in the attachment suit. This court held against the validity of the title, resting its decision on two points, as we understand the case: First, that the bill was not properly framed to reach the equitable estate; and, second, that King, holder of the legal title, was not made a defendant to the bill.

Upon the first ground above stated, *Lane* v. *Marshall* was followed and applied in *Rice* v. *O'Keefe*, 53 Tenn. (6 Heisk.), 638, and *Lyle* v. *Longley*, 65 Tenn. (6 Baxt.), 288. And, upon the second ground above stated, *Lane* v. *Marshall* has been followed and applied in *Fulghum* v. *Cotton,* 74 Tenn. (6 Lea), 596, where the contract was between a judgment creditor, with an execution returned *nulla bona,* on the one hand, and a mortgagee on the other., as to the right of the judgment creditor by a bill in equity to force a sale of the land mortgaged, where the mortgage debt was due, and unpaid, and the purpose of the creditor's bill was to sell the fee-simple or whole estate in the land, and out of the proceeds pay the mortgage debt and appropriate the balance upon the debt of the judgment creditor. The chancellor had held that the judgment creditor was entitled to a sale of the interest of the mortgagor, but not to a sale of the property itself, without the consent of the mortgagee. This holding of the chancellor seems to have been based on the doctrine of the English cases. But this court declined to follow the English rule, pointing out that, under their practice, a decree of foreclosure was not for the sale of the property, but was one cutting off the equity of redemption. See, also, on this point, *Cloud* v. *Hamilton,* 11 Tenn. (3 Yerg.), 82; *Craig Miles* v. *Hays,* 75 Tenn. (7 Lea), 720; *Schultz* v. *Blackford,* 77 Tenn. (9 Lea), 431; *Hall* v. *Fulgham,* 86 Tenn. (2 Pickle), 451, 7 S. W., 121; *Bridges* v. *Cooper,* 98 Tenn. (14 Pickle), 382, 39 S. W., 720; *McClurg* v. *McSpadden,* 101 Tenn. (17 Pickle), 434, 47 S. W., 698. Whereas, in this State foreclosure was accomplished by a sale of the whole property, and not the mere equity of the debtor, so as to vest the purchase with an absolute title, and to

apply the proceeds according to the priorities of in-
cumbrances. We quote from that opinion as follows:

"In fact, it was held in *Lane* v. *Marshall* that an
attachment levied upon land to which the debtor had
only an equitable title, fixed no lien upon it, and the
purchaser acquired nothing, not merely because it was
not described as an equitable title, but because, to attach it, the holder of the legal title was a necessary
party, so that the sale would pass the entire title. That
was a case where the debtor held the land by title bond,
subject to unpaid foreclosure money. It was held that
an attachment and sale, without making the holder of
the legal title a party, so as to effectuate the object had
in view—that is, a sale of the property—passed nothing to the purchaser. A vendor by title bond, holding
the legal title as security for unpaid purchase money,
it has been often said, occupies a position very similar
to a mortgagee." There is nothing in the line of
cases above cited following *Fulghum* v. *Cotton* in conflict with the doctrine of *Lane* v. *Marshall*. Certainly,
there is nothing in this case but the most unqualified
approval of *Lane* v. *Marshall*. That case was again
approved by this court in *Blackburn* v. *Clarke*, 85
Tenn. (1 Pickle), 506, 3 S. W., 505. The title to land
there involved depended on attachment issuing out of
the circuit court at the suit of Clarke against Blackburn and others. It was held that Clark acquired no
lien by virtue of his attachment, because Blackburn
had only an equitable interest in the land attached, and
the holder of the legal title was not before the court.

The case last above cited and *Lane* v. *Marshall* were each approved by this court in *Jackson* v. *Coffman*, 110 Tenn. (2 Cates), 272, 75 S. W., 718, where, by bill in equity and an attachment thereon issued and levied on land, without making the trustees named in a trust deed on the land parties to the bill, though the holders of a second incumbrance evidenced by mortgage were made parties, a creditor at large sought to acquire a lien on the land of his debtor, and later, by an amended and supplemental bill and another attachment and a garnishment, sought to reach the surplus proceeds of the land originally attached, which had in the meantime been sold by the trustees for a price which paid the trust deed debt, and left a surplus in their hands. It was held, upon the authority of *Lane* v. *Marshall* and *Clarke* v. *Blackburn*, that the attaching creditor took nothing by his original attachment, because he had failed to make the trustees parties to his bill; and, be it noted this holding against him applied not only to his contest with the trustees, but also to his contest with the mortgagee. This case, in so far as the opinion of the court dealt with the rights of attaching creditor under his original bill, turned on the doctrine of *Lane* v. *Marshall*. The amended and supplemental bill was disposed of on other grounds.

Mr. Gibson in his Suits in Chancery, sec. 127, says: "A creditor who seeks to reach an equitable interest or estate, or to enforce a lien or equitable interest of his own, must make the owner of the legal title a party as well as the owner of the equitable interest"—citing

Jackson v. *Coffman,* supra; *Railroad* v. *Todd,* 58 Tenn.
(11 Heisk.), 556; A. & E. Ency. of Law, 1116, 1128.

The reasons underlying the doctrine of *Lane* v. *Marshall* are sound, and are as follows: (1) That the
holder of the legal title may assert his rights in the
premises; (2) that the purchaser at the court sale may
get a full title; and (3) that the property may bring
the better price. See Gibson's Suits in Chy. sec. 882.

Analysis of the reasons above given by Mr. Gibson
may not be amiss. In the first place, how is the court
to know the quality and extent of the estate of the
holder of the legal title, unless he be brought into court
as a party? The record may show his estate to be
one in fee. His assurance of title may be a deed absolute on its face, yet, in fact, he may not own the fee.
The deed may be a mortgage only, when the facts of
the transaction between him and the holder of the
equitable title are disclosed. Again, as to the extent
or quantity of the estate of the holder of the legal
title: It may appear on the face of his written evidence of title to be large; that is to say in the case
of a mortgage the amount of the indebtedness appearing in the face of the instrument may be large, but
the amount of the real indebtedness of the holder of
the equitable estate may be very small. The holder
of the legal title cannot be bound by the proceedings
to subject the equity, in which there is necessarily involved the ascertainment both of the amount and quantity of the estate held by the holder of the legal title,
unless that holder be brought before the court as a

party to the cause. In the second place, it is manifest
from what has been said that the purchaser of the
equity at a sale made by decree of court cannot get a
full title both to the legal and the equitable estate,
unless the holder of the legal title be brought before
the court as a party. In the third place, it is equally
manifest that, if the holder of the legal title be brought
before the court as a party to the cause, and the quality and extent of his rights and of the rights of the
holder of the equitable title be fully disclosed in the
proceeding in such way as to bind the holder of the
legal title and the holder of the equitable title, the property, when sold, will bring a better price than if all
these matters should be left in uncertainty and doubt
by failure to make the holder of the legal title a party
to the cause.

The cases cited have firmly established in our jurisprudence the doctrine of *Lane* v. *Marshall*. There
is nothing in the case at bar to save it from the application of that doctrine, and it results that there is no
merit in the first question arising under complainants'
assignments of error, and it must be overruled. Nor
do we think there was error in the action of the chancellor in the taxation of costs, or in overruling the motion of complainants for leave to make the holder of
the legal title a party defendant to the various attachment suits brought by the complainants in the consolidated cause after the rights of other attaching creditors had accrued, when the effect of such action on
his part would have been to rob them of the fruits of

their superior diligence in the race to acquire valid
liens. Liberal as our statute of amendments is, it did
not authorize the court to disregard the rights of jun-
ior attaching creditors, who had acquired a priority
of lien in a fair race of diligence.

What we have just said disposes of the third and
fourth questions arising under the assignments of error made by complainants.

It is insisted for complainants that the motion to
quash the attachments and the exceptions to the report
as to priority of liens came too late, and that these
objections were waived, and were not made in the
proper way. Manifestly there is no merit in this insistence. The defendant attaching creditors were not
parties to the separate attachment bills brought by
the complainants. The motion to quash and the exceptions to the report were seasonably made in the
consolidated cause. The question of the validity of the
complainants' attachments was raised in the answer
of defendants, and the motion to quash and the exceptions to the report were proper methods of raising the
question and calling on the court for its decree thereon.

Of the questions arising on complainants' assignments of error, the only one left undisposed of is the
second, which raises the question that the chancellor
was in error in dismissing the bill, in so far as it
sought a marshaling of assets and securities. On this
point, the chancellor's decree recites as follows:
"Came the complainants herein and moved the court

to refer this cause to the master to report from the record what properties, both real and personal, have been levied on by each of the complainants in each of the cases herein mentioned and consolidated herewith, that decree may be had under the prayer of the bill to marshal the securities and liens in this and said consolidated causes. This motion having been considered by the court, the court is of the opinion that complainants in the causes are not entitled to said relief prayed in the bill for marshaling said liens and securities, and said motion is accordingly overruled; to which action of the court said complainants making this motion severallly excepted.''

The doctrine of marshaling securities is thus stated in one of our cases: ''When one creditor has a security upon two funds, another having a security on one of them may, if necessary to the protection of his security, compel the other to resort to the fund not embraced in it, if it can be done without perjudice to the other creditor or injustice to the common debtor or third person having interest in the fund.'' *Gilliam et al.* v. *McCormack et al.*, 85 Tenn. (1 Pickle), 610, 4 S. W., 521.

In a later case, *White* v. *Fulghum*, 87 Tenn. (3 Pickle), 282, 10 S. W., 501, the doctrine is again stated as follows: ''Where one creditor has a lien upon two funds or two parcels of property, and another creditor has a lien upon but one of them, the former creditor will, in equity, be required to seek satisfaction first out of that fund or property upon which the other

creditor has no lien''—citing Story's Equity Jur., sec.
633; 3 Pomeroy, Eq. Jur., sec. 1414. But it is later in
the opinion said that: ''While that doctrine is well
recognized and far reaching in its effect, it has distinct
and plain limitations. It will not be enforced to the
prejudice of any creditor or third person, or in such
a manner as to do injustice to the holder himself''—
citing authorities among which are *Gilliam* v. *McCormack,* supra. One general principle deducible from
our cases above referred to and others, and also from
the section cited from Mr. Pomeroy, is that the marshaling of assets by a creditor is an equity pure and
simple, and, as such, must always yield to a legal right
where the two conflict, and this whether the legal right
be one existing in another creditor or one existing in
the common debtor. The dominance of the legal right
over the equity of marshaling was again enforced by
this court in *Meek* v. *Thompson,* 99 Tenn. (15 Pickle),
732, 42 S. W., 685. On the same point, see, also, *Whitmore* v. *Roscoe,* 112 Tenn. (4 Cates), 623-636, 85 S. W.,
860; *Gwynne* v. *Estes,* 82 Tenn. (14 Lea), 673. And in
Parr v. *Fumbanks,* 79 Tenn. (11 Lea), 394, there is in
the opinion of the court a statement of the doctrine of
marshaling taken from Waites' Actions and Defenses,
vol. 3, p. 174, as follows: ''Where parties, whose legal
rights being confined to one fund would fail to obtain
satisfaction of their just claim if left to the course of
law, equity interferes, in order to afford complete relief, by means of what is called marshaling of assets,
which is such an arrangement of the different funds,

under administration, as that they may, as far as possible, without injustice, be applied in satisfaction of
the various claims, notwithstanding certain parties
have a right to priority of satisfaction out of some
one or more of such funds." There is nothing in the
above definition in conflict with the doctrine as stated
in the other cases, but, in so far as the decision in
Parr v. *Fumbanks* denied the homestead right, that
case was overruled by *White* v. *Fulghum,*. 87 Tenn. (3
Pickle) 289, 10 S. W., 501. It was said in *Allen, Trustee,* v. *Gilliland,* 74 Tenn. (6 Lea), 534, that "as between successive attachments, the priority depends upon the actual levy, and the first levy must prevail."
Applying the foregoing principles to the case at bar,
we are unable to see any error in the holding of the
chancellor. The nonresident debtor's entire estate was
laid bare to attachment when he abandoned his residence in this state. He was then indebted beyond the
value of the estate which he left. No creditor filed a
general creditor's bill, but each creditor for himself
sought a priority of lien by attachment. If some of
his creditors were left behind in the race for priority,
they only suffered the fate which they sought to impose on other creditors. Such part of the debtor's estate as has been covered by attachment liens to the
extent of its value cannot be subjected by those creditors who were left behind in the race under the doctrine of marshaling because that equity yields to the
legal right of prior attachment liens fixed upon that
part of the debtor's estate by other creditors, and such
part of the debtor's estate as was not so covered by

prior attachment liens of other creditors the complainants to this cause or any creditor left behind in the
race for priority had the legal right to fix a lien upon
by attachment, and therefore did not need to invoke the
doctrine of marshaling. The court sustained the bill
in so far as its purpose was to consummate one sale
of all the land attached, and in so far as its purpose
was to determine in one suit the priorities of attaching creditors. This, we think, is as far as the bill
should have been sustained, and, under the bill as thus
sustained, we think the court may, upon the remand
and by its final decree, administer full relief to all attaching creditors according to the priority of their liens
acquired by the several attachments successively levied.

Passing now to a consideration of the points raised
by the assignments of error on behalf of the defendants, we dispose of one of these questions by saying,
as we have heretofore in this opinion, that we find no
error in the chancellor's decree in so far as it provided for the taxation of costs in this cause. The only
remaining question made on behalf of the defendant
attachment creditors in this consolidated cause is the
objection made by them in each of their motions to
quash, and in each of their objections to the report
of the clerk and master, based upon the ground that
each of the bills of complaint of the attaching creditors, was multifarious. There is no merit in this insistence, as it is clearly covered by our statutes. Section
6137 of Shannon's Code provides as follows: ''The
uniting in one bill of several matters of equity distinct

and unconnected against one defendant, is not multifariousness.''

It is insisted for defendants, however, that this statute does not apply to the several attachment suits brought by complainants, for the reason that complainants were, while in a court of equity, really invoking only legal remedies in that court. Even if it be true that the demands on which complainants' attachment suits were based were legal demands, yet our statute (section 6135, Shannon's Code) provides: ''Multifariousness, misjoinder, or nonjoinder of parties, is no sufficient cause for the dismissal of a bill in equity, unless objection is made by motion to dismiss or demurrer.'' No such objection was made in the several attachment suits brought by the complainants, and in this consolidated cause equitable remedies were invoked.

It results that the decree of the chancellor is affirmed, and the cause will be remanded for further proceedings.

MENIHAN CO. *v.* HOPKINS.

(*Nashville.* December Term, 1913.)

1. **MASTER AND SERVANT. Actions for wrongful discharge. Nature and form.**

   Where a contract of employment for one year at an annual salary of $1500, but payable in monthly installments of $125, was breached by the employer, the remedy of the employee was an action for damages for the breach, and not for salary for the period after the discharge, since readiness of the employee to perform after discharge is not equivalent to performance, and such a contract is to be treated on breach as an entire and individual one, for the breach of which only one action will lie. (*Post,* p. 26.)

   Cases cited and approved: Tarbox v. Hertenstein, 63 Tenn., 78; East Tennessee, etc., Co. v. Staub, 75 Tenn., 397; Pierce v. Tennessee, etc., Co., 173 U. S., 1; Clark v. Manchester, 151 N. H. 594; James v. Allen County, 44 Ohio St., 226; Doherty v. Schipper, 250 Ill., 128.

2. **JUDGMENT. Merger and bar. Contract of employment. Recovery for breach.**

   Where a servant is wrongfully discharged before the expiration of his contract of employment, any recovery in a suit by him for services for a part of such unexpired period before the period has expired becomes *res adjudicata,* barring a subsequent action for services during a subsequent portion of the period. (*Post,* p. 27.)

   Case cited and distinguished: Olmstead v. Bach, 78 Md., 132.

3. **MASTER AND SERVANT. Actions for wrongful discharge. Other employment as ground for reduction of damages.**

   Where plaintiff was employed by defendant as its salesman for one year, and was wrongfully discharged before that time, defendant could, in an action for the wrongful discharge, set off in mitigation of damages any compensation received by plaintiff under other employment during the unexpired period. (*Post, pp.* 28, 29.)

Cases cited and approved: Children of Israel v. Peres, 42 Tenn., 620; Allen v. Maronne, 93 Tenn., 161.

FROM DAVIDSON.

Appeal from the Circuit Court of Davidson County to the Court of Civil Appeals and by *certiorari* from the Court of Civil Appeals to the Supreme Court.— M. H. MEEKS, Judge.

G. B. KIRKPATRICK, for plaintiff.

STOKES & STOKES, for defendant.

MR. JUSTICE WILLIAMS delivered the opinion of the Court.

The defendant in error, plaintiff below, Hopkins, was employed by the Menihan Company as a salesman for one year, at compensation of $1500, salary to be paid monthly at the rate of $125 a month. He was wrongfully discharged near the middle of the contract year (about June 1st), but his salary up to that date was paid. He obtained other employment of a similar nature on September 15th, and for the remainder of the year received salary from his new employer at the rate of $150 per month.

This suit was begun December 8th to enforce compensation for ''salary account for the months of June,

July, August and September 15, 1911, at the rate of $125 per month, making total due $437.50."

The question is duly raised on the record whether the employer company is entitled to have deducted from the amount thus sued for, if due the employee for the period he was out of employment, the excess sums of $25 per month for each of the subsequent months of his employment by another, aggregating $87.50.

In the circuit court this claim of the company was disallowed, and the court of civil appeals in affirmance states that, so far as its investigation extended, the question was, on the facts, one of first instance.

We are of opinion, however, that on principle and on test by the analogies of the law these rulings are erroneous.

A contract of employment for a specific period, such as for a year, is to be, on breach, treated as an entire and indivisible one. *Tarbox* v. *Hertenstein,* 4 Baxt., 78.

And this is true notwithstanding a provision therein for payments in monthly insallment, or at fixed intervals within the year. *East Tennessee, etc., Co.* v. *Staub,* 7 Lea, 397, cited and followed in *Pierce* v. *Tennessee, etc., Co.,* 173 U. S., 1, 19 Sup. Ct., 335, 43 L. Ed., 591; *Clark* v. *Manchester,* 51 N. H., 594; *James* v. *Allen County,* 44 Ohio St., 226, 6 N. E., 246, 58 Am. Rep., 821; *Doherty* v. *Schipper,* 250 Ill., 128, 95 N. E., 74, 34 L. R. A. (N. S.), 557, 23 Ann. Cas., 364, and notes; 1 Labatt, Master and Serv. (2 Ed.), sec. 347.

In this state the doctrine of constructive service has been rejected, and the rule is, in accord with the majority of the courts of other jurisdictions, that readiness to perform on the part of the employee is not to be construed to be equivalent to performance, for remedial purposes. *Railroad* v. *Staub,* supra.

It follows that, so far as regards the period following a wrongful discharge, the contract being entire, only a single action based on the breach is maintainable. Authorities, supra. And that the bringing of suit by the employees for services during a part of such period before the year has expired (and damages thus ascertained) becomes *res adjudicata,* barring a second action for services during a subsequent portion of the period.

The fact that the employee has set forth in his pleading that his suit was for "salary for the months" above indicated cannot avail to split the entire contract so as to defeat the employer's right of set-off. The action in behalf of the employee was one for damages incident to the breach of the contract as an entire one, and not, after breach, for salary for any given month or months. In *Olmstead* v. *Bach,* 78 Md., 132, 27 Atl., 501, 22 L. R. A., 74, 44 Am. St. Rep., 273, the true rule is well stated: "The employee had no option as to the remedies which he might pursue. He was confined to an action for the recovery of damages which he had sustained by a breach of the contract, because successive actions instituted for the recovery of fractions of the same aggregate damages cannot be supported. His suit before the magistrate was, whatever it purported to be, a suit for the breach of the contract of hiring. . . . There was but one dismissal and but one breach, and the plaintiff could not split up his cause of action, recovering a part of his damages in one suit and the remainder afterwards in other suits, for that single breach." A right of action arose, not for unearned wages or salary as such, but for damages for the breach of the contract.

We hold, therefore, that when the contract in question was broken, the employee's cause of action was not for salary, but one for damages growing out of the breach of the contract, which was, as seen, an entire one.

In ascertaining these damages, they will be viewed as being aggregate for the entire term, for the purposes of the complaining employee; and, by virtue of the same principle, any right to deduction, by way of mitigation of damages, arising at any time during the year in behalf of the employer, must be taken into reckoning. Otherwise the employee as plaintiff would be permitted to elect to segregate and include for remedial purposes that part of the year during or in respect of which no factor of mitigation arose, and exclude a subsequent portion of the period in which such counterright did arise.

It is, of course, the rule that whatever the employee has, during the term, in fact received as compensation under a contract with another employer, after dismissal, must be deducted. *Children of Israel* v.

Peres, 2 Cold., 620; *Allen* v. *Maronne,* 93 Tenn., 161, 23 S. W., 113; 1 Labatt, M. & S. (2 Ed.), sec. 390.

For error thus indicated, the writ of *certiorari* is granted, and the cause remanded for a new trial; costs of the appeal will be paid by appellee.

PHILIP CAREY ROOFING & MANUFACTURING CO. *v.* BLACK.

(*Nashville.* December Term, 1913.)

1. **MASTER AND SERVANT.** Injuries to servant. Defective ladder. Simple tool. Assumed risk.

Where plaintiff was injured by the breaking of a section of a ladder used to reach the roof of a house, such ladder as so used was a simple tool, the defective character of which was a risk which the servant ordinarily was required to assume as incident to his employment. (*Post. pp.* 32, 33.)

Case cited and approved: Sivley v. Nixon Mining & Drill Co., 128 Tenn., 675.

2. **MASTER AND SERVANT.** Injuries to servant. Defective ladder. Master's knowledge of defect. Effect.

Where defendant's superintendent had been notified of a defect in a ladder, by the subsequent breaking of which plaintiff was injured, but notwithstanding such notification the superintendent insisted that the ladder was safe, defendant would be liable for plaintiff's injury while using the ladder without notice of the defect, which was not of such a nature as to be discoverable by observation which would naturally accompany its use. (*Post, p.* 34.)

Cases cited and approved: Guthrie v. Railroad, 79 Tenn., 372; Stork v. Charles Stolper Cooperage Co., 127 Wis., 318; Mercer v. Atlantic Coast Line R. Co., 154 N. C. 399.

3. **MASTER AND SERVANT.** Injuries to servant. Tools. Duty to furnish. Inspection.

Although the master is not required to inspect simple tools, previously furnished to the employee, to discover defects of which the employee using such implements should be aware, and although generally no inspection of a simple tool may be necessary at the time it is delivered to an employee, yet if the master furnishes such a tool, with a dangerous defect of which he has actual knowledge, he is negligent. (*Post, p.* 35.)

Roofing & Mfg. Co. v. Black.

4. **MASTER AND SERVANT.**   Injuries to servant.   Descending ladder.   Contributory negligence.

A servant, who was injured by the breaking of a defective ladder, was not negligent as a matter of law because he descended the ladder with his back to the ladder, instead of backwards, which would have been more safe, under the rule that where an employee has two methods of doing his work, one of which is safe and the other dangerous, he is negligent if he adopts the dangerous method and is injured. (*Post*, *pp*. 35, 36.)

5. **NEGLIGENCE.**   Contributory negligence.   Questions for court or jury.

Questions of negligence and contributory negligence are ordinarily for the jury, though the facts are undisputed, if intelligent minds may draw different conclusions as to whether, under the circumstances conceded, plaintiff's conduct has been that of an ordinary prudent man. (*Post*, *pp*. 36, 37.)

Cases cited and approved: Traction Co. v. Carroll, 113 Tenn., 514; Traction Co. v. Brown, 115 Tenn., 323; Cummings v. Wichita R., etc., Co., 68 Kan., 218; Vindicator Consol. Gold Min. Co. v. Firstbrook, 36 Colo., 498; Merchants' Ice Co. v. Bargholt, 129 Ky., 60; Burch v. Sou. Pacific Co., 32 Nev., 75.

6. **MASTER AND SERVANT.**   Injuries to servant.   Request to charge.

Where plaintiff was injured by the breaking of a defective ladder, and defendant claimed that the ladder was a simple tool the defective character of which was a risk that plaintiff assumed, it was error to refuse requests submitting the doctrine of simple tools. (*Post*, *pp*. 37, 38.)

FROM DAVIDSON.

Appeal from Circuit Court, Davidson County,— M. H. MEEKS, Judge.

THOMAS H. MALONE and LARKIN E. CROUCH, for appellant.

PARKS & BELL and R. B. C. HOWELL, for appellee.

MR. JUSTICE GREEN delivered the opinion of the Court.

The defendant in error, Black, brought this suit to recover damages for injuries alleged to have been sustained by him while he was in the employ of the plaintiff in error. He was foreman of a painter's crew, and when descending a ladder from the roof of a house on which he was at work, one of the rounds broke and he had a fall, as the result of which he sues.

There was a judgment in his favor for $700 in the court below, which was affirmed by the court of civil appeals. The case is before us on writ of *certiorari,* granted, to the action of the latter court.

A motion for peremptory instructions in its favor was made by the defendant below, which was overruled by the trial court. It is with reference to this action of the trial court that the principal controversy has been waged in this court and in the court of civil appeals.

The first ground upon which the motion is predicated is that a ladder, such as the one used by defendant in error, is a simple tool, and it is insisted that defendant in error assumed the risk of its use, and the master owed him no duty of inspection in regard to the same.

The ladder which broke seems to have been a portion of a sectional ladder. There was nothing complicated about it, and only this particular section was in use when defendant in error had his fall. Such a ladder so used is a simple tool, and a servant ordinarily does assume any risk incident to its employment. We have expressly so held in the late case of *Harry Sivley* v. *Nixon Mining & Drill Co.*, Knoxville, 128 Tenn., 675, 165 S. W., —, 1913.

It was said in this case that: "An ordinary ladder falls within the class of simple tools, in respect of a defect in which the employer is held not liable on the ground that a defect in such a simple tool must be obvious to its user by whom any risk of danger therefrom must be held to be assumed."

In the case under consideration, however, proof was introduced by plaintiff below tending to show that the superintendent of plaintiff in error had been notified of a defect in this ladder by another foreman who had formerly used it. This foreman testifies he discovered that the ladder was defective, and refused to employ it in his work, that he was questioned by the superintendent as to why he put it aside, and that he (the foreman) then called the attention of the superintendent to the defects. The foreman testifies, further, that the superintendent differed from him as to the condition of the ladder, and insisted that it was safe. All this happened a short while before plaintiff below sustained his fall.

This proof takes the case out of the authority of *Silvey* v. *Nixon Mining & Drill Co.*, supra, in so far as peremptory instructions are concerned.

The general principle is that a master is bound to inspect tools or appliances furnished by him to his workmen, and to keep them in sufficient repair. If, however, the tools or appliances are common or sim-

ple tools, there is an exception to this general rule.
The presumption in such cases is that the servant is
equally conversant with the nature of such simple or
common tools, and is in as good a position as the master to discover any defects therein.

The master's opportunities for learning of a fault
in a tool of this kind are no better than the opportunities of the servant. By reason of the character of such
an implement, no superiority of knowledge on the part
of the master exists, or can be presumed, as to defects
therein. The foundation of the simple tool doctrine
is the assumption that the knowledge of the master
and servant must be equal.

Such a presumption cannot be indulged where the
master has actual notice of a defect, where the proof
shows his knowledge is superior. If the master is, as
a matter of fact, cognizant that a tool with which he
furnishes an employee is in such a condition as to render it use by the employee dangerous to the latter, he
will be liable for an injury sustained by the employee
in the use of such an implement, where the defect is
not known to the employee, and is not of such a nature
as to be discovered by that observation which would
naturally accompany its use. *Guthrie* v. *Railroad*, 11
Lea, 372, 47 Am. Rep., 286; *Stork* v. *Charles Stolper
Cooperage Co.*, 127 Wis., 318, 106 N. W., 841, 7 Ann.
Cas., 339; *Mercer* v. *Atlantic Coast Line R. Co.*, 154
N. C., 399, 70 S. E., 742, Ann. Cas. 1912A, 1002.

In the latter case it is apparently held that the duty
of a master to exercise ordinary care to furnish rea-

sonably proper tools to his servants applies to simple, as well as to complicated tools, and the rule is relaxed only as to the duty of inspection thereafter. See, however, cases in note following report of this decision in Ann. Cas. 1912A, 1002-1004.

Although the master is not required to inspect simple tools, previously furnished to the employee, to discover defects of which the employee using such implements should be aware, and although generally no inspection of a simple tool may be necessary at the time it is delivered to an employee, yet if the master furnishes such a tool, with a dangerous defect of which he has actual knowledge, he is negligent. He should not be permitted to expose the servant to such a risk, particularly if the defect is of such a character that it might be overlooked by the servant. There is testimony in this record that the defective condition of the round of the ladder which broke was not readily discoverable.

For the reasons above stated the trial judge properly overruled the first ground of the motion to direct a verdict.

It is next urged that the injuries of the defendant in error were sustained as a result of his contributory negligence. It is said that he was descending this ladder at the time he fell, face foremost; that in this way, he put all his weight on the rounds of the ladder, and was not in a position to hold to the sides of the ladder with his hands when the round broke, as he would have been if he had come down backwards.

It is urged that when an employee has two methods in which to do his work, one of which is safe and the other dangerous, he cannot hold the master liable when he adopts the latter method and is injured. This is a correct principle; but, in the absence of proof, the court is not willing to say, as a matter of law, that the defendant in error was guilty of such contributory negligence in descending the ladder in the manner he did as to bar his recovery.

It is insisted that the proper use of a ladder is of common knowledge, and that the court should view the act of defendant in error as it would the act of a person who jumps from a moving train, and hold him guilty of contributory negligence without proof. We think, however, there might be some reasonable difference of opinion as to the proper manner in which workmen may use a ladder. They frequently ascend and descend with material and tools in their hands, without holding, and are expected so to do. While we know it would have been safer for defendant in error to have descended this ladder backwards, with his hands on the rails, yet we would not be justified, upon our own knowledge, in imputing such negligence to him on account of the manner of his descent, under the facts and circumstances of this case, as to defeat his action.

The question of contributory negligence, as well as the question of negligence, is ordinarily for the jury. Even though the facts be undisputed, if intelligent minds might draw different conclusions as to whether, under circumstances conceded, the conduct of a plaintiff was that of an ordinarily prudent man, the matter should be left to the jury. The court should draw no inference when in doubt, but only in those cases where the evidence is without material conflict, and such that all reasonable men must reach the same conclusion therefrom. It is only in cases where the evidence is susceptible of no other fair inference that the court is justified in instructing the jury, as a matter of law, that the plaintiff has been guilty of contributory negligence which would bar his recovery. *Traction Co.* v. *Carroll,* 113 Tenn., 514, 82 S. W., 313; *Traction Co.* v. *Brown,* 115 Tenn., 323, 89 S. W., 319; *Cummings* v. *Wichita R., etc., Co.,* 68 Kan., 218, 74 Pac., 1104, 1 Ann. Cas., 708; *Vindicator Consol. Gold Min. Co.* v. *Firstbrook,* 36 Colo., 498, 86 Pac., 313, 10 Ann. Cas., 1108; *Merchants' Ice Co.* v. *Bargholt,* 129 Ky., 60, 110 S. W., 364, 16 Ann. Cas., 965; *Burch* v. *Sou. Pacific Co.,* 32 Nev., 75, 104 Pac., 225, Ann. Cas., 1912B, 1166.

We must decline, therefore, to say that the defendant in error as a matter of law was guilty of such contributory negligence as to defeat his suit. This question should have been left to the jury under a proper charge.

The defendant below offered several requests presenting its theory as to the use of simple tools, and as to the contributory negligence of the plaintiff there. These requests were refused by the circuit judge. While, for reasons stated above, a verdict should not have been directed, the doctrine of simple tools should have been charged, with the qualifications herein indicated. His honor did not charge the doctrine of simple tools at all, and his charge upon contributory negligence was quite meager; the theory of plaintiff in error was not fairly submitted, and the whole case went to the jury under a charge insufficiently stating the rules of law applicable thereto.

The case will accordingly be reversed, for errors in the charge, and remanded for another trial.

McMillan *et al. v.* McKee *et al.*

(*Nashville.   December Term, 1913.*)

1. EASEMENTS.   Selection of way.   Selection by owner.

Where a way by necessity, such as a way over private grounds
to a burial ground, has not been selected, the owner of the
servient estate has a prior right to select the way, provided
it be reasonable; but the route is to be determined by the
reasonable convenience of both parties, and not by the sole
interest of either.   (*Post, pp.* 41, 42.)

Cases cited and approved: Osborne v. Wise, L. R., 2 Ch. Div.,
968; Holmes v. Seley, 19 Wend. (N. Y.), 507, 510; Russell v.
Jackson, 2 Pick. (Mass.), 574; Ricley v. Welsh, 149 Ind., 214.

2. EASEMENTS.   Way by necessity.

A way by necessity passes by the presumed intention of the
grantor, and hence should ordinarily be over such a route as
the grantor would reasonably select.   (*Post, pp.* 42, 43.)

3. EASEMENTS.   Jurisdiction.   Selection of way.

A court of equity has jurisdiction to locate a way by necessity.
(*Post, p.* 43.)

Cases cited and approved: Pearne v. Coal Co., 90 Tenn., 619;
Ballard v. Titus, 157 Cal., 673; Blum v. Weston, 102 Cal., 362;
Gardner v. Webster, 64 N. H. 522.

Certiorari from the Chancery Court of Wilson County to the Supreme Court.—J. W. STOUT, Chancellor.

WALTER S. FAULKNER, for plaintiffs.

H. F. STRATTON, for defendants.

MR. JUSTICE.WILLIAMS delivered the opinion of the Court.

Complainants' bill was filed to invoke the aid of equity in the location of an easement of way over their lands to a private burial ground situate thereon, and in the bill complainants define the route deemed by them proper and convenient for the use of defendants, entitled to resort to the graveyard where their dead are buried and may be buried; and complainants pray for the adoption of this route by the court.

It appears that burial parties attending interments in this burial ground had not pursued any definite route so as to define the course of the way by user. The complainants seek to have the court locate a route that would avoid going over their tillable lands, but would follow, broadly speaking, the property lines around to the cemetery; while defendants insist that this route is unreasonable, and more than twice as long, starting from the point of entry on the tract of land to the public highway, as the direct line contended for by them.

It is urged by the defendants that they, as owners of the dominant estate, are entitled to locate the route of the way.

The burial ground is of the character of that dealt with in *Hines* v. *State,* 126 Tenn., 1, 149 S. W., 1058, 42 L. R. A. (N. S.), 1138, and the easement of way arises as an easement by necessity, to be used for ingress and egress for the purposes of burial, visiting, repairing, and keeping in proper condition the graves and grounds around same, to be exercised in a reasonable manner so as not to unnecessarily injure the owner of the farm in its cultivation and use.

The contention of defendants that the right of location, in the first instance, is with them is an erroneous one.

After much fluctuation in the early decisions, the English Court of Chancery, in *Osborne* v. *Wise,* L. R., 2 Ch. Div., 968, announced the rule to be that the primary right of selecting the route of an easement of necessity was with the grantor, but was one to be exercised in a way that would respond to the interests of the grantee, as well as his own.

In America the same rule obtains, and has been thus declared:

"Appellants (the landowner) contend that they had a right to choose where the way should be located. When no prior use of the way has been made, and the same is to be located for the first time, the owner of the land over which the same is to pass has the right to choose it, provided he does so in a reasonable manner, having due regard to the rights and interests of the owner of the dominant estate. But, if the owner of the land fail to select such way when requested, the party who has the right thereto may select a suitable route for the same, having due regard to the convenience of the owner of the servient estate." *Holmes* v. *Seely,* 19 Wend. (N. Y.), 507, 510; *Russell* v. *Jackson,* 2 Pick. (Mass.), 574; *Ritchey* v. *Welsh,* 149 Ind., 214, 48 N. E., 1031, 40 L. R. A., 105.

Where, as in the present case, there has been no location, and prior travel has been along no particular or definite route, it would seem that the court when called on to locate should defer to the selection of the landowner, if that be reasonable, as it is found to be in fact on the record.

The route when thus fixed by the court is to be determined, however, not by the sole interest of either of the parties, but by the reasonable convenience of both.

The rule, thus declared, is logical, as well as just, in that such way of necessity, arising by implication as an incident of grant, passes by the presumed intention of the grantor, and therefore should be over such a

McMillan v. McKee.

route as could be attributed reasonably to the grantor.

The jurisdiction of a court of equity to locate the route, not fixed by contract or user, is clear. If the location be contested, the controversy might not be settled by the negative results of many actions at law. Equity can move to fix the route affirmatively and specifically. This court, in *Pearne* v. *Coal Co.*, 90 Tenn., 619, 631, 18 S. W., 402, assumed, without discussion, the existence of jurisdiction, and exercised the power.

That a court of equity will entertain a bill for the location of the route of such a way is held in *Ballard* v. *Titus,* 157 Cal., 673, 678, 110 Pac., 118; *Blum* v. *Weston,* 102 Cal., 362, 369, 36 Pac., 778, 41 Am. St. Rep., 188; *Gardner* v. *Webster,* 64 N. H., 522, 15 Atl., 144; Jones on Easements, sec. 337.

Writ of *certiorari* granted; affirmed.

KING *v.* TENNESSEE CENTRAL RAILROAD CO.

(*Nashville.*   December Term, 1913.)

1. **CARRIERS.** Accidents to persons on track. Statutory lookout and warning.

Plaintiff and his companion, desiring to board a train in the nighttime at a flag station, signaled it to stop. By reason of the fact that the signal was not given in time, the train ran about 100 yards beyond the station before it stopped. Plaintiff started down the track toward the train, but was struck by it as it was backing to the station at the rate of 3 or 4 miles an hour. The train had the usual rear lights, and the light inside the coach shown out through the glass of the rear door; but plaintiff testified that he did not see that the train was in motion until it struck him. *Held* that, in such a case, Shannon's Code, secs. 1574-1576, requiring certain lookouts on, and warnings to be given by, moving trains, does not apply, since the movement of the train in this case was a switching in its depot grounds, to which the statutes are not applicable. (*Post, pp.* 50-53.)

Code cited and construed: Secs. 1166, 1167, 1168 (T. & S. and 1858); secs. 1547, 1575, 1576 (S.).

Case cited and distinguished: Patton v. Railroad Co., 89 Tenn., 372.

Cases cited and approved: Railroad Co. v. Rush, 83 Tenn., 150; Cox v. Railroad Co., 2 Leg. Rep., 168; Railroad v. Pugh, 95 Tenn., 421.

2. **CARRIERS.** Injuries to person on track. Contributory negligence.

The railroad was not liable to the plaintiff under the common law, for the plaintiff had no legal right to suppose that the company would receive him as a passenger at the point where the train first stopped, and his action in walking down to meet the train, without taking any care or precaution, was gross contributory negligence. (*Post, pp.* 53, 54.)

FROM WILSON.

Appeal from the Circuit Court of Wilson County to the Court of Civil Appeals and by *certiorari* from the Court of Civil Appeals to the Supreme Court.— JNO. E. RICHARDSON, Judge.

WALTER S. FAULKNER, for plaintiff.

J. R. SMITH, and JULIAN CAMPBELL and LILLARD THOMPSON, for defendant.

MR. JUSTICE BUCHANAN delivered the opinion of the Court.

This suit was begun in the circuit court, and was there prosecuted to judgment in favor of King for the sum of $2500 and costs. It was then taken to the court of civil appeals by the railroad company. That court reversed and remanded the cause for a new trial; and, based on that judgment, two petitions for *certiorari* have been filed in this court—one by King, insisting that the judgment of the trial court should have been affirmed; and one by the railroad company, insisting that both the trial court and the court of civil appeals were in error in not holding that it was entitled to a directed verdict, which was seasonably requested by it at the close of the evidence in chief offered by King, and again at the close of all evidence in the trial of the case in the circuit court.

The cause of action is predicated on personal injuries sustained by King as the result of a collision with a passenger coach, to wit, loss of an arm and other less serious injuries. The declaration was in two counts—the first averring a breach by the company of its common law duty; the second averring a failure on its part to observe the statutory precautions as the proximate cause of the injuries. To this declaration the company pleaded not guilty.

By the evidence of King, and otherwise, it appears that, at the time he was injured, he was living with Mr. Smith, who resided about one mile from Eagansville, a flag station on the line of the railroad company, and in company with Henry Wood, colored (King being also colored), he went to Eagansville to take passage on the passenger train bound for Lebanon, where he expected to attend a supper; that he had often prior to that time taken passage on that train at Eagansville, his habit being to go to Labanon from that station every two weeks; that he knew how to get on the train, which way was by flagging the train by means of lighting a piece of paper, which was done on the night he was injured, the flagging being done on that night by Henry Wood, who stood in the middle of the track and lighted the paper; that on the former occasions the train had always stopped at the station, but on the night he was injured it ran beyond the station about 100 yards and stopped. He saw it when it stopped, knew it had stopped, and, instead of waiting where he was until the train came back, he concluded that it was waiting for him, and that he would go up and board it where it stood; and so he and his companion, Henry Wood, left the station and walked up the track toward the train without notice to those in charge of the train; and the latter, expecting to find those intending passengers who had flagged the train at the flag station, began to back the train to that point, and while so backing the rear car of the train collided with King, knocked him down, cut off his arm, and otherwise injured him. No comprehensible reason is given either by King or his companion, Wood, for their failure to observe the backing train as it moved slowly back at the rate of three or four miles an hour to the flag station. It was after dark; the back door of the rear car was open; there were lights in the car. King and his companion do not deny these facts, and yet they say they did not see the rear car as it backed down the track toward them; and King says that the first knowledge he had of its movement toward him was when it struck him. He testifies that after his injuries, and manifestly while the car was still in motion, he crawled out from under it, and laid beside the track while the train passed on, and while it stopped at the flag station; and while, after it stopped at the flag station, it again started on its way to Lebanon, during all this time he was lying close to the rails, where he had received his injury.

King testifies that the point where he was struck by the train was "mighty nigh 100 yards" from the flag station. He admits that he made no outcry to attract the attention of employees in charge of the train when he received his injury, while the train passed on its way to the flag station, and during its stop at the flag station, or during the time the train passed him after it stopped at the flag station on its way to Lebanon. His companion Henry Wood, also admits that he in no way made his presence known to the train crew during the time the train was making the movements aforesaid. He testifies that, when the train struck King, he (Wood) sprang from the track, and thus escaped injury; and after the train had gone on its way to Lebanon, he found his injured companion, and with him went back to the farm of Mr. Smith about one mile from the flag station, where King had been living, and where during the same night King received surgical attention.

The failure of King and Wood to make known to the employees in charge of the train the injuries which King had received is entirely unexplained upon this record. The explanation which King offers is that he was in misery. No such explanation can be offered for Wood, and so far as King is concerned, it is an explanation which does not explain. Their apparent concealment of their presence, and of the injury which King had sustained, at a time when he was manifestly in desperate need of immediate surgical attention, brings seriously into question the truth of their entire evidence in the cause.

The flagman on the train testifies in substance that he was on the rear end of the rear car as the train was

backed toward the flag station with a white light in his
hand, and that, as the train backed, the air whistle on
the rear end was blown at short intervals from the
time the train started backing until it reached the station; that during all this time he was looking ahead
to see if anyone was on the track and saw no one; that
he could see some ten or twelve feet down the track
by means of the reflection from the light in his hand
and of the light from the rear coach; that there were
lights on the rear of the train, which showed red from
the rear and green from the front; that the inside of
the coach was lighted; that the rear door of the rear
coach was glass above the handle; that when the train,
upon backing up, reached the flag station, it stopped,
and that he was still on the rear platform; that nobody
got on at the flag station, and the train pulled out therefrom.

His evidence is corroborated on most of these points
by other employees in charge of the train, but the evidence of these witnesses was contradicted by evidence
introduced on behalf of King; but it is undisputed in
the record that the train was backing very slowly toward the station, the rate of speed being not more than
three or four miles an hour. King says "it was eased
along."

The first point for decision under these facts is
whether the rights of the parties to this suit should be
determined under sections 1166, 1167, 1168, of the Code
of 1858, now appearing as sections 1574, 1575, 1576,

Shannon's Code or whether such rights are to be determined according to the principles of the common law.

We think the statutes above mentioned do not apply in the present case.

In *Patton* v. *Railroad Co.,* 89 Tenn. (5 Pickle), 372, 15 S. W., 919, 12 L. R. A., 184, where the person injured was walking upon the track, and was overtaken by a train of freight cars, and stepped aside until the train passed, when he returned to the track and resumed his journey in the rear of the train which had passed him, and was overtaken and killed by some freight cars which had belonged to the train which had just passed him, but had become detached therefrom, and were following downgrade at the time of the injury, this court, speaking through Judge Lurton, held that the statutes above mentioned did not apply, saying: "The case provided for by the statute is that of a train pulled by a locomotive, and the precautions are those required to be observed by those servants upon the engine, and have regard to obstacles on the track in front of or ahead of the engine," etc.

In *Railroad Co.* v. *Rush,* 83 Tenn. (15 Lea), 150, construing these statutes, it was pointed out by Judge Cooper, speaking for this court, that in view of the stringent terms of the statutes and the manifest object of the legislature the court had not extended their provisions to every case which might be embraced in their general language; and it was there said that the statutes were intended for the benefit of the general public, and not for the servants of the company whose negligence caused or contributed to cause the accident. Cases illustrative of the exceptions to the operation of the statutes are cited in the opinion, and it is there noted that the statutes do not apply for the benefit of a stranger when the company is making up a switching train within its yards; the case of *Cox* v. *Railroad Co.*, 2 Leg. Rep., 168, 1 Shan. Cas., 475, being cited to sustain the point.

The case of *Railroad* v. *Pugh,* 95 Tenn. (11 Pickle), 421, 32 S. W., 311, is very much in point. There the plaintiff relied in his declaration upon an averment that he was struck and seriously injured by certain detached cars of the defendant while he was walking between the sidetrack and depot platform at Charleston, and that the collision and injury resulted from the making of a running switch, by which the cars were driven by the depot at an excessive rate of speed, having no one on the lookout ahead. This court, in disposing of that case, held that the statutory precautions did not apply, in cases where employees of a railroad company were engaged in the distribution of cars "in the 'making up' of trains, and in other necessary switching in and upon its yards, depot grounds, and sidetracks;" the reason given for the ruling being that "it is not possible, in such cases, to have the engine always in front of the moving portions of the train, yet the doing of the things indicated is absolutely indispensable to the efficient operation of railroads."

We think the present case falls clearly within the principle announced in the case last above referred to. In that case, as above shown, the injury occurred to one not an employee of the company, but who was at the time of receiving the injury at one of the depot places of the company. In the present case, the movement of the train by which King was injured was, within the meaning of our cases, a movement of the train at one of the depots of the company. The station at which the injury occurred was, to be sure, a flag station; but this fact can make no difference in the application of the principle. To that station King had gone for the purpose of taking passage upon the train which injured him. To his signal given at that station the engineer of the train had responded by stopping the train. It is an undisputed fact in the record that the failure to stop in the first instance immediately at the flag station was due entirely to the fault of complainant and his companion, who gave the signal to the engineer when the train was only 150 feet from the station, and after receiving the signal the train was stopped as soon as practicable. It is also clear that, in obedience to this signal which the engineer had received, the train at the time of the injury was backing to receive as passengers King and his companion, who had given the signal.

King had no legal right to suppose that the company would accept him as a passenger at a point 150 yards beyond the platform, where he says the train stopped in obedience to his signal; nor had he the right to act upon this supposition, in the absence of an express invitation of the company so to do. It was the right of the company to select the place where it would receive King as a passenger.

The movement of the train backward from the point where it first stopped was, within the meaning of *Railroad* v. *Pugh,* supra, a switching in and upon its depot grounds, and in the execution of that movement, and in the injury which King suffered, the common law, and not the statutes, measure the rights of the parties. It is clear that the legislature, in the passage of the statutes, never intended them to apply to a case like this. In proper cases for their application the statutes are wise and beneficient, but to apply them here would work a gross and manifest miscarriage of justice.

Turning now to a consideration of the rights of the parties under the principles of the common law, we hold that under the facts of this record the gross negligence of King was the proximate cause of the injuries which he received. Had he remained at the flag station, as it was right and his duty to do, his signal would have been obeyed, and he would have been able to board the train without injury. We have already observed that he had no right to suppose or act upon the supposition that the company would receive him as a passenger at the point where the train first stopped.

His act in abandoning a place of safety, walking down to meet an approaching train, without heed or care apparently of the consequences, can only be characterized as one of gross negligence, and clearly the proximate cause of his injuries.

It results that the company was entitled to the peremptory instruction which it requested at the trial of this cause, and therefore the petition for *certiorari* filed by King is denied. The petition of the company is granted, the judgment of the court of civil appeals is reversed, and the suit dismissed at King's cost.

ST. PAUL FIRE & MARINE INSURANCE CO. *et al. v.* KIRK-
PATRICK *et al.*

(*Nashville.* December Term, 1913.)

1. INSURANCE.   Fire Insurance.   Waiver of forfeiture.

Forfeiture of a fire policy by the sale by insured of the damaged
property, when the policy gave the company the option of
taking the part of the articles saved from the fire at the appraised value, was waived by the company by thereafter demanding an arbitration and appraisement of the loss; such
demand being equivalent to an admission of liability on the
policy. (*Post, p.* 63.)

2. INSURANCE.   Fire Insurance.   Admission of liability.

A demand by a fire insurance company for an appraisement and
arbitration pursuant to the policy is equivalent to an admission
of liability thereon. (*Post, p.* 64.)

Cases cited and approved: Hickerson v. Insurance Companies,
96 Tenn., 193.

**3. INSURANCE.   Fire Insurance.   Arbitration of loss.   Refusal
to arbitrate.   Effect.**

If insured fails to comply with a demand by the company for
arbitration of the loss pursuant to an arbitration clause, he
cannot sue thereon, and such refusal, if unreasonably persisted
in, forfeits the policy, and, if the company refuses such a demand, insured may sue on the policy at once. (*Post, p.* 64.)

4. INSURANCE.   Fire Insurance.   Appraisement.   Fraud.

If an arbitration of the amount of loss fails because of fraud or
intermeddling by insured, he cannot sue on the policy; and,
if it fails by the fraud, etc., of the company, insured may
abandon the arbitration and sue on the policy. (*Post, pp.* 64, 65.)

5. **INSURANCE.** **Fire Insurance.** **Arbitration of loss.** **Reappraisement.**

If the parties have appointed appraisers to determine the loss pursuant to an arbitration clause in a fire policy, and the appraisement has failed without fault of either party, insured cannot be required to select another arbitrator. (*Post, pp.* 65-68.)

Cases cited and approved: Jerrils v. German American Insurance Co., 82 Kan., 320; Spring Garden Insurance Co. v. Amusement Syndicate Co., 178 Fed., 519; Western Assurance Co. v. Decker, 98 Fed., 381; Connecticut Fire Insurance Co. v. Cohen, 97 Md., 294; Shawnee Fire Insurance Co. v. Pontfield, 110 Md., 353; Bretzfelder v. Merchant's Insurance Co., 123 N. C., 164; Bernhard v. Insurance Co., 79 Conn., 388; Globe, etc., Insurance Co. v. Johnson (Ky.), 127 S. W., 765; Coffin v. German Fire Insurance Co., 142 Mo. App., 295; Western Assurance Co. v. Hall, 120 Ala., 547; Niagara Fire Insurance Co. v. Bishop, 154 Ill., 9.

6. **INSURANCE.** **Fire Insurance.** **Arbitration.**

Upon the filing of a bill by a fire insurance company to set aside an award of arbitrators, the court acquired jurisdiction of the controversy, and could set aside the award and enforce the policies under a cross-bill praying for their enforcement, without the selection of new arbitrators. (*Post, p.* 68.)

Cases cited and approved: Dixie Fire Insurance Co. et al. v. American Confectionery Co., 124 Tenn., 247; Continental Insurance Co. v. Garrett, 125 Fed., 590.

7. **INSURANCE.** **Fire Insurance.** **Award of arbitrators.** **Actions to set aside.** **Cross-bill.**

In a suit by fire companies to set aside an award of arbitrators, defendant could file a cross-bill to enforce the award, or, in the alternative, to enforce the policies, if the award was set aside. (*Post, p.* 68.)

Acts cited and construed: Acts 1901, ch. 141, sec. 1.

Insurance Co. v. Kirkpatrick.

8. INSURANCE.   Fire insurance.   Nonpayment of premiums. Penalties.   Demand for payment.

Under Acts 1901, ch. 141, sec. 1, providing that insurance companies who refuse to pay the loss within 60 days after demand by the policy holder shall be liable to pay the holder, in addition to the loss, a sum not exceeding 25 per cent, on the liability for said loss, if such refusal to pay is not in good faith, a formal demand for payment must be made by the insurer after maturity of the policy, and, if the company fails to pay within 60 days thereafter, insured may sue on the policy or award and recover the penalty, if the refusal was not in good faith. (*Post, p.* 69.)

9. Insurance.   Fire insurance.   Payment of loss.   Demand.

If no demand is made for arbitration of the loss under a fire policy, it matures, for the purpose of authorizing a formal demand for payment in order to fix the penalty pursuant to Acts 1901, ch. 141, sec. 1, at the expiration of the number of days fixed in the policy for maturing; but, if the policy provides for payment a certain number of days after the filing of an award, the date of maturity would be governed by the number of days so fixed. (*Post, p.* 70.)

Cases cited and approved: Mutual Reserve Fire Insurance Co. v. Tuchfeld, 159 Fed., 833; Lester v. Insurance Co., 55 Ga., 475, 480; Iowa Insurance Co. v. Lewis, 187 U. S., 335.

10. INSURANCE.   Fire insurance.   Nonpayment of loss.   Penalties.

If an award of arbitrators as to the amount of loss under a fire policy was defective, and the company sued to set the award aside, no penalty could be imposed under Acts 1901, ch. 141, sec. 1, imposing a penalty on the company for a bad-faith refusal to pay the loss within 60 days after demand; the time for making a formal demand for payment not having arrived. (*Post, p.* 71.)

ON PETITION FOR A REHEARING.

11. INSURANCE.   Penal statute.   Strict construction.

Acts 1901, ch. 141, sec. 1, imposing a penalty on insurance companies refusing in bad faith to pay the loss within 60 days after demand is made, is penal, and must be strictly construed. (*Post*, *p.* 72.)

12. INSURANCE.   Fire Insurance.   Nonpayment of loss.   Penalty.

Under Acts 1901, ch. 141, sec. 1, providing that, upon the refusal of an insurance company to pay the loss within 60 days after demand, it shall be liable to pay a certain sum as a penalty, if the refusal was not in good faith, the failure to pay the loss within 60 days after demand would place the burden on the company of showing that such failure or refusal was in good faith. (*Post*, *p.* 73.)

FROM BEDFORD.

Appeal from Chancery Court, Bedford County.— W. S. BEARDEN, Chancellor.

R. LEE BARTELS, for appellants.

THOMAS N. GREER, for appellees.

MR. CHIEF JUSTICE NEIL delivered the opinion of the Court.

The original bill was filed for the purpose of setting aside an award of arbitrators appointed by the respective parties under five several policies on the property of the defendant, which had been destroyed by fire. The property consisted of a stock of goods and fixtures in the town of Shelbyville, Tenn. The complainants were four of the insurance companies that had issued policies on the property. The fifth one of the companies submitted to the award and paid its part of the loss. A cross-bill was filed by Mrs. Kirkpatrick against the original complainants, seeking in the first place to enforce the award, and, in the alternative, to enforce the policies irrespective of the award, in case the court should set aside the award under the application for that relief made in the original bill. The cross-bill also sought to enforce the penalty which is authorized under the Acts of 1901, ch. 141, against insurance companies which refuse to pay the loss when such refusal is not in good faith. A jury was demanded by one of the parties, and the case was tried by the chancellor and the jury, in accordance with the forms of law appertaining to that subject.

The issues were in the form of questions submitted to the jury. They were as follows, together with the answers which the jury made thereto:

"(1) What was the amount of loss or damage to the stock of merchandise of Mrs. Ada Kirkpatrick, caused by the fire referred to in the pleadings? A. $5,100. (2) What was the amount of loss or damage to the furniture and fixtures of Mrs. Kirkpatrick, caused by the fire referred to in the pleadings? A. $500. (3) Have all the valid stipulations of the policies required to be performed before action can be maintained to recover loss under the policies been either complied with by the cross-complainant, Mrs. Kirkpatrick, or waived by the insurance companies? A. Yes. (Peremptory instruction of court.) (4) Was the refusal of the insurance companies to pay the loss of the property insured under the policies made in good faith? A. No. (5) What expense, loss, and injury has Mrs. Kirkpatrick incurred on account of the refusal of the companies to pay the amount of the loss? A. $1,000. (6) Should the insurance companies be required to pay interest? A. Yes. (7) Did the insurance companies waive their right to take the stock of goods or salvage remaining after the fire? A. Yes. (Peremptory instruction of court.) (8) Was the refusal of the insurance companies to pay the amount of the award made in good faith, after demand therefor made more than sixty days after the award rendered? A. (Peremptorily instructed by the court to answer this issue as follows:) (1) That there was a demand for payment, and refusal to pay after that demand; (2) that there was no demand for payment, etc., made more than sixty days after rendition of award.''

The chancellor set aside the award and rendered judgment on the policies in accordance with the responses of the jury, and also for $1,000, the penalty referred to in the fifth issue.

The insurance companies prayed an appeal to this court, and have here assigned errors upon both branches of the case.

Several errors are assigned upon the admission of evidence, but these matters have been disposed of orally, and are not included in this opinion.

The only matters that will be here considered are those which arise under the peremptory instructions which the chancellor gave under issues 3 and 8.

In order to properly understand the matters arising under the third issue, it is necessary to state the facts with some degree of particularity:

The fire occurred on the 7th of June, 1911. Immediately thereafter notice was given to the insurance companies, and they sent their adjusters to the place. After making their inspection, they suggested to Mrs. Kirkpatrick, the insured, that she have an inventory made. This she did, showing a loss nearly the amount which the jury subsequently found. The adjusters, not being satisfied with this, appointed an agent of their own, Mr. Page, to prepare an inventory, and his inventory showed the loss to be about $1,500 less than that shown by the inventory of Mrs. Kirkpatrick. Here the matter rested for a time. The inventory made by Mr. Page showed something over $1,000 worth of goods saved from the fire, though in a damaged condition. The attorney for the insured wrote to the adjuster representing three of the companies, stating that, if the companies desired to further examine the goods so saved, they would be preserved for that purpose, but, if this was not desired, they would be advertised and sold. Quite a number of days elapsed without any reply being received. Thereupon the insured advertised the goods for sale. A day or two before the sale took place, which was on July the 8th, the adjuster wrote to the attorney for the insured that he had heard that the goods were to be sold, and that he was now writing for the purpose of saying he wished

it to be understood the companies were not consent-
ing to the sale. In the letter complainants' attorney
requested the companies to say whether they objected
to the sale. The response was in the form stated; no
direct objection being made. Taking the letter as a
refusal on the part of the companies to object, and
therefore as an indirect form of assent, the goods were
sold.

Thereupon considerable correspondence ensued, the
purport of which was that the insured desired the companies to say what they considered the loss to be. After much sparring the companies finally demanded an
appraisal. There was a clause in each of the policies
to the general effect that, in case a difference should
arise between the parties as to the amount of the loss,
it should be submitted to arbitrators, one to be selected by each of the parties, and the two arbitrators
to select an umpire. The arbitration agreement was
drawn up, and under this the arbitrators were to estimate and appraise the loss, stating separately sound
value and damage. They filed their report, in which
they found the damages in a round sum at $4,300. They
also required in the submission agreement to estimate
the loss on the fixtures, but their report contained nothing on this subject.

When this report was filed, the insured, through her
attorney, wrote to the companies, inquiring whether
the award was satisfactory, and whether payment
would be made thereunder. The reply was the original bill in this case to set aside the award because it

did not comply with the submission. Thereupon the insured, through her attorney, wrote to the adjuster who had the matter in charge, suggesting and asking that the arbitrators be recalled, in order that they might supply the deficiencies complained of. This was referred to the counsel for all the companies, and he declined the offer. Then the cross-bill was filed, which has already been mentioned.

There was a clause in the policies to the effect that it should be optional with the companies to take the whole or any part of the articles saved out of the fire at the appraised value within a time fixed.

It is insisted that, by the sale of the recovered property, the insurance companies were deprived of this option, and hence the policies were all forfeited, and there could be no recovery in this case on that ground.

To say nothing of the equivocal response made by the insurance companies to the inquiry as to whether the goods should be retained or sold, we are of the opinion that the subsequent demand for an arbitration and the appraisal of the loss waived the forfeiture. Such demand was equivalent to an admission of liability on the policies, and, being made after the companies knew that the goods had been sold, was necessarily a release of their option to demand the goods themselves. The demand for arbitration in this aspect of the matter could have meant nothing else than that the damages should be ascertained by the testimony of those who had seen and examined the stock, by the books, and by the inventories.

That a demand for an appraisal and arbitration is equivalent to an admission of liability on the policy see *Hickerson* v. *Insurance Companies*, 96 Tenn., 193, 199, 200, 33 S. W., 1041, 32 L. R. A., 172, and cases cited.

It is insisted on behalf of the insurance companies that, on the failure of the award, without fault of the companies, it was the duty of the parties to select new arbitrators, and that no suit could be brought on the policies until this should be done. The companies, however, did not, in fact, ask for the appointment of new arbitrators, but only that the award should be set aside because not in compliance with the submission. It does not appear that any demand was made on the insured for the appointment of a new arbitrator, nor was any new arbitrator selected by her.

The rules applicable to this general subject supported by the weight of authority are as follows: When there is an arbitration clause in substance like the one we have described, it is the duty of either party to comply and appoint an arbitrator, when requested so to do by the other party. If the insured fails to comply with this demand, he cannot sue on the policy, and, if the refusal be persisted in for an unreasonable time, it will amount to a forfeiture of the policy. If the refusal be on the part of the insurer, the insured may bring suit on the policies at once. There are cases to the effect that, where the insured at first refuses, and then complies, the policy is not forfeited. Where appraisers are appointed and the arbitrator fails, by reason of the fraud or intermeddling of the insured, the right to sue on the policies is lost. Where the fraud of intermeddling with the appraisers is at the instance of the insurer, the insured may abandon the arbitration and sue on the policies. Where the appraisers or arbitrators are appointed, but the arbitration falls without the fault of either party, the authorities differ as to the result. There are many authorities to the effect that it is the duty of the parties to agree upon new arbitrators, and continue again and again to select new arbitrators, as occasion requires, until a board be chosen which will bring in a valid award. There are other authorities to the effect that, where the insured has complied with the arbitration clause by appointing an appraiser,. and the arbitration has failed without his fault, he has discharged his duty, and he cannot be required to select another arbitrator, or to participate in the choosing of a new board. This latter view is sustained by the following authorities: *Jerrils* v. *German American Insurance Co.*, 82 Kan., 320, 108 Pac., 114, 28 L. R. A. (N. S.), 104, 20 Ann. Cas., 251; *Spring Garden Insurance Co.* v. *Amusement Syndicate Co.*, 178 Fed., 519, 102 C. C. A., 29; *Western Assurance Co.* v. *Decker*, 98 Fed., 381, 39 C. C. A., 383; *Connecticut Fire Insurance Co.* v. *Cohen*, 97 Md., 294, 55 Atl.., 675, 99 Am. St. Rep., 445; *Shawnee Fire Insurance Co.* v. *Pontfield*, 110 Md., 353, 72 Atl., 835, 132 Am. St. Rep., 449; *Bretzfelder* v. *Merchants' Insurance Co.*, 123 N. C., 164, 31 S. E., 470, 44 L. R. A., 424; *Bernhard* v. *Insurance Company*, 79 Conn., 388, 65

Atl., 134, 8 Ann. Cas., 302, and note; *Globe, etc., Insurance Co.* v. *Johnson* (Ky.), 127 S. W., 765; *Coffin* v. *German Fire Insurance Co.,* 142 Mo. App., 295, 126 S. W., 253; *Western Assurance Co.* v. *Hall,* 120 Ala., 547, 24 South., 936, 74 Am. St. Rep., 48. And see *Niagara Fire Insurance Co.* v. *Bishop,* 154 Ill., 9, 39 N. E., 1102, 45 Am. St. Rep., 105. The subject is discussed, and the authorities collected on both sides of the question in a note to 15 L. R. A. (N. S.), 1055 *et seq.* We believe the view sustained by the cases we have just referred to is the sounder one. One needs only to read the cases showing the trickery employed by both the insured and by insurance companies to be convinced that the arbitration clause is productive of but little good in actual practice, and is more productive of delay than conducive to speedy justice. Generally the arbitrators regard themselves as the agents and champions of the persons who appoint them, and there is very often great difficulty in choosing the umpire, because the respective arbitrators desire to secure some one supposed to be favorable to the side of the controversy which appointed him. This sometimes appears in such way as to be incapable of legal proof, yet the conclusion forces itself upon the mind of the careful investigator that partisanship is really involved. It is supposed that these boards cheapen and shorten the ascertainment of the amount of the loss. The purpose evidently was, in the beginning, that two fair-minded men should be selected, and they should select a third of like disposition, and that these two should inspect the loss, and return a reasonable finding. We have no doubt that in many cases this result is obtained. Really, however, the arbitrators so selected are a legal board, and their conclusions may be questioned by the writ of *certiorari* in this State, just as those of any other board of arbitrators, and hence there is likely to be, in any given case, a long litigation over the award. It seems to us more conducive to justice that after one board has been appointed, that this should satisfy the agreement, entered into at the issuance of the policy, that such board should be appointed. This view enables the parties to go directly into court for settlement of the questions involved, on failure of the arbitration board. Arbitrators, even of the limited kind under examination, to some extent oust the courts of their jurisdiction of causes, or have a tendency to do so, and should not be encouraged, or, at least should be subjected to a strict construction. This view will lead more certainly to the quick and just settlement of controversies than the continued forced submission of rights to raw and inexperienced tribunals, to say nothing of the prejudices and predilections with which they are likely to be imbued.

Furthermore, even on the opposite theory, it seems to us it would have been the duty of the insurance companies to agree to the recall of the arbitrators in order that they might correct the error they had fallen into, inasmuch as no charge of fraud was made against them, nor was there any intimation that they had acted in an unfair manner, or had been influenced by unfair motives. But it is unnecessary to go further into this particular phase of the matter, since we believe that neither party, under the principles already stated, was bound to go further with the arbitration after it had failed, in the manner stated, without fault of either party.

Furthermore, we are of the opinion that, when the bill was filed in the chancery court to set aside the award, that court immediately obtained jurisdiction of the whole controversy, and it had the right to settle it under a cross-bill in any view, without the selection of new arbitrators. *Dixie Fire Insurance Co. et al.* v. *American Cofectionery Co.*, 124 Tenn., 247, 249, 136 S. W., 915, 34 L. R. A. (N. S.), 1897; *Continental Insurance Co.* v. *Garrett*, 125 Fed., 590, 593, 60 C. C. A., 395.

We are of the opinion, on the grounds stated, that the chancellor committed no error in instructing the jury as he did under issue No. 3. The stipulations referred to had reference to the arbitration. We are further of the opinion that the cross-complainant had the right to file such a cross-bill as was filed, and the evidence sustaining the amount of the loss fixed by the jury under issue No. 1, the decree is affirmed on that branch of the case.

Second, as to the penalty: The Acts of 1901, ch. 141, sec. 1. provides:

"That the several insurance companies . . . in all cases when a loss occurs and they refuse to pay the same within sixty days after a demand shall have been made by the holder of said policy on which said loss occurred, shall be liable to pay the holder of said policy, in addition to the loss and interest thereon, a sum not exceeding 25 per cent. on the liability for said loss; provided . . . the refusal to pay . . . was not in good faith," etc.

The eighth issue deals with this subject. The jury were instructed to find that, while there was a demand for payment of the award, and a refusal to pay after that demand, yet there was no demand for payment made for more than sixty days after the rendition of the award.

The true construction of the act in question is this: A formal demand must be made on the insurer for the payment of the amount due after the maturity of the policy is fixed according to its terms. If, after such formal demand, the insurer fails to pay for the space of sixty days, or within the sixty days refuses to pay, then the insured may sue on the policy, or on the award, if there be one, and recover the penalty, if it appears, in addition to the lapse of time, that the refusal or failure to pay was not in good faith. This statute was so construed in *Mutual Reserve Fire Insurance Co.* v. *Tuchfeld*, 159 Fed., 833, 834, 86 C. C. A., 657. The Georgia statute, which is, in substance, the same as our own, was likewise so construed in the case of *Lester* v. *Insurance Co.*, 55 Ga., 475, 480. See, also, *Iowa Insurance Co.* v. *Lewis*, 187 U. S., 335, 23 Sup. Ct., 126, 47 L. Ed., 204, construing a Texas statute very much like our own. Where proofs of loss are

furnished, and no demand is made for arbitration, the
policy matures at the expiration of the number of days
fixed for maturement in the policy after such submission of proofs. Where the policy provides for payment after the lapse of a given number of days after
the filing of an award, where an arbitration has been
demanded, the date of maturity, for the purposes of
the present statute, would be governed by the number
of days so fixed in the contract. After the expiration
of this time so fixed, the duty devolves on the insurance
company to pay the amount of the loss. If it does not
pay, the formal demand required by the penalty statute above quoted should be made. A failure to pay
for sixty days thereafter would justify a recovery of
the penalty upon its further being made to appear that
the failure was not in good faith. Likewise a refusal
within the sixty days after such formal demand would
justify suit, and the penalty would be incurred, provided, as in the previous case, it should be made to appear that the refusal to pay was not in good faith.

The formal demand not having been made, as required by the statute, there can be no recovery of the
penalty. The formal demand not having been made
in this case, it is not necessary to consider the question of good faith or the contrary. It is true there was
a demand made in the present case, but it does not
appear when it was made. Furthermore, it cannot be
said that the time for the formal demand to initiate
the liability for the penalty had arrived; since an arbitration had been demanded and submitted to, and had

been partly executed by the arbitrators, but not fully, and a bill had been filed by the insurance companies to set aside the award. The award being defective, the insurance companies had the right to file a bill to set it aside, and therefore the time for making the formal demand never really arrived.

The result is that the decree is affirmed as to the amount due on the policies, but reversed as to the penalty.

The costs will be divided in the following proportions: Five-sixths will be paid by the complainant companies, and one-sixth by the cross-complainant.

ON PETITION FOR A REHEARING.

The petition makes the point that the opinion upon the subject of the penalty is in conflict with the case of *Thompson* v. *Interstate Life & Accident Insurance Co.,* dcided by this court at its recent Knoxville term, and reported in 128 Tenn., 526, 162 S. W., 39. A comparison of the two cases will so readily show the absence of conflict that we deem it unnecessary to make any comment on the point further than to say the opinion in that case shows there was a demand and a refusal of that demand within sixty days. In the case before us, it does not appear that any demand was made after the obligation of the company to pay had accrued. There was a demand, whether formal or not in the sense of the statute does not appear, to pay the amount fixed by the arbitrators, but the companies' failure to comply with that demand was justified by the subsequent decree of the chancery court setting aside the award on the grounds stated supra, as to which there was no appeal. So it is not shown that the insurers remained in default for the period of sixty days after formal demand made to pay a loss duly fixed on them pursuant to the terms of their contracts; nor that they refused to pay within such sixty days.

It is urged by the complainant that the construction we have given the statute affords litigants against insurance companies no relief. This suggestion is based, as we think, on a misconception of the purpose of the statute. It is a penalty statute, and must be strictly construed. The demand provided for in the statute is intended to operate as a fair warning to the insurer that the penalty will be claimed, on failure to pay within sixty days. It is not improper or unjust that such warning should be required. This requirement does not have any bearing upon the right of the insured to enforce the contract itself. Immediately upon the maturing of the policy under its terms, the arising of the duty to pay, the insured may bring suit to enforce the contract. The penalty statute gives an additional right. Its purpose was to supersede the necessity of suit, or, in case suit should finally have to be brought as a result of the delinquency of the insurer, then to indemnify the insured against delay interposed and defense made in bad faith; the underlying thought being that the insurers on formal demand so made would, noting the warning, thereby be induced to pay the loss without suit, in the absence of some real and *bona fide*

defense. Is it not better that the insured should in
this simple manner hasten the payment of the loss
within two months than that suit should be brought
immediately on the maturity of the policy, and then
that the insured should be compelled by the necessary
delays of litigation to wait many months, or a year, or
longer? Is the insured not fully protected by the right
to recover the penalty, at the expiration of such sixty
days, if the failure or delay of the insurers has not
been in good faith? True it is that the mere failure of
the insurers to pay, for the sixty days referred to,
would not of itself, as suggested supra, conclusively
fix the penalty, because there might be circumstances
which would show that the delay or failure or refusal
to pay was not in bad faith, even though the insurer
should ultimately be cast in the suit; but certainly the
burden would be on the insurer to make this appear.

It is insisted that the insurance companies in the
case before us refused to pay before the obligation to
pay matured, and that such refusal was a waiver of
the right to have a formal demand made upon them as
a preliminary to a claim for the penalty. The facts
elready stated sufficiently show that this contention is
not well based. There was a fire. The companies did
not deny liability. There was no controversy except
as to the amount of the loss. The insurers and the
complainant endeavored to ascertain the amount by inspection and by inventories. They could not agree.
Arbitration was then demanded and agreed to. An
award was filed. Complainant demanded payment of

the award. The companies answered by a bill to set aside the award because not in compliance with the arbitration agreement between the parties, and succeeded in obtaining that relief, and complainant acquiesced in this. In the meantime complainant filed a cross-bill to recover on the award, and, in the alternative, on the policies. She failed on the first and succeeded in the second; but no formal demand was ever made for the payment of the policies, irrespective of the award, prior to the filing of the cross-bill. If it was the contention of complainant that the companies were liable irrespective of the arbitration proceedings, formal demand on that basis should have been made before action brought and the pleadings framed accordingly.

Petition overruled.

BOND *v.* STATE.*

(*Nashville.* December Term, 1913.)

1. CRIMINAL LAW. Admission of evidence. Insanity.

Accused was charged with having obtained money in November,
1908, by false pretenses, and pleaded insanity as a defense.
In November, 1909, a lunacy inquisition was held, and it was
adjudged that accused was of unsound mind, and that he had
been so since the spring of 1908; and on May 12, 1910, he was
put to trial on his plea of present insanity, and the jury returned a verdict that he was then insane and incapable of
defending the charge against him. *Held,* that the lunacy proceedings and the verdict on the plea of present insanity were
admissible in evidence. (*Post, pp.* 83-85.)

2. CRIMINAL LAW. Responsibility. Insanity.

Under a plea of insanity the question for determination is,
whether accused had capacity and sufficient reason to enable
him to distinguish between right and wrong as to the particular
act, and a knowledge and consciousness that the act was
wrong and criminal. (*Post, pp.* 83-85.)

Cases cited and approved: Hughes v. Jones, 116 N. Y., 67;
Davidson's Appeal, 170 Pa., 96; Hopson v. Boyd, 6 B. Mon.
(Ky.), 296; Hutchinson v. Sandt, 4 Rawle (Pa.), 234; Christmas
v. Mitchell, 38 N. C. 535.

3. CRIMINAL LAW.: Evidence of insanity.

Evidence of insanity after the commission of the offense
charged is competent to enable the jury to determine the state
of accused's mind at the time the offense was committed.
(*Post, p.* 85.)

4. FALSE PRETENSES. Prosecution. Sufficiency of evidence.

In a prosecution for obtaining money from a national bank by

---

*On the question of insanity after commission of criminal
act, see note in 38 L. R. A. 577. And for the method of raising
insanity supervening after conviction, see note in 10 L. R. A. (N. S.)
1129.

Bond v. State.

false pretenses, evidence *held* to sustain a finding that the
bank was at least a *de facto* corporation. (*Post, pp.* 86, 87.)

5. **FALSE PRETENSES. Ownership of property. Proof of
ownership.**

It is sufficient to sustain a conviction for obtaining money by
false pretenses from a corporation that the proof showed a
de facto corporation. (*Post, pp.* 86, 87.)

Cases cited and distinguished: Trice v. State, 39 Tenn., 591;
Jones v. State, 37 Tenn., 347; Owen v. State, 37 Tenn., 493.

6. **FALSE PRETENSES. Possession of property. Sufficiency.**

The possession, by persons assuming without authority to be a
bank, of money left with them by depositors, would give them
such a title as would support a prosecution for obtaining
money by false pretenses, in fraudulently obtaining the money
from them. (*Post, pp.* 87, 88.)

Cases cited and approved: State v. Misseo, 105 Tenn., 218.

FROM DAVIDSON.

Appeal from Criminal Court, Davidson County.—
A. B. Neil, Judge.

John T. Lellyett and Edwin A. Price, for appellant.

F. M. Thompson, attorney general, and F. M. Bass,
for the State.

Mr. Justice Lansden delivered the opinion of the
Court.

The plaintiff in error, B. B. Bond, was indicted at
the January term, 1909, in the criminal court of Davidson county, upon an indictment containing five counts;
and he was convicted under the first count, which

charged in substance that he falsely pretended to R.
E. Donnell, assistant cashier of the First National
Bank of Nashvill‚e Tenn., that he, the said B. B. Bond,
doing business under the style and name of the Bond
Produce Company, had on November 23, 1906, shipped
and consigned from the city of Nashville, Tenn., to
Griffin-Thomas-Payne Company, Boston, Mass., 20C
cases of eggs via the Louisville & Nashville Railroad;
that he then and there had in his possession the bill of
lading covering said shipment, which had been regularly signed by G. F. Clark, agent at Nashville of said
Louisville & Nashville Railroad Company; that the
said B. B. Bond had drawn a draft on the said Griffin-
Thomas-Payne Company, payable to the order of the
Bond Produce Company, for the sum of $1,200, cover-
ing the said shipment, and requested said bank to advance said sum of $1,200 to him in cash, in considera-
tion of which he indorsed and transferred to the bank
the said draft with the bill of lading attached thereto;
that the said B. B. Bond then and there exhibited to
the said R. E. Donnell, assistant cashier, a draft as
aforesaid, dated November 23, 1908, payable to and
indorsed by the Bond Produce Company, and attached thereto was what purported to be, and what the
said B. B. Bond falsely pretended was, a bill of lading
of the Louisville & Nashville Railroad Company covering a shipment of eggs as aforesaid, which bill of lading purported to have been signed by G. F. Clark,
agent of said railroad company.

The said R. E. Donnell, relying on the pretenses and representations aforesaid, and being deceived thereby, then and there advanced to the said B. B. Bond $1,200, and received in return the said draft and bill of lading indorsed as aforesaid. The said $1,200 was then and there placed on deposit in said bank to the credit of said B. B. Bond subject to his immediate check, and the said B. B. Bond thereafter checked and drew out of said bank the sum of $1,200. By means of said false, unlawful, and felonious pretenses the said B. B. Bond did obtain from the First National Bank $1,200, good and lawful money of the United States, property of the First National Bank, with the unlawful and felonious intent of defrauding said bank thereof; whereas, in truth and in fact, the said B. B. Bond had not on that day shipped or consigned any eggs to the Griffin-Thomas-Payne Company by way of said railroad company as aforesaid, and the said bill of lading had not been issued and signed by G. F. Clark, agent of said road, nor by any one authorized to do so. The said B. B. Bond then and there made such representations and pretenses, well knowing at the time that they were false, fraudulent, and felonious.

The defendant pleaded "not guilty" to the indictment, but interposed as his chief defense a plea of insanity at the time of the alleged false pretenses.

The case was tried September 24, 1913, and defendant was convicted as stated and sentenced to serve a

term of three years in the state penitentiary. Defendant has appealed and assigned errors.

It appears from the evidence that the defendant
below has been engaged in the produce business at
Nashville for a great many years and the principal
part of his business has been in handling eggs. He
had his banking connections with the First National
Bank of Nashville for eighteen or twenty years of
this time, and had an agreement with the bank by
which the bank would advance money to him on drafts
drawn on Eastern commission houses when there was
attached to the draft a bill of lading issued by the railroad company covering a shipment of produce consigned to a particular house. It was the custom for
the defendant to ship or consign a carload of eggs to
an Eastern customer and receive from the railroad
company a bill of lading covering the shipment, drawn
to "order notify" such customer. The defendant
would thereupon draw a draft in the name of and
payable to the order of the Bond Produce Company
for an amount sufficient to cover the value of the shipment, and attach to the draft the bill of lading received from the railroad company, and when this
draft and bill of lading were presented to the bank
the bank would advance to the defendant the amount
of the draft, either by paying cash over the counter
or by placing the amount of the draft to his credit
subject to hisimmediate check. These transactions
would be completed, so far as his dealing with the
bank was concerned, when the defendant would pre-

sent the draft with a bill of lading attached to some officer of the bank, who would approve the transaction by marking "O. K." on the draft, and the defendant would then present the draft with the bill of lading attached to the teller of the bank, who would pay the cash or place the amount of the draft to defendant's credit. On November 23, 1908, the defendant presented a draft to the First National Bank, through its assistant cashier, R. E. Donnell, drawn by the Bond Produce Company on Griffin-Thomas-Payne Company, of Boston, Mass., for the sum of $1,200, payable to the order of, and indorsed by, the Bond Produce Company. Attached to this draft was what purported to be a bill of lading issued by the Louisville & Nashville Railroad Company, made out on one of its regular forms, and dated November 23, 1908, covering a shipment of 200 cases of eggs by the Bond Produce Company "to order notify Griffin-Thomas-Payne Company, Boston, Mass.," and signed"Louisville & Nashville Railroad Company, by G. F. Clark, Agent."   This bill of lading was indorsed: "Bond Produce Company. B. B. Bond, Manager."

These papers were approved by the bank's officers, after proper examination, and according to the long-standing custom existing between the bank and the defendant the amount of the draft was placed to defendant's credit, and, within a short time, he drew the entire sum out of the bank upon his individual check.

The bill of lading was a forgery. No such amount of eggs was delivered to the railroad company by the defendant, and the bank never received either the eggs or the amount of the draft from the supposed consignees, although demand was made for both.

This proof is made by the testimony of the assistant cashier, who says that the defendant presented the draft with bill of lading attached, indorsed as stated, and he approved it, believing the papers to be genuine. The cashier of the bank introduced the original deposit slip made out by the defendant, and identified it, together with checks drawn by defendant on the credits received from the deposit of the draft and the bill of lading as the original papers. The agent of the railroad company testified that the bill of lading was not signed by him, nor by anyone authorized to sign his name, and that the railroad company did not receive the consignment of eggs represented by the bill of lading.

A short time after this transaction with the bank, the defendant fled from Nashville to Hamilton, Ontario, Canada, and was there arrested. He had on his person, sewed up in his clothing, the sum of $6,186 in cash. Soon after the defendant was returned to Nashville from Canada he fell into a prolonged stupor, which lasted from about April 18, 1909, until about June 29, 1910, when he suffered a severe hemorrhage from the nose and kidneys, soon after which he regained consciousness. The evidence of his attending physician is in part as follows:

"Every time I saw him he was lying in bed on his back, and with his eyes shut, and simply breathing. Nothing I could say or do could make him show any manifestation of knowing I was there. I would open his eyelids and rub my finger on his ball, and he wouldn't even wink his eye, no more than rubbing it on the table. I would jab pins into him, jab them in his thigh, breast, and arms, and he wouldn't move any more than this chair. I can't see how he was feigning under those circumstances."

There is evidence of other witnesses introduced by defendant tending to show that, some months prior to the commission of the crime charged, the defendant's whole nature changed, so that he became irritable, fractious, and abusive to his family, whereas prior to that time he was aimable and agreeable with friends, and affectionate and indulgent with his family. The state offered proof to the contrary, indicating that, just prior to and on the day of the commission of the offense charged, the defendant was sane and of sound mind, and these witnesses give it as their opinions that he knew right from wrong, and could appreciate the quality of his act.

After the commission of the offense, and in November, 1909, an inquisition of lunacy was held concerning the defendant, and he was adjudged "a person of unsound mind, and that he has not capacity of mind sufficient for the government of himself or his property, and that he has been of unsound mind for the period since the spring of 1908."

It is also shown on the record that the defendant was put to trial May 12, 1910, upon his plea of present insanity, before the court and jury, and the jury returned a verdict that "the defendant is at present insane, and that it would endanger the peace of the community to set him at liberty, and that he is incapable of defending the charge against him."

Upon this verdict, the court committed the defendant to the superintendent of the hospital for the insane for the middle district of Tennessee; but on account of his physical condition the execution of the order of commitment was suspended until further orders of the court. No further order in respect of the defendant's custody seems to have been made. It appears that he remained at home under the care of his family until he was placed upon this trial in September, 1913. On the trial the defendant offered to introduce the lunacy proceedings and the plea of present insanity, together with the verdict and judgment of the court thereon, in support of his plea of insanity. Upon exceptions by the State, these documents were excluded, and the action of the trial judge thereon is assigned as error.

We think the exclusion of this evidence was error. The inquiry under the plea of insanity was whether the defendant had capacity and reason sufficient to enable him to distinguish between right and wrong as to the particular act he was then doing—a knowledge and consciousness that the act he was doing was wrong and criminal, and would subject him to punishment. Evidence of his conduct and condition before, at the time of, and subsequent to the doing of the thing charged is admissible to enable the jury to arrive at a proper conclusion as to the defendant's mental *status* at the time he did the thing complained of. This is true generally as to statements and acts of the defendant. This rule would seem to include an inquisition upon reason, and there is much authority in support. Greenleaf on Evidence, vol. 2, sec. 371. Mr. Greenleaf says: "An inquisition taken under a commission of lunacy is admissible evidence, but not conclusive for the party's own favor." In support of the text, numerous English and American cases are cited. The rule is stated in substantially the same terms in 22 Cyc. 1133. In this authority it is said that an inquisition finding a person is insane at the time of the finding has been held to afford no evidence that he was insane at a previous time; but it is further said, if the inquisition overreaches an anterior period of time during which the person is found to have been insane, it raises a presumption of the existence of insanity during that period, which presumption, however, is not conclusive, but may be rebutted by evidence of sanity during the period overreached by the finding. The text is supported by *Hughes v. Jones,* 116 N. Y., 67, 22 N. E., 446, 5 L. R. A., 637, 15 Am. St. Rep., 386, in which many cases are cited to the same effect. See, also, *Davidson's Appeal,* 170 Pa., 96, 32 Atl., 561; *Hopson v. Boyd,* 6 B. Mon. (Ky.), 296; *Yauger v. Skinner,* 14 N. J. Eq., 389; *Hutchinson v. Sandt,* 4

Rawle (Pa.), 234, 26 Am. Dec., 127; *Christmas v. Mitchell*, 38 N. C., 535.

The principal to be deduced from these authorities seems to be that, after an inquisition is regularly held on which it is found that the person is insane, the finding of. the inquisition is substituted for the legal presumption of sanity for the period of time covered by the inquiry and finding. In *Hughes v. Jones*, supra, the admissibility of the inquisition was admitted on the briefs of counsel, and it was conceded that the inquisition and findings "are *prima facie* evidence of the lunacy and incompetency of the party to contract from the time at which the inquisition finds the lunacy to have begun," and the court held that "contracts . . . made by this class of persons before office found, but within the period overreached by the finding of the jury, are not utterly void, although they are presumed to be so until capacity to contract is shown by satisfactory evidence."

To the same effect is Wigmore on Evidence, vol. 1, sec. 234; vol. 2, sec. 233; vol. 3, p., 2076.

Upon the foregoing authorities, we also think that the court should have admitted the verdict of the jury and the judgment of the court upon the defendant's plea of present insanity. This was a judicial declaration that the defendant was insane. It is true that it established his insanity at a period of time subsequent to the date of the alleged offense; but evidence of subsequent insanity is competent for the consideration of the jury in determining the state of the defendant's mind at the time of the offense. Greenleaf on Evidence, supra.

It is also assigned as error that there is no proof
of the corporate existence of the First National Bank
of Nashville, Tenn. It is proven without exception
by defendant that the defendant has been doing a
banking business with the First National Bank for a
period of eighteen or twenty years; that this bank had
a cashier and assistant cashier, a teller and bookkeep-
ers, who engaged in banking transactions with the defendant in the manner heretofore stated in this opinion. It is proven that the defendant presented the
draft with the bill of lading attached, and received
from the persons assuming to act as officers and employees of this bank $1,200 of good and lawful money
of the United States. This, we think, establishes that
the First National Bank is at least a *de facto* corporation, and such proof is sufficient to support a conviction. The absence of exception to the testimony showing the transactions of the bank with the defendant as
a bank, and the claim of the officers of that bank that
they were acting in their capacity as such, dis-
tinguishes this case from the case of *Trice v. State,* 2
Head, 591. The case is also distinguishable from the
case of *Jones v. State,* 5 Sneed, 347, and *Owen v.
State,* 5 Sneed, 493. The first of those cases was an
indictment and conviction for passing a counterfeit
bank note purporting to have been issued by the Iron
Bank, Ironton, Ohio, and the second case was an indictment and conviction of fraudulently having in pos-

session a counterfeit bank note of the Bank of Tennessee and certain Kentucky banks. It was held in the *Jones Case* that the incorporation of the bank could not be shown by parol, but that its incorporation upon proper objection must be proven by the introduction of its charter. In the *Owen Case* the court took judicial knowledge of the charter of the Bank or Tennessee and its authority to issue notes. But as to the Kentucky banks it was held that the court could not take such judicial notice, and its *de jure* existence must be proven by the introduction of its charter. The reason of this holding is manifest. Only such banks as were especially authorized to do so could issue notes which would circulate as money, and before anyone could be convicted for counterfeiting, or having in possession counterfeit notes of such banks, the authority of the bank to issue notes under the law would have to be proven. The offense would necessarily depend upon the authority of the bank in law to issue the notes, because a counterfeit of an illegal or unauthorized note could not defraud anyone receiving it.

In this case, however, the principal ingredients of the offense are the fraudulent pretenses of defendant, by which the officers of the bank were deceived, and upon which he received money from the possession of the bank. The bank's possession of the money would support the conviction, whether it were legally authorized to do a banking business or not. If depositors or stockholders or other persons should leave money in the custody of those unauthorized but assuming to be a bank, its possession thereof would be such a special title in the money as would make it larceny for anyone to steal and take it away, or to obtain its possession by false and fraudulent pretenses. The gist of this offense is the fraud and deceit by which possession of the money was wrongfully obtained. *State v. Misseo*, 105 Tenn., 218, 58 S. W., 216.

Other errors assigned were disposed of orally. For the errors indicated, the case will be reversed and remanded for· a new trial.

DIES ET AL., v. WILSON COUNTY BANK.

(*Nashville.* December Term, 1913.)

1. PRINCIPAL AND SURETY. Discharge of surety. Taking additional security. Note of principal debtor.

The sureties on a note, which expressly stipulated that they should not be discharged by an extension of time granted to the principal, are not released by the acceptance by the payee of an additional note from the principal debtor payable at a later date, not as a renewal of the former note, but as an additional evidence of the debt. (*Post,* p. 94.)

2. PRINCIPAL AND SURETY. Discharge of surety. Reservation of rights against surety. Statutory provision.

The Negotiable Instruments Act (Acts 1899, ch. 94, sec. 120, subsection 6), providing that a surety is not discharged by the taking of a renewal note from the principal extending the time of payment, where the extension is given under an express reservation of the right of recourse against the surety, applies where the original note is retained in posession by the payee, and the right of action thereon against the surety is thereby reserved. (*Post,* p. 94.)

Acts cited and construed: Acts 1899, ch. 94, sec. 120, subsec. 6.

Case cited and approved: Meredith v. Dibrell, 127 Tenn., 387.

3. NOVATION. Burden of proof.

The burden of proving novation of a note by a later note is upon him who asserts it. (*Post,* p. 95.)

Cases cited and approved: Sharp v. Fly, 68 Tenn., 4; Lover v. Bessenger, 68 Tenn., 393.

4. BILLS AND NOTES. Payment. New note. Presumption. Express agreement.

Where a new note is given to represent the original consideration and the old note is retained, while it is presumed that the

old note is extinguished by the later one, an express agreement by the parties as to the payment or nonpayment of the
old note will control. (*Post, pp.* 95-100.)

Case cited and approved: Bowman v. Rector, 59 S. W. 389, 393.

5. **BILLS AND NOTES. Collateral securities. Notes representing the same debt.**

Two notes representing the same debt may be outstanding at
the same time, the one as collateral to the other, and either
the original or the renewal note may be held as collateral to
the other. (*Post, p.* 96.)

Cases cited and distinguished: Continental Life Ins. Co. v.
Barker, 50 Conn., 567; National Park Bank v. Koehler, 137 App.
Div., 785.

Cases cited and approved: Ripley v. Greenley, 2 Vt., 129; Bank
v. Parriott, 125 Cal., 472; Fisher v. Denver Nat. Bank, 22 Colo.,
373; Weakly v. Bell, 9 Watts (Pa.), 273; Peninsular Savings
Bank v. Hosie, 112 Mich., 351.

6. **BILLS AND NOTES. Collateral security. Notes of same
maker.**

While the maker of a note, which was signed by two others as
sureties, cannot pledge the note as collateral for a note
executed by himself alone and evidencing the same debt, since
that note is a liability of his and not an asset which may be a
subject of a pledge, that rule does not prevent the payee of
the secured note from holding it as collateral for the second
note. (*Post, p.* 99.)

Cases cited and approved: International Trust Co. v. Union
Cattle Co., 3 Wyo., 803; *In re* Waddell-Entz Co., 67 Conn., 324;
Easton v. Bank, 127 U. S., 532; Dibert v. D'Arcy, 248 Mo., 617.

7. **JUDGMENT. Separate notes for same debt. Collateral satisfaction.**

In such a case the creditor can make but a single proof against
the debtor and have but one satisfaction. (*Post, p.* 101.)

Cases cited and approved: International Trust Co. v. Union
Cattle Co., supra; In re Waddell-Entz Co., supra.

Dies v. Bank.

8. **BILLS AND NOTES. Collateral security. Notes of the same maker. Different debts.**

The fact that the subsequent note included other indebtedness, or a new one in addition to that represented by the old note, does not affect the rule. (*Post, p.* 101.)

Case cited and approved: Ripley v. Greenleaf, supra.

Case cited and distinguished: Cotton v. Atlas Nat. Bank, 145 Mass., 49.

9. **PRINCIPAL AND SURETY. Discharge. Note held as collateral. Part payment of principal note.**

Where the payee of a note, signed by a principal and two sureties, accepted another note from the principal representing the same and additional indebtedness, under the express agreement that the old note was to be retained as collateral for the new, the proceeds of property mortgaged as security for the new note, which were applied to the payment of the debt represented thereby, released *pro tanto* the sureties on the old note. (*Post, p.* 101.)

Cases cited and approved: Bussey v. Grant, 29 Tenn., 238; Mason v. Smith, 79 Tenn., 67, 74.

FROM WILSON.

Appeal from the Circuit Court of Wilson County to the Court of Civil Appeals, and by *certiorari* from the Court of Civil Appeals to the Supreme Court. —JNO. E. RICHARDSON, Judge.

W. R. CHAMBERS, for plaintiff.

LILLARD THOMPSON, for defendants.

Mr. Justice Williams delivered the opinion of the Court.

This case was brought upon a note dated September 30, 1910, in terms as follows:

"Four months after date we promise to pay to the order of the Lebanon National Bank, one hundred ninety-eight & 35/100 dollars. Renewal of note due Wilson County Bank.

"The drawers and indorsers severally waive presentment for payment, protest and notice of protest, and nonpayment of this note, and in case of suit agree to pay court costs and all reasonable attorney fees for collecting same, and the principal may be granted further time, after due, from period to period, on payment of interest, without releasing sureties.

"[Signed]   "R. A. Denton.

                      "J. R. Odum, Security.

                      "J. L. Dies, Security."

The case was tried before the circuit judge without the intervention of a jury; and the court on request filed a written finding of facts, among which are the following:

That after the above note became due the defendant, R. A. Denton, principal, executed to the bank another note of $779.01, which covered all of the indebtedness of Denton to the bank, including the amount due on the above note in suit, as well as some other notes and some items of money at the time borrowed, and that a mortgage upon certain personalty of Denton was taken to secure the payment of the $779.01 note.

The last note embodied an agreement that the note in suit "shall be held by the bank as collateral security."

That no agreement for delay or extension of time by the note in suit was entered into unless, as a matter of law, the execution of the $779.01 note which matured six months after its date, April 11, 1911, amounted to such agreement.

That the execution of the new and larger note was not accepted by the bank as renewal of the note in suit, nor as payment of same, but it was taken and held as additional evidence of the indebtedness, the same in part as that evidenced by the note in suit.

That the proceeds of the sales under the mortgage, $277, were paid and credited on the $779.01 note.

That the two sureties, Dies and Odom, did not know of the execution of the $779.01 note until some time thereafter, when their principal, Denton, informed them that the old note had been settled by the new note, with other security, to wit, the mortgaged personalty.

The circuit judge thereupon rendered judgment against the principal and the sureties for the full amount of the note, and the sureties appealed to the court of civil appeals, which modified the judgment as below indicated.

Petition for *certiorari* was filed to bring the cause before this court for review.

The grounds urged for reversal are: (1) That the sureties were released from liability on the note in suit by the bank's action in extending the time of payment in taking the larger note; (2) because the note sued on was or should be deemed to be fully paid by the proceeds of the mortgage, $277.

It is clear that, even if the second note is to be deemed a renewal or extension of the first, the appellant sureties cannot successfully claim that they were released from liability by reason of such renewal or extension granted by the bank to their principal, since, first, the note in suit expressly stipulated that the principal might be granted further time after the note was due, from period to period without releasing the sureties.

Second, under our Negotiable Instruments Act (Acts 1899, ch. 94, sec. 120, subsec. 6) a surety on a note is not discharged by the taking of a renewal note of the principal, extending the time of payment, without notice to the surety, where the extension is given under an express reservation of the right of recourse against the surety. And this principal is operative if we can construe the finding of facts to be that the note in suit was retained in possession by the bank, and that the right of action thereon against the sureties was thereby reserved. *Meredith v. Dibrell,* 127 Tenn., 387, 155 S. W., 163, 46 L. R. A. (N. S.), 92.

In the event first above stated (without discussion of or specific ruling on the second ground above) the sureties were not released; it appearing that the second note was in point of fact not accepted by the bank even as a renewal, but only as an additional evidence of the indebtedness.

A contention of appellant sureties, however, is that the second note amounted to a novation or payment of this note in suit, as a necessary legal deduction or consequence.

The burden of proof to show novation of a note by a later note is upon him who asserts that there has been a novation. *Sharp v. Fly*, 9 Baxt., 4; *Lover v. Bessenger*, 9 Baxt., 393; 29 Cyc., 1139.

The rule is established by the weight of authority that where a new note is given to represent the consideration of a former note, and the original is retained, the new note operates only as a suspension of the debt evidenced by the original, and is not a satisfaction of it until paid. Daniel, Neg. Inst., sec. 1266. This author declares that there would be no cancellation of the older note by the later one if such were not the intention of the parties, and that it should be shown that it was expressly agreed that the old one should be extinguished, in order to have the effect of extinguishment.

The rule has been modified in this State to the extent that a presumption is raised that the old note is extinguished by the later one; but, if this presumption could prevail at all in cases where the old note was retained, it has been held that proof of an express agreement of the parties touching extinguishment or payment or the reverse will control. *Bowman v. Rector*, 59 S. W., 389, 398.

The intention of the obligor that the existing debt should be discharged by the new obligation must be concurred in by both debtor and creditor; and where the intention is shown, as in the case at bar, to have been to the contrary, it seems clear that neither novation nor payment resulted.

The fact that two evidences of one debt in the two notes outstand at the same time should not confuse the determination of the real rights of the parties. Such practice is not uncommon in business operations; and it is well recognized by the law that one of such evidences of the same debt may be treated as collateral to the other, and the only point of difficulty in the cases has been in relation to a surety on the paper, and as to when an agreement embodied or implied in the later obligation operates to postpone the remedy against the principal, which factor, we have seen, is not a determining one in this litigation.

The cases are numerous that illustrate the rule that two evidences of the same debt may outstand, the one as collateral to the other; and they are partially collated in 7 Cyc., 894, 895, to support the doctrine of the text to the effect that there is no extension of a note, so as to postpone suit or discharge a surety, where another note of the maker is taken merely as such collateral.

In *Continental Life Ins. Co.* v. *Barker*, 50 Conn., 567, it appeared that there was a renewal note (not in payment or satisfaction) secured by a mortgage on realty taken from the maker of a prior note, on which prior note there was an indorser, who did not agree to the renewal. The court said: "It is expressly found that the second note was taken as additional security for the balance due on the original note, and not in satisfaction of it nor as a substitute for it. Both notes were liable to be sued at any time; the one being overdue and the other on demand. Of course the indorser could have paid the first note and could at once have brought a suit against the maker. He was also entitled to the additional security, and could at once have brought a suit on that note, and could also have proceeded to foreclose the mortgage. Instead of being prejudiced by the transaction it was, in theory at least, a benefit to him."

In *Ripley* v. *Greenleaf*, 2 Vt., 129, where it appeared that the holder of a note, having advanced other sums to the maker, took a new note and a mortgage, which new note and mortgage were to secure both the old note and the subsequent advance, nothing being said as to the holder suing on the old note, it was held that the transaction did not suspend the holder's right to sue on the old note. See, also, *London, etc., Bank* v. *Parriott*, 125 Cal., 472, 58 Pac., 164, 73 Am. St. Rep., 64; *Fisher* v. *Denver Nat. Bank*, 22 Colo., 373, 381, 45 Pac., 440.

Some of the cases present the phase of the new note of the same maker being taken as collateral to an earlier note, while others present the converse phase, the maker's executing a new note, and the payee retaining, under agreement, the earlier note as collateral; but both are as one so far as the point here under discussion is concerned.

A case presenting the latter phase is that of *National Park Bank* v. *Koehler,* 137 App. Div., 785, 122 N. Y. Supp., 490, decided by the supreme court of New York. It there appeared that the maker of a note on which Koehler was indorser, shortly before maturity of that note requested an extension or renewal. The indorser being out of the country, the maker suggested to the holder bank, which had declined to accept a new indorser on the renewal note, that the old note with Koehler's indorsement be held by the bank as collateral until the new note was paid. This was acceded to. The court held that plainly the first note, sued on, was not paid; that the fair inference from the entire transaction (including the fact of the protest of the first note) was that the bank reserved its right to proceed forthwith against Koehler, as indorser; that Koehler could have taken up the indorsed note and sued the maker. The court further said: "Each case turns on the intention of the parties, which is a question of law if their acts and words are unequivocal, a question of fact if different inferences may be drawn." See, also, Brannan, Neg. Inst. 122; *Weakly* v. *Bell,* 9 Watts (Pa.), 273, 36 Am. Dec., 116, 124; *Peninsular Savings Bank* v. *Hoise,* 112 Mich., 351, 70 N. W., 890.

As will be noted, the only difficulty the court had in the above New York case was on the point whether there was fairly inferable a reservation by the bank of a right of action against the indorser (a point of discussion of which under the Negotiable Instruments Act we have already waived as unnecessary), but the court conceived that the first note was clearly collateral to the second.

But it is argued that, since the first note was recited in the second to be held as collateral security, by operation of law the first note was necessarily extinguished, since in order to a pledge thereof by the maker as pledgor it must be conceived of as being in his possession to pledge; and, when in his possession, it would be extinguished as to the sureties thereon.

In a true sense one personal obligation of a debtor proper cannot become the subject-matter of a pledge or collateral security proper, or in the sense of *pledged* collateral, for the security of another obligation of the same debtor, for the reason that a debtor's own personal obligation is no part of his personal property, and cannot be the subject of such a pledge—is a liability and not an asset. *International Trust Co.*, v. *Union Cattle Co.*, 3 Wyo., 808, 31 Pac., 408, 19 L. R. A. 640; *In re Waddell-Entz Co.*, 67 Conn., 324, 35 Atl., 257; 31 Cyc., 794; Jones, Coll. Sec., sec. 1.

There is nothing in these cases (and the authorities so treat of them) that militates against the rule, above recited, that one evidence of the same debt may stand as collateral to another evidence of the same debt.

In the case at bar there was no pledge of the first note attempted to be made as proceeding from the possession of the maker, Denton. The agreement was, as found, that the bank retained possession, and the second note only recited that it was "*held* by the bank as collateral security," which, as we have seen, was competent to be done. Further, the trial judge found that the new note was not even held as a renewal, but "was taken, and held as an additional evidence of indebtedness." In other words, both evidences were to exist, each collateral to the other. The finding of fact negatives the possession of the note on the part of Denton for any attempted pledge purpose proper.

Mr. Jones, in his work on Collateral Securities, at the section cited supra, after stating the rule that the personal obligation of the principal debtor is not, strictly speaking, pledgeable as collateral security to that debtor's obligation, proceeds to say that where the note placed as collateral was one signed by the maker *and indorsed by three others,* "it is difficult to see any good reason why this note should not have been regarded as collateral security. The indorsed note may have had the effect of extending the time of payment," and for that reason have released the surety. But the phase of release is one we are to leave aside in the case at bar, we repeat. When thus left, nothing can be urged, as we conceive, to effect a discharge of the sureties.

It has, quite unanimously we believe, been held that a note of A., which has collateral securities attached or a lien incident, may be treated as collateral to another note of A., and both the note and its collateral or lien enforced so far as to preserve to the creditor the benefit of the collateral or lien. *In re Waddel-Entz,* supra; *Easton* v. *Bank,* 127 U. S., 532, 8 Supp. Ct., 1297, 32 L. Ed., 210; *Dibert* v. *D'Arcy,* 248 Mo., 617, 154 S. W., 1116. Why not then the benefit of the incident of the suretyship of a personal surety?

While it is true two notes may thus exist, the creditor can make only a single proof against the debtor and have but one satisfaction. Jones, Coll. Sec., sec. 588d. It is really in substantiation of this rule that the decisions in *International Trust Co.* v. *Union Cattle Co.,* supra, and *In re Waddell-Entz Co.,* supra, are directed. A reading of these cases will make plain that on principle they are not in opposition to the other line of authorities above quoted and cited.

The fact that the new note of $779.01 included other indebtednesses, or a new one along with that evidenced by the earlier note sued on, cannot work a difference in principal. That feature was treated of in *Cotton* v. *Atlas Nat. Bank,* 145 Mass., 49, 12 N. E., 850, 856, where it was said: "In regard to giving time on the $50,000 debt, the effect upon that debt and its security by renewing the note as part of a larger note was the same as if it had been renewed alone. . . . The amount of the debt can be ascertained, and the payments made properly applied, with as much certainty, and by the same computations, as if the new note had not been given." *Ripley* v. *Greenleaf,* supra.

In regard to the right of the sureties in or by reason of the proceeds of the mortgaged personalty: The creditor bank applied these as credits on the last note

secured by the mortgage. In so doing the sureties obtained *pro tanto* satisfaction, which was the true and
just measure of their rights. This second note represented in part the indebtedness on which they were
sureties, and when there was a realization on the personalty conveyed to secure the large note in all its
constituent parts, and the proceeds were thus credited
thereon, the sureties cannot complain.

We have not for consideration the doctrine of application by a court of law of payments, since here
the bank as creditor has itself made the appropriation.
Bussey v. *Grant*, 10 Humph., 238; *Mason v. Smith*, 11
Lea, 67, 74; 30 Cyc., 1240.

The court of civil appeals, in modifying the judgment of the trial court so as to adjudge *pro tanto* satisfaction, did not err; affirmed.

KEELIN V. GRAVES *et al.**

(*Nashville.* December Term, 1913.)

1. EXEMPTIONS. Persons entitled to benefit.

The exemption laws, both as to personalty and realty, are exclusively for the benefit of citizens of the State having a domicile herein. (*Post, pp.* 109, 110.)

Cases cited and approved: Hawkins v. Pearce, 30 Tenn., 44; Lisenbee v. Holt, 33 Tenn., 50; Vaugh v. Ballentine, 1 Tenn. Cas., 596; Hicks v. Pepper, 60 Tenn., 42, 46; Emmett v. Emmett, 82 Tenn., 369, 370, 371; Doran v. O'Neal (Ch. App.), 37 S. W. 563, 565; Carrigan v. Rowell, 96 Tenn., 185; Faris v. Sipes, 99 Tenn., 298; Coil v. Hudgins, 109 Tenn., 217; Hascall v. Hafford, 107 Tenn., 355; Beeler v. Nance, 126 Tenn., 589; Grier v. Canada, 119 Tenn., 17; Prater v. Prater, 87 Tenn., 78; Graham v. Stull, 92 Tenn., 673; Whitly v. Steakly, 62 Tenn., 393.

2. ATTACHMENT. Grounds. Nonresidence.

One may be a temporary nonresident of the state, so as to authorize an attachment, though his domicile is still in the State. (*Post, pp.* 110, 111.)

Cases cited and approved: Smith v. Story, 20 Tenn., 420; Foster v. Hall & Eaton, 23 Tenn., 345; Stratton v. Brigham, supra; Klepper v. Powell, 53 Tenn., 503; People's Bank v. Williams (Ch. App.), 36 S. W., 983, 985, 986.

3. EXEMPTIONS. Nonresidence.

The exempt property of one whose domicile is in Tennessee, though he may be personally absent from the State for a considerable time on business, is free from attachment or execution for debt, even though he be absent long enough to author ize an attachment in lieu of personal service as to other kinds of property. (*Post, pp.* 111, 112.)

---

*As to when nonresidence of person intending to leave permanently begins for purpose of attachment or exemption, see note in 1 L. R. A. (N. S.), 778.

4. DOMICILE. "Change of domicile,"

Every one has a legal domicile, which is not changed until a new one is acquired, and to work a "change of domicile" he must have removed to another State to make his home there; a mere removal for business purposes, though long continued, not changing his domicile, if he intends to return to this State upon the completion of his business, though a mere floating purpose to return to the state at some indefinite time will not destroy the presumption that his change of residence changed his domicile (citing Words and Phrases, vol. 3, title "Domicile"; see, also, Words and Phrases, vol. 2, pp. 1053, 1054). (*Post, pp.* 111, 112.)

Cases cited and approved: Foster v. Hall & Eaton, supra; Allen v. Thomason, 30 Tenn., 536; Layne Ex. v. Pardee and Wife, 32 Tenn., 232, 235; Pearce v. State, 33 Tenn., 66; White v. White, 40 Tenn., 402; Williams v. Saunders, 45 Tenn., 60, 79, 80; Kellar v. Baird, 52 Tenn., 39; Sparks v. Sparks, 114 Tenn., 666.

5. ATTACHMENT. Grounds. Nonresidence.

In an action to replevy goods, attached by defendant on the ground that plaintiff was a nonresident, the court instructed that the plaintiff went to North Carolina to engage in business, with no definite idea as to when he would return, to make that state his residence, or if, after he got there, he determined to make it his residence, and actually resided there when the attachment was levied, he would be a nonresident, though he might not have carried his family with him, but if he went on a visit, with the intention of returning when his visit was was out, he would not be a nonresident, and that if plaintiff left Tennessee with the intention of obtaining employment, and did so without any definite idea of returning to that state, and found such employment, he was thereafter a nonresident. *Held* that, while the instruction did not refer to domicile and involved only the idea of nonresidence, it was substantially correct on the question of change of domicile. (*Post, pp.* 113, 114.)

Keelin v. Graves.

6. REPLEVIN. Judgment.

Under Shannon's Code, sec. 5144, requiring the judgment in replevin to provide for the return of the goods to the defendant,
or, on failure to do so, that defendant recover their value, with
interest and damages for their detention, and Acts 1905, ch. 31,
prescribing substantially the same form of judgment in actions
before a justice, in an ordinary action of replevin originally
brought before a justice, it was error to render a money judgment for defendant on the bond, in absence of evidence as to
the value of the property. (*Post, pp.* 114, 115.)

Acts cited and construed: Acts 1905, ch. 31.

Code cited and construed: Sec. 5144 (S.).

FROM DAVIDSON.

Appeal from the Circuit Court of Davidson County to the Court of Civil Appeals and by *certiorari* from
the Court of Civil Appeals to the Supreme Court.
—M. H. MEEKS, Judge.

C. H. RUTHERFORD, for plaintiff.

A. F. WHITMAN, for defendant.

MR. JUSTICE NEAL delivered the opinion of the Court.

The plaintiff in error, just prior to the time this controversy began, was a citizen and resident of this State, but, on obtaining employment in North Carolina, went there in the early part of February, 1912, and had been gone less than a month when his household furniture was attached, by defendant Graves, for a debt due to him, on the ground that plaintiff in error was a nonresident. He replevied the property before a justice of the peace, and, after trial before that officer and judgment in his favor, the case was appealed to the circuit court of Davidson county, where judgment was rendered in favor of the defendant Graves, from which an appeal was prosecuted to the court of civil appeals, and, on reversal of the judgment in that court, the case was brought here by the writ of *certiorari*.

The property involved was exempt from debt under the laws of this State, unless this right had been abandoned by reason of the removal of Keelin to North Carolina. In behalf of defendant in error it is insisted that this removal was of such a character as to effect such abandonment, and on behalf of the plaintiff in error it is urged that the facts show it was only a temporary removal. The case comes before us on the charge of the trial judge; but, in order that we may understand the application of the instructions complained of, it is necessary that the facts should be set out. They are practically undisputed with one exception.

It is shown by the officer who made the levy that at the time this levy was made there was a man present from Bond's warehouse for the purpose of packing the goods; that some of them had already been packed and marked for shipment to Raleigh, N. C., and some had been taken out of the house.

The plaintiff in error testified that he went to Raleigh, N. C., in February, 1912, on invitation of Edwards & Broughton Printing Company of that city, with a view to obtaining employment; that he was offered and accepted employment by the week, which still continues on the same terms; that he has no contract with his employers, except by the week; that he has rented a house by the month and moved his family into it; that at the time the attachment was levied he was in Raleigh, but his family was in Nashville, Tenn.; that when he went to Raleigh he had no definite plans as to the time of his return, but expected to return to Tennessee as soon as his business matters would justify—that is, as soon as he could secure employment that would justify his return; that his present employment is satisfactory, but the town is not; that he will not stay in his present place of employment at the salary now being paid, but he has not intimated to his employers his purpose to return to Tennessee; that he has not been back to Tennessee since he left; that, but for this lawsuit, he would not have removed his personal property to Raleigh; that it was his intention when he left Nashville to store his household goods in Nashville; that he has no contract, nor has he any prospect of making any contract, with any other person than his present employers; that he claims Nashville as his home, and expects to remain in Raleigh until he can secure employment in Tennessee; that he has not permanently taken up his residence in North Carolina; that he expects to return to Tennessee. Other witnesses testify that the household goods in controversy were, at the time the levy was made, in the house occupied by his wife and family in Nashville, and in due order.

The trial judge, among other things not excepted to, charged the jury as follows:

"The question which is submitted to the jury for decision is: Was the plaintiff in this case, J. N. Keelin, at the time of the levy of the attachment, a nonresident of the State of Tennessee? If he was, your verdict should be for the defendant; if he was not, your verdict should be for the plaintiff.

"If the jury should believe from the evidence that the plaintiff, Keelin, went to North Carolina to engage in business there, with no definite idea as to when he would return, to make that State his residence, or if, after he got there, he determined to make it his residence, and actually resided there when the attachment was levied, he would be a nonresident, although he might not have carried his family with him; but if he went on a visit, with the intention of returning when his visit was out, or had not changed his residence, he would not be a nonresident.

"Exempt property is protected as long as it is in the State, and the head of the family is in the State, and a resident thereof, but is not protected if he is a nonresident of the State.

"The jury should look at all the evidence bearing upon the intention and conduct of the plaintiff as to his purpose and intention, to the situation of the goods and the statements and conduct of parties in charge of them at the time the levy was made, to the letters introduced, to the length of time the plaintiff was in North Carolina, and to all the evidence submitted to them in deciding the question."

After the delivery of the foregoing charge the court gave to the jury the following special instruction at the request of the defendant below, which is also objected to by the plaintiff in error, viz.:

"If you should find that plaintiff had left the State of Tennessee with the intention of obtaining employment, and he did so obtain employment, without any definite idea of returning to this State, and that he found such employment in accordance with his intention and expectation at the time he left this State and went to North Carolina, then I charge you he was a nonresident at the time of suing out the writ of replevin."

Our exemption laws, both as to personalty and realty, are exclusively for the benefit of our citizens. *Hawkins* v. *Pearce,* 11 Humph., 44; *Lisenbee* v. *Holt,* 1 Sneed, 50. Citizens in the sense of these laws are only such persons as are domiciled in this State.

Vaughn v. *Ballentine,* 1 Tenn. Cas., 596; *Hicks* v. *Pepper,* 1 Baxt., 42, 46; *Emmett* v. *Emmett,* 14 Lea, 369-370-371; *Doran* v. *O'Neal* (Ch. App.), 37 S. W., 563, 565; *Carrigan* v. *Rowell,* 96 Tenn., 185, 34 S. W., 4; *Farris* v. *Sipes,* 99 Tenn., 298, 301, 41 S. W., 443; *Coile* v. *Hudgins,* 109 Tenn., 217, 70 S. W., 56; *Hascall* v. *Hafford,* 107 Tenn., 355, 65 S. W., 423, 89 Am. St. Rep., 952; *Beeler* v. *Nance,* 126 Tenn., 589, 150 S. W., 797. All the foregoing cases place the right squarely upon the existence and continuance of a domicile in the State. In *Grier* v. *Canada,* 119 Tenn., 17, at page 41, 107 S. W., 970, it is said generally that the homestead is abandoned by nonresidence; but this was said only in passing, and was not intended to overrule prior cases fixing domicile as the test, and, if so, it would itself be overruled by subsequent cases on the point. In *Prater* v. *Prater,* 87 Tenn., 78, 9 S. W., 361, 10 Am. St. Rep., 623, the term "nonresidence" is used; but it is apparent from the opinion that the word was used as the equivalent of domicile. In *Graham* v. *Stull,* 92 Tenn., 673, 22 S. W., 738, 21 L. R. A., 241, a case on the subject of the widow's year's support, the exemption was disallowed because the claimant was the widow of a nonresident; but no distinction was drawn between nonresidence and domicile in a foreign State, and this was not in the mind of the court. However, the court does refer to Arkansas as the domicile of the claimant. In *Whitly* v. *Steakly,* 3 Baxt., 393, a case wherein there was a levy on personalty claimed to be exempt, Whitly was held not entitled to the exempt property, because it appeared he had removed to Texas "without any intention of returning to Tennessee," which was equivalent, of course, to saying he had acquired a domicile in Texas.

In this State nonresidence is one of the grounds of attachment; but within the sense of our attachment laws one may be a nonresident for the time being, so as to justify an attachment, although his domicile may be in this State. Said Chancellor Cooper in *Cain* v. *Jennings,* 3 Tenn., Ch., 131, 136, 137: "The distinction between residence and citizenship is well established in the construction of the foreign attachment laws of the different states. A person may be a citizen of a State, and at the same time a nonresident of the State, within the attachment laws. This was held in New York, in a case where a citizen had been absent three years, attending to a lawsuit at New Orleans. *Haggart* v. *Morgan,* 5 N. Y., 422 [55 Am. Dec., 350]. The doctrine of this case has been substantially followed in New Jersey, Maryland, Mississippi, and Wisconsin. *Weber* v. *Weitling,* 18 N. J. Eq., 441; *Risewick* v. *Davis,* 19 Md., 82; *Alston* v. *Newcomer,* 42 Miss., 186; *Wolf* v. *McGavock,* 23 Wis., 516. The same principle, though not perhaps to the same extent, has been recognized by our supreme court in *Foster* v. *Hall,* 4 Humph., 346; *Stratton* v. *Brigham,* B *Sneed,* 420, and *Kellar* v. *Baird,* 5 Heisk., 46." Still it is difficult to draw the line of distinction, as will be seen from the following cases in this State: *Smith* v. *Story,* 1 Humph., 420; *Foster* v. *Hall &*

Eaton, 4 Humph., 345; *Stratton* v. *Brigham,* supra; *Klepper* v. *Powell,* 6 Heisk., 503; *People's Bank* v. *Williams* (Ch. App.), 36 S. W., 983, 985, 986.

But, at all events, one who is domiciled in Tennessee, although he may be temporarily absent from the State for a considerable length of time on business, is entitled to hold his exempt property free from attachment or execution for debt, even though such absence be so prolonged as to justify an attachment, in lieu of personal service as to other kinds of property. What are the characteristics of domicile in its several aspects it is difficult to state. There are many definitions which seem simple enough in form, but they are not easy to apply to the varying facts of cases as they arise. We have in this State several cases presenting the question from various points of view, viz.: *Foster* v. *Hall & Eaton,* supra; *Allen* v. *Thomason,* 11 Humph., 536, 54 Am. Dec., 55; *Layne Ex.* v. *Pardee and Wife,* 2 Swan, 232, 235; *Pearce* v. *State,* 1 Sneed, 66, 60 Am. Dec., 135; *White* v. *White,* 3 Head, 402; *Williams* v. *Saunders,* 5 Cold., 60, 79, 80; *Kellar* v. *Baird,* 5 Heisk., 39; *Sparks* v. *Sparks,* 114 Tenn., 666, 88 S. W., 173. The numerous definitions appearing under the heading of "Domicile" in Words and Phrases, vol. 3, fully illustrate the difficulty of making a clear statement of the principles involved. We believe, however, that the rule is settled that every one must have a legal domicile somewhere, and that this legal domicile is not changed in law until a new one is acquired. We think the substance of our cases is that, in order to destroy the *status* of a party as the possessor of a domicile once acquired in this State, it must appear that he has removed into another State for the purpose of making it his home, and that his removal for purposes of business, though long continued, will not have the effect of changing his domicile, if he has the purpose of returning to this State upon the completion of the business, but that a mere floating purpose to return to this State at some time will not be sufficient to destroy the presumption that his change of residence imported also a change of domicile.

Now, although the charge of the trial judge is based simply upon the idea of nonresidence without mentioning the subject of domicile, yet it contains in substance the thought that if the plaintiff in error went to North Carolina for the purpose of making it his home, without any definite intention of returning to Tennessee, his property would be subject to attachment as the property of a nonresident; that it to say, that he could not hold his *status* under such circumstances as the possessor of a domicile in Tennessee. So, in the special intsruction given, the same thought appears— that if he left Tennessee to obtain employment without any definite idea of returning, and did so obtain employment in the State to which he went, he would be a nonresident, and his property subject to attchment, even though of a kind exempt to those having a domicile or home in this State. While these instructions were not technically accurate, yet they were substantially so, and we therefore cannot sustain the error assigned upon the charge.

It is next assigned that the trial judge committed error in the form of the judgment. The verdict of the jury was in favor of the defendant below for the sum of $331.93. On this the trial judge rendered judgment as follows:

"It is therefore considered that the defendant C. A. Graves recover of J. N. Keelin the sum of $331.93, also the costs of this cause, for which amount, less that paid upon the bond in this cause, let *fi. fa.* issue; and it appearing to the court that J. N. Keelin, as principal, and T. L. Leatherwood, as surety, executed a bond in this cause to defendant J. M. Allen, deputy sheriff, February 28, 1912, in the sum of $300, for the recovery and possession of certain personal property then in the possession of J. M. Allen, deputy sheriff, under and by virtue of the writ of attachment then in his hands, issued by R. R. Caldwell, justice of the peace, in the case of *C. A. Graves* v. *J. N. Keelin*, February 27, 1912, and it further appearing that the conditions of said bond were to abide by and perform the orders of the court, and C. A. Graves having been substituted in the place and stead of the said J. M. Allen, deputy sheriff, and the court being of the opinion that the writ or replevin in this cause was wrongfully sued out by said Keelin, and the property wrongfully taken out of the possession of said officer, it is therefore ordered and adjudged by the court that

C. A. Graves recover of the said J. N. Keelin and T. L. Leatherwood the sum of $300, the same being the penalty of said bond, the same to be applied upon the above recovery of $331.93. It is ordered that said amount be paid into court within thirty days from this date, and, in case of failure so to do, execution will issue therefor."

The verdict and judgment were both fatally defective. The bond was not of the character described in the judgment, viz., a "replevy bond" to obtain possession of property under attachment. There was a distinct and independent action of replevin instituted before a justice of the peace, and an ordinary replevin bond was executed by Keelin, with Leatherwood as surety. The only judgment that could have been rendered on this bond was that the goods should be returned to the defendant, or on failure that the defendant recover their value, with interest thereon and damages for the detention. Shan. Code, sec. 5144. See, also, Acts 1905, ch., 31, prescribing substantially the same form of judgment before a justice of the peace. But no evidence was offered as to the value of the property.

The judgment must therefore be reversed, and the cause remanded for new trial.

PALMER v. SOUTHERN EXPRESS CO.

(Nashville.   December Term, 1913.)

1. **COMMERCE. Interstate commerce. State regulations. Validity.**
Acts 1913, 2d Extra Sess., ch. 1, sec. 5, forbidding any interstate
carrier of intoxicating liquor to deliver liquor to the consignee
unless the latter delivers a statement giving his name and
address, and stating the use for which the liquor was ordered,
directly interferes with interstate commerce as imposing a
condition precedent, on the exercise by the carrier of the
right to make delivery of an interstate shipment, and on the
right of the consignee to receive delivery, and cannot be sustained as an exercise of the police power, or as authorized by
the Wilson Act, which subjects liquor to State regulation, but
which does not apply before actual delivery to the consignee.
(*Post, pp.* 133-138.)

Acts cited and construed: Acts 193, sec 5.

Constitution cited and construed: Act 1, sec. 10.

Cases cited and approved: State v. Kelly, 123 Tenn., 567-575;
Louisville & Nashville Railroad Co. v. Brewing Co., 223 U. S.,
82.

Cases cited and distinguished: L. & N. R. R. Co. v. Brewing Co.,
supra; Leisy v. Hardin, 135 U. S., 100; Rhodes v. Iowa, 170 U.
S., 412, 419; Welton v. Missouri, 91 U. S., 281; Minnesota Rate
Cases, 230 U. S., 352.

2. **COMMERCE. Interstate commerce. State regulations. Validity.**
Acts 1913, 2d Extra Sess., ch. 1, sec. 9, subsec. 2, declaring that
nothing in the act prohibiting the carrying into the State of
intoxicating liquor shall make it unlawful for one to order, and
have shipped and delivered to him from without the State, for
his own use, intoxicating liquor in quantities not exceeding one
gallon, operates as a regulation of interstate commerce so as
to restrict deliveries to one gallon at a time where liquors are
intended for the personal use of the consignee, and is invalid.
(*Post, pp.* 138-143.)

Palmer v. Express Co.

Cases cited and approved: Hennington v. Georgia, 163 U. S., 299; Lakeshore, etc., R. R. v. Ohio, etc., 173 U. S., 285; Gulf Colorado & S. F. R. Co. v. Hefley, 158 U. S., 98; Rhodes v. Iowa, 170 U. S., 425; People v. Hawkins, 157 N. Y., 1; Arnold v. Yanders, 56 Ohio St., 417; Adams Express Co. v. Kentucky, 206 U. S., 129.

Cases cited and distinguished: Minnesota Rate Cases, supra; Oklahoma v. Kansas Nat. Gas Co., 221 U. S., 255; Adams Express Co. v. Kentucky, 214 U. S., 219.

3. COMMERCE. Interstate commerce. Congressional regulations. Effect.

The Interstate Commerce Act (Act Feb. 4, 1887, ch. 104, 24 Stat. 379 [U. S. Comp. St. 1901, p. 3154]), which applies to all corporations engaged in the transportation of property, and which declares that the term "transportation" shall include cars, facilities of shipment, etc., and the Wilson Act (Act Aug. 8, 1890, ch. 728, 26 Stat. 313 [U. S. Comp. St. 1901, p. 3177]), subjecting intoxicating liquors transported into the State to the State laws on arrival, and Crim. Code U. S. (Act March 4, 1909, ch. 321, 35 Stat. 1136 [U. S. Comp. St. Supp. 1911; pp. 1661, 1662]) secs. 238, 239, prohibiting a carrier from delivering liquor to any person except the consignee, and prohibiting carriers from collecting the price, or carrying C. O. D. shipments of liquor, etc., regulate interstate commerce in intoxicating liquors, and exclude all State action on the subject, and Acts 1913, 2d Extra Sess., ch. 1, sec. 5, forbidding the delivery of an interstate shipment of liquor to any person other than the consignee, and section 8, applying to interstate shipments, and section 9, subsec. 5, prohibiting an interstate carrier from delivering intoxicating liquors, unless the consignee presents a statement setting forth enumerated facts, are void, because they conflict with the federal stautues on the subject. (*Post, pp. 143-145.*)

4. COMMERCE. Interstate commerce. Congressional regulations. Effect.

The Webb-Kenyon Act (Act March 1, 1913, ch. 90, 37 Stat. 699), prohibiting the transportation from one State into another of

liquor for sale in violation of any law of the State where received, does not apply to a liquor shipment for the personal
use of the consignee and his family. (*Post, pp.* 146-148.)

5. **CONSTITUTIONAL LAW. Validity of statutes. Right to
raise questions.**

A party having no interest in provisions of a statute cannot require the court to determine the constitutionality of such provision. (*Post, pp.* 148, 149.)

Cases cited and approved: Kelly v. State, 123 Tenn., 516;
Richardson v. Young, 122 Tenn., 524.

6. **COMMERCE. Interstate commerce. State regulations.**

Acts 1913, 2d Extra Sess., ch. 1, sec. 3, requiring carriers of interstate shipments of liquor to file with the county court clerk
of the county in which the liquor is delivered a statement giving the name and address of the consignee, the place of
delivery, the kind and amount of liquor delivered, though imposing a new duty on interstate carriers of liquor, does not
impose a direct burden on interstate commerce, and is not in
conflict with the interstate commerce clause of the federal constitution, or with the federal statute making it unlawful for
any carrier to disclose any information which may be used to
the prejudice of a shipper or consignee, but not preventing the
giving of such information to any officer of any State in the
exercise of his powers. (*Post,* pp. 149-154.)

Cases cited and approved: Hennington v. Georgia, supra; Lakeshore, etc., R. R. v. Ohio, etc., supra; Gulf Colorado & S. F. Co.
v. Hefley, supra.

7. **STATUTES. Title. Constitutional provisions. Construction.**

The purpose of Const. art. 2, sec. 17, providing that no bill shall
embrace more than one subject, which shall be expressed in
the title is to prevent omnibus legislation; but particulars
leading directly or indirectly to the furtherance of the purpose
appearing in the title may be embodied in the body of the act. .
(*Post, pp.* 154-156.)

Constitution cited and construed: Art. 2, sec. 17.

8. CONSTITUTIONAL LAW. Statutes. Validity.

Where one construction of a statute will make it void, and another will render it valid, the latter will be adopted, though the former at first view is the more natural interpretation of the words used. (*Post, p.* 156.)

Case cited and distinguished: Hardaway v. Lilly, supra.

9. STATUTES. Title. Constitutional provisions.

Though the title of an act is double, in violation of Const. art. 2, sec. 17, the act will be upheld where only one of the subjects is embraced in its body.

Case cited and approved: Knoxville v. Gass, 119 Tenn., 438.

10. STATUTES. Title. Constitutional provisions.

Acts 1913, 2d Extra Sess., ch. 1, prohibiting the transportation into the State of intoxicating liquor except in the manner prescribed, is but a regulation, and not a prohibition, of transportation of intoxicating liquors, and is not broader than the title entitled "An act regulating the shipment and delivery of intoxicating liquor," etc. (*Post,* p. 157.)

11. STATUTES. Title. Constitutional provisions.

Acts 1913, 2d Extra Sess., ch. 1, prohibiting the transportation into the State of intoxicating liquor except in the manner provided, and requiring an interstate carrier to file with the county court clerk of the county in which the liquor is delivered a statement giving the name and address of the consignee, place of delivery, and the kind and amount delivered, and declaring that a certified copy of the statement shall be "competent evidence in any of the courts of this State upon the trial of any cause whatsoever in which the same may be material," does not embrace more than one subject, since the provision as to the competency of a certified copy of a statement applies only to a cause arising under the act. (*Post, pp.* 157-162.)

Cases cited and approved: Manufacturing Co. v. Falls, 90 Tenn.,

Cases cited and approved: Manufacturing Co. v. Falls, 90 Tenn., 469; State, ex rel., v. Schlitz Brewing Co., 104 Tenn., 715;

Railroad v. Byrne, 119 Tenn., 278; Darnell v. State, 123 Tenn., 663; Kirk v. State, 126 Tenn., 7.

Case cited and distinguished: Samuelson v. State, 116 Tenn., 470.

FROM DAVIDSON.

Appeal from Chancery Court, Davidson County— JOHN ALLISON, Chancellor.

VERTREES & VERTREES, for appellant.

FRANK M. THOMPSON, attorney general, and CHARLES C. TRABUE, for appellee.

MR. CHIEF JUSTICE NEIL delivered the opinion of the Court.

The bill in the present case was filed to test the constitutionality of chapter 1 passed by the general assembly at its second extra session, on October 16, 1913. The act is as follows:

"An act regulating the shipment of intoxicating liquor into this State or between points within this State; regulating the delivery of such liquor; providing for the filing of statements with the county clerk showing such shipments, and providing that certified copies of each statement may be used as evidence, and for the fees to such county clerk for making such copies; prescribing penalties for violation of the provisions of this act; and conferring jurisdiction for the trial of violations of this act upon the courts of the county from or to which such shipments may be made, and regulating the procedure in relation thereto.

"Section 1. Be it enacted by the general assembly of the State of Tennessee, that it shall be unlawful for any person, firm, or corporation to ship, carry, transport, or convey any intoxicating liquor into this State, or from one point to another within this State, for the purpose of delivery, or to deliver the same to any person, firm, company, or corporation within the State, except as hereinafter provided.

"Sec. 2. Be it further enacted, that the term 'intoxicating liquors' used in the first section hereof shall be deemed to cover and include, and shall cover and include, all liquors—spirituous, vinous, or malt—containing more than one-half of one per cent. alcohol, and which are used, or intended to be used, as a beverage.

"Sec. 3. Be it further enacted, that it shall be the duty of any railroad company, express company, or any other common carrier or person, who shall carry any intoxicating liquors into this State, or from one point to another within this State, for the purpose of delivery, and who shall deliver such intoxicating liquors to any person, company, or corporation, to keep a record of such liquor and file with the county clerk of the county in which such liquor is delivered a statement in writing, setting forth the date on which such liquor was received and delivered, the name and post

office address of the consignor and consignee, the place
of delivery and to whom delivered, and the kind and
amount of intoxicating liquor delivered, such statements to be filed within three days after the date of
the delivery of such liquor.

"Sec. 4. Be it further enacted, that it shall be the
duty of the county clerk to immediately file such statement as a part of the files of his office, and permit any
and all persons so desiring to inspect the same at any
time his office may be open; and it shall be the further
duty of the county court clerk to give a certified copy
of such statement to any person requesting or demanding the same upon the payment of the legal fees therefor, and said certified copy shall be competent evidence
in any of the courts of this state upon the trial of any
cause whatsoever in which the same may be material.

"Sec. 5. Be it further enacted, that it shall be unlawful for any railroad company, express company,
corporation, or other common carrier, or the agent of
any railroad company, express company, corporation,
or other common carrier, to deliver any intoxicating
liquor to any person other than the consignee; and in
no case where there are reasonable grounds for believing that any consignment or package contains intoxicating liquors shall any railroad company, express company, corporation, or other common carrier, or the
agent of such railroad company, express company, corporation or common carrier, or person, deliver such
consignment or package without first having such consignee sign and deliver to the person in whose charge

such consignment or package may be for delivery, a written statement in substance as follows:

" 'I hereby state that my name is——; that my post office address is——, Tenn.; that I am more than twenty-one years of age; that I am the consignee to whom a packing containing——of intoxicating liquors was consigned at——, on the——day of——19—, to be used for (set out the use for which such liquors are ordered or the purpose for which they are to be used).

" 'Signed and dated at——, Tenn., this——day of ——, 19—.'

"And in no case shall any railroad company, express company, corporation, or common carrier or person, or agent of such railroad company, express company, corporation, or other common carrier or person, be liable for damages for not delivering such intoxicating liquor or package supposed to contain the same until such statement is executed and delivered as herein provided.

"And in no case shall any such railroad company, express company, corporation or other common carrier, person or the agent of any such railroad company, express company, corporation, or other common carrier, or person, be held liable or subject to the penalties prescribed in this act for delivering such intoxicating liquors or package to the consignee without requiring such a statement when such statement is executed and delivered as herein provided, unless the party taking such statement knows the same to be false, in which case he may refuse to deliver such intoxicating liquors or package.

"Sec. 6. Be it further enacted, that any person who shall make the statement provided in section 5 of this act, knowing the same to be false, shall be deemed guilty of a misdemeanor, and, on conviction thereof, shall be fined not less than one hundred dollars nor more than five hundred dollars, and be imprisoned in the county jail not less than thirty days nor more than ninety days, in the discretion of the court.

"Sec. 7. Be it further enacted, that it shall be unlawful for any railroad company, express company, corporation, or other common carrier or person, to deliver any intoxicating liquor to any minor.

"Sec. 8. Be it further enacted, that it shall be unlawful for any person to ship any intoxicating liquor from any point within this State without marking on the outside of the package containing such intoxicating liquors, where it can be plainly seen and read, the words: 'This package contains intoxicating liquor.'

"Sec. 9. Be it further enacted, that nothing in this act shall make it unlawful:

"1. For any person, for the use of himself or the members of his family residing with him, to personally carry and transport to his own home such intoxicating liquor in quantities not exceeding one gallon.

"2. For any person to order and have shipped and delivered to him, from without the State, for his own use or the use of the members of his family residing with him, such intoxicating liquor in quantities not exceeding one gallon.

"3. For any person, for his own use and the use of his family residing with him, to order from and have shipped and delivered to him such intoxicating liquor, in quantities not exceeding one gallon, from any point in this State where such liquor can be lawfully sold for the purpose for which it is ordered; provided, the person, firm, or corporation from whom such liquor is ordered or bought or by whom it is shipped is authorized by the laws of this State to sell liquor for the purpose for which it is ordered.

"4. For any priest or minister of any religious denomination or sect to order, ship, or have shipped, carried, and delivered wine for sacramental purposes; or for any common carrier, corporation, or ship, transport, carry or deliver wine for said purposes to any priest or minister of any religious denomination or sect.

"5. For any person, firm or corporation to order, ship, transport, carry, or deliver intoxicating liquor into and within this State for purposes for which such liquor can be lawfully sold under the laws of this State, and to a person lawfully authorized to sell such liquors. But in all cases where any person, firm or corporation, carries and delivers any such intoxicating liquor for the purposes covered by subsections 2, 3, 4, 5 of this section, said person, firm, corporation, or carrier or the agent of any such firm, person, corporation, or carrier, shall require of the consignee a statement in writing, to be signed by such consignee, similar in form to the statement set out in section 5 hereof, showing the purpose for which said liquor has been ordered and is to be used, and, in cases covered by subsection 5 of this section, that the consignee is authorized by law to sell such liquor for the purpose for which it was ordered and delivery is sought; and any person who shall make a false statement in regard to the purpose for which said liquors are sought and are to be used or are used, shall be subject to the penalties prescribed in section 6 hereof.

"Sec. 10. Be it further enacted, that the delivery for shipment, the shipment, carriage, transportation, and delivery to the consignee of such liquors within the prohibition of this act from one point in this State to another point within this State, shall be deemed a continuing offense; and both the circuit and criminal courts held in the county from or to which such shipments are made, or in which delivery of any such shipment is made, shall have jurisdiction for the trial of any and all violations of this act, and the grand juries of said counties shall be vested with inquisitorial powers over violations of this act, and the circuit and criminal judges shall call attention to this act in charging the grand jury.

"Sec. 11. Be it further enacted, that any person, firm, or corporation violating any of the provisions of this act, except as hereinbefore expressly provided, shall, upon conviction, be fined not less than one hundred dollars and not more than five hundred dollars for each offense, and, in the discretion of the court, may be confined not less than thirty nor more than sixty days in the county jail.

"Sec. 12. Be it further enacted, that no person shall be excused from testifying either before the grand jury or on the trial in any prosecution for violating this act; but no disclosure or discovery made by such person shall be used against him in any penal or criminal prosecution for and on account of the matters disclosed.

"Sec. 13. Be it further enacted, that a conviction for violation of any of the provisions of this act may be had on the unsupported evidence of any accomplice or participant, and such accomplice or participant shall be exempt from prosecution for any offense under this law about which he may be required to testify.

"Sec. 14. Be it further enacted, that if for any reason any section or part of this act shall be held to be unconstitutional or invalid, then that fact shall not invalidate any other part of this act, but the same shall be enforced without reference to part so held to be invalid.

"Sec. 15. Be it further enacted, that in any indictment or presentment for any violation of this act it shall not be necessary to negative the exceptions herein contained or that the intoxicating liquor was ordered, shipped, transported, or delivered for any of the purposes set out in section 9 hereof; but such exception may be relied upon as a defense, and the burden of establishing the same shall be upon the person claiming the benefit thereof.

"Sec. 16. Be it further enacted, that all acts and parts of acts in conflict with the provisions of this act are hereby repealed.

"Sec. 17. Be it further enacted, that this act shall take effect from and after its passage, the public welfare requiring it.

"Passed October 16, 1913."

The original bill was filed on November 6, 1913, by Walter O. Palmer, a resident of Davidson county, and was brought against the Southern Express Company, which was described as "one of the few large express companies serving the public in this section of the United States."

The bill alleged that the complainant had ordered and purchased by mail order from dealers in liquors in Louisville, Ky., one gallon of a certain kind of intoxicating liquors, and fifteen gallons of a certain other kind of intoxicating liquors, and had directed them to be shipped to him by express to Nashville, and that this order was received and accepted at Louisville, and that the liquors were thereupon shipped to complainant at Nashville over the Southern Express Company in seven packages, one containing the one gallon of liquors first mentioned, and six "cases" containing each about 2½ gallons, constituting the other fifteen gallons, said liquors being of the value of $3.50 a gallon, and that these packages reached Nashville over the Southern Express Company about November 5, 1913, and that complainant was promptly notified, and called at defendant's office to receive them, and pay the express charges.

The bill further alleged that complainant is engaged in farming and live stock breeding, and is not engaged in the liquor business, and that he purchased these liquors solely for his own use, and for the use of his family residing with him.

Complainant further alleged that the defendant offered to deliver the one-gallon package of liquors to him only upon condition that he would make and deliver the statement required of consignee by the fifth section of the act, and that he protested against this, but finally made and delivered a written statement in conformity with the terms of the act, and thereupon received the one-gallon package.

He alleged that the defendant refused to deliver to him either of the six cases containing 2½ gallons each unless he would make and deliver a statement in writing that he was and is authorized by law to sell such liquors for some stated and specific lawful purpose, and which statement should further contain all the recitals prescribed by sections 5 and 9 of the act, and that he declined to sign any such statement, for which reason the delivery of the six cases was withheld.

The bill alleged that section 3 of the act, requiring express companies and other carriers, when they transport intoxicating liquors from another state into Tennessee, to file "a statement in writing" showing the facts therein mentioned, does not prescribe any rule for the government of the consignee, or regulate the use or disposition of the liquors transported, but imposes on such carriers duties with respect to transportation which have been ended and completed, duties which are onerous and expensive to carriers, vexatious and annoying to consignees, and which not only constitute burdens on interstate commerce, but violate the liberty of the citizen, his right of privacy, and is in violation of section 8 of article 1 of the constitution of Tennessee, and of the fifth and fourteenth amendments of the constitution of the United States.

It was further alleged that the contents of said packages are marked thereon; also the name of the complainant as consignee; likewise the name of the Paul Jones Company, the consignor; and that they could be identified thereby.

The bill prayed for an injunction to restrain defendant from filing the above-mentioned "statement in writing," and such an injunction was granted and executed on the filing of the bill.

The bill further alleged that so much of the terms of the act as assumed to prohibit a person from having shipped and delivered to him from without the State, for his own use, or the use of the members of his family residing with him, intoxicating liquors in quantities exceeding one gallon, was unconstitutional and void, for the reason that such provision was an interference with, and burden on, interstate commerce, and because it was lawful, under the laws of Tennessee, for a citizen of Tennessee to own and keep intoxicating liquor in an unlimited quantity, and because it was lawful, under the laws of the United States, for a citizen of Tennessee to purchase by interstate commerce intoxicating liquors in unlimited quantity; and complainant averred that, for these reasons, he was entitled to receive the six cases hereinabove referred to on demand and payment of the charges, and that he could not lawfully be required to make and deliver the statement prescribed by sections 5 and 9 of the act as demanded of him by the defendant express company.

Upon this ground complainant sought a writ of replevin to recover the six cases, and such writ was granted upon the filing of the bill, and the officer executing the writ took the cases and delivered them to complainant.

The bill further averred that the entire act was void' upon the ground that it contained two subjects.

The defendant demurred, challenging the correctness of the legal conclusions on which the bill was predicated, and assserting the validity and constitutionality of the act in all of its parts.

More particularly the demurrers asserted the validity of the two provisions of the act that were primarily attacked in the bill, namely: The provision requiring carriers to file "statements in writing" with the county court clerks, and the provision in regard to the "one-gallon" limitation.

The cause was heard on the demurrers.

The chancellor was of opinion and decreed that the two provisions of the act that were primarily attacked were, in respect of interstate shipments into Tennessee of intoxicating liquors for personal use and consumption, an unlawful burden upon and interference with interstate commerce, and were therefore unconstitutional and void, and that, upon the facts stated in the bill, complainant was entitled to the relief prayed for. The decree entered broadly sustained the bill, and overruled the demurrers.

Defendant, through its counsel, thereupon stated in open court—as appears in the decree—that "the averments of fact in the original bill were not and would not be controverted, and that it desired to stand on the demurrers," whereupon the chancellor granted an appeal to this court.

The general contentions of the complainant on the brief filed may be thus summarized: That certain provisions of the act are void under the constitution of the United States because they regulate interstate commerce; that one provision is void because it violates an act of congress regulating the duties of interstate carriers; that the recent act of congress, known as the Webb-Kenyon Act, has no application to the case, and that in any event that act is void; that the whole act of 1913, reproduced supra, is void as being in violation of article 2, sec. 17, of the constitution of Tennessee. The other questions suggested in the bill were not discussed in the brief.

1. It is insisted that section 5 is an attempted regulation of interstate commerce by the State, and therefore void, in that it imposes as a condition of delivery of the goods the making by the consignee of the written statement therein required.

We are unable to perceive any sound answer to this contention. Intoxicating liquor is recognized in the federal authorities as a lawful subject of interstate commerce. In *L. & N. R. R. Co.* v. *Cook Brewing Co.*, 223 U. S., 82, 32 Sup. Ct., 191, 56 L. Ed., 355, it is said: "By a long line of decisions, beginning even prior to *Leisy* v. *Hardin,* 135 U. S., 100 [10 Sup. Ct., 681, 34 L. Ed., 128.], it has been indisputably determined: (a) That beer and other intoxicating liquors are a recognized and legitimate subject of interstate commerce; (b) that it is not competent for any State to forbid any commerce carrier to transport such articles from a consignor in one state to a consignee in another." In *Leisy* v. *Hardin,* it is said: "That ardent spirits, distilled liquors, ale, and beer are subjects of exchange, barter, and traffic, like any other commodity in which a right of traffic exists, and are so recognized by the usages of the commercial world, the laws of congress, and the decisions of courts, is not denied." 135 U. S., 100, 110, 10 Sup. Ct., 681, 684 (34 L. Ed., 128). In *Vance* v. *Vandercook Co.,* it is said: "Equally well established is the proposition that the right to send liquors from one State into another, and the act of sending the same, is interstate commerce, the regulation whereof has been committed by the constitution

of the United States to congress, and hence that a
State law which denies such a right, or substantially
interferes with or hampers the same, is in conflict with
the constitution of the United States." 170 U. S.,
444, 18 Sup. Ct., 676, 42 L. Ed., 1100. Delivery is an
essential part of interstate commerce in any article
transported from one State to another in course of
that commerce, and cannot be interfered with by the
State. In *Rhodes* v. *Iowa*, 170 U. S., 412, 419, 18 Sup.
Ct., 664, 666 (42 L. Ed., 1088), the court, referring to
Bowman v. *Chicago & Northwestern R. Co.*, 125 U.
S., 465, 8 Sup. Ct., 689, 1062, 31 L. Ed., 700, said: "The
fundamental right which the decision in the *Bowman
case* held to be protected from the operation of State
laws by the constitution of the United States was the
continuity of shipment of goods coming from one State
into another from the point of transmission to the point
of consignment, and the accomplishment there of the
delivery covered by the contract." In *L. & N. R. R.
Co.* v. *Cook, supra*, it is said that one point clearly
settled by prior decisions is: "That, uutil such transportation is concluded by delivery to the consignee,
such commodities do not become subject to state regulation, restraining their sale or disposition." In *Welton* v. *Missouri*, 91 U. S., 281, 23 L. Ed., 347, it is
said: "The power which insures uniformity of commercial regulation must cover the property which is
transported as an article of commerce from hostile or
interfering legislation until it has mingled with and
becomes a part of the general property of the country,

and subjected like it to similar protection, and to no
greater burdens. If, at any time before it has thus
become incorporated into the mass of property of the
State or nation, it can be subjected to any restrictions
by State legislation, the object of investing the control in congress may be entirely defeated." In *Bowman* v. *Chicago & Northwestern R. Co.*, 125 U. S., 465,
8 Sup. Ct., 689, 1062, 31 L. Ed., 700, above referred to,
it appeared that the plaintiffs had tendered to the railway company sundry barrels of beer, in Chicago, for
the purpose of having the beer transported to a point
in Iowa for sale. The company refused to receive
the beer on the ground that there was a statute in Iowa
(Code 1873, sec. 1553, as amended by Acts 21st Gen.
Assem., ch. 66, sec. 10) which forbade any carrier to
transport "between points," that is, to any point in
the State, "any intoxicating liquors, without first having been furnished with a certificate from and under
the seal of the county auditor of the county to which
said liquor is to be transported or is consigned for
transportation, or within which it is to be conveyed
from place to place, certifying that the consignee or
person to whom said liquor is to be transported, conveyed, or delivered, is authorized to sell such intoxicating liquors in such county;" that the certificate had
not been furnished; and that the statute provided that
the offense denounced in it should be held complete,
and should be held to have been committed in any county of the State through or to which said intoxicating
liquors should be transported, or in which they should

be "unloaded, for transportation, or in which said liquors are conveyed from place to place or delivered." The plaintiff sued the railway company in damages because of its refusal to receive and transport the barrels of beer offered. The case finally reached the Supreme Court of the United States, and that court held that the State statute was void so far as it applied to interstate commerce, and, in so holding, said:

"It is conceded, as we have already shown, that, for the purposes of its policy, a State has legislative control, exclusive of congress within its territory, of all persons, things, and transactions of strictly internal concern. For the purpose of protecting its people against the evils of intemperance it has the right to prohibit the manufacture within its limit of intoxicating liquors; it may also prohibit all domestic commerce in them between its own inhabitants, whether the articles are introduced from other State or from foreign countries; it may punish those who sell them in violation of its laws; it may adopt any measures tending, even indirectly or remotely, to make the policy effective until it passes the line of power delegated to congress under the constitution. It cannot, without the consent of congress, expressed or implied, regulate commerce between its people and those of the other States of the Union in order to effect its end, however desirable such a regulation might be.

"The statute of Iowa under consideration falls within this prohibition. It is not an inspection law; it is not a quarantine or sanitary law. It is essentially a regulation of commerce among the States within any definition heretofore given to that term, or which can be given; and, although its motive and purpose are to perfect the policy of the State of Iowa in protecting its citizens against the evils of intemperance, it is none the less on that account a regulation of commerce." 125 U. S., 493, 8 Sup. Ct., 702, 31 L. Ed., 700.

We have seen that this case was referred to in a subsequent case as protecting the fundamental right of transporting goods by continuous shipment from a point in one State to a point in another State, "and the accomplishment there of the delivery covered by the contract."

It seems clear that section 5 of the act of 1913, in so far as it requires the certificate therein provided for, falls within the authorities referred to', and is void as a regulation of interstate commerce, imposing as it does a condition precedent, upon the exercise by the carrier of the right to make delivery, and upon the right of the consignee to receive delivery of the goods.

It is perceived, from the passage we have quoted out of *Bowman* v. *Railroad*, that the provision in question cannot be upheld on the ground that it is an exercise of the police power of the State, since that power in a state cannot transcend the constitution of the United States. *State* v. *Kelly*, 123 Tenn., 567-575, 133 S. W., 1011, 36 L. R. A. (N. S.), 171.

Nor can it be said that it has a mere incidental effect upon interstate commerce, and therefore, under the authorities on that subject, must be held a harmless invasion of national power. Its action is direct, since it arrests delivery until the certificate is executed.

It cannot be treated as a means of inspection, with a view to excluding an impure article, and thus falling within the power conceded or reserved to the States, under article 1, sec. 10, of the Constitution, to pass inspection laws, subject to the revision and control of the congress. *Bowman v. Chicago, etc., Railroad, supra,* 125 U. S., 488, 8 Sup. Ct., 689, 1062, 31 L. Ed., 700. No claim, indeed, is made that the act was passed for any such purpose.

Nor truly can the claim be made that the provision falls within any of the other recognized exceptions to the operation of the interstate commerce clause of the constitution. The whole subject is luminously discussed in the recent opinion of Mr. Justice Hughes, in the *Minnesota Rate Cases* 230 U. S., 352, 398-412, 33 Sup. Ct., 729, 57 L. Ed. 1511, wherein the rule and its recognized exceptions or qualifications are stated.

The Wilson Act, which subjects intoxicating liquors to State regulation, although in the original packages, does not apply before actual delivery to the consignee, where the shipment is interstate, and hence has no bearing upon the question we have before us. *Louisville & Nashville Railroad Co.* v. *F. W. Cook Brewing Co.,* supra.

2. It is insisted that subsection 2 of section 9, when read and properly construed in connection with sec-

tion 1, operates also as a regulation of interstate commerce, so as to restrict deliveries to consignees of
liquors shipped from other States into this State to
one gallon at a time, where the liquors are intended
for the personal use of the consignee, or the use of his
family.

We see no escape from the conclusion that it is such
regulation. The ultimate quantity to be obtained by
multiplying separate shipments is not restricted. So
far as anything appears in the act, the consignee can
have made to him any number of separate shipments
of liquors for his own use, or the use of himself and
family; but no single shipment must exceed one gallon
in quantity, and the shipments may be concurrent or
successive. What is this but a regulation of commerce? It can be nothing else. There can be no
doubt that such regulation would be very useful to
the State in the enforcement of its prohibition laws,
the requirements as to the certificate in section 3 being sustained, since many would hesitate to go on record for numerous shipments, and such as would dare
to do so would, by the accumulation of multiplied gallons, aggregating a large and unreasonable quanity
for alleged personal and family use, furnish ground
for a strong inference, or violent presumption, that
the real purpose was to store the liquors for illegal
and surreptitious sale. But the question is, not alone
whether it would be useful as a State police measure,
but whether, although thus useful, it would be an un-

constitutional attempt at regulating interestate commerce.

That it is a regulation is indubitable; is it an unconstitutional regulation? Every new question must be determined on its own facts; but these facts must be brought to the test of recognized principle. The States have no power to impose a regulation on interstate commerce merely because it is a reasonable or judicious one. That is a function of the congress. It is a mere truism, of course, that the states have no right to regulate a subject of interstate commerce within the exclusive jurisdiction of congress because the congress has failed to act. The decisions of the supreme court of the United States are to the effect that, where congress has failed to impose any regulation in such cases, there is a conclusive presumption that it is the will of that body that the traffic shall remain free until such time as it shall see proper to act in the matter. There is, it is true, a broad field, embracing a great variety of subjects, in which the powers of the federal and State governments are concurrent, and in these the States may control until congress acts, and, when the latter acts, it is said to take possession of the subject, to the exclusion of the states, in respect of the special aspect so legislated on. There is also, as already indicated, an exclusive field into which the States cannot enter at all. The point is thus expressed by Mr. Justice Hughes in the *Minnesota Rate Cases,* supra:

"The grant in the constitution of its own force . . . established the essential immunity of interstate commercial intercourse from the direct control of the States with respect to those subjects embraced within the grant which are of such a nature as to demand that, if regulated at all, their regulation should be prescribed by a single authority. It has repeatedly been declared by this court that as to those subjects which require a general system or uniformity of regu- lation the power of congress is exclusive.

"In other matters admitting diversity of treatment according to special requirements of local conditions, the states may act within their respective jurisdictions until congress sees fit to act, and when congress does act, the exercise of its authority overrides all conflict- ing legislation." 230 U. S., 399, 33 Sup. Ct., 740, 57 L. Ed., 1511.

Instances of the latter class are seen in *Hennington v. Georgia,* 163 U. S., 299, 16 Sup. Ct., 1086, 41 L. Ed., 166; *Lakeshore, etc., R. R.* v. *Ohio, etc.,* 173 U. S., 285, 19 Sup. Ct., 465, 43 L. Ed., 702, and cases cited. The case of *Gulf Colorado & S. F. R. Co.* v. *Hefley,* 158 U. S., 98, 15 Sup. Ct., 802, 39 L. Ed., 910, was a case in which such regulation in the concurrent field by the State was superseded and rendered nugatory by an act of congress in conflict therewith.

The special questions we have before us, arising on the one-gallon regulation, and the regulation in respect of the certificate required by section 5, previously dis- cussed, fall within that portion of the field which relates to interstate commerce in its fundamental aspect, in which, as stated, the power of congress is exclusive. In the constitution of the United States it is provided: "Congress shall have power . . . to regulate commerce with foreign nations, and among the several States, and among the Indian tribes." It has been said over and over again, in the federal authorities, that the purpose of the provision was to secure uniformity of regulation. In *Oklahoma* v. *Kansas Nat. Gas Co.*, 221 U. S., 255, 31 Sup. Ct., 571, 55 L. Ed., 716, it is said: " 'In matters of foreign and interstate commerce there are no State lines.' In such commerce, instead of the States, a new power appears, and a new welfare, a welfare which transcends that of any State." In *Rhodes* v. *Iowa*, 170 U. S., 425, 18 Sup. Ct., 669, 42 L. Ed., 1088, it is said that the right to contract for the transportation of merchandise from one State into or across another involves "interstate, commerce in its fundamental aspect," and imports "in its very essence a relation which necessarily must be governed by laws apart from the laws of the several States," since it embraces "a contract which must come under the laws of more than one State."

Some illustrations may be useful. A statute of Kentucky made it unlawful to sell or furnish liquor to a known drunkard. A drunkard, named Tharp, residing in Kentucky, ordered liquor from Nashville, and the express company conveyed it and delivered it to him. It was held that Kentucky could not punish the company and its agent, both having been indicted, because they were but performing an interstate commerce act, which the State could not regulate. The court said: "If such regulation of interstate commerce is deemed advisable, it must proceed from congress." *Adams Express Co.* v. *Kentucky,* 214 U. S., 219, 29 Sup. Ct., 633, 53 L. Ed., 972. A statute of New York required convict-made goods to be so branded before being exposed to sale. It was held to be void as to goods from other States because it was a regulation of interstate commerce. *People* v. *Hawkins,* 157 N. Y., 1, 51 N. E., 257, 42 L. R. A., 490, 68 Am. St. Rep., 737. A statute of Ohio required a license to be taken out for the sale of convict-made goods. It was held void as a regulation of commerce as to goods from other States. *Arnold* v. *Yanders,* 56 Ohio St., 417, 47 N. E., 50, 60 Am. St. Rep., 753. A statute of Kentucky forbade C. O. D. shipments of intoxicating liquor. It was held to be void as a regulation of interstate commerce. *Adams Express Co.* v. *Kentucky,* 206 U. S., 129, 27 Sup. Ct., 606, 51 L. Ed., 987.

It is apparent from the principles stated and authorities cited that the one-gallon regulation is wholly void in so far as it applies to interstate commerce.

In what has been said we have treated the question from the standpoint, which we believe to be the true one, that the regulations in question invade that field which is within the exclusive power of congress, interstate commerce in its fundamental aspect; but, if we err in this, the same result follows from viewing them

as falling within the concurrent field, since congress
has already entered this field with sundry regulations,
and has thus occupied the field, excluding any conflicting State regulations.   First is the Interstate Commerce Act.   Its provisions apply to all corporations
engaged in the transportation of persons and property, and declares that the term "transportation"
shall include "cars, . . . facilities of shipment or carriage, . . . all services in connection with the receipt,
delivery, . . . and handling of property transported."
Congress has regulated interstate commerce in intoxicating liquors as follows: The "Wilson Act," subjecting such liquors to the State laws upon arrival,
that is, immediately upon delivery (3 Fed. Stat. Ann.,
853); by a provision making it unlawful for a carrier
to deliver to any person except the consignee, or on
his written order (Crim. Code U. S., sec. 238); also
making it unlawful to deliver to a fictitious person
(Id.); also a provision making it unlawful for any
carrier to collect the purchase price, or carry C. O. D.
shipments of such liquors (Id., sec. 239); a provision
making it unlawful for any person to ship any package of intoxicating liquors not so labeled on the outside
as to show the name of the consignee, the nature of the
contents, and the quanitity; and, finally, the Webb-
Kenyon Act, to which we shall presently refer with
more particularity. As complainant's brief soundly insists: Interstate transportation "is regulated by the
Interstate Commerce Act—that is to say, all services

in connection with the receipt, delivery, and handling of the property transported. Necessarily that excludes all State action. But, specifically, congress has regulated the labeling; has provided that it may be delivered on the order of the consignee, that the liquor shall be subject to State laws on 'arrival,' which the courts have construed to mean delivery, and thereby necessarily declaring that the State laws shall not attach prior to delivery. Congress has provided against C. O. D. shipments; against shipments with intent to violate State laws by sale or use. It has placed no limit on quantity, and, instead of requiring a statement from the consignee, has provided what shall be marked on the outside of the package itself.''

3. That part of section 5 which forbids the delivery of intoxicating liquors ''to any person other than the consignee is void so far as it applies to interstate shipments, because in conflict with the federal statute on the same subject.

4. So far as section 8 applies to interstate shipments it is likewise void, because the subject is regulated by the federal statute.

5. The certificate provided for in subsection 5 of section 9 is likewise void in so far as it applies to interstate shipments, on the ground that it is a regulation of interstate commerce; the reasons being the same as those set forth in disposing of the question raised on the certificate required by section 5 of the act.

6. It is insisted in behalf of the state that the various provisions are saved by the Webb-Kenyon Bill, or Act. That act is as follows:

"An act divesting intoxicating liquors of their inter-state character in certain cases.

"Be it enacted by the senate and house of representatives of the United States of America in congress assembled, that the shipment or transportation, in any manner or by any means whatsoever, of any spirituous, vinous, malted, fermented, or other intoxicating liquor of any kind, from one State, territory, or district of the United States, or place noncontiguous to but subject to the jurisdiction thereof, into any other State, territory or district of the United States or place noncontiguous to but subject to the jurisdiction thereof, or from any foreign country into any State, territory, or district of the United States, or place noncontiguous to but subject to the jurisdiction thereof, which said spirituous, vinous, malted, fermented, or other intoxicating liquor is intended, by any person interested therein, to be received, possessed, sold, or in any manner used, either, in the original package or otherwise, in violation of any law of such State, territory, or district of the United States, or place noncontiguous to but subject to the jurisdiction thereof, is hereby prohibited."

It is perceived that the thing which the act prohibits is the interstate shipment or transportation of the liquors mentioned therein, when "intended by any person interested therein, to be received, possessed, sold, or in any manner used, either in the original package or otherwise, in violation of any law of the State, etc., into which the shipment is made.

It is enough to say, for the disposition of the case before us, that it does not appear that the liquors shipped were intended to be sold, or used in violation of any law of the State; and therefore the act does not apply to the present controversy. It appears from the facts stated in the bill, confessed by the demurrer, and agreed to on the record at the hearing in the court below, that the liquors were purchased for the personal use of complainant and his family. This was a lawful use, and indeed permitted by the statute in question. And see, generally, Woolen & Thornton on Intoxicating Liquors, sec. 203, and cases cited. The fact that the purchase was in excess of one gallon cannot change the conclusion, or alter the result, because that regulation is void as being in violation of the interstate commerce clause of the federal constitution, and of the Interstate Commerce Act passed thereunder. If the said Webb-Kenyon Act can be held operative for the purposes designed, it must be on the ground that liquors shipped tainted by the intention designated are, by the act, withdrawn from interstate commerce; that is, are, by the existence of the illegal intention, rendered noncommerce articles. Such seems to be the thought indicated by the caption of the bill. But this bill has no reference to quantity, but only to *sale,* or *use,* in violation of any law of the State. The act, therefore, does not apply to the present controversy.

A vigorous attack is made on the constitutionality of the act, supported by a very interesting and able discussion by the point; but we do not deem it essential, or even proper, to go into this question, since the view already stated is sufficient to dispose of the case in so far as the Webb-Kenyon Act relates to it.

But, before passing from this phase of the case, we desire to add, in order that the present opinion may not be misunderstood, that what we have just held as to the inapplicability of the Webb-Kenyon Act to the case before us is not intended to cover those instances in which sales of liquors are made in a foreign State for shipment into this State to be sold or used in violation of the prohibition laws of this State. A discussion of the illegal nature of such contracts, and the circumstances under which they are to be held illegal, is found in section 1015 of Woolen & Thornton on the Law of Intoxicating Liquors, and the cases cited in the notes. What we have said as to the certificates, or statements, or supercriptions on the packages, we apply in the present opinion only to intoxicating liquors shipped into this State for the personal use of the consignee and his family; that only being the nature of the case before us. Nor do we desire to be understood as expressing any opinion as to whether there can be constitutionally withdrawn from the operation of the interstate commerce laws, an article otherwise of a commercial nature, where the illegal intent is not found either directly or circumstantially to have existed at the time in the mind of the seller, as well as in the mind of the buyer. How far such power exists in the congress we have not considered. In short, the present opinion is confined only to the cases wherein the shipment is for the personal use of the consignee or his family. It is for the personal use of the consignee or his family. It is our duty to so confine the decision. Woolen & Thornton, Intox. Liq., sec. 186, and cases cited. The complainant belonging only to the class of those who buy for personal and family use has no interest in any other phase of the questions involved, and cannot call on the court for a decision in respect thereof. *Kelly* v. *State,* 123 Tenn., 516, 553-555, 132 S. W., 193; *Richardson* v. *Young,* 122 Tenn., 524, 125 S. W., 664.

7. It is insisted that the provisions of section 3 of the act in question are void as a regulation of interstate commerce. We are of a contrary opinion. The section referred to prescribes the ''statement in writing'' therein required of the carrier to be filed after delivery, and therefore after the interstate transaction has been completed. It is true that it imposes a new duty on an interstate carrier. States, however, have this right, when such duty does not impose a direct burden upon interstate commerce, and when congress has not itself legislated upon the special question. Congress has not so legislated, and the provision can have only a very incidental effect on interstate commerce. *Hennington* v. *Georgia,* supra; *Lakeshore, etc., R. R.* v. *Ohio, etc.,* supra; *Gulf Colorado & S. F. R. Co.* v. *Hefley,* supra. The provisions in question, there-

fore, are valid so far as concerns the operation of the interstate commerce laws.

8. But it is insisted that section 3 is in conflict with the following congressional legislation, viz.:

"It shall be unlawful for any common carrier subject to the provisions of this act, or any officer, agent, or employee, of such common carrier, or for any other person or corporation lawfully authorized by such common carrier to receive information therefrom, knowingly to disclose to or permit to be acquired by any person or corporation other than the shipper or consignee, . . . any information concerning the nature, kind, quantity, designation, consignee, or routing of any property tendered or delivered to such common carrier for the interstate transportation, which information may be used to the detriment or prejudice of such shipper or consignee, or which may improperly disclose his business transactions to a competitor; and it shall also be unlawful for any person or corporation to solicit or knowingly receive any such information which may be so used: Provided, that nothing in this act shall be construed to prevent the giving of such information in response to any legal process issued under the authority of any State or federal court, or to any officer or agent of the government of the United States, or of any State or territory, in the exercise of his powers, or to any officer or other duly authorized person seeking such information for the prosecution of persons charged with or suspected of crime; or information given by a common carrier . . .

or its duly authorized agent, for the purpose of adjusting mutual traffic accounts in the ordinary course of business of such carriers.''

We do not think section 3 is in conflict with this federal legislation. Its provisions are fairly within one of the exceptions of the federal act, viz.: ''That nothing in this act shall be construed to prevent the giving of such information . . . to any officer or agent . . . of any State or territory, in the exercise of his powers.'' Sections 3 and 4 impose upon the county court clerk the duty of receiving and filing such statements for the information of the public. The information thus obtained is obtained by him ''in the exercise of his powers'' pursuant to a duty imposed on him by law. It is true that he is the mere recipient of the information, not being required to go out of his office and demand it of the carrier. But we do not conceive that this could make any sort of difference. It could not be doubted, we think, that, if sections 3 and 4 had required the county court clerk to demand the information, it would have been the duty of the carrier to give it, within the exception mentioned. How can the substance of the matter be altered by the fact that the State statute itself, the whole State in its organized capacity, makes the demand of the carrier to give the information, and makes it the duty of the county court clerk to receive and file it? Moreover, the federal statute in question does not, in the exception we have quoted, require as a condition precedent to its effectiveness that any demand shall be made by an officer of the State. The heart of the matter, the substance, is that the information may be given to a State, through an officer or agent in the exercise of his powers. The method by which the State shall require that information or signify its desire to receive it is not material. In what more authoritative manner could it be required or could such desire be signified than by a solemn public act of the legislature of the State, making it the duty of the carrier to communicate the information to a designated officer of the State, and making it the duty of that officer to receive and file the certificate or statement containing the information?

Furthermore, we are of the opinion that the statute quoted can have but a limited application to an article of commerce as to which a federal law requires that the packages containing it shall "be so labeled on the outside cover as to plainly show the name of the consignee, the nature of its contents, and the quantity therein." Crimes Act, ch. 1, sec. 240. This act evinces a purpose on the part of the congress that the traffic in intoxicating liquors shall have the greatest publicity.

9. It is insisted that the act under review is void, because the body is broader than the title, and because it contains two subjects in violation of article 2, sec. 17, of the State constitution.

Article 2, sec. 17, provides: "No bill shall become a law which embraces more than one subject, that subject to be expressed in the title."

The proposition that the body of the act is broader than its title is founded on the criticism that, while the title purports only regulation, the body of the act imports prohibition. If this be a sound criticism, the act is necessarily void. It is true the title indicates regulation only. Does the body contain prohibition?

The cases in our books construing and applying article 2, sec. 17, of the Constitution are very numerous. Those up to 90 Tenn. are collected in *Hardaway* v. *Lilly* (Ch. App. 1898), 48 S. W., 712. Those appearing in 90 Tenn. to 116 Tenn., inclusive, are catalogued in *Malone* v. *Williams,* 118 Tenn., 438, 103 S. W., 798, 121 Am. St. Rep., 1002. The cases which have been published since that time on this important subject are *Dixon* v. *State,* 117 Tenn., 79, 94 S. W., 936; *Gilley* v. *Harrell,* 118 Tenn., 115, 101 S. W.. 424; *Malone* v. *Williams,* 118 Tenn., 390, 103 S. W., 798, 121 Am. St. Rep., 1002; *State ex rel.* v. *Taylor,* 119 Tenn., 229, 104 S. W., 242; *Railroad* v. *Byrne,* 119 Tenn., 278, 104 S. W., 460; *Knoxville* v. *Gass,* 119 Tenn., 438, 104 S. W., 1084; *Rhinehart* v. *State,* 121 Tenn., 420, 117 S. W., 508, 17 Ann. Cas., 254; *Acklen* v. *Thompson,* 122 Tenn., 43, 126 S. W., 730, 135 Am. St. Rep., 851; *Ledgerwood* v. *Pitts,* 122 Tenn., 570, 125 S. W., 1036; *Ransom* v. *Rutherford County,* 123 Tenn., 1, 130 S. W., 1057, Ann. Cas., 1912B, 1356; *Coke & Coal Co.* v. *Steel Co.,* 123 Tenn., 428, 131 S. W., 988, 31 L. R. A. (N. S.), 278; *Kenny* v. *State,* 123 Tenn., 516, 132 S. W., 193; *Darnell* v. *State,* 123 Tenn., 663, 134 S. W., 307; *State ex rel.* v. *Folk,* 124 Tenn.,

119, 135 S. W., 776; *Scott* v. *Marley,* 124 Tenn., 388, 137 S. W., 492; *Jackson* v. *Manufacturing Co.,* 124 Tenn., 421, 137 S. W., 757; *State ex rel.,* v. *Powers,* 124 Tenn., 553, 137 S. W., 1110; *Kirk* v. *State,* 126 Tenn., 7, 150 S. W., 83, Ann. Cas., 1913D, 1239; *Weil* v. *Newbern,* 126 Tenn., 223, 148 S. W., 680, Ann. Cas., 1913E, 25; *Railroad* v. *Memphis,* 126 Tenn., 267, 148 S. W., 662, 41 L. R. A. (N. S.), 828, Ann. Cas., 1913E, 153; *Brown* v. *Sullivan County,* 126 Tenn., 689, 151 S. W., 50; and see *Harris* v. *Hamby,* 114 Tenn., 361, 84 S. W., 622.

The principles on which the court acts are thus laid down in *Hardaway* v. *Lilly,* supra, after a review of the decisions up to that time, viz.:

"The foregoing affirmative and negative cases comprise substantially all of the decisions upon the subject appearing in the published volumes of our State reports. We think it is apparent, from an examination of these cases, that the rule laid down in *Cannon* v. *Mathes,* supra [8 Heisk. (Tenn.), 504], has been very thoroughly adhered to, and that in furtherance of that liberal construction in favor of the validity of the acts of the legislature, which is the declared policy of this State, upon the question in hand, occasionally a somewhat strained interpretation has been given both to the title and to the subject-matter of the acts under consideration. Very few instances, if any, can be found among the cases cited where the body of the act was declared to be repugnant to the title, unless such repugnancy was in fact clear and unmistakable.

On the other hand, we have instanced several cases in which the court with painstaking care has extricated a simple and general title out of more or less irrelevant matter, and has found the body of the act to be in conformity with such general subject, · and sometimes has exercised its power of construction upon the body of the act. In all of these cases the evident purpose of the court is apparent to yield to a co-ordinate branch of the government the consideration which is due to it as the immediate representative of the people to declare policies and give them the force of law. The court has kept before it always in these cases, as the pole star of construction, that the purpose of the constitutional provision governing the inquiry was to prevent omnibus legislation and confusion in the minds of members of the legislature, and misleading as to the real purpose and scope of acts brought before the legislature. It is clear, from a perusal of the above-mentioned cases, although the precise point may not be fully brought out in the excerpts we have made, that while no act can constitutionally have in its title more than one subject, and while that subject as it appears in the body of the act must fall under the title, yet that a multitude of particulars may be thus embraced under a general subject, each of them in some way leading, directly or indirectly, to the furtherance of the general purpose appearing in the title.

"It is also clear that, in construing both the title and the body of an act, the court must not manifest

a narrow and jejune purpose, but rather must have in
view the sustaining of the act under consideration, if
it can be done in harmony with the fair meaning of the
language, viewed in a large and generous relation to
the subject-matter of the legislation. This results
from the settled policy of the court upon constitutional
questions, to resolve all doubts in favor of the constitutionality of an act of the legislature assailed for
unconstitutionality. As said by the supreme court,
speaking through Mr. Justice Caldwell, in *Manufacturing Co.* v. *Falls,* 90 Tenn., 469, 16 S. W., 1046: "It
is well to observe in the outset that all intendments
are in favor of the constitutionality of an act of the
legislature passed with the forms and ceremony
requisite to give it the force of law, and that, where
one construction will make a statute void on account
of conflict with the constitution, and another would
render it valid, the latter will be adopted by the courts,
even though the former, at first view, be otherwise
the more natural interpretation of the language
used.' "

The foregoing principles have been substantially
adhered to in all subsequent cases. The only addition
that need be made is that the court has since held (in
Knoxville v. *Gass,* 119 Tenn., 438, 104 S. W., 1084)
that, even if the title be double, the act will be saved,
if only one of the subjects be embraced in the body of
the act, since the body need not be as broad as the
title.

Recurring, now, to the question whether the body of the present act is broader than the title: It is insisted for the complainant that, while the title expresses only regulation, the body embraces prohibition. We think it very clear that the body of the act imports merely regulation. It is true that section 1 provides "that it shall be unlawful" for any person, firm, or corporation to ship or transport any intoxicating liquors into the State, or to deliver it within the State, "except as hereinafter provided;" but the subsequent sections make clear that what is meant is that it shall be unlawful to do so except in the manner prescribed, that it to say, pursuant to the regulations therein provided. There is, to be sure, the provision concerning the one-gallon shipments for personal use; but in what has been said in a previous part of the opinion we believe it has been fully shown that this was only a regulation, and not a prohibition, since there was no limit to the quantity that might be obtained by contemporaneous or successive shipments.

10. Does the body of the act embrace more than one subject? It is insisted that a distinct subject appears in section 4 in these words: "And said certified copy shall be competent evidence in any of the courts of this State upon the trial of any cause whatsoever in which the same may be material." The reasoning runs thus: That section 3 requires a statement to be made out by the carrier, and filed with the county court clerk, showing certain facts, among others, the name and post office address of the consignor and con-

signee; that there are numerous cases in which the
name or post office address of a person mentioned in a
shipment as consignee will be very material, and which
cases have no relation whatever to shipments and deliveries of intoxicating liquors; and that yet this act
makes that copy admissible and competent evidence to
prove such facts. For example, the question whether
notice of the protest of a note was sent to the indorser
involves an inquiry as to his post office; a bequest in a
will to a man by a certain name involves an inquiry
as to the man's name. It is said that here is a new
species of evidence created by this act, and made competent in all cases in which it may be material; that
it is a distinct subject, a distinct rule of substantive
law; that, if the act had said that the statement should
be evidence in all prosecutions of the consignee for
making a false statement, or for violating the act, or
even that it might be evidence in suits between the
consignor, consignee, and carrier about the transaction, there might be ground upon which to say that
it was germane, but that it goes far beyond this, to the
extent already stated.

The rule of law applicable to this subject is that, if
there be two constructions to which an act is
susceptible, one of which will make it unconstitutional, and the other of which will save it, the
duty of the court is to adopt the latter, although it is
not the most obvious or natural construction. *Manufacturing Co.* v. *Falls,* 90 Tenn., 469, 16 S. W., 1045;
State ex rel., v. *Schlitz Brewing Co.,* 104 Tenn., 715,

59 S. W., 1033, 78 Am. St. Rep., 941; *Samuelson v. State.* 116 Tenn., 470, 498, 95 S. W., 1012, 115 Am. St. Rep., 805; *Railroad* v. *Byrne,* 119 Tenn., 278, 291, 292, 104 S. W., 460; *Darnell* v. *State,* 123 Tenn., 663, 134 S. W., 307; *Kirk* v. *State,* 126 Tenn., 7, 150 S. W., 83, Ann. Cas., 1913D, 1239. In *Samuelson* v. *State* it is said: "While it is true that, in arriving at the meaning of the legislature, primarily, the grammatical sense of the words used is to be adopted, yet if there is any ambiguity, or if there is room for more than one interpretation, the rules of grammer will be disregarded where a too strict adherence to them would raise a repugnance or absurdity, or would defeat the purpose of the legislature. *Garby* v. *Harris,* 7 Exch., 591; *Met. Bo. Wks.* v. *Steed,* L. R., 82, B. Div., 445; *George* v. *B. of E.,* 33 Ga., 344; *State* v. *Heman,* 70 Mo. 441. Many cases might be cited in which the future tense has been read as including the present and the past, where that was necessary to carry out the meaning of the legislature. Thus an enabling act relating to married women who 'shall come into the state' may apply to one who came into the state before the passage of the law. *Maysville & L. R. Co.* v. *Herrick,* 13 Bush (Ky.), 122. Where an act provided that certain land 'shall be allotted for and given to' an individual named, it was held that the words passed an immediate interest. *Rutherford* v. *Green,* 2 Wheat., 196, 4 L. Ed., 218. In *Babcock* v. *Goodrich,* 47 Cal., 488, the phrase 'current expenses of the year' was made to read, 'expenses of the current year;' it being evident

that the latter form of words more correctly expressed
the legislative intent. These cases are but a recognition of an old and well-established rule of the common
law, applicable to all written instruments, that *verba
intentioni, non e contra debent inservire';* that it to
say, words ought to be made subservient to the intent,
and not the intent to the words.'' The case of *Darnell*
v. *State,* supra, furnishes a strong example in close
analogy. In that case the court, after mentioning the
fact that there were only two assignments that needed
to be considered, said: ''The first of these is that
the act under which the jury was impaneled, commonly
known as the 'jury law of Franklin county' (Acts 1905,
ch. 233), is unconstitutional, because the body of the
act is broader than its title. The contention is based
upon the following: The act is entitled 'An act to
create a board of jury commissioners for counties in
this State having a population of not less than 20,292,
and not more than 20,400 inhabitants according to
the federal census of 1900, or that may have that
number of inhabitants by any subsequent federal census.' After making various and sundry provisions to
carry out the purposes indicated by the title, section
19 follows, near the close, in this language: 'Be it
further enacted, that the provisions of this act shall
apply to all grand and petit juries in circuit and criminal courts of this State.' The same question was decided against plaintiff in error's contention in the case of
Allen Damron v. *State,* from Bedford county, at the

December term, 1909. *Damron's Case* involved the jury law of Bedford county (chapter 355 of the Acts of 1907), which was a substantial copy of the Franklin county jury law involved in the present case. That case was thoroughly considered by the court, after full argument, oral and written, and a second time on petition to rehear filed by the plaintiff in error. The court held, upon a consideration of the whole statute, that it was the evident intention of the legislature that the section just quoted should be construed as if it read as follows, viz.: 'That the provisions of this act shall apply to all grand and petit juries in all circuit and criminal courts of this State in counties of the population herein prescribed.' We are of the opinion this was a sound construction, and we adhere to it.''

So, in the case before us, we construe the provisions complained of as applying to any cause or controversy whatsoever arising under the act. This is also a natural and reasonable construction, as we think, because it applies the language of the legislature to the subject about which, and in which, that body was engaged, and to which the minds of its members were directed. While it is true the language employed would bear the meaning attached to it in the argument, we think the more reasonable view would be to confine its generality to the subject which the legislature has in hand.

We hold, therefore, that the act is not void under our State constitution.

The result is the decree of the chancellor is affirmed in part, and reversed in part, and a decree will be entered here in accordance with this opinion.

The costs of this court and of the court below will be equally divided between the parties.

By consent of defendant express company the State of Tennessee was permitted to intervene in this court and take charge of and conduct the defense. A brief was therefore filed by Hon. F. M. Thompson, attorney-general of the State, and the case was also argued orally by him at the bar of the court.

DUNLAP LUMBER CO. v. NASHVILLE, C. & ST. L. RY. CO.*

(*Nashville.* December Term, 1913.)

1. **RAILROADS. Switching services. Right to discontinue.**

If a shipper denies his liability for demurrage, the railroad company cannot discontinue its switching services on account of the nonpayment of demurrage. (*Post, pp.* 173-175.)

Case cited and distinguished: Yazoo & M. V. R. Co. v. Searles, 85 Miss., 520.

2. **CARRIERS. Freight. Demurrage.**

If a railroad company knew that a shipper would not accept logs in cars placed on a certain track, before the cars were delivered there, the shipper could not be charged with demurrage for not receiving the cars at that point. (*Post, p.* 175.)

Case cited and approved: Railroad v. Hunt, 83 Tenn., 261.

3. **CARRIERS. Freight. Point of delivery.**

It is implied in a contract for the shipment of logs that they shall be delivered at a point enabling the shipper to receive without delay or inconvenience. (*Post. pp.* 175, 176.)

Case cited and approved: Railroad v. Hunt, supra.

4. **TROVER AND CONVERSION. Conversion by carrier.**

The sale of logs shipped by a railroad company for demurrage when the freight charges due had been paid, so that no demurrage was chargeable, was a conversion of the logs by the company. (*Post, p.* 176.)

Case cited and approved: M. & P. R. Co. v. Jacobson, 179 U. S., 287.

5. **CARRIERS. Freight. Facilities for shipment. Discrimination.**

Since railroad companies are organized primarily for the public interest and convenience, a railroad company cannot arbitrarily prevent the use by a shipper of the instrumentalities of other

*On the question of discrimination by carrier as to delivery of freight, see note in 12 L. R. A. (N. S.), 510. And upon the duty of a carrier to deliver car at consignee's place of business, see note in 41 L. R. A. (N. S.), 678.

roads beyond its own lines which it has acquired the right to use. (*Post, p.* 176.)

Cases cited and approved: Post v. Railroad, 103 Tenn., 202; M. P. R. Co. v. Larabee Flour Mills Co., 211 U. S., 614.

6. CARRIERS. Freight. Discrimination against shippers.

It is the common law duty of a railroad company to serve the public without discrimination in service or charges. (*Post, pp.* 177, 178.)

7. COMMERCE. Interstate commerce—State regulation.

While the State courts cannot directly interfere with interstate transportation, by regulating its conveniences or charges, they may control intrastate transportation, and the fact that a railroad company carries interstate freight, would not deprive the State courts of jurisdiction to compel it to switch cars for a shipper on an industrial siding. (*Post, pp.* 178, 179.)

Case cited and approved: M. P. R. Co. v. Larabee Flour Mills Co., *supra.*

8. CARRIERS. Freight. Common-Law duties. Discrimination.

Acts 1897, ch. 10, secs. 15, 17, prohibiting carriers from discriminating as to charges or services or from giving any unreasonable preferences, are merely declaratory of the common law. (*Post, pp.* 179, 180.)

9. RAILROADS. Freight. Performance of duties. Remedy.

Injunction is the proper remedy to compel a railroad company to deliver to a shipper on a spur track the freight shipped to it, where it appears that the discontinuance of switching services to the shipper would be destructive of its business; the legal remedy being inadequate. (*Post, pp.* 180, 181.)

10. RAILROADS. Freight. Remedy of shipper. Injunction.

In a suit to compel a railroad company to switch cars shipped to complainant on its industrial siding, the injunction issued was properly framed so as to require the company to receive and deliver to complainant on its spur track all freight, etc., according to complainant's reasonable needs and consistent with the company's duties to other shippers it was required to serve. (*Post, p.* ——.)

FROM DAVIDSON.

Appeal from the Chancery Court of Davidson County to the Court of Civil Appeals and by *certiorari* from the Court of Civil Appeals to the Supreme Court.— JOHN ALLISON, Chancellor.

PENDLETON & DE WITT, for plaintiff.

FRANK SLEMONS and CLAUD WALLER, for defendant.

MR. JUSTICE LANSDEN delivered the opinion of the Court.

This bill was filed by the complainant against the defendant railway to compel it to perform certain switching operations for the complainant and to recover in trover the value of four carloads of logs. The complainant sought a mandatory injunction commanding the defendant to deliver logs and merchandise in carload lots to its private track adjacent to its mill. The defendant answered the bill and denied its obligation to perform the switching operations demanded by complainant, and denied its liability for the value of the four carloads of logs sued for, and filed a crossbill by which it sought to recover $4 alleged to be due it from complainant as demurrage upon two certain cars which it claimed the complainant had held out of service longer than the rules of the Traffic Association permitted.

The chancellor granted the relief prayed for, except that he imposed, as a condition precedent to the defendant's switching operations, that the complainant should be required to unload all cars which were standing on the switch track belonging to it. From this part of the chancellor's decree the complainant appealed to the court of civil appeals, and from the other parts the railway appealed. The court of civil appeals affirmed the decree of the chancellor in all respects, except that it allowed the railway a recovery under its crossbill for the demurrage claimed, and it modified the decree of the chancellor in so far as he undertook to determine the hours of the day and the number of times each day that the railway should be required to perform switching services for the complainant; that court decreeing in general terms that the railway should be required and commanded to receive, transport, and deliver to complainant on its spur track at its mill all carloads of logs and merchandise to a just and equal extent, according to complainant's reasonable needs and consistently with the railway's duties to other industries which it was obligated to serve. Both parties have filed petitions for *certiorari* to the decree of the court of civil appeals and have assigned errors. The complainant insists that that court erred in requiring it to unload all cars which were placed upon its track east of Wall street before defendant is required to remove any of the cars which have been placed at that point for unloading, and that it was error for that court to give the railway company a decree for the demurrage claimed, and to tax complainant with any part of the costs.

The railway company complains at that part of the decree of the court of civil appeals which requires it to perform the switching operations demanded by complainant, and which awarded the complainant a recovery for the value of the four carloads of logs, and adjudged costs against it. The material facts necessary to be stated are as follows:

Many years ago the Louisville & Nashville Railroad Company constructed a spur track along Front street in the city of Nashville, connecting with its main line, and extending to within 500 feet of the present site of complainant's mill. The complainant operates a sawmill, and saws logs for itself and for other dealers and users of lumber, and requires in its business about four carloads of logs daily. It caused a sidetrack to be constructed connecting its millyard with the spur track of the Louisville & Nashville Railroad just referred to. This sidetrack is built upon a sharp curve so as to describe approximately a semicircle, and is about 480 feet in length. It will accommodate at one time about twelve cars of the length of cars usually employed by defendant in hauling logs. This sidetrack of complainant crosses a street known as Wall, or Mill, street, and is intersected by Wall street at a point about equidistant between the terminus of the sidetrack at the millyard and the intersection of the spur track with the Louisville & Nashville Railroad. When the sidetrack is filled with cars, there will be about six cars west of Wall street. For a considerable period of time prior to the filing of the bill, complainant demanded that the defendant switch the cars on its sidetrack about twice every day. This was deemed necessary by the complainant because it was convenient for it to unload only two cars at a time. Its millyard was so constructed that more than two cars could not be conveniently and economically handled at a time in the operation of its mill. When two cars would be unloaded, the complainant would demand that the defendant switch these cars out and place in their room two other cars. This switching operation made it necessary for the defendant to move all of the cars on the sidetrack onto the spur track, switch out the empty cars, and replace the loaded cars at the millyard where the empties had been, and place other loaded cars on the sidetrack. The defendant acquiesced in this mode of operation for a considerable period of time before the filing of the bill. In May, 1909, the defendant received two cars consigned to the complainant, and after weighing them and holding them in its yards for probably two days, it transported them along the spur track, and tendered them to the complainant on its sidetrack. These two cars were tendered on different days, and, at the time each car was tendered, the complainant was not in a position to receive it because its sidetrack was occupied by other loaded cars.

The various railroads entering the city of Nashville have formed what is called the Nashville Demurrage & Storage Bureau. This bureau was placed in charge of a manager, and it was his duty to see that each railroad charged each shipper the proper amount of demurrage due on cars, and to see that each shipper paid the demurrage due, and to adjust any differences that might arise between shippers and the railroads concerning demurrage. It was the practice of the Demurrage Bureau not to require shippers to pay demurrage upon delivery of cars, but delivery was made and accounts for the demurrage were rendered shippers and collected by the bureau. One of the rules of the Demurrage Bureau is a follows:

"In case consignee or consignor shall refuse to pay or unnecessarily defer the settlement of bills for demurrage charges, which have accrued upon private or specially designated tracks, the agent, after notice to such consignee or consignor, shall refuse to switch future cars to such private or specially designated tracks, but will make deliveries only from the railroad's public delivery tracks until such charges have been paid."

Another rule of the Demurrage Bureau is as follows:

"When delivery of cars consigned or ordered to private tracks cannot be made on account of inability of consignee to receive, delivery will be considered to have been made when the car was tendered. The agents must give written notice for all cars which they have been unable to deliver because of the condition of the private track or because of other conditions attributable to consignee. This shall be considered constructive placement.''

Under the authority conferred by the foregoing rules; the defendant demanded of complainant $6 demurrage on the two cars last referred to. A controversy arose about the matter, and it was finally referred to the manager of the Demurrage Bureau, who reduced the claim of the defendant to $4. This payment was demanded by defendant and was refused by complainant. The complainant took the position in respect of the demurrage that the free time allowed it for the use of cars did not begin to run until the cars were delivered on the switch track, and therefore it was not chargeable with demurrage for the time that the cars in question remained on the spur track. Soon thereafter the defendant gave notice to the complainant in conformity with the rules of the bureau that it would not deliver any more loaded cars of logs upon complainant's private track, but that it would make delivery of such cars at its general delivery tracks. Subsequently four cars of logs were shipped from Camden, Tenn., consigned to the complainant at Nashville. These cars arrived in Nashville over defendant's road and were delivered at its general delivery tracks. The complainant was notified of this fact and paid the freight charges on the four cars of logs and demanded that they be delivered on its private track. This the defendant declined to do, and the complainant declined to receive the logs. Defendant unloaded them at its team track, and they

lay on the ground for a number of months, when defendant sold them to enforce a claimed lien for accrued
demurrage while standing at the team track and because the logs were deteriorating.

The defendant railway has no line of road which
connects with the sidetrack of the complainants. Its
line of road, however, does connect physically with
the line of the Louisville & Nashville Railroad and the
lines of the Louisville & Nashville Terminal Company,
and they conect with complainant's switch track. This
latter company owns a number of tracks upon and
adjacent to a large number of streets in the city of
Nashville and constitutes practically the terminal
facilities of the Louisville & Nashville and Nashville
& Camden Railway Company. The Nashville Terminals is a joint organization of the Louisville & Nashville Railroad and the Nashville, Chattanooga & St.
Louis Railway, and has control over the terminal facilities of both of those roads and the Louisville &
Nashville Terminal Company within certain prescribed limits, and including the spur track heretofore referred to where it connects with the complainant's
sidetrack. The Louisville & Nashville Terminal Company has leased its property to the Louisville & Nashville Railroad and the Nashville, Chattanooga & St.
Louis Railway. All of these terminal properties are
maintained and operated for the benefit of the two
principal railroads. Business received over either
road is delivered to any private industrial track,
whether such track belongs to private persons, or

whether it belongs to or is operated by either of the
railroads, as if all of the tracks were owned jointly by
both roads. The Nashville Terminal Company was
designated by the two railroads as a convenient working arrangement between them for the handling of
traffic coming into or going out of the city of Nashville,
or passing through the city over the lines of either
road. The defendant company makes delivery of
freight in carload lots in Nashville through the agency
of the Nashville Terminals, and, as stated, the arrangement is such that delivery can be made to any point in
the city, regardless of whether the point of delivery is
served by the defendant or by the Louisville & Nashville Railroad Company. In pursuance of the arrangement referred to, it has been the custom and course
of dealing for some years prior to the filing of the bill
for the defendant to deliver freight in carload lots to
the complainant through the agency of the Nashville
Terminals. These deliveries would be made upon general instructions received by the terminals, and, as
a matter of course, arising from the business of the
Nashville Terminals and the customary dealings of the
defendant with the complainant and other shippers.
No distinction is made in delivering cars on industrial
tracks between cars destined to points on the line of
the defendant and cars destined to points on the line of
the Louisville & Nashville Railroad, whether such cars
are shipped into Nashville over the lines of the defendant or over the lines of the Louisville & Nashville Railroad. The evidence does not indicate the ex-

act length of time that the arrangement referred to has been in force, nor any particular length of time which it is to remain in force. The proof is clear, however, that the arrangement exists, and there is nothing to indicate that it is to cease.

1. The reasonableness of the regulations of the Demurrage Bureau is not questioned by the complainant. As we have seen, the rules of that organization provide that a delivery upon the spur track shall be deemed a delivery to the consignee if the condition of the side-track which serves the consignee is not such that carload lots can be delivered thereon. This being true, it is clear that the complainant was liable for the demurrage, and the decree of the court of civil appeals so adjudging is correct.

It does not follow, however, from this conclusion that the defendant railway was justified in suspending the switching service demanded by complainant on account of the dispute about the demurrage. Complainant is solvent, and any judgment which the railway might have recovered against it for the demurrage would have been good. We cannot say from the facts stated that the complainant's claim that it did not owe the demurrage was in bad faith. There is no direct proof to indicate a lack of good faith, and nothing upon the point except the facts out of which the controversy arose. We think therefore that if the complainant in good faith denied its liability for the demurrage that the railway company could not for that reason discontinue its switching services to the complainant. The

point was expressly decided by the supreme court of
Mississippi in *Yazoo & M. V. R. Co.* v. *Searles,* 85
Miss., 520, 37 South., 939, 68 L. R. A., 715, in which it
was said:

"No carrier has the right, on acount alone of a dispute arising from a doubt as to the correctness of a
particular bill or several bills for demurrage already
past due, or an honest difference of opinion as to the
justice of the charge on any number of cars already
received and delivered, to refuse to 'switch and place'
other cars subsequently received. No carrier can refuse its services to anyone desiring them on the ground
alone of an adjusted claim then pending, or on account
of any previous violation of contract by such person,
no matter how flagrant and inexcusable, if such person, at the time the service is demanded, is legally entitled thereto."

The remedy adopted by the defendant railway to enforce the collection of its demurrage charges was unreasonable and destructive of the business of the complainant. If such action should be allowable, as a
means of enforcing payment of disputed charges, the
practical effect of it would necessarily be to prevent
shippers from disputing items of charge with the carrier. The team track of the defendant to which it delivered logs consigned to the complainant after the controversy over the demurrage arose is more than a mile
from complainant's mill, and for complainant to be
compelled to receive logs at this point and transport

them in wagons to its mill would destroy its business. This is the undisputed evidence.

In addition, the defendant did not have any claim for demurrage upon the carloads of logs to be delivered to the team track, and therefore it had no lien upon these logs for any item of charge. The complainant paid the freight on these carloads in advance and demanded delivery to its switch track. The complainant accepted the freight, but declined to deliver the logs at the switch track and and delivered them at the team track. Later, and after the bill was filed in this case, the defendant sold the logs to enforce a claimed lien for demurrage accruing upon the cars while remaining at the team track. Plainly the defendant could not charge demurrage upon cars delivered at this point after the consignee had given notice, as in this case, that the shipment would not be received at the point of delivery. The defendant knew that the complainant would not accept the logs at the team track before the cars were delivered there, and of course complainant could not be charged demurrage for not receiving them at that point. *Railroad* v. *Hunt,* 15 Lea, 261.

We think, also, that the defendant was guilty of a conversion of the logs when it sold them. It was implied in the contract of shipment between complainant and defendant that the logs should be delivered at a point which would enable the complainant to receive them ''without inconvenience, delay, or interruption.'' *Railroad Co.* v. *Hunt, supra.*

The freight having been paid, and there being no proper charges for demurrage, the sale of the logs by the railway company was gratuitous and unwarranted and clearly a conversion.

2.   From the facts stated, it is made to appear that the defendant railway is equipped to deliver freight at the complainant's switch track, although it is beyond the terminus of the lines actually owned by it. The defendant has provided a means of such delivery to enable it to more effectually discharge its duty to the public as a carrier of freight and passengers. Railroad companies "are organized for the public interest and to subserve primarily the public good and convenience." *M. & P. R. Co.* v. *Jacobson,* 179 U. S., 287, 21 Sup. Ct., 115, 45 L. Ed., 194.

This law of their creation enters into and controls every facility of transportation which the railroad company acquires to aid it in the discharge of its duty to the public. Therefore, if it acquires the right to serve all of its patrons through the instrumentalities of other roads beyond the termini of its own lines, it cannot arbitrarily withhold such facilities from any shipper. Its duty to serve all shippers equally and alike upon the payment of proper and reasonable charges must extend to every right acquired by it in the lines of other roads for the purpose of aiding it in the general discharge of its duty to the public to the same extent and in the same degree as if the service were performed through its own instrumentalities. The right of every member of the public to receive equal service attaches to the right acquired by the carrier to render the service.

There is nothing in *Post* v. *Railroad,* 103 Tenn., 202, 52 S. W., 301, 55 L. R. A., 481, in conflict with the holding. It is true that it was held in that case that a railroad company cannot be required as a legal obligation to carry freights beyond its own terminal points. It is manifest, however, that the court was not speaking with reference to the title by which the railroad company held, or the degree of interest which it possessed in the terminal points referred to. It was speaking alone of a case in which the initial carrier had no right to use the termini under consideration. We cannot conceive that it could affect the duty of the carrier to deliver freight at points on terminals which it had a perfect right to use, whether it owned the terminals or not. The determinative point is the right of ingress and egress which the carrier has to and from the terminals upon which delivery is to be made. If it has such right, and has acquired the right in aid of the performance of its duty to the public as a common carrier, it must render the service to every member of the public in furtherance of its duty. *M. P. R. Co.* v. *Larabee Flour Mills Co.,* 211 U. S., 614, 29 Sup. Ct., 214, 53 L. Ed., 352.

The case last cited is direct authority for the doctrine that it is the common law duty of the defendant railway to serve the public equally and alike and without discrimination in service or charges by virtue alone of the fact that it is a common carrier of freights and passengers. In fact, we do not understand that it is denied that such a duty rests upon the defendant railway. The point made is not that the railway does not owe the duty to serve the public in its capacity of a common carrier of freights and passengers, but that it has no line of road connecting with the complainant's switch track, and therefore it cannot be compelled to deliver freights beyond its own line. This contention cannot be sustained.

It is not shown in the evidence that the complainant receives freight, or has ever received freight, from the defendant's line of road at a point outside of this State, or that it ships the products of its mill to any point beyond the limits of this State. The only shipment that is shown in the proof is the shipment of the four car loads of logs from Camden, Tenn., to Nashville, Tenn.

There is a suggestion on the brief of counsel for the railway that inasmuch as it is an interstate road, and therefore necessarily engaged in interstate transportation, there is no jurisdiction in the State courts to grant the relief awarded by the court of civil appeals and the chancellor to the complainant. The suggestion seems to have been made for the first time in the court of civil appeals, and then later in this court. In the various disputes between the complainant and the Demurrage Bureau, and the officers of defendant railway, there seems to have been no suggestion of inconvenience to or interference with the duties of the railway as a carrier of interstate freights. It is settled beyond dispute that the State courts cannot interfere directly with interstate transportation, either to regulate its conveniences or its charges. But it is also well settled that the State courts can control intrastate transportations of freight and passengers. The fact that a defendant is a carrier of interstate freights is not alone sufficient to oust the State courts of their jurisdiction to enforce the demand made in this case. Just how far the courts of a State may be authorized to go in regulating intrastate shipments when commingled with interstate shipments is not necessary for decision in this case. However, the *Mills Case,* supra, and the later case of *Grand Trunk Railroad Commission,* decided December 8, 1913, are very interesting cases upon this question. In the last case cited, it was held that the congress has not so taken over the whole subject of terminals, team tracks, switching tracks, siding, etc., of interstate railways as to invalidate all State regulations relative to the interchange of traffic.

By chapter 10, Acts of 1897, all discriminations between shippers by railroads is forbidden, and expressly made unlawful in this State. Jurisdiction of the punishment of violations of the act in criminal matters is directly conferred upon the circuit and criminal courts of the State, and jurisdiction of all suits of a civil nature arising under the act is conferred upon the chancery courts. By section 15, rebates, drawbacks, and all other devices by which railroads may charge,

demand, or collect a greater or less compensation for
any service rendered in the transportation of property
within this State than it charges from any other person for a like service is forbidden. And so, also, by
the same section, are railroads prohibited to make any
preference between shippers in "furnishing cars or
motive power," and by section 17 it is made unlawful
for any corporation "to make or give any undue or
unreasonable preference or advantage to any particular person, . . . or any particular description of
traffic, or to subject any particular person, company,
firm, corporation or locality, or any particular description of traffic, to any undue or unreasonable prejudice or disadvantage."

The sections of the statute just referred to are declaratory of the common law. They merely define
the common law duty of public carriers to serve equally
and alike all shippers who pay reasonable charges for
services required and comply with the carriers' reasonable regulations to enable it to perform its functions as such.

We think, too, that the complainant's remedy is injunction. A discontinuance of the switching services
required by it and a delivery of its logs at the team
track of the defendant is shown by the proof to be destructive of the complainant's business. If it should
be compelled to resort to an action for damages against
the railway for its refusal to deliver logs at the complainant's switch track, such a course would result in
a great multiplicity of suits, the accumulation of large

and unnecessary bills of costs, and judgments for damages in small amounts, the collection of which would be delayed to such periods that they would not aid the complainant in the operation of its mill like the profits it would receive in the orderly conduct of its business when logs are delivered at its yards. Being entitled to the service, it is entitled to earn and receive its profits. We think it clear therefore that the complainant's legal remedy is inadequate, and the only relief fully adequate to compensate it in the premises is the remedy of injunction to compel the defendant to perform the services which complainant is entitled to demand. As to the nature of the injunction which should be awarded to complainant, we are content with the decree of the court of civil appeals. Defendant will pay the costs of this court.

Affirmed.

WEBB *et al. v.* CARTER *et al.**
STATE *ex rel.* CARTER *et al. v.* WOOLLEN.
THOMAS *et al. v.* CANNON *et al.*

(Nashville.   December Term, 1913.)

1. **STATUTES.** Enactment. Legislative quorum.

In determining whether a quorum was present when a bill was
considered by the house of representatives, the court may
look to the journal of the house. (*Post, p.* 186.)

Cases cited and approved: Gaines v. Horrigan, 72 Tenn., 610;
Telegraph Co. v. Nashville, 118 Tenn., 8; State, ex rel., v. Base
Ball Club, 127 Tenn., 292.

2. **CONSTITUTIONAL LAW.** Judicial power. Validity of enactment.

The constitutionality of the passage of an enrolled bill or act
of the legislature may be inquired into by the courts, though
the enrolled bill is an act of a co-ordinate branch of the State
government. (*Post, pp.* 186, 187.)

Constitution cited and construed: Art. 3, sec. 18.

Cases cited and approved: State v. McConnell, 71 Tenn., 334;
Gaines v. Horrigan, supra; Nelson v. Haywood County, 91 Tenn.,
608; Atchison, T. & S. F. R. Co. v. State, 28 Okl., 94.

Cases cited and distinguished: Williams v. State, 74 Tenn., 553;
State, ex rel., v. Algood, 87 Tenn., 163.

3. **STATES.** Legislature. Journals. Enactment. Legislative
quorum.

House Bill No. 759, subsequently purported to have been enacted
as Pub. Laws 1913, ch. 37, was reconsidered by the house of
representatives on April 3, 1913, after being disapproved by
the governor. The journal of the house on that day showed
that 52 representatives were present and voted, "Aye," in favor
of passing the bill notwithstanding the governor's objections,

---

*The authorities on the conclusiveness of an enrolled bill, are
gathered in elaborate notes in 23 L. R. A., 340; and 40 L. R. A.
(N. S.), 1.

Webb v. Carter.

and that 4 representatives present voted, "No," and 2 representatives answered, "Present, but not voting"; and further
showed that when the names of 35 other representatives were
called the speaker answered, "Not voting." A representative
who voted, "No," offered an explanation of his vote which is
not set out in the journal, which shows, however, that when the
explanation was being read another member made the point
of order that the question of "no quorum" could only be determined by a roll call, whereupon the speaker ruled that the
explanation was out of order. *Held*, that the journal, when
read in the light of all permissible presumptions in its favor,
showed that there was no quorum of 66 members present when
the bill was attempted to be passed; presumptively showing
that the 35 members answered for by the speaker were not
present. (*Post, pp.* 189-193.)

Constitution cited and construed: Art. 2, secs. 11, 12.

4. STATUTES. Enactment. Vote of legislature.

In view of Const. art. 2, sec. 21, requiring each legislative house
to record in a journal the "ayes" and "noes" upon the final
passage of every general bill, the act of the speaker of the
house in answering, "Not voting," when the names of certain
representatives were called, would have no greater effect than
the same announcement by any other member of the house;
that not being a part of his duties as speaker. (*Post, pp.* 193-
201.)

Constitution cited and construed: Art. 2, sec. 21; art. 3, sec. 18.

5. STATUTES. Enactment. Journal of house of representatives.
Entry of vote.

Const. art. 3, sec. 18, requiring the votes of both houses upon
reconsideration of a bill after its disapproval by the governor
to be determined by "ayes" and "noes" and the names of all
members voting for or against the bill entered upon the
journals of their respective houses, is mandatory, so that the
"aye" and "no" vote must be entered upon the legislative
journals. (*Post, pp.* 201, 202.)

Constitution cited and construed: Art. 3, sec. 18.

Case cited and approved: Williams v. State, supra.

6. **STATUTES. Enactment. Disapproval by governor. Re-Enactment. Order of procedure.**

Const. art. 3, sec. 18, provides if the governor refuse to sign a bill he "shall" return it with his objections to the house in which it originated, and said house "shall" cause said objections to be entered upon its journal and proceed to reconsider the bill, and, if "after such reconsideration a majority of all the members elected to that house shall agree to pass the bill notwithstanding the objections, it shall be sent with said objections to the other house by which it shall be likewise considered." *Held*, that the provision as to the order in which a bill must be reconsidered by the legislative houses is mandatory, so that a bill originating in the house of representatives was not validly passed over the governor's veto, where it was reconsidered and passed by the house, acting without a quorum, and was then sent to the senate, which also passed it over the veto, and subsequently, in an attempt to cure the defect in the action of the house, the house passed it again with a quorum present, but did not thereafter send it to the senate for its action. (*Post*, pp. 203-226.)

Constitution cited and construed: Art. 3, sec. 18.

Case cited and distinguished: State v. McCann, 72 Tenn., 11.

Cases cited and disapproved: Furnace Co. v. Railroad Co., 113 Tenn., 731; Muse v. Lexington, 110 Tenn., 655.

LANSDEN AND GREEN, JJ., dissenting.

FROM DAVIDSON.

Appeal from Chancery Court, Davidson County.— JOHN ALLISON, Chancellor.

JOHN A. PITTS, FOSTER V. BROWN, W. H. SWIGGART, SAM HOLDING, L. J. RUST and F. M. THOMPSON, attorney-general, for appellants.

VERTREES & VERTREES and JOHN T. LELLYETT, for appellees.

MR. JUSTICE BUCHANAN delivered the opinion of the Court.

The controlling question in each of the above cases is the constitutionality of chapter 37 of the Public Acts of the year 1913. This act originated in the house of representatives as House Bill No. 759.

It is admitted that the bill on three readings, and according to the requirements of the constitution, was passed by the house of representatives and by the senate, and was, as required by the constitution, transmitted by the governor for his approval. In the attack here made, all the questions raised relate to what happened and what did not happen after the bill reached the governor. The governor disapproved the bill, refused to sign it, and returned it with his objections to the house in which it originated within five days after it was presented to him.

Under section 18, art. 3, of the constitution, the next step required was that the house in which the bill originated should cause said objections to be entered at large upon its journal. This requirement was never complied with. After the requirement last above mentioned, the next step authorized by section 18, art. 3, above, was that the house should proceed to reconsider the bill.

At this point, one of the main controversies in the case originates. On one side, it is insisted that the house of representatives did proceed to reconsider the bill on April 3, 1913, and that the same was then validly passed, notwithstanding the veto of the governor. On the other side, it is said that no valid action was taken by that house on that day for the reason that no quorum was present in the house on that day.

The house of representatives, under the constitution, was entitled to ninety-nine members, and by article 2, section 11, of the constitution, it is provided that "not less than two-thirds of all the members to which each house shall be entitled shall constitute a quorum to do business; but a smaller number may adjourn from day to day, and may be authorized, by law, to compel the attendance of absent members."

To determine the question of facts as to whether a quorum was present in the house on April 3, 1913, it is well settled under our cases that we may look to the journal of the house of representatives. *Gaines v. Horrigan*, 72 Tenn. (4 Lea), 610; *Telegraph Co.* v. *Nashville*, 118 Tenn. (10 Cates), 8, 101 S. W., 770, 11 Ann. Cas., 824; *State, ex rel.*, v. *Base Ball Club*, 127 Tenn. (19 Cates), 292, 154 S. W., 1151.

The doctrine which obtains in some jurisdictions that an enrolled bill or act of the legislature cannot, as to the validity or constitutionality of its passage be inquired into by the judicial department of the State, because the enrolled bill is an act of a co-ordinate branch of the government of the State, has·never been accepted by this court.

In one of our cases, where it was conceded that the bill under consideration was signed by the speakers of both houses and by the governor and duly enrolled and published, it was said that the presumption in favor of its regular passage through all its stages was so strong that the mere failure of the journal of the senate to show a second reading would not affect the validity of the act, but the failure would be treated as a clerical omission. *State* v. *McConnell,* 71 Tenn. (3 Lea), 334.

In another case, it is held that, notwithstanding the fact that the act is verified by the signature of the two speakers and of the governor, and has been published by proper authority, "nevertheless, the court may look to the journals of the two houses; and if from them it appears that the bill was not constitutionally passed, the act must be declared void. Such seems to be the decided weight of authority." *Gaines* v. *Horrigan,* 72 Tenn. (4 Lea), 611.

In another case, it was said: "The rule is that the journals may be looked to in order to determine whether the bill was in fact passed, but every reasonable presumption must be made in favor of the action of a legislative body acting in the apparent performance of its legal functions. The courts will not presume, from the mere silence of the journal, that the house had disregarded the constitutional requirements, unless where the constitution expressly requires the fact to appear on the journals." *Williams* v. *State,* 74 Tenn. (6 Lea), 553.

In another case, it is said: "We think the rule well settled that, where the journal does not affirmatively show the defeat of the bill, every reasonable presumption and inference will be indulged in favor of the regularity of the passage of the act subsequently signed in open session by the Speaker." *State, ex rel.,* v. *Algood,* 87 Tenn. (3 Pickle), 163, 10 S. W., 310.

In another case, where the question was whether the bill under consideration had been reconsidered in the senate after having been in the hands of a conference committee from both houses to consider certain amendments, this court, assuming that it was necessary to the valid passage of the bill that it should have been reconsidered in the senate, said: "The journals show no reconsideration; they are silent on the subject. Such silence will be treated as a case of omission." *Nelson* v. *Haywood County,* 91 Tenn. (7 Pickle), 608, 20 S. W., 4.

The cases above quoted from are referred to in *Telegraph Company* v. *Nashville,* 118 Tenn. (10 Cates), 8, 9, 101 S. W., 770, 11 Ann. Cas., 824.

In that case, in disposing of the question as to whether the section of our constitution which provides that no bill shall become a law, until it shall have been signed by the respective speakers in open session, the fact of such signing to be noted on the journals, this court held that the requirement was directory and not mandatory; but in reaching this conclusion it is clear that the court considered the journals of both the house of representatives and of the senate. This court also examined the house and senate journals for the purpose of determining the constitutionality of the act under consideration in *State, ex rel.,* v. *Baseball Club,* 127 Tenn. (19 Cates), 296, 154 S. W., 1151.

It is to be noted that in neither of the foregoing cases was this court considering article 3, section 18, of the constitution.

The case of *Atchison, T. & S. F. R. Co.* v. *State,* 28 Okl., 94, 113 Pac., 921, 40 L. R. A. (N. S.), 1-39, is accompanied by a note presenting an exhaustive review of the rulings in different jurisdictions respecting the conclusiveness of an enrolled bill. The note discloses a great diversity of judicial opinion. Some of the cases decided by this court appear in subdivision 10, of this note, among a large number of cases from other jurisdictions which do not recognize the absolute conclusiveness of an enrolled bill.

Reverting now to the controversy upon the question whether there was or was not a quorum or sixty-six members of the house of representatives present on April 3, 1913, and turning to the journal of the house for that day, we find it showing that fifty-two representatives were present and voted, "Aye," when their names were respectively called in favor of passing the bill notwithstanding the objections of the governor. It shows four representatives present who voted, "No," when their names were called; and two representatives present, each of whom answered when their names were called, "Present, but not voting." Thus, it affirmatively appears from the journal that fifty-eight representatives were present when the vote was taken. The names of thirty-five representatives are set out on the journal in addition to the fifty-eight, but the journal as to these thirty-five shows that, when the name of each of them was called, Mr. Speaker Stanton answered for each, "Not voting."

It is clear that the journal does not affirmatively show that the thirty-five representatives were present when the vote was taken. It is likewise clear that the journal does not affirmatively show that any one of them was present when the vote was taken; but it is said for one side of this controversy that, while the journal does not affirmatively show the presence of a quorum, it does inferentially, or by reasonable presumption, show the fact that a quorum was present when this vote was taken.

We cannot agree to this insistence. As we see the journal, the reasonable presumption is to the contrary of this insistence, and, in determining the question as to what the reasonable presumption is arising from this journal, we think it clear that the weight of authority establishes the rule that in those jurisdictions where an enrolled bill is not considered conclusive, but open to attack, judicial notice will be taken by the courts of legislative journals, both of the house and of the senate, whenever a consideration of such journals sheds light upon the question at issue.

A large array of cases to this effect may be found under subdivision 13, of the note referred to supra, in 40 L. R. A. (N. S.), at page 38.

Therefore, looking to the journal of the house of representatives for the day April 3, 1913, we see it recites the meeting of the house at 10 a. m. the calling of the same to order by the speaker, and, after prayer by the chaplain, the following: "On motion, the calling of the roll was dispensed with." After dispensing, by motion, with the calling of the roll, the latter being the proper method by which to ascertain and make the journal show whether a quorum was present or no, House Bill No. 759 was put upon its passage, "notwithstanding the objections of the executive." The bill was read, and then the roll was called, not for the purpose of ascertaining the presence of a quorum, but for the purpose of taking the vote and recording the same.

During the call of the roll for that purpose, when the name of Mr. Dorsey was called, he voted, "No," and offered no explanation, the purport of which is not set out on the journal, but nevertheless appears with sufficient clearness. That explanation was sent to the desk, and on request of Mr. Cox, the clerk proceeded to read the explanation; but its reading was interrupted by Mr. Cox, who made the point of order that the question of no quorum could not be determined except by a roll call. We think it evident that the explanation raised the question that no quorum was present. Mr. Speaker Stanton, however, ruled the point of order well taken, and declared the explanation out of order.

What reasonable inference or presumption arises from this circumstance? If a quorum had been present, it is extremely improbable that the question would have been made by Mr. Dorsey. If a quorum was present, it is certain that his point would not have been met as it was, but would, on the contrary, have been met by a call of the roll and a showing upon the journal that a quorum was present.

In this connection, it is clear that no ordinary matter of legislation was involved; it was one of extraordinary public interest, and we cannot escape the conclusion from the circumstance above discussed that the reasonable inference arising therefrom is that no quorum was present at the time of this occurrence.

A second fact appearing on the journal is the action of Mr. Speaker Stanton in answering, "Not voting," when the name of each of the thirty-five members was called.

The question arising is: Why did Mr. Speaker Stanton do this? Certainly, not in the exercise of any power or duty conferred on him by the constitution or any statute of the State. Article 2, section 11, of the constitution, enjoins upon the house and senate, respectively, the duty of choosing a speaker. His duties and powers are not outlined or defined by the constitution. Article 2, section 12, of that instrument provides that each house may determine the rules of its proceedings; but no rule of the house appears to have existed authorizing the speaker to answer for the thirty-five members.

The mandate of the constitution in respect of a quorum is "not less than two-thirds of all the members to which each house shall be entitled shall constitute a quorum to do business," and the only power possessed by less than that number is to adjourn from day to day, and, if authorized by law, to compel the attendance of absent members. So says article 2, section 11, of the constitution.

Article 2, section 21, of the constitution, enjoins upon each house the duty of keeping a journal, and of recording therein the "ayes" and "noes" upon the final passage of every bill of a general character, etc. Bill No. 759 was of a general character, a measure of public importance, and of the utmost moment. The duty was laid by the constitution upon the house, and not upon the speaker, to make a journal; and therefore we conclude that the act of the speaker in answering, "not voting," when each name of the thirty-five members was called, amounted to no more in legal effect than the same announcement would have, if made by any other member of the house.

However, since the words appear upon the journal and must be given due weight as the words of the house used in its journal, we will proceed to consider what effect these words "not voting" are entitled to in the construction of the journal. In other words, do they import or imply the presence or the absence of a quorum? The most evident meaning of the words "not voting," and in fact the only evident meaning they can be said to have, is that each of the thirty-five members, when his name was called from the roll, did not

129 Tenn. 13

vote. It is, however, insisted that a presumption may
be said to arise from these words that each of them
was present, though not voting. The only basis for
such a presumption is the legal duty resting upon each
of the thirty-five members to be present; but, whatever force this presumption may be entitled to, we
think is overthrown by the legal duty resting on each
of the thirty-five members, if present, to answer when
his name was called and to vote *pro* or *con*, or to announce for himself that he was not voting, to the end
that, by his vote or his announcement that he was not
voting, it might at least appear upon the journal that
he was present, and that it might appear from the
journal whether the house was proceeding in its business with or without the presence of a quorum. A
further reasonable presumption arises that each of
the thirty-five members, if present, would have answered for himself in the representation of his constituency. So we think the presumption based upon
his duty to be present is met and overthrown by the
conflicting stronger presumptions above set out.

It is, to be sure, possible that each of the thirty-five
members was present and sat mute, and heard the
answer of the speaker for him; but this possibility
does not, in our opinion, rise to the dignity of a legal
presumption upon which this court is authorized to
act, for this possibility is opposed by a presumption
of undoubted weight, to wit, that if each of the thirty-
five members had been present and had sat mute, and
had heard the speaker answer for him, the answer of

the speaker would have been, "Present and not voting," instead of the words he used, "Not voting."

So, upon the whole, we think that, giving the journal the full weight to which it is entitled upon its face, and giving it the benefit of every reasonable presumption arising from its recitals, and from its character, it does not show the presence of a quorum.

But what we have said is not all that may be said respecting the journal of April 3, 1913, and the insistence that it discloses a quorum present when action was had on House Bill 759. It remains to be noted that what occurred on that day was not all that transpired in the house on the subject of the passage of that bill, notwithstanding the objections of the governor; for, although the bill after the action shown by the journal was transmitted to the senate on April 3, 1913, and by that body on that day passed, notwithstanding the objections of the governor, and thence passed into the custody of the secretary of state for enrollment as a law, yet on June 21, 1913, a copy of House Bill No. 759 was again read in the house, and put upon its passage notwithstanding the objections of the governor. The vote as recorded on the House journal of that day showed fifty-three members voting, "Aye," and eighteen members voting, "No." Thus, the journal of that vote shows seventy-one members present and voting upon the roll call. Here is a showing by the journal of more than a quorum of the members of the house voting a second time to pass the same bill notwithstanding the objections of the governor.

The question arises: Why was this done? The journal of the house of that day affords an answer. It shows that a copy of the bill was read, attached to which were the certificates of the respective speakers of the house and senate that the bill had been passed in each of those houses, notwithstanding the objections of the executive, on April 3, 1913, and then it recites: "Whereas, it has been objected by the governor and others that the bill did not pass the house for the alleged reason that less than the number of members necessary to be present to enact laws was then present; and whereas, in view of the public nature and the importance of the bill, all matters of controversy as to its enactment should be determined: Now, therefore, the said bill is hereby repassed, the governor's veto notwithstanding." Then follows on the journal the record of the vote, as already stated.

From the quotation above, the pith and substance of the reason given for again passing the bill over the veto of the governor was that it had been objected by the governor and others that the bill had not passed the house on April 3d, because less than a quorum of members was present on that day. The only reasonable presumption which can arise from this extraordinary action on the part of the house is that the house knew that the objections made by the governor and others above stated were well founded in fact.

Under article 3, sec. 18, of the constitution, after House Bill 759 was disapproved by the governor, and returned with his objections to the house of representatives in which it originated, it could not become a law until passed notwithstanding the objections of the governor first in the house where it originated and next in the senate. It is clear that it did not pass the house over the objections of the governor on April 3, 1913, for the reason, as we think, that the journal of the proceedings of the house on that day not only fail to show the presence of a quorum, but, on the contrary, show that a quorum was not present. This result is reached by the process of eliminating the recital of the journal in respect of the thirty-five members. By the process of elimination, we mean that no reasonable presumption arises from the recitals of the journal in respect of the presence of the thiry-five members which is not met and overthrown by stronger presumptions to the contrary; and that, recital of the journal being thus eliminated, the journal is left standing with the affirmative showing that fifty-eight members, and no more, were present.

On the senate journal of April 3, 1913, it appears that House Bill No. 759 was transmitted to the senate by the clerk of the house together with the veto message of the governor; whereupon, Mr. Crawford made the point of order that the senate had no right or authority under the laws or constitution to receive any matter whatsoever transmitted from the house for the reason that there was not, and had not been, a con-

stitutional quorum of the house of representatives
since March, 1913; which point of order the speaker
of the senate declared to be not well taken. Thereupon it was moved by Mr. Stewart that the bill be
passed, the governor's veto to the contrary notwithstanding; whereupon, a copy of the governor's veto of
the bill was read. Mr. Williams then made the point
of order that the paper purporting to be the veto of
the governor was only a copy and not the paper required by the constitution. The speaker declared this
point of order not well taken; and thereupon the bill
was put on its passage, notwithstanding the veto of
the governor, resulting in a vote which the journal
shows to have been seventeen "ayes" and fifteen
"noes." The names of each senator voting, "Aye,"
and of each senator voting, "No," are shown upon the
journal. Thereupon the journal shows explanations of
votes by members of the senate on House Bill No. 759.

One of the explanations is signed by seven senators,
and it recites in substance that those senators voted,
"no," for the reason that the house transmitting the
bill to the senate was doing business without a quorum.
Sen. Thomas offered an explanation of his vote against
the passage of the bill over the veto of the governor
to the effect that it was a matter of such common and
public knowledge that no quorum existed in the house
at the time of the passage of the bill over the veto of
the governor by that body that the fact could not be
ignored by the senate, and in his explanation he set
out the names of thirty-nine members of the house,

and stated that those members of the house had been absent from the house from and including Tuesday, the 1st day of April, and that this fact was a matter of public knowledge, known to the house and to the senate, but concealed on the house record; and that it therefore followed that House Bill No. 759 had not by the house been constitutionally passed over the governor's veto.

Prior to all we have above stated in connection with the passage of House Bill No. 759 by the senate on April 3, 1913, over the veto of the governor, the journal shows that Sens. Underwood and Williams jointly made a parliamentary inquiry of the speaker of the senate. By this inquiry, those members stated to the speaker, in substance, that they were informed that there was no quorum in the house for the transaction of business, as required by the constitution, and that portion of the constitution relative to the number of members necessary to constitute a quorum was quoted in the inquiry; and the members making the inquiry requested the speaker of the senate to communicate with the speaker of the house, and to ascertain if there was a quorum of the house present for the transaction of legislative business, and that the speaker of the senate inform the senate as to the result of that inquiry.

There was also presented to the senate prior to its consideration of House Bill 759, as shown by the senate journal of April 3, 1913, a message of the governor of the State, by which the governor informed the senate that the house had that day undertaken to pass over the veto of the governor House Bills numbered 751 and 759, and the governor officially notified the senate by that message that said bills were passed without the presence of a constitutional quorum. The governor then proceeds to set out the names of the representatives who were not present upon the reconsideration of the bill in the house. And his message recited that all of the representatives named had been absent from the house from, and including, Tuesday, April 1st, and that the fact of their absence was a matter of public knowledge, known to the house and to the senate, but concealed upon the house record; and that it therefore followed that said bills had not been as a matter of fact passed over the governor's veto by the house. This message of the governor was presented to the senate by Messrs. Underwood, Morrell, and Butler, members of the senate, as explanation of their reason for voting, ''No,'' to the passage of House Bill No. 751, which was called up for reconsideration in the senate prior to its reconsideration of House Bill 759, on April 3, 1913.

If. as we have held, the journal of the house of April 3, 1913, showed no quorum present in that body upon its reconsideration of House Bill No. 759, then it is clear that the action of the senate was unconstitutional and void in reconsidering the bill; the same having originated in the house and not having there been reconsidered as required by the constitution in order to pass the same over the veto of the governor. And the action of the senate being for the above reason void, it cannot be considered for any purpose in any judicial inquiry where the purpose is to determine whether or no the act was passed as required by the constitution, notwithstanding the veto of the governor.

It is admitted that no consideration of House Bill 759 was ever had in the senate after the second consideration of that bill in the house of representatives, which occurred, as we have already stated, on June 21, 1913.

We think it clear that the purpose of the constitutional requirement that the journal should show the "ayes" and "noes" upon the reconsideration of a bill for passage over the veto of the governor was twofold: First, that it might thereby appear that a majority of all the members elected to that house had agreed to pass the bill over the veto; second, that it might appear from the "ayes" and "noes" that when the vote was taken a quorum was present. We cannot describe to the framers of the constitution less than these two purposes.

We hold that "ayes" and "noes" were not taken on April 3, 1913, within the meaning of the constitution, as to thirty-five of the members of the house. It was by no means a compliance to show that thirty-five members were not voting without also showing whether they were present or absent.

The result of this construction is the conclusion that the constitution requires the journal to show the presence of a quorum when such vote is taken; and this

showing must be an affirmative one, and not one arising merely by presumption from some fact appearing
on the journal, or from silence of the journal on the
point, or from a state of facts set out on the journal
which leaves the matter in doubt. It is true that our
cases from which we have quoted, have settled the
rule to be different from that above stated in cases
where certain of the requirements of section 18, art.
2, are involved; but the rule which applies in those
cases rests upon the reason that the latter section does
not require the journal to show that certain of its requirements have been complied with. No such reason
can exist, however, in respect of the requirement of
section 18, art. 3, that the journal show the "ayes"
and "noes"; that requirement is mandatory, and the
result of its nonobservance is the invalidity of the act.

In *Williams* v. *State,* supra, from which we have
quoted, the above principle was recognized; and,
paraphrased, what is quoted therefrom amounts to
this: That, where the constitution expressly requires
the fact to appear on the journal, mere silence on the
point is fatal. There, the question was whether the
bill on its third reading received the constitutional
majority. It will not be presumed in any case from
the mere silence of the journals that either house has
exceeded its authority, or disregarded a constitutional
requirement in the passage of legislative acts, unless
where the constitution has expressly required the
journals to show the action taken, as for instance

where it requires the "ayes" and "noes" to be entered. Cooley, Constitutional Limitations, 195.

There was no such connection between the reconsideration of Bill 759 in the senate on April 3, 1913, and the reconsideration of that bill by the house of June 21, 1913, as to be a compliance with article 3, sec. 18, of the constitution. Neither this court nor the legislature was authorized to change the order which the constitution prescribed, as that its framers thought best. We are not authorized to hold that order directory; the constitution says it shall be done in a certain order. If we essay to change that order, there is no limit to what may follow. No more mandatory words could be used than are employed in fixing the order in which bills must be reconsidered by that section.

In the construction of constitutions, it has been said: "The great majority of all constitutional provisions are mandatory, and it is only such provisions as from the language used in connection with the business in view may be said to be addressed to some person or department that courts have held to be directory; and these provisions in most cases have been those addressed to the legislative department with reference to the mode of procedure in the enactment of laws as above stated. But provisions of this kind will be treated as mandatory if the language used justifies it, even though the proceedings to which they refer are but formal. Whatever is prohibited or positively enjoined must be obeyed. Therefore all prohibitions and restrictions are necessarily mandatory. So, also, all provisions that designate in express terms the time or manner of doing particular acts, and are silent as to performance in any other manner, are mandatory, and must be followed." Cyc. vol. 8, p. 762.

In *State* v. *McCann*, 72 Tenn. (4 Lea), 11, this court, quoting from Judge Cooley in his work on Constitutional Limitations, said: "For the will of the people, as declared in the constitution, is the final law; and the will of the legislature is only law when it is in harmony with, or at least not opposed to, that controlling instrument which governs the legislative body equally with the private citizen. . . . To say a provision is directory seems, with many persons, to be equivalent to saying that it is not a law at all. That this ought not to be so must be conceded; that it is so, we have abundant reason and good authority for saying. . . . A constitutional provision, if it is to be enforced at all, must be treated as mandatory; and, if the legislature habitually disregards it, it seems to us that there is all the more urgent necessity that the courts should enforce it."

This court, following the above quotation in that opinion, added: "These are words of wisdom from the pen of the ablest constitutional jurist now in our midst, and well deserve to be pondered by those whose duty it is to administer the law and enforce its mandates, especially in the court of last resort."

Delicate, indeed, is the duty, and important the power which rests upon this court whenever called on to pass judgment upon the validity of an act of a co-ordinate department of the government of the State.

The exercise of such a judgment in its results may be large in good or evil. The law which stands above the three co-ordinate departments of the government and over-shadows all is the constitution; to its mandates, all must bow. Its command by the use of the word "shall" in prescribing the exact and formal procedure to be pursued when a bill has been disapproved by the governor excludes the idea that any other order of procedure may be recognized as a compliance with its terms. There is no room for the exercise of discretion by those agencies of the State to which it intrusted the execution of section 18 of article 3. The acts to be done by the chief of the executive department, and by that house of the general assembly in which the bill originated, and by the other house, are each and all laid down with specific attention to detail. It is easy enough to say that some other mode of procedure would have done as well, but it is not possible to conceive that any variation from the plain and simple form of procedure laid down with such exactness was intended. In such a case, no one of the three departments of the government can do aught but obey. Over the other two departments of the state government, this court of last resort is set to check and declare void any of their acts which, by appropriate proceedings, are brought to its bar for judgment. The result of such judgments, in so far as they affect the interests of the parties to the particular cause, are of minor importance, as compared with such results in so far as they affect the welfare of the State. If the mandatory provisions of the supreme law here involved should by us be held directory or discretionary, if we by our judgment say that this legislature in that order of reconsideration which it employed in this case found a way in substance the same or just as good and not materially different from that prescribed by the constitution, or that common sense or any other consideration should move us to construe the mandate of the constitution prescribing the particular order designated to mean some other order, then where does such a judgment lead! Clearly, it would be but a step or precedent toward a nullification of any other mandatory provision which may be brought in judgment, and against which some plausible argument may be leveled. By maintenance of the fundamental law of the land are the rights and liberties of citizens of all governments, founded on the will of the governed, preserved; and by judgments reckless of the sacred or mandatory provisions of that law, such rights and liberties are ultimately destroyed.

Among our adjudicated cases, we find no precedent to which we can point as authority for holding the constitutional mode of procedure laid down in section 18, of article 3, as directory.

Reasons plausible enough may be given for upholding the act of the majority of the general assembly in both of the houses composing that body, such as that, if the act be declared void, a minority of that body will have been allowed to defeat the will and judgment of the majority, etc.; but, after all is said that may be said on the line of expediency, the fact stands clearly out that to do the thing expedient is to set aside and hold as directory only, a clearly mandatory constitutional provision, and that a multiplication of such precedents must and can only result in in a destruction of the basic law of the State. Where such a condition exists, the duty of this court is to uphold, by its judgment, the fundamental law of the State.

The argument that the reconsideration of the bill by the house of representatives on June 21, 1913, may be treated as a ratification of what the journal shows was done on April 3, 1913, by members of the house amounting in number to less than a quorum for the transaction of legislative business, is, while plausible, we think wholly unsound. There was no house present on April 3, 1913, capable under the constitution of transacting legislative business. The only power possessed by those members of the legislature who undertook to make the journal show a reconsideration of House Bill 759 was to adjourn the house to the following day, or, if authorized by law, to compel the attendance of absent members. And being wholly without power to reconsider the bill and pass the same over the governor's veto, the action of that body was void in law. It was as a thing not done at all, and not an act defectively performed by a body possessing the power and the right to perform it perfectly; and therefore there was nothing upon which the doctrine of ratification could operate. And our cases (*Furnace Co.* v. *Railroad Co.*, 113 Tenn. [5 Cates], 731, 87 S. W., 1016; *Shields* v. *Land* Co., 94 Tenn. [10 Pickle], 123, 28 S. W., 668, 26 L. R. A., 509, 45 Am. St. Rep., 700; *Muse* v. *Lexington*, 110 Tenn. [2 Cates], 655, 76 S. W., 481) do not apply.

For the reasons above stated, we hold that House Bill No. 759 never became a law, and that chapter 37 of the Public Acts of 1913, as published, is unconstitutional and void.

Mr. Chief Justice Neil delivered a concurring opinion as follows: The first question in these cases is whether there was a quorum in the house on April 3, 1913.

Our constitution (article 2, sec. 11) provides: "The senate and house of representatives, when assembled, shall each choose a Speaker and its other officers; be judges of the qualifications and election of its members, and sit upon its own adjournments from day to day. Not less than two-thirds of all the members to which each house shall be entitled . . . shall constitute a quorum to do business; but a smaller number may adjourn from day to day, and may be authorized, by law, to compel the attendance of absent members."

In my judgment, this can mean nothing else than that two-thirds of the number to which each house is entitled are necessary to make a quorum; and that a less number can transact no business except to adjourn from day to day until a quorum shall assemble; there being no law in existence authorizing the body assembled, being less than a quorum, to compel the attendance of absent members.

That two-thirds are necessary to make a quorum is not only clear from the language quoted, but this construction is made stronger even by the fact that both of the prior constitutions, those of 1796 (article 1, sec. 8) and 1834 (article 2, sec. 11), phrased the matter thus: "Two-thirds of each house shall constitute a quorum to do business." It is perceived the present constitution changed this language into "not less than two-thirds," etc. It is also noted that the language "of each house" is changed into "of all the members to which each house shall be entitled." It is apparent, by comparing the three instruments, that the two prior constitutions were before the convention of 1870, and were examined at every step; and their language was, in many instances, adopted. The change from that language to the language used in the present constitution shows how solicitous the convention was to place beyond controversy the requirement that two-thirds should be necessary to make a quorum.

It is insisted that this requirement was not mandatory, but merely directory, in view of the fact that it

129 Tenn. 14

is provided in section 18 of the same article that in
order to become a law every bill must, upon its third
reading, receive, in each house, "the assent of a majority of all the members to which that house shall be
entitled under this constitution"; and that a similar
provision occurs in article 3, sec. 18, respecting the
passage of a bill over the governor's veto. Article 2,
sec. 5, provides that the membership of the house of
representatives shall never exceed nighty-nine, and
this is the number which now composes that house.
Sixty-six members are required to constitute a
quorum, but under article 2, sec. 18, and article 3, sec.
18, a majority of this quorum cannot pass any bill, and
make it a law; but, in order to effect this result, a
majority of all of the members to which each house is
entitled must vote for it. It is urged that the real,
effective body, therefore, is the majority of each house
voting for a bill. In view of the specific terms in which
the quorum was provided for, it is a singular thing,
it is true, that a majority of the quorum was not permitted to control, and that control was vested in the
majority of the whole membership. I cannot say, however, that this would evince a purpose to make the
provisions concerning the quorum merely directory.
Rather, the two provisions indicate a sedulous purpose on the part of the convention, and of the people
ratifying the constitution, that all legislative business
should receive the careful attention of at least two-
thirds of the membership of each house. To secure

that attention, it was required that two-thirds should at all times be present, and that of these, in case only that many should be present, a number equal to a majority of the whole membership of each house should vote for a bill before its passage could be effected. I do not think it can be gainsaid that the two requirements acting together would be more likely to secure an efficient execution of the business of the legislature, than if either were omitted. It is true that those in excess of the majority of the whole membership can have no effect, by their votes, as against that majority; but, pending the consideration of all legislation, it is furthermore true that, by the presence of the large number required to make a quorum, the constituents of all of the members will have the benefit of the consideration which the large quorum could give, a consideration necessarily superior to that which could be given by a smaller number, because the larger number represents a wider experience, and a wider range of views. This is all I deem it necessary to say at this time on the subject of directory and mandatory provisions in the constitution. Further along in this opinion I shall state my views on the general subject a little more at length.

Was there a quorum in the house on April 3d?

The journal of the House on that day, at the time Bill 759 purports to have been passed, shows the following:

"Mr. Cox made the following motion: Mr. Speaker, I move that House Bill No. 759 be passed, notwithstanding the objections of the executive.

"On request of Mr. Thompson, House Bill No. 759 was read by the clerk.

"On request of Mr. Todd, the message of the governor vetoing House Bill No. 759 was read by the clerk.

"Thereupon the roll was called upon the adoption of the motion of Mr. Cox, with the following result:

"Representatives voting aye were: Messrs. Acree. Babb, Barnett, Bejach, Boyer, Bryant, Byron, Cardwell, Chamlee, Cochran, Collier of Humphreys, Collier of Summer, Cox, Davis, Drane, Dunn, Emmons, Gilbert, Greene, Hill, Hunt, Johnson of Madison, Johnson of Shelby, Kirkpatrick, Larsen, Lefever, Link, Love, Malone, Matthews, Mayes, McCormick, McDade, McFarland, Miller of Marshall, Moore, Morris, Murphy, Myers, Nichols, O'Brien, Quenichet, Royston, Schmittou, Shaw, Stone of Cheatham, Taylor of Madison, Todd, Weldon, Wilson, Winchester, and Mr. Speaker Stanton—52.

"Representatives voting no were: Messrs. Dorsey, Fuller, Miller of Lauderdale, and Thompson—4.

"When the name of each of the following representatives was called, Mr. Speaker Stanton answered for each, 'Not voting': Messrs. Abernathy, Albright, Bullard, Campbell, Childs, Creswell, Denton, Duncan,

Emert, Fisher Fleeman, Fox, Gallagher, Harpole, Hughes, Koffman, Mitchell, Mullens, Park, Parkes, Pierce, Raulston, Rickman, Riggins, Roberts, Robin-son, Scott, Smith, Stephenson, Stone of Lincoln, Spears, Testerman, Walker, West, Williamson—35.

"Representatives answering, 'Present but not voting,' were: Messrs. McWherter and Taylor of Jefferson—2.

"When the name of Mr. Dorsey was called he voted, 'No.' and offered an explanation, which was sent to the desk, and on request of Mr. Cox the clerk proceeded to read the explanation.

"The reading of the explanation was interrupted by Mr. Cox, who made the point of order that the question of a quorum could not be determined except by a roll call.

"Mr. Speaker Stanton ruled the point of order well taken, and declared the explanation out of order.

"Mr. McWherter answered, 'Present but not voting,' and offered an explanation.

"Mr. Speaker Stanton ruled the explanation out of order.

"Mr. Thompson offered the following explanation, which was declared in order by Mr. Speaker Stanton:

"Mr. Speaker, I vote no on the motion to pass House Bill No. 759 over the veto of the governor notwithstanding, for the reason that the Republicans, or the minority party, is not permitted in this bill to name their choice on the board, and for the reason I am pledged to the maintenance of the present election law. J. R. Thompson.

"Mr. Todd made the following motion: Mr. Speaker, I move you that, whereas, House Bill No. 759 has passed the house, the objections or veto of the executive to the contrary notwithstanding, that the clerk be instructed by the house to transmit said bill to the senate, together with the governor's veto message, as having passed the house, the veto or objections of the executive to the contrary notwithstanding.

"The motion prevailed."

What weight should be accorded the journal? What authority, under the constitution, has the judicial department of our State government in respect of such a matter?

When called upon to accredit any apparent act of the legislature, we should feel sure it is indeed such an act. There is no duty to obey an act which is not genuine. If we find it in the book of the acts for the current legislative year published by authority, we should always, nothing else appearing, give it due credit. But recognizing the right, accorded by our constitutional law, to parties litigant to question whether such supposed act really passed the legislative bodies, we should always, when such question is made, examine the legislative journals to solve the doubt so raised. If the point made be that one of the houses was not duly organized, on a given day, we will examine that point in the light of the evidence which our law justifies. We will examine the journals. But right here it seems to me that a very important distinction arises. It is this. Where there is no question that the body making the journal is composed of a quorum, capable of legislating, the language of the journal made by it should be given the benefit of every reasonable doubt as to things done, or attempted to be done, in such houses, in the passage of bills, or other acts done in course of legislation, or in the progress of the two bodies towards legislation; and even silence on the part of the journal should not be counted against it as to any particular thing, but every presumption should be in favor of regularity, and, if possible apparent omissions should be supplied by inferences from those things which appear. In short, in such a case the journals must affirmatively show some constitutional defect in the manner of the legislation. Such is the effect of our decisions. *Brewer* v. *State,* 86 Tenn., 732, 737, 9 S. W., 166; *State* v. *Algood,* 87 Tenn., 163, 168, 10 S. W., 310; *Nelson* v. *Haywood Co.,* 91 Tenn., 596, 604, 20 S. W., 1; *State* v. *McConnell,* 3 Lea, 333; *Williams* v. *State,* 6 Lea, 553; *State, ex rel.,* v. *Baseball Club,* 127 Tenn., 309, 154 S. W., 1151, and cases cited; *Telegraph Co.* v. *Nashville,* 118 Tenn., 1, 101 S. W., 770, 11 Ann. Cas., 824, and cases cited; *State* v. *Swiggart,* 118, Tenn., 556, 102 S. W., 75, and cases cited; *Richardson* v. *Young,* 122 Tenn., 565-569, 125 S. W., 664; *Jackson* v. *Manufacturing Co.,* 124 Tenn., 424-425, 137 S. W., 757. But in none of these cases was any question made as to the existence of a quorum in the legislature at the time a bill was passed. It is manifest that this high grade as evidence should not be accorded to the journal of a body challenged as not duly constituted for want of a quorum. When the body is in this nascent form, it has, under our constitution, no right except to adjourn from day to day, and wait the coming of a quorum. To say that a body challenged as being in this incomplete form should have accorded to its record all of the presumptions attaching duly to a constituted body is tantamount to cutting off all inquiry, and so saying that any number of persons elected to membership in a legislative body (if at the beginning of the legislative term there has been effected an organization, with a speaker and clerk) may, on any day subsequent to the original organization, assemble with the speaker and clerk, at the ascertained place, and assume to be a quorum, and by such mere assumption prevent all investigation of their claims. Such assupmtion is but saying, in another form, "We who are assembled here claim to be a quorum, therefore we are a quorum." If such assumption could ever be indulged under our constitution, there would be no need for the provision that, when a number less than a quorum are present, they have the right to "adjourn from day to day, and may be authorized by law, to compel the attendance of absent members." Even a majority of one of the houses has no power to declare a quorum when none exists. A quorum is determined by a call of the roll. It is not a matter of judgment, or one requiring a technical decision. An assumption by a majority, or even a distinct declaration that it is two-thirds of the whole, or a quorum, cannot make it so. It is true that where one of the houses assumes that a quorum is present (in cases where the constitution does not require the ayes and noes to be entered on the journals), and proceeds with business on that assumption, unchallenged, the court will be bound to indulge the same presumption; but that will not prevent the ascertainment of the real facts, on proper evidence. The nature of that evidence has been already indicated. Whether there can be any other, or whether lapse of time, even a comparatively brief time, with the journal remaining unquestioned, would so obscure all the sources of knowledge as to render practically impossible all reasonable inquiry into such a matter, need not now be considered. Obviously the doings of a body challenged at the time as not being a quorum must be closely examined, with a view to fair, just, and reasonable interpretation. If, in the previous history of the body during the legislative term, as shown by the journal, the custom, as alleged in the bill in this case, had been each day up to March 28th, when an adjournment to April 1st was taken, to call the roll for the purpose of ascertaining the existence of a quorum, and on the special day in question the roll was not called, this fact would immediately arrest the attention of any

investigator. But if no question was made at the time
by anyone, and the body proceeded as if complete,
nothing else appearing, there would be ground for in-
ferring, and the presumption would be, that the presence of a quorum had been ascertained in some other
manner, and existed. But if we find, as appears in
the case before us, that some member of the body, in
the exercise of his constitutional right, attempted to
make the question of no quorum, and to have it entered on the journal, as his objection, or protest under
the constitution, and that this was refused, and sup-
pressed, and instead of calling the roll, and ascertaining the fact, in this simple way, all investigation was
cut off, and the body proceeded as if a quorum was
present, and attempted to show that enough members
were present to make a quorum by the mere fact of
the speaker's "answering for" such and such members, when their names were called on the ayes and
noes in the passage of a bill saying simply, "Not voting"—there can be no doubt that such a so-called
journal discredits itself. Here we have, without any
reason apparent except to make the semblance of a
quorum, the violation of a daily practice of calling the
roll, the suppression of all inquiry, as to the existence
of a quorum, and the speaker, without venturing to
name them as "present," simply announcing, "Not
voting," when the names of thirty-five members were
called. We can give no credence to such a record. It not
only fails to show a quorum present, but furnishes a

convicting basis for the conclusion that there was no quorum. The concurrence of all of these facts is consistent with no other conclusion.

I do not doubt that either of our legislative chambers would have the right to pass a rule giving the speaker power to note the presence of members actually present, but not answering to their names. This is fully established by the reasoning in the case of *United States* v. *Ballin*, 144 U. S., 1, 12 Sup. Ct., 507, 36 L. Ed., 321.

Whether the speaker, without such rule, would have the power, is another question. The constitution does not prescribe what the power of the speaker should be. It must therefore be true that, being a servant of the house over which he presides, he can have only such power as it confers on him, and may have all such powers as may be thus conferred, not in violation of some provision of the constitution. It may also be laid down as true that where there is no rule conferring a power exercised by the speaker, in a given instance, but a duly constituted house submits to the exercise of a power by him, that power must be held to have been rightly exercised, if not in violation of some provision of the constitution.

But it is obvious that this principle could not obtain or hold good where there was no previous rule conferring the power, and it does not appear that the house was at the time duly organized so as to confer the power by its acquiescence. In brief, such a power

could not exist for the purpose of organizing the
house, in the absence of a rule, or for the purpose of
ascertaining a quorum at any time in the absence of
such rule. And for this good reason: We cannot assume in any given case that members are present and
will not answer, because the contrary presumption in
favor of duty must prevail, in favor of all members.
If this presumption is to be overturned by the decision
of one man, he must have that great power conferred
on him from some source, power to witness conclusively the presence and the failure of duty. That power
can be conferred upon that single person only by the
houses. It might be conferred on the clerk, or on any
other person, but it could not exist without being so
conferred.

The power, it is observed, is to note the presence of
one who is actually present but who does not answer
to his name. Suppose a rule should be passed attempting to confer upon the speaker the power to declare a quorum by simply calling the names of members and noting them as "not voting," without regard
to whether they were present or absent. I think that
such a rule would be unconstitutional, as putting it
within the power of the speaker to declare a quorum
when none existed, and thus giving over legislative
power to a number of members less than that prescribed by the constitution. *A fortiori,* the mere act
of the speaker in having certain names called, and
.noting the persons bearing those names simply as not

voting, could not be held equivalent to "present and not voting," or to an announcement that these persons were present but were not voting. *State, ex rel.*, v. *Ellington*, 117 N. C., 158, 23 S. E., 250, 30 L. R. A., 532, 53 Am. St. Rep., 580.

I am of the opinion therefore that the journal shows that no quorum was present on April 3d.

The next question arises on the action of the house on June 21st.

Bill 759 was passed on March 27th by the house, was transmitted to the senate and passed in that body, and was thence transmitted to the governor of the State for his signature. On April 1st, Gov. Hooper vetoed the bill, transmitting it with his veto message to the house of representatives, in which body it had originated. On April 3d, when no quorum was present, the house undertook to pass the bill over the governor's veto and, assuming that this had been accomplished, transmitted the bill to the senate, and it was there passed and then transmitted by the latter body to the secretary of state for enrollment, as a law of the State.

Subsequently the bill of *Webb* v. *Carter* was filed attacking the constitutionality of the action of the two bodies on April 3d, on the ground that no quorum was in the house when the bill was passed over the governor's veto in the latter body.

After this, the action of June 21st was taken, which is thus evidenced by a copy of the journal of the house of that date:

"Mr. Cox sent a written statement to the clerk's desk, and upon request of Mr. Cox the clerk read the motion, and the bill as therein set out, as follows:

"Mr. Speaker:

"I move the following procedure of the house:

"Whereas the bill known as 'House Bill No. 759,' which is as follows:" (Here followed a copy of the bill in full) "was passed by this house on the third day of April, 1913, the governor's veto notwithstanding; and

"Whereas, it has been objected by the governor and others that the bill did not pass the house for the alleged reason that less than the number of members necessary to be present to enact bills were then present; and

"Whereas, in view of the public nature and the importance of this bill all matters of controversy as to its enactment should be determined:

"Now, therefore, the said bill is hereby repassed, the governor's veto notwithstanding (here result of vote), and it is ordered that the clerk of the house transmit to the secretary of State a duly certified copy of these proceedings.

"Mr. Cox moved the previous question.

"The motion prevailed.

"Thereupon the clerk called the roll on the adoption of the motion of Mr. Cox, with the following result:"

Then followed the names of fifty-three representatives voting, "Aye," and eighteen voting, "No."

It is perceived that a copy of the proceedings was directed to be sent to the secretary of State, and it is not directed that the bill should be transmitted to the senate, nor does it appear that the bill was thereafter so transmitted. From the fact that a copy of the proceedings was thus ordered to be transmitted to the secretary of State, that nothing is said about transmitting the bill, and from the further fact that Bill No. 759 appears in the published acts as chapter No. 37, and as passed on April 3, 1913, in both houses, we think the inference is irresistible that the house was never in actual possession of Bill No. 759 after April 3d, when it was placed in the hands of the senate; that on June 21st it was in the hands of the secretary of State; and that the house, on June 21st, acted only on a copy of the bill which had been procured, or was in possession of some member of the house. No other conclusion will fit all of the facts stated.

However, I shall consider the question on the assumption that the bill was itself in the house on June 21st; that although on April 3d it had been bodily, though illegally, placed in the hands of the senate, and thence in the hands of the secretary of State, it had been procured and had come into the possession of the house, that is, the original bill and not a copy merely.

The question to be determined on the basis is whether the due passing of the bill on June 21st could have any effect towards making it a law without its subsequent passage in the senate, on lawful transmission to that body by the house.

In order to make clear my view upon this matter, I shall briefly sketch, in the language of the constitution the course of a bill from its inception through the two houses to the governor, a veto by the governor, and then the passage of the bill over the governor's veto.

"Constitution, art. 2, sec. 17.

"Bills may originate in either house; but may be amended, altered or rejected by the other.

"Sec. 18. Every bill shall be read once, on three different days, *and be passed each time in the house where it originated, before transmission to the other.*"

This section further provides:

"No bill shall become a law until it shall have been read and passed, on three different days in each house, and shall have received, on its final passage in each house, the assent of a majority of all the members to which that house shall be entitled under this constitution; and shall have been signed by the respective speakers in open session, the fact of such signing to be noted on the journal; and shall have received the approval of the governor, or shall have been otherwise passed under the provisions of this constitution."

"Art. 3, sec. 18. Every bill which may pass both houses of the general assembly, shall before it becomes a law, be presented to the governor for his signature. If he approve, he shall sign it, and the same shall become a law; but if he refuse to sign it, he shall return it with his objections thereto, in writing, to the house in which it originated; and said house shall cause said objections to be entered at large upon its journal, and proceed to reconsider the bill. If *after such reconsideration* a majority of all the members elected to that house shall agree to pass the bill, notwithstanding the objections of the executive, *it shall be sent,* with said objections, to the other house by which it shall be likewise reconsidered. If approved by a majority of the whole number elected to that house, it shall become a law. The votes of both houses shall be determined by yeas and nays, and the names of all the members voting for or against the bill shall be entered upon the journal of their respective houses. If the governor shall fail to return any bill, with his objections, within five days (Sundays excepted) after it shall have been presented to him, the same shall become a law without his signature, unless the general assembly, by its adjournment, prevents its return, in which case it shall not become a law."

It is thus perceived that a bill must originate in one of the houses, must be read and passed on three different days in that house, before its transmission to the other house, must then be transmitted to the other house, where it must go through the same course, must be signed by the respective speakers, must then be transmitted to the governor, must be acted on by his signature, or his retaining the bill without signature for five days, or must be vetoed by him; that, in case of his veto, he must transmit the bill to the house wherein it.orginated, and must accompany its transmission with his veto message; that the house to which it is so transmitted must enter the governor's veto at large upon its journal, and must again act upon the bill; if that house again pass the bill notwithstanding the veto, the bill then "shall be sent with said objections to the other house, by which it shall be likewise reconsidered." If approved by both houses in this manner, the bill shall then become a law.

It is perceived that the exact sequence of events is laid down in precise terms in the constitution. After the bill was passed on June 21st, as already stated, it was not thereafter transmitted to the senate, nor passed on by the senate; hence, under the terms of the constitution, it could not become a law, since it requires the action of both houses to convert a bill into a law, along with the functions of the governor above indicated.

But it is insisted that inasmuch as there was a quorum in the senate on April 3d, and that body passed the bill by the usual three readings, the absence of a duly constituted house, that is, a house composed of a quorum, to pass the bill on April 3d, could be cured by the action of that body had on June 21st. The position taken, as we understand it, is that the order or sequence of events provided for in the constitution is immaterial, that these provisions are merely directory and not mandatory. The effect of this contention is that a bill originating in the house may be passed on in the senate before it is voted on in the house, and vice versa; likewise, that a bill originating in the house, and vetoed by the governor, may be voted on in the senate before it is voted on in the house after such veto.

If a bill must follow the order of progress laid down in the constitution, Bill No. 759 never legally passed out of the control of the house of representatives. That house having no quorum on April 3d had no constitutional power to send the bill to the senate, and the senate had no constitutional power to receive it, hence had no constitutional power to act on it, and hence its attempt to act on that bill was void. The senate having thus obtained possession of the bill without authority of the constitution, and hence in a manner that conferred no jurisdiction upon it, the constitutional custody of the bill remained with the house until June 21, 1913, on which day it was passed by a quorum. It should then, and not until then, have been transmitted to the senate. This was not done, so it remains a bill passed only by one house, the house of representatives.

The foregoing conclusions are sound if it be material that the exact order be followed as laid down in the constitution. If that order can be varied, and if it only be necessary that the bill shall have been passed by both houses over the veto regardless of whether both houses had legal possession of the bill, then it became a law when subsequently passed in the house on June 21st. The question then to be considered is whether the exact order laid down in the constitution is essential.

Is that provision of the constitution directory which declares that when the governor disapproves a bill he shall transmit it to the house in which it originated, and that that house, on passing it over the veto, shall transmit it to the other house?

If one part is directory, all of the parts are. But the word "shall" is used with each step. If the house can constitutionally transmit such a bill to the senate before itself acting on it, or a number of members less than a quorum can do this, then it seems with equal reason the governor may in his discretion transmit a senate bill with his veto to the house, or a house bill to the senate. Is there any good reason underlying the constitutional order? There is. It is evident that those who originated any legislation in question on any occasion are in the house where the bill was first introduced. They are more particularly interested than any others in seeing the bill become a law, and are therefore more likely to be vigilant and active in securing its passage over the veto. The great personal interest which a member takes in a bill originated by him, "his bill," is a matter of common knowledge. If the governor can send the bill to the other house, the house in which it did not originate, he can, for a time, at least, stifle this earnest, personal advocacy. The bill may linger in the house to which he has sent it until the ardor of its special advocate cools or dies out. Furthermore, the governor may be stronger in the house to which he has chosen to send it, and his friends there may be able to so obstruct the bill that it will not be acted on at all during the session, or action on it may be so delayed that, through the intervention of other legislative business, it may reach the other house too late for action there before the close of the session. The effect of holding constitutional such a course would be to add to the personal power of the governor, and to detract much from the power of the legislature.

View the question from another angle: Suppose the governor properly transmits a bill with his veto to the house in which it originated, and suppose it is a measure of monmentous importance on which parties are closely divided, and on which popular feeling is running high, and suppose the governor's reasons for the veto are weighty, and evoke strong popular support, and suppose the house in which the bill originated, and to which it had been so returned, wishes to avoid the responsibility of taking the initiative in overriding the veto and thereby repudiating the reasons given in the veto message, which we may suppose as stated, to be very strong and very popular, and from such motives that house wishes to place the responsibility on the other house of acting first. If the matter is discretionary, as suggested, this could be done. This would result, if valid, in the imposition by one house on the other of a duty for no other reason than that the first wished to escape the responsibility of performance. Let us suppose the body so wishing to escape or postpone responsibility is the house. It avoids the duty and hands it over to the senate, and that body is called on to act. But that body is co-ordinate and may insist the duty cannot be imposed. It has the power to refuse, and there is no authority known to our system which could compel it to act. Suppose it does refuse. We then have the spectacle of a bill being thrown from one house back to the other, and from that back to the first, and so on indefinitely. On the other hand, if the order laid down in the constitution be binding, there never can be any doubt in any instance as to the duty of each body and the method that should be pursued.

If the constitutional order can be departed from—that is, if it is directory instead of being mandatory—the people can never fix responsibility or impute blame to their legislative representatives, since, if each body has the discretion suggested, no one can say which is in the wrong. Yet the only court of appeal which the body of the people have for the correction of error, or the punishment of faithlessness on the part of their representatives, is the ballot box. But if the courts hold that the criteria of action which the people have prescribed in the constitution are simply directory and may therefore be obeyed or disobeyed as the legislature may see fit, what is there left by which the people can judge their representatives? This consideration is of the greatest importance, because it lies at the very foundation of representative government.

The danger in holding constitutional provisions directory is great, in any instance, but especially so as to those which concern action by the legislature. The courts, by so doing, can quickly destroy every barrier which the people have erected for their protection against usurpation by the lawmaking body. ''One of the first things a student of our system of government learns is that it is a system of checks and balances. One of the principal checks upon legislative power is the authority of the court to enforce obedience to the mandates of the constitution by adjudging void enactments which conflict with its provisions. History proves, and experience demonstrates, the necessity of such a check, for without it the legislative department arrogates to itself every substantial governmental function and power that it can grasp. . . . The change wrought by legislative usurpation and encroachment justifies the statement of Mr. Bagehot that 'a legislative chamber is greedy and covetous. It acquires as much, it concedes as little, as possible. The passions of its members are its rulers; the lawmaking faculty, the most comprehensive of the imperial faculties, is its instrument. It will take the administration if it can take it.' Eng. Const. (Am. Ed.), 95. The great men who framed our constitutional system knew and provided against the dangers of legislative usurpation of power, and the wisest among them united in devising checks upon it. The declarations of Madison and Washington are strong and clear, and no reader of history can misunderstand their meaning, or doubt their purpose. Jefferson thus expressed his conviction: 'An elective despotism was not the government we fought for, but one which should not only be founded

on free principles, but one in which the powers of
government should be so divided and balanced among
several bodies of magistracy as that no one should
transcend their legal limits without being effectually
checked and restrained by others.' 'To preserve
these checks,' said a greater thinker than Jefferson,
'must be as necessary as to institute them.' Washington's Farewell Address.'' Elliott, J., in *Parker* v.
State, 133 Ind., 178, 209, 32 N. E., 836, 845, 18 L. R. A.,
578, 579.

I am of the opinion, therefore, that the court
should deal most sparingly, and exercise the very
greatest caution, in holding any constitutional provision directory.

Such is the rule laid down, in substance, in Black's
Constitutional Law, p. 78, where it is said:

"The provisions of a constitution are almost invariably mandatory. It is only in extremely plain cases,
or under the pressure of necessity, that they can be
construed as merely directory."

In 8 Cyc., p. 762, it is said:

"The great majority of all constitutional provisions
are mandatory, and it is only such provisions as from
the laguage used in connection with the objects in
view may be said to be addressed to the discretion of
some person or department that courts have held to be
directory, and these provisions in most cases have been
those addressed to the legislative department with reference to the mode of procedure as to the enactment
of laws as above stated. But provisions of this kind

will be treated as mandatory if the language used justifies it, even though the proceedings to which they refer are but formal. Whatever is prohibited or positively enjoined must be obeyed; therefore all prohibitions and restrictions are necessarily mandatory. So also all provisions that designate in express terms the time or manner of doing acts, and are silent as to performance in any other manner, are mandatory and must be followed."

Judge Cooley, in his work on Consttiutional Limitations (5th Ed.), pp. 93, 94, gives it as his view that the whole doctrine of directory provisions in a constitution is inadmissible, using the following language:

"But the courts tread upon very dangerous ground when they venture to apply the rules which distinguish directory and mandatory statutes to the provisions of a constitution. Constitutions do not usually undertake to prescribe mere rules of proceeding, except when such rules are looked upon as essential to the thing to be done; and they must then be regarded in the light of limitations upon the power to be exercised. It is the province of an instrument of this solemn and permanent character to establish those fundamental maxims, and fix those unvarying rules by which all departments of the government must at all times shape their conduct; and, if it descends to prescribing mere rules of order in unessential matters, it is lowering the proper dignity of such an instrument, and usurping the proper province of ordinary legislation. We are not therefore to expect to find in a constitution provisions

which the people, in adopting it, have not regarded
as of high importance, and worthy to be embraced
in an instrument which, for a time at least, is to control alike the government and the governed, and to
form a standard by which is to be measured the power
which can be exercised as well by the delegates as by
the sovereign people themselves.   If directions are
given respecting the times or modes of proceeding in
which a power should be exercised, there is at least
a strong presumption that the people designed it should
be exercised in that time and mode only; and we impute to the people a want of due appreciation of the
purpose and proper province of such an instrument,
when we infer that such directions are given to any
other end.   Especially when, as has been already said,
it is but fair to presume that the people in their constitution have expressed themelves in careful and measured terms, corresponding with the immense importance of the powers delegated, and with a view to
leave as little as possible to implication.''

The author admits that there are a few reported
cases to the contrary, and these he discusses in the
succeeding pages and expresses the opinion that they
are against the weight of authority. He quotes with
approval our case of *Cannon* v. *Mathes,* 8 Heisk., 517,
wherein Nicholson, C. J., said:

''In the present case, we do not deem it necessary to
express an opinion as to the question whether any provision of the constitution can be properly treated otherwise than as mandatory.   The essential nature and

object of constitutional law being restrictive upon the powers of the several departments of government, it is difficult to comprehend how its provisions can be regarded as merely directory.''

It is true that in a later case (*Telegraph Co.* v. *Nashville*, 118 Tenn., 1, 101 S. W., 770, 11 Ann. Cas., 824) this court, in an opinion by Mr. Justice Wilkes, did hold a certain provision of the constitution directory; but it is apparent from an examination of the opinion that the court did so only after the most careful scrutiny, and with a full appreciation of the danger attendant upon holding any constitutional provision directory, and in view of the fact that there had been a practical construction of the point by the legislature for a long period during which nearly 200 acts, many of them very important, covered by the provision and practice in question had been passed; and further in view of the fact that an attentive examination of the very language of the constitution in which the subject involved was expressed seemed to clearly indicate that that provision was intended to be directory; and further reinforced by the consideration that a contrary view would place it in the power of a negligent or corrupt clerk of the senate or house, without the knowledge of either, to nullify the most important legislation. It was not deemed that the people in establishing the constitution could have intended to subject legislation to such constant menace of negligence or fraud, on the part of subordinate officers of the body having no part in the making of laws.

The last expression of the court on the subject is
found in *State* v. *Burrow,* 119 Tenn., 376, 104 S. W.,
526, 14 Ann. Cas., 809. In this case the court quotes
with approval the language of Judge Cooley, supra, and
lays down the general rule that every provision of
the constitution should be held mandatory, and admits
an exception to that rule only in the case where it can
be ascertained unmistakably and conclusively from the
language of such special provision that it was intended
to be directory only. The opinion on the subject, delivered by our former chief justice, now United States
senator, Shields, is couched in terms so appropriate and
so strong that we deem it proper to reproduce his language, in part, at least:

"Constitutions are expressions of the sovereign will
of the people, the fountain of all power and authority.
The several departments of the government are created
and vested with their authority by them, and they must
exercise it within the limits and in the manner which
they direct. The provisions of these solemn instruments are not advisory, or mere suggestions of what
would be fit and proper, but commands which must be
obeyed. Presumably they are all mandatory. Certainly no provision will be construed otherwise, unless the intention that it shall be unmistakably and
conclusively appears upon its face. The supremacy of
and permanency of republics depend upon the maintenance of the fundamental law, in its integrity, as written in constitutions adopted by the people; and it is
the solemn duty of all those temporarily vested with

power, in all departments of the State, to do this. The necessities of a particular case will not justify a departure from the organic law. It is by such insidious process and gradual encroachment that constitutional limitations and government by the people are weakened and eventually destroyed. It has been well said:

" 'One step taken by the legislature or judiciary in enlarging the powers of government opens the door for another, which will be sure to follow, and so the process goes on until all respect for the fundamental law is lost, and the powers of government are just what those in authority please to make or call them.' "

It may be useful to quote some observations in point from the decisions of other States.

In *Varney* v. *Justice,* 86 Ky., 596, 601, 6 S. W., 457, 459, it is said:

"Whenever the language (of the constitution) gives a direction as to the manner of exercising a power, it was intended that the power should be exercised in the manner directed, and in no other manner. It is an instrument of words, granting powers, restraining powers, and reserving rights. These words are fundamental words, meaning the thing itself; they breathe no spirit except the spirit to be found in them. To say that these words are directory merely is to license a violation of the instrument every day and every hour."

This language was quoted with approval in the opinion of Bennett, J., in the later case of *Norman* v. *Ken-*

tucky Board of Managers, 93 Ky., 537, 20 S. W., 901, 18 L. R. A., 560.

In *Parker* v. *State,* 133 Ind., 178, 196, 32 N. E., 836, 841, 18 L. R. A., 567, 574, it is said:

"Constitutional provisions are seldom, if ever, to be construed as merely directory."

The supreme court of West Virginia said:

"Constitutional provisions are organic. They are adopted with the highest degree of solemnity. They are intended to remain unalterable except by the great body of the people, and are incapable of alteration without great trouble and expense. They are the framework of the State as a civil institution, giving cast and color to all its legislation, jurisprudence, institutions, and social and commercial life by confining the legislature, the executive, and judiciary within prescribed limits. All the great potential, dominating, creative, destroying, and guiding forces of the State are brought within their control so far as they apply. Thus, to the extent of their duration, they define and limit the policy of the State more rigidly and unalterably than the sails and rudder of the ship when set govern and control its course. A more apt figure is made up of the great system of highways, including railroads, fixing the mode, courses, and extent of travel and transportation." *Capito* v. *Topping,* 65 W. Va., 587, 591, 64 S. E., 845, 846, 22 L. R. A. (N. S.), 1091, 1092.

What has been said in the preceding paragraphs, whether by way of reasoning, or in the language of authorities quoted, seems to me to present insuperable

objections to our holding as merely directory the provisions of our constitution referred to.

But I wish to add a few words more. I wish to call
special attention to the use of the word "shall." All
through the provisions quoted the people of the State
in making their constitution use that authoritative and
compelling word—a word which leaves no doubt of the
purpose of one who uses it, having at the same time
power to enforce his will. Thou shalt, and thou shalt ·
not. These are the dominant expressions of a controlling will. It is most interesting, instructive, and
impressive to read the constitution through, and note
how often the people use therein the expressions we
have just referred to—"shall," and "shall not," or
their equivalents. A few instances will suffice: "That
no political or religious test, other than an oath to
support the constitution of the United States and of
this State, shall ever be required as a qualification to
any office or public trust under this State." Article
1, section 4. "That the right of trial by jury shall remain inviolate, and no religious or political test shall
ever be required as a qualification for jurors." Id., sec.
6. "That the people shall be secure in their persons,
houses, papers and possessions, from unreasonable
searches and seizures; and that general warrants,
whereby an officer may be commanded to search suspected places, without evidence of the facts committed,
or to seize any person or persons not named, whose
offenses are not particularly described and supported
by evidence, are dangerous to liberty, and ought not

to be granted." Id., sec. 7. "That no man shall be
taken or imprisoned, or disseised of his freehold, liberties or privileges, or outlawed, or exiled, or in any manner destroyed, or deprived of his life, liberty, or property, but by the judgment of his peers or the law of
the land." Id., sec. 8.

But why need I go further, and furnish other ex-
amples? It is already perceived that by these words,
"shall" and "shall not," the people have endeavored
to preserve, and save from harm, their most sacred
rights of life, liberty, property, and the pursuit of
happiness; that by these they have sought to guard
every man from oppression and to guarantee right and
justice to all. Can we hold these words as merely directory in the passages we have quoted? If not, what
warrant have we that their imperative meaning is lost
in subsequent parts of the constitution?

It may be said that the result would have been the
same in the present instance, if the constitutional order had been followed, that the senate would have
again passed the bill by substantially the same vote as
before; therefore that the question is immaterial. Who
can say that a change of opinion might not have occurred among the members of the senate? But grant
that no change would have occurred, and that the result of another vote would have been the same. Would
this be true of every future violation of the constitutional order? It must not be overlooked that we are
not only deciding the case before us, but laying down
also a rule of constitutional duty to be followed in suc-

ceeding cases, and by the legislature in its future conduct. Is it a sound and true principle that the legislature and this court will be justified in disregarding a command embraced in the constitution, when we are satisfied the result will be the same as it would be if we obeyed it? It is provided in article 1, section 9, that "in all criminal cases the accused hath the right to be heard by himself and his counsel." We may conceive a case wherein the accused, though a weak and ignorant man, employed very able and competent counsel who represented him in the trial court. On his conviction and appeal to this court, and error assigned to the effect, and sustained by the record, that he had demanded to be heard in person, and this right had been denied him in the trial court, would this court consider it a sufficient answer that he was weak and ignorant, his speech, or talk to the court and jury would have done him no good, the evidence was conclusive, and the result would have been the same? Assuredly, no. The same section provides that the prisoner has the right to a copy of the indictment. Would a refusal of this right, on demand from him, be excused in this court on the ground that it would have done him no good, that the indictment was read in his presence when he was put on trial before the jury? This court has held to the contrary. *Moses* v. *State*, 9 Baxt., 230; *Nokes* v. *State*, 6 Cold., 297. In the same section it is provided that the accused has the right to a "speedy public trial, by an impartial jury of the coun-

ty in which the crime shall have been committed.''
Suppose the trial was had in secret over the prisoner's objection, and his demand for the public trial
guaranteed him by the constitution, would this court,
for one instant, excuse that denial on the ground that
the result would have been the same? Suppose he had
been tried by an ''impartial jury'' of another county
than the one in which the crime had been committed,
when he had not asked for a change of venue, would
this court fail to promptly reverse the judgment? The
court has answered this question in no uncertain way.
Kirk v. *State*, 1 Cold., 344; *State* v. *Donaldson*, 3
Heisk., 48. In article 6, section 12, it is provided that
all indictments shall conclude, ''against the peace and
dignity of the state.'' Could a failure to so conclude
an indictment be excused by us on the ground that it
was an immaterial matter, and the result would have
been the same? This court has answered, no, that the
constitutional provision is imperative, and must be
obeyed. *Rice* v. *State*, 3 Heisk., 215, 221. Yet it is
difficult to see why the constitution required this language to be used. The same section provides that ''all
writs and other process shall run in the name of the
State of Tennessee.'' Why could not a case be tried
just as well with the writ running in the name of one
of the great cities of the State? But this court has
said, no, such a writ is void. *Mayor and Aldermen* v.
Pearl, 11 Humph., 249, 250. Why could it not run in
the name of one of the courts of the State? This court
has said such a writ is void. *McLendon* v. *State*, 8

Pick. (92 Tenn.), 520, 525, 22 S. W., 200, 21 L. R. A., 738.

What is the principle underlying all of these cases? Simply, that our duty is not to ask the reason why, when the mandate is plain; not to question why another way would not do as well, but simply to obey. As said by Mr. Justice Buchanan, quoting with approval an author mentioned by him: " 'Where the legislature has used words of plain and definite import, it would be very dangerous to put upon them a construction which would amount to holding that the legislature did not mean what it had expressed.' In a recent . . . work on Statutory Law, it is said that the intention of the legislature is to be learned from the words it has used; . . . and, if that intention is expressed in a manner devoid of contradiction and ambiguity, there is no room for interpretation or construction, and the judges are not at liberty, on consideration of policy or hardship, to depart from the words of the statute; that they have no right to make exceptions or insert qualifications, however abstract justice or the justice of the particular case may seem to require it." *Heiskell* v. *Lowe*, 126 Tenn., 475, 499, 153 S. W., 284, 290.

If this order was immaterial, why was section 18, of article 3, laying down in precise terms what shall be done in case of a veto by the governor, embraced for the first time in the constitution of 1870, when it did not appear in that of 1796, or that of 1834? A comparison of the three instruments shows that the constitution of 1796 was before the convention of 1834, and that changes and additions were made, matters omitted, and matters added, when the latter constitution was made; likewise it is apparent that both constitutions were before the constitutional convention of 1870, and that other excisions and additions were made. The constitution of 1870 established the new matter covered in article 3, section 18. Can this be regarded as an immaterial circumstance, and the new matter likewise immaterial, to be obeyed or disobeyed as may seem proper or convenient to the legislature? Why was the convention of 1870 at so much pains to add this new matter, after an inspection and comparison of the two former constitutions, if it was to be disregarded at will? By this new matter the governor was for the first time given the veto power. By it that power was regulated, and the action of the legislature in respect thereof as well. One is as imperative as the other. I have shown in a former part of this opinion that there are excellent reasons for the rule of legislative action thus laid down; but, even if there were no such reasons, still it was the simple duty of the legislature to obey the directions given. Having failed to obey the constitution, their act was nugatory, and it is the duty of the court, as I conceive, to so hold and decide.

If I am correct in the proposition that the order of events, the due course of legislation, is essential, the action of the senate on April 3d was, as previously said, void because there had been no previous constitutional

action in the house, in which the bill originated. For
a like reason, the action of the house on June 21st could
not cure the previous void action of the senate, and
could have no effect at all because there was no subsequent action of the senate. On the same principle, the
action of the house on June 21st could not relate back
to April 3d so as to make the action of the house in
legal effect antedate that of the senate. If such fiction of relation should be indulged, it would subvert
the constitutional order as effectually as an open and
designed effort on the part of the two legislative bodies
to subvert that order. Such supposed curative action
would as surely violate the constitutional policy as if
there had been no previous attempt in the house. The
thing to be cured would be the fact that the senate had
acted prior to the house; the latter under the constitution being required to act first. The cure on the assumption of relation is to be effected, if at all, by the
house still acting subsequent to the senate, but treating that action as if it had in fact been prior; in short,
by the operation of a legal fiction. Constitutional powers cannot be so conferred, or exercised. Again, the
right of the legislature to pass curative acts is based
on its authority to enact legislation, to make good now,
by an act of legislation, what it could have made good
prior thereto if called upon, or to correct some defective exercise of its own legislative power on some former occasion; but here, in the special case before us,
the difficulty is not in the exercise of legislative power,
but in the failure to occupy a certain constitutional

status, the absence of which *status* made the house, at
the time, being without a quorum, no legislative body
at all. By sustaining the proper *status* at a subsequent time, it could not change the fact that on a former day it did not have that *status,* or supply the lack
of that *status.* The power resides in the constitution
as an expression of the will of the people, not in the
legislature. By having a quorum and being organized,
a branch of the legislature stands in such relation to
the constitution as that it is a legislative body, and
capable of exercising constitutional power. A constitutional status on a subsequent day cannot relate to a
former day and cure a lack of *status* existing at that
time. The body purporting to act on the former day
without a quorum was simply no legislative body.
Nothing can alter that fact. Such was the assemblage
of men purporting to act as the house on April 3d.

Reference is made in the opinion of Mr. Justice Lansden to *Archibald* v. *Clark,* 112 Tenn., 532, 82 S. W.,
310. As I understand the reference, it is made for the
purpose of showing that the order in which the two
houses shall consider a bill is immaterial. In my judgment that case is incapable of that construction, and so
are the cases which subsequently cite it with approval.
The court was not considering, and did not have in
mind, in any degree, the subject which we are now discussing, but only whether the bill, under the practice
pursued, had had three readings in each house. It was
adjudged that it had, because the same bill had been
introduced in each body, had two readings in each, had

a third reading in the house, a transfer then to the senate, and a third reading there. The practice is not a wise one, and is more honored in the breach than in the observance, because it enables the passage of a bill through the two houses during three days' time instead of six; but there is nothing in the constitution that prevents the same bill being introduced simultaneously in the two houses, and thus being at the same time both a house bill and a senate bill. In such a case each house would proceed in the regular course to consider its own bill, but the one first succeeding in passing the bill upon its third reading would transmit its bill to the other house, and it would there be substituted for the bill of that house, and be passed; this passage in such other house being treated as a passage on its third reading in that house because it had already, in the form of a bill of that house, passed two readings. It is perceived that the question is not one of due progression from one house to the other, but only as to whether there had been three readings in each house. The due order of constitutional progression was recognized and followed, on final reading, when the house bill was transmitted to the senate, and was there passed. In such a case the bill is finally treated as a bill originated in the house in which it first passed its third reading. *Archibald* v. *Clark* is therefore not an authority for the proposition that the constitutional order is immaterial, but rather the contrary. The fact that this case is cited for such a purpose emphasizes the danger of departing from con-

stitutional provisions even in appearance, because
precedents of this kind may be the fruitful origin of
other precedents which will lead us far beyond real
constitutional bounds.

For the reasons stated, I am of the opinion that
House Bill 759 was never constitutionally passed, and
therefore that chapter 37 of the Acts of 1913 is void.

MR. JUSTICE WILLIAMS delivered a concurring opinion as follows:

My concurrence in holding that article 2, section 11,
and article 3, section 18, are mandatory in character
is compelled by the reasoning of Mr. Justice Buchanan and the chief justice in the opinions delivered in
this case, as well as by the admirable statement of the
rule by former Chief Justice Shields in *State* v. *Burrow*, 119 Tenn., 376, 104 S. W., 526, 14 Ann. Cas., 809.

When we view the nature and functions of a constitution, as the expression of the sovereign's will in
respect of the legislature and legislation, and as intended not merely to provide for the exigencies of a
few years but to endure stably throughout a long period, the limitations imposed by it upon the power of
the sovereign's agencies should not be deemed less
than mandatory.

Constitutional limitations of this character are of
necessity rigid, if they are truly to impose the sovereign's will upon the will of its agents.

The courts in their guardianship of the constitution,
should be slow to rule otherwise.

As said by Mr. Justice Lamar, in *Board of Lake Co. v. Rollins,* 130 U. S., 662, 9 Sup. Ct., 651, 32 L. Ed., 1060: "The liberty of the citizen, and his security in all his rights, in a large degree depend upon a rigid adherence to the provisions of the constitution and the laws, and their faithful performance. If courts, to avoid hardships, may disregard and refuse to enforce their provisions, then the security of the citizen is imperiled. Then the will, it may be the unbridled will, of the judge, would usurp the place of the constitution and the laws, and the violation of one provision is liable to speedily become the precedent for another, perhaps more flagrant, until all constitutional and legal barriers are destroyed, and none are secure in their rights. Nor are we justified in resorting to strained construction or astute interpretation, to avoid the intention of the framers of the constitution. . . . If unwise or hard in their operation, the power that adopted can repeal or amend, and remove the inconvenience."

If, then, we proceed upon the basis that article 2, section 11, stipulating that "not less than two-thirds of all members to which each house shall be entitled shall constitute a quorum to do business," is mandatory, what weight shall be given, the house journal as evidence of the fact that such quorum was present or lacking on April 3d?

When we look to the journal entries, we find that on previous legislative days in compliance with parliamentary procedure the house had, without variation, up to April 1st-3d undertaken to ascertain the existence of a quorum or no quorum by roll calls; that, for the first time, on April 1st-3d, it failed to do so, but on the contrary dispensed with the call. Further, that while the form of response, "Present but not voting," was used to indicate the physical presence in the house, but refusal to vote, of two representatives, the form, "Not voting," was used by the speaker in his effort to answer for thirty-five representatives. These two facts in conjunction tend strongly to raise affirmatively a showing of a lack of a quorum.

Yet further: It appears in the journal entry of April 3d that a representative offered an explanation, calling in question the matter of a quorum, and thereupon a point of order was made by another representative to the effect that the question of a quorum could not be determined except by a roll call. This point of order was sustained, and yet no roll call for the ascertainment of a quorum was ordered; and the explanation was denied entry on the journal.

Appellees properly treat of this attempted explanation as an attempted protest. The constitution, art. 2, sec. 27, provides: "Any member of either house of the general assembly shall have the liberty to dissent from and protest against, any act or resolve which he may think injurious to the public or to any individual, and to have reasons for his dissent entered on the journals."

It is insisted in behalf of appellees that "the only protest allowed by the constitutional provision is one against a bill or resolution which has passed.'' This is too narrow a view and would unduly restrict the right of protest and postpone it to a time when it would be less availing, if, indeed, not unavailing in instances.

When we consider that this explanation of protest was directed immediately at the lack of a constitutional quorum to proceed to the passage of the bill over the governor's veto, to my mind its suppression by the speaker and the house is pregnant with meaning, especially when viewed in conection with the two facts above commented on. I do not consider that a journal that shows that a protest, thus constitutionally raised to call in question the lack of power on the part of the house, has been stifled, is entitled to be accredited by the courts with verity by way of conclusive presumption of regularity in respect of the presence of a quorum.

If it be said that the journal is otherwise silent touching the presence or absence of quorum, it yet affirmatively appears that a mandatory provision in respect of the right of protest was violated in the suppression of that which tended to impeach the existence of the very thing we are asked to presume. We should refuse to so presume in favor of a body thus proceeding in disregard of a plain constitutional mandate. To do otherwise would be to place it in the power of a speaker and a few members by the fabrication of a journal to create *evidence of power* and then of power exercised in any manner they might will, silencing protest the while.

Manifestly, the journal, under the rule obtaining in this State, comes under review by us as *evidence*, and it is for the court to say what dignity in grade shall be assigned to it as evidence. If those who make such a journal leave upon it marks of manipulation in an effort towards showing apparent power, it is conceived that this should subtract from the dignity otherwise assignable to it, and leave the question open to proof.

What has been said by Mr. Justice Buchanan and the Chief Justice in regard to the effect of the proceedings in the house on June 21st is so comprehensive and convincing as to leave nothing to be here added, further than the statement of my concurrence.

MR. JUSTICE LANSDEN delivered a dissenting opinion as follows:

I am unable to concur in the opinions delivered by the majority of the court, and, because of the great importance of the case and the far-reaching effect of the questions decided, I deem it proper to express the grounds of my dissent. I shall only discuss the effect of the action of the two houses when quorums were admittedly present in passing the bills over the governor's veto, pretermitting the other questions made and discussed by counsel. So if it be conceded that there was no quorum present in the house on April 3d, and that the journals so show, it still remains a conceded fact that the senate passed the bill when a quorum was present in that body, and, upon a proper roll call, it received the votes of a majority of all the members to which that house was entitled. Afterwards it was passed by the house when a quorum was present in that body, receiving on proper roll call the votes of a majority of all the members to which the house was entitled.

As I understand the opinion of the majority, it was decided that the bill in question never became a law, notwithstanding it received the assent of both the house and the senate, for the reason that the two houses did not act in the sequence required by the constitution. Upon the passage of bills over the governor's veto, the constitution (article 3, sec. 18) provides as follows:

"Every bill which may pass both houses of the general assembly, shall before it becomes a law, be presented to the governor for his signature. If he approve, he shall sign it, and the same shall become a law; but if he refuse to sign it, he shall return it with his objections thereto, in writing, to the house in which it originated; and said house shall cause said objections to be entered at large upon its journal, and proceed to reconsider the bill. If after such reconsideration, a majority of all the members elected to that house shall agree to pass the bill, notwithstanding the objections of the executive, it shall be sent, with said objections, to the other house, by which it shall be likewise reconsidered. If approved by a majority of the whole number elected to that house, it shall become a law. The votes of both houses shall be determined by yeas and nays, and the names of all members voting for or against the bill shall be entered upon the journals of their respective houses.''

It should be observed that the foregoing provision of the constitution has for its object the passage of bills over the veto of the governor, and states in what event a vetoed bill shall become a law. All of the requirements of the constitution in respect thereto have been met by the action of the two houses except that the senate reconsidered the bill and passed it over the veto before it was legally reconsidered and passed in the house.

The governor has no power to defeat legislation. Under the constitutions of 1796 and 1834 he did not have power to even check legislation because the veto was entirely withheld from him. His right of veto originated in our present constitution, and section 18, art. 3, above quoted, relating to the passage of bills over the governor's veto, and the veto itself, are manifestly modeled from section 7 of article 1 of the constitution of the United States with the very important difference that our constitution permits bills to be passed over the veto of the governor by the same number of votes and the votes of the same members who are empowered to pass it originally. In other respects, the language of the two instruments on this subject is strikingly similar. The purpose of these provisions of the constitution manifestly is to require the general assembly to reconsider the proposed legislation upon the objection presented to it by the governor. The governor is authorized to counsel and advise the majority of the legislature, but he cannot defeat their will. He represents a majority of all the voters of the State acting *en masse*. A majority of the members of the legislature may or may not represent the will of a majority of all the voters of the State, but they do represent a majority of the majorities of certain subdivisions of the State composing the counties and the floterial and senatorial districts from which the members are chosen. So when an issue is joined upon the passage of a bill between the governor opposed and the general assembly in favor of such passage, the constitution requires the general assembly to reconsider the bill in the light of the governor's objections.

From these considerations, I think there can be no doubt but that the meaning and purpose of these provisions of the constitution are to compel the general assembly to receive counsel from the governor and reconsider the bill in view of his specific objections. The procedure by which the reconsideration is to be had and the sequence in which the two houses are to act are merely means to the chief end in view. These purposes of the constitution, and especially the fact that the governor has no power to defeat legislation, should be borne constantly in mind in determining the legal existence of the bill under consideration. This is true because the final question to be decided is whether the governor's veto has defeated this legislation. It inevitably comes to this because the two houses passed the bill and transmitted it to the governor and he vetoed and returned it to the house of its origin. Both

houses have since reconsidered it in the light of his
objections with quorums present and have passed it
over the veto by requisite majorities.

The power of the legislature to enact laws and the
absence of power in the governor to defeat laws are
emphasized here to show that each one of those departments has exercised the full power belonging to
it in respect to this bill, and therefore the power of
both has been exhausted in the effort upon the one hand
to enact the law and upon the other to defeat it.

The balance of the powers given to the different
departments of government must be rigidly maintained. It is the duty of this court in construing the
constitution to require a strict adherence of each department of government to the sphere of action assigned to it by that instrument. A construction cannot
be given it which would enable one department to
exercise a power not conferred or that would enable
it to defeat the exercise of a power by another department which is conferred.

If the action of the two houses has failed to result
in the constitutional enactment of the bill, it must be
because of a failure to observe some sequence in their
action made necessary by the constitution. The general assembly had the power to pass the bill. It also
had the purpose to do so. The objection taken to the
validity of its action is not to its power to do the thing
attempted, but to the manner, form, and time in which
the thing was done. So it is not a question of the
power of the legislature to do it, but the mode of pro-

cedure by which it attempted to exercise its admitted power. A distinction has always been taken in the construction of the constitution between power and procedure. I believe it has never been held before that an admitted power to do a thing has been defeated by a mere failure to comply with the exact order of. sequence in which it was to be done. No cases are cited for such a holding, and there are numerous cases in our own reports which are to the contrary. The fundamental difference between power and procedure is thus admirably stated on the brief of learned counsel for appellants:

"This purely American idea, of the courts standing as the final guardians of the constitution, is the crowning glory and excellence of the American system of government, state and national; and yet this system, wise and beneficent as it is, could not endure for a day without a constant recognition of the fundamental difference between power and procedure. If every lapse in the mode or manner of action by the agents of government within the legitimate spheres of their powers operated to defeat such action, the system would lose all efficiency and fall of its own weight—the people would not endure it.

"And, on the other hand, if the same liberality which it is necessary to indulge for practical purposes with respect to the mode and manner of doing things were extended also to the powers and their limitations, then indeed would the constitution become a dead letter, and every agent of government be invested with a discretion to do not only as he pleased, but what he pleased; and the whole government become at once, not a government of law, but a government of men. Throughout the whole system, the substance is ever and always to be exalted over mere form.

"And so the courts, from the beginning, in.dealing with both constitutions and statutes, have been found constantly recognizing this fundamental distinction between power and the mode of its exercise; treating certain provisions as mandatory, and others as directory; certain things as matters of substance and other things as matters of form."

The language of the constitution pointing out the procedure of the two houses in passing bills over the governor's veto is positive and not negative. It is:

"If he refuse to sign it, he shall return it with his objections thereto, in writing to the house in which it originated; and said house shall cause said objections to be entered at large upon its journal and proceed to reconsider the bill. If, after such reconsideration, a majority of all the members elected to that house shall agree to pass the bill, notwithstanding the objections of the executive, it shall be sent with said objections to the other house by which it shall be likewise reconsidered. If approved by a majority of the whole number elected to that house, it shall become a law."

It is sought to construe this language as though it read: "The house in which a bill originates shall retain exclusive custody of it when vetoed by the govern-

or and returned to it by him, and shall not send it
with the governor's objections to the other house until
it reconsiders it.   And such bill shall not be reconsidered in the other house until it is finally disposed of in
the house of its origin.''

It is apparent upon the slightest consideration that
no such negative words are found in the constitution.
The prohibition against the senate acting in advance
of legal action upon the part of the house is found by
inference only. The majority have concluded that because the constitution says that ''if after such reconsideration,'' it shall be passed by the house of its
origin, ''it shall be sent with said objections to the
other house by which it shall be likewise reconsidered,''
therefore the bill did not become a law because this is
in effect a command to the senate forbidding it to act
upon the bill unless a quorum were present in the house
when that body reconsidered the bill. Carried to its
logical conclusion, the majority opinion must also hold
that if the house should have passed the bill with a
quorum present, but had failed to cause the governor's
objections to be entered at large upon its journal, that
the senate would not be authorized to reconsider the
bill upon receiving it from the house, and its action in
such event would be void. I think there are two fundamental errors in this position. The first is in requiring the senate to sit in judgment upon the validity of
the proceedings of the house as a condition precedent
to its right to reconsider the bill. The second is in
drawing an inference from a mere form of procedure

which has for its inevitable effect the defeat of the main objects and purposes for which this clause of the constitution was written. On the first point I can only reply to the holding of the majority by saying that I have never before heard of any case which held that one branch of a legislative body either could or should undertake to determine, or in any manner sit in judgment upon the validity of the action of the other branch. It is true that we have cases in which this court has looked to the journals of both the senate and the house to determine whether a given measure had been constitutionally enacted. But we have no case in which the court has looked to the journal of one house for the purpose of determining that the other house had acted unconstitutionally. The validity of the action of each house must be measured solely and alone by its journals. The constitution expressly provides that each house of the general assembly shall keep its journal and shall have all the powers necessary to a branch of the legislature of a free State.

Upon the second point there are numerous authorities which hold that positive words in a constitution will not be given a negative meaning when such a construction would destroy some of the most important objects for which the power was created. *Cohans v. Virginia,* 6 Wheat., 395, 5 L. Ed., 257. The case cited was brought to the supreme court of the United States on a writ of error to the quarterly sessions court of the borough of Norfolk. It was maintained that the supreme court had no appellate jurisdiction of any suit to which a state was party; that the affirmative words of the constitution conferring upon that court original jurisdiction of such suits were exclusive in their operation and denied to the court appellate jurisdiction of these suits. The court said:

"But although the absence of negative words will not authorize the legislature to disregard the distribution of the power previously granted, their absence will justify a sound construction of the whole article, so as to give every part its intended effect. It is admitted that 'affirmative words are often, in their operation, negative of other objects than those affirmed,' and that where 'a negative or exclusive sense must be given to them, or they have no operation at all,' they must receive that negative or exclusive sense. But where they have full operation without it, where it would destroy some of the most important objects for which the power was created, then, we think, affirmative words ought not to be construed negatively. . . . .

"It is, we think, apparent, that to give this distributive clause the interpretation contended for, to give to its affirmative words a negative operation, in every possible case, would, in some instances, defeat the obvious intention of the article. Such an interpretation would not consist with those rules which, from time immemorial, have guided courts, in their construction of instruments brought under their consideration. It must therefore be discarded. Every part of the article must be taken into view, and that construction adopted which will consist with its words and promote its general intention. The court may imply a negative from affirmative words, where the implication promotes, not where it defeats, the intention.''

Cohans v. *Virginia,* supra, applied a familiar and generally accepted rule of construction laid down almost universally by writers on constitutional law, but of course stated in different terms by many of them. The rule was stated by this court in the case of *Prescott* v. *Duncan,* 126 Tenn., 130, 148 S. W., 234, as follows:

. ''Powers conferred, as well as restraints upon inherent power, may be supported by such implications as are necessary to give effect to the intent of the people in conferring the one or setting the bounds of restraint upon the other. . . .

''No implication of intention with respect to one part of the instrument can be justified which does violence to a plainly expressed intention to be found in another part. . . . Necessary implications may be made, but unnecessary ones, however probable or plausible, cannot. And the necessity for the implication must be found in the constitution.''

The implication with respect to the procedure of the two houses drawn by the majority is not to support the exercise of a power conferred on them, but it is an implication to defeat the exercise of a power plainly created. Omitting the words in the constitution which prescribe the procedure of the two houses, it clearly appears that if they reconsider the bill in the light of the governor's objections, and take the yeas and nays and a majority of all the members elected to each house shall agree to pass the bill, notwithstanding the objections of the executive, "it shall become a law."

I think it clear that the jurisdiction of either house to pass a bill must arise from the introduction of the bill by a member thereof, or by receipt of it from the other house with a *prima facie* showing that the bill has been passed by the house of origin. But the same bill may be introduced in both houses simultaneously, and they may consider it concurrently on the first and second readings; and a bill so considered and passed by one house on its first, second, and third readings and sent by it to the other house, where it has been passed on two readings and there substituted and passed a third time, is a law. *Archibald* v. *Clark*, 112 Tenn., 533, 82 S. W., 310. And in *Railroad* v. *Memphis*, 126 Tenn., 292, 148 S. W., 662, 41 L. R. A. (N. S.), 828, Ann. Cas., 1913E, 153, a bill was held to have been constitutionally enacted which was passed by the house on two separate readings, and was then referred to a committee. The committee substituted another bill for the original bill, the body of which was essentially different from the original; the title remaining the same. Upon recommendation of the committee, the house passed the substituted bill upon its third and final reading, treating the passage of the original bill upon its two separate readings as sufficient to make the final passage of the substituted bill a passage upon its third reading. It was then sent to the senate, and there passed upon three separate readings.

The holdings just referred to were made, notwithstanding the procedure in such matters pointed out by the constitution, section 18 of article 2, is that "every bill shall be read once, on three different days, and be passed each time in the house where it originated, before transmission to the other house. These cases are in absolute conflict with the holding of the majority. Neither the bill considered in *Archibald* v. *Clark*, supra, nor the one in *Railroad* v. *Memphis*, supra, was read once on three different days in the house of its origin before it was transmitted to the other house. Still the bills were read three times in each house on three different days, and the cases cited hold, in effect, that this is a reasonable and substantial compliance with the procedure of the constitution, and that is all that ought to be required.

These cases show that this court has never strictly construed the requirements of the constitution as to matters of procedure, and has always regarded the substance of the requirement rather than its form. The main objects and purposes of these provisions are to secure a reading and a consideration of the questions of legislation, rather than a particular order or sequence in which the houses are to act. They also show that this court has never considered the presence of the identical paper on which a bill is written as necessary to the power of either house to act upon the legislative proposition embodied in the measure.

After the house assumed to pass the bill over the governor's veto, on April 3d, it ordered the bill to be transmitted to the senate for its reconsideration. The clerk of the house appeared at the bar of the senate and said:

"I am directed by the house by motion to transmit to the senate House Bill No. 759, to amend the election laws, as having passed the house, the objection or veto of the executive to the contrary notwithstanding."

After receiving this message, the senate, with a quorum present, reconsidered the bill in the light of the governor's objections and passed it over the veto by the requisite majority. It is held by the majority that this action of the senate was void because a quorum was not present in the house when that body attempted to pass the bill over the veto. I do not understand the opinion of the majority to expressly say that the senate must determine the validity of the action of the house in such cases before it is authorized to enter upon a reconsideration of the bill, but, whether stated in terms or not, this is the necessary result of the conclusion reached. This, of course, leaves out of consideration a principle of universal application in governments like ours, which is that each house acts separately upon the passage of laws, and independently of the other. Indeed, that is the sole purpose of dividing the general assembly into two branches. It is to secure separate, distinct, and independent action in each branch, that such a division is made. Each house for the same reason is required to keep its own journal. The constitution requires each house to select its own speaker, clerks, and other officials. If either

house fails in some constitutional particular to properly enact a law, the law is just as invalid as if both
houses should fail in the same particular. However,
this does not mean that the two houses shall act jointly, or that the validity of the action of one must depend upon the validity of the action of the other. It
only means that they must both concur in the constitutional sense in the passage of a measure before it
can become a law.

So I think when the senate received House Bill No.
759 from the clerk of the house with the statement
from him that the house had passed it over the governor's veto and had directed him to transmit the bill
to the senate, it had a right to enter upon its reconsideration. The senate is not compelled to go beyond
this apparent showing of legal action on the part of
the house before it can act. It is not required, and it
has no power, to determine the presence of a quorum
in the house. The house was in session and transmitted the bill to the senate with a certificate from the
proper officials that the bill had been reconsidered and
passed. Literally, the bill (paper) was "sent" to the
senate by the house, and it was its duty as "the other
house" to reconsider it. The house claimed to have
legally reconsidered the bill. It turns out by our adjudication in this case that this was not true.

But in what possible view can this affect the action
of the senate? Its action must be adjudged from its
own journal. Its journal shows that it properly and

legally received the bill from the house, and that it reconsidered and passed it as the constitution requires.

What is said by the majority upon the dangers of holding any provision of the constitution to be directory, and the references made to the warnings of great political and constitutional writers might be all right in a case to which they had application; but, without deciding this, I can safely appeal from the *dicta* of the constitutional and political writers referred to in the opinion of the chief justice to a solemn decision of this court in the case of *Telegraph Co.* v. *Nashville,* 118 Tenn., 1, 101 S. W., 770, 11 Ann. Cas., 824, in which it was held that a plain and unambiguous direction of the constitution is directory and not mandatory. The opinion appears to have been rendered by a unanimous court, but Brother Shields says in *State* v. *Burrow,* 119 Tenn., 376, 104 S. W., 526, 14 Ann. Cas., 809, that he did not concur.

In the case of Burrow, the court was considering a constitutional objection to the enactment of the Pendleton Bill, which it was claimed violated section 20 of article 2, providing "the style of the laws of this State shall be 'Be it enacted by the general assembly of the State of Tennessee.'" The act assailed was styled "Be it enacted by the general assembly of Tennessee," omitting the words "the State of." Much is said in this opinion against holding any provision of the constitution directory, and the court held in that case that the clause under consideration was mandatory, but it also held that the assailed act was valid, because, although the words used in styling the act were not the same as those prescribed by this mandatory provision of the constitution, still they meant the same thing and the law was good. This case is authority against the holding of the majority. Its real meaning can only be that the constitution should receive a reasonable and sensible construction in matters of form and procedure, so as to uphold and sustain the power to enact laws conferred upon the general assembly. The clause must be held mandatory because it canot be given any effect, and would be entirely defeated if construed otherwise. *Cohans* v. *Virginia,* supra. In the opinion of the chief justice it is held that if the house of origin can constitutionally transmit a bill after veto to the other house before acting on it itself, with equal reason the governor may in his discretion transmit a senate bill with his veto to the house or a house bill to the senate, and from this conclusion many things are supposed to result which the framers of the constitution did not contemplate.

After sketching the order of sequence provided by the constitution, and concluding that it must be literally observed by the two houses, it is said with the confidence of conclusiveness that, "If one part is directory, all parts are." This opinion also supposes that the framers of the constitution had in mind the preservation of the ardor and zeal of the members of the legislature. I think both assumptions are erroneous. There is a reason found in the constitution for requiring the governor to return a vetoed bill to the house in which it originated. The reason is that the constitution does not require the governor to either sign or veto a bill. If he holds it for more than five days without signifying either his approval or disapproval, it shall become a law. Therefore it is not only proper, but it is necessary in order to preserve the genealogy of a bill, that the governor should be required to return it to the house in which it originated if he disapproves it. If it should be returned to the other house, the history of the bill could not be obtained from an inspection of the journal of that house. So I think there is a clear distinction found in the constitution itself, and imbedded there for the purpose of preserving the power of veto conferred upon the governor, between the requirement that he shall return vetoed bills to the house in which it originated and the supposed requirement as to the sequence in which the two houses shall act.

And as to the other supposed purposes of the constitution—that is, the preservation of the zeal and ardor of legislators—I must concede to it the virtue of originality. It had always supposed before that State constitutions were made for the sole purpose of curbing and abating, not only the zeal, but the power, of legislators.

Now I do not say that the procedure under consideration prescribed by the constitution is directory, but I do say it should receive a reasonable construction so as to preserve and not to defeat the undoubted powers of the general assembly to which it relates. The sen-

ate had the unquestioned right, and it was its plain
duty, to receive the bill from the clerk of the house
and reconsider it as having been "sent" to it by the
house. The right of the senate to enter upon a reconsideration of the bill cannot be assimilated to an appeal from an inferior to a superior court. Its right to
act did not depend upon the legality of the action of
the house, but upon the bill being sent to it by the house
with a claim of legal action against the veto. The
transmission of the bill from the house to the senate
is not jurisdictional, but is procedural. The bill—that
is, the proposition of legislation, and not the paper
upon which it was written—was pending before both
houses after it was vetoed by the governor until it
was finally disposed of. It was far advanced on the
way of becoming a law before it was transmitted to
the governor. Had he signed it, it would have become
a law. But when he vetoed it, the only effect upon the
passage of the bill which his veto could have under the
constitution was to require a reconsideration of it in
both houses. This opened up the whole question in
both houses and made it pending before them, and it
remained a question of undisposed-of legislation until
one of the houses legally acted unfavorably, or until
both houses legally passed it over the veto, or until the
general assembly adjourned *sine die*. Therefore I
think it is but fair to say that the senate had authority
to reconsider the bill and pass it over the veto. If this
is true, of course the bill was a law, in so far as the
action of the senate was necessary to make it so. But

at this time the house had not constitutionally reconsidered the bill and passed it over the governor's veto,
but later, and on June 21st, the house did reconsider
the bill in such manner that we all agree was valid,
and therefore it is my opinion that House Bill No.
759 is a valid law.

The only right which the governor can insist upon
in respect of his veto is the right to have the bill reconsidered in connection with his objections by a legally
constituted house with a quorum present. The time,
the order, the sequence of the action of the two houses
are not of the governor's right.

This case legalizes the filibuster. As its results are
upheld and apparently approved by the court of last
resort, it will become the trick of the politician and the
resort of the spoilsman. It is most doubtful if a time
will come within our generation when a combination
of spoilsmen, special interests, and petty political
bosses cannot be made which can muster votes enough
in one house or the other to break a quorum. Under
the holding of the majority, when that event occurs,
all that is necessary to thwart the majority will is to
defeat the sequence of action in the two houses. So
the framers of our constitution, instead of establishing
a government in perpetuity with a system of checks
and balances, have embodied in that instrument the
germs of its own destruction, and have placed it within the power of a minority in the government to destroy organized society and inaugurate a reign of an-
archy. In the face of threats which could be made by

designing men, although a minority, when entrenched behind the power which this decision gives them, it is not difficult to imagine that a majority of the people's representatives must either cease to act or act in obedience to the demands of the minority, however wicked and selfish they may be.

Justice Green and myself also dissent from the holding that Reichman was not validly elected successor to Stratton. Without elaborating our views, we think this feature of the case falls directly within, and is controlled by, *Williams* v. *State,* 6 Lea, 549. The majority have not in terms overruled this case, but I think in frankness they should do so. They do not follow it.

PARRISH *v.* STATE.

(Nashville. December Term, 1913.)

1. **CRIMINAL LAW. Evidence. Other offenses.**

In a prosecution for placing in the yard of a negro, a note telling him that he was given twenty days to leave the State, or he would otherwise be killed, evidence of other outrages against the negroes in that vicinity, and of the fact that the trial of accused upon a charge of shooting into the prosecutor's house was interrupted by force, was inadmissible as showing the intent of the threats; the note being unequivocal, and there being no showing of a general scheme on the part of accused to intimidate the negroes of that community. (*Post,* pp. 274-278.)

2. **CRIMINAL LAW. Appeal. Review. Harmless error.**

In a prosecution for placing in the yard of a negro a communication warning him to leave the country, or that he would be killed, the admission of evidence of other outrages committed upon negroes in that vicinity, and of the trial of accused for shooting into the prosecutor's house, was prejudicial, where the evidence tending to show accused's guilt was nicely balanced. (*Post, pp.* 274-278.)

Cases cited and approved: Coleman v. People, 55 N. Y., 81; Peek v. State, 21 Tenn., 78; Queener v. Morrow, 41 Tenn., 123; People v. Molineux, 168 N. Y., 264; Price v. Clapp, 119 Tenn., 430.

FROM SMITH.

Appeal from Criminal Court of Smith County.—J. M. GARDENHIRE, Judge.

McGINNESS & LIGON, for appellant.

WM. H. SWIGGART, JR., assistant attorney general, for the State.

MR. JUSTICE LANSDEN delivered the opinion of the Court.

The prisoner was indicted and convicted for violating section 4633 of the Code of Tennessee (Shannon's Code, sec. 6474), which is as follows:

"If any person, either verbally or by written or printed communication, maliciously threaten to accuse another of a crime or offense, or to do any injury to the person or property of another, with intent thereby to extort any money, property, or pecuniary advantage whatever, or to compel the person so threatened to do any act against his will, he shall, on conviction, be punished by imprisonment in the penitentiary not less than two nor more than five years."

It was alleged in the indictment, and the State offered evidence to prove, that the prisoner deposited in the prosecutor's yard a note which contained the following:

"Sid Harvey: You are given twenty days to get out of the State. Otherwise you will be killed."

The prisoner denied that he deposited this or any other note in the yard of the prosecutor, and offered witnesses whose testimony tended to establish an alibi for him.

In the view which we have taken of the case, it is not necessary to express an opinion upon the weight of the testimony as to the prisoner's guilt, further than to say that the evidence of the prosecutor, his wife, and son tended to establish guilt, while the evidence of the prisoner, his daughter, and other witnesses, who appear to be disinterested, tend to show his innocence. The trial judge permitted the State to prove, in addition to the fact that the prisoner deposited a note in the prosecutor's yard, the further fact that the prosecutor's house had been dynamited on previous occasions, and that his house had been shot into. It is also shown that considerable excitement and feeling existed between the white and colored races in the neighborhood where the prosecutor and the prisoner live, and that some parties had been "night-riding" the negroes of that neighborhood, so much so that numbers of negroes had moved away. It was also proven by the State that on the day preceding the night on which it is claimed the prisoner deposited the note in the prosecutor's yard there was a trial of the prisoner before a justice of the peace upon a charge lodged against him by the prosecutor of shooting into the prosecutor's house, and that on that day certain parties unknown assaulted counsel for the prosecution and broke up the trial. It was further proven that the white people of that community had employed detectives to apprehend the persons perpetrating the outrages on the colored people. This evidence was objected to by counsel for the prisoner, and the trial judge admitted it over the objection for the purpose, as stated in the bill of exceptions, of explaining the state of mind of the negroes, and to shed light upon the probable effect of the note on the minds of the negroes, and to further explain their actions and conduct in remaining up all night watching their house.

But in his charge to the jury the court said, speaking of this evidence:

"You will bear in mind that the defendant is not on trial for such offenses, and this evidence can only be looked to as illustrating the purpose and intent of the threats, and in shedding light on the same."

There can be no doubt but that the general rule in this country is that a person accused of crime cannot be convicted of one offense upon proof that he committed another. *Coleman* v. *People*, 55 N. Y., 81. This general rule has an exception in this state to the effect that, where knowledge of the accused of the quality of the particular act for which he is being tried is an element of the offense, evidence of other acts of like character is competent to show such knowledge. The same exception, in many cases, obtains as to motive and intent. *Peek* v. *State*, 2 Humph., 78. But where the collateral fact offered in evidence is incapable of elucidating the principal matter in dispute, it is error to admit it. *Queener* v. *Morrow*, 1 Cold., 123. A full discussion of the general rule with its exceptions is found in *People* v. *Molineux*, 168 N. Y., 264, 61 N. E., 286, 62 L. R. A., 193, and the very elaborate notes thereto.

It is not contended in the State's testimony that the prisoner had any connection directly or indirectly with the collateral crimes which were proven upon the trial. He denies that he had any such connection, and the witnesses for the State expressly disclaim any knowledge that he did have. In view of the absence of such connection by the prisoner, it is impossible to see how the proof of these collateral crimes could illustrate the prisoner's purpose and intent in making the threats. There is no question of a general scheme upon the part of the prisoner to terrorize or intimidate the negroes of that community, and, as stated, no claim that he had connection with such scheme upon the part of others. In addition, the note itself, from the language employed, precludes any possible discussion or dispute as to the intent with which it was written. It was held in *Price* v. *Clapp*, 119 Tenn., 430, 105 S. W., 864, 123 Am. St. Rep., 730, that, where there could be no doubt of the intent or purpose with which the letter was written, evidence of collateral crimes committed by the person on trial could not be received to show intent. It should be observed that, in all of the cases in which evidence of collateral crimes has been admitted, the testimony tended to show that the person accused and upon trial was the author of the collateral crimes. In this case it is not claimed that the prisoner was the author of the collateral crimes, or that he had any connection with them directly or indirectly. We think it clear, therefore, that the admission of this evidence was incompetent. This testimony opened up to the consideration of the jury the general condition of hostility existing between the races in the community where the prisoner and the prosecutor live, and we think that, in view of the closeness of the evidence, it must have injuriously affected the rights of the prisoner.

For this error, the judgment of the criminal court is reversed, and the case remanded for a new trial.

STATE, *ex rel.* COLLEGE OF BISHOPS OF M. E. CHURCH, SOUTH, *et al. v.* BOARD OF TRUST OF VANDERBILT UNIVERSITY *et al.*

(Nashville. December Term, 1913.)

1. **COLLEGES AND UNIVERSITIES. Governing boards and officers.**

The action of the board of trust of a denominational university in adopting resolutions accepting a report of a commission appointed by a general conference to inquire into the relations of the university to the denomination, recognizing the ownership of the church in the university and welcoming any supervision by the college of bishops, so as to insure observance of the charter, etc., was not an acceptance of the commission's conclusion that since 1898 the general conference, as assignee of the annual conferences is the sole member of the corporation, that the university was founded by the annual conferences, and not by an individual donor, and that the college of bishops had no other rights or powers than that of common-law visitation. (*Post, pp.* 322-324.)

2. **CORPORATIONS. Incorporation and organization. Statutes.**

Acts 1871, ch. 54, secs. 1, 9, passed in pursuance of Const. 1870, forbidding charters by special act, providing by section 1 that persons desiring to be incorporated shall file a petition in the chancery court of the county in which the largest number of them reside, setting forth the purposes of the corporation, prescribing publication of the petition, and directing an *ex parte* hearing thereof, and a decree or charter enumerating such usual powers of corporations as might be necessary to carry out the corporate objects, and by section 9 providing that the court may incorporate educational, religious, and charitable institutions with powers and privileges as prescribed in Code 1858, secs. 1470-1473, was a general act covering the whole

subject and superseding the Code provisions, except so far as
they were adopted thereby, and as to institutions of learning
expressly gave the same powers as enjoyed by like corporations under the Code. (*Post, pp.* 324-326.)

Acts cited and construed: Acts 1870-71, ch. 54.

Code cited and construed: Secs. 1471-2-3 (M. & V. and 1858).

Cases cited and approved. Terrell v. State, 86 Tenn., 523; Malone v. Williams, 118 Tenn., 445; Heck v. McEwen, 80 Tenn.,
97; *ex parte* Chadwell, 62 Tenn., 98.

3. CORPORATIONS. Incorporators. Conferences.

Acts 1871, ch. 54, requiring incorporators to file a petition in the
chancery court, which, after publication and *ex parte* hearing,
shall by decree or charter enumerate the usual powers of corporations necessary to carry out the corporate objects, and which
extends the power of the court to incorporation of institutions
of learning, etc., contemplated the incorporation of actual persons and not of corporations or voluntary associations, so that
conferences composed of delegates from the several churches
within their limits were not competent to associate with each
other for incorporation, or without express statutory authority
to act as members of a corporation, nor were the delegates to
such conferences competent to act as incorporations. (*Post,
pp.* 326-328.)

Cases cited and approved: Mallory v. Oil Works, 86 Tenn., 598;
Rhodes v. Rhodes, 88 Tenn., 637; Green v. Allen, 24 Tenn., 170.

4. COLLEGES AND UNIVERSITIES. Incorporations and organizations. Ratification.

Where the action of a religious convention did not intend to incorporate any but individuals composing the board of trust
thereby appointed, and where a by-law adopted in furtherance
of the convention's action, declared that the charter should
leave "the perpetuity of the board in its own power," and requested the several co-operating conferences to nominate four
members for election thereto, which by-law was certified, to-

gether with the charter obtained by such trustees, to the conferences, their ratification of such action, even if they understood that they thereby became incorporators, could not change the legal effect of the charter, which made the trustees the incorporators. (*Post, pp.* 328, 329.)

5. **COLLEGES AND UNIVERSITIES. Petition for Incorporation. Incorporators.**

The petition to the chancery court for incorporation is the basis and measure of the charter, and while the court may grant less, it may not grant more, than is sought by the petition; and hence the petition for a charter for a denominational university, filed by the designated board of trustees as individuals and not as representatives, made them and no others the incorporators, with the right of perpetual succession; the fact that they were described in the charter as representatives of certain annual conferences being immaterial. (*Post, pp.* 328, 329.)

6. **CORPORATIONS. Incorporation by chancery court. Ministerial Act.**

The chancery court, in granting a decree or charter under Acts 1871, ch. 54, though acting according to judicial forms, acted ministerially, and could not depart in substance from the petition. (*Post, pp.* 328, 329.)

Cases cited and approved: Wilson v. Schaefer, 107 Tenn., 300; Gilreath v. Gilliland, 95 Tenn., 383.

7. **CORPORATIONS. Charter. Incorporators. Choice of Successors.**

Where neither the general incorporation act nor the charter itself provided how successors to the individual incorporators should be chosen, such right in the case of a corporation aggregate, by necessary implication, vested in the persons so incorporated. (*Post, p.* 329.)

8. **CONTRACTS. Construction. Practical Interpretation.**

The practical interpretation of a contract by the parties thereto is intitled to great, if not to controlling, influence. (*Post, p.* 329.)

9. **COLLEGES AND UNIVERSITIES. Incorporation. Charter.**

Under the general incorporation act (Acts 1871, ch. 54), requiring that the petition to the chancery court set forth the objects of the corporation, it was proper for the court, upon petition for incorporation "for the purpose of soliciting subscriptions and donations for the erection and maintenance of an institution of learning of the highest order, . . . together with the rights, powers, and privileges which, by law, may belong to literary institutions chartered by the laws of the State," to inquire into its objects and to include in the decree or charter the amplified and particular terms found in the resolutions of a denominational convention constituting the plan upon which the institution was to be incorporated and built. (*Post*, *pp.* 330, 331.)

Acts cited and construed: Acts 1870-71, ch. 54.

10. **COLLEGES AND UNIVERSITIES. Incorporation. Amendment of charter.**

Resolutions of a denominational convention looking to the establishment and incorporation of a denominational university and stating the number of and character of the schools, its name, location, and board of trustees, and providing for general supervision by the bishops of that denomination, included in a charter incorporating the designated individual trustees, were not eliminated by an amendment empowering it to change its name and to increase or diminish the members of the board of trust, and passing to the university under its new name all rights, franchises, etc., originally conferred, but were rather confirmed by the amendment. (*Post*, *pp.* 331, 332.)

11. **COLLEGES AND UNIVERSITIES. Organization. Foundation.**

A convention of a religious denomination composed of delegates from participating conferences, without power to bind such conferences by its action, framed "articles of foundation" for a university for such denomination, named the board of trust to procure an act of incorporation, and authorized and enjoined such board, when incorporated, to seek and find a founder who would supply the necessary funds, and which prescribed $500,000 as the minimum amount upon which it could be founded, in pursuance of which efforts to raise the needed amount were only partially successful, including a comparatively small amount given to secure a location. An individual donor gave it the amount necessary for foundation and afterwards gave the full endowment. *Held* that, in so far as the donor's conditions of his gift were valid, he, and not the individual incorporators, or the conferences they represented, was the founder and original patron of the university upon the plans outlined by the convention. ' (*Post, pp.* 332-335.)

Cases cited and approved: Dartmouth College Case, 4 Wheat., 574; Attorney-General v. Pierce, 2 Atk., 87; Nelson v. Cushing, 2 Cush. (Mass.), 527; State v. Toledo, 23 Ohio Cir. Ct. R., 327.

12. **COLLEGES AND UNIVERSITIES.** Organization. Incorporators as trustees.

Persons chosen by a convention of a religious denomination as a board of trustees to incorporate a denominational university and to administer it according to a plan formulated by the convention, who were incorporated by charter including such plan in full and describing the individual incorporators as representatives of the several conferences from which they came, were, under the charter and the law, trustees of the property for the purposes of the corporation, with all the lawful conditions imposed by the donor of the fund by means of which the university was established; the charter itself constituting a declaration of trust. (*Post, pp.* 335, 336.)

Case cited and approved: Church v. Hinton, 92 Tenn., 188.

Case cited and distinguished: Nelson v. Cushing, 2 Cush. (Mass.), 527; State v. Toledo, 23 Ohio Cir. Ct. R., 327.

13. **COLLEGES AND UNIVERSITIES.** Incorporation. Governing boards and officers.

The convention of a religious denomination, composed of delegates without authority to bind their conferences, adopted resolutions looking to the establishment of a denominational university to be called the "Central University of the Methodist Episcopal

Church, South," consisting of different schools, and to the raising of a minimum amount as a foundation, and appointed a
board of. trust to obtain a charter which should provide for a
fair representation in its management to any patronizing conference, and that the board of trust should make all by-laws
necessary to carry out such resolutions. After incorporation
the board first allowed each conference four members, which
number was subsequently reduced to one, and changed their
election from nomination by the conferences and confirmation
and election by the board to nomination by the board and confirmation by the conferences, and afterwards admitted members not representing or confirmed by the conferences, and
finally terminated relations with the conferences by mutual
consent, and substituted therefor the general conference of the
whole denomination, which was to confirm members elected
by the board. *Held* that, under such resolutions and by-laws
and their practical construction, the relation between the board
and the conferences, and afterwards between it and the general
conference, was not one of ownership by the conferences, but
of co-operation and representation in its management, and that
such relation was a trust relation, which neither party could
ignore or violate. (*Post, pp.* 337-341.)

14. **COLLEGES AND UNIVERSITIES. Powers. By-Laws.**

A denominational university, incorporated for educational purposes and the management of property by officers and trustees,
had the implied power to pass by-laws and to enter into agreements relating to the appointment and election of members of
its board of trustees. (*Post, p.* 341.)

15. **CORPORATIONS. By-Laws. Requisites and effect.**

The by-laws of a corporation must be consistent with the spirit
and terms of its charter, and while in force they become as
much a part of the law of the corporation as though they had
been made a part of the charter; and a by-law of a nonstock-
holding corporation entering into a declaration of trust between
the corporation and its beneficiaries, could not be repealed, so
as to deprive the parties of their rights thereunder. (*Post, pp.*
341, 342.)

State, ex rel. v. Vanderbilt University.

Cases cited and approved: Kent v. Quicksilver Mining Co., 78 N. Y., 179; Matthews v. Associated Press, 136 N. Y., 333.

16. **CHARITIES. Administration. Visitation.**

At common law visitorial power was a property right belonging to the first donor and founder of a charity, arising by implication from the gift, and which might be vested by him in his appointee. (*Post, pp.* 342-347.)

17. **COLLEGES AND UNIVERSITIES. Governing boards.' Officers. Visitation. Supervision.**

Under a charter of a denominational university founded by an individual donor, including a resolution of a previous convention to the effect that the bishops of the Methodist Episcopal Church, South, be and be requested to act as a board of supervision of the university or any of its departments and jointly with the board of trust to elect officers and professors and prescribe the course of study and plan of government, etc., but without appointing the bishops to anything, the college of bishops was not vested with the common-law right of visitation over the corporation; the power of "supervision" not being equivalent to or necessarily including that of visitation. (*Post, pp.* 342-347.)

Acts cited and construed: Acts 1857-58, ch. 32.

Cases cited and approved: Dartmouth College Case, 4 Wheat., 563; Allen v. McKean, 1 Sumn., 276; Sanderson v. White, 18 · Pick. (Mass.), 328.

Cases cited and distinguished: Phillips v. Bury, 2 Term R., 352; Green v. Rutherforth, 1 Ves. Sen., 471.

18. **COLLEGES AND UNIVERSITIES. Right of Visitation. Estoppel.**

In such case the college of bishops, who had assumed and exercised uncertain and occasional rights and privileges, and a part of whose number had at one time been elected to active membership in the board of trust, and who for nearly forty years after the charter was granted and they had declined all official relations to the corporation had asserted no common-law right of visitation, were estopped from asserting such right. (*Post.* p. 347.)

Acts cited and construed. Acts 1895, ch. 6.

19. **STATUTES. Subjects and titles. Statute relating to corporations.**

Acts 1895, ch, 6, entitled "An act for the benefit of incorporated educational institutions," by section 1 empowering such institutions to acquire and hold property, and by section 2 providing that any religious denomination maintaining or patronizing such institution should have certain powers in the election of directors and trustees, in filling vacancies, and in increasing or diminishing the number of members thereof and authorizing the consolidation of two or more such institutions, did not violate Const., art. 2 sec. 17, providing that no bill shall embrace more than one subject, to be expressed in the title; such title being general enough to include all the provisions of the act, within the rule that generality of title is not objectionable, so long as it is not made to cover legislation incongruous in itself, or which may not be considered as having a necessary or proper connection with the subject expressed. (*Post, pp.* 349-351.)

Constitution cited and construed: Art. 2. sec 17.

Case cited and approved: State, ex rel. Dobson v. Washington & Tusculum College. (Mss., Knoxville, September Term, 1912).

Case cited and distinguished: State v. Yardley, 95 Tenn., 546.

20. **COLLEGES AND UNIVERSITIES.** Officers and governing boards. Statutes. "Patron."

Acts 1895, ch. 6, by section 1 empowered educational institutions to acquire and hold property, and by section 2 provided that, whenever such institution was established and was being maintained and patronized, or, having been otherwise established, was being maintained and patronized by any religious denomination, the representative governing board of such denomination might, at its option, elect its board of directors or trustees, or fill vacancies therein, or change the number of members thereof. A denominational university, designated as the "Central University of the Methodist Episcopal Church, South," was incorporated on petition of the individual members of its board of trust, and an effort to raise by subscriptions from the conferences and churches the required endowment of $500,000 resulted in subscriptions for about $100,000, from which about $15,000 was realized, devoted to an incidental "sustentation fund" for students, and in contributions of about $50,000 for the purchase of its campus and erection of its buildings, and about $325,000 for specific endowments of chairs, lecture courses, and scholarships, nearly all of which were in the theological school, without to any extent relieving the general endowment from allowances to that department. Soon after its incorporation a wealthy layman, through the bishop, gave to the university $500,000, and an equal amount to complete its entire endowment, members of his family also giving another $1,000,000, whereupon the name of the university by resolution was then changed to that of such donor. *Held*, that according to the dictionary definitions of "establish," "maintain," and "patronize," and of "patron" as an endower or a perficient founder, to establish, maintain, and patronize meant to found and support, he was its patron and founder, and that the denomination had not maintained and patronized the university, so as to entitle its general conference to elect the board of trust or fill vacancies therein. (*Post, pp.* 351-356.)

Cases cited and distinguished: Phillips v. Bury, 2 Term R., 346; Dartmouth College Case, 4 Wheat., 563; Carson v. Carson. 115 Tenn., 50.

21. **COLLEGES AND UNIVERSITIES. Officers and governing boards. Statutes.**

Acts 1895, ch. 6, entitled "An act for the benefit of incorporated educational institutions," by section 2 provided that whenever any such institution shall be maintained and patronized by any religious denomination, the representative governing body of such denomination shall have power to elect its board of

directors or trustees to fill vacancies therein, and, with the
consent of such board, to change the number of members thereof, did not apply to a denominational university chartered under the general incorporation act (Acts 1871, ch. 54), providing
by section 9 that the chancery court might incorporate institutions of learning with the powers and privileges prescribed by
Code 1858, sec. 1471, *et seq.*, which authorized members of a
corporation to fix the number of trustees, subsequently required
by Shannon's Code, sec. 2520 to be not less than five nor more
than thirty-three, all of whose incorporators chose to act as
trustees, but dealt only with the election of directors or trustees, and not with members of the corporation, and applied
rather to educational institutions organized under Acts 1875,
ch. 142, sec. 2, or similar acts, and under the patronage of some
religious denomination. (*Post, pp.* 356-364.)

Acts cited and construed: Acts 1889, ch. 181; Acts 1875, ch. 142.

Code cited and construed: Sec. 2520 (S.).

22. **COLLEGES AND UNIVERSITIES. Claim of parties. Renunciation.**
If the general conference should voluntarily renounce the right
to confirm persons elected to the board of trust, or cease to co-
operate with the university, its right to membership in the
board of trust and in its management, the board could act independently of the conference in the election of members of
the board. (*Post, p.* 364.)

23. **COLLEGES AND UNIVERSITIES. Officers and governing
boards. Tenure.**
Under the inherent power of the board of trust of an incorporated
denominational university to fill vacancies in its own body, new
members elected and installed by it were entitled to their seats
on the board *ad interim* until such time as they should be rejected by the general conference, or its general board of education, acting for it and under its authority, in pursuance of an
agreement between the board of trust and the general confer-

ence whereby the board was to appoint and the general conference to confirm the trustees. (*Post, p.* 365.)

LANSDEN, J., dissenting in part.

FROM DAVIDSON.

Appeal from Chancery Court, Davidson County.—
JOHN ALLISON, Chancellor.

JOHN BELL KEEBLE, J. J. VERTREES, J. C. BRADFORD,
and CHAS. C. TRABUE, G. T. HUGHES, and J. M. ANDER-
SON and JORDAN STOKES, SR., for appellants.

A. B. ANDERSON and P. D. MADDIN, FITZHUGH &
BIGGS, E. C. O'REAR, and HARRIS & HARRIS, for appellees.

MR. JUSTICE TURNER delivered the opinion of the
Court.

The bill in this case was filed by the State, on the
relation of the College of Bishops of the Methodist
Episcopal Church, South, and three gentlemen, who
had been elected by the General Conference of the
Church to fill vacancies in the Board of Trust of Vanderbilt University, against the University, as a corporation, and its Board of Trust, and three other
gentlemen who had been elected by the Board of Trust
to fill the aforesaid vacancies in that board, and seeks

to enjoin the board from admitting its own appointees, and to compel it to seat those elected by the General Conference.

Two answers are filed, one by the majority of the trustees, their appointees, and the University, contesting the bill, and the other by a minority of the trustees, admitting the rights claimed by the complainants, and joining in the prayer of the bill.

On the hearing in the court below, the chancellor granted the relief prayed for by the bill, and the University and. majority trustees and their appointees have appealed and assign errors in this court.

Two questions are involved, to wit: Whether the General Conference had the right to elect the members of the Board of Trust, and whether the College of Bishops had visitorial power over the University and the right to veto the action of its Board of Trust.

The pleadings and proofs are very voluminous. On the hearing below, exceptions were taken to much of the evidence as hearsay, irrelevant, and immaterial. The chancellor overruled the exceptions and admitted all the evidence. The objection is not preserved or made in this court, and hence the whole proof is before us for what it is worth. A large part of it is immaterial to the real issues in the cause.

The essential facts, appearing in the pleadings and proof, are as follows:

In the fall of 1871, eight or nine of the annual conferences of the Methodist Episcopal Church, South, appointed committees "to confer" with each other, "in reference to the establishment and endowment of a Methodist University of high grade and large endowment," but, as stated in one of the resolutions appointing such committee, "it being understood that said committee shall not have authority to pledge this conference to any action." Some of these annual conferences were incorporated and some not; but all were composed of the ministers and lay delegates from the churches within certain territory assigned to each, and each had jurisdiction over the churches within the district so assigned.

In January, 1872, the several committees appointed by these annual conferences met at Memphis, were presided over by some of the bishops, and, after conferring and discussing the subject for three days, adopted certain resolutions prepared by Bishop McTyeire, as follows, to wit:

"Resolved by the Convention: 1. That measures be adopted looking to the establishment, as speedily as practicable, of an institution of learning of the highest order, and upon the surest basis, where the youth of the church and country may prosecute theological, literary, scientific, and professional studies to an extent as great, and in a manner as thorough as their wants demand.

"2. That the institution shall be called the Central University of the Methodist Episcopal Church, South.

"3. That it shall consist, at present, of five schools or departments—viz.: A theological school, for the training of young preachers, who, on application for

admission, shall present a recommendation from a
quarterly or annual conference, and shall have obtained
a standard of education equal to that required for
admission on trial into an annual conference; and instruction to them shall be free, both in the theological
and the literary and scientific departments. Secondly,
a literary and scientific school. Thirdly, a normal
school. Fourthly, a law school. Fifthly, a medical
school.

"4. That the sum of one million dollars is necessary in order to realize fully the object desired, and
not less than five hundred thousand dollars must be
secured as a condition precedent to the opening of any
department of the university.

"5. That the location of the university shall be left
to the decision of the College of Bishops of the Methodist Episcopal Church, South,

"6. That the carrying out of this whole scheme is
hereby committed to the following persons, viz.: Wil-
liam C. Johnson, Robert J. Morgan, Smith W. Moore,
Milton Brown, Alexander L. P. Green, Jordan Stokes,
David C. Kelley, Edward H. East, Robert A. Young,
Landon C. Garland, Phillip Tuggle, John M. Steele,
James H. McFerrin, Christopher D. Oliver, William
Dickson, Edward Wadsworth, William Byrd, William
L. C. Hunnicutt, Thomas Christian, James L. Borden,
William H. Foster, Andrew Hunter, James L. De
Yampert, and David T. Reynolds, who shall take im-
mediate steps for securing a suitable charter of incor-
poration, and shall be a Board of Trust, with power to .

solicit and invest funds, appoint an agent or agents, and to do whatever else is necessary for the execution of this scheme.

"7. That seven of the Board of Trustees, at any meeting regularly called, shall constitute a quorum.

"8. That provision be made in the charter for giving a fair representation in the management of the university to any annual conference hereafter co-operating with us.

"9. That the bishops of the Methodist Episcopal Church, South, be, and are hereby, requested to act as a board of supervision of the university or any of its departments, and jointly with the Board of Trust to elect officers and professors, and prescribe the course of study and plan of government."

On the day after the Memphis convention adjourned, this Board of Trust, so designated and appointed, met and organized by electing a president, secretary, treasurer, and executive committee. The latter were "requested to prepare a code of by-laws, defining the duties of officers and standing committees, and such other by-laws as may be necessary for the government of the operations of the Board of Trust." They adjourned to May 8, 1872, at which time they met at Nashville, where the College of Bishops was then in session. They addressed to the bishops the following communication, to wit:

"Whereas, the convention left the location of the university to the decision of the College of Bishops of the M. E. Church, South, and also requested the bishops to act as a board of supervisors of the university, or any of its departments, and jointly with the Board of Trust to elect officers and professors, and prescribe the course of study and the plan of government:

"Resolved: (1) That the secretary be and is hereby directed to address the bishops with the view of obtaining their acceptance of the foregoing official relation to the university.

"(2) That the secretary invite the bishops to attend the present meeting of the Board of Trust."

On the next day the bishops made the following reply (having first voted down a motion to decline the request outright) to wit:

"Resolved: (1) That the College of Bishops accede to the request, made by the Board of Curators of the contemplated university, to locate the institution whenever the sum of $500,000 shall be pledged for the enterprise.

"(2) That, by this act, we are not to be understood as implying that the said institution is to be considered connectional, to the damage of existing colleges and universities. We can take no official relation to the Central University that will discriminate between it and any and every other institution of the church. Nevertheless, we feel free to give our decided approval to the combination of the several annual conferences represented in the convention in Memphis, or so many of them as shall agree together, acting through respective bodies in getting up an institution of the highest grade.

"(3) That, as the question of theological schools is in a controversy among our people, we propose no action that may be construed into an expression of our collective opinion on the subject, but it is made a condition of the first resolution that the theological department, to be comprised . . . with the literary and professional departments of the proposed Central University, be such as is consistent with the action of the General Conference held in Memphis in 1870, in the words following:

" 'Resolved, that we indorse the action of the last General Conference, in reference to Biblical chairs, in connection with out existing colleges, as the best available means for training young preachers.' "

To this the board responded:

"Resolved, that the terms and conditions upon which the bishops of the church are willing, in due time and proper form, to accede to the request made of them by the late educational convention, held in Memphis, to locate this proposed university, are, in the judgment of the board, sufficient to encourage it in the prosecution of this scheme of education, contemplated by said convention, and as such they are hereby accepted and will be observed in good faith by this board."

On June 29, 1872, the individuals named by the Memphis convention as the Board of Trust filed their petition in the chancery court at Nashville, praying the court "to incorporate them under the name and style of the Central University of the Methodist Episcopal Church, South, for the purpose of soliciting sub-

scriptions, donations, and for the erection and maintenance of an institution of learning of the highest
order, containing all the schools belonging to a university of that character, together with the rights,
powers, and privileges which by law may belong to
literary institutions chartered by the laws of the
State. They pray to this end that the required publication may be made and all other necessary and proper
steps may be taken.''

Publication was duly made in accord with the petition and as prescribed by law.

On August 6, 1872, decree was entered on this petition, constituting the charter of the university, as follows, to wit:

"The Central University of the Methodist Episcopal

Church, South. *Ex parte.*

"This matter came on this day to be heard before
the Hon. Nathaniel Baxter, judge, etc., of the circuit
court of Davidson county, sitting by interchange with
Hon. Edward H. East, the chancellor presiding, but
who was incompetent to preside and hear this cause, for
the reason that he was interested herein, and the same
was heard upon the petition of W. C. Johnson, Robert
J. Morgan, Smith W. Moore, and Milton Brown, citizens and residents of the State of Tennessee, and
representatives of the Memphis Conference of the
Methodist Episcopal Church, South; and Alexander L.
R. Green, Jordan Stokes, David C. Kelley, Edward H.
East, David T. Reynolds, and Robert A. Young, citi-

zens and residents of Tennessee, and representatives
of the Tennessee Conference; and Landon C. Garland,
a citizen and resident of Mississippi, and Phillip
Tuggle, a citizen and resident of Tennessee, the two
latter representing the North Mississippi Conference;
and James H. McFerrin and John M. Steele, citizens
of the State of Arkansas, and representatives of the
White River Conference; and Christopher D. Oliver,
and William Dickson, citizens of the State of Alabama
and representatives of the North Alabama Conference;
and Edward Wadsworth and W. M. Byrd, citizens
of the State of Alabama, and representatives of
the Alabama Conference; and W. L. C. Hunnicutt
and Thomas Christian, citizens of the state of Mississippi, and representatives of the Mississippi Conference; and James L. Borden and William H. Foster, citizens of the State of Louisiana, and representatives of the Louisiana Conference; and Andrew
Hunter and J. L. De Yampert, citizens of the State of
Arkansas, and representatives of the Little Rock Conference. And it appearing to the court that said persons,
in their said petition, prayed to be incorporated under
the name and style of the Central University of the
Methodist Episcopal Church, South, the object and
plan of said university having been fully set forth in
resolutions passed by the delegates of said conferences,
at a convention of the same, held in the city of Memphis on the 24th, 25th, 26th, and 27th of January, 1872,
and which resolutions are in words and figures as fol-
·lows: [Here follow the Memphis resolutions.]

"And it appearing to the court that, upon the filing
of said petition, the clerk and master of this court
caused, by an order at rules, the same to be advertised,
in pursuance of the statutes in such cases made and
prescribed; and it further appearing to the court that
no one has appeared and made known any objection to
the granting of the prayer of the petition; and the
court, upon inspection of the designs and objects of
said corporation, finds nothing therein contained to be
against public policy or good morals, or in conflict with the Constitution and laws of the State or of
the United States, is pleased to grant the prayer of the
same, and doth hereby order and adjudge and decree
that the petitioners be declared a body politic and corporate under the name and style of the Central University of the Methodist Episcopal Church, South, and in
that name may sue and be sued, plead and be implead-
ed, in the courts of this State or of the other States of
the Union, or of the United States of America; may
have a common seal, which may be altered at pleasure;
shall have perpetual succession; may solicit and receive subscriptions, donations, legacies, and devises;
may hold real estate and personal property in such
amounts as the business of the corporation requires,
and may receive the same by contract, gift, will, or
devise, and shall hold the same for the purpose of
said corporation, with all the lawful conditions imposed by the donor; may appoint such subordinate
officers and agents as the business of the corporation
requires, prescribe their duties, and fix their compensa-

tion; to make by-laws not inconsistent with the laws of the land or this charter, or the resolutions of the convention at Memphis, as set out hereinbefore, which resolutions are hereby adopted as a part of this charter, but shall make all by-laws necessary and proper to carry out the object of said resolutions, as well as for the management of its property and the regulation of its affairs, and may also have power to pass all by-laws necessary to the use of the powers herein given, or which by law may hereafter be conferred, and all said powers, rights, and privileges, together with such others as are not herein specially given and referred to, are hereby conferred upon said corporation in as full, complete, and ample manner as by the laws of the State the same can or might be; and said corporation shall have the power to confer all the degrees of merit and honor usually conferred by universities. It is further decreed that petitioners pay the costs of this proceeding, and that the clerk and master issue to them a certified copy of this decree.''

On August 22, 1872, at Iuka, Miss., the board met, accepted the charter, confirmed the previous election of officers and executive committee, and adopted by-laws, one of which was as follows:　　　　·

"No. 2. Since the charter leaves the perpetuity of the board in its own power, we request the several annual conferences co-operating to nominate at least four representatives from each. So soon as this shall be done, the present board will reorganize in such manner as to secure the election of trustees so nominated, and that thereafter, when vacancies shall occur, they shall be filled by nominations by the several annual conferences and confirmed by the board; it being understood that the board will not be enlarged beyond the first number, except so far as shall be necessary to give four members to each one of the conferences co-operating.''

They also: ''Resolved, The executive committee are empowered, through such agents as they may employ, to adopt such scheme, or schemes, as they may deem best in order to obtain the endowment, with the single reservation that none of the principal shall be used for any purpose other than that originally intended by the donor, and that we advise that interest, in all available cases, be collected semiannually. That the executive committee be required to get up definite printed forms for notes, gifts, bequests, etc.''

They also formulated and adopted a report or address to the bishops and annual conferences, soon to be assembled, in which they recited the previous appointment of committees, their meeting and proceedings at Memphis, the appointment of this Board of Trust, and its proceedings as hereinbefore stated, setting out in full the charter, the communications to and from the bishops, and said by-law No. 2, above quoted, and saying, among other things:

''There was secured the cordial approval of the College of Bishops in behalf of an enterprise which promises, in connection with our other institutions of learning, to accomplish a great work for Christian education under Methodist direction and control.

"It remains for the action of the convention and the Board of Trust appointed by it to receive the sanction, not only formal, but hearty, of the several annual conferences represented in the convention, and not only their sanction, but their co-operation in the use of all the means at their command. . . .

"The action of the convention and of the Board of Trust is now before you.

"It has all been taken with the best light at hand, and, at the same time, in deference to the fact that it requires your sanction and co-operation, as well that it may be binding upon you as that it may result in the success of the enterprise itself, the importance of which, we doubt not, is estimated very highly by you, as it is by ourselves. . . .

"Asking your sanction and co-operation with us, in behalf of the university, and particularly your aid in the organization of a system of agencies for procuring an endowment fund of $500,000, we now commit this whole subject to your deliberation and action."

This report, or address, was printed in pamphlet form, and furnished, during the fall of 1872, to the several annual conferences concerned. Six of the conferences in question approved, nominated trustees as provided in by-law No. 2, most of whom were already members of the board, and agreed to co-operate in efforts to raise the required endowment. The other conferences failed to act or approve.

On January 16, 1873, the board met at Brownsville, Tenn., elected the new members, nominated by the conferences, reduced the number, representing the Tennessee Conference, from six to four, by requesting and accepting the resignations of two of their number, that each conference should have an equal representation in the board, and passed the following resolutions:

"Resolved: (1) That the members previously in the board under the charter, with those now elected, are hereby in due form recognized as the representatives of their several annual conferences which have resolved to co-operate in behalf of the Central University, there being four from each annual conference, viz.: Tennessee, Memphis, North Mississippi, White River, Little Rock, and Arkansas.

"(2) That we hereby declare vacant the seats as members of the board under the charter of those persons, all of them now absent, heretofore recognized as representatives of the North Alabama, Alabama, Mississippi, and Louisiana Conferences; those conferences having failed to take action in favor of the Central University."

They also revised their code of by-laws, substituting for former by-law No. 2 new by-law VII: "Each co-operating conference, being entitled to four members or representatives in the Board of Trust, should any vacancy or vacancies occur the board shall fill the same upon the nomination of the conference to be represented"—and added No. VIII: "These by-laws may be amended at any annual meeting of the board by a two-thirds vote of all the members present.''

On March 26, 1873, at a called meeting of the board in Nashville, Bishop McTyeire, ''after an explanation highly satisfactory to the board,'' submitted a letter from Mr. C. Vanderbilt, dated March 17, 1873, as follows, to wit:

''To Bishop H. N. McTyeire, of Nashville:

''I make the following offer through you to the corporation known as the Central University of the Methodist Episcopal Church, South:

''First—I authorize you to procure suitable grounds, not less than from twenty to fifty acres, properly located, for the erection of the following work:

''Second—To erect thereon suitable buildings for the uses of the university.

''Third—You to procure plans and specifications for such buildings and submit them to me, and, when approved, the money for the foregoing objects to be furnished by me as it is needed.

''Fourth—The sum included in the foregoing items, together with the 'endowment fund' and the 'library fund,' shall not be less in the aggregate than five hundred thousand ($500,000) dollars, and these last two funds shall be furnished to the corporation as soon as the buildings for the university are completed and ready for use.

''The foregoing being subject to the following conditions:

"First—That you accept the presidency of the Board of Trust, receiving therefor a salary of three thousand ($3,000) dollars per annum and the use of dwelling house, free of rent, on or near the university grounds.

"Second—Upon your death or resignation, the Board of Trust shall elect a president.

"Third—To check hasty and injudicious appropria- tions or measures, the president shall have authority, whenever he objects to any act of the board, to signify his objections in writing within ten days after its en- actment, and no such act to be valid unless, upon re- consideration, it be passed by a three-fourths vote of the board.

"Fourth—The amount set apart by me as an endow- ment fund shall be forever inviolable, and shall be kept safely invested, and the interest or revenue only used in carrying on the university. The form of invest- ment which I prefer, and in which I reserve the privi- lege to give money to said fund, is in seven per cent. first mortgage bonds of the New York Central & Hud- son River Railroad Company, to be registered in the name of the corporation, and to be transferrable only upon a special vote of the Board of Trust.

"Fifth—The university is to be located in or near Nashville, Tennessee.

"Respectfully submitted,
"C. VANDERBILT."

Thereupon, with a suitable preamble, the board adopted the following resolutions:

"Resolved, 1. That we accept with profound gratitude the donation, with all the terms and conditions specified in said proposition.

"Resolved, 2. That, as an expression of our appreciation of this liberality, we instruct the committee, hereinafter mentioned, to ask the honorable chancery court to change the name and style of our corporation from the 'Central University' to the 'Vanderbilt University,' and that the institution thus endowed and chartered shall be, from henceforth, known and called by this name.

"Resolved, 3. That the Hon. M. Brown, the Hon. E. H. East, and the Rev. D. C. Kelley, D. D., be and they are hereby authorized and requested to obtain at the earliest practicable day such modifications of our charter as will enable this board to conform its future operations to the conditions aforesaid.

"Resolved, 4. That the secretary is requested to convey to Mr. C. Vanderbilt the sincere thanks of this board and a copy of these resolutions."

Bishop McTyeire had not solicited this donation, but, while lately in New York, was a guest of Mr. C. Vanderbilt in his home (their wives being cousins), and evidently had acquainted Mr. Vanderbilt with the project of this university, and probably furnished him a copy of the printed pamphlet, hereinbefore referred to, containing its charter, by-laws, etc., which had been submitted to the conferences; and Mr. Vanderbilt was so impressed with the enterprise that he voluntarily made the proposition aforesaid.

Thereupon the then president, Judge Milton Brown, resigned, and the board elected Bishop McTyeire, not previously a member, president of the Board of Trust, which position he held during his life.

On April 23, 1873, in the chancery court at Nashville, a petition to amend its charter was filed by the university, as follows:

"The Central University of the Methodist Episcopal Church, South.   Ex parte.

"To the Hon. W. F. Cooper, Chancellor, etc.:

"The petition of the Central University of the Methodist Episcopal Church, South, a corporation chartered heretofore by the chancery court at Nashville.

"Petitioner would state to your honor that heretofore, by a decree of record in this court, it was chartered as a university of learning. A certified copy of its charter is here filed, marked 'Exhibit B,' and made a part of this petition. Since it has obtained its charter, its condition is so altered that it now desires to have an amendment to its said charter, which amendments are as follows:

"It having been thought politic to limit the number of the Board of Trust to four from each co-operating conference, the names of Jordan Stokes and Robert A. Young be dropped from the list. Some conferences not having co-operated in the purposes of said institution, it is now desirable to omit from the list of trustees the names of the persons heretofore incorporated, and who represented said conferences, as follows, viz.: Christopher D. Oliver and William Dickson, of the North Alabama Conference; Edward Wadsworth and W. W. Byrd, of the Alabama Conference; W. L. C. Hunnicutt and Thomas Christian, of the Mississippi Conference; and James L. Borden and William H. Foster, of the Louisiana Conference.

"A large donation having been made to petitioner by C. Vanderbilt, of New York, of not less than $500,-000, as set out in 'Exhibit C,' herewith filed, and made a part of this petition, petitioner prays that its name and style be changed to that of the 'Vanderbilt University,' and that the terms and conditions of said gift be incorporated as a part of said charter.

"Petitioner also prays that the words, 'or the resolutions of the convention at Memphis, set out herein, which resolutions are hereby adopted as a part of this charter,' on page 12 of the printed charter here filed, be stricken out and omitted, and that said charter may be so altered and amended as to read as set out in 'Exhibit D,' here filed and made a part of this petition. Petitioner asks that this be done, in order that the ends of its creation may be the more readily attained.

"Petitioner prays general and full relief in the premises.

"EDWARD H. EAST, Solicitor."

Publication was duly made as required by law, and on June 16, 1873, Chancellor Cooper pronounced and entered the following decree:

"In the Matter of the Central University of
    the Methodist Episcopal Church,
              South.

"This matter came on this day to be heard before
the chancellor upon the petition heretofore filed, and
publication of the matter thereof having heretofore
been made according to the statutes in such cases made
and provided, the court is pleased to order and decree
that the name and style of the Central University of
the Methodist Episcopal Church, South, a corporation
heretofore chartered under the Constitution and laws
of this State as a university of learning, and with all
the powers, rights, and privileges of such corporations
as are now given and conferred by the laws of the
State of Tennessee, or may hereafter be given or conferred, be changed to the name and style of the Vanderbilt University, by which name it shall hereafter be
known, and sue and be sued, hold and receive property,
confer degrees, and do any and all things which, by
the present and future laws of Tennessee, it may be
empowered to do.

"It is further decreed that all the rights of property,
powers to contract, privileges, immunities, and franchises, which heretofore by law, under the decree of
this court were conferred upon the said corporation
under the name and style of the Central University of
the Methodist Episcopal Church, South, and the property or rights thereof which have heretofore been secured to said corporation, pass to the Vanderbilt University, and its assigns and successors, forever, for the

purposes of said corporation, and that it have the power to pass by-laws, resolutions, etc., not inconsistent with the laws of the land, and to increase and diminish the number of its trustees and directors, and do and perform any and all acts allowable by law to corporations of learning. It is further decreed that the said Vanderbilt University pay the cost of this proceeding, for which *fi. fa.* issue.''

In the meantime, Bishop McTyeire and the board proceeded to acquire the grounds, procure plans for buildings, etc., as provided by Mr. Vanderbilt's offer and otherwise carry out its terms and conditions.

Citizens of Nashville contributed about $30,000 toward the purchase of the campus of the university.

From time to time within the next year or two Mr. C. Vanderbilt increased his donations to a million dollars, and subsequently other members of the Vanderbilt family added to the funds of the university, for its enlargement and endowment, in round numbers, another million dollars.

At the time of Mr. C. Vanderbilt's first gift, subscriptions from other persons in small amounts and of no very considerable aggregate had been procured by the financial agents of the university, but little or nothing had been paid thereon. The whole amount promised fell far short of the minimum upon which, under the Memphis resolutions, the board was authorized to open any department of the university. Hence, at that time the board resolved ''that our agents be requested to double their diligence to secure, if possible, the remaining half million of endowment, by the ensuing sessions of the annual conferences." This, however, they never succeeded in doing.

It further appears that whatever funds were realized from subscriptions previous to the Vanderbilt gifts were subsequently devoted to the "sustentation fund" to pay the personal expenses of students in the theological department.

After the original Vanderbilt gift, other donations were made to purchase the campus, for special endowments of particular chairs, scholarships, and other specific purposes; but it does not appear that anything was added to the general endowment of the university, except by Mr. C. Vanderbilt himself and other members of the family.

Now, reverting to the proceedings of the Board of Trust, we find that at a meeting on January 14, 1874, they accepted the amended charter, again resolved to exclude members from the nonparticipating conferences, and that the six co-operating were entitled to representation.

At their meeting on September 30, 1874, Bishop McTyeire announced the death of Dr. Green, one of their members, and in his address stated:

"Another vacancy or two will occur in the board by the transfer of members beyond the patronizing conferences. I suggest that it is very important so to amend the by-laws that this board may have the initiative in filling vacancies by nominations of the successors, the conferences confirming. This reverses the order followed in originally making up the board. For obvious reasons, while as yet the patronizing conferences were to be determined by their own action, it was left to them, as they concurred in the plan outlined by the convention at Memphis, to name persons to represent them in organizing.

"But since the charter leaves the perpetuity of tne board in its own power, we should keep up the conference representation on the principle here suggested The constituency, the fitness and the safety of the board, having this vast and growing interest in trust, will be very uncertain if, by popular election on hasty and perhaps ill-considered grounds of choice, its future members are to be supplied; whereas, the board knows its own wants, is familiar with the nature of the work to be done, has the university and its interests in mind and on heart, and is ever watchful of its welfare and on the lookout for suitable instruments and agents to promote it. As the whole matter is covered by a resolution of your body, it may be adjusted readily; and a precedent should now be set in filling the first vacancies. If possible, this board should send up its nominations to the ensuing conferences. This course is not only demanded by provident wisdom, but is in analogy with other and the oldest institutions of learning under the care of the church. The board elects or nominates, and the annual conference confirms."

Whereupon the board passed what is known as the Garland Resolution:

"Forasmuch as the charter of Vanderbilt University confers upon its Board of Trust the exclusive right and power to fill vacancies that may occur in its own body, and as this power cannot be delegated to any other body of persons whatsoever: Therefore, be it

"Resolved, that this board will now proceed to fill the vacancies which have been created by the death of the late Dr. Green and by the transfer of the Rev. W. C. Hearn to the Denver Conference.

"But in order to maintain the closest connection with the patronizing conferences, the board submits these and every other election to fill a vacancy in its own body to the confirmation of the annual conference from which the election is made."

They then elected two trustees to fill these vacancies, and instructed the secretary to convey this information to the two conferences concerned, and ask for the confirmation of these elections; also to send a copy of the recorded action of the board, to wit, the Garland Resolution. The records of one of these conferences (Tennessee) show that this was done, and it made the following response:

"Resolved, 1. That in view of the relations already established by contract between the Tennessee Conference and Vanderbilt University, we proceed now to nominate one of our members to fill the vacancy in the Board of Trust, caused by the death of Dr. Green, and that we nominate Dr. R. A. Young.

"2. That, in response to the request of the Board of Trust, we consent to modify the original contract so that hereafter, when a vacancy occurs, the board may nominate one of our members to us for confirmation, . the nominee not to be a member of the board until confirmed by us."

In the fall of 1874, the Alabama Conference, theretofore excluded for failure to co-operate under the charter, decided to come in, and nominated four members to represent it on the Board of Trust.

In May, 1875, the board rescinded its former action excluding members from the Alabama Conference, and elected the four named by that conference. At the same time, they amended their by-law VII to conform to the Garland Resolution, elected two new members to fill vacancies from the North Mississippi Conference, and directed that this action be reported to that conference for confirmation.

In 1880 the president, Bishop McTyeire, recommended that the members of the board be reduced from four to two from each conference, and that Louisville Conference, not heretofore connected with the enterprise, be admitted and represented on the board, as one of the co-operating conferences.

In 1881 a committee reported in favor of the proposed reduction and that it be referred to the conferences for concurrence.

This report was tabled and the matter referred to another committee, of which Judge East was chairman.

In 1882 this committee reported, "contrary to the view it first entertained that this matter was a charter question, that it is simply a by-law question, the charter being silent on the subject, and the whole matter is subject to by-law VII, and the by-laws may be changed or amended at any annual meeting of the board by a two-thirds vote of all the members present," and recommended a change of the by-law to that effect. The report was adopted and the by-law so amended. No action of the conferences was asked or taken on the subject.

In 1884 two members from the Louisville Conference were elected by the board and reported to the conference for confirmation.

In 1888 the term of membership was reduced by the board from life to eight years. This action was referred to the conferences for concurrence, and they approved.

In 1894 the board amended its by-laws so as to admit to membership, *ex officio,* the chancellor of the university and the bishops of the church, also "four additional members without regard to their location in any particular one of the patronizing conferences." Their election was not made subject to confirmation, and the board declined to make its amended by-law subject to the concurrence of the patronizing conferences.

In 1895 Chancellor Kirkland, in his address to the board, suggested that some change in the method of electing trustees and in the constitution of the board should be made so as to relate the university more closely to the whole church and constitute it the Central University of Southern Methodism. This was referred to a committee who, in 1896, reported as follows:

"I. We think it very important that Vanderbilt University should be closely allied to the whole church as the Central University of Southern Methodism.

"II. We believe this can be partially effected, even now, by increasing the number of trustees who are selected independently of our eight patronizing conferences.

"III. We recommend that the by-laws be amended so as to give only one representative to each of the eight patronizing conferences, and that the eight vacancies thus created be filled by the selection of representative men without regard to geographical limitation.

"IV. As the best method of effecting this result we suggest as the terms of the present members expire, the board select only one representative for each patronizing conference, and we suggest that each patronizing conference be requested to approve this change in the by-laws and accept the reduction from two to one representative."

The board adopted this report and amended its by-laws accordingly. The conference approved this action.

In 1897 the chancellor in his address suggested further changes along this line, and a committee, to whom the subject was referred, reported:

"We recommend that, in order that Vanderbilt University may be related to the church as the Central University of Southern Methodism, and may assume a connectional relationship to the whole church as the crowning feature of our educational system, the consent of the patronizing conferences be asked to the proposition that hereafter the Board of Trustees be selected from the entire church without regard to geographical limitation and to be confirmed by the General Conference. In order to secure such consent, the chancellor of the university is requested to submit this proposition to the several patronizing conferences at the next annual sessions. We furthermore suggest that a resolution be submitted to the next General Conference asking the adoption of this university as the central institution of the Methodist Episcopal Church, South."

This report was adopted, and a committee, composed of three bishops, appointed to prepare a memorial to the General Conference. This matter was referred to the annual conferences, and all except the Louisville Conference, which deferred action, passed resolutions expressing willingness to transfer to the General Conference "all rights, title, and interest that we have in said university, and hereby solicit the co-operation of all the conferences represented, and the Board of Trust, in securing this desirable end.

"2. That until this is accomplished we adhere to the *status* secured to us by contract, which gives us a controlling voice in the appointment of our representatives on the Board of Trust."

In 1898 the Louisville Conference took similiar action.

In the meantime the committee of the Board of Trust, composed of three bishops, presented to the General Conference of the M. E. Church, South, which met in Baltimore in May, 1898, a memorial as follows:

"The undersigned, constituting a committee appointed by the Board of Trust of Vanderbilt University, to make a special report to the General Conference of the M. E. Church, South, beg leave to present this communication with reference to the university and its relation to the whole church. Vanderbilt University, as is well known, has heretofore been the central institution of eight patronizing conferences. The title to the property is vested in a board, to be held in trust for these conferences of the Methodist Episcopal Church, South. For several years the board has had under consideration a plan to make the university entirely connectional and relate it directly to the whole church. The plan proposed is to have the patronizing conferences transfer their rights in the university to the General Conference, and to have the General Conference, by proper resolution, accept the patronage of the university and consent to assume toward this enterprise the same relation heretofore held by the separate conferences. The Board of Trust has officially expressed its approval of this plan, and most of the patronizing conferences have done the same thing.

"By the charter of the university the Board of Trust is vested with the power and obligation to fill its own vacancies; but the election of any member is not valid under the law of the university until said member has been confirmed by the conference which he is designed to represent. Under the new plan the board would be at liberty to select its members without geographical restrictions of any kind, and the General Conference would confirm or reject the appointment. This duty could be exercised either by the General Conference as a body, or it could be delegated by the conference to some board, itself the creature of the General Conference. Naturally the Board of Education will be thought of in this connection. This board meets every year, and is likely to be charged more and more with the oversight of our institutions of learning. It is now trying to devise methods for correlating all our colleges and universities, and it would be appropriate for the General Conference to exercise its control of Vanderbilt University largely through the board. In that manner vacancies in the Board of Trust of the university could be filled every year, and it would not be necessary to wait four years for action that might be promptly needed.

"As a committee, therefore, of the Board of Trust of Vanderbilt University, we beg to present this matter to the General Conference, and invite such action as may be adjudged right and proper.

"[Signed] A. W. WILSON.
"CHARLES B. GALLOWAY.
"EUGENE R. HENDRIX."

The General Conference accepted this proposal in the following resolutions:

"First, that the General Conference of the M. E. Church, South, hereby accepts the proposed relation and control of the Vanderbilt University and commits to the General Board of Education the confirmation of all trustees, selected by the Board of Trust of Vanderbilt University.

"Second. That this resolution take effect as soon as the consent of all the present patronizing conferences has been obtained, all the necessary legal steps taken, and preliminary details arranged."

This relation between the university and the General Conference was maintained from 1898 to 1910.

In 1905 the board repealed the by-law making the chancellor and bishops, thirteen in number, *ex officio* members, and adopted in lieu one making the chancellor and five bishops, selected according to their seniority, regular members of the board, and made nominations accordingly to the General Board of Education for confirmation.

The board at the same time determined to take out an amended charter, under Acts 1875, ch. 142, prepared and signed an application therefor, but some of the members subsequently withdrew their names and it was not filed. These and other matters created some dissatisfaction in the minds of some of the bishops and members of the General Conference, and hence at its session in 1906 the General Conference

so as to insure the observance of the charter, the conditions of specific gifts, and the statutes of the State.''

Complainants now insist that this was an acceptance by the board of the conclusions of the commission. The chairman of the commission did not so construe it, and in this view the General Conference and its Committee on Education seem to have agreed with him, and so do we. We need not inquire what effect, if any, such an acceptance would have.

The General Conference adopted the report, and resolved, in part, as follows:

''Resolved, first, that this General Conference hereby accepts the report of the Vanderbilt Commission as a definition of the rights of the Methodist Episcopal Church, South, to Vanderbilt University; moreover, that it accepts the judgment of the commission that the College of Bishops is a board of common law visitors of the university; and, furthermore, that it accepts the finding of the commission that the General Conference has the right to select the Board of Trustees in such manner as it may elect, either by direct election by the conference itself or through such agency, or agencies, as it may designate.

''Resolved, second, that it is the sense of this General Conference that its right to select the Board of Trust of Vanderbilt University and fill vacancies in the same now be exercised, and hereafter at its discretion; and it being ascertained that vacancies now exist in the Board of Trust of said university, the following named members of the Methodist Episcopal

Church, South, are hereby elected to fill said vacancies, namely: ————.

"Resolved, third, that following this election the General Conference will, for the future, continue the method of choosing the trustees adopted by the General Conference held at Baltimore in 1898, when it committed 'to the General Board of Education the confirmation of all trustees elected by the Board of Trust of Vanderbilt University.'

"Resolved, fourth, that the General Conference approves the action of the bishops in entering upon the discharge of their duties as visitors of the university."

In pursuance to said second resolution, it elected the relators, V. A. Godbey, N. E. Harris, and Albert W. Biggs as trustees, and ordered their election certified to the board. At the next meeting of the Board of Trust in June, 1910, said parties, so elected, applied to be admitted as members; but the board refused their application, and resolved, by a vote of 19 to 8, that the General Conference had no right to elect members to fill vacancies in the board, that the board itself had that right, that it amend its by-laws accordingly, and proceed to fill the existing vacancies. Therefore it elected for that purpose, and seated, the defendants, Claude Waller, R. F. Jackson, and Jas. A. Robbins, instead of the persons elected thereto by the General Conference. Afterwards, on July 12, 1910, the College of Bishops met as visitors of the university, vetoed this action of the board, declaring it illegal, null, and void, and sustained the right of the General Conference to

elect, and of its appointees to membership in the board.
Thereupon this bill was filed by the State, at the relation of the College of Bishops and Messrs. Godbey,
Harris, and Biggs, against the University, the Board
of Trust, and Messrs. Waller, Jackson, and Robbins,
seeking to establish and enforce the alleged rights of
the relators, as hereinbefore indicated.   •

The controversies in this case are not so much of
fact as of proper construction of documents and written records of various kinds offered in evidence, and
of questions of law arising thereon. We will now
pass to a consideration and decision of these questions.

The University was incorporated under the Acts of
1871, ch. 54· Section 1 thereof provides: "Hereafter,
when persons in this State shall desire to be incorporated with the powers and privileges of a corporate
body, they shall file a petition in the chancery court of
the county in which the largest number of petitioners
reside, setting forth the purposes and objects of the
corporation prayed for." Then, after prescribing the
publication required to be made, the court is directed
to proceed to an *ex parte* hearing of the petition, and
"it appearing to the court that the objects of the corporation prayed for are not in conflict with the laws
of the land, nor detrimental to public interests or
morals, the court shall so adjudicate and decree,
. . . and, shall enumerate such usual powers and
privileges of corporate bodies as may be necessary
to carry out the legitimate objects of said corporation."
Section 9 thereof provides: "That the powers granted

to chancery courts by this act, shall extend to the incorporation of institutions of learning, churches, religious and charitable institutions; and the powers and the privileges of such corporations shall be as prescribed in sections 1470, 1471, 1472, and 1473, of the Code of Tennessee."

Code, sec. 1470, applies to corporations with stockholders.

Section 1471 provides: "If the members are not interested as stockholders, each member is entitled to vote at all elections one vote, and to bear an equal voice in all the deliberations of the whole body. Such members may fix the number of trustees, the officers of the association, their terms of service, and compensation."

Section 1472: "Corporations created under this article may hold real and personal property not exceeding in value $50,000, may receive property by gift, will, or devise, holding the same for purposes of their incorporation, with all the lawful conditions imposed by the donor, and may exercise such powers as are incident to private corporations."

Section 1473 provides for service of process on the corporation in case of suits, etc.

The Code of 1858, from which these sections are taken, had provided for the organization of corporations of various kinds by proceedings quite different from those provided by the act in question. The Constitution of 1870 had forbidden the granting of charters by special act, and required that all charters of corporations should be granted by general laws. In pursuance to this provision of the Constitution, the Legislature of 1870-71 passed the act in question as a general corporation act, providing for the organization of various kinds of corporations. We have quoted so much thereof as is appliable to the class of corporations to which this educational institution belongs. This is a general act, covering the whole subject, and therefore superseded the Code provisions except so far as they were adopted and re-enacted thereby. *Terrell* v. *State*, 86 Tenn., 523, 8 S. W., 212; *Malone* v. *Williams*, 118 Tenn., 445, 103 S. W., 798, 121 Am. St. Rep. 1002.

It changed entirely the method of procedure necessary to obtain a charter and organize a corporation, but as to institutions of learning, etc., section 9 of the act gave them the same powers as were given to like corporations organized under the Code. *Heck* v. *McEwen*, 12 Lea, 97; *Ex parte Chadwell*, 3 Baxt., 98.

Whether that act would authorize representative incorporation, that is to say, the incorporation of a certain body or class of individuals as an educational institution upon the application of a few acting as their representatives, it is not necessary in this case to decide, for the reason that the applicants for this charter had not been authorized to represent for that purpose any one other than themselves, unless, perchance, it were the members of the Memphis convention by whom they had been named. The members of that convention formed a mere temporary body, without permanence or succession, and clearly they did not contemplate their own incorporation. The insistence in this case is not to this effect, but that they represented the annual conferences, whose committees constituted that convention. We cannot agree with this contention, for several reasons. The conferences had not authorized that convention to bind them, and the convention did not undertake to do so. The conferences, whether incorporated or mere voluntary associations, were not competent to form an association with each other for the purpose of incorporation, or, without express statutory authority, to act as members of a corporation. 1 Thomp. Corp. (2d Ed.), sec. 176; 1 Wilgus, Corp., 56, 553; 1 Clark & Marsh. Corp., p. 127; 1 Meacham, sec. 130. See, also, *Mallory* v. *Oil Works,* 86 Tenn., 598, 8 S. W., 396; *Rhodes* v. *Rhodes,* 88 Tenn., 637, 13 S. W., 590; *Green* v. *Allen,* 5 Humph., 158.

The Tennessee act in question clearly contemplates the incorporation of natural persons, and not corporations or voluntary associations. These annual conferences, whether incorporated or not, were representative bodies composed of delegates from the several churches within their bounds, and the churches were composed of individual members. It has been suggested that, if the conferences could not act as incorporators, the delegates of whom they were composed might do so; but it is clear that they had no such intention, or that the individual members of the several churches could do so. It is equally clear that they had no such intention. The Memphis convention and its Board of Trust entertained no such thought. This would be carrying representative incorporation beyond the limit. If such were permissible, a large class of persons who had never even dreamed of the subject, might wake up and find themselves incorporated. The act provides only for persons so desiring to be incorporated.

The subsequent ratification of the action of the convention, and the Board of Trust, could not change the result, for the action taken did not purport to incorporate any but the petitioners, and the by-law adopted in furtherance of the Memphis Resolutions proclaimed that "the charter leaves the perpetuity of the board in its own power," and requested the several conferences co-operating to nominate four members for election, etc. This was certified, along with the charter and the Memphis Resolutions, to the conferences, and when they ratified they could not possibly have understood that they thereby became incorporators, and such ratification could not, in any event, change the legal effect of the charter already granted. Moreover, the petition for the charter was filed by the applicants as individuals, and not as representatives of any one, and the publication thereon was made accordingly. The fact that they are described in the decree or charter as representatives of certain annual conferences does not in this respect change the result. While the court in pronouncing this decree was acting not judicially, but ministerially (*Ex parte Chadwell*, 3 Baxt., 108), yet the proceeding was according to judicial forms, and the decree, or charter, cannot depart in substance from the petition. The petition is the basis and measure of the thing to be granted. The court might grant less, but not more, than was sought by the petition. *Wilson v. Schaefer,* 107 Tenn., 300, 64 S. W., 208; *Gilbreath v. Gilliland,* 95 Tenn., 383, 32 S. W., 250.

Therefore we are of opinion that, under this act and these proceedings, the persons applying for the charter became the incorporators, the body politic or corporate, in other words, the members of the corporation; and had the right of perpetual succession. Neither the act, nor the charter, provides how their successors shall be chosen, and, in the absence of such provision, in the case of a corporation aggregate, that right, by necessary implication, would be vested in the persons so incorporated. 1 Blackst. Com., 475-576; Taylor on Corp., sec. 14; Kyd on Corp., 69; Ang. & Ames on Corp., 70, 89; Fowler on Charitable Uses, 138, note 3.

Such, indeed, for a period of thirty-five years or more after the organization of this corporation, was the uniform construction of its charter by all parties concerned.

It is to be observed that many members of the Board of Trust from its inception have been eminent lawyers, not only of Tennessee, but also of other states.

The practical interpretation of a contract by the parties thereto is entitled to great, if not controlling, influence. *Chicago v. Sheldon,* 9 Wall., 54, 19 L. Ed., 594.

There is great contention in this case as to the effect of the Memphis Resolutions, which are embodied in this charter. Complainants insist that they constitute the essence, or soul, of the charter, and the defendants that they are mere surplusage, and of no effect whatever. It seems that, throughout the history of this institution, much doubt on this question has arisen in the minds of the Board of Trust, and other parties concerned, and to settle that doubt more than one effort was made to eliminate them from the charter; and it is now contended by the defendants that this was in fact done by the amended charter of 1873. We do not regard it as very material whether they became technically a part of the charter or not. At any rate, they were not improperly incorporated therein. The Acts of 1871, ch. 54, requires, among other things, that the petition shall set forth the purposes and objects of the corporation prayed for, to the end that the court may adjudge and decree that the objects of the corporation are not in conflict with the laws of the land, etc. The objects of this corporation, as stated in the petition, were "for the purpose of soliciting subscriptions [and] donations, and for the erection and maintenance of an institution of learning of the highest order, maintaining all the schools belonging to a university of that character, together with the rights, powers and privileges which, by law, may belong to literary institutions chartered by the laws of the State." It was altogether proper for the court under this petition to inquire into, find, and insert

into the decree the objects and purposes of this corporation, not merely in the general terms of the petition, but
the more amplified and particular form as stated
in these Memphis Resolutions, which constitute the
plan and specifications upon which this institution was
to be built, and then, as directed by the statute, "enumerate such usual powers and privileges of corporate
bodies as may be necessary to carry out the legitimate
objects of said corporation," and so the court did in
this charter.

Mr. Thompson, in his work on Corporations, says:
"The statute of perhaps every State in the country
authorizing the organization of corporations requires
the articles to state definitely and clearly the objects
and purposes of the proposed corporation. This is
regarded in some respects as the most important requirement, for by this the powers of the corporation
are to be determined, and its acts, to be legal and binding, except as otherwise hereinafter shown, must be
measured by the objects and purposes stated." 1
Thomp. Corp. (2d Ed.), sec. 191. See, also, Id., sec.
40.

We are of opinion that the Memphis Resolutions
were not eliminated from the charter by the amendment thereto of 1873.

The petition asked, not for a new charter, but for
certain specific amendments to the existing charter.
The decree shows that only two of these were allowed,
to wit, the change of name and the power to increase
or diminish the number of members of the board.

Nothing is said of the others. However, the decree passes to Vanderbilt University all rights, powers, privileges, immunities, and franchises "which heretofore by law under the decree of this court were conferred upon said corporation" under its former name and style, and so seems to confirm, rather than eliminate, the provisions of the original charter in regard to the Memphis Resolutions. But whether they had ever been incorporated in the charter or not, or whether they had been eliminated therefrom by this decree of 1873 or not, we think they would still constitute, in so far as their provisions are legal, the underlying plan of this institution, and their character and effect would, in either event, be the same, to wit, its so-called "Articles of Foundation."

This leads up to the much discussed question as to who is the founder of this institution.

The Memphis convention, composed of delegates from the several annual conferences, without power, however, to bind them by its action, was the original designer, architect, as it were, of this educational enterprise. It devised and formulated the general plans and specifications, or so-called "Articles of Foundation," upon which it was to be built. It named a Board of Trust, who should procure an act of incorporation, in order to give it permanence and carry out the founder's intention with more convenience. 2 Perry on Trusts, sec. 742; *Dartmouth College Case*, 4 Wheat., 574, 4 L. Ed., 629; *Atty. Gen.* v. *Pierce*, 2 Atk., 87; Tudor on Charities, sec. 63; *Nelson* v. *Cushing*, 2 Cush.

(Mass.), 527; *State v. Toledo,* 23 Ohio Cir. Ct. R., 327.

It also authorized and enjoined on this Board of Trust when so incorporated to seek and, if possible, find a founder or builder who would supply the necessary funds to accomplish its objects. It had prescribed a million dollars as the amount desired, and a half million dollars as the minimum amount upon which it could be founded or begun.

In pursuance to this authority and injunction, the Board of Trust at first sought this founder and funds necessary to its projects among the co-operating annual conferences and the members of the Methodist Episcopal Church, South. In this effort they succeeded in raising but a fraction of the minimum amount required, and that fraction rested only in promises. Possibly those promises, or subscriptions, were not binding, or, in law, collectible, until the minimum required had been procured. They had about despaired of success from this source when Mr. Vanderbilt made his first donation of not less than half a million dollars, the full minimum required, and directly afterwards doubled the amount, thus making the full endowment called for by said Memphis Resolutions.

With these funds so donated by Mr. Vanderbilt, and a comparatively small amount contributed by citizens of Nashville in order to secure a particular location of the institution, the Board of Trust provided a campus, buildings, outfit, and endowment for the university. Such amounts as they realized from antecedent subscriptions were subsequently devoted to the so-called "sustentation fund," for defraying personal expenses of students attending the theological department of the university.

Then, so far as money was concerned, it was Mr. Vanderbilt, and not the church, who breathed the breath of life' into this corporate body, if not dead, at least until then inert and powerless. Hence on this issue we find that Mr. Vanderbilt, and not the annual conferences or the church, was the founder and original patron of this institution.

Nevertheless, in so far as their provisions are valid and legal, he founded the institution upon the plans and specifications, or so-called "Articles of Foundation," contained in the Memphis Resolutions, except so far as he saw fit to append other legal conditions to his gifts. He did impose on·these gifts some conditions which modified to some extent these Memphis Resolutions, the chief of which was that Bishop McTyeire, through whom the gift was communicated to the corporation, should be made president for life, at a fixed salary, and the use of a dwelling house free of rent; that as such president he (and possibly his successors in office) should have a veto power over the acts of the Board of Trust, the legality and validity of which is open to very serious question, and that the university should be located in or near Nashville. It will thus be seen that they did not supplant the main body of the Memphis Resolutions, but were ingrafted thereon.

Whether the seventh and ninth of these resolutions do not attempt an·unwarrantable and illegal interference with the normal and legitimate powers of a Tennessee corporation and its governing body of directors, or trustees, presents a very serious question, but is not in issue here, and for that reason is not discussed and decided.

The petitioners for this charter were incorporated as a Board of Trust, or trustees. Trustees for what purposes and trust? Originally, to administer this charity as planned by the Memphis convention, or, in the language of the resolutions, for "the carrying out of this whole scheme . . . with power to solicit and invest funds . . . and do whatever is necessary for the execution of this scheme." This trust was recognized by incorporating in the charter these resolutions in full, also by describing therein the petitioners or Board of Trust as representatives of the several annual conferences from which they came. The law, as well as their charter, imposed upon them the further trust of holding such real estate and personal property as they may receive by contract, gift, will, or devise "for the purposes of said corporation, with all the lawful conditions imposed by the donor."

A charitable corporation is in itself a trustee, and its charter constitutes a declaration of trust. 2 Morawetz on Corp., sec. 1046, cited in *Church* v. *Hinton*, 92 Tenn., 188, 21 S. W., 321, 19 L. R. A., 289.

In Perry on Trusts, cited above, it ·is said: "The trustees of a charity frequently procure an act of incorporation in order to carry out the intention of their donor with more convenience."

In *Nelson* v. *Cushing,* supra, where trustees appointed by will for the establishment of a free school had become incorporated, the court said: "This act, in our judgment, does not vary the powers or the duties of the trustees, or change the character of the school placed under their management. It enables them to act in a corporate name, and to have a corporate seal; and it affords them the facility of taking conveyances, obligations, and securities, in their corporate name, and avoids the necessity of changing such securities upon a change of individual members composing the board."

In *State* v. *Toledo,* supra, a corporation had been formed for the purpose of carrying out a trust founded by one Scott, and the court held that "a person establishing an institution of learning of such a character and for such purposes as he deems proper, and such as he deems useful and beneficial to his fellowmen, has a right to place such restrictions or conditions upon the trust which he creates as he sees fit; and the act of incorporation, while made under general laws, for the purposes of carrying out the trust, is subordinate and subsidiary to such trust. The purposes and objects of the donation must govern the institution, unless by some act of those who have power over the fund some change is made. The legislature has no independent power to change or alter the trust."

This brings us to the consideration of the eighth of the Memphis Resolutions. We find in it nothing that contravenes the express provisions, or policy, of the law. It is in furtherance of the general objects and purposes of this corporation, as expressed in its charter and the petition therefor.

Then what was the effect upon the constitution of the Board of Trust, of this eighth of the Memphis Resolutions? "That provision be made in the charter for giving a fair representation in the management of the university to any annual conference hereafter co-operating with us." With us? With whom? Not the annual conferences from whom the delegates came, for they were not bound by the convention's action, and might not, any or all, co-operate in this enterprise. Therefore "with us" means primarily the convention, who was speaking, and ultimately the Board of Trust—the corporation, the university itself, the sole survivor and heir of that convention. What "annual conferences hereafter co-operating with us?"   Not merely those which were not then represented in the convention, but any annual conference, whether there represented or not, which ratified the action of the convention and thereafter would co-operate with the Board of Trust in the "carrying out of this whole scheme."   This, then, calls for giving "a fair representation in the management of the university to any [and all] conferences hereafter co-operating," thereby recognizing that none were at the present time bound to do so.

This scheme was not conditioned upon the ratification of the conferences. The very first resolution was to the effect "that measures be adopted looking to the establishment, as speedily as practicable, of an insti-

tution of learning," etc.; and the sixth provided "that
the carrying out of this whole scheme is hereby committed to the following persons," to wit, the Board of
Trust named, "who shall take immediate steps" to
carry it out; and this eighth resolution does not contemplate ownership of the intsitution by the conferences, but merely co-operation by them "with us"—
the Board of Trust—the university itself, and in return for such co-operation each conference should have
a fair representation in the management of the university; that is to say, on the Board of Trust.   The
second resolution, "that the institution shall be called
the Central University of the Methodist Episcopal
Church, South," does not necessarily mean ownership
of the university by the church.   If it stood alone, it
might imply as much; but, in connection with the other
resolutions, it is intended merely to define the character of the institution, and invite the affiliation and influence of the church.   Such, too, was the purpose of
the fifth resolution as to its location by the bishops,
and the ninth, as to the relation of the bishops to the
university.   The effect of the latter resolution will be
hereinafter more fully noticed in connection with another matter.   The charter expressly provided that the
Board of Trust "shall make all by-laws necessary and
proper to carry out said resolutions." The board properly construed this "fair representation" to mean
equal representation, and originally provided for it
by by-law No. 2, allowing to each conference four members of the board.   The number was subsequently re-

duced, first to two, and finally to one, from each. Originally they provided that the conferences should name their representatives and the board would elect. Then, for very good reasons, wisely suggested by Bishop McTyeire, they reversed this rule, and provided that the board should elect subject to confirmation by the conferences. They excluded members from conferences, represented in the Memphis convention and the charter, but failing afterwards to ratify and co-operate. One such conference subsequently approved and named representatives, who were then admitted to membership. They also admitted members from one co-operating conference not represented in the convention and charter. They reduced the terms of members from life to eight years. At first, the whole board was made up of representatives of the several conferences. Then, as these representative members were reduced in number, others were admitted who did not represent and were not named or confirmed by the conferences. All of these changes were originated and made by the board, but most of them, at least the more radical ones, affecting the representation of the conferences, were submitted to and approved by the conferences. This arrangement from the first was referred to by the conferences as a contract, and usually by the board as a by-law relation between the parties. We think both were right, and that it amounted, in fact, to a trust relation between them. The relation, both by the Memphis Resolutions, and the practical interpretation thereof by the parties, was not that of ownership by

the conferences, but of co-operation with the university
and fair representation in its management. What this
fair representation should be, considering the best interests of the university, was from time to time settled and fixed by mutual agreement. Neither party was
at liberty to violate these agreements.

Finally, in 1898, this relation between the annual conferences and the university was by mutual consent terminated, and the General Conference of the whole
church was substituted to the rights and privileges
theretofore enjoyed by the annual conferences. It was
agreed between the General Conference and the Board
of Trust that the board should elect and the General
Conference confirm all members of the board. This
arrangement was entirely consonant with the original
plans and purpose of the corporation, and with the
Memphis Resolutions. It was merely an acknowledgment of the underlying principle that the church should
co-operate with the university and have fair representation in its management. In this way, this relation
was to be extended from a part of the annual conferences, theretofore co-operating, to the General Conference, composed of delegates from and having jurisdiction over all annual conferences and the church at large.
The by-laws of the university and the practice of the
parties were conformed to that agreement until 1910,
when this controversy arose. Then both parties, the
General Conference first, and the board afterwards,
undertook to repudiate that arrangement without consent of the other, and each asserted the right to elect

members independently of the other. Unless controlled by Act of 1895, ch. 6, hereafter to be noticed, that agreement could no more be ignored or violated by the parties thereto than those formerly existing between the annual conferences and the university.

The power of this corporation to enter into such agreements and pass such by-laws appears to be expressly given by the charter; but, if not, it is so consistent with the charter and its declared purposes and objects that it may well be implied. 3 Thompson on Corp. (2d Ed.), secs. 2108-2112. In section 2112 it is said: "When an express power is granted to do a particular act, or to engage in a stated business, this carries with it by' implication the right to do every act which may be found reasonably necessary to give effect to the power expressly granted. On this principle every corporation, at least in the absence of restrictive language, possesses the powers found necessary, not only to its existence and self-preservation, but, as already said, to powers expressly granted, or to effectuate the purposes and objects of the incorporation."

The by-laws of a corporation must be consistent with the spirit and terms of the corporate charter, and when such a by-law is adopted it becomes, while in force, as much a part of the law of the corporation as though its provisions had been a part of the charter. When a by-law enters into a compact between the corporation and its shareholders, it is in the nature of a contract between them, and is not revocable to the prejudice of the shareholder. So, too, a by-law of a nonstockholding corporation which enters into or constitutes a contract or declaration of trust between that corporation and its beneficiaries, cannot be repealed, so as to deprive the parties of their rights under such contract or declaration of trust. See 5 Am. & Eng. Enc. Law (2d Ed.), 88, 91, 95; *Kent* v. *Quicksilver Mining Co.*, 78 N. Y., 179; 1 Thomp. Corp., sec. 1017; *Matthews* v. *Associated Press*, 136 N. Y., 333, 32 N. E. 981, 32 Am. St. Rep. 741; 1 Cook, Corp., sec. 4a and notes.

We will next inquire into the effect and operation of the ninth of the Memphis Resolutions: ''That the bishops of the Methodist Episcopal Church, South, be and are hereby requested to act as a Board of Supervision of the University or any of its departments, and, jointly with the Board of Trust, to elect officers and professors, and prescribe the course of study and a plan of government.''

It is claimed by complainants that this vested in the College of Bishops the common-law right of visitors over this corporation. At common law, this visitorial power was a property right, belonging to the first donor and founder of a charity, and arose by implication from the gift, or it might be vested by him in his appointee. There is no claim in this case that the bishops were donors to and founders of this charity, and hence no such right can arise on that ground; but it is said that they were appointed by the founder to be the visitors. As we have already said, the founder of this charity, by gift of its endowment, was Mr. C. Vanderbilt, and he did not appoint the College of Bishops visitors. If he appointed any visitor, it was a limited appointment of Bishop McTyeire (and possibly his successor in office), who was, as a condition of his gift, made president of the board for life, with veto power over its action. Whether this was a lawful condition, or an unwarranted interference with the power and authority of the directors of a Tennessee corporation, it is not necessary in this case to inquire or decide. The condition was made, and complied with, and, by the death of Bishop McTyeire, has been treated as terminated. Whether this is so is not in issue here.

But it is insisted that, by providing the plan or "Articles of Foundation," the Memphis convention or the Methodist Church founded this institution, and by this ninth resolution appointed the bishops visitors, and it may be asserted that Mr. Vanderbilt, as founder, adopted this appointment, if such it was. Let us inquire into the meaning and effect of this resolution. As to what, if any, relation other than that of visitors, it created between the College of Bishops and the corporation, it is not necessary to decide, as no issue of that kind is made in this case. Hence we limit the inquiry to the question as to whether it vested in the College of Bishops this common-law visitorial power.

By Private Acts 1857-58, ch. 32, certain persons named were granted a charter and incorporated under the name and style of "The Board of Trustees of Central University of the General Conference of the Methodist Episcopal Church, South." Several of those named therein as incorporators were also members of the Memphis convention, and it is asserted by both parties to this case, and seems altogether probable, that the committee of that convention who drafted its resolutions had before it as a precedent this act of 1857-58. Section 2 thereof provides "that the General Conference of the Methodist Episcopal Church, South, shall have supervision over the above incorporated Board of Trustees; they shall have and possess power of visitation, and also power to fill vacancies in the board by death, resignation or removal."

A comparison thereof with this ninth resolution is significant, in that both provide for "supervision" of the corporation, while the former confers the additional power of "visitation" and "to fill vacancies in the board," and the latter omits both.

The act of 1857-58 thus makes a decided distinction between the power of "supervision" and of "visitation."

That the Memphis Resolutions adopted the one and rejected the other can mean nothing less than an intention not to give the power of "visitation." Moreover, we think the power of "supervision" is not equivalent to and does not necessarily include that of "visitation." The latter was probably omitted for the very good reason that it was not pertinent to the corporation contemplated by the Memphis Resolutions. At common law, the right of visitation vests only where the persons interested in the charity were themselves incorporated, and not where disinterested trustees were appointed and incorporated to administer the trust for the beneficiaries.

In the leading case on this subject it is said by Lord Holt:

"For it is fit the members, that are endowed and that have the charity bestowed upon them, should not be left to themselves (for divisions and contests will arise amongst them about the dividend of the charity), but pursue the intent and design of him that bestowed it upon them."

"Now, indeed, where the poor or those that receive the charity are not incorporated, but there are certain trustees who dispose of the charity according to the case in 10 Coke, there is no visitor; because the interest of the revenue is not vested in the poor that have the benefit of the charity, but they are subject to the orders and direction of the trustees. But where they who are to enjoy the benefit of the charity are incorporated, then, to prevent all perverting of the charity, or to compose differences that may happen among them, there is by law a visitorial power."

Phillips v. *Bury*, 2 Term. R., 352.

In *Green* v. *Rutherford*, 1 Ves. Sen., 471, Lord Hardwicke said: "If the charity is not vested in the persons who are to partake, but in the trustees for their benefit, no visitor can arise by implication."

A like rule is recognized in the *Dartmouth College Case*, 4 Wheat., 563, 565, 566, 645, 675, 676, 4 L. Ed. 629; *Allen* v. *McKean*, 1 Sumn. 276 Fed. Cas. No. 229; *Sanderson* v. *White*, 18 Pick. (Mass.) 328, 29 Am. Dec. 591.

In 2 Kent's Commentaries (13th Ed.) 300, it is said: "Where governors, or trustees, are appointed by a charter, according to the will of the founder, to manage a charity (as is usually the case in colleges and hospitals), the visitorial power is deemed to belong to the trustees in their corporate capacity."

There is yet another reason why we think the visitorial power did not vest in the College of Bishops. This ninth resolution did not appoint the bishops to anything, but merely requested them to act as a Board of Supervision, etc. Soon after the convention adjourned, the Board of Trust communicated this resolution, together with the fifth, in regard to locating the university, to the College of Bishops then in session, "with the view of obtaining an acceptance of the foregoing official relation to the university." The bishops first considered a motion to decline the request outright, but on second thought resolved: First, that they would locate the institution when the $500,000 shall be pledged for the enterprise. Second, "that by this act we are not to be understood as implying that the said institution is to be considered connectional to the damage of existing colleges and universities. We can take no official relation to the Central University that will discriminate between it and any and every other institution of the church. Nevertheless, we feel free to give our decided approval to the combination of the several annual conferences represented in the convention in Memphis, or so many of them as may agree together, acting through their respective bodies, in getting up an institution of the highest grade.'' And, third, withholding any opinion upon the subject of a theological department, about which there was grave controversy among the churchmen. It does not appear that the bishops had any official relation to any other educational institution of the church, so that their acceptance in this case would apparently operate as a discrimination in its favor. The board (as do we also) construed this answer of the bishops as a declination of all official relations with the university contemplated by that ninth resolution. This is manifest from their reference to the bishops' conditional promise to locate the university and their significant silence as to what the bishops say about assuming no official relations to the institution.

After Mr. Vanderbilt had endowed the university, and the board by means of his gifts had established it, the bishops seem to be ready and willing to adopt the enterprise. All parties seemed to be in doubt about what relation they bore to the institution. They assumed and exercised very uncertain and fitful rights and privileges. After a time the board resolved to admit them as members *ex officio,* and later rescinded that action and elected five of their number to active membership. Not until after the so-called Vanderbilt Commission had reported that they had no right to membership in the board, but that they held the right of visitation, were they heard to claim such a right, or did they attempt to exercise it; and this was nearly forty years after the charter was granted to the uni-

versity, and after they had in the outset declined all
official relations to the corporation. If there ever had
been any merit in the claim, we think they had long
since abandoned it, and were then estopped to assert
it.

Whether this resolution invests them with legal
power of any kind we very much doubt; but, as hereinbefore stated, the alleged visitorial power is all that
is here in issue, and for that reason we limit our decision to that point.

We turn now to the consideration of the Act of 1895,
ch. 6, entitled "An act for the benefit of incorporated
educational institutions."

Section 1 empowers such institutions to acquire, receive, and hold property for educational purposes, without limit of amount.

Section 2 provides: "That wherever any such educational institution has been established, and is being
maintained and patronized by, or having been otherwise established, is now being maintained and patronized by any religious society or denomination, or shall
hereafter be so established, maintained and patronized,
the representative governing body of such society or
denomination shall have the power and authority as
its option, to elect its board of directors or trustees,
or fill vacancies occuring therein, and, with the consent
of such boards, to increase or diminish the number of
members thereof, as may seem to such body best for the
welfare and judicious management of the institution;
provided, that in case such governing body shall fail

or refuse to exercise the power given herein, then the vacancies shall be filled as now provided by law.''

Section 3 authorizes the consolidation of two or more such institutions.

Complainants claim that section 2 of this act authorizes and empowers the General Conference of the Methodist Episcopal Church, South, at its option to elect the Board of Trust or fill vacancies therein of Vanderbilt University. The defendants upon several grounds deny this claim. They say that this act violates article 2, sec. 17, of the state constitution, which provides that ''no bill shall become a law which embraces more than one subject, that subject to be expressed in the title.''

They further say that the title to this act is so vague and indefinite that it does not express or indicate the subject, and that the act itself contains three distinct subjects, and hence is void. If this were an open question, the writer of this opinion would regard it as very serious, but in the case of *State ex rel. Dobson* v. *Washington & Tusculum College* (Mss., Knoxville, September Term, 1912), involving the validity or invalidity of an attempted consolidation of two incorporated educational institutions under section 3 of this act, the same attack was made on its constitutionality, and the court, by a majority opinion, sustained the act.

It is now said in argument that the case was decided on another question, rendering it unnecessary to pass on the validity of this act, but that the court did hold the title sufficient, and that the point that the act contained more than one subject was not raised, discussed, or passed upon, and therefore is yet an open question.

It is true that the case turned principally upon another question, but the decision of this question was not an improper or unnecessary one in the case. The discussion of this act in the opinion is rather meager, but the court states, not only the title, but also the substance, of the act. It says its constitutionality is attacked upon several grounds. It then refers particularly to the question raised on the title, and the subject expressed therein, and says: "The majority of the court is of the opinion that the caption of the statute in question does sufficiently express the subject of the legislation, and that therefore complainant's contention must be overruled. The authorities upon which the majority rest their decision on this subject are *State* v. *Yardley,* 95 Tenn., 516, 32 S. W., 481, 34 L. R. A. 656, *State* v. *Brown,* 103 Tenn., 450, 53 S. W., 727, *Furnace Company* v. *Railroad,* 113 Tenn., 728, 87 S. W., 1016, *Scott* v. *Marley,* 124 Tenn., 390, 137 S. W., 492, and other cases in these cited and referred to."

It is only fair to presume that both questions here made were there made by counsel in that case and considered by the court, although the second point is not particularly discussed by the court. The one almost necessarily involved the other. Then we think that if the title to this act is sufficient, as was distinctly held in that case, it is general enough to include all the provisions of this act. In *State* v. *Yardley,* supra, this court has said: "Generality of title is not objectionable, so long as it is not made to cover legislation incongruous in itself, or which by fair intendment may not be considered as having a necessary or proper connection with the subject expressed"—citing authorities.

We therefore think that this objection to the act is precluded by these authorities, and we overrule it.

Defendants also contend that this university does not come within the purview of this statute. That is to say, that it had not been established and was not being maintained and patronized by, or having been otherwise established, was not being maintained and patronized by, any religious society or denomination (particularly, the Methodist Episcopal Church, South), within the meaning of this act, at the time of its passage or thereafter, and particularly at the time the General Conference undertook to elect its trustees, and hence it was not subject to the operation of this act.

The most significant terms of this act are defined by the Standard Dictionary as follows:

"Establish"—"To settle or fix firmly; place on a permanent footing; settle securely, as in a business; found."

"Maintain"—"To support; to supply with means of support; provide for; sustain; keep up."

"Patronize"—"To act as a patron; extend patronage; lend countenance; encourage; favor."

"Patron"—"One who protects, countenances, or supports some person or thing; one who habitually extends material assistance; a regular customer; a protector or benefactor.''

At common law, as applied to charities such as universities, the patron was the founder, the endower.

''*Patronum faciunt dos, aedificatio, fundus* (Black's Law Dictionary); this is to say: Endowment, building, and land make a patron. So, in the leading case of *Phillips* v. *Bury,* 2 Term, R., 346, Lord Holt said: 'It is now admitted on all hands that the founder is patron.' ''

''And again, in the *Dartmouth College Case,* Judge Story said: ''The patron, or endower, is the perficient founder.''

From these various definitions, it will be seen that to establish, to maintain, to patronize, mean, in short, to found and support. Now, did the church establish—found—this University? We have already answered this in the negative.

Has it maintained and patronized it? In the sense of lending countenance, encouragement, and favor, and being a regular customer, it has undoubtedly patronized it. The university has drawn probably half or more of its students from Southern Methodists; but its doors have always been open to all, and many other denominations have in this sense patronized it. If this were sufficient, a number of denominations might set up similar claims under this statute. This is clearly not the maintenance and patronage contemplated by this act.

Has the Methodist Episcopal Church, South, then, maintained and patronized this institution in the more substantial way and legal meaning of said terms of providing the means of support, founding, endowing, sustaining?

To answer this question, let us again briefly review the facts. The original effort to raise by subscriptions from the conferences and churches and their members the endowment called for and required was an acknowledged failure. Altogether, from first to last, about a hundred thousand dollars of subscriptions, or promises, were had from these sources, of which about fifteen thousand dollars have been realized, and the whole has been devoted to the "sustentation fund," as hereinbefore explained. Outside of the Vanderbilt gifts and Nashville's contributions to the purchase of the campus, and about $23,000 from the same source for rebuilding after destruction by fire of some of the buildings, there has been received at various times from the church, churchmen, and all other cources, excepting tuition and fees of students, about $325,000 for specific purposes, such as endowing certain chairs or professorships, lecture courses, and scholarships, most or all in the theological department, and to enlarge that department, without, however, relieving to any extent the general endowment from allowances made therefrom to that department. Nothing from these sources has been realized and applied to the general endowment and support of the university in any of its other departments. Mr. Cornelius Vanderbilt gave the original endowment of a million dollars and other members of the family subsequently

added another million, partly to pay expenses, but
chiefly to add to the general endowment, and this endowment has provided the blood, bones, and sinews of
this body corporate, properly and justly called, after
his first gife, "Vanderbilt University."

It is now claimed that the church is entitled to credit
for these Vanderbilt gifts. The original endowment
was given by Mr. C. Vanderbilt through Bishop Mc-
Tyeire, without solicitation, to the corporation itself.
It was not given to or through the church. Mr. Vanderbilt was not a churchman. At the time of his gift he
must have been acquainted with the charter, including
the Memphis Resolutions and the by-laws of the University. He made his gifts to the corporation by its
corporate name.

In *Carson* v. *Carson*, 115 Tenn., 50, 88 S. W. 178, this
court has said: "The devise and bequest being made
direct to a corporation which is charitable, the trusts
need not be set out so specifically and definitely as if
made to individuals, in order to make them valid. The
reason is that a corporation organized for charitable
purposes has these purposes and trusts set out in its
charter and articles of foundation, so that the trusts
are thus made certain and will control; due deference
being paid to the directions of the testator, if any are
given. But no trusts in such case need be declared, as
they are set out in the charter and articles of foundation. To illustrate: If a bequest be made to the Vanderbilt University, or Cumberland University, by name,
the trust to which the fund is to be applied need not be

further specified by the grantor, since these are well-known charitable corporations, whose objects, purposes and trusts are fully set forth in their charters and other instruments of foundation.''

Hence, subject to the particular conditions imposed by him in his deed of gift, his endowment was impressed by the trusts specified in the charter and by-laws of this institution. He knew that the Board of Trust claimed, and in fact had, the right of selfperpetuation by electing its own members, subject however, to the condition imposed by the by-laws in pursuance of the Memphis Resolutions, to the effect that the conferences co-operating with the university should have a fair representation in its management, to wit, on its Board of Trust, and doubtless relied upon that fact for the proper administration and application of the endowment so provided, subject, of course, to such other legal conditions as he imposed in his deed of gift. The same is doubtless true of the subsequent gifts by other members of his family.

Upon these facts, we hold that the church cannot properly lay claim to the Vanderbilt gifts as coming from it.

From the time of these gifts until this present controversy arose, and the report of the Vanderbilt Commission was made, not only the university and its Board of Trust, but the church at large, its bishops, conferences, and members, recognized Mr. Vanderbilt as the founder, the patron, of this institution. His birthday was early declared to be Founder's Day, and was ever afterwards celebrated as such. The present claim that the church was the founder first took form, if it did not originate, with the report of the Vanderbilt Commission. We repeat our holding that Mr. Vanderbilt, and not the church, was the true founder and patron of this university, and now further hold that he and his family, by their endowments, have maintained and patronized this institution in the true and proper sense and meaning of those terms, and that therefore this university does not come within the purview and operation of this statute.

There are yet other reasons to support this view. It must be remembered, as we have heretofore held, that this Board of Trust are not only the directors or trustees of this corporation, but also the incorporators themselves. By their charter and the code (section 1471, hereinbefore quoted) they are authorized as members of the corporation to fix the number of trustees, the officers, etc., and under this authority they might have fixed the number of trustees or directors at less than their whole body, but not less than the minimum number required by statute (at present, not less than 5 nor more than 33—Acts 1889, ch., 181; Shannon's Code, sec. 2520); but, as their whole body did not exceed the maximum allowed by law, they all chose to act as directors or trustees. This, however, cannot affect their character as incorporators, nor can they be deprived of any of their rights as such by dealing with them as directors or trustees. This act deals only with the election of directors or trustees, and not members of the corporation.

It was not intended to apply to corporations like this, but rather to such as are organized under Acts 1875, ch. 142, sec. 2 (or similiar acts), which provides: "If said corporation is organized as a literary or educational institution, under the patronage of any Christian or Jewish denomination, the corporation shall have the power to increase the number of directors or trustees; to regulate the mode and manner of appointments of the same, on expiration of terms of service; to regulate the number, duties and manner of election of officers, either actual or *ex officio*; to appoint executive agencies, and to pass all other by-laws, for the government of said institution as may be required by the denomination establishing the same: Provided, said by-laws are not inconsistent with the Constitution and laws of this State."

Such was the case of *Southwestern Presbyterian University* v. *Presbyterian Synods of Tennessee*, decided by this court at Nashville March 31, 1905, referred to by complainants as authority for their contentions in this case. In that case the university was chartered under the last act mentioned, and as an institution under the patronage of the Presbyterian Church in the United States, and in pursuance to a certain plan of union entered into by certain synods of that church for the purpose of establishing, maintaining, and patronizing said university. This court, in its decree, decided "that the said university is under the patronage of the Presbyterian Church in the United States, and that in this relation of patronage the state synods of Tennessee, Mississippi, Louisiana, and Alabama act for said church, and for it and in such capacity have the right to elect each two directors of the said university corporation, according to the plan of union adopted by the synods originally co-operating in the establishing of said Southwestern Presbyterian University, which provided in substance that the government of the university shall be in the hands of the directorate, consisting of two members from each synod, one elected each year after the first, and that therefore the trustees or directors of the said university have no power or authority to select their successors and perpetuate the said board, regardless of the will and desire of the said synods as hereinbefore stated, and that the trustees and directors are rightfully to be selected or chosen in accordance with the customs and by-laws of said university adopted in pursuance of said plan of union, and in practice before the 21st of June, 1904, when this bill was filed.''

The case seemed to turn more upon the construction of the charter and the plan of union upon which it was based than upon this act of 1895 in question; but the decision might well be supported by that act. The case, however, is not controlling, or, indeed, applicable to the facts in the case at bar. This case at bar would be quite different if the university were chartered under the act of 1875, or if, as contended by complainants' counsel, its charter could be construed so as to make

the annual conferences in the first instance, and afterwards the General Conference as their sole assignee
and successor, the incorporators of this institution, and
the Board of Trust merely its directors or trustees.
In that event, however, as is well said by defendants'
counsel, they would have no need to appeal to the act
of 1895 for authority to elect members of the board of
directors or trustees.   They would already have that
power, as did the synods in the *Southwestern Presbyterian University Case,* by virtue of their charter. This
case is more like that of *State ex rel. Duncan* v. *Martin
Female College,* decided by this court at Nashville
February 25, 1888, referred to by both parties as
authority for their respective contentions. In that case
it appears that the testator, Thomas Martin, in 1870
had bequeathed a fund "to the officers of the Methodist Episcopal Church, South, established in the town
of Pulaski," to be used "for the purchasing of grounds
and erecting suitable buildings for a female school."
The officers of the local church met and accepted the
bequest, and in conformity with the procedure prescribed by the Code of 1858, elected trustees to procure
a charter, and a charter was accordingly procured. The
charter, among other provisions, contained the following:

"Item 3. The trustees herein named shall hold their
offices   until   their   places   become   vacant   by   death,
resignation, or removal from the county, or removal
by the board for cause, and any vacancy occurring shall
be filled by the board at a regular meeting from nomina-

tions made by the officers of the said Methodist Episcopal Church, South, established at Pulaski; that is to
say, by the present officers and their successors of the
Methodist Episcopal Church, South, now established
at Pulaski, and by whom the present trustees were
elected.''

The insistence of the bill in that case was that this
church was under the control of the quarterly conference and of the Tennessee Annual Conference, and that
this school was for that reason under the same control,
but that the charter as taken out had denied this right.
It also appears that for many years the school was
regularly reported to the Tennessee Conference as a
church school and an endowed institution belonging
to the conference, and its president was ''appointed'';
that is to say, being a minister of that conference, was
assigned by the conference to that position. The issue
for decision in the case was whether this school corporation was under the control of the church, or,
rather, the Tennessee Annual Conference representing
the church, as an ecclesiastical body. The court decided and decreed ''That there is nothing in the will
of Thomas Martin, or in the charter of Martin Female
College, or in the resolutions of the officers of the
Methodist Episcopal Church, South, at Pulaski, invoking and putting said charter into existence, which
requires or contemplates that the female school founded
thereunder should be under the dominion, control, or
direction of the Methodist Episcopal Church, South,
through its annual or quarterly conference, or other-

wise, or under the dominion, control, or direction of any religious denomination or sect whatever; that it was not the object of Thomas Martin by his will to place the school founded thereby under the control of the local officers of the Methodist Episcopal Church, South, at Pulaski, as a church organization and in a church capacity; but said officers were designated as a body of individuals who were to inaugurate such school in conformity with the will of said Thomas Martin by invoking and putting on foot a corporate organization with the proper founding, establishment, and subsequent control and management of said school, which they did in the incorporation of Martin Female College, · and that the charter of said college is in conformity with said will and not in conflict with same.'' See the citation of this case in *Johnson* v. *Johnson*, 92 Tenn., 567, 23 S. W. 114, 22 L. R. A. 179, 36 Am. St. Rep. 104.

This case appears to be authority for the following propositions: That the local officers of the Methodist Episcopal Church, South, at Pulaski, not as a church organization or in a church capacity, but as a body of individuals, were members of this corporation by virtue of their charter and the provisions of the Code under which it was granted, and as such were entitled to name the trustees or directors of the corporation; that the charter proceedings, although had under the Code provisions, which expressly allowed representative incorporation, incorporated them as natural persons, and not the church of which they were officers; and that the court, in order to determine the purpose and plan of government of the charity, will look to the articles of foundation.

Our view of this matter, to wit, that this statute does not apply to this particular corporation, is reinforced by the common understanding and conduct of all the parties. Notwithstanding the fact that this act was passed in 1895, yet the annual conferences co-operating with the university up to 1898 made no claim of right or power under this statute to elect members of the Board of Trust of Vanderbilt University. In 1898, in the memorial addressed by the Board of Trust to the General Conference, it was said: "By the charter of the ·university the Board of Trust is vested with the power and obligation to fill its own vacancies; but the election of any member is not valid under the law of the university until said member has been confirmed by the conference which he is designed to represent. Under the new plan the board would be at liberty to select its members without geographical restrictions of any kind, and the General Conference would confirm or reject the appointment."

In accepting the proposal of the university through this memorial, the General Conference resolved "that the General Conference of the M. E. Church, South, hereby accepts the proposed relation and control of the Vanderbilt University, and commits to the General Board of Education the confirmation of all trustees selected by the Board of Trust of Vanderbilt University." It asserted at that time no claim of right under the act in question to elect these trustees. and at no time subsequent, until after this controversy arose and the Vanderbilt Commission had made its report. Here were twelve years of acquiescence in the former relation existing between the university and the conference, and thereby an acknowledgment and tacit admission that this university did not fall within the provisions of this act of 1895. In fact, at the time this controversy culminated in the election by the General Conference of three members of the board upon the assertion of its exclusive right to do so, this action appears to have been taken, not from a dissatisfaction with the former relation existing between the General Conference and the university, but merely to force and test the issue as to its exclusive right to elect members of the board, for at the same time it adopted a resolution to the effect "that following this election the General Conference will for the future continue the method of choosing the trustees adopted by the General Conference held at Baltimore in 1898, when it committed to the General Board of Education the confirmation of all trustees [elected] by the Board of Trust of Vanderbilt University." This rather indicates that the real quarrel or controversy between these parties was not in fact upon this issue.

Other objections are made by the defendants to this act of 1895, but in the view which we have taken of this case it is not necessary to take further notice thereof.

From the foregoing conclusions, it results that in the opinion of this court the relations maintained by the university with the annual conferences from its birth to 1898, and afterwards with the General Conference to 1910, were their proper and legal relations under the charter and by-laws of the university and its contracts and agreements with the conferences, and that the General Conference in 1910, when it undertook to elect members of the Board of Trust, was not acting within its rights, and its appointees are not entitled to seats in that board; that the action of the Board of Trust in rescinding its existing by-law and electing members independently of the General Conference was likewise unauthorized, except upon the assumption that the General Conference had surrendered its relation of co-operation with and representation in the Board of Trust. We think that the General Conference did not mean to do this, or to abandon any part or right it had in the management of the university, but was asserting a right to more than it was entitled to.

"If one party to the contract claims, as contract rights, thereunder, more than he is given by the contract, such claim does not, of itself, amount to a renunciation of the contract." 3 Page on Contract, sec. 1439, and cases cited. Of course, at any time, if it should voluntarily surrender or renounce this relation. or contumaciously refuse to confirm members elected, and cease to co-operate with the university, its rights to representation in its Board of Trustees, and in its management, would, as a consequence, cease; and, in that event, the Board of Trust could proceed, independently of the General Conference, to the election of members, to fill vacancies in its own body.

We are further of opinion that the inherent power of the Board of Trust to fill vacancies in its own body authorizes it to elect and install members to fill such vacancies and that such new members are entitled to their seats on the board ad interim, until such time as they may be rejected by the General Conference, or its General Board of Education, acting for it and under its authority. It has the right to keep its membership full, and cannot legally divest itself of that power and duty, except conditionally upon the refusal of the General Conference to confirm its appointees. The rejection of such member, or members, by the General Conference would at once create a vacancy to be again filled by the board, subject to the like condition.

We therefore conclude that the relators, Messrs. Harris, Godbey, and Biggs, are not entitled to membership in the Board of Trust; that the defendants, Waller, Robbins, and Jackson, are entitled to such membership, subject to the action of the General Conference, or its General Board of Education, to whom it has committed the duty of confirming, or rejecting, the members elected by the board; and that they are entitled to act as such members, until such time as they may be rejected by that conference or board. Since their election has not been so rejected, they cannot be ousted under this proceeding from their seats in the Board of Trust. It results, therefore, that the chancellor's decree will be reversed, and the complainants' bill will be dismissed, at their costs.

Let decree be drawn accordingly.

LANSDEN, J. I concur in the result reached, but I do not concur in all of the reasoning of the opinion.

MITCHELL *et al. v.* DENNY *et al.*

(*Nashville.*   December Term, 1913.)

1. HOMESTEAD. Conveyance between spouses. .

A conveyance by a husband to his wife of an undivided one-third
interest of land owned by him when he was married, and in
which he had a homestead right after marriage, did not de-
story the wife's right of homestead in the entire tract. (*Post,*
p. 368.)

Code cited and construed: Sec. 3798 (S.).

Constitution cited and construed: 1870, art. 11, sec 11.

Cases cited and approved: Avans v. Everett, 71 Tenn., 77; J. I.
Case Co. v. Joyce, 89 Tenn., 337; Adcock v. Adcock, 104 Tenn.,
154.

Case cited and distinguished: Hicks v. Pepper, 60 Tenn., 44.

2. HOMESTEAD.   Land subject.

A homestead does not attach to undivided interests in land. (*Post,*
p. 370.)

3. HOMESTEAD.   Floating right of homestead.

If the value of land owned by the husband at his marriage exceeded $1,000, the wife's homestead right therein was a mere
floating right; but if its value did not exceed that sum, she had
a vested right of homestead therein.   (*Post, p.* 371.)

4. HOMESTEAD.   Conveyance.   Joint deed.

Under Const., art. 11 sec. 11, providing that the homestead property shall not be alienated without the joint consent of husband
and wife, and Shannon's Code, sec. 3798, containing substantially the same provision, homestead property can only be
conveyed by the joint deed of husband and wife, whether the
homestead be vested or a mere floating right.   (*Post, p.* 371.)

Mitchell v. Denny.

Code cited and construed: Sec. 3798 (S.).

Constitution cited and construed: 1870, art. 11, sec. 11.

Cases cited and approved: Briscoe v. Vaughn 103 Tenn., 314; Hall v. Fulgham, 86 Tenn., 451; Cox v. Keathley, 99 Tenn., 523.

Case cited and distinguished: Beeler v. Nance, 126 Tenn., 592.

FROM PUTNAM.

Appeal from the Chancery court of Putnam county to the Court of Civil Appeals, and by *certiorari* from the Court of Civil Appeals to the Supreme Court.— A. H. ROBERTS, Judge.

B. G. ADCOCK, for plaintiffs.

O. K. HOLLADAY, and JOHN TUCKER, for defendants.

MR. JUSTICE BUCHANAN delivered the opinion of the Court.

The bill was filed by complainants, as heirs at law of Isaac M. Scudder, and sought to sell a certain tract of land comprising about seventy acres for partition. Jack Denny and wife, Edna Denny, were made defendants, and along with them certain of the heirs at law of Scudder, who had conveyed their respective interests in the land to Alcorn, who in turn had conveyed to Jack Denny. Alcorn was also made a defendant, and so were certain minor heirs at law of Scudder; these heirs being his children by defendant Edna Denny, who was his wife at the time of his death, and who married defendant Denny some four years after the death of Scudder.

The bill was met by an answer and cross-bill filed by Denny and wife, and by answer on behalf of the other defendants. Proof was taken, and on final decree complainants appealed to the court of civil appeals, where the decree of the chancellor was affirmed. The case is before us on the complainants' petition for *ceritorari*.

The chancellor and court of civil appeals decreed that Edna Denny was entitled to a homestead interest in the land. That holding is here assailed, and is the main question in the case. The point made against this decree is that, some years prior to the death of Scudder, and in consideration of the sum of about $350 advanced by her to Scudder to enable him to pay off an incumbrance on the land, and under which it was about to be sold, he conveyed to Edna Denny, then his wife, an undivided one-third interest in this land by a deed of general warranty, executed in due form and delivered to her for record. This deed was never recorded, and was lost or mislaid, but was under proper pleadings and proof in this cause set up and established by the decree of the chancellor; and it is insisted for complainants that this deed created between this husband and wife the relationship of tenants in common in the ownership of this land, and wrought a destruction of her right to a homestead in the entire tract.

It is clear from the proof that at the time the deed was made and prior thereto the husband and wife resided on the land as a homesead, and that neither of them owned any other land, and they lived on this land from the date of that deed until his death, and from that time until the date of the decree she continued to reside upon it with her three minor children, whom she had supported and cared for after his death. Her present husband, Denny, owns no land except that interest in the land in suit acquired by the deed from Alcorn as heretofore stated.

We will now proceed to examine the question made. Article 11, sec. 11, of the constitution of 1870, provides that: "A homestead in the possession of each head of a family and the improvements thereon, to the value of one thousand dollars, shall be exempt from sale under legal process during the life of such head of a family, to inure to the benefit of the widow, and shall be exempt during the minority of their children occupying the same, nor shall said property be alienated without the joint consent of husband and wife, when that relation exists. This exemption shall not operate against public taxes, nor debts contracted for purchase money of said homestead, or improvements thereon." This section of the constitution is in substance embodied in section 3798, Shannon's Code, with the addition: "And shall be exempt from sale in any way at the instance of any creditor or creditors. Said real estate may be sold by the joint consent of husband and wife, where that relation exists, to be evidenced by conveyance duly executed as required by law for married women."

It has been said by this court that "the controlling object of the constitutional provision is to protect the possession or occupancy of the homestead, the home of the family, from legal process, or from alienation of the husband without his wife's consent during the life of the husband, and while this relation exists, and after his death during the life of the widow, and upon her death to the minor children of the deceased husband, and until the youngest child reaches the age of twenty-one years." *Hicks* v. *Pepper*, 60 Tenn. (1 Baxt.), 44.

It is true that in the above case it was held that after the death of the husband and father the homestead right was abandoned and lost by a removal of the widow with her minor son to the state of Kentucky with no intention to return and occupy the homestead in this state. Such, however, are not the facts of this case. But the insistence of complainants is mainly rested upon three of our cases. These are *Avans* v. *Everett*, 71 Tenn. (3 Lea), 77, *J. I. Case Co.* v. *Joyce*, 89 Tenn. (5 Pickle), 337, 16 S. W. 147, 12 L. R. A. 519, and *Adcock* v. *Adcock*, 104 Tenn. (20 Pickle), 154, 56 S. W. 844.

The doctrine of the two former cases, as interpreted in *Adcock* v. *Adcock*, was "that homestead does not attach to undivided interests in land." Now, accepting this as the settled rule, the question is: Does it apply to the facts of this case? Suppose we grant that, if the tract of land in question had been in the first instance conveyed to the husband and wife as tenants in common, the homestead right would not have attached, for the reasons stated in *Avans* v. *Everett,* supra, and in *Case Co.* v. *Joyce,* supra, does it follow that right did not attach in this case, where the land was in the first instance not conveyed to husband and wife, as tenants in common, but was conveyed to the husband alone? There would seem to be a sound distinction here. When the husband and wife were married, the land was his property; he owned it, was in possession of it, and it was the only land he did own. He was the head of the family, and, as against his creditors, beyond all question he had a homestead right either vested in or hovering over the land from the date of his marriage to the date of the deed, by which he conveyed an undivided one-third interest in the land to his wife. It is also clear that from the date of the marriage to the date of the deed, the wife had a homestead right hovering over or vested in the land. Now, whether this homestead right was a vested estate in the land or a mere floating right in an unassigned homestead depended on the value of the land. If its value was in excess of $1,000, the right was a floating one; if its value was not in excess of $1,000, then under our cases the right was a vested one. See *Beeler* v. *Nance,* 126 Tenn. (18 Cates), 592, 150 S. W. 797, and cases cited. But, as said in that case, whether the right "be a mere floating right in an unassigned homestead, or such right as under our cases has arisen to the dignity of an estate for life in the specific tract of land by reason of facts which the law will treat as an assignment of homestead in that tract," it is clear that it

"can only be conveyed by the joint deed of husband
and wife when that relation exists." Section 11, art.
11, Const. 1870; section 3798, Shannon's Code; *Cox* v.
Keathley, 99 Tenn., 523, 42 S. W. 437.

It is not claimed that the homestead right of this
husband and wife was ever divested out of either of
them by their joint deed. The husband exercised the
right until his death, which occurred many years after
the date of his conveyance to the wife of the undivided
one-third interest in the land. But the argument is
that the legal effect of that deed was to cut off the
homestead right. Well! why should that be? Certainly such a result was not dreamed of by the parties to
the deed; nothing in the deed indicates such a purpose.
The whole conduct of the parties indicates a contrary
purpose; that is to say, no right was ever asserted
under the deed hostile to the homestead right. The
deed cannot be regarded as a waiver or abandonment
of the homestead right, because a material element in
either of those acts would be the intent to waive or
abandon, and such intent nowhere appears. So, upon
the whole, we think the deed must be held as matter
of law to have been made subject to the homestead
right; and from this it would follow that the execution
of the deed had no effect upon the homestead right.
The husband could not convey that right without the
joinder of the wife in the conveyance in the manner
required by the statute. The rule that "homestead
does not attach to undivided interests in land" is not
effective to destroy such a right, which became fixed in

or upon, or was hovering over, a specific tract of land at the time the owners of it became tenants in common. For to permit the deed to have that effect would be either to say that the deed which created the tenancy in common operated to convey the homestead right, or that it operated as a waiver or abandonment of that right, neither of which, as we have seen, would be a correct view of the legal effect of that deed. The true view is that the homestead right here claimed did not attach to a tract of land held by tenants in common after the execution of the deed from the husband to the wife, but, on the contrary, that the right antedated the deed and was in no wise affected by the execution of that instrument. This view is in harmony with the reasoning of the opinion in *Briscoe* v. *Vaughn*, 103 Tenn. (19 Pick.), 314, 52 S. W. 1068; *Hall* v. *Fulgham*, 86 Tenn. (2 Pickle), 451, 7 S. W. 121, and in fact, we think with all our cases.

We find no error in the decree of the chancellor or the court of civil appeals, and therefore the decree of the latter court is affirmed.

CUMBERLAND TELEPHONE & TELEGRAPH CO. *v.* PEACHER
MILL CO.

(*Nashville.* December Term, 1913.)

1. **EVIDENCE. Subjects of expert testimony. Matter directly in issue.**

In an action by a mill company for damages from the burning of its storehouse and the stock therein, on the theory that lightning struck the telephone line of the defendant about three-quarters of a mile from the storehouse, and that the current of electricity followed the wire into the building in which a telephone was installed, causing the ignition, and alleging defendant's negligence in failing to have ground connections and appliances near the point of the wire's entrance into the building to arrest such a current, in which the defendant claimed that the building was directly struck by lightning without the intervention of its wire as a conductor, the answer of plaintiff's expert that, assuming that the hypothesized fact were true, the fire was probably due to the lightning discharged from the wire, was inadmissible as an opinion on the ultimate fact to be determined, invading the province of the jury. (*Post, p.* 376.)

2. **EVIDENCE. Subject of expert testimony. Negligence.**

Though there are exceptions, an expert witness may not give an opinion as to what is imprudent or negligent, by way of exception to the general rule that experts may not testify in the form of an opinion as to an ultimate fact to be determined by the jury. (*Post, p.* 376.)

Cases cited and approved: Bruce v. Beall, 99 Tenn., 303; Camp v. Ristine, 101 Tenn., 534; Pointer v. Klamath, etc., Co., 28 Ann. Cas., 1077; Castner v. Davis, 154 Fed., 938; Crane Co. v. Construction Co., 73 Fed., 984; Goddard v. Enzler, 222 Ill., 471; Keefe v. Armour, 258 Ill., 28; State v. Hyde, 234 Mo.

200; Sever v. Minneapolis, etc., R. Co. (Iowa), 137 N. W., 937; Lacas v. Detroit, etc., R. Co., 92 Mich., 112; Maitland v. Gilbert Paper Co., 97 Wis., 476; Hamann v. Milwaukee Bridge Co., 127 Wis., 550.

3. **EVIDENCE. Subjects of expert testimony. Cause and effect.** Where the cause of an existing condition or injury is in dispute, and where the jury must determine which of the causes urged by the respective parties is the right one, an expert opinion is generally admissible to the effect that a certain cause could or might produce the condition. (*Post, p.* 381.)

FROM MONTGOMERY.

Error to Circuit Court, Montgomery County.—W. L. Cook, Judge.

J. M. Anderson, for plaintiff in error.

H. N. Leech, for defendant in error.

Mr. Justice Williams delivered the opinion of the Court.

This is an action by the Mill Company against the Telephone Company to recover damages for the alleged negligent burning of the Mill Company's store-house and the stock of merchandise contained therein. The suit has been twice before tried; the first trial resulting in a failure of the jury to agree on a verdict, the second resulting in a verdict for the Telephone Company, and the last in a verdict in favor of the Mill Company, on which the court rendered judgment. An appeal was prayed to the court of civil appeals, and that court affirmed the judgment of the lower court.

The sole assignment of error to be here treated of relates to the admission of the testimony of an expert witness, Prof. Daniel, who holds the chair of physics in Vanderbilt University.

The declaration and the Mill Company's proof went on the theory that a stroke of lightning struck the line of telephone wire and a pole of the Telephone Company, about three-fourths of a mile distant from the store-house, and that the current of electricity followed the line of wire into the building, in which a telephone was installed, causing the ignition and destruction of the storehouse. The negligence averred was in the failure of the Telephone Company to have ground connections and appliances near the point of the wire's entrance into the building, for the purpose of arresting such a current.

A warmly contested question of fact was whether a current so brought in over the wires could or did so arc as to reach the point in the basement of the building where the fire originated; and the Telephone Company's contention, further, was that the building was struck immediately by lightning, without the intervention of its wire as a conductor.

Prof. Daniel was introduced as a witness in behalf of the plaintiff below, and, after qualifying as an expert, was asked a question, the first part of which was framed in hypothetical form, but which terminated as follows: "Taking that state of facts, and assuming them to be true, state whether it was probable or not that the fire was the result of lightning coming in on that wire? Ans. Then the question is: Was that fire probably due to the lightning discharged from this wire? I say it was." Objection was interposed, on the ground that the question called for a determination of a question that was for the jury, and was an attempt to invade the domain of the jury by an expert witness.

The trial judge overruled the exception, and the court of civil appeals has affirmed that ruling.

The Telephone Company insists that the case of *Bruce* v. *Beall,* 99 Tenn., 303, 41 S. W., 445, is conclusive of the question in its favor. We do not conceive that the court in that case passed directly upon the point thus raised in the present case. In that cited case an expert witness was permitted to testify that it was not prudent to operate an elevator with wire cables, under conditions described, longer than six or seven years; and the court held that the witness, thus testifying to what was not prudent, virtually pronounced upon the culpable negligence of the defendant sued, and that this was tantamount to determining an issue the jury was sworn to try, and for that reason was incompetent.

It is true that Mr. Justice Beard in the opinion used broadly the expression: "We think it clear that in no case can the witness be allowed to give an opinion upon the very issue involved. To permit this would be to substitute the opinion of the expert for that of the jury, whose duty it is to find the facts.''

In the later case of *Camp* v. *Ristine*, 101 Tenn., 534, 47 S. W., 1098, the same able judge had occasion to qualify the broad statement just quoted, and to show that there are exceptions to the rule that experts may not testify in the form of opinion as to an ultimate fact to be determined by the jury. In the later case the opinion of a physician was held admissible as to the value of the professional service of a physician—a fact to be found by the jury. This by way of exception to the general rule.

There are exceptions to the rule which grow out of necessity or compelling convenience. It is argued by counsel for appellee, and was held by the court of civil appeals, that there is here presented such an exception.

Bruce v. *Beall*, supra, in establishing that an expert may not give an opinion as to what is imprudent or negligent, by way of exception to the general rule, is in accord with the decided weight of authority on that point in other jurisdictions. *Pointer* v. *Klamath, etc., Co.*, 28 Ann. Cas., 1076, note.

The court of civil appeals in its opinion said: ''This question, in view of some of the holdings of our supreme court, especially *Bruce* v. *Beall*, has given us much concern. We are of the opinion, however, that when properly understood no error was committed. It is true that the jury was called upon to determine the cause or origin of the fire; but, as pointed out in the numerous cases brought to our attention by counsel of appellee (*Transportation Line* v. *Hope*, 95 U. S., 297, 24 L. Ed., 477; *Texas, etc., C. R.* v. *Watson*, 190 U. S., 291 [23 Sup. Ct., 681], 47 L. Ed. 1059; *Gila Valley, etc. R. Co.* v. *Lyon*, 203 U. S. 465 [27 Sup. Ct., 145], 51 L. Ed., 276; *Goddard* v. *Enzler*, 222 Ill., 462 [78 N. E. 805]), the ultimate fact was the negligence of the plaintiff in error in not installing or using devices or appliances. It will be noticed that this distinction was not observed by Judge Beard in *Bruce* v. *Beall*, supra.   Hence it should not be construed as conclusive authority upon this point.''

Bruce v. *Beall* does not lack conclusiveness for the reason assigned by the court of civil appeals. That case, along with the majority of cases in other jurisdictions, runs counter to the doctrine announced by the supreme court of the United States in the cases cited by the court of civil appeals in the above excerpt, and is not to be held inconclusive on the point it does immediately treat.

Bruce v. *Beall*, supra, however, did not deal with the admissibility of experts on the point of showing that a certain effect was produced by a certain cause, where that matter is a contested one. No case decided by the supreme court of the United States has gone to the extent of holding that expert evidence as to causation is admissible. The rule in the federal courts appears, rather, to be in accord with appellant's contention: *Castner* v. *Davis*, 154 Fed., 938, 83 C. C. A.,

510; *Crane Co.* v. *Construction Co.*, 73 Fed., 984, 20 C. C. A., 233.

The supreme court of Illinois, instead of supporting such a doctrine, has declared to the contrary in several recent cases.

In *Illinois, etc., R. Co.* v. *Smith*, 208 Ill., 608, 617, 70 N. E., 628, 631 it was said: "The appellee has referred to a number of decisions of this court, . . . and of the courts of last resort in other states, which, it is insisted, sustain the position that the opinion evidence above referred to is competent. An examination of those cases discloses the fact that they, generally, are cases where physicians have been allowed to express an opinion as to what might have caused the injury the cause of which was being investigated, but none of them, so far as we have been able to discover, sustain a course of examination which calls for an opinion from the expert as to the cause of the injury, and they all recognize the fact that the question of what did cause the injury is a question of fact for the jury, and not for the witness." The later cases of *Goddard* v. *Enzler*, 222 Ill., 471, 78 N. E., 805, and *Keefe* v. *Armour*, 258 Ill., 28, 34, 101 N. E., 252, are in accord.

In *Martin* v. *Light Co.*, 131 Iowa, 724, 739, 106 N. W., 359, 364, the rule is well declared: "It was the theory of the defendant that Bass was not killed by an electric shock, but died from heart disease or other natural cause. A witness on the stand was asked by plaintiff's counsel the following question: 'You may state, Mr. Spry, from your knowledge of electrical laws, and from the machinery there, and from what you saw, what is your opinion as to whether or not Bass received an electric shock before he fell?' Defendant's objection to the competency of the testimony was overruled, and the witness answered: 'My opinion is that he did.' We think the objection to the question should have been sustained. It is an accepted rule that, while experts may testify as to what in their opinion may or may not have been the cause of a given result or conditions, it is not permissible for them to give their opinion as to the ultimate fact which the jury was organized to determine. . . . The question now under consideration required the witness to enter the domain of the jury and pass upon one of the ultimate propositions inhering in the verdict." See, also, *State v. Hyde,* 234 Mo., 200, 136 S. W., 316, 25 Ann. Cas., 191; *Sever v. Minneapolis, etc., R. Co.* (Iowa), 137 N. W., 937, 44 L. R. A. (N. S.), 1200; *Lacas v. Detroit, etc., R. Co.,* 92 Mich., 412, 52 N. W., 745; Rogers, Expert Testimony (2d Ed.), 128.

Courts holding to the contrary of *Bruce* v. *Beall,* on the point of the establishing by experts of imprudence or lack of due care, hold against the admissibility of such evidence in establishing what is the producing cause. For example: *Maitland* v. *Gilbert Paper Co.,* 97 Wis., 476, 72 N. W., 1124, 65 Am. St. Rep., 137; *Hamann* v. *Milwaukee Bridge Co.,* 127 Wis., 550, 106 N. W., 1081, 7 Ann. Cas. 458.

Generally speaking and without stopping to define exceptions, it may be said that where the cause of an existing condition or injury is in dispute, and where the jury must determine which of the causes urged by the respective parties is the right one, an expert's opinion may be admitted to the effect that a certain cause could or might produce the condition; but to permit him to testify as to what in his opinion probably did it would be to supplant the jury by the witness. In this case the jury might well have concluded that the testimony of Prof. Daniel, admitted by the trial judge over objection, imposed on it a peculiar deference to the expert's opinion as to the true cause of the conflagration.

For this error, the judgment of the court of civil appeals is reversed, with remand for a new trial.

STATE EX REL. HULL *v.* RIMMER.

(*Nashville.*   December Term, 1913.)

1. **RAPE. Assault with intent to rape. Female under age of consent. Statutory provisions.**

   In view of the history of the legislation which makes a distinction between carnal knowledge of a female forcibly and against her will, which is rape, and carnal knowledge of a female under the age of consent, where the character of the act is not affected by the consent of the female, Shannon's Code, sec. 6459, making any person who assaults a female with intent, forcibly and against her will, to have carnal knowledge of her, punishable by imprisonment for not less than ten years nor more than twenty-one years, applies only to assaults upon females over the age of consent, while Shannon's Code, sec. 6471, imposing a different punishment upon one who assaults another with intent to commit any felony, etc., where the punishment is not otherwise prescribed, applies to assaults with intent to have carnal knowledge to a female under the age of consent. (*Post, p.* 385.)

   Acts cited and construed: Acts 1829, ch. 23; Acts 1871, ch. 56; Acts 1879, ch. 63.

   Code cited and construed: Secs. 6451, 6459, 6471 (S); secs. 4614, 4615, 4630 (M. & V. and 1858).

   Cases cited and approved: Murphy v. State, 47 Tenn., 516; Mayfield v. State, 101 Tenn., 673; Fitts v. State, 102 Tenn., 141; Wright v. State, 23 Tenn., 196; Wyatt v. State, 32 Tenn., 394; Brown v. State, 65 Tenn., 424.

2. **RAPE. Statutory rape. Repeal.**

   Code 1858, sec. 4614, later codified as Shannon's Code, sec. 6455, made punishable any person who should carnally know and abuse a female under the age of ten years. It was amended

by Act 1871, ch. 56, as to the punishment, and again amended
by Act 1879, ch. 63, so as to read that any person who should
assault a female under the age of ten years with intent to
carnally know her should be punishable as in the case of
rape. Act 1893, ch. 129, amended section 4614 as amended in
1871 so as to change the age to twelve years, and re-enacted
it as amended, but made no reference to the act of 1879, and
did not incorporate its provisions. *Held*, that the amendment
by the act of 1879, which was an addition to, and not a substitution for, section 4614, was repealed by the amending
act of 1893. (*Post*, p. 391.)

Acts cited and construed: Acts 1871, ch. 56; Acts 1893, ch. 129.

Code cited and construed: Sec. 6458 (S.); sec. 4614 (M. & V.
and 1858).

FROM DAVIDSON.

Appeal from the Criminal Court of Davidson county
to the Court of Civil Appeals, and by *certorari* from the
Court of Civil Appeals to the Supreme Court.—
A. B. NEIL, Judge.

JOHN T. ALLEN, and LYTTON TAYLOR, for plaintiff.

F. M. THOMPSON, attorney-general, for defendant.

MR. JUSTICE BUCHANAN delivered the opinion of the
Court.

The controlling question in this case is which of two
sections of Shannon's Code declared the offense and

fixed the punishment for a crime charged against John Carter by indictment at the November term of the circuit court of Henry county, for the year 1911, upon which he was tried and convicted by a jury at the November term, 1912.

Upon Carter's appeal therefrom, the judgment based on the above conviction was affirmed by us at our April term, at Jackson, in 1913, and Carter was committed to the penitentiary to serve out the term of four years imposed by the verdict of the jury. In August, 1913, this *habeas corpus* proceeding was set on foot against the warden, Rimmer, drawing into question the legality of the imprisonment of Carter under the judgments aforesaid; the insistence being that, on the face of the record, he is entitled to be discharged from custody. This insistence was denied by Judge Neil, of the criminal court of Davidson county, and, on appeal from his judgment, by the court of civil appeals, and is now before us on petition for *certiorari*.

The statutes in question are: First, section 6459 of Shannon's Code. The history of the legislation culminating in this statute may be traced in detail by examination of Acts of 1829, ch. 23, sec. 53; Section 4615, Code of 1858; and Acts of 1871, ch. 56, sec. 3. It is sufficient to say that this legislation is correctly codified in the section of Shannon's Code above mentioned; and, as there found, it reads: "Any person guilty of committing an assault and battery upon any female with an intent, forcibly and against her will to have carnal knowledge of her, shall, on conviction be imprisoned in the penitentiary not less than ten nor more than twenty-one years.''

The second statute in question is section 6471 of Shannon's Code, reading as follows: ''If any person assault another with intent to commit, or otherwise attempt to commit, any felony or crime punishable by imprisonment in the penitentiary, where the punishment is not otherwise prescribed, he shall, on conviction, be punished by imprisonment in the penitentiary not exceeding five years, or by imprisonment in the county jail not more than one year and by fine not exceeding five hundred dollars, at the discretion of the jury.''

This section is an exact reproduction of section 4630 of the Code of 1858.

Now, petitioner insists that Carter was indicted, tried, and convicted under section 6459 of Shannon's Code, and, assuming this hypothesis to be correct, he maintains that the verdict of the jury, and all of the judgments thereon depending, are illegal and void, because he says the lowest measure of imprisonment which could have been inflicted under section 6459, Shannon's Code, was ten years, and therefore there resided no power in the jury, by its verdict, to impose a term of four years' imprisonment upon him and no power in any court to enforce by its judgment or sentence such unauthorized verdict of the jury, upon which point he cites as authority our cases: *Murphy v. State*, 47 Tenn., (7 Cold.), 516; *Mayfield v. State*, 101

Tenn. (17 Pickle), 673, 49 S. W., 742; and *Fitts* v. *State,* 102 Tenn. (18 Pickle), 141, 50 S. W., 756.

It will not become necessary for us to consider the point last mentioned, and the cases cited above to support it, if we reach the conclusion that the primary insistence is unsound. In the outset, it is well to note that, as early in our legislation as the act of 1829, a distinction was taken between unlawful carnal knowledge of a female under the age of ten years and such an act committed upon one over that age. By the terms of the statute, to constitute the offense of rape, as defined in the thirteenth section, twenty-third chaper, Acts of 1829, the carnal knowledge must have been had forcibly and against the will of a woman. By the fifteenth section of the same act, there are no words used to indicate that will or consent on the part of a female under ten years of age would affect the character of the act. One of these offenses the statute names, rape; the other it does not so name.

In respect of the distinction above pointed out, our statutes are closely analogous to Westminster II, ch. 34, and 18 Eliz., ch. 7, referred to by Mr. Blackstone (book 4, ch. 15, p. 212), where he speaks of what he calls the offense of "forcible rape," and another offense which he speaks of as "the abominable wickedness of carnally knowing and abusing any woman child under the age of ten years," in which case, he says: "The consent or nonconsent is immaterial, as by reason of her tender years she is incapable of judgment and discretion."

Another distinction between rape and unlawful carnal knowledge of a female under the age of ten years noticeable in the statutes above named is that force is a necessary element in the crime of rape, but not so in the other crime. This distinction is apparent in the language of the act by which each offense is defined: "Rape is the unlawful carnal knowledge of a woman, forcibly and against her will." See section 13, ch. 23, Acts 1829; section 6451, Shan. Code. But the other crime is thus defined: "Any person who shall unlawfully and carnally know and abuse a female under the age of ten years, shall, on conviction, be punished as in case of rape." See section 15, ch. 23, Acts 1829; section 4614, Code 1858.

The two distinctions above pointed out are recognized in our cases. See *Wright* v. *State,* 23 Tenn. (4 Humph.), 196; *Wyatt* v. *State,* 32 Tenn. (2 Swan), 293; *Brown* v. *State,* 65 Tenn. (6 Baxt.), 424.

Following the distinctions above indicated, this court, in a case where the indictment charged an assault and battery, with intent to commit rape upon a female child four years old, said the only question presented was whether the facts constituted the offense created by section 4615 of the Code of 1858. This section in that Code is the same, in substance, as section 6459 of Shannon's Code, which is the section under which petitioner insists Carter was charged and convicted. But the court in that case said: "Yet we are of opinion that this section has reference only to cases where, if the intent was carried out, the offense would be rape.

That would not be so if the female was under ten.''
And in that case, the judgment of conviction was reversed. See *Rhodes* v. *State*, 41 Tenn. (1 Cold.), 352.

In another case, where the indictment charged the
same offense as in the case last cited, and the age of
the female was five years, and there was a conviction,
the judgment based on a verdict of guilty was reversed,
for the reason that the circuit judge told the jury that
the section 4615, Code 1858, applied to the facts of
that case; in other words, this court in that case held
clearly and expressly against the insistence of petitioner in the present case. See *Brown* v. *State,* 65
Tenn. (6 Baxt.), 422. And the holding in that case
goes even further than we have indicated, for it is an
express holding in favor of the insistence of the State
in the present case, which is, in brief, that, when properly construed, the words ''any female,'' used in section 4615, Code 1858, section 6459, Shan. Code, do not
include or refer to a female who is under the age of
consent, or, as put by Mr. Blackstone, who is, ''by reason of her tender years, incapable of judgment and
discretion,'' but do include and refer only to any female
above that tender and indiscreet age fixed by the law
as the boundary line between subjects of the crime of
rape and the other and more heinous crime, to wit,
carnal knowledge of a child in whom the law recognizes
no capacity to will or consent, or to resist force. The
court in that case pointed out that, in the description
of the crime intended to be committed, the indictment
used the words which define rape, where the intent

must be to have carnal knowledge of the female forcibly
and against her will, and adds: "This would not be
necessary to create the offense perpetrated on a female under ten." By the above quotation, the court
did not mean that rape could be committed on a female
under ten; it only meant to say that in such case it
would not be necessary to show that the carnal knowledge was accomplished by force, or that it was done
against the will of the female. The court then proceeds
to say that it did not follow from its view "that there
was no provision made in the Code for the punishment of the offense of which the proof" seemed to show
that defendant was guilty (and then the opinion sets
out the substance of section 6030 of the Code of 1858,
which we have already set out herein, which is now
section 6471 of Shan. Code, and is the section under
which the state insists that Carter was indicted, tried,
and convicted); and the opinion in that case then proceeds: "The proof in the case would tend to show
that defendant was guilty of an assault with intent to
commit the offense described in section 4614, for attempting to commit which offense the punishment is not
otherwise prescribed."

Thus we have in the last paragraph of that opinion
a clear determination of the precise point on which
this case turns, a clear adjudication that the state's
insistence in this case is correct, and a foreclosure of
further controversy. At the time the indictment against
Carter was found, the only change which had been
made in section 4614 of the Code of 1858 appears, by

section 6455 of Shannon's Code, to be the substitution of the word "twelve" for the word "ten," as indicating the age of the female; and, as already stated, section 6030 in the Code of 1858 appears word for word as section 6471 of Shannon's Code. It was true when the *Brown Case,* supra, was decided, when the indictment was returned and tried in that case, and it was also true when Carter was indicted, tried, and convicted in this case, that there was a statute denouncing as guilty of a felony punishable by imprisonment in the penitentiary any person who should unlawfully know and carnally abuse a female under the age of 10 years at the time of the *Brown Case,* under the age of 12 years at the time of the *Carter Case.* But there was no statute at the time of either event which prescribed the punishment for an assault upon such a female with the intent to commit such an offense, and the absence of such a statute *ipso facto* brought into operation in each case the same statute, numbered 6030 in the Code of 1858, and numbered 6471 in Shannon's Code.

It is urged, on behalf of Carter, that a suggestion was made in *Hill* v. *State,* 73 Tenn. (5 Lea), 725, to the effect that chapter 63 of the Acts of 1879, was intended to be an amendment of section 4614 of that Code. Such a suggestion was made in that case *arguendo,* but the point was not decided, and we think the suggestion was clearly refuted by the plain terms of the amending act.

Our attention has been called to section 6458 of Shannon's Code. This statute became a part of our legislation in a clumsy effort to amend section 4614 of the

Code of 1858 at a time when the age of the female
stood in section 4614 at ten years, and no doubt, the
purpose was to add to that section of the Code what
now appears as section 6458 of Shannon's Code; but
the act of 1879 as passed, omitting the enacting and
concluding clause was as follows: "That section 4614
of the Code be so amended as to read, that any person
who shall commit an assault and battery upon a female,
under the age of ten years, with intent to unlawfully
and carnally know her shall, on conviction, be punished as in case of rape." But, for the manifest purpose to add the quotation above to the section 4614 of
the Code, the language of the act would convey the
meaning that a substitution was intended. That question is, however, immaterial in the light of subsequent
legislation, which was chapter 129 of the Acts of 1893,
which, omitting the enacting clause, so far as material
reads: "That section 5365 of Milliken & Vertrees
Compilation of the Laws of Tennessee, the same being.
section 4614 of the Code, as amended by chapter 56
of the Acts of 1871, be, and the same is hereby, amended
so as to read as follows: 'Any person who shall unlawfully and carnally know and abuse a female under
the age of twelve years shall, on conviction, be punished
as in case of rape.'" Then follows other provisions
of this act not material to the present subject.

Thus it becomes apparent that the act of 1879 took
no note of the act of 1871, and the act of 1893 paid no
heed to the act of 1879. Now the act of 1871 (see sections 1 and 2) amended section 4614 of the Code of

1858 in respect of the punishment to be inflicted, the details of which need not be discussed. In this state of the legislation, a prudent codifier may well have followed the course pursued by Mr. Shannon in carrying into his Code the section 6458, but nevertheless we think the act of 1893 repealed the act of 1879, and that section 6458 of Shannon's Code was not an existing statute in 1896, when that compilation occurred, and has not been such since the act of 1893. Manifestly the legislature could not have intended the act of 1879, fixing the age of discretion at 10 years, and the act of 1893, fixing that age at 12 years, to stand together. The two cannot coexist by reason of their repugnancy.

We think there was no error in the judgment of the court of civil appeals, and it is affirmed at the cost of petitioner.

PUTNAM COUNTY v. SMITH COUNTY.

(*Nashville.*   December Term, 1913.)

1. **ESTOPPEL. Persons estopped. Municipal corporations.**

The doctrine of estoppel due to laches and acquiescence is applicable, in certain cases, to a county, as a *quasi* municipal corporation. (*Post, p.* 396.)

Acts cited and construed: Acts 1870, ch. 84; Acts 1873, ch. 66; Acts 1877, ch. 115; Acts 1881, ch. 142; Acts 1883, ch. 99.

Cases cited and approved: County of Boone v. Railroad, 139 U. S., 684; Louisville v. Cumberland Tel. Co., 224 U. S., 649; McMillan v. Hannah, 106 Tenn., 689.

2. **COUNTIES. Boundaries. Estoppel by conduct.**

A county which acquiesces for twenty years, the common law period of prescription, in the detachment of a part of its territory, so as to reduce its territory to less than 500 square miles in area, contrary to Const. 1870, art. 10, sec. 4, will be estopped by laches from maintaining a suit to recover the detached territory. (*Post, p.* 397.)

3. **COUNTIES. Division of territory. Taxes.**

A county suing to recover territory which had been detached from it and added to another county by unconstitutional statutes was entitled to recover taxes collected by such other county, after the original bill was filed in the suit, on lands affected by the unconstitutional statutes. (*Post, p.* 397.)

Cases cited and approved: McMillan v. Hannah, 106 Tenn., 689; Cheatham County v. Dickson County (Ch. App.), 39 S. W., 734.

FROM PUTNAM.

Appeal from Chancery Court, Putnam County.—
A. H. ROBERTS, Judge.

ALGOOD & FINLEY, W. BRYANT, and O. K. HOLLADAY, and E. H. BOYD, and LON EDWARDS, for plaintiff.

J. N. FISHER and L. A. LIGON, for defendant.

MR. JUSTICE WILLIAMS delivered the opinion of the Court.

The complainant, Putnam county, filed its bill attacking Acts 1905, ch. 370, Acts 1897, ch. 148, and Acts 1895, ch. 98, as unconstitutional on the ground that each attempted to effect a deduction of territory from complainant county and to add the same to Smith county, whereas, it is alleged Putnam county had at the dates of passage less than 500 square miles of area; the constitutional provision invoked being article 10, sec. 4, of the Constitution of 1870, which stipulates: "Nor shall such old county be reduced to less than five hundred square miles."

Complainant county also sought to collect from Smith county the taxes for county purposes collected by the latter which were assessed upon the lands attempted to be detached by the several acts.

Later an amended bill was filed which incorporated a like attack on the following acts, by which it was attempted to detach further lands from Putnam county, and to attach same to Smith county. Acts 1883, ch. 99; Acts 1881, ch. 142; Acts 1877, ch. 115; Acts 1873, ch. 66; and Acts 1870, ch. 84.

The county of Smith defended by answer on grounds: (1) That Putnam county had not, in point of fact, been reduced below the constitutional area; (2) gross laches and long acquiescence estopping complainant county. The chancellor decreed in favor of complainant, Putnam county, as to the territory involved, but allowed no recovery of taxes against Smith county. Both counties have appealed and assigned errors.

The question of fact as to the reduction of the area of Putnam county below the constitutional standard is by us resolved against Smith county, with result that the detachment acts are to be treated as unconstitutional.

. This leaves for determination whether that county may prevail on its second defense. Estoppel due to laches and acquiescence is applicable, in certain conditions, to a county, as a quasi municipal corporation. *County of Boone* v. *Railroad*, 139 U. S., 684, 11 Sup. Ct. 687, 35 L. Ed. 319; *Louisville* v. *Cumberland Tel. Co.*, 224 U. S., 649, 32 Sup. Ct., 572, 56 L. Ed., 934.

The doctrine has been applied in this State to a county which acquiesced for a long period in the attempted detachment from its area and jurisdiction of lands by void legislative acts, of the character of those involved in the present contest. *Roane County* v. *Anderson County*, 89 Tenn., 258, 266, 14 S. W., 1079, and cases therein cited.

We have for determination what period of time, during which there has been such acquiescence, will suffice to work an estoppel by reason of laches. In *McMillan* v. *Hannah*, 106 Tenn., 689, 61 S. W.. 1020, it was held that a complainant county would not be estopped by such quiescent course for a period of fourteen years; but a period of "about eighteen years" was held sufficient to work such estoppel in the case cited in *Roane County* v. *Anderson County,* supra.

It seems proper that, for the guidance of the profession and future contestants, we should define the period requisite to an estoppel of the nature indicated, having application to such a case. We are of the opinion that the common law period of prescription, twenty years, furnishes the best analogy, and that it would be a just standard to adopt. This we do.

It should be noted that we are not dealing with a question of boundary line location, in which class of cases other considerations may or may not appear, such as the concurrent, recurrent, or mixed exercise of jurisdiction by each county within the limits of the territory in dispute, or negotiations between the authorities for settlement of the controversy. Here, the county of Putnam acquiesced in the conditions apparently wrought by the five legislative acts, last referred to, as fully as if they had been valid acts.

The chancellor erred, also, in denying to complainant county the recovery of taxes collected by Smith county, after the original bill was filed, on lands affected by the legislative acts therein attacked. *McMillan* v. *Hannah,* supra; *Cheatham County* v. *Dickson County* (Ch. App.), 39 S. W., 734.

Modified, with decree here accordingly.

GRANT *et ux. v.* LOUISVILLE & NASHVILLE RAILWAY
COMPANY, *et al.* *

(*Nashville.* December Term, 1913.)

1. NUISANCE. Persons liable. Landowners.

An owner of real property is not responsible for a nuisance
erected thereon without his knowledge, actual or constructive,
and generally it must have been created by his authority.
(*Post, p.* 403.)

Case cited and approved: Railroad v. Cheatham, 118 Tenn., 160.

2. RAILROADS. Persons liable. Landowners.

Where parties, who had contracted with a railroad company to
construct an underpass beneath its tracks 100 or more feet
from the street, about 6 oclock in the morning placed a portable forge, which made much noise and emitted a good deal of
smoke, at a point near the street, and an accident, resulting
from a horse becoming frightened, occurred about four hours
later, before the railroad company or any person connected
with it had any knowledge of such location, the lapse of time
was insufficient to charge it with constructive notice. (*Post, p.*
404.)

Cases cited and approved: Skelton v. Fenton Electric Light, etc.,
Co., 100 Mich., 87; Moore v. Townsend, 76 Minn., 64; Gulf, etc.,
R. Co. v. Chenault, 31 Tex. Civ. App., 558.

Case cited and distinguished: Davis v. Lumber Co., 126 Tenn.,
584.

**3. MASTER AND SERVANT. Independent contractors. Nui-
sance.**

Where a railroad company employed an independent contractor

---

*As to the liability of an employer for nuisance committed
by independent contractor, see notes in 65 L. R. A., 751; and 66
L. R. A., 146, 948.

On the question of the power of the trial court to cure an
excessive verdict by requiring or permitting a renduction where
true measure of damages not ascertainable by mere computation,
see note in 39 L. R. A. (N. S.), 1064.

Grant v. Railroad.

to construct an underpass beneath its tracks 100 or more feet from the street, and the contractor placed a portable forge near the street on the railroad company's land, though not directed by the railroad company, which did not know thereof, to do so, and though the forge might have been, and ordinarily would have been, located near the work, the contractor alone, and not the railroad company, was liable for the damages resulting from a horse becoming frightened at such forge. (*Post, p.* 405.)

4. DAMAGES. Excessive damages. Reduction.

The power of the trial court to suggest a remittitur, in a case of tort involving unliquidated damages, may be exercised where the verdict is merely excessive, and is not limited to cases where passion, prejudice, or caprice on the part of the jury appears. (*Post, p.* 406.)

Cases cited and approved: Branch v. Bass, 37 Tenn., 366; Railroad v. Jones, 56 Tenn., 27; Young v. Cowden, 98 Tenn., 577; Massadillo v. Railway Co., 89 Tenn., 661; Northern Pacific R. R. Co. v. Herbert, 116 U. S., 642; Ark Cattle Co. v. Mann, 130 U. S., 73; Koenigsberger v. Richmond Silver Mine Co., 158 U. S., 53; Hayden v. Sewing Machine Co., 54 N. Y., 221; Doyle v. Dixon, 97 Mass., 218; Blunt v. Little, 3 Mason, 102; Burdict v. Mo. Pac. R. Co., 123 Mo., 221; Railroad v. Roberts, 113 Tenn., 488; Tunnell Hill, etc., Co. v. Cooper, 50 Colo., 390; Telegraph Co. v. Frith, 105 Tenn., 167; Moore v. Burchfield, 48 Tenn., 203; Nashville & Chattanooga R. Co. v. Smith, 53 Tenn., 174; Railroad v. Roddy, 85 Tenn., 400, Railroad v. Stacker, 86 Tenn., 343; Railroad v. Griffin, 92 Tenn., 649.

5. DAMAGES. Excessive damages. Reduction.

Though a verdict is so excessive as to indicate that it was influenced by passion, prejudice, or caprice, it may be cured, and will stand, if a remittitur is accepted by plaintiffs, and the verdict reduced to a reasonable amount. (*Post, p.* 408.)

Cases cited and approved: Railroad v. Roberts, 113 Tenn., 488; Railroad v. Roddy, 85 Tenn., 400.

Grant v. Railroad.

6. DAMAGES. Excessive damages. Reduction.
The trial judge, in an action for personal injuries, who saw
plaintiff and heard her injuries described, might infer passion,
prejudice, or caprice on the part of the jury from an excessive
verdict alone. (*Post*, p. 409.)

7. APPEAL AND ERROR. Review. Amount of damages.
Under Acts 1911, ch. 29, providing that, when the trial judge suggests a remittitur because of prejudice, partiality, or unaccountable caprice, plaintiff may accept the remittitur under
protest, and appeal, the supreme court will not ordinarily interfere with the decision of the trial court. approved by the court
of civil appeals, as to the amount of damages. (*Post*, p. 410.)
Acts cited and construed: Acts 1911, ch. 29.

FROM MAURY.

Appeal from the Circuit Court of Maury County,
to the Court of Civil Appeals, and by *certiorari* from
the Court of Civil Appeals to the Supreme Court.—
W. B. Turner, Judge.

Figuers, Holding & Garner, for plaintiffs.

Hughes & Hughes and E. H. & C. P. Hatcher, and
Thomas H. Malone, for defendants.

Mr. Justice Lansden delivered the opinion of the
Court.

This was an action for damages, brought by W. Y.
C. Grant and his wife, Mrs. Susie Grant, against the
Louisville & Nashville Railroad Company, the Nash-

ville, Chattanooga & St. Louis Railway Company, and W. N. McDonald and W. J. Thompson, partners doing business under the name of the Nashville Concrete Company.

McDonald was never served with process. A nonsuit was taken as to the Nashville, Chattanooga & St. Louis Railway Company, and upon the trial the court directed a verdict in favor of the Louisville & Nashville Railroad Company, and submitted the case to the jury as to W. J. Thompson, and the jury returned a verdict against Thompson for $3,500. The court suggested a remittitur of $1,500, which the plaintiffs accepted under protest.

The plaintiffs below appealed in error to the court of civil appeals, and in that court assigned as error the action of the trial judge in directing a verdict in favor of the railroad company, and also his action in suggesting a remittitur of $1,500. The court of civil appeals, in a majority opinion, approved the reduction of the verdict, but reversed the judgment of the court below in the matter of the directed verdict, and remanded the case for further proceedings against the railroad company.

Grant and wife have filed a petition for *certiorari*, in which they again challenge the propriety of the reduction of their verdict against Thompson. The railroad company has filed a petition for *certiorari*, in which it assigns as error the action of the court of civil appeals in reversing the judgment of the circuit

court embodying a directed verdict in its behalf. Both
of these petitions have been granted, and the case has
been fully argued in this court.

The Louisville & Nashville Railroad Company had
a contract with McDonald & Thompson, whereby the
latter firm was to construct an underpass beneath certain tracks of the railroad company near the city of
Columbia. The railroad company seems to have owned
a considerable plot of ground at this point, through
which its tracks ran. The proposed underpass was 100
or more feet from the street. The property of the
railroad company, however, it being vacant land, extended to the street. These contractors were engaged
in this work, and in connection with the work were using a portable forge, which made much noise and
emitted a good deal of smoke.

On the morning of the accident, the contractors had
located this forge at a point very near the street, and
a gentle horse, attached to a buggy driven by Mrs.
Grant, took fright at this object as she was passing,
ran away, and overturned the vehicle, inflicting upon
her the injuries on account of which this suit was
brought. This runaway occurred about 10 o'clock in
the morning. It appears that there was no necessity
for locating the forge at the particular point which it
occupied on this occasion. The proof shows that it
was put at this place on this morning for the first time,
and the railroad company had no notice that the forge
had been so located. There seems to have been no necessity for placing the forge so close to the street. It

might have been more conveniently operated nearer to the work, 100 feet away.

The defense urged in behalf of the railroad company is that McDonald & Thompson were independent contractors, and that the company is not liable for damages resulting from their negligence.

There is a great controversy in the case as to whether McDonald & Thompson were in fact and in law independent contractors in the prosecution of this work. The contract between them and the railroad company is set out in the record and has been the subject of much discussion. The circuit judge was of opinion that McDonald & Thompson were independent contractors. The court of civil appeals took the opposite view.

We think the circuit judge was correct. We are unable to distinguish the present case from the case of *Railroad* v. *Cheatham*, 118 Tenn., 160, 100 S. W., 902. The contract in this case and the one construed in *Railroad* v. *Cheatham* appear to be essentially the same. We have discussed this contract orally, and it is unnecessary to consider it in this opinion. Our comment would be but a repetition of what the court has previously said in *Railroad* v. *Cheatham,* supra.

It is nevertheless contended, on behalf of the plaintiffs below, that the railroad company owed a nondelegable duty to the public to see that its premises were kept free from any nuisance that would endanger persons traveling near by.

It is insisted that, inasmuch as this forge was located on the property of the railroad company, the company was liable, whether McDonald & Thompson were independent contractors or not.

We cannot agree to this contention on the facts of this case.

The bare fact that a person owns real property does not impose upon him responsibility for a nuisance erected thereon. 29 Cyc. 1203. The owner cannot be liable in respect to such a nuisance unless he has some knowledge of it, either actual or constructive. Generally, in fact, it must have been created by his authority.

The proof in this case shows that the forge was placed at this point near the street at 6 o'clock in the morning, and the accident occurred about four hours later. Neither the supervising engineer of the railroad, nor any other person connected with the company, seems to have had any knowledge of this location of the forge. The accident occurred within too short a time after the forge was placed there to justify an implication of constructive notice.

In those cases which hold the owner of property liable for damage caused by a nuisance created thereon by an independent contractor, it appears that the owner authorized the location of the nuisance at the particular place, had knowledge of its location, or the nuisance was a necessary incident of the work to be performed. *Skelton* v. *Fenton Electric Light, etc., Co.,* 100 Mich., 87, 58 N. W., 609; *Moore* v. *Townsend,* 76

Minn., 64, 78 N. W., 880; *Gulf, etc., R. Co.* v. *Chenault,* 31 Tex. Civ. App., 558, 72 S. W., 868.

This court has said in a recent case:

"It may be now generally stated as a correct proposition of law that an employer is not liable for an injury resulting from the performance of work given over by him to an independent contractor unless the work was unlawful in itself, or the injury was a necessary consequence of executing the work in the manner provided for in the contract, or subsequently prescribed by the employer, or was caused by the violation of some absolute nondelegable duty which the employer was bound at his peril to discharge, or was due to some specific act of negligence on the part of the employer himself." *Davis* v. *Lumber Co.,* 126 Tenn., 584, 150 S. W., 545.

This underpass might have been built in such a manner as not to have interfered with the traveling public. The portable forge might have been located, and ordinarily would have been located, at a point near the work itself, a considerable distance from the street. Its location was not directed by the railroad company, or known to it. The nuisance was not a necessary incident of the work to be performed, but resulted from the improper execution of it. In such cases the contractor is alone liable for damages resulting from the nuisance, unless knowledge of the existence of the nuisance can be charged to the employer. Ward on Nuisance (1st Ed.), 81; *Davis* v. *Lumber Company,* supra.

So we think the circuit judge properly directed a verdict in favor of the railroad company, and the court of civil appeals erroneously reversed this action.

The other question presented is on the remittitur suggested by the trial judge and accepted by the plaintiffs below under protest.

It is said in behalf of Mrs. Grant that her injuries were serious; that there was nothing to indicate that the jury were moved by passion, prejudice, or caprice in returning a verdict for $3,500; and that the court improperly suggested the remittitur of $1,500.

While the majority of the court of civil appeals affirmed this action of the trial court, the learned judge who delivered the opinion entered into an elaborate discussion of the subject of remittiturs, and vigorously assailed the course taken by the circuit judge. It is argued in that opinion, and in briefs of counsel for Mrs. Grant here, that the circuit judge merely substituted his judgment for that of the jury, without anything to justify him in saying that the jury were actuated by passion, prejudice, or caprice, and that such a practice violates the fundamental principles underlying the right of trial by jury and is without justification in law. It is urged that the trial court is without power to suggest a remittitur, in a case of tort involving unliquidated damages, unless it appears to him that the jury were moved by passion, prejudice, or caprice in fixing their verdict.

We cannot agree that the trial judge is without power to suggest a remittitur, unless there is an ap-

pearance of passion, prejudice, or caprice in the verdict of the jury. The power to suggest remittiturs
was long ago established in Tennessee, in cases of tort
involving unliquidated damages, as well as in other
cases. There is no intimation in our earlier decisions
that this power can be exercised only when passion,
prejudice, or caprice appears in the verdict of the
jury, nor is the right to suggest a remittitur restricted
to such cases in other jurisdictions. *Branch* v. *Bass,*
5 Sneed, 366; *Railroad* v. *Jones,* 9 Heisk., 27; *Young*
v. *Cowden,* 98 Tenn. 577, 40 S. W., 1088; *Massadillo*
v. *Railway Co.,* 89 Tenn., 661, 15 S. W., 445; *Northern
Pacific R. R. Co.* v. *Herbert,* 116 U. S., 642, 6 Sup. Ct.,
590, 29 L. Ed., 755; *Ark. Cattle Co.* v. *Mann,* 130 U. S.,
73, 9 Sup. Ct., 458, 32 L. Ed., 855; *Koenigsberger* v.
Richman Silver Mine Co., 158 U. S., 53, 15 Sup. Ct., 751,
39 L. Ed., 893; *Hayden* v. *Sewing Machine Co.,* 54 N.
Y., 221; *Doyle* v. *Dixon,* 97 Mass., 218, 93 Am. Dec.,
80; *Blunt* v. *Little* (Judge Story), 3 Mason, 102, Fed.·
Cas., No. 1,578; *Burdict* v. *Mo. Pacific R. Co.,* 123 Mo.,
221, 27 S. W., 453, 26 L. R. A., 384, 45 Am. St. Rep.,
528. See annotations; also see cases collected in notes
to *Railroad* v. *Roberts,* 113 Tenn., 488, 82 S. W., 314, 67
L. R. A., 495, 3 Ann. Cas., 937; *Tunnell Hill, etc., Co.*
v. *Cooper,* 50 Colo., 390, 115 Pac. 901, Ann. Cas., 1912C,
504; and note to last case in 39 L. R. A. (N. S.), 1064;
Sutherland on Damages, vol. 2, sec. 460.

Telegraph Co. v. *Frith,* 105 Tenn., 167, 58 S. W., 118,
was the first case in which this court distinctly held
that a verdict so excessive as to show passion, preju-

dice, caprice, or corruption might be cured by a remittitur. Prior to that time such verdicts were set
aside. *Moore* v. *Burchfield,* 1 Heisk., 203; *Nashville
& Chattanooga R. Co.* v. *Smith,* 6 Heisk., 174; *Railroad* v. *Roddy,* 85 Tenn., 400, 5 S. W., 286; *Railroad*
v. *Stacker,* 86 Tenn., 343, 6 S. W., 737, 6 Am. St. Rep.,
840; *Railroad* v. *Griffin,* 92 Tenn., 694, 22 S. W., 737.

The rule still prevailing in most jurisdictions is that
verdicts so excessive as to indicate they were the result of prejudice, passion, or caprice should be set
aside. It is said that in such cases the passion or
prejudice permeates the whole verdict, that none of it
should be allowed to stand, that parties are entitled
to a trial by a fair jury, and that verdicts appearing to
have resulted from improper motives should be rejected in toto. See notes to *Railroad* v. *Roberts,* 113
Tenn., 488, 82 S. W., 314, 67 L. R. A., 495, as reported
in 3 Ann. Cas., 937, and to *Tunnell Hill, etc., Co.* v.
Cooper, 50 Colo., 390, 115 Pac., 901, as reported in Ann.
Cas., 1912C, 504, and 39 L. R. A. (N. S.), 1064; also
see *Ark. Cattle Co.* v. *Mann,* 130 U. S., 73, 9 Sup. Ct.,
458, 32 L. Ed., 855.

Telegraph Co. v. *Frith,* supra, is referred to by Mr.
Sutherland, in his work on Damages (volume 2, sec.
460), as being an exceptional case, and it is said to
carry the doctrine of curing verdicts improperly influenced to a further extent than other courts have
gone.

The practice now, however, is firmly established in
Tennessee, and although a verdict is so excessive as

to indicate that it was influenced by passion, prejudice, or caprice, it may be cured, and will stand, if a remittitur is accepted by the plaintiffs, and the verdict reduced to a reasonable amount.

The case of *Railroad* v. *Roberts*, 113 Tenn., 488, 82 S. W., 314, 67 L. R. A., 495, 3 Ann. Cas., 937, merely announces the adoption of the practice of suggesting remittiturs in the appellate courts and holds that the appellate courts may cure an excessive verdict in the same manner as the trial courts do. The law, therefore, has long been settled in Tennessee that a remittitur might be suggested by the court in cases where the verdict was merely excessive. That a verdict due to passion and prejudice may also be saved by remittitur is the later doctrine. *Railroad* v. *Roddy*, 85 Tenn., 400, 5 S. W., 286, does not consider the question of remittitur at all, but deals with the duty of the court as to setting aside verdicts in toto.

In the present case, the trial judge found that the verdict was so excessive as to indicate passion, prejudice, or caprice, so that, even according to the view of the law taken by Mrs. Grant's counsel, the court was authorized to suggest a remittitur. It is said, however, that there was nothing to indicate passion, prejudice, or caprice on the part of the jury, that it was a body of fair-minded men, subjected to no improper influence, etc.

The deliberations of a jury are in secret, and no one can ordinarily know what considerations move them. The only evidence the court usually has of passion, prejudice, or caprice is the amount of the verdict. He is authorized to infer the existence of such improper influence from an excessive verdict alone. In this case, the trial judge, who saw the plaintiff and heard her injuries described, said that the verdict was so large as to indicate passion, prejudice, and caprice.

Under chapter 29 of the Acts of 1911, when a remittitur is suggested because the trial judge is of opinion a verdict is so excessive as to indicate passion, prejudice, corruption, partiality, or unaccountable caprice, the plaintiff below may accept the remittitur under protest, and appeal to the court of civil appeals. Mrs. Grant took this course, and the court of civil appeals sustained the trial judge.

This is not a proper case in which to undertake a general discussion of the scope and meaning of the Act of 1911. This remittitur was suggested because of passion and prejudice appearing to the circuit judge, and under the very terms of the statute plaintiff below was entitled to accept under protest and appeal. The court of civil appeals affirmed the lower court, and this action was likewise justified by the very terms of the statute.

It has been our practice in cases like this, when the trial court and the court of civil appeals have agreed on damages, to acquiesce in the amount so found. The concurrent finding of both lower courts on such a question should be well-nigh conclusive here. We see no reason to depart from our custom on this occasion, and the damages to which the two courts have agreed will be accepted.

Any further effort at interpretation of this statute in the case at bar would be beside the questions presented for our determination herein.

The circuit judge was correct in directing a verdict for the railroad company, and, in so far as the decree of the court of civil appeals reversed him, the decree of that court will be reversed; otherwise, the decree of the court of civil appeals will be affirmed.

Ward Seminary v. City Council.

WARD SEMINARY FOR YOUNG LADIES *v.* MAYOR AND CITY
COUNCIL OF NASHVILLE *et al.**

(*Nashville.*   December Term, 1913.)

**TAXATION. Exemptions. "Educational Institution". Property
used for educational purposes.**

Const. art 2, sec, 28, provides that all property shall be taxed,
but the Legislature may except such as may be held and used
for purely religious, charitable, scientific, literary, and educational purposes, etc. Acts 1907, c, 602, sec. 2, subsec. 2, exempts
all property belonging to any educational institution when used
exclusively for educational purposes, or is unimproved or yields
no income, but that all property belonging to such institution
used in secular business shall be taxed on its whole or partial
value in production as the same may be used in competition
with secular business. *Held* that the words "educational institution" should be construed to mean school, seminary, college,
or educational establishment, not necessarily a chartered institution, so as to limit the exemption to educational corporations, and that under such act all property, whether owned
by a corporation or a private individual, used exclusively for
educational purposes, without reference to whether a profit
was made therefrom or not, was exempt from taxation, but
vacant real property, used for no purpose connected with the
institution and property belonging to the institution, on which
stores were erected and rented for business purposes, was
subject to taxation.

(Williams J., dissenting.)

Acts cited and construed: Acts 1881, ch. 58; Acts 1883, ch.
105; Acts 1907, ch. 602;

Code cited and construed: Secs. 2199-2200 (S.).

---

*On the question of the effect of using the property of a relig-
ious, charitable, or educational institution in secular business or for
revenue, upon its right to exemption from taxation, see note in
19 L. R. A., 289.

Ward Seminary v. City Council.

Constitution cited and construed: Art. 2, sec. 28; Art. 11, secs. 8, 12.

Cases cited and approved: Mayor, etc., of Nashville v. Ward, 84 Tenn., 27; State v. Railroad, 124 Tenn., 16; State v. Fisk University, 87 Tenn., 241; University of the South v. Skidmore, 87 Tenn., 156; Methodist Episcopal Church, South, v. Hinton, 92 Tenn., 188; Vanderbilt University v. Cheney, 116 Tenn., 259; Governor v. Allen, 27 Tenn., 176; Polk v. Plummer, 21 Tenn., 500; Gerke v. Purcell, 25 Ohio St., 229; Nobles County v. Hamline University, 46 Minn., 316; Engstad v. County, 10 N. D. 54; Morris v. Lone Star Chapter, 68 Tex., 698; Academy v. Bohler, 80 Ga., 162; Kentucky, etc., School v. Louisville, 100 Ky., 486; Leagon Transportation Co. v. Detroit, 139 Mich., 1; Mobile v. Stonewall Ins. Co., 53 Ala., 581; Adams v. Yazoo, etc., R. Co., 77 Miss., 194; Wey v. Salt Lake City, 35 Utah, 504; State v. Johnston, 214 Mo., 656; New Haven v. Sheffield Scientific School, 59 Conn., 163; Webster City v. Wright County, 144 Iowa, 502; N. W. University v. People, 80 Ill., 333; Phillips Academy v. Andover, 175 Mass., 118; Detroit Home v. Detroit, 76 Mich., 521; Railroad Co. v. Harris, 99 Tenn., 684; Berryman v. Board of Trustees, 222 U. S., 334.

Cases cited and distinguished: State v. Fisk University, 87 Tenn., 233; Jackson v. Preston, 21 L. R. A. (N. S.), 165; Cemetery Co. v. Creath, 127 Tenn., 6861; Parsons Business College v. Kalamazoo, 166 Mich., 305; Dodge v. Williams, 46 Wis., 100.

FROM DAVIDSON

Appeal from Chancery Court, Davidson County.— JOHN ALLISON, Chancellor.

EWING & GARARD, and H. L. SCOTT, for appellants.

JAS. C. BRADFORD and R. T. SMITH, for appellee.

Mr. Justice Green delivered the opinion of the Court.

The complainant is a private corporation organized under the laws of Tennessee for the purpose of teaching any useful profession, trade, business, or art, and of giving instruction in any branch of learning, practical or theoretical. It was chartered under the provisions of chapter 58, sec. 3, of the Acts of 1881, Shannon's Code, secs. 2199-2200. It is a corporation organized for profit, and not an eleemosynary corporation, or corporation organized for general welfare.

Ward Seminary has for many years been conducted as a boarding school for girls, and has become quite a famous institution.

An attempt was made by the city of Nashville to tax its property within the limits of that city, and this bill was filed to enjoin the city from so doing. The complainant claimed to be exempt as an educational institution under a statute that will be hereafter noted. The chancellor rendered a decree in favor of the complainant, and the city of Nashville has appealed to this court.

The complainant owned, in addition to its school equipment, several pieces of real estate. Upon some of these were buildings used for dormitories and recitation rooms; some of the land was used for exercise and playgrounds; some was vacant and used for no purpose connected with the school, and upon some were stores rented out for business purposes.

The provisions of our constitution and of our statute regarding exemption of educational institutions from taxation are as follows: Article 2, section 28, of the constitution of the State contains this language:

"All property, real, personal or mixed, shall be taxed, but the legislature may except such as may be held by the State, by counties, cities or towns, and used exclusively for public or corporation purposes, and such as may be held and used for purposes purely religious, charitable, scientific, literary or educational, and shall except one thousand dollars' worth of personal property in the hands of each taxpayer, and the direct product of the soil in the hands of the producer, and his immediate vendee."

The act of 1907, ch. 602, sec. 2, subsec. 2, contains this exemption from taxation:

"All property belonging to any religious, charitable, scientific, or educational institutions when used exclusively for the purpose for which said institution was created, or is unimproved and yields no income. All property belonging to such institution used in secular business and competing with a like business that pays taxes to the State shall be taxed on its whole or partial value in proportion as the same may be used in competition with secular business."

The various revenue acts passed since the adoption of the constitution of 1870 are quite similar in the provisions they contain respecting the exemption of property used for religious, charitable, scientific, literary, and educational purposes.

We have only one reported case dealing with an effort to assess the property of educational institutions when that property was actually used for school purposes. This is the case of *Mayor, etc., of Nashville v. Ward,* 16 Lea, 27. In this case the court construed the acts of 1882 and 1883. The court held that the act of 1882 exempted from taxation property which belonged to private individuals, if used for educational purposes. It held, however, that the act of 1883 exempted such property only in case it belonged to incorporated institutions of learning, and did not exempt the same if it belonged to private individuals, although used for educational purposes.

The latter holding was based on the use of the word "institution" in the act of 1883; the exemption in that act being to property belonging to religious, charitable, scientific, literary, or educational institutions. The court said that the word "institution" meant a chartered institution, or a corporation, and that the exemption, therefore, did not include the property of individuals which might be used for educational purposes.

This construction cannot be adhered to. Such a construction exempts from taxation property belonging to corporations for profit, if used for educational purposes, but holds the property of individuals used for identical purposes liable for such taxes. If subsection 2 of section 2, Ch. 602, Acts of 1907, be so construed, it would be clearly unconstitutional. The court has recently considered the question of discrimination between individuals and private corporations in the case of *State* v. *Railroad*, 124 Tenn., 16, 135 S. W., 773, Ann. Cas., 1912D, 805, where the authorities are reviewed at length. As pointed out in *State* v. *Railroad*, there must be some natural and reasonable basis for discrimination in legislation between individuals and corporations. Such classification must have some natural and reasonable basis. No reason whatever has been suggested for a discrimination between an individual and a corporation for profit, both engaged in educational work, and any attempt of the legislature to make such a distinction as between the two in the matter of exemption from taxation would be invalid. This court, therefore, cannot suppose that the legislature had any such intention, unless the language used coerces this conclusion.

This question of arbitrary classification was not called to the attention of the court in *Mayor, etc., of Nashville* v. *Ward*, supra.

We are of opinion, therefore, that the above-quoted provisions of the act of 1907 exempt from taxation all the property of educational institutions, whether the property or the institution be owned by corporations or individuals if the property is exclusively used for educational purposes.

Such is the construction given like acts in most of the States. In a note to *Jackson* v. *Preston*, as reported in 21 L. R. A. (N. S.,) 165, the annotator says:

"In the majority of cases, legislative intent has been construed as including private schools within such terms as 'school,' 'educational institution,' 'seminary,' 'college,' or other similar term, whether such schools are conducted for profit to the owners, or because of charitable or religious considerations, and whether they are incorporated or not incorporated.'

A number of cases are collected in this note which fully sustain the quotation made.

It is not worth while to undertake a review of the cases from other jurisdictions, since at last the decision of this court must rest upon our own constitution, statutes, and public policy.

Our constitution of 1870, art. 11, sec. 12, says:

"Knowledge, learning and virtue, being essential to the preservation of republican institutions, and the diffusion of the opportunities and advantages of education throughout the different portions of the State being highly conducive to the promotion of this end, it shall be the duty of the general assembly in all future periods of this government, to cherish literature and science."

This court said in State v. Fisk University, 87 Tenn., 233, 10 S. W., 284, speaking of the foregoing section:

"And while it is true that this language is found in the section which treats of the common school fund, it is not confined to it, but is declaratory of the sense of the constitutional convention on the subject of education, and the duty of subsequent legislatures to cherish."

We think, therefore, in view of this constitutional admonition and the necessity of schools, that it was the intention of the legislature to exempt property used in educational work, whether such property was owned and such work conducted by individuals or corporations. We know of no one who has accumulated riches in educational endeavor. No abuse is likely to arise if the exemption be confined to property actually used in school work. School teachers have to live, and their property should not be denied exemption when employed in educational work merely because the owners of the property derive some profit from it. In the great majority of cases, this profit is meager, and not at all commensurate with the work done for the youth of our State and the consequent benefit to the whole body politic.

The natural construction of our constitution and revenue statutes is to exempt from taxation all property physically used for religious, charitable, and educational purposes, or actually occupied for such purposes. We think the words "educational institution" as used in the act of 1907 mean school, seminary, college, or educational establishment, not necessarily a chartered institution. If the word "institution" be interpreted as in *Mayor, etc., of Nashville* v. *Ward,* supra, this section of the act, as we have seen, would be unconstitutional, and it is our duty to give the act a construction that will save it. The exemption is to the owner of the institution, whether corporate or individual.

In regard to vacant property owned by the complainant and the property which complainant rents out, we are of opinion that such property is not exempt from taxation.

In *State* v. *Fisk University*, 87 Tenn., 241, 10 S. W., 284; *University of the South* v. *Skidmore*, 87 Tenn., 156, 9 S. W., 892, *Methodist Episcopal Church, South*, v. *Hinton*, 92 Tenn., 188, 21 S. W., 321, and *Vanderbilt University* v. *Cheney*, 116 Tenn., 259, 94 S. W., 90, it was held that certain income-bearing property and vacant property not actually used for religious, charitable, or educational purposes was exempt from taxation. These cases proceeded on the theory that, inasmuch as the profit derived from such property was applied exclusively to educational, charitable, and religious purposes, the property was entitled to immunity from taxation. In all these cases, however, the property belonged to eleemosynary corporations, or corporations for the general welfare.

A distinction was taken in the cases referred to between such property so held by such corporations and such property so held by individuals or corporations for profit. It was concluded that while certain property belonging to Vanderbilt University, the Methodist Church, Fisk University, and the University of the South was not physically employed in educational, religious, and charitable work, nevertheless, inasmuch as all the income arising from the property was so applied, and the ultimate use of the property was for such purposes, an exemption arose under our Constitution and statutes. Such a question is not presented in this case.

The complainant here is a corporation for profit. Its net earnings or ultimate gains go to its stockholders, not to educational, charitable, or religious ends. Therefore the only portion of its property which is entitled to immunity from taxation is that portion physically used and actually occupied in educational work.

The doctrine of *Methodist Episcopal Church, South,* v. *Hinton,* and of other cases above cited, was announced by divided courts, and has been subjected to criticism. It certainly will not be extended. It must be confined to the property of corporations organized for the general welfare.

That portion of the act of 1907, undertaking to exempt the property of educational institutions which "is unimproved and yields no income," must be held unconstitutional in so far as it applies to the property of such institutions operated by private corporations or individuals. There is no warrant in the constitution for such an exemption. The constitution authorizes the legislature to exempt property "used for purposes purely religious, charitable, scientific, literary or educational." Vacant property and property held merely as an investment by an institution, such as complainant, a corporation for profit, cannot be exempt. Neither the direct use of such property nor the ultimate use is for purely educational purposes.

It is suggested that the word "institution" in the act of 1907 should be construed to mean corporations organized for general welfare alone. It is urged that, so construed, the act would be constitutional; it being insisted that a discrimination and distinction between an eleemosynary corporation on the one hand and a private corporation or individual on the other rests on a sound basis.

This contention is plausible, but such an interpretation of the act would subject to taxation all school property in the State owned by corporations for profit. Such property has been considered exempt for thirty years, since the decision of this court in *Mayor, etc., of Nashville* v. *Ward*, supra. On the faith of this case, thousands upon thousands of dollars have been invested in school property in Tennessee, held and operated by private corporations. Scarcely a state in the South compares with Tennessee in the number, efficiency, and value of educational institutions so owned. Such institutions have thus been fostered and built up, and it has been the policy of our State to encourage them. It would be disastrous for the court at this time to reverse the attitude of the State and to adopt a construction of our revenue statute that would subject such institutions to taxation on the property physically used and actually employed in educational work.

Although recognizing the force of the contention made by learned counsel for the city, we are unwilling to adopt such a construction of the Revenue Act as he urges. If a different policy along these lines is to be inaugurated in Tennessee, the legislature should adopt it and not the courts.

The result of the whole case is that we hold the property of the complainant which is in reality used in educational work, such as the school buildings, dormitories, exercise grounds and the usual and appropriate equipment of this character of institution, to be exempt from taxation. All of its property which is vacant, and all of its property which is rented out, is liable for taxation.

Thus modified, the decree of the chancellor will be affirmed, and the costs will be divided between the city and the complainant in the proportion that the property held exempt bears to the property held subject to taxation.

MR. JUSTICE WILLIAMS delivered a dissenting opinion.

In this cause a bill in equity was filed by complainant corporation to enjoin the collection by the city of Nashville of municipal taxes levied for the year 1910 upon certain of its property in that city, on the ground that the property was, under the constitution of the State and the applicable statute, exempt from taxation. A cross-bill was filed by the city to enforce the lien claimed to have been fixed by the levy.

The facts were agreed upon in the form of a stipulation, and such as are pertinent to the present determination are as follows:

(1) Ward's Seminary is a Tennessee corporation, organized by virtue of and under the provisions of

chapter 58, section 3, of the Acts of 1881, carried into Shannon's Code, at sections 2199 and 2200. It was chartered on April 27, 1888, for the purpose of teaching "any useful profession, trade, business or art, and of giving instruction in any branch of learning, practical or theoretical." It conducts a school or seminary for girls and young women and has been engaged in this business ever since its incorporation, including the year 1910.

(2) When first organized, the Seminary's capital stock was $20,000, but on the 15th day of August, 1906, it was increased to $40,000. All of its stock has not yet been issued, but such as has been issued is held by the following parties in the following amounts: J. D. Blanton, 239 shares; Eustice A. Hall, 122 shares; W. E. Ward, 1 share; R. T. Smith, 1 share, M. G. Buckner, 1 share; and J. Harry Howe, 1 share.

(3) Complainant has never earned in the conduct of its business enough money to more than conduct and carry on its school, and has never paid or undertaken to pay any dividends or profits to its stockholders. It has, however, the legal right to declare dividends whenever the profits justify such action on the part of its board of directors.

(4) The total market value of complainant's property is $240,520; total amount of indebtedness, $105,000; net value of property, real and personal, $135,520; authorized capital stock, $40,000; stock issued, $36,500.

(5) All of property set forth in the stipulation, except such as was vacant and unimproved, was physic-

ally used during the year 1910 exclusively in connection with the operations of the Seminary, and it was used for no other purpose; and all of said property, except that noted above, was, during the year 1910, and is now, exclusively used for the purpose of its business. No actual use for educational purposes is made of the excepted property.

(6) Ward's Seminary is not supported by public taxes; tuition fees are charged, all of which are devoted to maintaining said school anl paying its necessary expenses; it maintains no free scholarships; its patrons are drawn from nearly every State in the Union and some from foreign countries.

The errors assigned by the city, as appellant, may be reduced to four in number:

(1) The court erred in holding that the complainant was an educational institution under the meaning of the Revenue Acts of the State and under the State constitution.

(2) The court erred in holding that section 2, subsection 2, of the Revenue Act of 1907, chapter 602, was constitutional, in the following particulars, to wit: In that it exempted all property belonging to any educational institution when used exclusively for the purpose for which said institution was created or is unimproved and yields no income, for the reason that this statute in this particular discriminates oppressively, unreasonably, and unfairly against private individuals, and only seeks to exempt the property of corporations, although used for the same purpose.

(3) The court erred in sustaining so much of section 2, subsection 2, Revenue Act of 1907, chapter 602, as exempted unimproved property that yields no income. This part of said act is, it is insisted, unconstitutional and void, in that it goes beyond the exemption allowed by the State constitution, art. 2, sec. 28.

(4) The court erred in sustaining complainant's bill and dismissing the cross-bill of the city, and in refusing to decree in its behalf for the collection of the taxes assessed against complainant. The constitution of this State (1870) in article 2, sec. 28, provides:

"All property real, personal or mixed, shall be taxed, but the legislature may except . . . such as may be held . . . and used for purposes purely religious, charitable, scientific, literary or educational. . . . All property shall be taxed according to its value, that value to be ascertained in such manner as the legislature shall direct, so that taxes shall be equal and uniform throughout the State. No one species of property from which a tax may be collected, shall be taxed higher than any other species of property of the same value."

Article 11, sec. 8, of the same constitution provides:

"The legislature shall have no power . . . to pass any law . . . granting to any individual or individuals, rights, privileges, immunitie [immunities] or exemptions other than such as may be, by the same law extended to any member of the community, who may be able to bring himself within the provisions of such law."

The act of the legislature under which complainant Seminary claims exemption from taxation is the Revenue Act of 1907, ch. 602, sec. 2, subsec. 2, as follows:

"Section 1. That all property—real, personal and mixed shall be assessed for taxation for State, county, and municipal purposes, except such as is declared exempt in the next section.

"Sec. 2. That the property herein énumerated and none other shall be exempt from taxation. . . .

"Subsec. 2. All property, etc., belonging to any religious, charitable, scientific, or educational institutions when used exclusively for the purpose for which said institution was created, or is unimproved and yields no income. All property belonging to such institution used in secular business and competing with a like business that pays taxes to the State shall be taxed on its whole or partial value in proportion as. the same may be used in competition with secular business."

It is conceded by counsel of the Seminary and of the city that the provision of the constitution (article 2, sec. 28) is not a self-executing provision exempting property from taxation, and is permissive and not mandatory on the legislature.

When the constitutional convention met in 1870, they found that, as the result of the waste of the war between the States and of the depression incident to the period of reconstruction following the war, the educational interests of the State were in a deplorable condition. The public school fund had been dissipated; there was scarcely a college the doors of which had

not been closed, some never to be opened again; and
the public school system had been swept away, and the
sources of support had, practically speaking, dried
up. A feeble and abortive effort had been made by the
legislature in 1867 to re-establish the State's system
of public schools, but this act had been repealed in
1870. The convention, therefore, wisely decided to
provide for immunity from taxation in behalf of. property "held and used for purposes purely educational,"
and as wisely left this provision elastic, so that the
legislature could make the immunity broad so long as
it might deem the true policy of the State to be one of
encouraging individuals and private and public bodies
to aid the sovereign power in educating its citizenship;
and also so that the legislature might narrow the scope
of the immunity of exemption as the need of the
State's efforts being supplemented grew less.

It is not to be doubted that, under this constitutional
provision for tax exemption or property held and used
for purposes purely educational, it is within the power
of the legislature to grant the immunity to the property of individuals, and of created institutions, corporate or noncorporate in form. *Nashville* v. *Ward,*
16 Lea, 27, 34.

A further point was involved for decision in the
case of *Nashville* v. *Ward,* supra, that an individual
(W. E. Ward, then the owner of the Seminary now
belonging to complainant corporation) was not within
the purview of Act 1883, ch. 105, sec. 2, subsec. 2,
which provided for exemption from taxation of "all

property belonging to any religious, charitable, scientific, literary or educational *institution*, and actually
used for the purpose for which such *institution was
created*," the court holding that such individual was
not an "institution . . . created." That was, it
is conceived, the sole queston there decided, so far
as the questions raised in the present case are concerned.

The complainant Seminary bases, on language used
by Chief Justice Deaderick in the opinion in that case,
its contention that it was there further held that, in
order to the exemption, the claimant need only be an
institution in the sense of a corporation, created by
the legislature, and that, since complainant is such
a corporation, it is entitled to claim immunity in this
case under Act 1907, ch. 602, quoted above, in which
the phraseology is somewhat similar to that found in
Act 1883, ch. 105, and identical as to the words "institution created."

It is true that Chief Justice Deaderick, in *Nashville
v. Ward*, said that the word "institution," fairly construed, meant one created by act of incorporation, but
it is evident that what was thus said did not bear
upon and had no necessary relation to the point the
court there had before it for decision, as is noted above.

That able jurist used this language, more by way
of illustration than of application, and as if to say:
An "institution" cannot be an individual but must
have inhering in its foundation the element of permanency, such as bodies created by acts of incorporation.

The unfairness of imputing more to the language so used becomes the more apparent when we consider that, if it was there meant to be held that only educational corporations created by legislative act were so entitled, the same word from Act 1883, ch. 105, "created," would have applied to and qualified "religious institutions" as well as "educational institutions," with result that no church that was not at that date incorporated by legislative act would have been entitled to tax exemption. An infinitesimally small number of churches were then so incorporated. To assign to the court's opinion in *Nashville* v. *Ward* a meaning that would have so resulted is not fair, particularly so since it is unnecessary. Further, to impute to the court a holding in that case that the immunity was granted to corporations aggregate or corporations by legislative creation, and denied to corporations sole, as complainant's insistence would require, would place the court in an attitude of having there enforced an act, which embodied a classification for immunity purposes, that approximated being arbitrary and vicious, if indeed it was not truly such, including corporations aggregate created by legislative enactment, and excluding corporations sole which are not so created, but which are recognized as corporations in our system of jurisprudence. *Governor* v. *Allen*, 8 Humph., 176; *Polk* v. *Plummer*, 2 Humph., 500, 506, 37 Am. Dec., 566; 1 Thomp. Corp., sec. 8.

A familiar example of a corporation sole makes what is here said all the more pertinent—a bishop of a diocese in whom, and whose successors in perpetuity, often titles to educational and religious properties are vested, which holder is as justly due, under any test of reason or equity, the immunity as any corporation created by legislative enactment.

It is repeated that what the court in *Nashville* v. *Ward* meant to thus imply, by way of illustrating example, was that it was requisite, in order to immunity, that the "institution" be one "created" under terms that fixed upon it permanency as to the use of the given property, which element was lacking in an individual.

The word "institution" has often been before courts for construction and definition, but quite as often from various angles of vision and side lights furnished by the particular act under review, in which the word was found, therefore, with discordant results in definition.

Thus some of the courts have held, under particular acts, that the word was used as descriptive of the establishment, place, or physical plant where the business of the association was carried on. *Gerke* v. *Purcell*, 25 Ohio St., 244, 16 Am. & Eng. Ency. Law (2d Ed.), 823.

In other jurisdictions (basically differing) the word is held referable to the organized body, itself, and to *ownership* by it. *Nobles County* v. *Hamline University*, 46 Minn., 316, 48 N. W., 1119; *Engstad* v. *County*, 10 N. D., 54, 84 N. W., 577; *Morris* v. *Lone Star Chapter*, 68 Tex., 698, 5 S. W., 519; *Academy* v. *Bohler*, 80 Ga., 162, 7 S. E., 633; *Kentucky, etc., School* v. *Louisville,*

100 Ky., 486, 36 S. W., 921, 40 L. R. A., 119. With the latter decisions our cases accord. *M. E. Church, South,* v. *Hinton,* 92 Tenn., 188, 196, 201, 203, 206, 21 S. W., 321, emphasized by the dissenting opinion of Snodgrass, J., and cases cited; *Vanderbilt University* v. *Cheney,* 116 Tenn., 259, 94 S. W., 90.

In respect of the limitations upon the word "institution" tending to confine it, it is conceived that, as used in our tax exemption statute, the definition should exclude an organization lacking in permanency of nature, as contradistinguished from an undertaking that is transient and temporary, and should imply foundation by law, whether the mode of its creation be by way of legislative enactment, common law fiction (corporation sole), or a trust, but imposing always an irrevocable use of the property for the purposes the law granting the immunity holds in regard.

The complainant Seminary contends that while this element of permanency is requisite, yet such inheres in it as a body corporate, and that, so inhering, there was warrant for the legislature's granting it the benefit of exemption from taxation while withholding it from individuals; its further insistence being that Act 1907, ch. 602, sec. 2, subsec. 2, is constitutional if and when construed to so grant and withhold immunity; the element of permanency justifying the classification which excludes alike the individual and the creation by way of trust.

The counter contention of the city is that such a classification is arbitrary and vicious, and would under test recently applied by this court, make the subsection unconstitutional and void. *State* v. *Railroad*, 124 Tenn., 1, 135 S. W., 773, Ann. Cas., 1912D, 805; *Daly* v. *State*, 13 Let, 228; *Teagan Transp. Co.* v. *Detroit*, 139 Mich., 1, 102 N. W., 273, 69 L. R. A., 431, 111 Am. St. Rep., 391; *Mobile* v. *Stonewall Ins. Co.*, 53 Ala., 581; *Adams* v. *Yazoo, etc., R. Co.*, 77 Miss., 194, 24 South., 200, 317, 28 South., 956, 60 L. R. A., 33, 95. The two last-named cases related to a classification for tax exemption excluding individuals and including corporations for profit. It may be remarked in passing that Mr. Gray, in his work on Limitations of the Taxing Power, secs. 1721-1722, 1323, indicates his opinion to be that the rule of the Alabama and Mississippi cases, cited above, was a sound one, and that it would apply in all States where, as in Tennessee, the constitution demands the application of the test of uniformity and equality. Article 11, sec. 8.

This contention of defendant city we all agree to be well taken.

We should, in my opinion, hold that complainant, being a body corporate for profit, whose incorporators had the option of taking out a charter for educational purposes under our general incorporation law (a) for general welfare (Acts 1875, ch. 142), or (b) for private profit (Acts 1881, ch. 58), chose the latter mode; and since it is optional with its stockholders to have declared, through a board of directors, and to receive current dividends, and, further, to terminate by dis-

solution the corporation's existence, distributing its assets to themselves at will, the Seminary here involved
is lacking in such permanency, and its property is not
used "exclusively" for educational purposes within the
meaning of the exemption act here under review. This
phase was commented on as a determining element in
the recent tax exemption case of *Cemetery Co.* v.
Creath, 127 Tenn., 686, 157 S. W., 412, 413, where it was
said:

"We have not here involved, it should be specially
noted, a corporation for profit, that is, free at will to
throw off or terminate the responsibility of the charity, but one on which rests during corporate existence
a law-imposed trust," etc.

The argument *contra* in behalf of the Seminary is
that the *actual* use of its property and income during
the given tax year was for educational purposes only,
and that this suffices. In the early statutes the words
"used actually" were employed instead of the phrase
"used exclusively," which appears in the later acts,
and it seems clear that in the change in phraseology
there was a purposed meaning.

The fact that the income referred to in the stipulation may have been, for the given year, used for the
Seminary's needs and purposes, and not for personal
profit, was due to self-imposed and not law-imposed
limitation. Besides, the capital stock, represented by
$37,500 of outstanding shares, is shown to have in-
creased in value to $240,520, thus affording a basis for
the declaration of a stock dividend, as distinguished

from current or installment dividends. It is not made clear by the stipulation whether the increase in capital stock from $20,000 to $40,000, therein referred to, was or was not by way of a declaration of such a stock dividend. Further, if we consider it to be an agreed fact that no sort of dividends have ever been paid, still it cannot be said that personal profit is excluded, because of the further consideration that the shares in the hands of the stockholders, having a value very far above par, are most practically usuable by the stockholders to personal advantage by way of collateral security.

Since the change in the phrasing of the tax exemption acts to the expression "used exclusively," this court has consistently treated of the exemption as an immunity granted to educational institutions created for general welfare, and not for profit.

Thus, in *State* v. *Fisk University*, 87 Tenn., 233, 241, 10 S. W., 284, 286, where a liberal construction was declared proper to be indulged in respect of a corporation for public welfare, it was said:

"The same strictness of construction will not be indulged when the exemption is to religious, scientific, literary, and educational institutions that will be applied in considering exemptions to *corporations created and operating for private gain or profit.*"

In *M. E. Church, South,* v. *Hinton,* supra, the court said:

"There is a material difference between charitable and business corporations. In the former *there are no*

*stockholders, and there is no element of individual
gain or profit, but a public trust.''*

Logically leading to the conclusion that the immunity from taxation is not by the cited statute granted
to complainant Seminary, are these further considerations:

In *State* v. *Fisk University*, supra, *M. E. Church,
South*, v. *Hinton*, supra, and *Vanderbilt University* v.
Cheney, supra, it was held that it was not requisite to
the claim of exemption by a corporation for general
welfare that the property used be such as is directly
and immediately held and devoted to educational purposes, or charitable purposes, and that it is permissible for real estate used to produce rentals, or a publishing plant used for income, to be protected as im-
mune, provided the product or income from the property thus indirectly held be devoted to such purpose.
In line with these Tennessee cases are decisions of the
courts of other States. *Nobles County* v. *Hamline University*, 46 Minn., 316, 48 N. W., 1119; *Wey* v. *Salt
Lake City*, 35 Utah, 504, 101 Pac., 381; *State v. Johnston*, 214 Mo., 656, 113 S. W., 1083, 21 L. R. A. (N. S.),
171; *New Haven* v. *Sheffield Scientific School*, 59 Conn.,
163, 22 Atl., 156; *Webster City* v. *Wright County*, 144
Iowa, 502, 123 N. W., 193, 24 L. R. A. (N. S.), 1205;
Kentucky, etc., School v. *Louisville*, 100 Ky., 470, 36
S. W., 921, 40 L. R. A., 119.

We so recently as 1913 reaffirmed the doctrine in
the case of *Cumberland Lodge* v. *Nashville*, 127 Tenn.,
248, 154 S. W., 1141.

The principle upon which our cases proceed is that the test applicable is the *ultimate use,* whereas those courts which hold to the contrary doctrine look only to the *direct use,* disallowing the tax exemption to property not held immediately as parts of the physical plant. *N. W. University* v. *People,* 80 Ill., 333, 22 Am. Rep., 187; *Phillips Academy* v. *Andover,* 175 Mass., 118, 55 N. E., 841, 48 L. R. A., 550; *Detroit Home* v. *Detroit;* 76 Mich., 521, 43 N. W., 593, 6 L. R. A., 97.

If educational corporations created for profit be admitted, under the statute, into the class of educational corporations for general welfare and not profit, it could be argued that, by parity of reasoning they would have to be accorded all the incidents of immunity held to inure to the general welfare corporations, inclusive of the right to have protected in their hands property held incidentally and indirectly for income. Such contention, if followed, would result in the grant of exemption from taxation to property not *immediately* held for educational purposes, and the holding of which is not vindicated by the *ultimate* use, which is seen to be one for profit. The abuses that would be incident to such a ruling are of easy contemplation.

If corporations for profit be allowed entrance into the class with corporations for public welfare, it is not improbable that, in this age of promotion, enterprises will be launched in corporate form under the guise of educational corporations, having in view yet more patently private profit, such as business colleges. The Supreme Court of Michigan in the case of *Detroit, etc., School* v. *City of Detroit,* 76 Mich., 521, 43 N. W., 593, 6 L. R. A., 97, held, under the Michigan statute providing exemption from taxation of the property of "scientific institutions incorporated under the laws of this state . . . and occupied by them for the purposes for which they were incorporated," that a seminary incorporated for profit was entitled to the benefit of the exemption. But in the later case of *Parsons Business College* v. *Kalamazoo,* 106 Mich., 305, 131 N. W., 553, 33 L. R. A. (N. S.), 921, it was held that a business college so incorporated was not within the protection of the act; it having become incorporated chiefly to avoid taxation. Such entrance, if permitted, would lead to attempted differentiations, in respect of institutions that lie in the debatable zone, in classification, where the line of cleavage could not be easily or satisfactorily drawn.

If the rule of classification is placed, as indicated, upon the nature of the institution as one for public welfare, we have at once a practical and just test, and one that cannot be said to be arbitrary or lacking in reasonableness.

In reference to an insistence and the holding of the majority that the word "institution" in the Revenue Act may be construed to relate to property held as an institution, whether by a body corporate, noncorporate, or an individual, thus meeting the point of arbitrary classification, I conceive this to be based on two fundamental misconceptions or errors; and, further, it is admitted that the construction so contended for would, on adoption, work an overruling of the case of *Nashville* v. *Ward*. And herein:

Let us assume that, for test of exemption from taxation, we should thus refer the claimed exemption to *property* held as such; that is, in the sense of a physical plant or establishment where educational work is carried on. This would be, as indicated, directly in the face of the decision of this court in *Nashville* v. *Ward,* where under a statute (1883) identical in its immediately pertinent phraseology with the act we have here under review the court said:

"In the Act of 1883, the terms used in describing the ownership in respect of 'institutions' are 'belonging to', and these terms were intended to and do import ownership."

As we have seen, this is in harmony with the later holdings of this court, the strongest illustration and application being that embodied in the decision of the case of *University of the South* v. *Skidmore,* 87 Tenn., 156, 9 S. W., 892. Such a ruling would be, furthermore, directly out of accord with the act in question which refers the test to ownership of the property, rather than to the property per se.

Again, this court in *Nashville* v. *Ward,* directly ruled that the phrase "corporations created" did not include an individual owner of property. Much authority might be cited in support of the proposition that the word "institution" (standing alone) cannot be construed to cover an individual; and we believe that no case can be cited which holds that an individual owner can be brought within the meaning of the phrase "institutions *created.*" The Supreme Court of Wisconsin (*Dodge* v. *Williams,* 46 Wis., 100, 50 N. W., 1107) said:

"A private school or college may by courtesy be called an 'institution,' according to the American fashion of promoting people and things by brevit names. But, in legal parlance, an 'institution' implies foundation by law, by enactment or prescription. One may open and keep a private school; he cannot be properly said to institute it."

And, for a stronger reason, an individual cannot in any legal sense be said to be an "institution *created.*" The language of the statute had in anticipation a creation not by one's own act, but by the act of another, binding the ownership under terms importing permanency in foundation.

I have, as above outlined, indicated a liberal construction for the phrase "institutions created" under the doctrine announced and applied by this court in holdings that where an institution for the public welfare is involved, an exemption statute, in respect of same, shall be given a liberal construction; but in the same connection it was declared that this rule of liberal construction will not be applied to institutions created and operating for private gain or profit.

Any attempted further liberality in construction in order to the inclusion of individual owners would be necessary to sustain the exemption clause of the act under consideration against the attack based on the constitutional inhibition against arbitrary classification; but if this construction were adopted, it would be to place this court absolutely alone, without the support of any precedent from another jurisdiction, in holding that an individual may be conceived of as being covered or included by the expression "corporation *created.*"

It would seem plain that the legislature in its every enactment subsequent to the decision in *Nashville* v. *Ward,* supra, in adopting the phraseology of the act of 1883 therein construed, did so having in mind that judicial construction which excluded individuals who engaged in educational endeavor for profit. The majority, therefore, do more than overrule that case; they reform the legislation presumably based thereon.

Under the contention here being combated, how would the property of complainant Seminary that is not *actually* used (but incidentally held) for educational purposes be treated? The ownership of such property on its part is shown to exist, by the terms of the stipulation. This is held by the majority to be nonexempt under the statute. It should be here noted that those courts which, under the peculiar legislative acts in their States, hold that the physical plant is the test also hold that the lands purchased and held by such holder for the purpose of removing thereto its buildings after a sale of the property then occupied by it is not exempt from taxation, a direct and immediate holding being requisite. But on what principle under our statutes and decisions could the complainant

Seminary be denied the right to have treated as exempt property incidentally held, if it be once admitted that it, equally with a corporation not for profit, is within the terms of legislative act of exemption?

Unless the majority means to overrule or undermine the cases of *M. E. Church, South,* v. *Hinton,* supra, *Vanderbilt University* v. *Cheney,* supra, and the *Cumberland Lodge Case,* and to adopt the doctrine of those courts which hold to the test of physical plant, rather than to the test of ownership, it is submitted that when the Seminary is granted immunity at all, it must be granted it in full measure; that to grant it in so far and to deny it in so far leaves our cases lacking in symmetry and the law of this State on the subject unique among the jurisdiction of the Union.

The firmly fixed doctrine of this court is that a statutory grant of exemption must be clearly shown by one who claims it. *Railroad Co.* v. *Harris,* 99 Tenn., 684, 43 S. W., 115, 53 L. R. A., 921. In the case of *Berryman* v. *Board of Trustees,* 222 U. S., 334, 350, 32 Sup. Ct., 147, 56 L. Ed., 230, the Supreme Court of the United States applied the rule of strict construction to college incorporated for public welfare; but, as we have seen, this court has been in that particular more liberal; but liberality stops at the point where a claimant is unwilling to subordinate self-gain to the public weal and to conduct the enterprise "exclusively" for that purpose which the State regards as entitled to the recognition of exemption privilege—education. True reciprocity may be said to be involved where property is devoted and used under terms of such subordination or abnegation. The State, in recognition of the fact that one of the duties incumbent on it as sovereign is thus being in part borne by others, with relief to her in so far, by way of reciprocity extends her immunity from taxation.

My dissent is therefore compelled. It might be admitted that the policy announced and result reached by the court are desirable of being compassed. That is a matter for the legislature to consider, not the court.

WALKER *v.* LEMMA *et al.*

(*Nashville.* December Term, 1913.)

SUPERSEDEAS. Jurisdiction. Supreme Court.

Under Acts 1907, ch. 82, sec. 8, providing for the review by the
supreme court upon *certiorari* of the cases appealed to the
court of civil appeals, the supreme court can take jurisdiction
of such cases only through that writ, and then only after final
decree or judgment in the court of civil appeals, and it has no
jurisdiction to issue a writ of *supersedeas* suspending or discharging a *supersedeas* granted by the court of civil appeals.

Acts cited and construed: Acts, 1907, ch 82.

FROM MARION

Appeal from Chancery Court, Marion County.—V.
C. ALLEN, Chancellor.

G. B. MURRAY, for plaintiff.

W. E. WILKERSON, for defendants.

MR. CHIEF JUSTICE NEIL delivered the opinion of the
Court.

The question to be determined arises under a petition filed before this court to supersede an order of
supersedeas granted by the court of civil appeals
against an order issued by the chancellor holding the
chancery court of Marion county.

It appears that a bill was filed in the chancery court referred to, enjoining the sale of land under a trust deed. The chancellor dissolved the injunction. The court of civil appeals, on petition of the complainant in that case, granted a *supersedeas* against the chancellor's decree of dissolution. A motion was afterwards made in the court of civil appeals to discharge the *supersedeas* and that court refused to do so. In the petition now filed before us, and its accompanying brief, it is insisted that the court of civil appeals committed grave error in granting the *supersedeas* to the chancellor's order, and we are asked by the writ of *supersedeas* to suspend or discharge the *supersedeas* which the court of civil appeals granted.

We express no opinion upon the merits of the question, because in the view we take of the matter we have no jurisdiction. The bill presents a case lying wholly within the jurisdiction of the court of civil appeals under section 7 of chapter 82 of the Acts of 1907 creating that court. We can take jurisdiction of cases in that court only through the writ of *certiorari*, and then only after final decree or judgment in that court. Acts 1907, ch. 82, sec. 8.

On the ground stated, the petition must be disallowed.

CASES

ARGUED AND DETERMINED

IN THE

SUPREME COURT OF TENNESSEE

FOR THE

WESTERN DIVISION.

JACKSON, APRIL TERM, 1914.

R. A. GRIFFIN & SON *v.* PARKER. *

(*Jackson.* April Term, 1914.)

1. **MASTER AND SERVANT. Liability for Injuries. Unsafe scaffolds.**

While the rule that an employer must use reasonable diligence to furnish a safe place and safe instrumentalities for the work to be done is subject to the exception that where he supplies ample material of good quality and competent labor for the construction of a scaffold, which he is not required to furnish in a completed state, and which the employees within the scope of their employment are themselves required to construct,

---

*As to the master's liability for negligence of coservant in respect to preparation of scaffolds, staging, etc., see note in 54 L. R. A., 142.

Upon the duty of the master to furnish safe appliances as affected by fact that defective appliances are prepared by fellow servants, see notes in 3 L. R. A. (N. S.), 500 and 4 L. R. A. (N. S.), 220.

Griffin & Son v. Parker.

he is not liable for the negligence of a fellow servant in the construction of the scaffold, the employer must either furnish the scaffold complete for use, or leave the employees unembarrassed in selecting the material from that furnished, and where the selection is intrusted to a foreman, he is deemed a vice principal. (*Post*, *p.* 451.)

Cases cited and approved: Killea v. Faxon, 125 Mass., 485; Kennedy v. Spring. 160 Mass., 203; Rose v. Walker, 139 Pa., 42; Kimmer v. Weber, 151 N. Y., 417; Noyes v. Wood, 102 Cal., 389; Lindvall v. Woods, 41 Minn., 212; Haakensen v. Burgess, etc., Co., 76 N. H., 443; Haskell v. Cape, etc., Co., 4 L. R. A. (N. S.), note, pp. 226-229; Lambert v. Missisquoi Pulp Co., 72 Vt., 278; Sowles v. Norcross Bros. Co., 195 Fed., 889; Olsen v. Nixon, 61 N. J. Law, 671; Blomquist v. Chicago, etc., R. Co., 60 Minn., 426; Lee v. Leighton Co., 113 Minn., 373; Arkerson v. Dennison, 117 Mass., 407; Donahue v. Buck, 197 Mass., 550; Dunleavy v. Sullivan, 200 Mass., 29; Richards v. Hayes, 17 App. Div., 422; Austin Mfg. Co. v. Johnson, 89 Fed., 677.

2. **MASTER AND SERVANT. Liability for injuries. Burden of proof.**

Where a scaffold, which an employer was bound to keep safe by the exercise of reasonable care, was not defective when constructed, but collapsed because of the negligence of a workman in dislodging a brace, thus permitting a board set on edge to turn flat and break, the burden was on an employee, suing for injuries, to overcome the presumption of due care on the part of the employer by proof that he had notice of the defective condition, or in the exercise of ordinary care should have known thereof. (*Post*, *p.* 454.)

Cases cited and approved: Railroad v. Lindamood, 111 Tenn., 463; Railroad v. Hayes, 117 Tenn., 680.

3. **MASTER AND SERVANT. Liability for injuries. Burden of proof.**

No presumption of negligence could arise from an employer's · failure to discover a defect in a scaffold within an hour and a

---

Griffin & Son v. Parker.

---

half after it became defective by the displacement of a brace. (*Post, p.* 454.)

. Case cited and construed: Box Co. v. Gregory, 119 Tenn., 537

FROM ————

.App^{eal} from the ——— court of ————county to the Court of Civil Appeals, and by *certiorari* from the Court of Civil Appeals to the Supreme Court.— —————————, Judge.

THOMAS H. MALONE and LARKIN E. CROUCH, for plaintiff.

J. B. DANIEL, for defendants.

MR. JUSTICE WILLIAMS delivered the opinion of the Court.

This suit was brought by Parker to recover damages for personal injuries incurred while in the service of the appellant firm of contractors as a carpenter. In the circuit court a judgment was recovered by Parker; but the court of civil appeals has reversed this judgment and remanded the case for a new trial.

Neither party is content with the action of the last-named court, with result that two petitions for *certiorari* are before us asking for a review of the judgment. Parker's contention is that there was error in the remand of the cause; the contracting firm insists that its motion for peremptory instructions to the jury in the lower court should have been sustained.

Parker, a carpenter of 35 years' experience, while in the employ of petitioner firm, was injured by the falling of a scaffold on which he was standing doing work on the ceiling of a church under course of erection in Nashville. The scaffold was about twenty-eight feet high, and was held up by boards of yellow pine about 28 feet in length which projected as supporting beams or arms. One of these arms, 6 inches wide and 2 inches thick, carried a knot (about 1½ inches in size) about the center of its length. This arm was in the construction of the scaffold set edgewise, and if held to that position was capable of sustaining a greater weight than it would if set flat. It was held firmly by braces when first placed; but, after so remaining for about five weeks, these braces or one of them had been displaced by material carried up by workmen striking against same. With the brace removed, the arm or beam careened under the weight of the floor, men, and material above it, and when it turned flat from upright the arm broke at the center, where the knot was, causing the collapse and Parker's fall.

The court of civil appeals held that the proximate cause of the breaking was not the knot, but the displacement of the bracing and the consequent careening of the beam. Parker himself testified that immediately preceding the collapse he felt this beam career and did not have time to protect himself.

The scaffold was built under the supervision of R. A. Griffin, Jr., who was not a member of the firm sued, but a general foreman employed by the firm, and who inspected the lumber that went into the scaffold. Parker was not engaged at this building when the scaffold was erected, but a boss of the firm on another job in the city. He had come to the church construction work one day before the scaffold fell.

The court of civil appeals found the fact to be, on the uncontradicted evidence, that the firm furnished ample suitable material with which to erect the scaffold; that, so far as disclosed, no one noticed the knot in the beam until after the break and collapse.

It is not shown when the bracing of the arm was displaced. The only evidence on the point elicited was to the effect that it might have occurred on the morning of the collapse. Work commenced at 7 a. m. and the fall of the scaffold occurred at 8:30 a. m.

The primary contention of the firm sued is that this scaffold was a temporary structure, intended only to be used by the carpentry crew in finishing the room where it was constructed; that it was but a part of the work in which the force (of which Parker claimed to be a member) was engaged; that they, as employers, furnished an ample quantity of suitable materials, employed a competent foreman, and did not themselves undertake to furnish the scaffold as a completed structure; and that, therefore, they are not answerable to Parker for his injury—citing *Killea* v. *Faxon,* 125 Mass. 485; *Kennedy* v. *Spring,* 160 Mass. 203, 35 N. E. 779; *Ross* v. *Walker,* 139 Pa. 42, 21 Atl. 157, 159, 23 Am. St. Rep. 160; *Kimmer* v. *Weber,* 151 N. Y. 417, 45 N.

E. 860, 56 Am. St. Rep. 630; *Noyes v. Wood,* 102 Cal. 389, 36 Pac. 766; *Lindvall v. Woods,* 41 Minn. 212, 42 N. W. 1020, 4 L. R. A. 793, and other cases in accord.

The general rule is that an employer is bound to use reasonable diligence to furnish the employee a safe place and safe instrumentalities for the work to be done; but an exception exists in case of a scaffold where the employer supplies ample material of good quality and competent labor for the construction of such appliance, which he is not required to furnish in a completed state, and which the employees, within the scope of their employment, are themselves required to construct. In such case the employer is not liable to one of the workmen for the negligence of a fellow servant in the construction of the scaffold. Authorities, supra; *Haakensen v. Burgess, etc., Co.,* 76 N. H., 443, 83 Atl., 804, Ann. Cas. 1913B, 1122, and note; *Haskell v. Cape, etc., Co.,* 4 L. R. A. (N. S.), note pp. 226-229.

A close question, touching which the authorities are not in accord, is whether an exception to the above-noted exception arises where the employer has engaged in the work of scaffold construction a foreman, to whom is assigned the selection of the material from the mass or the designing of the structure, and where by reason of the negligence of the foreman in regard to such matter injury to an employee occurs, and the doctrine of fellow servant is interposed as a defense by the employer.

In the case of *Ross v. Walker,* supra, it appeared that Walker, the employer, had in his employ as foreman one Duffey. The trial court instructed the jury that if Duffey was in the entire control of the work, determining what and where materials were to be used for the scaffolding, he was to be deemed to be a vice principal, and his negligence would be that of defendant Walker. The supreme court of Pennsylvania, holding this to be error, said:

"For an error in judgment, or neglect of duty on the part of any one of his employees, from the foreman down to the humblest unskilled laborer, he was not liable. It was not material to this inquiry to know whether 'Duffey had entire charge and control of the work' as a foreman or not; nor to know whether he selected from the mass furnished by the employer the materials to be used for any particular purpose, or not. . . . The inquiry is: Was it the employer's duty, after having provided materials ample in quantity and quality, to supervise the selection of every stick out of the mass for every purpose? To state the question is to answer it. This was not his duty, and for this reason Duffey, if he did select the timber, . . . did not represent Walker as a vice principal in such selection." See, also, *Lambert* v. *Missisquoi Pulp Co.*, 72 Vt., 278, 47 Atl., 1085; *Lindvall* v. *Woods*, 41 Minn., 212, 42 N. W., 1020, 4 L. R. A., 793; *Sowles* v. *Norcross Bros. Co.*, 195 Fed., 889, 115 C. C. A., 577; *Noyes* v. *Wood* 102 Cal., 389, 36 Pac., 766; *Olsen* v. *Nixon*, 61 N. J. Law, 671, 40 Atl., 694.

We are of opinion, however, that the cases ruling to the contrary announce the better doctrine. When the employer through such a foreman undertakes, as we must infer to have been the fact from the evidence in this case, to make the selection of the materials for use in the scaffolding, the foreman is to be deemed a vice principal. The fact of selection by him defined for the common employer what was fit for use; opportunity for the exercise of discretion on the part of workmen in the selection from any mass was withheld. Without such discretion coming into play, it is difficult to see how any of the workmen can be convicted of negligence in that regard, as a basis for a denial of relief to Parker. *Woods* v. *Lindvall*, 48 Fed., 62, 1 C. C. A. 37; *Blomquist* v. *Chicago, etc., R. Co.*, 60 Minn., 426, 62 N. W., 818; *Lee* v. *Leighton Co.*, 113 Minn., 373, 129 N. W. 767; *Arkerson* v. *Dennison*, 117 Mass., 407; *Donahue* v. *Buck*, 197 Mass., 550, 83 N. E., 1090, 18 L. R. A. (N. S.), 476; *Dunleavy* v. *Sullivan*, 200 Mass., 29, 85 N. E. 866; *Richards* v. *Hayes*, 17 App. Div., 422, 45 N. Y. Supp., 324; *Austin Mfg. Co.* v. *Johnson*, 89 Fed. 677, 32 C. C. A., 309.

We hold, therefore, that when the foreman exercised the function of making such election he acted as vice principal. It was the duty of the employer (1) to furnish the scaffold as an instrumentality complete for use; or (2) to leave the employee unembarrassed as to selection from a mass of character above defined.

We also conceive that the facts found establish that the scaffold when constructed was not a defective structure, and that the beam or arm as placed was sufficient to render the scaffolding superimposed secure. The

efficient cause of the collapse was not due to any defect
of construction, but to the negligent acts of the workmen thereafter in dislodging the bracing.   Treating
the scaffold as an instrumentality in reference to which
the employer firm owed the workmen the duty to keep
safe, by the exercise of reasonable care, yet under another firmly established rule it was incumbent on Parker, as plaintiff below, to overcome the presumption of
the exercise of due care on the part of the employer by
proof of fault, in that the latter had notice of this defective condition, or that in the exercise of ordinary
care he should have known of it.   *Railroad* v. *Lindamood,* 111 Tenn., 463, 78 S. W., 99; *Railroad* v. *Hayes,*
117 Tenn., 680, 99 S. W., 362.

For aught that appears in the proof, the displacement of the bracing occurred within 1½ hours before
the accident.   In *Box Company* v. *Gregory,* 119 Tenn.,
537, 542, 105 S. W., 350, 13 L. R. A. (N. S.), 1031, it
was held that no presumption of negligence could arise
from the employer's failure to inspect during a period
of 4½ hours covering the period of the existence of
the defect; and on that ground it was ruled that peremptory instructions should have been given on defendant's motion.

A like holding must here result.   The judgment of
the court of civil appeals will, on grant of the writ of
certiorari, be modified accordingly.

WOOLEN, *State Comptroller, v.* STATE, *ex rel.* PORTIS, *Sheriff.*

(*Jackson.*   April Term, 1914.)

1. COSTS. In criminal prosecutions. Liability of state.

Under Shannon's Code, secs. 7606, 7619-7622, declaring that costs shall include the safe-keeping of accused before and after conviction, and providing that costs in felony cases shall be paid by the State, the State is liable for costs for confining in the county jail one convicted of a felony; the commutation in the sentence not changing the grade of the offense. (*Post,* p. 456.)

Acts cited and construed: Acts Extra Session 1891, ch. 22.

Code cited and construed: Sec. 7606, 7619 (S.); secs. 5577, 5585 (M. & V. and 1858).

2. COSTS. In criminal prosecutions. Liability of State.

Acts 1891, ch. 123, sec. 11, providing that the State shall pay for the board of State prisoners, covers safe-keeping in a workhouse before and after conviction, on commutation from penitentiary confinement. (*Post,* p. 458.)

Acts cited and construed: Acts 1891, ch. 123.

FROM TIPTON.

Appeal from Circuit Court, Tipton County.—S. J. EVERETT, Judge.

NAT TIPTON, and STEELE & STEELE, for appellant.

WILLIAM H. SWIGGART, JR. assistant attorney-general, for appellee.

MR. JUSTICE WILLIAMS delivered the opinion of the Court.

This is an action in the name of the State of Tennessee, on relation of Portis, sheriff and jailor of Tipton county, against the comptroller of the State, seeking the grant of a writ of *mandamus* to compel the issuance of a warrant on the treasury for a sum alleged to be due from the State for the board of certain prisoners in the county jail, who were convicted of felonies, but whose sentences had been commuted by trial juries to imprisonment in jail from imprisonment in the State penitentiary.

The comptroller answered, denying liability on the part of the State to the jailor for such board, and contending that the county was liable. The circuit judge ruled against this contention, and granted the writ of *mandamus,* with result that an appeal was prayed by the comptroller to this court.

The Code of 1858, section 5577 (Shannon, sec. 7606), defines criminal costs as follows: "The costs which may be adjudged in criminal cases include all costs incident to the arrest and safe-keeping of the defendant before and after conviction, due and incident to the prosecution and conviction, and incident to the carrying of the judgment or sentence of the court into effect."

The Code in section 5585 (Shannon sec. 7619), provides that the State or the county, according to the nature of the offense, "pays the costs accrued in behalf of the State" in certain contingencies named.

Acts Extra Session 1891, ch. 22 (Shannon's Code, secs. 7620-7622), defined more closely on which of the named contingencies the payor should be the State or the county, as between themselves, and this act again defines criminal costs as follows: "What is meant by costs in the foregoing sections is all costs accruing under the existing laws on behalf of the State or county, as the case may be, for the faithful prosecution and safe-keeping of the defendant, including the cost . . . of the jailor."

By the last-named act, the test of liability, as between the state and the county, is placed on the grade of the offense. All costs of the prosecution of crimes punishable otherwise than by death or confinement in the penitentiary are made payable by the county.

We are of opinion, and hold, that in cases of felonies, where the punishment has been commuted from confinement in the penitentiary to confinement in a county workhouse or jail, there is worked by the commutation no change in the grade of the offense, so as to disturb the above test of liability for costs. They are payable by the State, except where the statute provides to the contrary.

As seen, "costs," within the purview of the earlier statutory provision, included "safe-keeping of the defendant before and after conviction," and, in the later act, the equivalent "costs of the jailor." Thus is made a legislative distribution of an entire burden as between State and county.

It is insisted by the comptroller, for the State, that the general county workhouse act (Acts 1891, ch. 123), in section 11, wrought a change in the measure of the State's burden. This contention is based on a construction of the word "safe-keeping," appearing in that section, which would assign to it a narrower meaning than did the earlier statute, and improperly confine it to a keeping of a defendant before conviction. The above section 11 provides that the State shall pay for the board of State's prisoners, and this we construe to cover a safe-keeping in work-house or jail, both before and after conviction, on commutation from penitentiary confinement.

It is insisted by counsel of the Comptroller that the ruling in the case of *Knox County* v. *Fox*, 107 Tenn., 724, is favorable to his contention. It was in that case ruled that costs accruing after conviction, such as jail fees, were not costs to be taxed against and worked out by a convicted defendant. This being so, it becomes all the more manifest that sections 7606 and 7622 of Shannon's Code, quoted above, govern the taxation of costs as between the State and county, rather than as between the State and a defendant. We have so construed them.

The circuit judge did not err in granting the writ. Affirmed.

UNION RAILWAY COMPANY *v.* CARTER.

(*Jackson.* April Term, 1914.)

1. DEATH. Actions for death. Damages.

Under Shannon's Code, secs. 4025-4028, authorizing an action for death by wrongful act, and the recovery of the damages suffered by the beneficiaries for the loss of decedent and such damages as decedent could have recovered had he survived, a widow, suing for the death of her husband by wrongful act, may recover, not only the damages she has sustained as the result of her husband's death, but such damages as he might have recovered had he survived. *Post, p.* 461.)

Code cited and construed: Secs. 4025-4028 (S.).

Cases cited and approved: Davidson Benedict Co. v. Severson, 109 Tenn., 572; Collins v. Railroad, 56 Tenn., 851; Railroad v. Shewalter, 128 Tenn., 368.

2. DEATH. Actions for death. Punitive damages.

In an action under Shannon's Code, secs. 4025-4028, for death by wrongful act, exemplary damages are recoverable. (*Post, p.* 462.)

3. DEATH. Actions for death. Damages. Excessive damages.

Where the declaration, in an action for death by wrongful act, demanded exemplary damages, and the court found that decedent was shot by an employee of defendant, acting as a special officer, while attempting to arrest decedent for the misdemeanor of stealing a ride on a train of defendant, a judgment for $2,000 would not be disturbed as excessive, for punitive damages were recoverable. (*Post, p.* 462.)

Cases cited and approved: Haley v. M. & O. Railroad, 66 Tenn., 239; Railroad v. Daughtry, 88 Tenn., 721.

FROM SHELBY.

Appeal from Circuit Court, Shelby County.—J. P. Young, Judge.

J. W. Canada, for Union Railway Co.

Bell, Terry & Bell, for Carter.

Mr. Justice Green delivered the opinion of the Court.

This suit was brought by Josie Carter to recover damages for the killing of her husband by an employee of the Union Railway Company. The case was tried without a jury, and the circuit judge rendered judgment in favor of the plaintiff below for $2,000. This judgment was affirmed by the court of civil appeals, and a petition for *certiorari* has been filed by the railway company to bring the case to this court.

The plaintiff in error, the Union Railway Company, is a common carrier, operating its lines in and near the city of Memphis. John Carter, the husband of plaintiff below, while stealing a ride on a train operated by the plaintiff in error, was put under arrest by one Earl Barnard, an employee of the railway company, who was also commissioned by the city of Memphis as a special police officer.

The circuit judge found that Carter was shot in the back of the head by this special officer while the former was running away trying to escape arrest. Carter was riding on top of a freight train with some other negroes, and for this misdemeanor Barnard attempted the arrest. Although there was a conflict in the evidence, and the special officer claimed that he shot Carter in self-defense, the proof introduced by the plaintiff below abundantly sustained the finding of the trial judge.

The principal question made in the petition for *certiorari* is that no evidence was introduced to support a judgment for as much as $2,000 damages.

The wife of deceased testified that her husband worked for certain coal dealers at Memphis and made $9 a week. His age, however, was not shown, nor was any proof offered as to the condition of his health, his expectancy, or his habits with reference to the support of his family.

A number of witnesses testified in behalf of the railway company that deceased was a worthless negro, of bad habits and dangerous character, and it is insisted that his wife has sustained no damages by reason of his death, and has not attempted to show any.

Under Shannon's Code, secs. 4025-4028, the damages recoverable by those authorized to bring suit on account of a wrongful killing are of two kinds: First, the damages suffered by the beneficiaries by reason of the loss of deceased; and, second, such damages as deceased himself would have been entitled to recover had he survived. *Davidson Benedict Co.* v. *Severson*, 109 Tenn., 572, 72 S. W., 967, and cases reviewed.

So the widow's claim for damages in this case under our statute is not limited to damages that she may
have sustained as the result of her husband's death,
but she may also recover damages for the injury done
to deceased himself. She may recover substantial damages in a suit like this without any special showing of
pecuniary loss to herself. Had deceased survived,
totally disabled, and brought suit, a verdict of $2,000
would scarcely have been deemed excessive, no matter what his age and expectancy were.

His beneficiaries under the statute are entitled to
include in their recovery all damages he could have
obtained under the circumstances just indicated. *Collins* v. *Railroad,* 9 Heisk., 851; *Davidson Benedict Co.*
v. *Severson,* 109 Tenn., 572, 72 S. W., 967. In other
words, our statute was not only enacted for the protection of designated beneficiaries, but is a survival statute as well. *Railroad v. Shewalter* (Knoxville, 1913),
128 Tenn., (1 Thompson), 363, 161 S. W., 1136.

Moreover, as we have stated, this case was tried without a jury, and the declaration laid ground for exemplary damages. Such damages are recoverable in suits
founded on our statute. *Haley* v. *M. & O. Railroad,*
7 Baxt., 239; *Railroad* v. *Daughtry,* 88 Tenn.. 721, 13
S. W., 698. On the findings of the trial judge, this is
a proper case for punitive damages. If the judgment
is in excess of compensatory damages, it should nevertheless be sustained, and the difference charged as
smart money.

It has become customary throughout the state for large enterprises of every character to have certain employees appointed special officers and clothed with police authority. While this practice may be desirable for the protection of the property of such concerns, it has led to many abuses. These men so clothed with official power lack the experience and discretion of regular State and municipal officers, and their conduct has very generally been oppressive and flagrant.

In view of the well-known tendencies of these special officers, parties so employing them will be held to a strict degree of accountability for the acts of such dangerous agents.

Other matters presented by the petition have been orally discussed, and the writ of *certiorari* will be denied.

Goodman *et al. v.* Wilson.

(*Jackson.* April Term, 1914.)

1. **MASTER AND SERVANT. Negligence of chauffeur. Joint liability.**

Where a brother and sister jointly own an automobile, each paying one-half of all expenses, including the wages of the chauffeur jointly employed, and with an equal right to the use of the machine, with the exception that the brother had a preference in being taken to and from work, the sister is liable for injuries sustained in a collision with a buggy while the chauffeur, alone in the machine, was racing with another machine on his way to take the brother home from work. (*Post,* p. 467.)

2. **MASTER AND SERVANT. Respondeat superior. Nature of doctrine.**

The doctrine of *respondeat superior* applies only when the relation of master and servant is shown to exist between the wrongdoer and the person shown to be charged with the injury resulting from the wrong, and in respect of the very transaction out of which the injury arose. (*Post,* p. 467.)

3. **MASTER AND SERVANT. Negligence of chauffeur. Liability of master.**

The mere fact that a driver of an automobile was defendant's servant will not make defendant liable. unless it is further shown that at the time of the accident the driver was in the master's business, and acting within the scope of his employment. (*Post,* p. 467.)

Cases cited and approved: Brow v. Boston, etc., R. Co. 157 Mass. 399; Illinois Central R. Co. v. King, 69 Miss., 852.

---

*As to the liability of the owner for injuries by automobile while being used by a servant or a third person for his own business or pleasure, see notes in 1 L. R. A. (N. S.), 235; 9 L. R. A. (N. S.), 1033; 14 L. R. A. (N. S.), 216; 21 L. R. A. (N. S.), 93; 26 L. R. A. (N. S.), 382; 33 L. R. A. (N. S.), 79; 37 L. R. A. (N. S.), 834; and 47 L. R. A. (N. S.), 662. And as to making *prima facie* case of responsibility for negligence of driver of automobile by proof of defendant's ownership of car or employment of driver, see note in 46 L. R. A. (N. S.) 1091.

4. NEGLIGENCE.   Dangerous Instrumentalities.   Automobile.

An automobile is not such a dangerous machine as would require
it to be put in the category with the locomotive, dangerous animals, explosives, and the like, so as to render the owner liable
from its use. (*Post, p.* 470.)

Cases cited and approved: Lotz v. Hanlon, 217 Pa., 339; Steffen
v. McNaughton, 142 Wis., 49; Eichman v. Buchheit, 128 Wis.,
385.

FROM SHELBY.

Appeal from Circuit Court, Shelby County.—
WALTER MALONE, Judge.

GEORGE HARSH, for appellee.

STEEN & KLEWER and D. W. DE HAVEN, for defendant Goodman.

MR. JUSTICE LANSDEN delivered the opinion of the
Court.

This suit was brought by Wilson against Goodman
and his sister, Mrs. Corinne A. Richardson, to recover
damages resulting from a collision with a buggy in
which Wilson was riding and an automobile owned by
Goodman and Mrs. Richardson. From the verdict and
judgment in the circuit court against both defendants,
an appeal was taken to, and the judgment of the circuit court was affirmed by, the court of civil appeals.
The case is presented to us upon the petition of Mrs.
Richardson alone. The facts which we consider material are that the automobile which collided with defendant in error is owned jointly and equally by Mrs.
Richardson and Mr. Goodman, who are brother and
sister. They live in the same residence, and jointly

employ one chauffeur, and each pays one-half of his
wages, and he serves them both in the operation of the
automobile. They equally bear the expense of operation and repair of the automobile, and each of them,
separately or jointly, may use it accordingly as their
needs or pleasures may require. They have an agreement by which Mr. Goodman has a right of preference
to the use of the automobile in being carried to and
from his office in the morning and afternoon, if he sees
proper to require the use of the car at this time, to
the exclusion of the right of Mrs. Richardson to use
it at these hours. When either party desires to use
the automobile, orders would be given by the one so
desiring to use it to the chauffeur for this purpose.
Occasionally they used it jointly, and occasionally Mrs.
Richardson would ride into town after her brother, or
would ride to town with him in the morning when he
would go to his office.

On the occasion of the accident, the automobile was
going into town to the office of Mr. Goodman, and was
going west on Union avenue. Wilson was driving west
on Union avenue in an open buggy with a horse attached. The automobile approached him from behind.
It was racing with another automobile moving in the
same direction, and was running at a rate of speed estimated by the witness for plaintiff at from twenty-five
to forty miles an hour. When Wilson saw the two
automobiles approaching him he drew his horse and
buggy close to the curb, and, as he did so, the automobile in front of that of plaintiff in error passed Wilson,

and plaintiff in error's automobile appeared to be trying to get in between the other automobile and Wilson's buggy. In this attempt, the automobile struck the wheel of the buggy, and knocked Wilson into the air; and he fell onto the asphalt pavement. The automobile ran ninety yards after striking the buggy, before it was stopped.

Upon these facts, it is insisted for Mrs. Richardson that she is not liable, because the evidence does not connect her with the accident, and that the chauffeur, at the time of the accident, was in the service of Mr. Goodman only, and therefore the rule of *respondeat superior* does not apply as between the chauffeur and Mrs. Richardson.

The court of civil appeals was of opinion that, although Mrs. Richardson was not in the automobile at the time, and may not have given orders to the chauffeur to proceed on the journey, still the chauffeur and the automobile at the time of the accident were on the business of the joint owners of the automobile.

It is undoubtedly true, as a general proposition of law, that the doctrine of *respondeat superior* applies only when the relation of master and servant is shown to exist between the wrongdoer and the person sought to be charged with the injury resulting from the wrong at the time and in respect of the very transaction out of which the injury arose, and the mere fact that the driver of the automobile was the defendants' servant will not make the defendant liable. It must be further

shown that at the time of the accident the driver was on
the master's business, and acting within the scope of
his employment. This rule was said by Blackstone to
be founded on the superintendence and control which
the master is supposed to exercise over his servant. 1
Bl. Com. 431.

The rule arises out of the relation of superior and
subordinate, and is applicable to that relation wherever
it exists, and is coextensive with the relationship itself.
It is founded on the power of control which the superior has a right to exercise, and which, for the safety
of other persons, he is bound to exercise, over the acts
of his subordinates, and in strict analogy to liability
ex contractu upon the maxim, *"Qui facit per alium facit
per se." Clark* v. *Fry,* 8 Ohio St., 358, 72 Am. Dec. 590.
This rule is not modified by the existence of the fact
that the negligent servant is jointly employed by two
or more persons. For instance, in the case of a flagman
at a railroad crossing jointly employed by two or more
railroads, the road in whose service he is negligent, or
otherwise commits a tort, is liable for his misconduct.
Brow v. *Boston, etc., R. R. Co.,* 157 Mass., 399, 32 N. E.
362; *Illinois Central R. R. Co.* v. *King,* 69 Miss., 852, 13
South. 824.

It is said in 26 Cyc., p. 1525, that: "Where a servant
is generally employed by several persons who are not
partners, each contributing to his wages, one of the
masters is not liable for the misconduct of the servant
while engaged solely in the service of another master."

For the text a case is cited from a circuit court in Ohio. From a note to the text, it appears that the case cited was where three persons hired a coachman and divided his wages, and the carriage belonged to one, and the horse to another, and a person was injured by the negligence of the coachman while driving one of his employers. It was held that the latter employer alone was liable for the injuries. Upon such a meager report of the case upon which the text is founded, we cannot determine its soundness. Upon principle, it would seem that if two or more persons, as the case under consideration, purchase an automobile in partnership and employ a driver, whose duty it is to drive the vehicle for the joint and separate use of the partnership, that both owners would be liable for injuries resulting from the negligence of the driver, whether they were both using the automobile at the time or not. In fact, neither owner was occupying the car at the time of this accident. It had left the residence of Mrs. Richardson, and was on its way to the office of Mr. Goodman for the purpose of conveying him to the residence of Mrs. Richardson, and it is conceded that this was one of the purposes for which the automobile was owned and operated by them. While it is entirely true that the driver and the automobile were going for Mr. Goodman, it is none the less true that the driver was doing the thing for which he was jointly employed, and the machine was being used for one of the purposes for which it was jointly owned. The machine is partnership property, and the driver was in the service of the partnership. There is no separateness of time at which the driver may serve, or of interest in the automobile, so that it could be said that the machine belonged exclusively to one, or the driver was exclusively in his service. The case might be different if the understanding between Mrs. Richardson and Mr. Goodman had been that at certain hours of the day one should have the exclusive use of the machine and the driver. But the proof is that each one has an equal right to the use of the machine and the services of the driver, with the slight exception stated heretofore.

Under the partnership arrangement, Mrs. Richardson could have directed the driver, when leaving for Mr. Goodman, to speed the car and return to her within a given time, and this shows that, as joint employer, she had control of the servant at the time of the accident.

We have examined *Lotz* v. *Hanlon*, 217 Pa., 339, 66 Atl., 525, 10 L. R. A. (N. S.), 202, 118 Am. St. Rep., 922, 10 Ann. Cas., 731; *Steffen* v. *McNaughton*, 142 Wis., 49, 124 N. W., 1016, 26 L. R. A. (N. S.), 382, 19 Ann. Cas., 1227; *Eichman* v. *Buchheit*, 128 Wis., 385, 107 N. W., 325, 8 Ann. Cas., 435. These cases and the annotator's notes indicate that the weight of authority is that an automobile is not a dangerous instrument, so as to be classed with locomotive engines, dangerous animals, explosives, and the like, and also that the liability of the owner of an automobile for acts or omissions of his chauffeur in handling the machine depends upon whether, at the time of the act or omission complained of, the chauffeur was acting within the scope of his employment; that the relationship between owner and chauffeur is not different from that existing between master and servant generally, and is governed by the same general rules of law which govern the relationship of master and servant. The cases referred to do not disclose the existence of any statutory regulation of the subject in the States in which they were decided, and the notes to those cases indicate that the authorities cited are speaking with reference to the general subject of master and servant, and proceeding upon the idea that an automobile is not a dangerous instrument, and falls within the general rule stated. In this case it is not necessary for us to say what effect chapter 173, Acts of 1905, would have upon the general rule, or whether this enactment of the legislature was intended to place the automobile in the category of dangerous instruments.

We believe the judgment of the court of civil appeals should be affirmed, for the reason stated, and that is that the driver and the automobile were employed directly in the execution of the purposes of the joint ownership of the automobile and the joint employment of the driver. It was a partnership arrangement, and not a separate interest which each had in the automobile and in the service of the driver.

STRONG, Superintendent of Workhouse, *v.* STATE, *ex rel.* BARRETT.

(*Jackson.* April Term, 1914.)

CONSTITUTIONAL LAW. Costs. Jury. Escape of prisoners. Working out costs of recapture. Due process of law.

Workhouse Act (Shannon's Code sec. 7423), providing that a prisoner, who escapes, when recaptured shall be made to work out the costs of the same, in addition to the other costs in the case, and making no provision for hearing and without fixing what is a reasonable amount for recapture, is unconstitutional as denying the right to trial by jury and due process of law guaranteed by Const. art. 1, sec. 8.

Acts cited and construed. Acts 1875, ch. 83; Acts 1891, ch. 123.

Code cited and construed. Sec. 7423 (S.).

Cases cited and approved: In re Mallon, 16 Idaho, 737; State v. State, 46 Tenn., 250; People v. Creamer, 30 App. Div., 624; State v. Sanders, 153 N. C., 627; State v. Everitt, 164 N. C., 399; Ughbanks v. Armstrong, 208 U. S., 481.

FROM SHELBY.

Appeal from Circuit Court, Shelby County.—H. W. LAUGHLIN, Judge.

R. LEE BARTELS and GREER & GREER, for appellant.

CLARENCE FRIEDMAN, for appellee.

MR. JUSTICE WILLIAMS delivered the opinion of the Court.

The relator, Barrett, was convicted in the criminal court of Shelby county and sentenced to serve a term of eleven months and twenty-nine days in the county workhouse, and to pay the costs of the prosecution. After serving a portion of the sentence period he escaped; but he was recaptured and again placed in the workhouse. After then completing the original term of service, he tendered to the proper official the amount of the costs of his prosecution, $114, which was refused on the ground that the county had expended the further sum of $125 in recapturing him, which sum was demanded, making the aggregate of $239 required to be paid as the condition of his release.

A writ of *habeas corpus* was sued out to enforce release upon the payment of the $114 and without payment of the $125. The circuit judge granted the relief sought by Barrett; and the relator, who is superintendent of the workhouse, has appealed.

The record shows no denial that there was an escape from custody, and there is neither denial nor admission that the expense of recapture was properly the sum stated.

The general workhouse act (Acts 1891, ch. 123, sec. 18; Code, Shannon, sec. 7423) provides: ''Should any prisoner escape, he or she shall forfeit all deductions (of good time) that have been allowed, and, when recaptured, shall be made to work out the costs of the same, in addition to the other costs in the case.''

It is the contention of the relator that Barrett was properly held to work out the cost of his recapture under the statute, while Barrett insists that this provision is unconstitutional in that it works a denial of trial by a jury of his peers and of due process of law.

The statute under review makes no provision for an opportunity to the prisoner to be heard, for representation by counsel, or for the production of evidence as to the fact or intent of the escape. The amount to be expended in recapture is not fixed by the statute, and the reasonableness of the same is not provided to be ascertained after an inquiry in which the prisoner may be heard, in which hearing the rules of procedure shall be the same as are applied in similar causes, as must be the case. *In re Mallon*, 16 Idaho, 737, 102 Pac., 374, 22 L. R. A. (N. S.), 1123.

It is conceded by relator that escape and prison breach are offenses at common law. The statute in question does not even undertake to declare such an escape a statutory crime and fix the payment of cost of recapture as punishment for its infraction. We have, then, to deal with an effort to enforce punishment for such an offense without a trial by a jury and without procedure that satisfies the requirement of the constitutional right of due process of law, under Constitution of Tennessee, art. 1, sec. 8, which provides that no free man shall be taken or imprisoned but by the judgment of his peers and the law of the land, nor shall any person be deprived of life, liberty or property without due process of law. *State* v. *Staten,* 46 Tenn. (6 Cold.) 250.

A kindred question arose in this State and was decided in *Knox* v. *State,* 68 Tenn. (9 Baxt.), 202. Acts 1875, ch. 83, sec. 4, provided that after working out the term in the workhouse fixed by the jury, and the costs in the case, the convict should be further held to work out "all costs which may accrue after conviction for clothing and other necessaries." The court, in an opinion by Judge McFarland, held that this quoted provision was void under the above section of the Constitution. See, also, *People* v. *Creamer,* 30 App. Div., 624, 53 N. Y. Supp., 1111; *State* v. *Sanders,* 153 N. C., 627, 69 S. E., 272; *State* v. *Everitt,* 164 N. C., 399, 79 S. E., 274, 47 L. R. A. (N. S.), 848.

The appellant relies upon a line of cases wherein, under prison rules, a board or some official has authority to determine how much good time should be allowed prisoners, and, after such time has been allowed to take it from them for cause not judicially passed on. It is held that such withdrawal is not a denial of due process of law. These rulings, perhaps, might have relation to that portion of the statute which makes the escape of a prisoner "forfeit all deductions of good time that have been allowed," since the allowance of good time was but the grant of a favor to a convicted criminal in confinement, and that grant may have attached to it such conditions, precedent or subsequent, as the legislature may see fit. The withdrawal of the favor so extended on violation of such a condition is held not to be a denial of due process of law. *Ughbanks* v. *Armstrong,* 208 U. S., 481, 28 Sup. Ct., 372, 52 L. Ed., 582.

The distinction between such a case and the one at bar is obvious.

There was no error in the judgment of the court below holding the particular provision herein questioned unconstitutional. Affirmed.

Lumber Co. v. Insurance Co.

ATLAS HARDWOOD LUMBER Co. *v.* GEORGIA LIFE INSUR-
ANCE Co.

(*Jackson.* April Term, 1914.)

INSURANCE. Employer's liability policy. Loss. Necessity of payments.

An employer's liability policy provided that no action would lie
  thereon unless brought in the name of assured for loss actually
  sustained and paid in money by the assured in satisfaction of
  a judgment after trial. *Held,* that payment by and loss to the
  insured were conditions precedent to a recovery on the policy,
  and hence, where the insured transferred a claim under the
  policy to an injured employee, and after judgment against it
  recovered by the employee brought suit for his benefit on the
  policy without having paid the judgment, insured could not recover.

Cases cited and approved: Finley v. Casualty Co., 113 Tenn.,
  592; Cayard v. Robertson, 123 Tenn., 382; Brick Co. v. Surety
  Co., 126 Tenn., 402; St. Louis Dressed Beef & P. Co. v. Maryland
  Casualty Co., 201 U. S., 173.

FROM SHELBY.

Appeal from Chancery Court, Shelby County.—F. H.
HEISKELL, Chancellor.

WILSON & ARMSTRONG, for appellant.

R. LEE BARTELS, for appellee.

MR. JUSTICE GREEN delivered the opinion of the Court.

The defendant insurance company which does an employer's liability business, issued a policy to the complainant whereby the insurance company agreed to indemnify the lumber company against loss arising or resulting from claims upon the insured for damages on account of bodily injuries accidentally sustained by any employee or employees of the insured.

One James H. Poag, claiming to have been an employee of the lumber company, and to have sustained injuries while in the service of the latter, brought suit against the lumber company and recovered a judgment by default for $15,000. By agreement between attorneys for Poag and for the lumber company, this judgment was set aside in consideration of the lumber company's assigning to Poag its rights or claim against the insurance company on account of this accident. Another trial was had which resulted in a judgment in favor of Poag against the lumber company for $5,000.

Upon the happening of the accident on account of which Poag sued, the lumber company gave due notice to the insurance company, and the insurance company investigated the accident and denied any liability therefor, for the reason that it concluded Poag was not in the service of the insured at the time of the accident, but was in the service of an independent contractor. The insurance company declined to assume the defense of the suit brought by Poag, or to have anything to do with it. Likewise, the insurance company has refused the demand of the lumber company to satisfy the judgment which Poag has obtained against the lumber company, to which reference has just been made. This suit is brought by the lumber company in its own right, and for the use of Poag to recover from the insurance company the amount of this judgment, together with costs and attorney's fees, expended by the lumber company in resisting suit. There was a decree in favor of the insurance company below, and the lumber company has appealed. The lumber company has not paid Poag's judgment, nor does it appear that payment of the other amounts included in its suit has been paid by it.

The policy issued to the insured recited that in consideration of a certain premium and statements made, the insurance company "hereby agrees to indemnify the assured designated in the said schedule against loss arising or resulting from claims upon the assured for damages on account of bodily injuries suffered or alleged to have been suffered while this policy is in force, including death resulting at any time therefrom by any employee or employees of the assured by reason of the operation of the trade or business described in the said schedule, and to defend the assured and pay expenses and costs subject to the following conditions."

The only conditions of the policy necessary to be considered in this opinion are conditions B and D which are as follows:

"Condition B. When any accident occurs the assured shall give immediate written notice thereof to the company at its home office in Macon, Georgia, or to its duly authorized agent. If any claim is made on account of such accident the assured shall give like notice thereof. If any suit is brought to enforce such a claim the assured shall immediately forward to the company at its home office in Macon, Georgia, every summons or other process as soon as the same is served on him, and the company shall defend such suit (whether groundless or not) in the name and on behalf of the assured. All expenses (legal and otherwise) incurred by the company in defending such suit, and all court costs assessed against the assured shall be paid by the company (whether the verdict is for or against the assured) regardless of the limits of liability expressed in condition N. The assured shall always give to the company all co-operation and assistance possible. The company shall have the right to settle any claim or suit at its own cost at any time.

"Condition D. No action shall lie against the company under the indemnity clause herein unless brought by and in the name of the assured for loss actually sustained and paid in money by the assured in satisfaction of a judgment after trial of the issue. No action shall lie against the company under any other agreement herein, unless brought by and in the name of the assured for money actually paid by him. In no event shall any action lie against the company, unless brought within two years after the right of action accrues. The company does not prejudice by this condition any defenses to any such action to which it may be entitled.''

It will be observed that by the terms of this policy the insurance company agrees to indemnify the assured against loss on account of accident covered thereby, and does not agree to indemnify the insured against liability from loss on account of such accidents.

This distinction is well recognized in law and has been taken by this court in two cases. *Finley* v. *Casualty Co.*, 113 Tenn., 592, 83 S. W., 2, 3 Ann. Cas., 962; *Cayard* v. *Robertson*, 123 Tenn., 382, 131 S. W., 864, 30 L. R. A. (N. S.), 1224, Ann. Cas. 1912C, 152.

In *Finley* v. *Casualty Co.*, supra, the authorities are reviewed at length, and this court said that under policies insuring against indemnity from loss, ''the amount of insurance does not become available until the assured has paid the loss and is not even then available unless proper notice has been given as provided in the policy.''

As stated above, the assured in this case has not paid the loss, and the authorities approved in *Finley* v. *Casualty Co.*, and upon which that case rests, hold that such payment is a condition precedent to the maintenance of a suit against the indemnity company on such a policy. In other words, the cases hold that until the claim or judgment against the assured has been paid by him, he has sustained no loss, and therefore, he has no claim under a policy insuring him against loss.

The policy under examination in *Finley* v. *Casualty Company,* supra, was in all essential particulars similar to the one here sued upon, and was held to be a policy against indemnity from loss, and not a policy against indemnity from liability on account of loss. *Finley* v. *Casualty Co.* was followed and approved by the later case of *Cayard* v. *Robertson,* supra, and we think the rule announced in these two cases is decisive of the present controversy.

Counsel for the complainant assumes that relief was denied the complainant in *Finley* v. *Casualty Co.* on account of a provision in the policy there construed similar to condition D of this policy heretofore set out. It is then argued that by repudiating liability in the outset, and refusing to undertake the defense of Poag's suit, this defendant insurance company waived the benefit of condition D, and should be held liable on the authority of *Brick Co.* v. *Surety Co.,* 126 Tenn., 402, 150 S. W., 92, Ann. Cas. 1913E, 107, and *St. Louis Dressed Beef & P. Co.* v. *Maryland Casualty Co.,* 201 U. S., 173, 26 Sup. Ct., 400, 50 L. Ed., 712.

The two cases just mentioned are to the effect that a provision in a policy of this kind, similar to condition D, may not be relied on by an insurance company in certain cases where it has breached its primary obligation under the contract of insurance, and repudiated all responsibility for a claim properly falling within the terms of its contract of indemnity. In both cases the losses were paid by the assured.

This court held in *Brick Co.* v. *Surety Co.*, supra, when the Surety Company refused to do any of the things it had contracted to do upon notice of an accident included in the terms of the policy issued, that by such action the company breached its contract of insurance and became liable to the insured for the legal consequences of this breach. We held that a provision like condition D did not apply to such a case; that the company had to pay the loss its default had occasioned, and which had been by the Brick Company discharged.

We adhere to the rule announced in *Brick Co.* v. *Surety Company*. In this case we may eliminate entirely condition D and its effect. We then have a case in which an insurer against loss breached its contract to defend a suit brought against the assured. The contract having been to indemnify against loss, the measure of damages for the breach would be the loss suffered by the assured. As we have heretofore seen, there has been no payment by the assured on account of this accident, and it has therefore sustained no loss. Payment by the assured, loss to the assured, must appear before there can be a recovery on this policy. This is true, regardless of condition D, and results from the nature of the obligation.

For the foregoing reasons, we think the chancellor correctly determined the case in favor of the defendant. The question upon which we decide the case was raised by demurrer, and later by a motion for peremptory instructions. The chancellor directed a verdict

in favor of the insurance company, the case having been
tried by a jury, but it does not distinctly appear upon
what ground he based his action. Several defenses
were interposed by the insurance company. Without
passing on the other points in the case, we must hold
that payment on account of this loss or judgment
against it is a condition precedent to any recovery
by the complainant upon the policy here sued on. The
chancellor's decree will be affirmed, with costs.

ARBUCKLE *v.* ARBUCKLE *et al.*

(*Jackson.* April Term, 1914.)

1. **GUARDIAN AND WARD. Ward's real estate. Sale. Purchase by witness. Statutes.**

Shannon's Code, sec. 5078, provides that on an application for sale of a ward's real estate the pleading shall set forth fully the age and condition of the ward, what other property, if any, he owns, and the reason why a sale was sought. Section 5088 declares that no guardian, next friend, or witness in such cause shall purchase at such sale, or afterwards until five years from removal of existing disabilities, and, if he does so, the sale shall be void. *Held,* that only such witnesses are deprived of the right to purchase as resort to their testimony as an artifice to bring about a sale of the infant's property in order that they may purchase, and hence a purchaser within the prohibition must testify to facts which would reflect in some material degree on the jurisdictional facts included in section 5078, and this testimony must have influenced the court's judgment in the decision of those questions. (*Post, p.* 487.)

Code cited and construed: Secs. 5072, 5078, 5088 (S.).

Cases cited and distinguished: Starkey v. Hammer, 60 Tenn., 445; Hunt v. Glen, 79 Tenn., 16.

2. **GUARDIAN AND WARD. Ward's realty. Purchase by witness.**

A witness having purchased certain undivided interests in land agreed with the guardian of a minor owning a one-sixth interest to purchase the same for $500. In proceedings to confirm the sale, the witness was subpoenaed by the guardian and testified that he was familiar with the property, that he owned five-sixths thereof, that he and the minor's guardian, who was an intelligent woman, had contracted for a sale of the minor's interest to a witness for $500, and, though he had paid $1,000 for an undivided one-third interest in the property and $650 for an undivided one-sixth interest, he thought the price he proposed to pay was fair. *Held*, that such testimony did not bar the witness from purchasing or authorize an avoidance of the sale under Shannon's Code, sec. 5088, declaring that no witness shall purchase at a guardian's sale, or at any time within five years after the removal of the existing disabilities, etc. (*Post*, p. 490.)

FROM SHELBY.

Appeal from the Chancery Court of Shelby County to the Court of Civil Appeals and by *certiorari* from the Court of Civil Appeals to the Supreme Court.— ✗✗✗✗✗✗✗✗✗✗ F. H. Heiskell, Chancellor.

Metcalf, Minor & Metcalf, for guardian.

W. H. Fitzhugh, for ward.

Mr. Justice Lansden delivered the opinion of the Court.

This case is before us upon a petition for writs of *certiorari* to a decree of the court of civil appeals, which reversed the decree of the chancellor confirming an agreed sale between the guardian and the defendant Frazer of an undivided one-sixth interest of a tract of land in which Frazer and Edith Arbuckle, a minor, were tenants in common.

It appears that Mrs. Arbuckle is now guardian in California of her daughter Edith, who was nine years old at the time of the filing of the original bill, and that they had removed their residence from Shelby county, Tenn., to Los Angeles, Cal., about one year prior to the filing of the bill. The bill seeks to confirm an agreed sale entered into between Mrs. Arbuckle, as guardian of her daughter, and the defendant Frazer, by which Frazer agreed to pay to the guardian $500 net for the ward's undivided one-sixth interest in the land. The proof is overwhelming that the sale was an advantageous one, because the price offered was the full value of the land, and the guardian was receiving a very small income from the investment in the land, and, she and her daughter having removed to California to reside permanently, it was inconvenient to her to look after the land in Tennessee. This is not questioned.

The sole error assigned in the court of civil appeals, and which that court sustained, was that the sale to Frazer was void because he testified in the case as a witness for the guardian in violation of section 5088 of Shannon's Code. Proceedings of the nature of this bill are regulated by chapter 3 of Shannon's Code, sec. 5072, *et seq.* Section 5078 requires that the pleadings should set forth "fully and particularly the age, circumstances, and condition of the party under disability; what other property, if any, such person owns, or is in any way entitled to, and the cause or reason why a sale of the particular property is sought."

Section 5088 provides:

"No guardian, next friend or witness, in such cause, shall purchase at such sale, or at any time afterwards, until five years from the removal of the existing disabilities; and if any such person shall make such purchase, the original sale shall become void, and the infant or married woman may bring ejectment for the land, as if no sale had been made."

In *Starkey* v. *Hammer*, 1 Baxt., 445, it was said:

"The object of the statute was to prevent purchases by witnesses who had given evidence tending to show the necessity of the sale, and for this purpose they are forbidden to buy, and their purchase declared void, and we can but enforce the provisions of the statute."

The case cited also held that the remedy of the infant or a married woman was not limited to ejectment as provided in the statute. The remedy enforced in that case, while not technical ejectment, was in effect so, as it was a bill to remove cloud. In *Hunt* v. *Glenn*, 11 Lea, 16, it was said that the purpose of the foregoing section of the Code "is to protect persons under disability from the artifices of persons who may desire to own their property and may resort to unfair means, even upon the witness stand, to bring it to a sale that they may purchase." In that case it was held that a witness who testified only that he agreed with the trustee to purchase, and was willing with the approval of the court to purchase at an agreed price, was not within the prohibited class described by section 5088, Shannon's Code. Certainly such a witness would not fall within the declaration of the purpose of that section of the Code made by the court in *Hunt* v. *Glenn.*

We hold that the statement of the purpose of the legislature in enacting the prohibition contained in section 5088 is correctly stated in *Hunt* v. *Glenn.* The statement of the legislative purpose made in *Starkey* v. *Hammer* was evidently not intended to be full or complete, and isolated from the remainder of the opinion; the statement quoted is too broad, and is certainly not in harmony with the later case of *Hunt* v. *Glenn.* *Hunt* v. *Glenn* expressly held that it was not every witness who gave testimony in such a case that was prohibited from buying. It is only witnesses who resort to their testimony in the case as an artifice to bring about a sale of the infant's property in order that they may purchase who are forbidden to buy. It is not meant that the artifice itself must appear from the testimony of the witness, or necessarily from extrinsic facts; but it would be sufficient if the witness who afterwards became the purchaser should testify to material facts which it could be seen would reasonably influence the judgment of the court in ordering or confirming a sale.

The jurisdictional facts and those which must control the discretion of the court are set out in section 5078, supra, and relate to the age of the minor, his circumstances in life, and his condition, what other property he owns or is entitled to, and the cause or reason why sale of the particular property is sought. A witness who becomes a purchaser, in order to fall

within the prohibition of section 5088, must testify to
facts which would reflect in some material degree upon
the jurisdictional facts included in section 5078, and
his testimony must have influenced the judgment of
the court in the decision of those questions.

The witness Frazer testified in substance that he
was familiar with this property, and was the owner
of five-sixths, and the minor was the owner of the other
one-sixth; that he and the guardian, who is the minor's
mother and an intelligent, competent woman, had made
a contract by which he agreed to pay $500 net for
the minor's interest in the land, and that he had deposited with the court $25 as earnest money; that he
had bought land in the neighborhood of this land both
before and since the filing of the bill; that for some
of his other purchases he had paid more, and for others
he had paid less, than he was agreeing to pay for
this land; that he had paid $1,000 for an undivided
one-third interest in this particular property, and he
had paid $650 for an undivided one-sixth interest; that
he thought the price he proposed to pay for this one-
sixth was fair, and the rental received by the guardian
is small. He exhibited with his deposition the correspondence he had had with the guardian, and which
resulted in the agreement of sale sought to be confirmed.

The court of civil appeals held that the purchase
by this witness was void because he testified as above
set out.

We think this was error. It should be stated that this witness was called by the guardian, and most all of the facts detailed by him were brought out by counsel representing the guardian. His testimony relates to facts which he could not in good faith have withheld from the court, whether he had been called by the guardian or not. One significant fact testified to by him is that only a few months previous to his making the contract with the guardian he purchased a one-sixth undivided interest of the identical tract for $150 more than he proposed to pay for this interest. This evidence would tend to show that it was not to the manifest interest of the minor that the agreed sale be confirmed, and we think it affirmatively negatives any artifice upon the part of the witness to bring the minor's property to sale in order that he might purchase it. We think the testimony of Mr. Frazer clearly shows that he acted in the very best faith, that he made a full and complete disclosure of all facts within his possession, and that he was in possession of material facts which the court should have known.

To allow the guardian and ward to avoid this sale upon the ground sustained by the court of civil appeals after the lapse of nearly eight years would be to allow them to use the law and the machinery of the courts as instrumentalities for the perpetration of fraud. As we have said, Mrs. Arbuckle and the defendant Frazer entered into an agreement for the sale and purchase of this interest in the land involved, and Mrs. Arbuckle, as guardian of her daughter, filed the original bill to have this agreement confirmed by the chancellor. She then subpoenaed Frazer as a witness, and he testified to the facts heretofore detailed by her procurement. He did not volunteer and could not have declined to testify, had he so desired. We are now asked to take away from him the land which he acquired by the decree of the chancellor, notwithstanding that the complainants have his money, and are themselves beyond the jurisdiction of the courts of this State; and the reason for inflicting this injury upon him, which we are asked to approve, is that he testified in the case as a witness called by the guardian. If such a result could be worked out through the courts, it would enable guardians and others occupying similar relationships to perpetrate frauds of the most vicious character.

The statute was not intended to apply to such cases. The decree of the court of civil appeals is reversed, and that of the chancellor is affirmed.

McDONALD AUTOMOBILE CO. *v.* BICKNELL.*

(*Jackson.* April Term, 1914.)

1. **Sales. Conditional Sales. Collateral Security.**

Where a seller under a conditional sale contract subsequently takes security, personal or collateral, he does not thereby divest himself of his retained title or authority to retake the goods for the buyer's failure to pay the price. (*Post, p.* 495.)

Cases cited and approved: Edgewood Distilling Co., v. Shannon, 60 Ark., 133; Thornton v. Findlay, 97 Ark., 432; Bierce v. Hutchins, 205 U. S., 340; Monitor Drill Co. v. Mercer, 163 Fed., 943; Kimball v. Costa, 76 Vt., 289; Pettyplace v, Groton, etc., Co. 103 Mich., 155; Standard Steam Laundry v. Dole, 22 Utah, 311; Bank v. Vandyck, 51 Tenn., 617; Manufacturing Co. v. Buchanan, 118 Tenn., 238; Byrns v. Woodward, 78 Tenn., 444; Murrell v. Watson, 1 Tenn., ch., 342; Fogg v. Rogers, 42 Tenn., 290; Anthony v. Smith, 28 Tenn., 508.

2. **Sales. Conditional Sales. Recovery of Property. Right to Sue.**

Where reservation of title to property conditionally sold was contained in the contract, and not in the notes for the unpaid price, the seller, though having indorser the notes, was still entitled to enforce the condition and recover the property in replevin; he being interested as indorser in securing satisfaction of the notes to the holder out of the proceeds of the sale. (*Post, p.* 495.)

Case cited and approved: McPherson v. Acme Lumber Co., 70 Miss., 649.

FROM SHELBY.

Appeal from the Chancery Court of Shelby County to the Court of Civil Appeals and by *certiorari* from the Court of Civil Appeals to the Supreme Court.— F. H. HEISKELL, Judge.

---

*The question of the effect of taking collateral security upon conditional sale is treated in a note in 33 L. R. A. (N. S.), 491.

H. H. BARKER, for plaintiff.

W. P. BIGGS, for defendant.

MR. JUSTICE WILLIAMS delivered the opinion of the Court.

This is an action of replevin involving the right to the possession of an automobile sold by complainant company to one McEachern under a sale contract in which title was retained by the vendor to secure seven notes of $100 each, representing unpaid balance of purchase money. These were plain promissory notes, and contained no reference to the automobile. They were indorsed by Smith and Collier, then by the payee company, and discounted in bank by the company. At maturity all of the notes were not paid, and the bank granted a renewal in the form of a consolidated note, of the same character, but with an additional indorser thereon, Moore.

A few days before indorsing the note last referred to Moore took from McEachern a power of sale chattel mortgage on the automobile to secure a note of $200 due from McEachern. On default this mortgage was foreclosed; defendant Bicknell becoming the purchaser.

It is the contention of Bicknell that the security by way of retention of title was waived by the taking of the renewal note without therein retaining title, but with the addition of a personal surety. Both the chancellor and the court of civil appeals ruled against this contention, and petition for writ of *certiorari* for review is before us.

There is a line of decisions cited and relied upon by petitioner Bicknell which cases tend to support his insistence.

In the case of *Edgewood Distilling Co.* v. *Shannon*, 60 Ark., 133, 29 S. W., 147, followed by *Thornton* v. *Findlay*, 97 Ark., 432, 134 S. W., 627, 33 L. R. A. (N. S.), 491, it was held that, where a vendor of personal property, sold conditionally, sued to recover its possession, and there was evidence tending to prove that, after the sale, the purchase money was paid partly in cash and by the execution of a new note, the vendee's title became absolute, unless there was an agreement for a reservation of title in the vendor at the time of the execution of the second note, citing 35 Cyc., 675.

It is stated by the writer of the article in Cyc. that:

"As a general rule, if the seller takes a mortgage or other security for the price, such act will be regarded as a waiver of the condition reserving the title and an election to consider the sale as absolute."

Whether or not this was a fair statement of the majority rule at the time it was written, we need not consider. We think it certain that at this date it may not be correctly said that the "taking of other security" operates as such waiver.

While, as indicated, the authorities are not harmonious on the question, the best and decided weight of authority we believe to be to the effect that the subsequent taking of security, personal or collateral, does not operate to divest such seller of his retained title. Thus in the leading case of *Bierce* v. *Hutchins*, 205 U. S., 340, 27 Sup. Ct., 524, 51 L. Ed., 828, such taking of additional security, contemporaneously with or subsequent to the execution of the contract of conditional sale, was not allowed to work such result, and that case was followed in *Monitor Drill Co.* v. *Mercer*, 163 Fed., 943, 90 C. C. A., 303, 20 L. R. A. (N. S.), 1065, 16 Ann. Cas., 214.

Other cases in accord are *Kimball* v. *Costa*, 76 Vt.. 289, 56 Atl., 1009, 104 Am. St. Rep., 937, 1 Ann. Cas., 610; *Pettyplace* v. *Groton, etc., Co.*, 103 Mich., 155, 61 N. W., 266; *Standard Steam Laundry* v. *Dole*, 22 Utah, 311, 61 Pac., 1103, and cases cited in the annotation of the case of *Monitor Drill Co.* v. *Mercer*, supra.

These are also cases in harmony with the rulings of this court in analogous cases. In this State such retention of title by a vendor is a mere security for the payment of the price, partaking of the nature of a lien (*Bank* v. *Vandyck*, 4 Heisk., 617; *Manufacturing Co.* v. *Buchanan*, 118 Tenn., 238, 251, 99 S. W., 984, 8 L. R. A. [N. S.], 590, 121 Am. St. Rep., 1002, 12 Ann. Cas., 707), and in cases of express vendor's liens the renewal with additional security does not effect a waiver (*Byrns* v. *Woodward*, 10 Lea, 444; *Murrell* v. *Watson*, 1 Tenn. Ch., 342).

The same rule applies in case real estate is involved, and the vendor retains the legal title. *Fogg* v. *Rogers*, 2 Cold., 290; *Anthony* v. *Smith*, 9 Humph., 508.

It is next insisted that the holder of the notes, the bank which discounted them, alone may replevin the automobile; that the vendor company has no interest or *status* to that end. The reservation of title in the company appeared in the contract, not in the notes, and manifestly the company was in a position to regain possession of the machine by the writ of replevin, and was interested as indorser in the holder of the notes being satisfied out of the proceeds of sale, following repossession. *McPherson* v. *Acme Lumber Co.*, 70 Miss., 649, 12 South., 857; 35 Cyc., 702.

Writ of *certiorari* denied.

SUGGS *v.* STATE.

(*Jackson.* April Term, 1914.)

BAIL. Liability of Surety.

Sureties upon a bail bond conditioned that accused should not depart without leave of court are not liable where, after conviction and sentence which provided for incarceration in the county jail pending the coming of proper authorities to carry accused to the penitentiary, and sheriff improperly allowed accused to go without custody for a few days, and he escaped, for, the sureties having delivered accused into the custody of the court, there was no further liability on the recognizance.

Cases cited and approved: State v. Whitson, 8 Blackf. (Ind.), 178; State v. Stewart, 74 Iowa, 336; Dennard v. State, 2 Ga., 137; Neininger v. State, 50 Ohio St., 394; Hawk v. State, 84 Ala., 466; Roberts v. Gordon, 86 Ga., 386; State v. Wilson, 14 La. Ann., 450; State v. Cobb, 44 Mo. App., 375; Fortenberry v. State, 47 Tex. Cr. R., 84; Phillips v. State, 100 Ark., 515; Miller v. State, 158 Ala., 73; Com. v. Skaggs, 152 Ky., 268; State v. Murman, 124 Mo., 502; State v. Charles, 207 Mo., 40.

Cases cited and distinguished: *Ex parte* Williams, 114 Ala., 29; Miller v. State, 158 Ala., 73.

FROM CROCKETT

Appeal from Circuit Court, Crockett County.—T. E. HARWOOD, Judge.

W. M. McCALL, and W. H. BIGGS, for Suggs.

W. H. SWIGGART, JR., assistant attorney-general, for the State.

MR. JUSTICE WILLIAMS delivered the opinion of the Court.

The single legal question to be herein treated of arises out of the facts following:

Suggs was charged with a felony, and Duffy and another were sureties on his recognizance for his appearance before the trial court on a day fixed to answer the State of Tennessee upon a charge of burglary, "defendant not to depart the court without leave." Suggs appeared and stood his trial, which resulted in a verdict of guilty, after entry of which sentence was pronounced by the court:

"It is considered that for the offense aforesaid the defendant be confined in the state penitentiary for one year, and that he be remanded to the county jail to await the proper authorities to take him to said penitentiary."

Due to a misunderstanding not induced by the sureties, the sheriff permitted Suggs to go without custody for several subsequent days of the term, after which defendant departed the jurisdiction. Following judgment *nisi* on the recognizance against the sureties, *scire facias* issued for the sureties to show cause why the same should not be made final.

The sureties defended on the ground, among others, that by the sentence and order for incarceration the convicted defendant had been taken out of their custody. Cast upon all defenses, one of the sureties has appealed to this court and renewed the defenses.

Hawkins, in his Pleas of the Crown, in stating the law as to the power and duty of the sureties, says:

"It must be confessed that, if a man's bail, who are his jailers of his own choosing, do as effectually secure his appearance and put him as much under the power of the court as if he had been in the custody of the proper officer, they seem to have answered the end of the law and to have done all that can be reasonably required of them."

This early statement of the rule by the eminent author may well be said to concisely summarize the best holdings in cases coming into adjudication since his day.

A line of demarcation in the decisions, exceptional cases disregarded, differentiates the sureties' liability following conviction or verdict from their nonliability following the pronouncement of sentence upon the principal.

Thus, where a bail bond stipulates that the principal is not to depart without leave of the court, the sureties are not exonerated by the mere conviction of the principal. *State* v. *Whitson*, 8 Blackf. (Ind.), 178; *State* v. *Stewart*, 74 Iowa, 336, 37 N. W., 400; *Dennard* v. *State*, 2 Ga., 137; *Neininger* v. *State*, 50 Ohio St., 394, 34 N. E., 633, 40 Am. St. Rep., 674; *Hawk* v. *State*, 84 Ala., 466, 4 South., 690. But when a conviction is followed by a pronouncement of sentence, such pronouncement, it has been held, has the legal effect of a direction to the sheriff to hold the convicted defendant in custody, and operates to exonerate the sureties. *Roberts* v. *Gordon*, 86 Ga., 386, 12 S. E., 648; *State* v. *Wilson*, 14 La. Ann., 450; *State* v. *Cobb*, 44 Mo. App., 375; *Fortenberry* v. *State*, 47 Tex. Cr. R., 84, 79 S. W., 538; *Phillips* v. *State*, 100 Ark., 515, 140 S. W., 734.

In many of the cases an actual taking of the defendant into custody by the sheriff following sentence appears. *Miller* v. *State*, 158 Ala., 73, 48 South., 360, 20 L. R. A. (N. S.), 861; *Com.* v. *Skaggs*, 152 Ky., 268, 153 S. W., 422, 44 L. R. A. (N. S.), 1064, and cases cited in notes.

For the State it is insisted that, in order to a release of the sureties following sentence, it must be made to appear that the officer did in fact take control or custody of the principal in the bond.

In *Ex parte Williams*, 114 Ala., 29, 22 South., 446, it was said:

"Whenever a party is convicted and sentenced, he is no longer in the custody of his bail, but is in the custody of the proper officer of the law, and the bail are thereby discharged by operation of law without a formal order to that effect. The condition of the bond then will have been fully complied with. . . . The obligation of a proper bail bond binds the sureties, at least, until after the verdict of the jury; but, when the sentence of the law is pronounced, the officer of the law is charged with its due execution. The bail have no further control over the custody of their principal, and can no longer be held responsible. . . . The bail bond became *functus* by the trial and sentence."

See, also, *State* v. *Murmann*, 124 Mo., 502, 28 S. W., 2, as construed in *State* v. *Charles*, 207 Mo., 40, 105 S. W., 609, 13 Ann. Cas., 565.

In the case at bar we find not only a sentence but a remand of the defendant and principal to the county jail to await the coming of the proper authorities to take him to the penitentiary. May the failure of the sheriff to give heed to this plain pronouncement following sentence, in not taking custody of the defendant, avail to hold the sureties liable to the State?

In the case of *Miller* v. *State*, supra, it appeared that there was no such express order of the court as to custody as appears in this case; but the court said:

"While there was no express order of the court that he [the sheriff] should do so, there is, under such circumstances, always an implied order that the sheriff shall take custody of the defendant, and the defendant was as effectually in the custody of the sheriff as if the bail had delivered him . . .. into such custody. It is the surrendering of the defendant into custody of the sheriff that exonerates the bail under the statute, and if, under a judgment of the conviction of the offense charged, the sheriff rightfully secures custody of the defendant, it must follow that the defendant is as rightfully withdrawn from the custody of his bail, so far as that offense is concerned, as if they had surrendered him."

We are of opinion that, for a stronger reason, the judgment entered, with its stipulation for remand to jail, operated to place the defendant within the control and custody of the court and sheriff. After its entry it can scarcely be contended that he was in the custody of the sureties. The defendant was "as much under the power of the court as if he had been in the custody of the proper officer," and, as Hawkins says, this answers the end of the law. If there was dereliction following the sentence and remand to jail, it was not the dereliction of the sureties.

Other questions have been debated; but all are to be solved by the above adjudication upon the basic contention.

Reversed.

MISSIO *v.* WILLIAMS.*

(*Jackson.* April Term, 1914.)

1. **ANIMALS:** Injuries to persons. Liability.

The owner of premises who permits another to harbor thereon dogs which the owner knows are vicious, is liable for injuries inflicted by the dogs upon another. (*Post, p.* 507.)

2. **ANIMALS.** Injuries to persons. Liability. Knowledge of vicious character.

The owner or keeper of a domestic animal is not liable for injuries inflicted by the animal, unless he has knowledge of its vicious habits; but, where he has such knowledge his liability is not limited to negligence in the custody of the animal, but he is bound to keep the animal from doing mischief. (*Post, p.* 507.)

3. **ANIMALS.** Personal injuries. Liability. Knowledge of Vicious Character.

Knowledge by the owner or keeper of a dog that it is vicious is sufficient to render him liable for injuries inflicted by the dog, without a showing that it had ever before bitten any person. (*Post, p.* 507.)

Cases cited and approved: Sherfey v. Bartley, 36 Tenn., 58; Smith v. Causey, 22 Ala., 568; Le Forest v. Tolman, 117 Mass., 109; Popplewell v. Pierce, 10 Cush. (Mass.) 509; Loomis v. Terry, 17 Wend, (N. Y.) 496; Empire Spring Co. v. Edgar, 99 U. S., 645; Frammell v. Little, 16 Ind., 251; Marsh v. Jones, 21 Vt., 378; Wilkinson v. Parrott, 32 Cal., 102; Rider v. White, 65 N. Y., 54; Gordeau v. Blood, 52 Vt., 251.

---

*As to the liability of the keeper of an animal known to be dangerous as affected by absence of negligence on his part, see notes in 6 L. R. A. (N. S.), 1164, and 2 B. R. C., 14. And on the question as to what scienter is necessary to charge owner with liability for injury inflicted by dog to person or property of another, see note in 24 L. R. A. (N. S.), 458.

The questin of the liability of a married woman for the use and safety of premises owned by her is treated in the note in 19 L. R. A. (N. S.), 531.

4. **ANIMALS.   Injuries to persons.   Liability.   Wild Animals.**
Owners or keepers of animals which are naturally vicious are
liable for the acts of such animals, even though no notice of
their vicious propensities is shown. (*Post, p.* 507.)

Cases cited and approved: Empire Spring Co. v. Edgar, 99 U
S., 645; Vrooman v. Lawyer, 13 Johns, (N. Y.) 339; Sherfey
v. Bartley, 36 Tenn., 58.

5. **HUSBAND AND WIFE.   Liability of wife.   Torts.**
A married woman who permitted, during her husband's absence,
another to keep vicious dogs on her premises is liable for the
injuries inflicted by them, since she is liable for her own personal torts not committed in the presence or under the supposed influence of her husband. (*Post, p.* 509.)

Cases cited and approved: Dailey v. Houston, 58 Mo., 361;
Marshall v. Oakes, 51 Me., 308; Collier v. Struly, 99 Tenn.,
241.

6. **HUSBAND AND WIFE.   Liability of Wife.   Negligence of
Husband.**
A married woman is not liable for torts committed through the
negligence of her husband under the rule *respondeat superior*,
since she is not liable *ex contractu*. (*Post, p.* 510.)

7. **HUSBAND AND WIFE.   Liability of Husband.   Torts of Wife.**
Where a married woman, during her husband's absence, permitted vicious dogs to be kept upon the premises, the husband
is liable jointly with her for the injuries inflicted by the dogs
upon another. (*Post, p.* 510.)

Cases cited and approved: Collier v. Struly, 99 Tenn., 241:
Price v. Clapp, 119 Tenn.,425.

FROM SHELBY.

Appeal from the Circuit Court of Shelby County
to the Court of Civil Appeals and by *certiorari* from
the Court of Civil Appeals to the Supreme Court.—
——————, Judge.

BELL, TERRY & BELL, for plaintiff.

L. T. M. CANADA, for defendants.

MR. JUSTICE LANSDEN delivered the opinion of the Court.

The defendant in error recovered judgment in the court below against the plaintiff in error and her husband, R. L. Missio, for $300 for personal injuries inflicted upon the .defendant in error by two bull dogs which were kept on the premises of the plaintiff in error. Motion for a new trial was made and overruled, and an appeal was taken to the court of civil appeals, where the judgment of the circuit court was affirmed. The case is before us upon a petition for *certiorari* to the judgment of that court.

The facts are that a brother of Mrs. Missio, one Coradini, procured two bull pups and kept them on the premises of Mr. and Mrs. Missio for protection to Mr. and Mrs. Coradini. The dogs were known by the Coradinis and Mrs. Missio to be dangerous, and they were kept because of their dangerous and vicious habits. A sign was put up on the yard fence where the dogs were kept, "bad dogs."

Before the dogs were brought upon the premises, Mr. and Mrs. Missio left Tennessee for a visit to Italy, and Mr. Missio did not know of the presence of the dogs on the premises until after the defendant in error was injured by them. Mrs. Missio, however, returned home in September, before the defendant in error was attacked by the dogs in October, 1911, and she knew that her brother had the dogs on the premises, and the purposes for which they were kept.

The house and lot constituting the premises are the property of Mrs. Missio. She and her husband, her father, and mother, and brother lived together in this house.

The defendant in error is a scrubwoman and worked at the Peabody Hotel at night. She finished her labors for the night and boarded a street car to go home about daylight of the morning of the accident. She alighted from the street car near the premises of the plaintiff in error, and started down the street known as Kings Highway, when the two dogs rushed out of the yard and assaulted her and inflicted serious injuries upon her person.

The questions made here are that Mrs. Missio's plea of coverture is good, and that Mr. Missio is not liable, because he did not know of the presence of the dogs on the premises, and hence did not harbor them. And also that the mere fact that the dogs were on the premises with the knowledge of Mrs. Missio would not make either her or her husband liable, because they were owned by the Coradinis, and were kept on the plaintiff in error's premises by Coradini, and not by them.

What is perhaps the earliest rule upon this subject is found in Exodus, chapter 21, 28th and 29th verses, as follows:

"If an ox gore a man or a woman, that they die: then the ox shall surely be stoned, and his flesh shall not be eaten; but the owner of the ox shall be quit.

"But if the ox were wont to push with his horn in time past, and it hath been testified to his owner, and he hath not kept him in, but that he hath killed a man or a woman; the ox shall be stoned, and his owner also shall be put to death."

But the general rule at this time respecting the liability of owners or keepers of domestic animals for injuries to third persons is that the owner or keeper of domestic animals is not liable for such injuries, unless the animal was accustomed to injure persons, or had an inclination to do so, and the vicious disposition of the animal was known to the owner or keeper. *Sherfey* v. *Bartley*, 4 Sneed, 58, 67 Am. Dec., 597; *Smith* v. *Causey*, 22 Ala., 568; *Le Forest* v. *Tolman*, 117 Mass., 109, 19 Am. Rep., 400; *Popplewell* v. *Pierce*, 10 Cush. (Mass.), 509. And where an animal is accustomed or disposed to injure persons, and the owner or keeper has notice or knowledge of that fact, he is liable for any injury which such animal may do to another person. As stated in *Sherfey* v. *Bartley*, supra, he is "bound to have so confined him as to prevent him from doing mischief." *Loomis* v. *Terry*, 17 Wend. (N. Y.), 496, 31 Am. Dec., 306. The gist of the action is the keeping of the animal with notice of its vicious disposition, and not the negligence of the owner in its custody. *Empire Spring Co.* v. *Edgar*, 99 U. S., 645, 25 L. Ed., 487. And if a person harbors a dog accustomed to bite, or allows it to frequent his premises, he is liable, although not the owner of it.

Frammell v. *Little*, 16 Ind., 251; *Marsh* v. *Jones*, 21 Vt., 378, 52 Am. Dec., 67; *Wilkinson* v. *Parrott*, 32 Cal., 102. Knowledge of the owner or keeper that the dog is vicious is sufficient to sustain liability, without showing that it had ever bitten anyone. *Rider* v. *White*, 65 N. Y., 54, 22 Am. Rep., 600; *Godeau* v. *Blood*, 52 Vt., 251, 36 Am. Rep., 751.

Owners or keepers are liable for injuries done by them, even without notice of their vicious propensities, if the animals are naturally mischievous; but, if they are of a tame and domestic nature, there must be notice of the vicious habits. *Empire Spring Co.* v. *Edgar*. And where injury is done by domestic animals kept for use or convenience, the rule is that the owner is not liable to an action on the ground of negligence, without proof that he knew that the animal was accustomed to injure persons. *Vrooman* v. *Lawyer*, 13 Johns. (N. Y.), 339. If the latter class of animals are rightfully in the place where the injury is inflicted, the owner is not liable, unless he knew that the animal was accustomed to be vicious. In such case he must confine the animal so as to prevent it from doing mischief. *Empire Spring Co.* v. *Edgar*, supra; *Sherfey* v. *Bartley*, supra.

The whole subject is fully covered in 1 R. C. L. under the title "Animals," and additional authorities, both early and late, will be found there.

The foregoing rules apply to persons who keep or harbor animals upon their premises with notice of their vicious disposition, whether they own them or

not. Applying these principles to the facts stated, it
is beyond doubt that Mrs. Missio, as the owner and
occupant of the premises upon which her brother har-
bored the vicious dogs with her knowledge and consent,
is liable for the injuries inflicted by them upon defendant in error, unless her plea of coverture is good. It
is well settled, however, that a married woman is liable in an action for her torts not committed in the
presence, or under the supposed influence of her husband. 2 Bishop on Married Women, 256; Schouler on
Husband and Wife, 134; *Dailey* v. *Houston,* 58 Mo.,
361; *Marshall* v. *Oakes,* 51 Me., 308; all cited and approved in *Collier* v. *Struby,* 99 Tenn., 241, 47 S. W., 90.

The rule of *respondeat superior* does not apply to
the torts of a married woman committed through the
negligence of her husband because married women are
not liable *ex contractu;* but the rule is otherwise, and,
as just stated, where the action arises out of her personal tort. *Collier* v. *Struby,* supra. In this case the
husband was not present and knew nothing of the action of the wife in harboring the vicious dogs, and of
course the tort committed was not his personally, nor
was it committed in his presence. Therefore the wife
is liable for her personal tort. The husband is jointly
liable with her because of their marriage relations.
Price v. *Clapp,* 119 Tenn., 425, 105 S. W., 864, 123 Am.
St. Rep., 730; 14 Am. & Eng. Ency. of Law, 647, *et seq.*

Other questions are made in the petition and assignments of error which we deem it unnecessary to
discuss in this opinion. The result is that the writ of
certiorari is denied.

HARDEE *v.* WILSON *et al.* *

(*Jackson.* April Term, 1914.)

RECEIVERS.   Foreign receivers.   Permission to sue.

While a receiver, at least an ordinary chancery receiver, has
no legal right to sue in a state other than that of his appointment, the privilege of doing so will be accorded, as a matter of
comity; the suit being neither inimical to the interest of local
creditors, or of anyone who has acquired rights under a local
statute, nor in contravention of the policy of the forum.

Code cited and construed: Sec. 6106 (S.).

Cases cited and approved: Relfe v. Rundle, 103 U. S., 222; Con-
verse v. Hamilton, 224 U. S., 243; Howarth v. Lombard, 175
Mass., 570; Howarth v. Angle, 162 N. Y., 179-182; Bank v.
Motherwell, etc., Iron Co., 95 Tenn., 172-181; Dillingham v.
Insurance Co., 120 Tenn., 302; Booth v. Clark, 17 How., 322;
Cagill v. Wooldridge, 67 Tenn., 580.

Cases cited and distinguished: Runk v. St. John, 29 Barb.,
(N. Y.), 585; Choctaw Coal, etc., Co. v. Williams, Echols, etc.,
Co., 75 Ark., 365; Newsum v. Hoffman, 124 Tenn., 369.

FROM SHELBY.

Appeal from Chancery Court, Shelby County.—
FRANCIS FENTRESS, Chancellor.

WILSON & ARMSTRONG, for appellant.

EDGINGTON & EDGINGTON, for appellees.

---

*Upon the power of a receiver to sue out of jurisdiction of
appointment, see note in 4 L. R. A. (N. S.), 824.

MR. JUSTICE GREEN delivered the opinion of the Court.

This bill was filed by the complainant to recover a certain indebtedness, consisting of notes and overdraft, alleged to be due from the defendants to the First State Bank of Shaw, Mississippi. The bill averred that the said bank was being wound up as an insolvent institution by the chancery court of Bolivar county, Miss., and that the complainant had been appointed receiver of said bank by said court, and was authorized by decree of that court to collect all the assets of the same, and to bring all necessary suits.

The defendants interposed a demurred, which challenged the right of complainant, as a receiver appointed in a foreign jurisdiction, to sue in the courts of Tennessee.

Subsequently the bill was amended by the following words:

"That said complainant was, by virtue of his appointment as receiver in Bolivar county, Mississippi, vested with title and possession of said notes and said account, and that the same were turned over to him in said Bolivar county, Mississippi, by virtue of his office as receiver, and that he holds same, having there received title and actual possession of said notes and said evidences of account, and that there are no creditors of the said bank nor of the parties in the State of Tennessee whose rights would be affected in any way by this suit; that there is no receivership pending here, and no necessity for one; and that the maintenance of this suit would be in every way without any prejudice or influence upon the rights of said parties, either in the State of Tennessee or elsewhere than in the State of Mississippi.''

On the bill as amended, the same point was made by another demurrer.

The chancellor sustained the demurrer and dismissed the bill, and complainant has appealed to this court.

There is a distinction between the right and power of a receiver in a foreign court, when that receiver is by statute or voluntary assignment or conveyance vested with title to the assets of the estate he is administering, and the right of such receiver when he is a mere chancery court appointee. This difference is pointed out in *Relfe* v. *Rundle*, 103 U. S., 222, 26 L. Ed., 337; *Converse* v. *Hamilton*, 224 U. S., 243, 32 Sup. Ct., 415, 56 L. Ed., 749, Ann. Cas., 1913D, 1292; *Howarth* v. *Lombard*, 175 Mass., 570, 56 N. E., 888, 49 L. R. A., 301; *Howarth* v. *Angle*, 162 N. Y., 179-182, 56 N. E., 489, 47 L. R. A., 725. The distinction is also recognized in *Bank* v. *Motherwell, etc., Iron Co.*, 95 Tenn., 172-181, 31 S. W., 1002.

It is not necessary to consider this question here, because we do not think that the complainant, even according to the averments of the amended bill, is the sort of receiver or *quasi* assignee referred to in the cases just cited, with authority to maintain suits in other jurisdictions. Although in the amendment to the bill it is said this complainant was vested with title to the assets of the defunct bank, the statement is a mere conclusion announced by the pleader. No statute, nor conveyance or assignment conferring title upon the receiver, is set out, and so far as we can see he is only an ordinary chancery receiver.

The question is, then, whether we shall permit such an officer of a foreign jurisdiction to maintain a suit of this character in Tennessee.

It is well settled that the receiver of a foreign court may not, as a matter of right, sue in the courts of this State. *Bank* v. *Motherwell Iron Co.*, 95 Tenn., 172, 31 S. W., 1002; *Dillingham* v. *Insurance Co.*, 120 Tenn., 302, 108 S. W., 1148, 16 L. R. A. (N. S.), 220. This rule as to foreign receivers was announced by the Supreme Court of the United States in *Booth* v. *Clark,* 17 How., 322, 15 L. Ed., 164, and is very generally accepted throughout all the states of the Union. See High on Receivers (4 Ed.), sec. 239.

In *Dillingham* v. *Insurance Co.*, 120 Tenn., 302, 108 S. W., 1148, 16 L. R. A. (N. S.), 220, there was a contest between the Illinois receiver of a foreign insurance company and a citizen of Tennessee, who was a creditor of this company. The property of Mrs. Dillingham, covered by a policy of insurance in said company, was destroyed by fire, and she attached certain assets of the insurance company in Nashville to satisfy her demand. The receiver of the company attempted to recover the assets, and was denied the right to sue by this court.

In *Bank* v. *Motherwell Iron Co.*, 95 Tenn., 172, 31 S. W., 1002, an Ohio judgment creditor of the Motherwell Iron Company, having exhausted his legal remedies against the said company in Ohio, filed a bill in the chancery court of Shelby county to subject to satisfaction of his judgment certain property of the iron company located in Memphis. This bill was filed under the provisions of Shannon's Code, section 6106. After the attachment had been levied, the receiver of the iron company, appointed by an Ohio court, filed a bill in Memphis to recover the said assets, which had been attached. This bill was dismissed by the court.

In *Dillingham* v. *Insurance Co.*, therefore, it will be seen that the suit of the foreign receiver, had it been allowed, would have prejudiced the rights of a local creditor.

In *Motherwell, etc., Iron Co.* v. *Bank,* the suit of the foreign receiver, had it been allowed, would have prejudiced the rights of a foreign creditor, upon whom our statute had conferred a standing equivalent to that possessed by a citizen of the State.

In both these cases the foreign receivers sought to assert claims in opposition to liens created by attachment under our laws.

So neither *Dillingham* v. *Insurance Co.* nor *Bank* v. *Motherwell, etc., Iron Co.* is in point here. The bill distinctly avers that the present suit can be maintained without prejudice to the rights of any other creditors protected by the laws of Tennessee.

It was said, generally speaking, in both of these cases, that a foreign receiver was without authority to bring a suit beyond the jurisdiction of the court appointing him. This is undoubtedly true as a question of legal right, and it was from this standpoint the question was considered in these cases. A foreign receiver is not entitled to *demand* a hearing in the courts of this State.

Other considerations control, however, when a foreign receiver comes into our courts and asks as a matter of comity to be allowed to sue here, and when it appears that the interests of no local creditor, nor any other creditor protected by our statutes, will be prejudiced.

The general expressions of the court in *Bank* v. *Motherwell, etc., Iron Co.*, supra, are founded on a quotation from the work of High on Receivers, sec. 239, in which the author lays down the principle that a receiver has no extraterritorial right of action. Following this language, in the last edition of his work, the author enumerates a great many instances in which the courts have been opened to foreign receivers in cases which did not involve the interest of local creditors. He concludes the discussion as follows:

"It is thus apparent that the exceptions to the rule denying to receivers any extraterritorial right of action have become as well recognized as the rule itself, and the tendency of the courts is constantly toward an enlarged and more liberal policy in this regard. And it is believed that the doctrine will ultimately be

established, giving to receivers the same rights of action in all States of the Union with which they are invested in the State or jurisdiction in which they are
appointed." High on Receivers (4 Ed.), sec. 241.

The New York court has well stated the prevailing
modern doctrine as follows:

"The plaintiffs are receivers of a corporation chartered in the States of Pennsylvania and New Jersey,
and were appointed under the decree dissolving the
corporation, made by the court of chancery in the latter State, and were confirmed by an act of the legislature of the former. The defendant's counsel denies
the capacity of receivers, appointed in other States
and countries, to sue in the courts of this State. The
laws and proceedings of other sovereignties have not,
indeed, such absolute and inherent vigor as to be effi-
cacious here under all circumstances. But in most
instances they are recognized by the courtesy of the
courts of this State; and the right of foreign assignees
or receivers to collect, sue for, and recover the property of the individuals or corporations they represent,
has never been denied, except where their claim came
in conflict with the rights of creditors in this State.
All that has been settled by the decisions to which
we have been referred on this subject is that our courts
will not sustain the lien of foreign assignees or receivers, in opposition to a lien created by attachment
under our own laws. In other words, we decline to extend our wonted courtesy so far as to work detriment
to citizens of our own State, who have been induced to

give credit to the foreign corporation.'' *Runk* v. *St. John*, 29 Barb. (N. Y.), 585.

In a note to *Choctaw Coal, etc., Co.* v. *Williams, Echols, etc., Co.*, 75 Ark., 365, 87 S. W., 632, as reported in 5 Ann. Cas., 569, it is said:

''While the courts have with unanimity denied the capacity of a receiver to bring suit in a foreign jurisdiction as a matter of right, the privilege or permission to sue is ordinarily accorded as a matter of comity, and in the absence of statutory regulations the appointment and title of the receiver will be recognized, and he will be allowed to sue, unless injustice or detriment will result therefrom to the citizens of the State permitting it, or the policy of its laws will thereby be contravened.''

Authorities are collected from twenty-seven States in support of the annotator's proposition.

See later note to the same effect under *Converse* v. *Hamilton*, 224 U. S., 243, 32 Sup. Ct., 415, 56 L. Ed., 749, as reported in Ann. Cas., 1913D, 1292. See, also, note to *Gilman* v. *Hudson River Boot & Shoe Mfg. Co.*, 84 Wis., 60, 54 N. W., 395, as reported in 23 L. R. A., 52, 36 Am. St. Rep., 899, and note to *Fowler* v. *Osgood*, 141 Fed., 20, 72 C. C. A., 270, as reported in 4 L. R. A. (N. S.), 824.

The privilege of suing in jurisdictions other than that of their appointment is almost universally conceded to receivers now, as a matter of comity or courtesy, unless such a suit is inimical to the interest of local creditors, or to the interest of those who have acquired rights under a local statute, or unless such a suit is in contravention of the policy of the forum. No such objection can be urged to the maintenance of the present suit, and we are of opinion it should be allowed to be prosecuted.

In *Cagill* v. *Wooldridge*, 8 Baxt., 580, 35 Am. Rep., 716, we permitted a receiver appointed by an Arkansas court to prosecute in this State an action of replevin to recover property taken from his possession.

In *Newsum* v. *Hoffman,* 124 Tenn., 369, 137 S. W., 490, speaking of chattel mortgages executed and registered in other States, this court held that they would be recognized as valid and effective here, if the mortgaged property was brought into the State without the consent of the mortgagee. The court said:

"It seems a churlish and ungracious course, if not an example of improvident judgment, to hold out against the generous comity of the many States which recognize the rule of interstate courtesy upon this subject."

This observation applies with even more force to the case of a foreign receiver who seeks to bring an action in our courts under circumstances such as are here existing. We have in Tennessee several border cities, Memphis, Chattanooga, Bristol, Clarksville, and others, the trade and business of which are largely, if not chiefly, in border States. These cities are in the main creditor cities, and it would therefore, as the court said in *Newsum* v. *Hoffman,* supra, be an exceedingly improvident course for Tennessee to deny recognition to the interstate comity and courtesy usually prevailing in such matters. Such a policy would provoke retaliation, and work to the detriment of our own citizens and business interests.

For the reason stated, we are of opinion that the chancellor erroneously sustained the demurrer to complainant's bill, and the decree below will be reversed, and the case remanded for answer. Other questions made have been disposed of orally. The costs of this court will be paid by defendants.

MAY *v.* ILLINOIS CENTRAL RAILROAD CO. *et al.*

(*Jackson.* April Term, 1914.)

PLEADING. Allegation of time. Pleading and proof.

Not only may plaintiff allege that the personal injury for which she sues was inflicted "on or about" a certain day, but, being unable to do so, she may not be required to allege the date with greater particularity, and may recover on her testimony that the accident occurred in the month alleged, and to the best of her recollection on the day alleged. (*Post, pp.* 522-534.)

Code cited and construed: Secs. 4605, 4606 (S.).

Cases cited and approved: Martin v. McNight, 1 Tenn., 380; Thompson v. French, 18 Tenn., 453 Rollins v. Atlantic City R. Co., 73 N. J. Law, 64; Gulf, T. & W. R. v. Lowrie, 144 S. W., 367; Florida East Coast R. Co. v. Welsh, 53 Fla., 145; Southern Railroad Co. v. Puckett, 121 Ga., 322; Richmond & Danville R. Co. v. Payne, 86 Va., 481; State v. Lewis, 69 W. Va., 472; Warfield v. State, 116 Md., 599; Washington & Va. R. Co. v. Boukright, 113 Va., 696; Watkins v. Cope, 84 N. J. Law, 143; Crowley v. Railroad, 108 Tenn., 74.

Cases cited and distinguished: Bogard v. Ill. Cent. R. R. Co., 116 Ky., 429; Tilton v. Reecher, 59 N. Y., 176; Mynott v. Mynott, 53 Tenn., 311.

FROM SHELBY.

Appeal from the Circuit Court of Shelby County to the Court of Civil Appeals and by *certiorari* from the Court of Civil Appeals to the Supreme Court.— —————, Judge.

LINDSAY B. PHILLIPS, for plaintiff.

A. W. BIGGS, T. A. EVANS, and C. N. BURCH, for defendants.

MR. CHIEF JUSTICE NEIL delivered the opinion of the Court.

This action was brought in the circuit court of Shelby county to recover damages for an injury alleged to have been inflicted upon the plaintiff by the defendant railway company.

The declaration alleged that "on or about the 12th day of September, 1912," plaintiff, while walking on defendant's track at a place which, for many years prior thereto, the public had been in the habit of using as a walkway, near the intersection of the said track and Iowa avenue, was negligently run upon by one of defendant's engines, after her danger became apparent to the defendant's servants, or by the exercise of ordinary care would have been apparent to them. It appears inferentially from an amendment made that a motion was entered by defendant to require the plaintiff to make her declaration more specific, but the order itself is not in the record. Thereupon the plaintiff filed the following amendment:

"Comes now the plaintiff in compliance with the order of the court heretofore granted herein, and amends her original declaration by inserting in the second paragraph, page 1 thereof, immediately after the words and figures 'that heretofore, to wit, on or

about the 12th day of September, 1912,' the following
words and figures, to wit: 'at about 5 p. m.' ''

The defendant interposed the general issue.

The plaintiff's testimony fully made out the case
as to the fact that an injury had been inflicted on her
by one of the defendant's engines while she was walking on the track as stated; that she was looking and
listening all the time; that the track was straight, and
she could have been seen by anyone upon the lookout;
and that she was run upon without warning. As to
the time of the injury, she said that it occurred in the
month of September, 1912, and, according to the best
of her recollection, it was on the 12th of the month;
but she could not be certain as to the day. She was
sure it was near that time.

The defendant introduced a claim agent, in its employment at the time of the accident. He testified
there was no report made of any accident by the employees of the company; that there were nineteen
tracks in the yard at the point where the accident is
said to have occurred, and there were nineteen switch
engines working at the place on September 12, 1912;
that he saw each of the trainmen, making 125 in all,
and they knew nothing of the occurrence; that he then
suggested to the company's attorney to put down a
motion to make the declaration more specific, and when
this was done he made a further investigation, but
could not find the crew that manned the engine that
is said to have struck the plaintiff; that the train
crews and the engines were changed each day, and if

the wrong day should be alleged in the declaration it would be impossible to find the right train crew.

The rest of the evidence was upon the extent of the injury.

The trial judge charged among other things not excepted to, the following:

"The plaintiff alleges that the accident occurred on the 12th day of September, 1912. In order for the plaintiff to be entitled to recover in this case, it is necessary for her to show by a preponderance of the evidence that the accident occurred on that day. Unless you find that the accident occurred on the 12th day of September, 1912, and not at a much later date, you must return a verdict for the defendant."

The jury returned a verdict for the defendant, and thereupon an appeal was prosecuted to the court of civil appeals. From that court the case has reached us by the writ of *certiorari*, and has been argued at the bar of the court.

In the court of civil appeals the above-mentioned charge of the trial judge was held erroneous, and it was likewise adjudged in that court that there was no evidence to sustain the verdict, and the cause was remanded for a new trial. These rulings of the court of civil appeals are assigned as error in this court.

The case turns upon whether the charge was correct. If it was necessary for the plaintiff to prove that the accident occurred on the 12th day of September, and on no other day, then there was no evidence to sustain the verdict, because, as already recited, the plaintiff was unable to state the date any more definitely than that it was either on the 12th or near that day.

The general rule is that it is not essential to prove with exactness the time as laid in the declaration. 7 Bac. Abridg., 477, 579; 1 Elliott on Ev., sec. 197; 31 Cyc., 706, 707. The point is ruled in the same way in one of our earliest cases, *Martin* v. *McNight,* 1 Tenn. (1 Overt.), 380, a *qui tam* action. In *Thompson* v. *French,* 18 Tenn. (10 Yerg.), 453, 458, the same proposition was laid down in a case involving a verbal or implied contract. See, also, the following cases cited in a note to *Hewitt* v. *Pere Marquette R. R. Co.,* 41 L. R. A. (N. S.), 635, viz.: *Rollins* v. *Atlantic City R. Co.,* 73 N. J. Law, 64, 62 Atl., 929; *Gulf, T. & W. R.* v. *Lowrie* (Tex. Civ. App.), 144 S. W., 367; *Florida East Coast R. Co.* v. *Welch,* 53 Fla., 145, 44 So.,250, 12 Ann. Cas., 210, 213, 214; *Southern Railroad Co.* v. *Puckett,* 121 Ga., 322, 48 S. E., 968. But where the date is an essential element of description in stating the cause of action it must be proved as laid. 1 Elliott on Ev., sec. 197; 31 Cyc., 706, 707.

In several cases it has been held that on application of the defendant, showing good cause, the complainant may be required to make the date more specific, or at least as specific as he is able to make it.

In *Bogard* v. *Ill. Cent. R. R. Co.,* 116 Ky., 429, 76 S. W., 170, 3 Ann. Cas., 160, the facts were that the declaration or petition stated the cause of action, a personal injury to the petitioner, as having occurred "within the last twelve months." The defendant moved the court in writing to require the plaintiff to state the date of the injury complained of, the point where it occurred, the number of the train producing it, and the parties in charge thereof. Over the objection of the plaintiff the motion was sustained, and, on plaintiff's declining to plead further, the action was dismissed and the case was appealed to the court of appeals. The court said:

"There is no uncertainty or indefiniteness with respect to the nature of the charge made against the defendant. The difficulty under which the defendant claims to labor is that the plaintiff has not sufficiently specified the facts as to the time and place where the alleged acts of negligence occurred to enable it to intelligently defend the action. The defendant operates a trunk line through McCracken county, and it has perhaps fifty miles of track within the county. In course of twelve months thousands of trains pass over its road, operated by hundreds of different employees, at all hours of the day and night. The plaintiff necessarily has information as to the time and place of the accident, whether it was day or night, whether the injury was inflicted by a freight or passenger train; and a state of case might exist when it would be impossible for the defendant to secure this information so necessary for the proper conduct of its defense. When such a case arises, the trial court has inherent power to require such information to be furnished. This question was very fully considered in the case of *Com.* v. *Snelling*, 15 Pick. (Mass.), 321. The opinion in that case was delivered by Chief Justice Shaw. It was held that, where a person is indicted for a libel containing general charges of official misconduct against a magistrate, the court was authorized to require him previously to the trial, in case he intended to give the truth of the publication in evidence, to file a bill of particulars specifying the instances of misconduct which he proposes to prove. After a thorough review of all the authorities, he says: 'The general rule to be extracted from these analogous cases is that where, in the course of a suit, from any cause, a party is placed in such a situation that justice cannot be done in the trial without the aid of the information to be obtained by means of a specification or bill of particulars, the court, in virtue of the general authority to regulate the conduct of trials, has power to direct such information to be seasonably furnished, and in authentic form.' "

Again, quoting from *Tilton* v. *Reecher*, 59 N. Y., 176, 17 Am. Rep., 337:

"In actions upon money demands consisting of various items, a bill of particulars of the dates and description of the transactions out of which the indebtedness is claimed to have arisen is granted almost as a matter of course; and this proceeding is so common and familiar that, when a bill of particulars is spoken of, it is ordinarily understood as referring to particulars of that character. But it is an error to suppose that bills of particulars are confined to actions . . . for the recovery of money demands

arising upon contract. A bill of particulars is appropriate in all descriptions of actions, where the circumstances are such that justice demands that a party
should be apprised of the matters for which he is to be
put for trial with greater particularity than is required
by the rules of pleading. They have been ordered in
actions of libel, escape, . . . trespass, . . .
trover, . . . and ejectment, . . . and even in
criminal cases . . . on an indictment for being
a common barrator, . . . on an indictment for nuisance, etc. . . . A reference to a few of the authorities upon which these decisions were founded will show
that in also every . . . case in which the defendant can satisfy the court that it is necessary to a fair
trial that he should be apprised beforehand of the particulars of the charge which he is expected to meet,
the court has authority to compel the adverse party to
specify those particulars so far as in his power.''

3 Ency. of Plead. & Prac., 517, was quoted as follows:

''There is no inflexible rule as to the class of cases in
which a bill of particulars will be granted, but it rests
within the sound judicial discretion of the court, to
be exercised only in furtherance of justice. But,''
continuing the quotation, ''the rule is quite well established that a party will not be obliged to furnish facts
already known to his adversary, nor when the means
of ascertaining the facts are equally accessible to both
parties.''

On these authorities the court of appeals of Kentucky said:

"We are of the opinion that, upon a proper showing that defendant did not have the information or the means of readily ascertaining the time when and place where the accident occurred, and whether it occurred during the day or night, or was inflicted by a freight or passenger train, the plaintiff should be required to furnish such information, if in his power. But it is not necessary or proper in an action for personal injuries that the petition should set out specifically the injuries complained of, or the details of the alleged acts of negligence of the defendant in inflicting the injuries. In our opinion, the trial court erred in sustaining the motion to require the plaintiff to give the number of the train producing the injury or the names of the parties in charge thereof. It is not at all probable that such information is in his possession, and, if the identity of the train inflicting the injury is established, the means of ascertaining these facts are more accessible to defendant than to the plaintiff. Nor should the motion have been sustained at all, without some showing by the defendant, by affidavit or otherwise, that it did not have the required information or reasonable means of obtaining it."

There is an extensive note to this case discussing bills of particulars in negligence actions.

Other general authorities are: *Richmond & Danville R. Co.* v. *Payne*, 86 Va., 481, 10 S. E., 749, 6 L. R. A., 849, 851, 852; *State* v. *Lewis*, 69 W. Va., 472, 72

S. E., 475, 26 Ann. Cas., (1913A), 1203, and note; *War-field* v. *State,* 116 Md., 599, 82 Atl., 1053, 28 Ann. Cas., (1913C), 824, and note; *Washington & Va. R. Co.* v. *Bouknight,* 113 Va., 696, 75 S. E., 1032, 30 Ann. Cas., (1913E), 546, 548; 31 Cyc., 699, 704; 59 L. R. A., note on pp. 218-221.

It is not our purpose to go further into the subject at this time than to· say, we approve the principles stated in *Bogard* v. *Ill. Cent. R. R. Co.,* supra, and to add a few general propositions which we find in the cases. These additional propositions are that, while the propriety of making the order is in the discretion of the trial judge, yet this discretion is subject to review; that the party is not to be required to state the evidence on which he rests his demand or defense; that the making the order must depend upon the special circumstances and situation of each case, the action of the court being guided solely by the purpose of effectuating justice between the parties, at the same time not imposing an undue burden upon either one; that where the party upon whom the order is made shows to the court that he is unable to furnish the particulars required the order should be vacated; that whenever the order is made, it is enforced by confirming the evidence to the particulars stated, construed with liberality to effect the ends of justice. Our statutes do not in direct terms provide for, or authorize, the requirement of a bill of particulars; but we deem this immaterial, since the power is inherent in courts of justice to enable them to properly conduct trials before them,

as held in *Com. v. Snelling,* supra. To the same effect
is *Watkins* v. *Cope,* 84 N. J. Law, 143, 86 Atl., 545.

We have three cases in this State bearing more or
less directly on the subject. We have *Smith, Exec.,* v.
Wilkinson et al., 45 Tenn. (5 Cold.), 157, wherein an
order was asked requiring the plaintiff to make the
dates of alleged collections by a constable more certain,
the suit being one against a constable and his sureties
on his bond; but the motion was denied, because the
matters referred to were necessarily more particularly
within the knowledge of the defendant. We have another case, *Mynatt* v. *Mynatt,* 53 Tenn. (6 Heisk.), 311,
wherein it appears a motion was made to strike out
a plea on the ground that it was too indefinite in its
statements as to the defense of the statute of limitations therein relied on. Instead of specifying the
time within which the action had been barred, the
plea averred that:

"The offense was not committed within such period
of time before the beginning of the suit as may be inquired of by the court."

The court said:

"If the motion was made because the plea failed to
carry a reasonable certainty of meaning, it was the
duty of the court, upon motion to dismiss, to direct
a more specific statement, but not to strike it out. If
the motion was made because the plea did not show
a substantial cause of defense, a demurrer, and not
a motion, was the mode prescribed for reaching the
defect, and, upon sustaining the demurrer, the party

should have the privilege of pleading over. Upon whatever ground, therefore, the motion was made and sustained, it was error to strike out the plea.''

There is also *Crowley* v. *Railroad,* 108 Tenn., 74, 65 S. W., 411, wherein it was held that plaintiff, having fixed the day and place in the declaration, could not be required to state the special hour of the day.

All of these Tennessee cases were based on Shannon's Code, secs. 4605, and 4606, which read as follows:

"Any pleading possessing the following requisites is sufficient: (1) When it conveys a reasonable certainty of meaning; (2) when, by a fair and natural construction, it shows a substantial cause of action or defense.

"If defective in the first of the above particulars, the court, on motion, shall direct a more specific statement; if in the latter, it is ground of demurrer.''

Perhaps it would be more accurate to say that they were based on that part of section 4606 which provides that, in case any pleading fails to contain a reasonable certainty of meaning, the court shall on motion direct a more specific statement.

For the reason already stated, we deem it unnecessary to express any opinion as to whether the bill of particulars could be treated or considered as falling within the sense and meaning of the sections quoted. Certain it is, however, that they go far in that direction. It may be conceded that in their ordinary application they refer to a case wherein the ambiguity is patent on the face of the pleading. However, it is not inconceivable that in many instances affidavits showing the surroundings of the subject-matter of the pleading with reference to one or the other of the parties, or to the cause of action, might develop a latent ambiguity requiring to be cleared up by a further and more particular statement. But, however this may be, we think, as already stated, that it is within the inherent power of the court to require, in a proper case, what is commonly known as a bill of particulars.

We are of the opinion that the parties may be required to furnish, in the form of such a bill or statement, a more particular reference to the day on which an injury or other material thing is alleged to have occurred. It is true that a plaintiff may allege in his declaration that the cause of action arose on or about a specified day, as was done in the present case, and may satisfy this averment by proving any date reasonably near the given day; but he may be required by order of the court, if he can do so, to fix the particular day, and the order may confine the evidence to the day so fixed. However, this must be understood with the qualification, already stated, that he cannot be so compelled if he show that he is unable to state the date more definitely than he has already done.

This aspect of the case finds illustration in the case now before us. The declaration averred that the accident occurred "on or about the 12th day of September, 1912." The sworn statement of the plaintiff showed that she could not fix the date of the injury with any more definiteness, and accordingly the court could not require it of her. He did require her to fix the hour of the day; but this was held error in the case of *Crowley* v. *Railroad,* supra.

Coming, now, to the specific errors assigned, we are of the opinion that the trial judge committed error in instructing the jury that it was incumbent on the plaintiff to prove that the injury was inflicted on the 12th day of September. This was erroneous, because the declaration was not so limited in its terms; nor had it been so limited by any order of the court, confining the evidence to that date; nor could such order have been made, in view of plaintiff's showing that it was impossible for her to fix the date with any more definiteness than she had already done.

We are of the opinion, therefore, that the portion of the charge complained of was erroneous, and the court of civil appeals acted correctly in reversing the judgment of the trial court, and remanding the cause for a new trial, and the action of the court of civil appeals in respect of this matter is affirmed.

STATE *v.* McTEER.*

(*Knoxville.*   September Term, 1913.)**

GAMING. Offenses. "Gambling Device." Slot Machine.

A slot machine inscribed "5 Cents" "Insert and receive a package of Liberty Bell Gum Fruit," at the top of which was an indicator showing the player each time he played and before he played what he would receive on each play and which always indicated either the word "Gum" on one of the even numbers from 2 to 20, so that, when it showed the word "Gum," the player received a package of gum on putting five cents into the slot, and if it showed a number, he received a corresponding number of checks worth five cents in trade at the place where the machine was located, was a gambling device, the use of which was an offense, since the lure and chance of gain induced players to continue, although without ultimate loss to the owner of the machine; it not being essential that there should be the chance of loss to the players as well as of extraordinary or greatly disproportionate gain. (*Post, pp.* 536-540.)

Cases cited and approved: Bell v. State, 37 Tenn., 507; Eubanks v. State, 50 Tenn, 488; Ferguson v. State, 178 Ind., 568; People, *ex rel.*, v. Jenkins, 153 App. Div., 512; Territory v. Jones, 14 N. M., 579; Muller v. Stoecker Cigar Co., 89 Neb., 438; Lang v. Merwin, 99 Me., 486; Meyer v. State, 112 Ga., 20; Loiseau v State, 114 Ala., 34; Horner v. U. S., 147 U. S., 449.

---

*On the question whether the operation of a slot machine constitutes gambling, see notes in 20 L. R. A. (N. S.), 239; 34 L. R. A. (N. S.), 573, and 42 L. R. A. (N. S.), 720.

**This case tried and decided at the September Term, 1913, at Knoxville, but opinion was not prepared and sent to publisher for publication until during the April Term, 1914, at Jackson.

FROM KNOX

Appeal from Criminal Court, Knox County.—
T. A. R. NELSON, Judge.

W. W. LAW, assistant attorney-general, for the State.

S. G. HEISKELL, for appellee.

MR. CHIEF JUSTICE NEIL delivered the opinion of the
Court.

The defendant was presented in the criminal court
of Knox county:

"For that he . . . on the ——— day of October,
1912, in the State and county aforesaid, unlawfully did
then and there encourage, promote, aid, and assist in
playing, betting, gambling, and putting in hazard five
cents each, in a certain gambling device, known as the
Mills O. K. Gum Vendor, which is a slot machine, and
is described as follows:

"Being about five feet and ten inches square, and at
the extreme top of the machine and across the front is
inscribed the following: '5 Cents;' 'Insert and receive
a package of Liberty Bell Gum Fruit.' Near the top of
the machine is an indicator which shows the player each
time he plays and before he plays what he will receive
on each play. This indicator always shows either the
word 'Gum' or one of the following numbers, to wit:

2, 4, 6, 8, 10, 14, 16, 18, 20. If the indicator shows the word 'Gum,' the player will receive a package of gum on putting five cents into the slot. If the indicator shows any one of the numbers aforesaid, the player will receive the number of checks shown by the number on the indicator, and these checks are worth five cents each in trade at the place of business where the machine is located.

"The machine is operated as follows, to wit: The player deposits a nickel or five-cent piece in the slot and pulls the lever attached to the side of the machine. This sets the mechanism of the machine in motion, which turns a large cylinder and causes the nickel or five-cent piece to pass through the machine and fall into a receptacle at the bottom on the inside of the machine, and causes a package of gum or checks, according as the indicator showed before the lever was pulled, to drop into a receptacle at the front of the machine, where the player can get the same.

"Immediately after the nickel or five-cent piece is deposited in the slot and the lever is pulled and the play is complete, the indicator shows what the next player will get on depositing a nickel in the slot. The player always gets for his nickel or five-cent piece so deposited what the indicator showed he would get for it."

The defendant moved to quash the presentment on the ground that it charged no offense. The trial judge sustained the motion, and the State thereupon appealed to this court.

The question raised is whether the slot machine described is a gambling device. We are of the opinion
that it is. It is insisted by the defendant that this is
not a sound conclusion, because the indicator always
shows what the player is to get before he deposits his
nickel; hence it is said there is no element of uncertainty, and no opportunity of obtaining disproportionate gains, or sustaining loss, by the hazard of anything of value. It is true there is no hazard of loss, if
we assume, as we think we should, that each package
of gum is the fair commercial equivalent of five cents;
but there is the prospect of obtaining very greatly disproportionate gains. The indicator may show a package of gum when the player deposits his nickel, and
this he will get when he works the lever, but at the
same time the indicator may present for the next play
either one of the numbers 2, 4, 6, 8, 10, 12, 14, 16, 18, or
20, representing checks of the value of five cents each.
If, for example, the number shown is 20, the player, by
depositing five cents, will obtain twenty checks worth
$1. So for the other numbers. The lure is the op-
portunity of winning from 10 to 100 cents by the deposit and expenditure of 5 cents. There must be at
least one play before any of the numbers mentioned is
shown on the indicator, and there may be many, and
it is not known which number will appear, nor at what
time, nor after how many plays. In case the checks are
shown on the indicator, the owner of the machine stands
to lose on that play the difference between 5 cents and
the denomination of the check which the machine may

show; that is, a loss of from 5 cents to 95 cents. We may assume that the dealer makes some profit on each package of gum, and that the profits thereon, and the profits on the goods to be sold in exchange for the checks, will show an ultimate profit for him on all the contents of the machine, and this whether the contents be exhausted by one player or by many successive players. So there will be no ultimate loss to him. However, there is always a chance that any single player, by the expenditure of 10 cents, through making two plays of 5 cents each, may obtain, not only a package of gum worth 5 cents, but checks worth from 10 cents to 100 cents, and so in proportion for many plays, and a corresponding loss to the owner of the machine on such individual deals. The player is induced to continue by the fact that he is getting 5 cents' worth of gum for each play, with always the chance just ahead that the next presentation of the indicator will give him the opportunity of making a profit of from 100 to many times that per cent. We think this shows the machine is a gambling device. It is not essential that there should be the chance of loss to the players, as well as of extraordinary or greatly disproportionate gain. *Bell* v. *State,* 5 Sneed, 507; *Eubanks* v. *State,* 3 Heisk., 488.

In substantial accord with these views are the following cases in other jurisdictions: *Ferguson* v. *State,* 178 Ind., 568, 99 N. E., 806, 42 L. R. A. (N. S.), 720; *People, ex rel.,* v. *Jenkins,* 153 App. Div., 512, 138 N. Y. Supp., 449; *Territory* v. *Jones,* 14 N. M., 579, 99 Pac.,

338, 20 L. R. A. (N. S.), 239, and note, 20 Ann. Cas., 128, and note; *Muller* v. *Wm. F. Stoecker Cigar Co.*, 89 Neb., 438, 131 N. W., 923, 34 L. R. A. (N. S.), 573; *Lang* v. *Merwin*, 99 Me., 486, 59 Atl., 1021, 105 Am. St. Rep., 293; *Meyer* v. *State*, 112 Ga., 20, 37 S. E., 96, 51 L. R. A., 496, 81 Am. St. Rep., 17; *Loiseau* v. *State*, 114 Ala., 34, 22 South., 138, 62 Am. St. Rep., 84; *Horner* v. *U. S.*, 147 U. S., 449, 13 Sup. Ct., 409, 37 L. Ed., 237.

The judgment must therefore be reversed, and the cause remanded for issue and trial.

MATTHEWS *et al. v.* CROFFORD. *

(*Jackson.* April Term, 1914.)

1. **APPEAL AND ERROR. Review. Question reviewable.**

Only those matters assigned in the motion for new trial can be reviewed on appeal. (*Post, pp.* 548-551.)

2. **LANDLORD AND TENANT. Surrender. Effect.**

Whil a surrender of demised premises, duly accepted, relieves the lessee, from any liability for rent subsequently accruing, yet where a lessee, who defaulted in payment and against whom the lessor had brought an action of unlawful detainer, retained possession pending a removal of the case to the circuit court, by giving the bond required by Shannon's Code, sec. 5111, a surrender pending the litigation did not relieve the lessee and her surety from liability on the bond, consequently, while it was unnecessary for the court to render judgment awarding the lessor possession, yet under section 4702, providing that judgment should be molded to suit facts, the judgment should recite the facts, including the surrender, and declare the lessor entitled to possession and assess damages on the bond. (*Post, pp.* 548-551.)

Code cited and construed: Secs. 4702, 5111 (S.).

Cases cited and approved: Hanaw v. Bailey, 83 Mich., 24; American Bonding Co. v. Pueblo Investment Co., 150 Fed., 17; Boyd v. Gore, 143 Wis., 531.

3. **LANDLORD AND TENANT. Rent. Forfeiture.**

In order to forfeit a lease for nonpayment of rent, the landlord must demand it on the day, due before sunset, and at the most public place on the land. (*Post, pp.* 551-554.)

4. **LANDLORD AND TENANT. Rent. Nonpayment. Forfeiture.**

The necessity of demand, which is a condition precedent to the forfeiture of a lease for nonpayment of rent, may be waived by agreement in the lease. (*Post, pp.* 551-554.)

---

*On the question of acceptance of rent accrueing after cause for forfeiture, with knowledge of such cause, as waiver of forfeiture, see note in 11 L. R. A. (N. S.), 831.

5. LANDLORD AND TENANT. Nonpayment of rent. Forfeiture. Re-entry.

Before a landlord can declare a lease forfeited for nonpayment of rent, re-entry must be effected. (*Post, pp.* 551-554.)

6. LANDLORD AND TENANT. Forfeiture. Nonpayment of Rent. Re-entry. What Constitutes.

In view of Shannon's Code, sec. 5090, declaring that no person shall enter upon any lands and detain or hold the same, but where entry is given by law, then only in a peaceable manner, the action of unlawful detainer is a substitute for an entry by a landlord to forfeit a lease for nonpayment of rent; the institution of the action having the same effect as an entry. (*Post, pp.* 551-554.)

Cases cited and approved: Parks v. Hays, 92 Tenn., 161; Lewis v. Hughes, 12 Colo., 208; Guffy v. Hukill, 34 W. Va., 49; Crean v. McMahon, 106 Md. 507; Allen v. Kelly, 17 R. I., 731; Whitney v. Brown, 75 Kan., 678, 468; Wilson v. Campbell, 75 Kan., 159; Davidson v. Phillips, 17 Tenn., 93, 95, 96.

7. LANDLORD AND TENANT. Nonpayment of rent. Forfeiture.

Where a tenant, against whom judgment for possession because of nonpayment of an installment rent, was rendered in unlawful detainer proceedings, begun in justice court, removed the proceedings to the circuit court, giving the *supersedeas* bond for the value of the rent of the premises during the litigation required by Shannon's Code, sec. 5111, it was unnecessary to institute successive actions to enforce the forfeiture for nonpayment of each installment of rent as it fell due, for the single *supersedeas* bond covered the whole contract. (*Post, pp.* 554, 555.)

Code cited and construed: Sec. 5111 (S.).

8. LANDLORD AND TENANT. Nonpayment of rent. Forfeiture.

Where a lessor declared a forfeiture of a lease for the nonpayment of an installment of rent, and instituted an action of unlawful detainer to recover possession, the lessee cannot, by a tender of the accrued rent, avoid the forfeiture. (*Post, pp.* 555, 556.)

Matthews v. Crofford.

Case cited and approved: Insurance Co. v. Diggs, 67 Tenn., 563, 569.

Case cited and distinguished: Lee v. Security Bank & Trust Co., 124 Tenn., 582.

9. **ABATEMENT AND REVIVAL.**   **Death of party.**   **Revival.** **Necessary parties. "Leasehold."**

Under Shannon's Code, sec. 511, "leaseholds" are interests in land descending to the heirs at law and hence where a lessee died pending an action of unlawful detainer by the lessor, the heirs at law of the lessee are necessary parties upon the revival. (*Post, pp.* 556, 557.)

10. **APPEAL AND ERROR.**   **Review.**   **Questions presented.**

Where the circuit court to which an action of unlawful detainer was appealed by the lessee, rendered judgment on the lessee's *supersedeas* bond, but failed to render judgment for possession against the heirs of the lessee, the action having been revived in the name of the heirs and administrator, of the lessee who died before judgment, the court of civil appeals may, upon appeal by the surety alone, reform the judgment and render judgment against the heirs.   (*Post, pp.* 556, 557.)

Code cited and construed: Sec. 63 (S.).

Cases cited and approved: Spillman v. Walt, 59 Tenn., 574.

FROM SHELBY

Appeal from Circuit Court, Shelby County.—H. W. LAUGHLIN, Judge.

LEHMAN, GATES & MARTIN, for Matthews and North Memphis Savings Bank.

FANT & MOORE, for Crofford.

MR. CHIEF JUSTICE NEIL delivered the opinion of the Court.

On the 1st day of September, 1910, T. J. Crofford leased to Mrs. W. C. Deatherage certain real estate in the city of Memphis, for the term of two years, ending on August 31, 1912, at the price of $3,600, payable monthly in advance in twenty-four installments, represented by twenty-four promissory notes, each for the sum of $150, payable the first day of each month. The lease contained the following provisions for forfeiture:

"It is further agreed that in default of either one or more of said payments or any part thereof at maturity . . . this lease may be declared forfeited by said party [lessor] at his option, in which case the second party [lessee] shall be liable for all rents until the possession be delivered, and for all damages done to the premises; and the first party [lessor] shall have the right to re-enter and retain possession of said premises without being required to make demand of the same, or demand the payment of rents due, or to give notice of the nonpayment of the rent; and the first party [lessor] shall not become a trespasser by taking possession as aforesaid. . . . In case of default of the second party, so as to forfeit her lease, in her absence from this city, service of process upon any white adult occupying or in possession of the premises shall be good and valid service upon the second party."

All of the rents were paid up to a note falling due September 1, 1911. Those falling due prior to the day just mentioned were, many of them, not paid promptly, but were generally paid from the 23d to the 25th of the month. The rent notes were deposited in one of the banks of Memphis, and it was expected that the lessee would pay them as they fell due. She became so constantly remiss, however, in this duty, that they were placed in the hands of the agent of the bank who had charge of its real estate matters, the witness, Elmer Harris. He testified that he visited the lessee two or three times a month, urging her to pay the money, but frequently had to content himself with collecting it about the 23d or 25th.

"Q. What would you tell her when she would put off paying the rent this way? A. I would tell her I was not going to wait any longer, and try to bluff her out of it each month until I got it. I would tell her I was not going to do it the next month. Q. Did you tell her that every month? A. Yes, sir; every month, but it didn't do any good. Q. Did you have to see her more than every month? A. Yes, sir; every day or two."

The note due the 1st of September, 1911, was demanded but not paid. Thereupon, on the 2d day of September, 1911, a suit of unlawful detainer was brought before George B. Coleman, a justice of the peace of Shelby county, by Crofford to recover possession of the property. The writ was duly served on Mrs. Deatherage on the same day, and on the 8th day of the month a judgment was rendered by the justice of the peace in favor of Crofford for the possession.

On the 13th of September Mrs. Deatherage filed her petition to obtain the writs of *certiorari* and *supersedeas* for the purpose of removing the cause into the circuit court of the county, and to restrain the enforcement of the writ of possession. Accompanying this petition she tendered into court $155.75, to cover the note and interest and costs.

She also executed a *supersedeas* bond with W. D. Matthews as surety in the penal sum of $3,600, conditioned to prosecute the petition with effect and, on default, to abide by and perform the judgment of the court trying the case; likewise to pay the costs.

On August 12, 1912, Mrs. Deatherage died, and the cause was thereafter duly revived in the name of her children, Charles Deatherage, James E. Lewis, and Mrs. J. I. Stewart, as her heirs at law, and in the name of the North Memphis Savings Bank as her administrator.

On August 14, 1912, possession of the real estate in controversy was surrendered to Crofford by the heirs.

The case came on for trial before his honor, H. W. Laughlin, one of the judges of the circuit court.

The court found the plea of no assets in favor of the administrator, also the tender made by Mrs. Deatherage as already mentioned, the execution of the bond by Matthews, the surrender of the possession of the property on August 14th, and proceeded to adjudge as follows:

"And thereupon the court adjudged that the plaintiff [Crofford] is entitled to no judgment either against the said heirs or said bank [the administrator], but is entitled to a judgment for the value of the rent of said premises against W. D. Matthews the surety on the bond of *certiorari* and *supersedeas* of Mrs. W. C. Deatherage, now deceased, from September 1, 1911, up to August 14, 1912, at the rate of $150 per month, with interest at six per cent. on each month's rent from the first of that month to this date."

After ascertaining the whole amount, principal and interest, $1,849.54, the judgment proceeds:

"The court further orders that the clerk of the court at once pay the plaintiff, or his attorney, the $155.75 paid into court by deceased defendant on September 13, 1911, when she prayed for the writs of *certiorari* and *supersedeas*, and that this amount be credited on the amount of this judgment.

"Wherefore it is ordered that the plaintiff, T. J. Crofford, have and recover of the said W. D. Matthews, surety on said bond, and the said North Memphis Savings Bank, administrator of the said Mrs. W. C. Deatherage, deceased, $1,849.54, and the costs of the suit, less the $155.75 mentioned, making a total of $1,693.79, for which execution will issue."

Matthews prayed an appeal to the court of civil appeals, and that court reversed the judgment as to the administrator, holding that the entry of judgment against it was evidently an inadvertence, and corrected the entry so as to render judgment for the possession against the heirs, but directed no writ of possession, inasmuch as this feature of the judgment of that court was based on a decision of this court (*Spillman* v. *Walt*, 12 Heisk., 574), in which it was held that a judgment on a *certiorari* bond, executed under our statute in forcible entry and detainer cases, could only follow as an incident to a judgment for possession. With these emendations the judgment of the trial court against Matthews for the rent was affirmed.

At this point Matthews filed a petition in this court for the writ of *certiorari* and *supersedeas* to remove the cause here for trial, and errors have been assigned.

Only two errors are available, however, in this court under our rules, viz., those which were embraced in a motion for a new trial. These are as follows:

"(1) The court erred in rendering judgment because it is established by the evidence that on the 14th day of August, 1912, the land for the possession of which this suit was instituted was surrendered to the plaintiff, and he then entered into possession of said premises and demised same to other tenants, leaving nothing really for controversy or decision in the suit.

"(2) The court erred in entering judgment in the suit for the further reason that, at the time of suing out the writ of *certiorari* and *supersedeas* as herein, the defendant, Mrs. M. C. Deatherage, with leave of the court tendered and paid all the rent in arrears for said premises, whereby the right of the plaintiff to forfeit the said lease and end the term was extinguished and the forfeiture became extinct, leaving nothing to be determined in this case.''

These assignments were repeated in the court of civil appeals and are urged again in this court.

We think the first should be overruled. At the time the surrender was made by the heirs of Mrs. Deatherage the situation of the parties was as follows: Crofford had brought an action to enforce the right of forfeiture secured to him in the lease, had obtained a judgment for the possession in the court of first instance, appellate proceedings had been instituted by Mrs. Deatherage, and in doing this she had been compelled, by the statute applicable to such cases (Shan. Code, sec. 5111), to give bond for the rents and the costs that might accrue during the continuance of the litigation. Pending the period between the filing of the *certiorari* petition on September 13, 1911, and the surrender of possession on the 14th of August, 1912, all of the rents had accrued for which judgment was given, likewise a bill of court costs. The surrender relieved Mrs. Deatherage, or her estate, from any liability accruing subsequently thereto, but not from any right which had accrued to Crofford. *Hanaw v. Bailey*, 83 Mich., 24, 46 N. W., 1039, 9 L. R. A., 801; *American Bonding Co. v. Pueblo*

Investment Co., 150 Fed., 17, 80 C. C. A., 97, 9 L. R. A.
(N. S.), 557, 10 Ann. Cas., 357 and note; *Boyd* v.
Gore, 143 Wis., 531, 128 N. W., 68, 21 Ann. Cas., 1263.
It is true that it was not essential, indeed it was
wholly unnecessary, to enter a formal judgment for
the possession after the surrender had taken place
pending the suit; but it was the duty of the court to
mold the judgment according to the facts; (Shan.
Code, 4702), and there should have been a judgment
entered reciting the facts, including the surrender
pending the litigation, and declaring the plaintiff Crofford's right to the possession at the beginning of the
action, and, as a consequence a recovery on the
bond for the rents and costs. It is a mistake to suppose, as argued by defendant's counsel in effect, that
the surrender could have a retroactive effect, and
blot out all of plaintiff's previously acquired rights.
It is true that the purpose of the suit was to recover the possession, and it may be well said, when
the matter is considered in its narrowest aspect, that,
the possession having been already obtained by consent of parties, it was idle to longer litigate to obtain it; that one cannot sue for what one already has.
Still, the matter must be viewed in the larger light;
that there was attached to the right of possession
the right to receive unpaid rents and the costs, and
these were not turned over when the possession of
the real estate was surrendered. Nor did the surrender bind the surety on the *certiorari* bond. He could
take advantage of it indeed, as to all subsequent rents,

but the principal could not, by making a surrender, determine against the surety the question whether the plaintiff was entitled to enforce the forfeiture, in so far as that concerned a judgment on the bond. The surety had the right to litigate that question for his own protection. After the surrender had been made, it had yet to be determined between the plaintiff and the surety at the beginning of the action.

The second assignment presents the point that the tender with the *certiorari* petition to the circuit court of an amount sufficient to pay the rent due September 1st, the interest thereon, and the costs accrued to the date of the petition, forced on Crofford the duty of acceptance, and destroyed his action for possession. It is insisted, in substance, that the maturity of each note, followed by failure to pay it, gave a separate right to forfeiture, but that the tenant could prevent this forfeiture in each instance by tendering the amount due each time, even after suit brought for possession; that it was the duty of the landlord, even pending the present suit, on the falling due of each note month by month, to declare a forfeiture for that, and so on to the end; and finally, that the surety on the *certiorari* bond became liable only for the amount of the first note, and not for all the rents that might accrue during the litigation, and that, inasmuch as the amount of this note and interest was tendered with the petition in the circuit court, there was no liability against him of any character.

The crucial question, as we think, is whether the forfeiture was made effective before the tender was made.

In this State we follow the old common-law rule that, in order to an effective forfeiture, the landlord must demand the rent on the day it is due, before sunset, and at the most public place on the land; that is to say, at the front door of the dwelling house of the tenant if there be such house on the land. *Parks* v. *Hays,* 92 Tenn., 161, 22 S. W., 3. But the necessity of such demand may be waived in the lease. Id. *Lewis* v. *Hughes,* 12 Colo., 208, 20 Pac., 621. There was such waiver in the present case. But the lease provides for a re-entry, and the authorities are that when such is the case a re-entry must be effected before the forfeiture can become operative. Taylor, Landlord and Tenant, secs. 288, 492, and note; *Guffy* v. *Hukill,* 34 W. Va., 49, 11 S. E., 754, 8 L. R. A., 759, 762, 26 Am. St. Rep., 901; *Crean* v. *McMahon,* 106 Md., 507, 68 Atl., 265, 14 L. R. A. (N. S.), 798, 804. Very many authorities hold that the entry by the landlord may be in person or by agent, and with such force as be necessary to expel the tenant, on expiration of the lease. *Allen* v. *Keily,* 17 R. I., 731, 24 Atl., 776, 33 Am. St. Rep., 905, 16 L. R. A., 798, and authorities cited in note; note to *Whitney* v. *Brown,* 11 L. R. A. (N. S.), 468. Quite a considerable number of other authorities are to the effect that the action of unlawful detainer is the legal substitute for personal entry. Same note, and authorities cited. *Wilson* v.

Campbell, 75 Kan., 159, 88 Pac., 548, 121 Am. St. Rep., 366, 12 Ann. Cas., 766, 8 L. R. A. (N. S.), 426, and notes; *Whitney* v. *Brown,* 75 Kan., 678, 90 Pac., 277, 12 Ann. Cas., 768, 11 L. R. A. (N. S.), 468 and note.

The reason underlying these' cases is that the statutes on this subject, and on forcible entry and detainer, were designed to preserve the peace and good order of society, and to prevent the collisions that are so likely to follow invasions of real estate.

We have such statutes, and we are of the opinion that the line of cases last referred to state the safer and better rule. This was recognized in *Davidson* v. *Phillips,* 9 Yerg. (17 Tenn.), 93, 95, 96, 30 Am. Dec., 393. Indeed we believe that any other form of entry would violate the first section of the chapter of our Code covering the subjects of forcible entry and detainer, forcible detainer, and unlawful detainer. That section (5090) reads:

"No person shall enter upon or into any lands, tenements, or other possessions, and detain or hold the same, but where entry is given by law, and then only in a peaceable manner."

This mode of procedure seems also to have been in the minds of the parties to the lease, since the last sentence quoted indicates on whom process shall be served in case the tenant shall be absent when the forfeiture occurs.

Similarly it has been held that:

"Wherever the action of ejectment is in force, no actual entry by the landlord is necessary to enable

him to take advantage of a condition broken, because
the constructive entry implied and confessed in the
action is sufficient for the purpose, even where the
estate to be avoided is one of freehold." Taylor's
Landlord and Tenant, sec. 298, citing *Doe* v. *Masters,*
2 B. & C., 490; *Little* v. *Heaton,* 2 Lord Raymond,
750; *Bear* v. *Whisler,* 7 Watts (Pa.), 149; *Jackson* v.
Crysler, 1 Johns. Cas. (N. Y.), 125; *Doe* v. *Alexander,* 2 M. & S., 525; *Garrett* v. *Scouten,* 3 Denio (N.
Y.), 334.

We are of the opinion on the grounds stated that
the service of process in the unlawful detainer suit
operated as a constructive re-entry, and an actual re-
entry by the landlord was unnecessary.

However, the tenant remained in the actual possession of the land pending the action, and was enabled
to maintain that possession by virtue of the *supersedeas* bond allowed by the statute, under which the writ
of *certiorari* was granted to remove the cause from the
court of first instance to the circuit court.

But the burden of the statute must be so borne along
with the enjoyment of its benefits. It requires that
the defendant's bond must bind him and his surety for
"the value of the rent of the premises during the litigation." Shannon's Code, sec. 5111. So while it is
true that after an actual entry by the landlord there
can be no subsequent rents, the case is necessarily different in a case where the defendant is held in possession, as here, by virtue of a statute on the execution of a bond of the kind we have mentioned.

From what has been said, it is apparent that there could be no need for successive actions to enforce the forfeiture as each successive installment of rent fell due. When default was made on the note due September 1st, and action was brought the next day to enforce the forfeiture, that action covered the whole contract.

Nor is it true that the tender which was made with the filing of the petition for the writs of *certiorari* and *supersedeas* availed to destroy the forfeiture. We had occasion to consider a similar question in *B. W. Lee* v. *Security Bank & Trust Co.*, 124 Tenn., 582, 139 S. W., 690. We there said:

"The authorities are in conflict upon the effect of a tender made after default. In our opinion, the better view, supported by the latest cases, is that where a tender is made after default, but before the mortgagee has exercised his option, the mortgagee is bound to accept the money, and the acceleration will not take place. There are some authorities which hold that the mortgagee is bound to accept the money if tendered at any time before sale made, even after suit brought, if the tender of the money and interest due includes also the costs accrued. We do not think these authorities state the true rule, and decline to follow them. As we have said, the question is not whether the court will enforce a penalty, or forfeiture, since no such matter is involved, but whether it will recognize a contract which the parties have made, for advancing the day of payment upon a contingency which they had provided for in terms agreed upon between them."

In that case we had under consideration the terms of a mortgage or trust deed, which provided that on failure of the debtor to pay any part of the indebtedness when due, all of the indebtedness, at the option of the creditor, should become due without notice to the debtor, and the trustees should enter and foreclose. The same principle is recognized as to leases in *Insurance Co.* v. *Diggs*, 8 Baxt. (67 Tenn.), 563, 569.

It is insisted that the court of civil appeals erred in awarding judgment for the possession of the real estate in controversy against the heirs at law of Mrs. Deatherage. The ground of the objection is that the trial court rendered no such judgment, and the plaintiff did not appeal from the judgment which was in fact rendered, but only the defendant, the surety on the *supersedeas* bond. Under our statutes leaseholds are interests in land (Shannon's Code, sec. 51), and as such descend to the heirs at law, and not to the personal representative, as chattels. Hence it was necessary to have the heirs of Mrs. Deatherage before the court, and they were, as already recited, brought in, and the cause was revived against them. The appeal of the surety brought up so much of the case as was required for the court to properly determine his rights, and therefore brought with it the plaintiff and the defendants, the heirs at law. The trial judge, in order to render a proper judgment against the surety, was required, under *Spillman* v. *Walt*, supra, to declare the right of possession. Having failed to correctly frame the judgment, the court of civil appeals, on the case being brought before that tribunal, acted within their jurisdiction in ascertaining the right of possession when modifying and affirming the decision of the trial court.

The result is the judgment of the court of civil appeals, on the grounds herein stated, is affirmed.

SOUTHERN RAILWAY CO. *v.* GRIFFIN.

(*Jackson.*   April Term, 1914.)

RAILROADS.   Statutory requirements.   Approaching city or town.
Shannon's Code, sec. 1574, subsec. 3, providing that, in approaching
a city or town, the bell or whistle of a train shall be sounded
when at a distance of one mile, and then at short intervals till
it reaches the depot or station, and also on leaving a town or
city, etc., applies to through trains which do not stop at a town
or city as well as to local trains that do stop.   (*Post, p.* 559.)

Code cited and construed: Sec. 1574 (S.).

FROM SHELBY.

Appeal from Circuit Court of Shelby County.—
WALTER MALONE, Judge.

BELL, TERRY & BELL, for Griffin.

CARUTHERS EWING, for Southern Ry. Co.

MR. JUSTICE WILLIAMS delivered the opinion of the
Court.

This suit was brought by Walter L. Griffin, as administrator of the estate of Mrs. Laura L. Griffin, alleging that Mrs. Griffin was killed by one of the trains
of the company which was being run through the vil-
lage of Germantown negligently, in that there was a
failure to observe the statutory precautions prescribed

by Code (Shannon) 1574 (3) which section is as follows:

"On approaching a city or town, the bell or whistle shall be sounded when the train is at the distance of one mile, and at short intervals till it reaches the depot or station; and on leaving a town or city, the bell or whistle shall be sounded when the train starts, and at intervals till it has left the corporate limits."

The train was a fast through train that did not stop at Germantown, which is an incorporated municipality. The proof of the railway company fails to show a compliance with the statute, if on proper construction it be applicable.

The contention of defendant company is that the quoted statute has reference to trains approaching and leaving a station at which it makes a stop, and not to through trains such as was this. We cannot accept this as the correct construction of the statute, which was applicable, in its protective features, to Mrs. Griffin at the crossing of the highway and the railroad.

There is more reason for the bell and whistle to be sounded by the enginemen of a through train, which does not slow down its speed on its approach to a depot, than by a train which comes to a stop. We do not conceive that this stronger reason was not in contemplation by the legislature when the statute was enacted.

Writ of *certiorari* having been granted, the judgment of the court of civil appeals is affirmed.

STATE *v.* RAGGHIANTI.

(*Jackson.*   April Term, 1914.)

1 INTOXICATING LIQUORS.   Nuisance.   Injunction.   Violation.
Erroneous Injunction.

Assuming that under Acts 2d Ex. Sess. 1913, ch. 2, sec. 4, relative
to injunctions against nuisances consisting of the conducting,
maintaining, or engaging in the sale of intoxicating liquors, a
temporary injunction should not have been issued without notice
to the defendant, an injunction issued without notice was merely
erroneous, as a matter of procedure, and was not void or in
excess of jurisdiction, and a violation thereof was punishable
as a contempt. (*Post, pp.* 565-568.)

Acts cited and construed: Acts 1913, ch. 2.

Cases cited and approved: McHenry v. State, 16 L. R. A. (N. S.),
1063; Weaver v. Toney, 107 Ky., 419.

2. NUISANCE.   Injunction.   Violation.   Erroneous Injunction.

That a bill for an injunction against the maintenance of a nuisance
brought in the name of the State did not allege that the State
sustained any special injuries by reason of the nuisance was
immaterial in a proceeding to punish a violation of the injunction as a contempt even if such an allegation was necessary.
(*Post, pp.* 568, 569.)

3. INTOXICATING LIQUORS.   Nuisance.   Abatement and Injunction.   Bill.   Sufficiency.

Acts 2d Ex. Sess. 1913, ch. 2, authorizing injunctions restraining
the continuance of a nuisance consisting of the carrying on of
the sale of intoxicating liquors on a bill filed by citizens and free-
holders or by the attorney-general or district attorney, changes
with respect to the nuisances to which it relates, the rule that
parties seeking to enjoin a nuisance must show special injury.
(*Post, pp.* 568, 569.)

State v. Ragghianti.

Acts cited and construed: Acts 1913, ch. 2.

Cases cited and approved: Weidner v. Friedman, 126 Tenn., 677; Weakley v. Page, 102 Tenn., 179.

4. INTOXICATING LIQUORS. Nuisance. Injunction. Violations. Proceedings to punish. Petition for attachment.

Where, upon a bill alleging that defendant was engaged in the sale of intoxicating liquors, a temporary injunction was issued enjoining defendant from further engaging in the sale of liquors, from moving or disturbing his stock of liquors and bar fixtures, or from entering the barroom of his building and interfering therewith, a petition for an attachment for contempt, charging that he had continued the sale of intoxicating liquors in willful disobedience of the injunction, showed a violation of the injunction; it is not being pretended that defendant supposed himself to be charged with selling liquors at any place other than his barroom. (*Post, p. 569.*)

5. INJUNCTION. Violations. Proceedings to punish. Petition for attachment.

Where defendant answered a petition for an attachment for contempt in violating an injunction by alleging various matters of excuse and avoidance, he could not attack the petition on appeal on account of its general averments and lack of specific allegations. (*Post, pp. 569, 570.*)

6. INTOXICATING LIQUORS. Nuisance. Injunction. Violation. Extent of punishment.

Shannon's Code, sec. 5919, providing that, where not otherwise specially provided, the circuit court, chancery, and Supreme Court are limited to a fine of $50 and imprisonment for not exceeding ten days in punishing contempts, does not apply to violations of injunctions issued under Acts 2d Ex. Sess. 1913, ch. 2, relative to enjoining the business of selling intoxicating liquors, as that act provides that any person violating any injunction shall be imprisoned not less than thirty days nor more than six months and be fined not exceeding $50. (*Post, p. 570.*)

129 Tenn. 36

State v. Ragghianti.

Acts cited and construed: Acts 1913, ch. 2.

Code cited and construed: Sec. 5919 (S.).

7. **INTOXICATING LIQUORS. Constitutionality of acts.   Abatement and injunction.**

Acts 2d Ex. Sess. 1913, ch. 2, making the conducting, maintaining, carrying on, or engaging in the sale of intoxicating liquors, and all buildings, fixtures, etc., used for such purpose, public nuisances, subject to abatement thereunder, and authorizing injunctions restraining the continuance of such nuisances and closing the building or place where it is conducted, is constitutional. (*Post, p.* 571.)

Acts cited and construed: Acts 1913, ch. 2.

Case cited and approved: State of Tennessee, *ex rel*, v. J. J. Persica *et al.*, 167 S. W., 689.

FROM SHELLY

Appeal from Chancery Court of Shelby County.—F. H. HEISKELL and FRANCIS FENTRESS, Chancellors.

ANDERSON & CRABTREE, for appellant.

FRANK M. THOMPSON, attorney-general, Z. N. ESTES, district attorney-general, and G. T. FITZHUGH, for the State.

MR. JUSTICE GREEN delivered the opinion of the Court.

This was a proceeding brought in the name of the State, on the relation of the district attorney-general, to abate as a nuisance the establishment of defendant

Ragghianti. It was alleged that he was engaged in the sale of intoxicating liquors at his place of business, and this bill was filed under the authority of chapter 2 of the Acts of the Second Extra Session of 1913, commonly known as the Nuisance Act.

The bill was filed on March 16, 1914, and in the second, third, and fourth paragraphs it was prayed that an injunction issue forbidding defendant from further engaging in the sale of liquors, from removing or disturbing the stock of liquors and bar fixtures, and forbidding him from entering the bar-room of his building and interfering with the stock of liquors or fixtures.

Before it was filed, the bill was presented to Chancellor Heiskell, who indorsed his fiat thereupon in the following language:

"To the Clerk & Master: File this bill and notify defendants that Chancellor Fentress and I will hear the within application for an injunction at 10 a. m. March 24th, 1914, and that pending the hearing of said injunction, they are enjoined as prayed in the second, third and fourth paragraphs of the prayer of the bill.

"This 16 day of March, 1914.

"F. H. HEISKELL, Chancellor."

The notice, the writ of injunction, copy of the bill, and subpoena were served on Ragghianti March 17th. Defendant did not answer, and there was no hearing on March 24th.

On April 3, 1914, the district attorney-general filed a petition alleging that defendant had violated the terms of the aforesaid temporary injunction and praying for an attachment for defendant that he might be punished for contempt. An attachment was issued; defendant was arrested and placed under bond for his appearance April 8th. On April 8th defendant appeared in person and filed an answer to the original bill, and also an answer to the petition averring him to be in contempt.

It is not necessary to set out the contents of either answer filed by defendant. The answer to the original bill was a general denial, and the answer to the petition for an attachment against his body consisted of various matters of excuse and avoidance. The whole case was heard before the chancellor upon oral testimony which has not been preserved in a bill of exceptions, and it is conceded by counsel for defendant that the proof offered was sufficient to sustain the judgment of the court.

The chancellors adjudged that defendant was guilty of willful violation of the temporary injunction aforesaid, and ordered that he be punished for such contempt by imprisonment in the county jail for three months, and that the cost of the proceedings be taxed to him. On the merits, the chancellors found him guilty of maintaining a nuisance, as averred, the temporary injunction was made perpetual, and defendant's stock, fixtures, and appurtenances were decreed to be dealt with as provided in section 6 of the Nuisance Act.

The defendant has appealed and assigned as errors:

1. That the temporary injunction herein was null and void for the reason that it issued upon the *ex parte* application of the state without notice to defendant, as required by section 4 of the Nuisance Act.

It is insisted that the court below was without jurisdiction to issue this temporary injunction except upon notice to the defendant, under the provisions of the act, and that accordingly defendant was under no obligation to respect and obey this order of the court.

It is not necessary in this case to construe section 4 of chapter 2, Acts of 1913 (Second Extra Session), and to determine whether a defendant is entitled to notice prior to the issuance of a temporary injunction against him.

In this case the injunction was issued without notice, and was duly served upon the defendant. This court has said that a party so served with an injunction "is not allowed to speculate upon the equity of the bill, or the legality or regularity of the writ, but his simple duty is to obey." *Blair* v. *Nelson*, 8 Baxt., 1-5.

If it be conceded that, under a proper construction of the Nuisance Act, a defendant is entitled to notice of an application for temporary injunction, nevertheless the failure to give him such notice is merely an error in procedure on the part of the court. Such an error is procedural only and not jurisdictional. By the act

in question, the chancery court is clothed with authority to deal with nuisances, such as plaintiff's business
is declared by the act to be, and of course the court
had jurisdiction of the defendant. That is to say,
the court below had jurisdiction of the subject-matter and of the person of defendant, and although the
action of the court in issuing the temporary injunction may have been erroneous, as a matter of practice, it was by no means a void order which the defendant was at liberty to disregard, but was an order
which the statute empowered the court to make. See
note to *McHenry* v. *State*, 16 L. R. A. (N. S.), 1063.

Speaking of the issuance of temporary injunctions,
after discussing the rules with reference to same, the
supreme court of West Virginia said:

"Violation of these rules regulating the exercise
of the jurisdiction does not, any more than any other
case of erroneous decision, make the action of the
court *coram non judice.* To grant such an injunction
when the state of the case, tested by the rules established for the exercise of jurisdiction, does not warrant it is nothing more than judicial error. It is not
an act in excess of jurisdiction." *Powhatan Coal &
Coke Co.* v. *Ritz*, 60 W. Va., 395, 402, 56 S. E., 257,
260, 9 L. R. A. (N. S.), 1225-1229.

Mr. High days down the rule as follows:

"With whatever irregularities the proceedings may
be affected, or however erroneously the court may have
acted in granting the injunction in the first instance,
it must be implicitly obeyed so long as it remains in

existence, and the fact that it has been granted erroneously affords no justification or excuse for its violation before it has been properly dissolved. . . . Upon proceedings for contempt in this class of cases, the only legitimate inquiry is whether the court granting the injunction had jurisdiction of the parties and of the subject-matter, and whether it made the order which has been violated, and the court will not, in such proceedings consider whether the order was erroneous." 2 High on Injunctions (4 Ed.), sec. 1416.

Mr. Joyce says:

"Unless an injunction order is void upon its face for lack of jurisdiction on the part of the judge who granted it, it must be obeyed, however erroneous the granting of it may have been, until it is dissolved on motion or appeal or some other method of direct review in the action in which it was granted." 1 Joyce on Injunctions, sec. 247.

So at most the action of the court in granting this temporary injunction, without notice, was a mere violation of a rule of procedure. The temporary injunction was not with respect to a matter and parties beyond the court's jurisdiction, and it was therefore not an order which the defendant was at liberty to disregard.

The authorities relied on by the defendant are not applicable to this case. The case of *Weaver* v. *Toney*, 107 Ky., 419, 54 S. W., 732, 50 L. R. A., 105, was one in which the temporary injunction granted without notice accomplished the whole relief obtainable in the

suit, and, had it been obeyed, the litigation would
have ended. It was a mandatory injunction issued
with reference to the holding of an election without
notice, on the day before the election, and the day on
which the defendants were required to answer was several days after the election had transpired. This injunction was therefore not one which effected a mere
temporary stay with the reservation of the rights of
the parties until they could be heard, but, as said before, it accomplished the whole purpose of the litigation. *Weaver* v. *Toney* is therefore readily distinguishable from the present case. It was no doubt decided correctly upon its facts, but the circumstances
are here quite different. The temporary injunction
here issued might have put the defendant to some inconvenience and slight pecuniary loss, but the subject-matter of the litigation was left open for future
investigation and determination.

Defendant also cites section 1425 of High on Injunctions, which is merely to the effect that injunctions issued respecting elections, legislative action,
and like matters, of which a court of equity has no
jurisdiction, are void, and need not be obeyed. The
cases referred to by Mr. High in this section are those
in which the court lacked jurisdiction of the subject-
matter.

It is further said on behalf of defendant that the
State of Tennessee did not aver that it sustained any
special injuries by reason of the nuisance, and was
not entitled to an injunction. This is not material in

a contempt proceeding, but the rule that parties seeking an injunction against a nuisance must show special injury, formerly laid down by this court in *Weidner* v. *Friedman,* 126 Tenn., 677, 151 S. W., 56, 42 L. R. A. (N. S.), 1041, and *Weakley* v. *Page,* 102 Tenn., 179, 53 S. W., 551, 46 L. R. A., 552, is changed by chapter 2 of the Acts of 1913 (Second Extra Session), with respect to nuisances of the character described in the act. ·No such averment is now necessary.

Defendant also maintains that the petition for an attachment for contempt does not aver that defendant has been guilty of any act punishable under the provisions of the act in question. The petition for attachment charges that, since the issuance of the temporary injunction, the defendant has continued the sales of intoxicating liquors in willful disobedience of said injunction. He was enjoined from entering the barroom of his building. The averment of the petition was that he continued the sale of liquors in disobedience of the injunction, by which was meant that he entered his barroom and sold liquors. It was not pretended by defendant that he supposed himself to be charged with selling liquors at a place other than his barroom. He in fact admitted the sale of liquor there, and the consequent entry into those premises. His answer merely undertook to offer excuses for his conduct.

Whatever objection might originally have been made to the petition for attachment on account of its general averments, and lack of specific allegation, was waived by the answer defendant filed. He cannot make such points now. The petition must be held to have charged that he entered and used his premises in violation of the preliminary injunction, and such a violation is an act punishable under the provisions of the statute.

The next assignment of error is that the chancellors exceeded their authority in fixing defendant's punishment at ninety days in prison. It is contended that the defendant is only punishable, if at all, under section 5919 of Shannon's Code, which section is as follows:

"The punishment for contempts may be fine or imprisonment, or both; but where not otherwise especially provided, the circuit, chancery, and supreme courts are limited to a fine of $50, and imprisonment not exceeding ten days, and all other courts are limited to a fine of $10."

Chapter 2 of the Acts of 1913 (Second Extra Session) fixes the punishment for violation of injunctions issued under its authority. Its provisions with respect to such violation are controlling, and it provides that upon conviction for contempt parties "shall be imprisoned in the county jail or workhouse not less than thirty days nor more than six months, and may also be fined not exceeding $50, at the discretion of the court." The punishment inflicted on this defendant therefore falls directly within the penalty prescribed by the statute.

State v. Ragghianti.

It is finally assigned as error that chapter 2 of the Acts of 1913 (Second Extra Session) is unconstitutional. The constitutionality of the act has been sustained by the court in the case of *State of Tennessee, ex rel., v. J. J. Persica et al.*, 167 S. W., —.

The judgment of the court below is in all things affirmed.

HUNTER *et al. v.* UNITED STATES FIDELITY & GUARANTY
· Co.*

(Jackson. April Term, 1914.)

1. **INSURANCE.** Employers' Indemnity Insurance. **Contracts.**
Construction.

A "continuation certificate" made by the president of a bank to
a guaranty company in contemplation of the renewal of a fidelity
bond, indemnifying it against losses due to the fraud or dishonesty of its cashier, certified that the books of the cashier
"were examined from time to time in the regular course of business and found correct in every respect, all moneys or property
in his control or custody being accounted for with proper securities and funds on hand to balance his accounts, and he is
not now in default." *Held,* that the certificate was not a warranty of the correctness of such accounts, but merely that examinations were made as represented, and no errors or falsifications were discovered; the phrase "and he is not now in default,"
not being a substantive and distinct warranty, independent of
the preceding language, but only expressing the result of the
examinations. (*Post, pp.* 578-580.)

Cases cited and approved: First National Bank v. Fidelity &
Guaranty Co., 110 Tenn., 10; United States Fidelity & Guaranty
Co. v. Citizens' Bank (Ky.), 143 S. W., 997; American Bonding
Co. v. Spokane Building & Loan Soc., 130 Fed., 737; Title
Guaranty & Surety Co. v. Bank of Fulton, 89 Ark., 471; Rem-
ington v. Fidelity & Deposit Co., 27 Wash., 429.

2. **INSURANCE.** Employers' liability Insurance. **Question for**
Jury.

In an action by a bank against a guaranty company upon a fidelity
bond indemnifying it against loss due to the fraud or dishonesty

---

*As to the construction of a bond or policy indemnifying em-
ployer against loss from negligence of employee, see note in 31
L. R. A. (N. S.), 775. And on the question whether employers'
indemnity contract constitutes insurance, see note in 47 L. R. A.
(N. S.), 294.

of its cashier, *held*, a question for the jury whether the bank had in good faith made reasonable examinations of the books and accounts of the cashier as required by the contract with the guaranty company. (*Post, p.* 580.)

3. INSURANCE. Employers' Indemnity Insurance. Contracts. Construction.

A fidelity bond indemnifying an employer against loss due to the dishonesty of an employee is to be construed as an insurance contract and, in cases of doubt, against the insurer. (*Post, pp.* 580, 581.)

Cases cited and approved: Railroad v. Fidelity & Guaranty Co., 125 Tenn., 690; Insurance Co. v. Dobbins, 114 Tenn., 239; Royal Ins. Co. v. Vanderbilt Ins. Co., 102 Tenn., 264.

4. INSURANCE. Employers' Indemnity Insurance. Contracts. Construction.

Words and phrases in an employers' fidelity bond are to be construed according to their context. (*Post, pp.* 581-584.)

Case cited and approved: Winkler Brokerage Co. v. Fidelity & Deposit Co., 119 La., 735.

5. INSURANCE. Policy. Construction. Warranties.

Warranties by the insured are not favored by construction. (*Post, p.* 584.)

FROM SHELBY

Appeal from Chancery Court of Shelby County.—J. P. Young, Judge.

Julian C. Wilson and W. P. Armstrong, for Hunter.

R. P. Cary and Wm. Hall, for United States Fidelity & Guaranty Co.

MR. JUSTICE GREEN delivered the opinion of the Court.

This bill was brought by the receivers of the Bank of Collierville to recover from the defendant guaranty company $25,000, the penalty of a certain fidelity bond executed by the company to cover losses to the bank occasioned by reason of fraud or dishonesty of the bank's cashier, L. T. Ward.

The Bank of Collierville was placed in the hands of a receiver as an insolvent institution, and the defalcation of Ward upon investigation turned out to be about $38,000. Premiums had been duly paid on this bond, notice was regularly given, and the facts concerning Ward's default are not in dispute. The controversy here arises upon certain language of the bond, the application therefor, and an employer's certificate, upon which a renewal of the bond was had. The case depends for decision upon a proper construction of the several instruments.

In April, 1904, the bond in question was issued by the guaranty company to the bank in the penalty stated, upon a written application of the employer in which certain representations were made respecting Ward and his employment.

Referring first to the material statements in the application for the bond, we find the following:

"11. To whom and how frequently will he account for his handlings of funds and securities?

"A. Twice a year, our auditing committee.

"12. (a) What means will you use to ascertain whether his accounts are correct?

"A. Audit.

"(b) How frequently will they be examined?

"A. Twice a year.

In the face of the bond occurs this paragraph:

"Whereas the employer has heretofore delivered to the company certain representations and promises relative to the duties and accounts of the employee and other matters, it is hereby understood and agreed that those representations and such promises, and any subsequent representation or promise of the employer hereafter required by or lodged with the company, shall constitute part of the basis and consideration of the contract hereinafter expressed."

This bond, executed by the guaranty company, as aforesaid, was renewed each year from the date of its issuance, May 1, 1904, until May 1, 1912, inclusive. Each renewal was to cover a period of twelve months from date. Ward was first ascertained to be a defaulter in the fall of 1912.

The guaranty company tendered to the receivers and subsequently paid into court the amount of Ward's shortages, ascertained to have occurred prior to May 1, 1910. The company, however, claimed to be released from liability for Ward's defaults after that date by reason of a certain certificate made by the bank to procure the 1910 renewal.

Prior to the 1910 renewal, Ward was advised by the general agent of the guaranty company that it

would be necessary for him to procure what was called
a "continuation certificate" from the bank before this
bond would be renewed for the ensuing year. A certificate was sent to Ward to be executed by his employer. The bank did execute it through its president,
J. M. Glenn, and, upon such execution and return of
the certificate, the bond was continued for another
year. This certificate was in the following language:

"This is to certify that the books and accounts of
Mr. L. T. Ward were examined by us from time to
time in the regular course of business, and we found
them correct in every respect, all moneys or property
in his control or custody being accounted for with
proper securities and funds on hand to balance his
accounts, and he is not now in default. He has performed his duties in an acceptable and satisfactory
manner, and no change has occurred in the terms or
conditions of his employment as specified by us when
the bond was executed.

"Dated Collierville, this 2d day of May, 1910.
          "Signature of employer:
                    "Bank of Collierville.
"By J. M. Glenn, Pres't [Official Capacity]."

In its answer to the bill of the receivers, the guaranty company admitted all the facts stated in the
bill, but averred that this certificate sent to it for the
1910 renewal was a false representation of facts material to the risk; that Ward was in default at that
time; and that it continued the bond for that year
and subsequent years on the faith of this certificate,

and was accordingly released from liability on account of the obligation it had thus been induced to assume.

A jury was demanded by the complainants, and certain issues framed by them were tendered for submission. These issues were:

"(1) Was the United States Fidelity & Guaranty Company induced to make the renewal of its bond, which renewal was dated April 1, 1910, by any substantial misrepresentation of facts, and which facts were material to the risk then assumed or continued by the United States Fidelity & Guaranty Company?

"(2) Did the Bank of Collierville fail, through its officers and directors, to use ordinary diligence and prudence in making in its regular course of business its examinations of the books and accounts of Mr. L. T. Ward, its cashier?"

After hearing the proof, the chancellor declined to submit either of these issues to the jury, and submitted to the jury only one issue which was tendered by the defendant as follows:

"Did J. M. Glenn, as president of the Bank of Collierville, sign the original employer's certificate dated May 2, 1910?"

There being no controversy upon the latter issue, the chancellor directed the jury to answer it in the affirmative, and thereupon rendered a decree in favor of the defendant, from which the complainants have appealed to this court.

It is virtually conceded by the learned counsel for the defendant that the submission of the second issue tendered by complainants would have been proper had not the certificate contained the phrase, referring to Ward, "and he is not now in default."

Leaving out of consideration the phrase above quoted, this certificate is a statement that the books and accounts of Ward were examined in the regular course of business and found correct. The words "all moneys or property in his control or custody being accounted for with proper securities and funds on hand to balance his accounts" constitute a parenthetical clause, qualifying and explaining the language previously used. They indicate the manner in which the books and accounts were found correct.

A certificate that books and accounts have been examined and found correct by an examining committee of a bank is not to be taken as a warranty of the absolute verity of said books and accounts. Such a statement merely means that an examination has been made as represented, and that no errors or falsifications have been discovered.

The supreme court of the United States has lately considered, in a similar case, the effect of a certificate such as this, and disposes of the matter thus:

"Finally it is said that the greater part of the loss occurred during the currency of renewal bonds, and that each renewal was made upon a certificate by the employer, which stated that just prior thereto the books and accounts of the employee 'were examined and found correct in every respect and all moneys accounted for.' It is said that this statement was untrue inasmuch as, at the date of such renewals, the books and accounts were not correct and the cashier was short in his cash. But the certificate was not to be taken as a warranty of the correctness of the accounts. The statement is that his books and accounts had been examined and found correct. The mere fact that the examination, if made by a reasonably competent person, failed to discover discrepancies covered up by false entries or other bookkeeping devices would not defeat the renewal. The case upon this point went to the jury upon the fact of reasonable examinations and the good faith of the bank in making the representation. The question of the weight or credibility of the evidence is not one for our consideration. There was evidence which the trial judge thought sufficient to carry the case to the jury. The supreme court of Arizona agreed with the trial court, and with both courts we concur." *Title Guaranty Co.* v. *Nicholls,* 234 U. S., 346, 32 Sup. Ct., 475, 56 L. Ed., 795.

The foregoing observations of the supreme court of the United States are in line with the current of modern authority, and with our own case of *First National Bank* v. *Fidelity & Guaranty Co.,* 110 Tenn., 10, 75 S. W., 1076, 100 Am. St. Rep., 765. See, also, *United States Fidelity & Guaranty Co.* v. *Citizens' Bank* (Ky.), 143 S. W., 977; *American Bonding Co.* v. *Spokane Building & Loan Soc.,* 130 Fed., 737, 65 C. C.

A., 121; *Title Guaranty & Surety Co.* v. *Bank of Fulton*, 89 Ark., 471, 117 S. W., 537, 33 L. R. A. (N. S.), 676; *Remington* v. *Fidelity & Deposit Co.*, 27 Wash., 429, 67 Pac., 989.

In this case, there is evidence tending to show that Ward's books and accounts were examined by the auditing committee twice a year, prior to the issuance of the certificate in question, in the regular course of business, as was represented in the application for the bond would be done. While a different character of examination would have disclosed the shortages, the legal sufficiency of the examinations made depended upon the good faith and care of the auditing committee. Evidence was offered tending to show that said examinations were made with reasonable care, in the manner customary in such banks, and in good faith, without the discovery of any shortage.

So, leaving out of consideration the phrase "and he is not now in default," the receivers were entitled to have their case submitted to the jury upon the fact of reasonable examinations and good faith of the bank.

Does the addition of the words "and he is not now in default" to this certificate change its character and call for the application of a different test with respect to defendant's liability?

It is contended in behalf of the guaranty company that the language "he is not now in default" is to be considered as a substantive representation, independent of the preceding language. It is argued that by these words the employer undertook to state a detached fact, or exact condition, and did not undertake by this language to state a conclusion drawn from foregoing statements made. As a matter of course, the representation that Ward was not in default was material to the risk, and had it been knowingly made, in another connection, if false, the bond would have been avoided. It is well settled that a bond of this character is to be construed as an insurance contract, and its language, carefully considered and prepared by the company, in all cases of doubt, is to be construed against the company. *Railroad* v. *Fidelity & Guaranty Co.*, 125 Tenn., 690, 148 S. W., 671; *Insurance Co.* v. *Dobbins*, 114 Tenn., 239, 86 S. W., 383; *Royal Ins. Co.* v. *Vanderbilt Ins. Co.*, 102 Tenn., 264, 52 S. W., 168.

Words and phrases are to be construed according to their context. The whole of the preceding part of this certificate constitutes a mere statement that investigations of Ward's books and accounts have been made and these books and accounts found correct.

We do not think that a new and distinct warranty can be incorporated into this certificate lawfully by the use of a conjunction and a few words of general import in this sort of connection. Fairly construed, the concluding phrase must be restricted to conform to the dominant meaning of the whole passage. The words "and he is not now in default," naturally interpreted, appear only to express the result of the investigations, which the certificate avouches to have been made.

If the guaranty company had intended to require the bank, as a condition precedent to the renewal of this bond, to warrant that Ward was not in default, good faith would have required a less equivocal method. Had a separate paragraph been incorporated in this certificate, and the bank officers therein required to warrant the *status* of Ward's accounts, the case would have been different. Inserted into the certificate in this manner, if construed as defendant insists, the words in controversy would be most deceptive.

The apparent meaning of this certificate is that examinations made in the usual course of business, in good faith, and with ordinary care, have disclosed no derelictions on the part of the employee. Almost in its entirety, the certificate has been so interpreted by the courts. Having collected from the whole certificate its seeming purpose, general words therein must be restrained so as to effectuate that purpose. If the defendant wishes to obtain an additional guaranty, and to have an absolute warranty that the employee is not in default prior to the issuance or renewal of its bonds, language must be used less susceptible of misinterpretation. Fair dealing demands that the attention of the employer be distinctly directed thereto, if it is expected to charge him with such an unusual and sweeping warranty. Such a warranty cannot be made effective when disguised and obscured by its context. It will not be countenanced, if it is masked.

We are of opinion that this whole certificate must be construed to mean that examinations of the employee's books and accounts were made in the regular course of business, in the manner indicated by the parenthetical clause, and said books and accounts were found to be correct and, from such examinations, the employer concludes and represents, as a result thereof, that the employee is not in default. So if it appears that the examinations were conducted in good faith, and with reasonable care, the mere fact that such examination failed to disclose the default will not defeat the bond. This certificate does not amount to an unqualified statement that no default exists, but is rather that none was found to exist.

Winkler Brokerage Co. v. *Fidelity & Deposit Co.*, 119 La., 735, 44 South., 449, is not in conflict with the views we have here expressed. The employer's certificate in the *Winkler Brokerage Company Case* did not purport to represent conditions as they were found, but represented conditions as they actually were. In that case it was certified that the employee had punctually accounted, and had always had proper securities, and was not now in default. The employer did not undertake to state what had been found or discovered from examination, but stated without qualification matters of fact. As said by the supreme court of Louisiana, there "was not a question of supposition or belief to which it was asked to certify, but a matter of fact.''

The difference between the two employer's certificates is plain enough.

The construction we have given this employer's certificate is fully justified by well-settled rules for the interpretation of legislative acts, written contracts, and insurance policies. Lewis' Sutherland Statutory Construction, sec. 347; Page on Contracts, secs. 1112-1113; Joyce on Insurance, sec. 1949.

Warranties are not favored by construction. Joyce on Insurance, sec. 1949; 19 Cyc. 684.

It results that the second issue tendered by the complainants should have been submitted to the jury.

Regarding complainants' first issue, inasmuch as the whole defense was based on the certificate, there was really no occasion to submit a question of material misrepresentations to the jury. The representations in this certificate are undoubtedly material. They are expressly made so by the contract of the parties. In so far as the first issue included a submission of the truth of the representations, it should have gone to the jury. We have undertaken in this opinion to explain the meaning of the representations embodied in this employer's certificate. Whether they were made in good faith is a vital question of fact in the case.

From what has been said heretofore, it is obvious that the chancellor was in error in submitting to the jury, as the only issue in the case, the issue tendered by the defendant as to whether the bank through its president, as a matter of fact, executed the renewal certificate. The third, fourth, and fifth assignments of error are accordingly sustained.

In view of the disposition made of the case, it is not necessary to comment on the sixth, ninth, and tenth assignments.

After full consideration, we overrule the seventh and eighth assignments of error.

The decree of the chancellor will be reversed, and the cause remanded for another trial. Defendant will pay the costs of this court.

GULF COMPRESS CO., *v.* INSURANCE CO. OF PENNSYL-
VANIA. *

GULF COMPRESS CO. *v.* COMMERCIAL UNION ASSUR-
ANCE CO. *

GULF COMPRESS CO. *v.* STUYVESANT INSURANCE CO.*

(*Jackson.* April Term, 1914.)

1. **APPEAL AND ERROR. Harmless error. Submission of unnecessary issues.**

Where, in an action on a fire policy, the issue was the amount
of the loss, the action of the court in submitting the issue of
insurer's good faith in refusing to pay the loss was not prejudicial to insurer, especially as the question of good faith was
found in favor of the defendant. (*Post, p.* 590.)

2. **INSURANCE. Fire insurance. Confession of liability.**

An insurer, agreeing to an arbitration to ascertain the amount
of a loss, thereby confesses its liability on the policy, and it
cannot escape from the admission by subsequently violating
the arbitration agreement, or by withdrawing from the arbitration. (*Post, pp.* 590-594.)

3. **APPEAL AND ERROR. Harmless error. Instructions.**

Where, in an action a fire policy stipulating that it should be void
if insured concealed any material fact, or in case of any fraud
touching any matter relating to the insurance before or after
a loss, it appeared that insurer agreed to arbitration, but subsequently withdrew therefrom, whereupon insured brought the
action on the policy, the refusal to charge that insurer could
withdraw from the arbitration whenever it saw fit to do so
without giving any reason therefor, which withdrawal did not
prejudice its rights under the policy either to contest the

---

*On the question of arbitration as condition precedent to action on
insurance policy, see note in 15 L. R. A. (N. S.), 1055.

The question of the law governing as to extent of recovery on policy
is discussed in a note in 63 L. R. A. (N. S.), 868.

Compress Co. v. Insurance Co.

amount of the loss or to question the good faith of insured in making proof of loss, was not prejudicial to the insurer, where it was allowed to introduce such evidence as it had on the question of the good faith of insured in making proof of loss and submitting the issue to the jury. (*Post, pp.* 590-594.)

Cases cited and approved: St. Paul Fire & Marine Insurance Co. v. Kirkpatrick, 129 Tenn., ——; Hickerson v. Insurance Companies, 96 Tenn., 193; North German Insurance Co. v. Morton-Scott-Robertson Co., 108 Tenn., 384.

4. TRIAL. Instructions. Laying stress on evidence.
A requested instruction, which lays stress on a special item of evidence, is properly refused. (*Post, pp.* 594-596.)

5. TRIAL. Instructions. Assumption of fact.
A requested instruction, which assumes a fact not shown by the evidence, is properly refused. (*Post, pp.* 596, 597.)

6. APPEAL AND ERROR. Harmless error. Admission of evidence.
Where, in an action on a fire policy, there was no evidence that insured had knowingly made a false statement of the value of the property destroyed, except in so far as the proof related to his supposed knowledge of another machine of substantially the kind destroyed by fire, but there was no evidence that he had any such knowledge at the time of making the proof, the error in permitting complainant to testify that insurer did not, up to the filing of its crossbill, state to him that a knowingly false proof of loss had been made to defraud insurer, was not prejudicial to insurer, and must be disregarded, as required by Acts 1911, ch. 32. (*Post, p.* 597.)

7. APPEAL AND ERROR. Harmless error. Erroneous rulings.
In an action on a fire policy against an insurer which had confessed liability, an issue whether insured furnished fraudulent proof of loss was immaterial, and rulings on the issue were not prejudicial. (*Post, p.* 598.)

8. APPEAL AND ERROR. Verdict. Conclusiveness.
A verdict sustained by any evidence cannot be disturbed by the court on appeal. (*Post, p.* 598.)

9. INSURANCE. Fire Insurance. Loss. Liability.

Where insurer refused to replace machinery destroyed by fire with another plant, which could then have been obtained cheap, or to furnish the money to buy it, it could not insist that the loss by the fire should be measured by the cost of the plant is refused to buy. (*Post, pp.* 598-601.)

10. INSURANCE. Fire Insurance. Total loss. "Cash value."

Where there was a total loss of property covered by a fire policy, and the property included a machine which insured purchased for $11,500 at a sacrifice sale, and which was as good as new at the time of the loss, and the machine was insured for $15,000, and insurer failed to settle by procuring an equally good machine for $15,000 several months after the fire, and there was no evidence that the latter machine could have been procured at that price at any earlier or later date, or any other machine of the kind for that price, insured could recover the actual cash value of the property destroyed; "cash value" meaning what it would cost to reproduce it in the same condition as before the fire. (*Post, pp.* 601-607.)

Cases cited and approved: McCready v. Hartford Insurance Co., 61 App. Div., 584, 585; Standard Sewing Machine Co. v. Royal Insurance Co., 201 Pa., 645; Everett v. Insurance Co. (Tex. Civ. App.), 36 S. W., 125; Frick v. Insurance Co., 218 Pa., 409; Mechanics' Insurance Co. v. C. A. Hoover Distilling Co., 182 Fed., 590.

FROM SHELBY.

Appeal from Chancery Court, Shelby County.— F. H. HEISKELL, Chancellor.

R. LEE BARTELS, for appellants.

G. T. FITZHUGH, for appellee.

MR. CHIEF JUSTICE NEIL delivered the opinion of the Court.

The bill in this case was filed at Memphis, Tenn., to recover on four several policies of insurance executed on the plant of the complainant, located in Argenta, Ark. The complainant corporation is domesticated in Tennessee. A judgment was rendered in complainant's favor on all the policies, and the defendants have appealed to this court, and assigned errors, fourteen in number.

A jury was demanded, and issues were framed for their consideration in the trial court. There were seven of these. They were in the form of questions. In No. 1 the jury was asked to state the amount of damages which the fire had caused to complainant's compress machine and boilers, and answered: "$34,492.-80." No. 2 the amount of damages to the other property of the complainant. They answered: "$37,833.-15." Nos. 3, 4, and 5 presented the question in various aspects as to whether the insurance companies, in refusing to pay the loss, had acted in bad faith. To this the jury responded: "No." The sixth and seventh issues asked the question whether complainant, or its receiver, furnished the insurance companies proofs of loss which were false or fraudulent, and knowingly so, and whether they knowingly made an exaggerated and false claim against the companies. The jury answered these two quesions: "No."

The various assignments of error arrange themselves around the several issues mentioned, and they
will be considered in relation thereto, rather than in
the order in which they appear in the briefs of counsel.

It is most convenient to first dispose of those bearing
solely upon the third, fourth, and fifth issues, concerning the good faith of the defendant companies.

Assignments Nos. 4, 5, 8, 9, and 10 bear solely on the
question of good faith presented by these issues. They
seem to us wholly immaterial, in view of the fact that
the response of the jury on these issues was favorable
to the defendants. It matters not, therefore, whether
the action of the chancellor in respect of the matters
covered by these assignments was correct or incorrect,
inasmuch as no injury was caused the defendants by
his action in respect of any of them. It is insisted, however, in behalf of the defendants, that the chancellor's
rulings upon these various points prejudiced the defendants generally before the jury. In the view we
take of the case the chief matters before us are the
questions arising under issues Nos. 1 and 2, and the
assignments based on them. We are unable to see how
the rulings of the chancellor on the other question could
prejudice the defendants on the subject of value, with
which issue Nos. 1 and 2 are wholly concerned.

Assignments Nos. 3, 11, and 12 bear solely upon the
matters covered by issues Nos. 6 and 7, concerning
the good faith of the complainant.

Before setting out the contents of assignment No.
3, it is proper to quote the exact language of issue No.

6, and state certain facts bearing thereon, and certain points in the pleadings in respect thereof.

Issue No. 6 reads:

"Did the Gulf Compress Company, or its receiver, C. C. Hanson, furnish to the defendant insurance companies proofs of loss which were false or fraudulent, and knowingly so, and did it (or he) knowingly make an exaggerated and false claim against the insurance companies?"

The defendants filed a cross bill, in which they charged the substance embraced in this issue, and this was denied by the complainant, and an issue was framed thereon as above. However, it appeared as an undisputed matter in the evidence that, after complainants had filed their proofs of loss, it called on the defendants to go into an appraisement or arbitration with it, pursuant to the terms of the respective policies on that subject. This was agreed to, and arbitrators were selected. Subsequently, a dispute having arisen over the selection of an umpire, the defendants receded from the arbitration, and notified the complainants they would proceed no further in that matter. Thereupon the original bill was filed.

The arbitration clause in one of the policies, which is in substance the same in all, reads:

"In the event of disagreement as to the amount of loss, the same shall, as above provided, be ascertained by two competent and disinterested appraisers, the insured and this company each selecting one, and the two so chosen shall first select a competent and disinterested umpire; the appraisers together shall then estimate and appraise the loss, stating separately sound value and damage, and, failing to agree, shall submit their differences to the umpire; and the award in writing of any two shall determine the amount of such loss. The parties thereto shall pay the appraiser respectively selected by them, and shall bear equally the expense of the appraisal and umpire.''

Assignment No. 3 makes the point that the chancellor committed error in refusing to charge the following special instruction which the defendant's counsel asked him to give to the jury:

''The insurance companies had a right, as a matter of law, to withdraw from the appraisal or arbitration agreement whenever they saw fit to do so, without giving any reason whatever therefor; and this withdrawal could in no way prejudice their rights under the policies, either to contest the amount of the loss, or to question the good faith of the insured in making the proofs of loss, or to make the claim that they did not truly and correctly represent the amount of the loss.''

This instruction would have misled the jury. When the defendants agreed to an arbitration, they thereby confessed their liability on the policies just as fully as if they themselves had proposed the arbitration, and it had been accepted by the insured, the complainants. That the demand of an appraisal is an admission of liability has been fully settled in this State. *St. Paul Fire & Marine Insurance Co.* v. *Kirkpatrick,* 129 Tenn.,—, 164 S. W., 1186; *Hickerson* v. *Insurance*

Companies, 96 Tenn., 193, 199, 200, 33 S. W., 1041, 32 L. R. A., 172; *North German Insurance Co. v. Morton-Scott-Robertson Co.,* 108 Tenn., 384, 390, 67 S. W., 816. having thus admitted liability, the insurer could not escape from the admission by subsequently violating the arbitration agreement. Upon such recession the insurer has the right to a trial in court for the purpose of ascertaining the amount of the damage, but not to question the liability. The fundamental basis of an agreement to arbitrate the amount of damages is necessarily a confession that there is such liability. It is as much a confession as if an admission of liability were in terms made in the agreement for arbitration. The rule is likewise based on the proposition of law that one cannot be permitted to maintain at the same time two inconsistent contentions. Conduct of this kind is indicative of fraud, or oppression, or both. To sanction it would be contrary to public policy and sound morals. The case is different, of course, where, before going into an appraisement or estimate, there is an agreement that neither party shall be bound by the result; the understanding being that the effort is to be made only with a view to a contemplated settlement. But to hold that the insurer can compel the insured to go into an arbitration on pain of the forfeiture of the policy for refusal, and at the same time incur no risk either by acceptance or refusal, or by withdrawing after it has once agreed, is to destroy the mutuality in the contract as to this special feature, and authorize the companies to pursue an unfair course of conduct towards the unfortunate victim of a fire loss. It is to sanction the unjust conduct of professional adjusters, who too often commend themselves to the good graces of the insurer by browbeating the distressed insured, and thereby forcing him to make ruinous concessions. While it is true that a single consideration, as, for example, the promise to pay on the happening of a loss may support many promises on the other side, and while it is likewise true that the insurance may be limited by conditions, yet it is furthermore true that when a loss has occurred, and the contract has become consummate, and the question is simply upon the method of ascertaining the amount to be paid, the way is open for the application of considerations based on public policy, and it is within the power of the court to refuse to enforce any stipulation which it regards as violative of those considerations. We have had occasion to point out in a recent opinion some of the abuses of the appraisement, or arbitration clause, in its practicable operation. *St. Paul Fire & Marine Insurance Co.* v. *Kirkpatrick*, supra.

However, regardless of the rule just stated, the chancellor permitted the defendants to not only contest the amount of the loss, but to question the good faith of the insured in making the proofs of loss, with a view to enabling the defendants to take advantage of a clause in a policy as follows:

"This entire policy shall be void if the insured has concealed or misrepresented in writing or otherwise any material fact or circumstance concerning this insurance, or the subject thereof, . . . or in case of any fraud or false swearing by the insured touching any matter relating to this insurance, or the subject thereof, whether before or after the loss.''

He permitted the defendants to introduce such evidence as they had bearing upon this subject, and submitted the issue to the jury. Therefore the defendants could not have been harmed by the failure of the chancellor to give the instruction quoted. The submission of this issue and the introduction of the evidence referred to on both sides necessarily meant that the jury were to decide the issue regardless of whether the defendants had withdrawn from the arbitration. It would therefore have been an idle thing, as we conceive it, for the chancellor to give the instruction mentioned. Moreover, it would have been laying stress upon a special item of evidence, viz., the effect of withdrawal from the arbitration as bearing upon the issue submitted, and this would have been contrary to the rule that the trial judge cannot emphasize special parts of the testimony to the exclusion of the other parts, laying stress now upon this, and now upon that, portion of the evidence.

In the discussion, however, to this assignment in the brief of defendants' counsel, it is applied to the issue of good faith on the part of the insurance companies; that is, the question arising under issues Nos. 3, 4, and 5, which were decided in their favor. So considered, we must apply what has already been said under that head, to the effect that, since the defendants were suc-

cessful under those issues, the question is now immaterial.

Assignment No. 11 claims that the chancellor erroneously refused to give the following special instruction:

"If you find that C. C. Hanson, receiver for the Gulf
Compress Company, furnished proofs of loss, making
a total claim against the insurance companies of $63,-
000, and you further find that the amount of this claim
did not truly and correctly represent the amount of
his loss, and if you find that at the time he made said
proofs of loss he knew that another compress, machinery, and boilers, etc., of a similar type in all respects, capable of doing the same amount of work as
the old damaged press, could have been purchased and
installed for $15,000, or less than the amount claimed
on item 1 (compress, machinery, etc.) then you will
answer No. 6: 'Yes.' "

Among other reasons not necessary to be stated,
the instruction assumed as a fact that at the time Hanson made the proofs of loss he knew that he could purchase another compress of similar type and capable of
doing the same work as the damaged press, when there
was no evidence of this kind in the record. The proofs
were made in April. It does not appear that Hanson
learned of the other press until some time in July. It is
not disputed that he then offered to take that press in
full settlement of the loss, if the insurance companies
would furnish it to him, or pay him in money a sum

which would purchase it and install it; that is, $15,000. This was refused by the companies.

Under assignment No. 12 the point is made that the chancellor erred in permitting the witness Hanson to answer the following:

"Did they [referring to the insurance companies] at any time, by letter or otherwise, up to the filing of the cross bill in this case, state to you that you had knowingly made a false statement as to the value of this property for the purpose of deceiving and defrauding the company? A. No."

The objection made on the trial was that the evidence was immaterial. We think the objection was well taken, but the evidence could not have injured the defendants, and the error was not, therefore, a reversible one, to say nothing of chapter 32, Acts of 1911, which forbids the court to reverse unless it affirmatively appears that the error affected the verdict. As stated, the contrary appears, because there was no pretense that Hanson had knowingly made a false statement as to the value of the property, except in so far as that matter was related to his supposed knowledge of another compress of substantially the same kind, procurable for $15,000. We have already stated in another connection that there is no evidence that he had any such knowledge. It is true that the insurance companies, even if they believed he had made a false statement, were not bound to make that charge to him, and no adverse inference could be properly indulged against them because of their failure to make the charge. But for the reason stated the error was innocuous.

We have thus considered all of the errors assigned which could under any kind of construction have a bearing upon issue No. 6; but, as already held, we are of the opinion that that issue was, for the reasons given, an improper one—that is, because of the confession of liability on the part of the insurance companies. Therefore all of the questions raised on the issue were really immaterial. Out of deference to the learned counsel, however, we have considered them, and stated our conclusion in respect of each of them.

This brings us to the main questions in the case, those falling under issues Nos. 1 and 2. The questions chiefly arise under issue No. 1.

Assignment No. 13 makes the point that there is no evidence to sustain the finding of the jury under these issues, and No. 14 makes the point that the amounts found were excessive. There was ample evidence under which the jury acted, and the rule is that, where there is any evidence to sustain the verdict on the facts, we cannot interfere.

It is complained under assignment No. 1 that the chancellor refused to charge the following special request, offered by defendant's counsel:

"If you find that a compress, machinery, boilers, etc., of a type similar in all respects to the compress, machinery, etc., that was injured in the fire on March 1st, could have been purchased at Natchez, Miss., at or immediately after the fire, for the sum of $10,000, plus the cost of dismantling, installing, and freight, about $5,000, according to the statement of Mr. Hanson, and you further find that the compress, boilers, and machinery were a total loss, then the amount for which the press at Natchez could be purchased, $15,-000, should be your answer to issue No. 1.''

This assignment also complains of the refusal of the chancellor to charge:

''The policies in question provide that loss or damage shall be estimated or ascertained according to the actual cash value with proper deduction for depreciation, and 'shall in no event exceed what it would then cost the insured to repair or replace the same with material of a like kind and quality.'

''Should you find that the compress, boilers, machinery, etc., at or immediately after the fire could have been purchased and installed in the Gulf Compress Company's plant at Argenta, Ark., for $15,000, that figure or amount should represent the amount of the insured's loss upon the compress, machinery, boilers, etc., and you should answer issue No. 1 accordingly.''

Both of the instructions were properly refused, because they assume a fact, as to which there is no testimony in the record, viz., that such a compress as is referred to in the instructions could have been purchased at or immediately after the fire for the sum of $10,000, plus the cost of installation, say about $5,000, in all about $15,000. As we have previously said, in disposing of another assignment, the opportunity to buy such machine at Natchez, Miss., because of the great devastation by the boll weevil in that country, did arise in July, 1913; but this was more than four months after the fire, and there is no evidence that this machine could have been purchased at that price at any time before July 5th, or at any time thereafter. The only evidence upon the point is that which appears in Mr. Hanson's testimony, which is as follows:

"When I made the proposition to Mr. Shafer [representing the insurance companies] to take that Natchez press, if he would dismantle it and bring it to Argenta and put it up, he did not accept the proposition. I put that to Mr. Shafer in this way: We had big cotton prospects in Arkansas, and I was anxious to rebuild. Our operations are profitable there, and I wanted to keep going, and the trade was after me to go ahead and rebuild, and now I said to Mr. Shafer: 'If you will take that Natchez plant and put it down at Little Rock, we will call the machinery part of it square. I estimate it will cost $5,000 to move it. It may cost you a little less, or a little more. Here is a telegram that says you can get it for $10,000. Now give me that plant in Little Rock and we will call the machinery part square, and we will take up the question of the buildings; or, if you don't want to go to the trouble of taking that plant and moving it and building it, give me $15,000, and I will go and buy it and move it myself'—because I was anxious to get this thing settled, to get the benefit of the particular advantages existing at that time. Q. Do you know whether you can get it at all, now? A. No, sir; he said I had insulted his intelligence, and he was rather hard to talk to on that account. He seemed to think it was insulting his intelligence, and he objected to it.''

Mr. Hanson further testified:

''I do not know where I could get a press at any such price now.''

Not only were the instructions properly disallowed, because of the incorrect assumptions of fact therein contained, but likewise on the ground that after such refusal the companies would be estopped to base any claims on the offer made at Natchez in July, 1913.

The second assignment of error complains of a certain portion of the charge. The assignment as drawn omits, supplying the blank with asterisks, certain words which we deem material to a proper understanding of the views of the trial judge as given to the jury.

The language of the charge complained of was as follows:

''You will find in the policies the provision that the actual cash value of the property damaged at the time of the fire is to be the test. Now actual cash value means the value of a thing upon the market—what it would cost to produce it in like condition, as it was before the fire. If you find that the press and machinery were a total loss under issue No. 1, you will ascertain at what figure another press, machinery, boilers, etc., similar in all respects to that destroyed, could have been purchased, and that figure will and should be your answer to issue No. 1.

"So far as the proof goes, gentlemen, as to another press that could have been purchased at Natchez, Miss., if that was a purchase that could have been made only at a particular time, and not one that could have been made on the open market at any time, and if that was meant merely as a matter of compromise, why you may consider that—you may look to that in determining the value of a new press; and, assuming this to be a total loss, the test is what another press —what it would cost to procure another press—just as good as the one in question before the fire."

The policy provision referred to reads:

"This company shall not be liable beyond the actual cash value of the property at the time any loss or damage occurs, and the loss or damage shall be ascertained or estimated according to such actual cash value, with proper deduction for depreciation, however caused, and shall in no event exceed what it would then cost the insured to repair or replace the same with material of like kind and quality."

The facts applicable to issue No. 1, as to which the instruction complained of applies, are as follows:

The Bierce compress, which was the subject of the insurance, was the best and likewise the most costly one made. It is true it was slower in its operation than others, and a little more expensive in the way of fuel, but less liable to accident, and an accident occurring by the breaking of any of its parts would rarely ever result in the death of any of the operatives, or in any injury to the plant. Though slower, as stated, this type of machine is very durable, and is sufficiently rapid in its movements to accomplish all needed work. The initial expense is a little over $40,000. By reason of this fact it is no longer made for the general market, and can be purchased only, if at all, on special order; that is, to be made for special order. Its place in the general market has been taken by cheaper machines doing practically the same work, although not so safely.

The history of the special compress in question is as follows:

It was bought six or seven years before the fire in question from a firm or concern in New Orleans that had used it but little, and had gone out of business. Complainants bought it at a sacrifice price of $11,500, including cost of removal and reinstallment, but it was as good as new. It was moved to Argenta, Ark., by complainants and set up there. It went through a fire in 1911, but comparatively slight in character, only the smaller parts of the machine being injured, and repairs were made which restored it to a condition as good as new. Then came the fire of 1912, which the evidence shows was a very great one; 7,000 to 9,000 bales of cotton, ranged near the machine, were burned; steel was melted and ran very close to this great compress, and the heat was so great, mounting up to 2,900 degrees, as that the machine was practically ruined.

The amount for which the machine was insured in 1911 was $15,000. The policy at that time was placed at the figure stated, because complainants had learned primarily where they could procure another machine as good as their own at second hand for the price named. But, the policies having a coinsurance clause, the companies proved by the appraisement of Coats and Burchard, well-known public appraisers in Chicago, that the machine was worth $40,000, and compelled complainants to account for it on that basis, by means of which they lost, under the coinsurance clause, between $7,000 and $8,000.

We have already referred, in another part of this opinion, to the nature of the opportunity to obtain another machine of the Bierce type after the fire of 1912. As stated, there was another machine just as good in Natchez, Miss., that could have been procured in July, 1913, for $15,000, because of the prevalence of the boll weevil in that part of the country, which had ruined the cotton crop. As already stated, this matter was brought to defendant's attention, and an effort was made by complainant to settle on procurement of that machine for them; but the defendants indignantly refused the offer.

There is no evidence to show that it could have been procured for that price at any earlier or later date, or any other machine of the kind for that price.

As applicable to these facts, we think the charge is correct. Certainly there is nothing in it of which the defendants could complain. It is substantially in accord with the rule contended for by them, for which they cite *McCready* v. *Hartford Insurance Co.*, 61

App. Div., 584, 585, 70 N. Y. Supp., 778, 779; *Standard Sewing Machine Co.* v. *Royal Insurance Co.*, 201, Pa., 645, 649, 650, 51 Atl., 354; *Everett* v. *Insurance Co.* (Tex. Civ. App.), 36 S. W., 125; *Frick* v. *Insurance Co.*, 218 Pa., 409, 67 Atl., 743 We shall quote from one of these cases, the first mentioned, as follows:

"The plaintiffs claim that there was a total loss, . . . and that the verdict should have been for the full sum of $5,000 [the amount of the policy]. They insist that upon a correct construction of the policy the underwriter was liable for a total loss. The real question upon this branch of the case is: What is the measure of liability of the defendant under its policy? The plaintiffs insist that it was the value of the building as it stood just before the fire. Under the terms and conditions of the policy in suit, which is . . . standard form, . . . the parties have . . . agreed [among themselves] upon the measure of liability. . . . It is provided . . . that 'the company shall not be liable beyond the actual cash value of the property at the time any loss or damage occurs, and the loss or damage shall be ascertained or estimated according to such actual cash value, with proper deduction for depreciation, however caused. Thus far, and if nothing more were contained in the policy, it is apparent that if there were a total destruction . . . the company would be liable for the actual cash value at the time [of the loss]; but the policy also provides that the liability of the underwriter 'shall in no event exceed what it then cost the insured to repair or replace the same with material of like kind and quality.' By this stipulation the parties settled for themselves the measure of damages in case of loss. Plaintiffs expressly agreed [thereby] that the indemnity to be furnished . . . should be the sum that it would cost the insured to repair or replace the building with material of like kind and quality.''

Complainant's counsel have insisted that, because defendant did not specially plead the second part of the standard clause, they cannot rely on it. citing *Mechanics' Insurance Co.* v. *C. A. Hoover Distilling Co.*, 182 Fed., 590, 105 C. C. A., 128, 31 L. R. A. (N. S.), 878.

Defendant's counsel insist that the rule stated in the opinion referred to is unsound in principle and not supported by the authorities cited therein. From what has been said it is apparent we have no need to consider this question.

It appears that complainant's plant was under mortgage to a trustee for the benefit of certain bondholders for an amount in excess of the whole insurance, and that the rights of the bondholders were fully recognized and protected in the policies; also that by an amendment to the bill the trustee for the bondholders came in and asserted his right and their rights. It is argued for them that as between them and the companies they occupy a certain *status* superior to that of the compress company, in that they are relieved of any derelictions and defaults charged by defendant against the complainant corporation. From the view we take of the case it is apparent that this question likewise needs no discussion or decision at our hands at the present time.

It results that there is no error in the decree of the chancellor, and it must be affirmed, with costs.

HESSIG-ELLIS DRUG Co. *v.* STONE *et al.*

(*Jackson.*   April Term, 1914.)

**MASTER AND SERVANT.   Wages.   Liens and preferences.
Enforcement.**

A petition for the establishment of the preferred lien for employees' wages given by Acts 1897, ch. 78, as amended by Acts
1905, ch. 414, was properly denied where it merely described
the property, which was in the hands of a receiver appointed
by the court, as the drug business at the corner of C. and M.
avenues in M., particularly as there were prior liens on part
of the property, as it should have described the property
specifically, with a statement of the nature of the lien, or an
attachment should have been issued and levied. (*Post, pp.*
609-613.)

Acts cited and construed: Acts 1897, ch. 78.

Constitution cited and construed: Art. 2, sec. 17.

Cases cited and approved: Luttrell v. Railroad, 119 Tenn., 507;
Bryan v. Zarecor, 112 Tenn., 511; Memphis Street Railway v.
State, 110 Tenn., 608; Burnett v. Turner, 87 Tenn., 124.

FROM SHELBY.

Appeal from Chancery Court, Shelby County.—
FRANCIS FENTRESS, Chancellor.

FITZHUGH & BIGGS, McKELLAR & KYSER, and ARTHUR
C. FANT, for appellants Hessig-Ellis Drug Co.

L. T. M. CANADA, for appellee Stone.

MR. JUSTICE LANSDEN delivered the opinion of the Court.

The only question necessary to be determined in this case is whether the appellants Sager and Brookover have acquired a lien asserted in their petition. The chancellor held that they had not perfected the lien claimed because no attachment was issued and levied upon the stock of drugs, and because the act of 1905 creating the lien is unconstitutional and void.

The petitioners were employees of Mrs. Stone, one the prescription clerk and the other a porter in her drug store. She is indebted to them for wages in the sum stated in the petition.

The original bill is a general creditor's bill against Mrs. Stone and was filed March 15, 1913. March 18th a receiver was appointed and given possession of the stock of drugs in controversy. The petitioners filed their petition April 16th after the appointment of the receiver, and before the sale of stock of drugs by the receiver. The property which came into the hands of the receiver consists of a stock of goods and certain fixtures in the drug store, including a soda fountain and "appurtenances," one roller-top desk, one iron safe, and one McCaskey cash register. There was also another cash register, a hot soda appurtenance, and perhaps some other articles. The title to the McCaskey cash register was claimed by J. B. Stone. The other cash register was not paid for in full, the title to which had probably been retained by the seller. The hot soda "appurtenance" was also incumbered by a purchase money debt. The soda fountain was claimed by the complainant for an unpaid balance of purchase price.

The description of the property upon which the petitioners claim their lien as contained in their petition is "the drug business at the corner of College and McLemore avenues in Memphis, Tenn.," and the petitioners "claim a prior and superior lien and equity under the statutes of the State over the other creditors to the proceeds derived from the sale when made of the fixtures and stock of drugs and other assets of said business which was conducted by the defendants at the corner of McLemore and College avenues."

The petitioners deny that the complainants have any title retained to the soda fountain described in their bill, "which soda fountain was used in said business at the corner of College and McLemore avenues."

The prayer of the petitioners, in part, is that petitioners have a decree for the amount of their claims and have been paid out of the assets or proceeds derived from the sale of the stock of drugs and fixtures and out of their assets of said business and that their lien "on all the assets of said business for what is found to be due them be declared, and that they have satisfaction in full for their indebtedness in preference to the general creditors of said estate."

Without deciding whether it is necessary, in a case like this, for attachment to actually issue and be levied upon the property upon which the lien is claimed, it is clear that the petition does not contain a description of such definiteness as will take the place of the attachment. It would seem to be an idle ceremony to have attachment issue and be levied upon property in the hands of a receiver appointed in the case in which the attachment is sued out, but it is necessary that the petitioners identify the particular property upon which the lien is claimed by description in the petition or by description in the writ of attachment if it is issued and levied. The necessity of this is well illustrated by the adverse claims in this case to different articles of fixtures, the proceeds of the sale of which go to make up the fund out of which petitioners desire to have their claims paid. The conditional vendor of the soda fountain would, of course, have prior claims for his unpaid purchase money over that of the petitioners, and this would be true of the other fixtures upon which there was unpaid purchase money. But the petition does not identify any particular article upon which the lien is claimed, and confines the claim of the petitioners to the assets of the defendants generally. With admitted superior claims to particular articles, the court could not decree a prior lien upon the assets generally. It is necessary either for the petitioner to specifically describe the property upon which the lien is claimed, together with the statement of the nature of the lien, or it is necessary that a writ of attachment issue and be levied.

Upon the grounds stated, we affirm the decree of the chancellor denying the petitioners the lien sought. *Luttrell* v. *Railorad*, 119 Tenn., 507, 105 S. W., 565, 123 Am. St. Rep., 737; *Bryan* v. *Zarecor*, 112 Tenn., 511, 81 S. W., 1252, Ency. Pl. & Pr., vol. 22, p. 722.

While it is not necessary to decide the constitutionality of chapter 414 of the Acts of 1905, it is not improper to say that a very serious question is made upon the validity of this statute. The title of the act is "An act to amend chapter 78 of the Acts of 1897, so as to give employees and day laborers of individuals engaged in mercantile lines of business a first lien upon the merchandise for their services." The amendment proposed in the act is to insert after the word "firm" in line 5 of section 1 of chapter 78, Acts of 1897, the following, "or of any individual engaged in mercantile lines of business," and to insert after the words in chapter 78 sufficient general words to make the act read, when amended, so as to include individuals as well as corporations and firms.

The criticism of the act is that it violates section 17 of article 2 of our constitution, which requires all acts which repeal, revise, or amend former laws to recite in their caption or otherwise the title or substance of the law repealed, revised, or amended. It was held in *Memphis Street Railway* v. *State*, 110 Tenn., 608, 75 S. W., 730, and *Burnett* v. *Turner*, 87 Tenn., 124, 10 S. W., 194, that the reference to the chapter number of the act to be amended is not a sufficient compliance with the provision of the constitution just referred to. It is further said in criticism of the act that its body does not recite either the caption or the substance of the act proposed to be amended, but only recites the proposed amendments. As stated, we do not determine the soundness of these criticisms, but we have set them out in this memorandum so that the attention of the next legislature may be directed to the questions made; and, if in its wisdom it is deemed proper, the whole subject of employers' liens may be re-enacted or the supposed infirmities of this act may be cured. Chapter 78 of the acts of 1897 is also criticised as being class legislation because the lien therein conferred upon the employees is limited to employees of corporations and partnership. If the act of 1905 is valid, the criticism made upon the act of 1897 would be removed because the latter act as amended would include individuals, firms, and corporations.

The decree of the chancellor is affirmed at the cost of the appellants.

SCHEIBLER *v.* STEINBURG. *

(Jackson.   April Term, 1914).

1. **MALICIOUS PROSECUTION.   Element of suit.   Termination
   of original case.**

   In order to maintain a suit for malicious prosecution, plaintiff
   must allege and prove that the original prosecution has
   terminated in his favor. (*Post, pp.* 616, 617.)

2. **CRIMINAL LAW.   "Nolle prosequi."**

   A *"nolle prosequi"* is a formal declaration of record by the prosecuting officer that he will no further prosecute the case either
   as to some of the counts of the indictment or as to some of
   the defendants, or all together. (*Post, pp.* 616, 617.)

   Cases cited and approved: Swepson v. Davis, 109 Tenn., 107;
   Pharis v. Lambert, 31 Tenn., 228; Sloan v. McCracken, 75
   Tenn., 626; Gas Co. v. Williamson, 56 Tenn., 314; Stewart v.
   Sonneborn, 98 U. S., 187; Crescent City Live Stock, etc., Co. v.
   Butchers' Union Slaughter House, 120 U. S., 141.

3. **MALICIOUS PROSECUTION.   Termination of original proceeding.   Nolle prosequi.**

   The entry of a *nolle prosequi* without procurement of the defendant is such a termination of the criminal prosecution in defendant's favor as to sustain a suit by him for malicious
   prosecution, though the suit for malicious prosecution is
   brought on the day following entry of the *nolle prosequi*, while
   the court had power to set the *nolle prosequi* aside, since the
   court, in an action for malicious prosecution, could look no
   further than the final judgment to determine whether the
   prosecution had terminated in favor of the defendant therein.
   (*Post, pp.* 617, 618.)

   Cases cited and approved: State v. Fleming, 26 Tenn., 154; Walton v. State, 35 Tenn., 687; Graves v. Scott, 104 Va., 372;

---

*On the question of termination of criminal prosecution by entry
of nolle prosequi so as to support suit for malicious prosecution, see
note in 2 L. R. A. (N. S.), 938, 942.

Stanton v. Hart, 27 Mich., 539; Southern Car & Foundry Co. v. Adams, 131 Ala., 147; Swepson v. Davis, 109 Tenn., 107.

FROM SHELBY.

Appeal from the Civil Court of Shelby County to the Court of Civil Appeals and by *certiorari* from the Court of Civil Appeals to the Supreme Court.— A. B. PITTMAN, Judge.

W. W. GOODWIN and BARTON & BARTON, for Scheibler.

LEO GOODMAN and ANDERSON & CRABTREE, for Steinburg.

MR. JUSTICE LANSDEN delivered the opinion of the Court.

This suit was brought in the circuit court of Shelby county by Steinburg against Scheibler to recover damages for the alleged malicious prosecution of Steinburg by Scheibler for knowingly receiving stolen property. There were verdict and judgment in favor of plaintiff below for $10,000. Upon appeal to the court of civil appeals, that court reversed and remanded the case for a new trial.

The case is before us upon the petition of Scheibler for writs of *certiorari*, and the only error assigned is the failure of the court of civil appeals to reverse the case because the trial judge held that the entry of a nolle prosequi in the criminal case was a sufficient termination thereof to authorize the commencement of this suit. As stated, the court of civil appeals held this to be the true rule, and, although the case was reversed and remanded upon other grounds, the plaintiff in error has presented this single question for our consideration.

It appears that the attorney-general announced, when the criminal case was called for trial, that, on account of the absence of a certain witness, he could not proceed to trial, and, the court having set the case peremptorily, the attorney-general asked leave of the court to *nol. pros.* the case. To this the defendant in error objected and insisted upon a verdict of not guilty; but, after a considerable argument between counsel for the prosecution and the defense, the court allowed the *nolle prosequi* to be entered and discharged Steinburg. The next day this suit was brought.

It is universally held that, in order to maintain a suit for malicious prosecution, it is necessary to allege and prove that the original suit on which the malicious prosecution is based has terminated, and that it resulted in favor of the defendant in that suit. *Swepson* v. *Davis*, 109 Tenn., 107, 70 S. W., 65, 59 L. R. A., 501; *Pharis* v. *Lamberts*, 1 Sneed, 228; *Sloan* v. *McCracken*, 7 Lea, 626; *Gas Co.* v. *Williamson*, 9 Heisk., 314; *Stewart* v. *Sonneborn*, 98 U. S., 187, 25 L. Ed., 116; *Crescent City Live Stock, etc., Co.* v. *Butchers' Union Slaughter House*, 120 U. S., 141, 7 Sup. Ct., 472, 30 L. Ed., 614. This rule, however, as stated by Judge Cooley in his work on Torts, vol. 1, p. 341, is merely "a technical prerequisite," and means that the particular prosecution must have been disposed of in such manner that it cannot be revived, and the prosecutor, if he desires to proceed further, will be put to a new action. A *nolle prosequi* is a formal declaration of record by the prosecuting officer by which he declares that he will no further prosecute the case, either as to some of the counts of the indictment or as to some of the defendants, or all together. Black's Law Dictionary; Clark's Criminal Procedure, 375; 12 Cyc., 374.

It was said by this court in *State* v. *Fleming*, 7 Humph., 154, 46 Am. Dec., 73, that a *nolle prosequi* is a discharge without acquittal, and can be awarded only by the attorney-general and the court. It being a discharge, it is necessarily a termination of the particular prosecution, although it is not a bar to a subsequent prosecution, unless it shall be entered after the defendant has been put to his trial upon a valid indictment before a jury duly sworn and impaneled. In such case, it is generally held that a *nolle prosequi* would terminate the prosecution, as the defendant would have been in jeopardy. *Walton* v. *State*, 3 Sneed, 687. It would seem that the entry of a *nolle prosequi* would terminate the particular prosecution at whatever stage of the suit it might be entered. We are of opinion, therefore, that the entry of a *nolle prosequi,* without the procurement of the defendant, is such a termination of the criminal prosecution in defendant's favor as is contemplated by the rule requiring that the original suit be terminated in favor of the plaintiff before he can commence his suit for malicious prosecution.

There is a division of authority upon the question. The following authorities are in accord with this holding: *Graves* v. *Scott,* 104 Va., 372, 51 S. E., 821, 2 L. R. A. (N. S.), 927, 113 Am. St. Rep., 1043, 7 Ann. Cas., 480; *Stanton* v. *Hart,* 27 Mich., 539; *Southern Car & Foundry Co.* v. *Adams,* 131 Ala., 147, 32 South., 503; Cooley on Torts, (3d Ed.), vol. 1, p. 341; American & Eng. Enc. of Law (2d Ed.), p. 681; Cyc., vol. 26, p. 60. Many other cases could be cited to the same effect, but the foregoing sufficiently illustrate the trend of authority.

It is further said by the petitioner that inasmuch as the present suit was brought the day following the entry of the *nolle prosequi,* and as it was within the power of the court to set aside the *nolle prosequi* during the term, or within thirty days, if the term should last longer, it does not sufficiently appear that the criminal prosecution is finally terminated, and for that reason this suit was prematurely brought. This contention, however, is not sound. It was settled in *Swepson* v. *Davis,* supra, in response to the petition to rehear, that the court could not look beyond the final judgment in the original suit, and whether the original suit was terminated in the plaintiff's favor would be determined alone by the final judgment therein.

We concur in the opinion and reasoning of the court of civil appeals and affirm its judgment.

STATE *v.* GREEN.

(*Jackson.* April Term, 1914.)

1. **CRIMINAL LAW.** **Trial.** **Assessment of punishment.**

Const., art. 6, sec. 14, providing that no fine shall be laid in excess of $50 unless assessed by the jury, requires the assessment by the jury of the fine for an offense finable in excess of $50 at discretion, if it merits more than that amount, and it was error for the court to assess the fine for transporting intoxicating liquor in violation of Acts 1913 (2d Ex. Sess.), ch. 1, imposing a fine of $100 to $500 therefor. (*Post, pp.* 621,622.)

Constitution cited and construed: Art. 6, sec. 14.

Cases cited and approved: France v. State, 85 Tenn., 478; Metzner v. State, 128 Tenn., 45; State v. Fleming, 26 Tenn., 152.

2. **CRIMINAL LAW.** **Appeal and error.** **Review.** **Harmless error.** **Sentence.**

Error in the court's assessing the fine for transporting intoxicating liquor in violation of Acts 1913 (2d Ex. Sess.), ch. 1, imposing a fine of $100 to $500 therefor, instead of submitting its amount to the jury, as required by Const. art. 6, sec. 14, was harmless, where the fine was made $100, as it could not be made less. (*Post, pp.* 622, 623.)

3. **INDICTMENT AND INFORMATION.** **Aider by verdict.** **Description of offense.**

The uncertainty of an indictment charging the unlawful transportation of intoxicating liquors "from one point or county in this State to Tipton county" was made certain by proof that the initial point was in Shelby county, and was cured by the verdict of conviction. (*Post, pp.* 623, 624.)

FROM TIPTON.

Error to Circuit Court, Tipton County.—S. J. EVERETT, Judge.

NAT TIPTON, for plaintiff in error.

WM. H. SWIGGART, JR., assistant attorney-general, for the State.

MR. JUSTICE LANSDEN delivered the opinion of the Court.

Plaintiff in error was indicted and convicted for unlawfully conveying, transporting, and carrying vinous, spirituous, malt, and other intoxicating liquors "from one point in this State, or one county in this State, to Tipton county, for his own use in quantities larger than one gallon," as set out in the first count of the indictment, and for unlawfully transporting, carrying, and conveying vinous, spirituous, malt, and other intoxicating liquors "from one point or county in this State to Tipton county, for the purpose of delivering to some person, whose name is to the grand jury unknown," as set out in the second count.

The evidence is that the plaintiff in error carried four gallons and one quart of whisky from Memphis to Tipton county; that one gallon of it was for his personal use, and the remainder, divided into four packages, was for friends who had requested him to bring the whisky to them on his return from Memphis. These friends had previously sent orders for the whisky to Memphis, and plaintiff in error carried no money to Memphis for them and had no connection with the sale of the whisky to those persons to whom he delivered it.

He was tried before the circuit judge without a jury, and was found guilty and fined $100 and costs. The conviction evidently was under the second count of the indictment, and the penalty provided for this offense by chapter 1 of the Acts of the Extra Session 1913 is a fine of not less than $100 nor more than $500 and imprisonment, at the discretion of the court, not less than thirty nor more than sixty days.

Two errors are assigned in this court: First, that the trial judge was without power to assess a fine of $100; and, second, that the trial judge erred in overruling the motion in arrest of judgment.

It is provided in section 14 of article 6 of the constitution that:

"No fine shall be laid on any citizen of this State that shall exceed $50, unless it shall be assessed by a jury of his peers, who shall assess the fine at the time they find the fact, if they think the fine should be more than $50."

It was held in *France* v. *State,* 6 Baxt., 478, that the foregoing provision of the constitution had no application to fines exceeding $50, where the legislature had prescribed a fine of more than that amount, to wit, $500, and in the application of which the court had no discretion. The court said in that case that neither the court nor the jury had anything to do in assessing the fine, inasmuch as the law fixed $500 as a flat penalty, and as a consequence of the verdict.

In the case of *Metzner* v. *State,* 128 Tenn., 45, 157 S. W., 69, it was said that the provision of the constitu-

tion under consideration "withholds from the court
or judge the right to inflict fines exceeding $50, and
confers upon the jury exclusive power or jurisdiction
to impose fines above that sum." That case also holds
that inflicting fines exceeding $50 is "a matter of ju-
risdiction." In *Metzner* v. *State,* the statute authorized a fine of not less than $50 nor more than $500. In
France v. *State,* the statute imposed a fine of $500. In
this case the statute fixes the fine at not less than
$100 nor more than $500. So this case is not exactly
within the facts of either of the cases referred to.
However, the principle recognized in both *France* v.
State and *Metzner* v. *State* is that, if the offense of
which the defendant is convicted is to be punished by
fine which may exceed $50 at the discretion of the court
and jury, the constitutional provision referred to requires that the jury must assess the fine, if the offense
merits more than $50. In *France* v. *State,* the ma-
jority of the court seem to consider that the fine prescribed in the statute under consideration there was a
legislative sentence against all who might be convicted
of violating that law. But see *State* v. *Fleming,* 7
Humph., 152, 46 Am. Dec. 73. It was said in the
France case that this provision of the constitution "re
fers to cases where the court has a discretion in fixing
the amount of the fine."

It cannot be doubted that the amount of the fine to
be imposed upon the plaintiff in error, within the minimum and maximum limits prescribed by the legislature, is within the discretion of the court and jury, and

the case would be controlled by the principles upon that subject stated in *Metzner* v. *State,* and evidently recognized in *France* v. *State.* However, the trial judge, in fixing the fine, fixed it at the minimum sum of $100. This is the least sum that the jury could have imposed upon plaintiff in error had the question of the amount of the fine to be inflicted been submitted to a jury. While it was error for the court to assess the fine without submitting the question of its amount to the jury, it is not reversible error, because he exercised his assumed power for the benefit of the plaintiff in error.

We cannot reduce the fine to the sum of $50, because the legislature has fixed the minimum fine at $100. It would be useless to reverse and remand the case, with directions to submit the question of the amount of the fine to a jury, because the jury could not reduce it to less than $100. This assignment of error is overruled.

It is next assigned as error that the trial judge erred in overruling the motion in arrest of judgment. The point made is that the indictment fails to charge that the initial point from which the plaintiff in error started with his cargo of intoxicating liquors was beyond the limits of Tipton county. The language of the indictment is: "From one point or county in this State to Tipton county." We think this criticism is cured by the verdict. The proof shows definitely the initial point at which plaintiff in error received his cargo of intoxicants to have been in Shelby county, and that he carried the whisky from Shelby county into Tipton county. Thus the uncertainty of the indictment is made certain by the proof, and the motion in arrest was properly overruled.

Judgment affirmed.

LEE *et al. v.* VILLINES *et al.*

(*Jackson.* April Term, 1914.)

1. WILLS.   Construction.   "Survivors."

Testator bequeathed certain real property to a trustee, to collect
the rents and apply the net income to testator's children, and
at the death of either of the children the child or children of
the one so dying should receive the portion of the rents and
profits that their father or mother enjoyed under the
will, and should any of testator's children so specified
die without child or children, then his or her portion should
be paid to the "survivors" in equal portions and the children
of such as may have died leaving issue. *Held*, that such clause
was divisible into two parts, the first providing for the vesting
of the fee in each portion of testator's estate held by his trustee
for either of testator's children in the event of the death of
of his children leaving a surviving child or children, in which
event such surviving grandchild or grandchildren took *per
stirpes* that part of the estate to the use of which the deceased
parent had been entitled for life, and the second part providing
for the vestiture of the fee in each portion of the estate so
held in the event either of testator's children died without
child or children surviving, in which event the fee vested *per
stirpes;* the word "survivors" being used to mean, not only
testator's children who survived, but also children of such
children as had theretofore died leaving children surviving
them. (*Post, p.* 629.)

Cases cited and approved: Davis v. Williams, 85 Tenn., 646;
Porter v. Lee, 88 Tenn., 783.

2. WILLS.   Construction.

Under such clause, on the death of either of testator's children,
the trust ceased as to the share of such children, and the absolute fee vested in the remaindermen. (*Post, p.* 630.)

Case cited and approved: Davis v. Williams, 85 Tenn., 646.

129 Tenn. 40

FROM SHELBY.

Appeal from the Chancery Court of Shelby County to the Court of Civil Appeals and by *certiorari* from the Court of Civil Appeals to the Supreme Court.— F. H. HEISKELL, Chancellor.

MAIDEN & MAIDEN, and WATSON & PERKINS, for plaintiffs.

GEORGE HARSH, W. P. ARMSTRONG, and JULIAN C. WILSON, and JEFF MCCARN, for defendants.

MR. JUSTICE BUCHANAN delivered the opinion of the Court.

This case is before us on three separate petitions for *certiorari*, drawing into question as many different phases of a decree rendered by the court of civil appeals, construing the last will and testament of Robert Williams, deceased. A copy of the will in full is as follows:

"I, Robert Williams, Sr., a citizen of the town of Grenada, State of Mississippi, being of sound mind and good health, do make and publish this, my last will and testament, revoking and annulling all others.

"Item 1. I do will and devise to my friend, H. E. Garth, of the city of Memphis, Tennessee, in trust for the uses and purposes hereinafter expressed, the following named real estate, situated in the city of Memphis, Tennessee, to wit: [Here follows a description of the property] with all the improvements on all the aforesaid lots.

"It is my will and desire that the said H. E. Garth, trustee, and his successors shall, at my death, take charge and possession of the said described property and real estate, and rent the same, and collect the rents and all the profits accruing in any manner from said property; and, after paying all necessary repairs and improvements that may be required to keep said property in good and tenantable condition, and all taxes that may be lawfully imposed upon said property, the said trustee shall pay over the remainder of rents accruing from said property to my son Edward P. Williams, my daughter Mary Lee, my daughter Rebecca Villines, my daughter Winny Davis, and my daughter Margaret Williams, equal portions to each.

"At the death of either of my said children, it is my will that the child or children of such one dying shall receive the part or portion of said rents and profits that their father or mother was entitled to under this will; and should any of my said children die without child or children, then, and in that event, his or her share or portion shall be paid over to the survivors in equal portions and the children of such as may have died leaving issue.

"It is my will and desire that the said H. E. Garth, trustee as aforesaid, shall retain and receive from the rents and profits of said property the sum of fifty dol-

lars per month as full compensation for his services in
attending to the execution of this will, he having agreed
to accept the trust upon these terms. This done 8th
day of April, 1878.

"ROBERT WILLIAMS, Sen."

This is the third time the above will has been before
this court. See *Davis v. Williams*, 85 Tenn. (1 Pick.),
646, 4 S. W., 8, and *Porter* v. *Lee*, 88 Tenn. (4 Pick.),
783, 14 S. W. 218. In *Davis v. Williams* supra, it was
insisted for the complainants that the effect of the will
was to carve out of the property of the testator (1) an
equitable life estate for the children of the testator,
who are mentioned in the will; (2) an equitable life
estate for the grandchildren of the testator; and (3)
that the testator died intestate as to the remainder in
fee. But to this insistence the court replied that such
a construction would result in a violation of the rule
against perpetuities, and for that and other reasons
declined to admit the insistence, and to the contrary
held that the devise made by this will of the rents and
profits or increase from the land was equivalent to a
devise of the land, and that, by this devise, the legal
title to the land passed into the trustee in order to
preserve the remainder for the grandchildren of the
testator; that the legal title in the trustee would cease
upon the termination of the equitable life estate created by the will in the children of the testator; and
that, upon the cessation of the legal title in the trustee,
the absolute and unlimited fee would vest in the grandchildren of the testator.

The clause of the will which we are now called on to construe is as follows:

"At the death of either of my said children, it is my will that the child or children of such one dying shall receive the part or portion of said rents and profits that their father or mother was entitled to under this will; and should any of my said children die without child or children, then, and in that event, his or her share or portion shall be paid over to the survivors in equal portions and the children of such as may have died leaving issue."

The clause in question is divisible into two parts; the first providing for the vestiture of the fee in each portion of the testator's estate held by his trustee for either of his children in the event of the death of either of his children leaving a surviving child or children, in which event it is clear that it was the purpose of the testator that such surviving grandchild or grandchildren should take *per stirpes* that part of the estate to which the deceased parent had been entitled for life. The second part provided for the vestiture of the fee in each portion of the testator's estate held by his trustee for either of his children in the event either of his children should die without child or children surviving, in which event the testator, as we think, also intended stirpital vestiture of the fee to take place, for he said that portion of his estate should go to the "survivors," meaning, as we hold, not only those of his children who survived, but also children of such children as had theretofore died, leaving children surviving them.

It is also clear from the whole will, and from the particular clause thereof in question, that it was the intention of the testator that, upon the death of either of his children, the power and title of the trustee should cease as to that share or portion of the estate which the trustee had theretofore held for such decedent, and that as to such portion the absolute and unlimited title in fee should vest in the remaindermen as above indicated.

We recognize the equity of the claims of the great-grandchildren of the testator, who are petitioners herein; but we think the language of the will and the former construction of it by this court in *Davis* v. *Williams*, supra, precludes them.

We think the questions made by the other petitioners were all decided against them in *Davis v. Williams*, supra; at all events, we find no merit in any assignment made upon either of the three petitions for *certiorari*, and each of them are accordingly denied at the costs of petitioners and their sureties.

BOND *v.* UNGERECHT *et al.* *

(*Jackson.* April Term, 1914.)

1. **LOGS AND LOGGING. Deed of standing timber. Defeasance. Tme for removal.**

A deed of standing timber, with provision that the grantee is to be allowed five years, but no longer, to cut and remove it, passes a title to the timber, subject to defeasance as to such of it as is not removed within the time specified; the grantee's title terminating as to timber not then removed. (*Post, pp.* 633-636.)

Cases cited and approved: Carson v. Lumber Co., 108 Tenn., 681; Box Co. v. Moore, 114 Tenn., 596; Zimmerman Mfg. Co. v. Daffin, 149 Ala., 380; U. S. Coal & Oil Co. v. Harrison, 71 W. Va., 217; Pierce v. Finerty, 76 N. H., 38.

Case cited and distinguished: Carson v. Lumber Co., 108 Tenn., 681.

2. **LOGS AND LOGGING. Deed of standing timber. "Removal."**

Within a deed of standing timber, allowing five years to cut and remove it, cutting and sawing into saw logs does not constitute a removal. (*Post, p.* 636.)

Cases cited and approved: Box Co. v. Moore, 114 Tenn., 596; Anderson v. Miami Lumber Co., 59 Or., 149; Rowan v. Carleton, 100 Miss., 177; Hitch Lumber Co. v. Brown, 160 N. C., 281.

FROM HAYWOOD.

Appeal from the Chancery Court of Haywood County to the Court of Civil Appeals and by *certiorari* from the Court of Civil Appeals to the Supreme Court.— C. P. McKinney, Judge.

---

*On the general question of conveyance of title to standing timber without title to land, see notes in 55 L. R. A., 513 and 47 L. R. A. (N. S.), 870.

H. J. LIVINGSTON and MOORE & SON, for plaintiff.

SIMONTON & GWINN, for defendants.

MR. JUSTICE WILLIAMS delivered the opinion of the Court.

The bill of complaint was filed to recover of defendants a number of saw logs which it is alleged were wrongfully cut on the lands of complainant, Bond.

It is alleged that complainant had conveyed standing timber to the Hatchie Manufacturing Company by deed, dated November 3, 1905, which contained, among others, the following provisions pertinent to this inquiry:

"I Sallie Bond, for the consideration of $5,500, cash, have sold and do hereby transfer and convey unto said Hatchie Manufacturing Company, all of the timber of every kind and description [on tract of land, described].

"To have and to hold all of said timber, unto said Hatchie Manufacturing Company, and its assigns forever. [Here are inserted covenants of seisin, unincumbrance and general warranty.]

"It is expressly understood and agreed by the parties hereto, that said Hatchie Manufacturing Company, and its assigns, are to be allowed five (5) years, but not longer, from this date, to cut and remove from said land the timber hereinbefore sold and conveyed."

The grantee corporation, shortly after this purchase, itself conveyed the standing timber so that its

rights therein were owned by the defendants, Ungerecht and others, long prior to the expiration of the
time limit of five years.

The chancellor and the court of civil appeals decreed in favor of complainant, and defendants are before us on petition for writ of *certiorari.*

The primary contention of defendants is that by the
deed the grantee took an absolute and indefeasible
title to the timber, so that regardless of the time limit
the trees were subject to be cut and removed at will
on payment of damages done to the lands of complainant on which the timber or logs were, in any effort to
remove the same.

They correctly contend that in no reported case has
this court passed on the rights of a grantee under such
a deed of conveyance. While this is true, the attitude of the court on the question was foreshadowed in
two cases and indicated to be against defendants' insistence. *Carson* v. *Lumber Co.,* 108 Tenn. (24
Pickle), 681, 69 S. W., 320; *Box Co.* v. *Moore,* 114
Tenn. (6 Cates), 596, 87 S. W., 415, 4 Ann. Cas., 1047.

In *Carson* v. *Lumber Co.,* supra, the nature of the
title passing in standing timber under such a conveyance was discussed; but in the contract of sale there
involved no time limit had been named for cutting and
removing the timber, and the court held that the
grantee had by implication a reasonable time for that
purpose, and that a reasonable period of time had not
expired, with result that the questions here raised
were expressly left open.

In *Box Company* v. *Moore,* supra, there was a similar discussion, but the contract was expressly held to be one granting permission or license and not one of conveyance.

The authorities cited and reviewed in those cases need not be recanvassed in this opinion. A large number of decisions on the subject in other jurisdictions have been reported since the dates of those decisions, and, while the lack of harmony in the cases has not passed, the decided trend of the recent authorities is towards the view signfied in our two cases referred to, and now by us held to be applicable to the deed in contest.

A typical and leading case relied upon by the defendants is that of *C. W. Zimmerman Mfg. Co.* v. *Daffin,* 149 Ala., 380, 42 South., 858, 9 L. R. A. (N. S.), 663, 123 Am. St. Rep., 58, in which the deed was almost identical with the one we have under review. It was there held that the deed vested a title in the trees in the grantee, not forfeited by a failure to remove the timber within the time limited; that the provision allowing a period of years within which to cut and remove the timber conveyed is to be treated as a covenant to cut and remove on the part of the grantee, who could still enter and remove the timber at his pleasure, being liable to the grantor for such damages to the freehold as he should cause in so doing; and that the grantor would also have a right of action against the grantee for a breach of the covenant in not removing as agreed. Other recent cases in accord with that view are collected by the annotator in notes to *U. S. Coal & Oil Co.* v. *Harrison,* 71 W. Va., 217, 76 S. E., 346, in 47 L. R. A. (N. S.), 871, along with the cases *contra.*

In our view, in this Alabama case and other cases cited by the defendants, the contract is construed technically and in a way to lead to results in declared rights that are inequitable and in remedies that are inadequate. The soundness of a construction that gives rise to so many and such remedies on breach of the contract may well be doubted. Some of the courts holding to the doctrine of indefeasible title declare that, although the grantee does not lose his title by failure to remove the timber from the land within the period limited, the court cannot give him authority to enter to remove after expiration of the period. In this view there would be an existing title barren of right to be enforced legally, to be enjoyed only by way of a trespass. *Pierce* v.`Finerty,* 76 N. H., 38, 76 Atl., 194, 79 Atl., 23, 29 L. R. A. (N. S.), 547.

The better conception of the rights of the parties appears to us to be that such a deed passes a title to the timber which is subject to defeasance as to such of the timber as is not removed within the time fixed for removal; that the title of the grantee terminates, except as to timber removed, with the termination of the grantee's right of entry. As was well said by Mr. Justice Beard in *Carson* v. *Lumber Co.,* supra, under the other rule:

"The standing timber may interfere with the use of the soil by its owner, practically oust him from its control and enjoyment, without" a contract in terms "for such extensive rights. The lumber company, claiming under the original grantees, purchased timber and the right to cut and remove it, and not land, and yet upon its contention . . . it has the right to use the soil for sustenance of standing trees, and the land as a depositary for the cut, and their removal, forever, if it pleases."

An element that may enter into consideration as inuring to the benefit of the grantor is the clearing of the land for tillage in the contracted removal of timber, and this advantage would be lost to the landowner under the doctrine we discard, if it should please the grantee to leave the timber standing beyond the time limit.

The stipulation allowing five years, but not longer, to cut and remove the timber from the land, was not complied with by a mere cutting. A severance from the soil is not a removal from the premises, and such as has been cut beyond the point of such severance into the form of saw logs is lost to the grantee if not removed from the land within the allowed period. *Box Company* v. *Moore*, supra; *Anderson* v. *Miami Lumber Co.*, 59 Or., 149, 116 Pac., 1056; *Rowan* v. *Carleton*, 100 Miss., 177, 56 South., 329; *Hitch Lumber Co.* v. *Brown*, 160 N. C., 281, 75 S. E., 714.

Other questions raised by the assignments of error have been considered, but discussion of same in this opinion is waived. Writ denied.

CHARLES B. JAMES' LAND & INVESTMENT Co. *et al. v.* VERNON *et al.*

(*Jackson.*   April Term, 1914.)

SPECIFIC PERFORMANCE.   Contract to convey land.   Separate tracts.   Partial failure of title.

Where a vendor contracted to convey separate tracts of land, and thereafter discovered that because of a failure of title as to a tract which formed an insignificant portion of the whole he was unable to perform as agreed, and the tract as to which the title failed was immaterial to the purchaser's enjoyment of the rest, the vendor was entitled to enforce specific performance of the part as to which he was able to perform, allowing a proportionate rebate in the price for the deficiency. (*Post,* 638-650.)

Cases cited and approved: Foley v. Crow, 37 Md., 51; De Wolf v. Pratt, 42 Ill., 198; Coleman's Ex'r v. Meade, 13 Bush (76 Ky.), 358; Shaw v. Vincent, 64 N. C., 690; Farris v. Hughes, 80 Va., 930; Creigh's Adm'r v. Boggs, 19 W. Va., 240; Morgan's Adm'r v. Brast, 34 W. Va., 332; Van Blarcom v. Hopkins, 63 N. J. Eq., 466; Keepers v. Yocum, 84 Kan., 554; McCourt v. Johns, 33 Ore., 561; Topp v. White, 59 Tenn., 165; Winfrey v. Drake, 72 Tenn., 293.

Cases cited and distinguished: Newman v. Maclin, 6 Tenn., 241; Wood v. Mason, 42 Tenn., 251; Cunningham v. Sharp, 30 Tenn., 116; Galloway v. Bradshaw, 37 Tenn., 70.

FROM SHELBY.

Appeal from the Chancery Court of Shelby County to the Court of Civil Appeals and by writ of *certiorari* from the Court of Civil Appeals to the Supreme Court. —FRANCIS FENTRESS, Judge.

BARTON & BARTON, for plaintiff.

HIRSH & GOODMAN, for defendant.

MR. CHIEF JUSTICE NEIL delivered the opinion of the Court.

The petition for *certiorari* must be granted, the decree of the court of civil appeals reversed, and that of the chancellor affirmed.

The case is this:

During the year 1908, Vernon sold and conveyed to the complainant two pieces of land in Shelby county, one embracing 139.17 acres, the other 6.82 acres, making 145.99 acres, and both together known as lot No. 3 and the north half of lot No. 2 of Burrow subdivision, and a part of Goodwyn subdivision. The price agreed to be paid, including about $500 worth of personal property on the land, was $15,300. To secure the payment of the purchase money, except $650 paid in cash, a trust deed was executed by the complainant to Samuel Morrow as trustee. This trust deed, by oversight of the parties, omitted to waive the equity of redemption. In course of time the complainant paid, including the original cash payment, $4,500 on the purchase price, but was unable to pay any more. Vernon thereupon set about to foreclose the trust deed by sale of the property, but was embarrassed by the fact that the equity of redemption had not been waived. As a result of this fact, Vernon felt the necessity of making some kind of an adjustment with the complainant, to the end that he might secure the complete title, or the title unincumbered by the equity when foreclosure should take place. The complainant insists that this was not the reason, but other facts existed as the inducing cause, arising out of negotiations between the two. Whatever the cause may have been, and we deem it immaterial, as it is not denied that the consideration was valuable, an agreement was made between Vernon and complainant that a friendly foreclosure should take place, and the complainant should have the benefit of the $4,500 previously paid in the way of an allowance to him on the purchase price of 127 acres of the land, which was to be reconveyed to complainant after the foreclosure should take place. Accordingly the following written agreement was executed by the parties:

"This agreement, entered into this 21st day of July, 1910, between J. W. Vernon and Charles B. James, is to the effect that in case said J. W. Vernon shall become the owner, within thirty days from this date, of a certain tract of land known as lot No. 3 of the Burrow tract in the Sixth civil district of Shelby county, Tennessee, containing 124.16 acres, and a small tract estimated at three acres, being immediately east and adjoining the said lot No. 3, bounded on the north and east by Wolf River, and extending south on a line with

the south line of the said lot No. 3, same being the
north line of Vernon avenue extended to Wolf River:

"Then in that event the said J. W. Vernon agrees
to sell and convey the above-described lands to said
Charles B. James for the sum of $8,000 as follows:
$500 cash, ten notes for $150 each, payable monthly,
beginning thirty days after date, also six notes for
$1,000 each, payable twelve, eighteen, twenty-four
thirty, thirty-six, and forty-two months after date, and
all notes bearing interest from date, and all to be secured by a trust deed upon said lands. And said
Charles B. James agrees to buy the above lands at the
price and upon the terms stated. Said sale is to be
closed on or before the 1st day of September, 1910.
This contract is signed in duplicate. Witness our
hands this 21st day of July, 1910.

"J. W. VERNON."
"CHARLES B. JAMES."

The foreclosure of the trust deed before referred to
was had, and Vernon became the purchaser of the
property at the sale, at a price representing about the
sum of the balance due on the purchase money notes
executed in 1908.

On October 20, 1910, Vernon addressed the following
letter to Mr. James:

"Dear Sir: In reference to our contract for the
sale of lot 3 of the Burrow tract, with the lights before me now. I have no clear title to the twelve acres
claimed by McCallum, Scheibler, King, and others, so
I could not sell it. I will, however close up as far as I

can by selling you all of said lot 3 except the twelve acres referred to for $7,700, on terms agreed upon, but this must be closed up by November 1, 1910, all payments dated September 10, 1910, or we will consider the whole trade off, and proceed to make other arrangements. I hope this will be entirely satisfactory to you, and that you will let me know without delay what I may depend upon.

"Hoping to hear from you soon, I am, as ever,
"Yours, etc., J. W. VERNON."

In order to properly understand this letter, it should be stated that the twelve acres, according to the weight of the evidence, was understood between the parties to be, and was, of the value of $300. It also lay across the river from the other land, and was low and swampy, and not material to the enjoyment of the rest of the land, and the title had failed. The difference between the price stated in the letter of October 20th, and that of the contract of July 21st, is represented by the $300, the value of the twelve acres.

Mr. James declined to accept this offer. After this the parties made numerous efforts to settle, but were unable to accomplish anything. Finally, the present bill was filed on July 8, 1912.

The immediate occasion of the filing of this bill was that the complainant investment company had, in 1908, in addition to the land already referred to, bought another tract of sixteen acres from Vernon at the price of $5,000, for which notes were executed, and also a trust deed to secure the notes. Vernon caused this land to be advertised for sale, and thereupon the bill was filed, claiming that Vernon was indebted to the investment company in the sum of $4,500, which should go as a credit on the purchase-money notes for the sixteen acres. The basis of the liability claimed was that, inasmuch as Vernon, in the adjustment made prior to the foreclosure of the trust deed on the other lands, had agreed to account to the investment company for the $4,500 already referred to, by way of conveying the land described in the contract of July 21, 1910, and had repudiated that contract, he became liable to pay the aforesaid sum of $4,500 in money, and it was insisted that this should be entered as a credit on the purchase-money notes of the sixteen acres; the interests of C. B. James and the investment company being blended.

The chancellor denied this relief, dissolved the injunction that had previously issued against the sale of the sixteen acres, but further adjudged as follows:

That inasmuch as Vernon had, in his answer and by statement in open court, professed himself as willing and ready to carry out the agreement of July 21, 1910, and the chancellor being of the opinion that under the prayer of general relief he had the power to require the parties to do justice to each other, "that upon the tendering to the said Vernon by the said Charles B. James' Land & Investment Company of the sum of $7,700 and interest, of which $5,000, with interest thereon from September 1, 1910, shall be cash, the balance shall be evidenced by notes of date September 1, 1910, one due March 1, 1913, for $1,000, one due September 1, 1913, for $1000, one due March 1, 1914, for $700, all bearing interest at the rate of 6 per cent. from date, and secured by a trust deed on the lands agreed to be reconveyed in the document of July 21, 1910, less the twelve acres, the title to which has failed, and also to execute a quitclaim deed to all the lands conveyed in the sale by Vernon to Charles B. James' Land & Investment Company under the sale of June 1, 1908, that the said Vernon is hereby required to reconvey back to the said James' Land & Investment Company the said lands mentioned in the document of July 21, 1910, less the twelve acres, the title to which has failed. Sixty days are given to the James' Land & Investment Company to make said cash payment, and to execute its notes and trust deed as above set forth. In all other respects the complainant's bill is dismissed.''

From this decree the complainants prayed an appeal to the court of civil appeals, and that court reversed the chancellor, and gave the complainants a decree for $4,500 and interest, and also for $300, the value of the twelve acres—in all, $4,800, with interest.

From this latter decree Vernon sought relief by his petition to this court for the writ of *certiorari* to remove the case from the court of civil appeals, to the end that the rights of the parties might be adjudged.

The complainants, however, proceeded on the assumption that it was the duty of Vernon, under the contract of July 21, 1910, to convey all of the land therein described, regardless of the failure of title to the twelve acres, and that on his failure to make this conveyance there was such a repudiation of the contract as made him liable, either for such a judgment as was entered by the court of civil appeals, or for a credit of the same amount on the notes given for the sixteen acres. It is said in the brief, in effect, that this result is so certain that it scarcely needs argument to support it.

We are unable to perceive the soundness of this proposition. We are of the opinion that, when Vernon found that he was unable to convey the twelve acres, he should have made just such a proposition as he did; that is, to comply with the contract of July 21, 1910, as far as he could, and to offer compensation for the deficiency. We are furthermore of the opinion that by a bill in equity for specific performance he could have compelled the complainants to execute the contract, because the amount he offered to allow by way of reduction in the price was the full value of the twelve acres to which title had failed, and that land was not material to the enjoyment of the rest of the land.

That under such circumstances a vendor can compel specific performance we think is very clear under the authorities bearing on that subject. It is laid down in 36 Cyc. p. 738:

"Where a vendor is unable, from any cause not involving bad faith on his part, to convey each and every parcel of the land contracted to be sold, and it is apparent that the part which cannot be conveyed is of small importance, or is immaterial to the purchaser's enjoyment of that which may be conveyed to him, in such case the vendor may insist on performance with compensation to the purchaser, or a proportionate abatement from the agreed price, if that has not been paid.''

This proposition is fully sustained by the following authorities: *Foley* v. *Crow,* 37 Md., 51; *De Wolf* v. *Pratt,* 42 Ill., 198; *Coleman's Ex'r* v. *Meade,* 13 Bush (76 Ky.), 358; *Shaw* v. *Vincent,* 64 N. C., 690; *Farris* v. *Hughes,* 89 Va., 930, 17 S. E. 518; *Creigh's Adm'r* v. *Boggs,* 19 W. Va., 240; *Morgan's Adm'r* v. *Brast,* 34 W. Va., 332, 12 S. E. 710; *Van Blarcom* v. *Hopkins,* 63 N. J. Eq., 466, 52 Atl. 147; *Keepers* v. *Yocum,* 84 Kan., 554, 114 Pac. 1063, Ann. Cas. 1912A, 748; *McCourt* v. *Johns,* 33 Or., 561, 53 Pac. 601. In *Farris* v. *Hughes,* out of a contract to convey 282 acres, there was a deficiency of seven acres and eighteen poles. In *Morgan's Adm'r* v. *Brast,* out of a sale of 300 acres, there was a failure of title to twenty acres. In *Van Blarcom* v. *Hopkins* it appeared a lot was advertised and sold at judicial sale as being 100 feet front and 255 feet deep, but was only ninety-three feet front and 255 feet deep, including the sidewalk. It appeared that the purchaser was not buying the property for a purpose requiring such an exact area, and he was required to specifically perform the contract, with a deduction for the deficiency. In *Keepers* v. *Yocum* the contract was for 114 acres, and there was a deficiency of two and one-half acres, which it appears was of small importance, and

not material to the purchaser's enjoyment of the rest
of the land. It was held that the purchaser could be
compelled to specifically perform the contract, with a
ratable deduction for the value of the two and one-half
acres. Other illustrations are given in the notes to the
text of Cyc. above referred to. The acreage in the
present case is somewhat larger than in any of these,
but the proportion of value is very small—$300 out of
a consideration of $8,000.

There are some cases in this State which, on first
impression, seem to hold that the vendor must be able
and willing to convey all of the land he contracted to
sell, but an examination of these cases discloses that
the special question we now have before us was not in
the mind of the court, or considered in either of them.

In *Newman* v. *Maclin*, 5 Hayw. (6 Tenn.), 241, 242,
decided in 1813, it was held broadly that the title to
part of the land being doubtful, the vendee could claim
rescission. Nothing was said about the proportion or
value of the defective acreage. In *Reed* v. *Noe*, 9 Yerg.
(17 Tenn.), 283, decided in 1836, it appeared there was
a contract to convey seventy and one-half acres, but
the complainant's title failed as to twenty-five acres.
It was held he was not entitled to specific performance
The court said:

"The bill admits that at the time it was filed the
complainant did not have a legal title to the entire tract
agreed to be conveyed. This being true, he was not in
a condition to perform the contract on his part, and, as
he could not ask the defendant to take an imperfect

title, he had no ground of equity upon which to come here for the enforcement of his contract.''

But in this case likewise the court said nothing on the question of proportion. However, as seen, the land to which the title failed was more than one-third of the acreage of the whole tract that was to be conveyed. In *Wood* v. *Mason,* 2 Cold. (42 Tenn.), 251, it appeared that the defect of title was as to a one-seventh undivided interest in the whole. The court held that a purchaser could not be compelled to take an undivided interest when he had purchased the whole. It was said that to compel him to execute the contract would make him a tenant in common against his will with a stranger; that the owner of the one-seventh of the estate would have the right to enter upon the land, use and enjoy it, and, if the owner of the six-sevenths attempted at any time to prevent his entry, he would be subjected to a suit; that, if improvements were erected, the land could at any time be sold for division, and hence the owner of the six-sevenths be put to great inconvenience and possible loss. There is a general statement in the opinion that the purchaser cannot be compelled to accept a part of the land purchased, with compensation for the failure to convey the residue; but in view of the special facts of that case, as just recited, the principle mentioned can have no application to the controversy before us.

We have several other cases which appear to recognize the general doctrine stated in the excerpt from

Cyc., but it is stated in these cases in its negative form arising under bills for recission. *Buchanan* v. *Alwell*, 8 Humph. (27 Tenn.), 516; *Cunningham* v. *Sharp*, 11 Humph. (30 Tenn.), 116, 121; *Galloway* v. *Bradshaw*, 5 Sneed (37 Tenn.), 70; *Topp* v. *White*, 12 Heisk. (59 Tenn.), 165, 181; *Winfrey* v. *Drake*, 4 Lea (72 Tenn.), 293, 295. A short excerpt from two or three of these cases will be sufficient for illustration. In *Buchanan* v. *Alwell* it is said:

"When a contract is for an entire tract of land, and a good title can only be made to part, the purchaser will not be compelled to take title, with an abatement of the price or compensation for the deficiency, especially if the defect of title be so considerable as to defeat the inducement to the purchase, but may disaffirm the contract altogether."

In *Cunningham* v. *Sharp*:

"The general rule is that the purchaser is entitled to the specific property for which he contracted; and if a good title can be made to part only, he will not be compelled to accept a title for such part, with an abatement of the purchase money, or compensation for the deficiency, unless the deficiency be so immaterial as not to affect the inducement to the purchaser."

In *Galloway* v. *Bradshaw*:

"The mere failure of title to a part of the land purchased, which materially affects its value, or constituted an inducement to the trade, gives the vendee the option to set aside and annul the whole contract, or retain the part to which the title is good, and have a de-

duction from the consideration, to the extent of the
value of the portion lost, in reference to the whole contract.''

So it appears that our cases are, on the whole, in accord with the current of authority.

We are of the opinion, therefore, that when Vernon
made the offer of October 20th he performed his full
legal duty, and Mr. James refused it at his peril. Vernon had agreed to refund the $4,500 in the way of a
reconveyance of the 127 acres, and in the reduction of
the price therefor. When he found that he was unable
to convey a small and immaterial part of it, he offered
to convey the rest, and make compensation for the deficiency. This was all he could do, and the deficiency
was so small the vendee should have accepted it. Not
having accepted it, he could not claim the $4,500 in
money.

It is true, as insisted by the complainant, that the
contract which the chancellor tendered with consent of
Vernon in his decree was not the same contract that
the parties had agreed upon in the paper of July 21,
1910, since, for one thing, the cash payment was very
much larger. But, inasmuch as complainants had lost
all right to any relief at all by failure to accept the
offer of October 20, 1910, they could not complain that
Vernon, through the chancellor's decree, offered them
a new contract, which they could either take or refuse.

The result is that the decree of the court of civil appeals should be reversed, and the cause remanded to
the chancery court, with leave to complainants to ac-

cept the offer contained in the chancellor's decree within sixty days after the *procedendo* shall be docketed in that court. The chancellor's decree is likewise, in all other respects, affirmed.

The costs of the appellate proceedings will be taxed to the complainants. The costs of the court below will be paid as decreed by the chancellor.

CALHOUN v. McCRORY PIANO & REALTY CO. *

(*Jackson.* April Term, 1914.)

PRINCIPAL AND AGENT. Unauthorized execution of note by agent. Liability of principal.

Where an agent, with authority to make sales and collect the price, but without authority to borrow money, was a defaulter, and then borrowed money and executed a note therefor in his principal's name, and remitted out of the loan a sum less than the amount of the defalcation, the principal, receiving the remittance as one on sales, was not liable on the note, under the equitable doctrine that, where a principal obtains the benefit of a loan procured by his agent acting without authority, he ratifies the same and makes himself liable to the lender. (*Post,* pp. 651-655.)

Cases cited and approved: Bannatyne v. McIver, 1 K. B., 103; Alton Mfg. Co. v. Garrett Bibical Institute, 243 Ill., 298; McAdow v. Black, 4 Mont., 475; Mundorff v. Wickersham, 63 Pa., 87.

Cases cited and distinguished: Blackburn Bldg. Soc. v. Cunliffe, 22 Ch. D., 6172; Reversion Fund, etc., v. Maison Cosway, Ann. Cases, 1913, 1106.

FROM SHELBY.

Appeal from the Chancery Court of Shelby County to the Court of Civil Appeals and by writ of *certiorari* from the Court of Civil Appeals to the Supreme Court. —F. H. HEISKELL, Chancellor.

---

*On the question of the liability of a principal on negotiable paper executed by an agent, see note in 21 L. R. A. (N. S.), 1046.

As to what will constitute an implied ratification of an unauthorized loan effected by an agent, see note in 6 L. R. A. (N. S.), 311.

SWEENEY & SWEENEY, for plaintiff.

G. J. McSPADDEN, for defendant.

MR. JUSTICE LANDSDEN delivered the opinion of the Court.

One Brown was an agent of the piano company, without authority to borrow money, but with authority to make sales of pianos and collect the purchase price of the pianos sold. He defaulted in his remittances for the sales of pianos, and to make good his defalcation borrowed $360 from Miss Banks and executed a note therefor, signed "The McCrory Piano & Realty Company, M. R. Brown, Mgr." After the maturity of the note, Miss Banks sold and indorsed it to Calhoun. Calhoun filed this bill against the piano company to recover the amount. The piano company did not know that Brown had borrowed the money, nor did it know that any part thereof had been received by it until after Brown absconded and left its service. Brown deposited the money received from Miss Banks in a bank to his own credit, and remitted $300 of the amount to the piano company by his own check, which the piano company credited to Brown's account.

The chancellor and the court of civil appeals held that the piano company is not liable to Calhoun upon the note. We denied a petition for writ of *certiorari* at a former day, and the case is now before us upon petition to rehear. It is earnestly insisted by the petitioner that the piano company is liable, because it received the benefit of the loan, and it is said that the actual money received from Miss Banks has been traced into the hands of the piano company. *Bannatyne* v. *McIver*, cited in the Court of Appeal of England, 1 K. B. 103, 3 Ann. Cases, 1143, is relied upon as authority to sustain the complainant's claim.

If liability against the piano company can be sustained at all, it must be upon some equitable principle. There is no liability at law, because Brown was without authority to borrow the money, and the defendant has not ratified his transaction.

Bannatyne's Case is based upon the judgment of Lord Selborne in *Blackburne Bldg. Soc.* v. *Cunliffe*, 22 Ch. D., 6172. In his judgment in that case, Lord Selborne thought that the equity allowed there was consistent with the general rule of law that persons "who have no borrowing powers cannot, by borrowing, contract debts to the lenders." He thought the principle of law stated and the equity enforced there could be harmonized upon the principle that, if the one without power to borrow should use the money to discharge liabilities of his principal, the amount of the principal's liabilities would not be changed, and therefore there was no substantial borrowing in the result, so far as the position of the principal was concerned. In substance, this is undoubtedly true, and in such a case the principal, who receives the benefit of the money borrowed, is liable to the lender. In *Bannatyne's Case* it appeared that the lender did not know of the want of authority in the agent to borrow money. In the

later case of *Reversion Fund, etc.,* v. *Maison Cosway,*
Ann. Cases, 1913, p. 1106, it appeared that the lender
knew that the agent was without power to borrow, but
the sums borrowed were used to discharge outstanding
liabilities of the principal, and the rule laid down by
Lord Selborne was applied as in *Bannatyne's Case.*
The underlying equity in those cases is that the principal has received the benefit of the borrowed money in
such way as not to enlarge his liability. But such is
not this case. The agent here borrowed the sum in controversy to discharge in part his own defalcation with
his principal. If the principal should be required to
pay the note in suit, its liabilities would be increased
in precisely the amount of the judgment.

It is a well-settled doctrine of equity that, where a
principal obtains the benefit of a loan procured by his
agent acting without authority, he thereby ratifies the
unauthorized contract, and makes himself liable to the
lender for the sum received. This is in fact a statement in another form of the doctrine announced by
Lord Selborne, supra. The principal, however, cannot be said to have received the benefit of an unauthorized loan, unless the sum borrowed is used to increase
his money in hand, or which he is entitled to receive
from the agent, or unless it is used to extinguish outstanding liabilities against him.

In this case Brown was due the piano company a
larger sum than that which he remitted to it out of the
loan procured from Miss Banks. The piano company
received this remittance from Brown in such manner

that, as between them, it was a remittance upon sales of pianos, and therefore was the company's money. Its liabilities were not decreased, and its money in hand was not increased. Therefore the mere act of retaining the sum remitted to it by Brown is not a ratification in equity of the unauthorized transaction.

Cases illustrating the general subject: *Alton Mfg. Co.* v. *Garrett Biblical Institute,* 243 Ill., 298, 90 N. E. 704; *McAdow* v. *Black,* 4 Mont., 475, 1 Pac. 751; *Mundorff* v. *Wickersham* 63 Pa., 87, 3 Am. Rep. 531.

WESTERN UNION TELEGRAPH CO. *v.* FRANKLIN *et al.*[*]

(Jackson. April Term, 1914.)

1. **TELEGRAPHS AND TELEPHONES.** Nondelivery of message. Actions. Evidence. Sufficiency.

In an action for damages for nondelivery of a death message, evidence *held* insufficient to show that defendant's messengers made inquiries at the address given in the message. (*Post, pp.* 658-660.)

2. **TELEGRAPHS AND TELEPHONES.** Delivery of messages. Inquiries.

Where a telegraph message contained no intimation that the addressee had an agent to receive it at the place to which it was sent, the telegraph company's messenger need not make inquiries as to whether there is such an agent, but the agent should reveal himself in case of inquiry at the place of address. (*Post, pp.* 660-661.)

Cases cited and approved: Western Union Telegraph Co. v. Redinger, 66 S. W., 485; Western Union Telegraph Co. v. Cobb, 95 Tex., 333; Western Union Telegraph Co. v. Barefoot, 97 Tex., 159; Western Union Telegraph Co. v. Mitchell, 91 Tex., 454; Lyles v. Western Union Telegraph Co., 84 S. C., 1; Telegraph Co. v. McCaul, 115 Tenn., 99.

3. **TELEGRAPHS AND TELEPHONES.** Messages. Delivery agent.

A telegram cannot be delivered to any one but the addressee, unless he has appointed an agent to receive it, or there is a custom warranting delivery to another. (*Post, pp.* 660, 661.)

4. **TELEGRAPHS AND TELEPHONES.** Delivery of messages. Duty of telegraph company.

_____

[*]On the contingency of possible action of sendee, or of some third person, as affecting liability for failure properly to transmit and deliver a telegram, see note in 12 L. R. A. (N. S.), 748.

A telegraph company should, if possible by a reasonable effort, deliver messages personally to the addressee. (*Post, pp.* 660, 661.)

5. **TELEGRAPHS AND TELEPHONES.** Nondelivery of messages. Actions. Defenses.

Where the addressee of a death message had an agent who was to bring it to her from the place of address, and the telegraph company's messenger failed to make inquiry or to offer the message for delivery at the place of address, the company cannot escape liability for nondelivery on the theory that the addressee's agent might not have performed her duty, or might not have been at the place of address when the inquiries were made. (*Post, pp.* 661, 662.)

FROM SHELBY.

Error to the Circuit Court of Shelby County from the Court of Civil Appeals, and error to the Court of Civil Appeals from the Supreme Court.—A. B. PIT-MAN, Judge

GREER & GREER for plaintiff in error.

BELL, TERRY & BELL for defendants in error.

MR. CHIEF JUSTICE NEIL delivered the opinion of the Court.

The defendants in error are husband and wife. They recovered a judgment in the circuit court of Shelby county against the plaintiff in error for $500 damages, for failure to deliver the following telegram, sent from Memphis, Tenn., to Mobile, Ala.:

129 Tenn. 42

"April 6, 1912.

To Mrs. Louis Franklin, 650 Davis Ave., Mobile, Ala.
Father dead. Let me know if you can come. Answer.

WALTER SOUTHALL.

The sendor of the telegram was the brother of the sendee.

The message reached Mobile the same night, and was placed in the hands of a night messenger boy at 11:30 p. m. He testified that he went to No. 650 Davis avenue and Oak street, that he saw several colored men standing at the corner, and inquired of them if they knew Mrs. Louis Franklin, and they replied that they did not, and that no one by that name lived in that neighborhood. He then inquired on the next corner, and at three or four houses in the same block—in the 650's spending in all about twenty-five minutes in the search. He then returned the message to the office. The next morning a day messenger boy went to the same corner and made inquiry. He testified that he went to a house two or three doors the other side of No. 650, and there found George Houston and Helen Carroll, and they both told him they did not know any such person as Mrs. Louis Franklin.

Discredit, however, is thrown upon the testimony of these messenger boys by the fact that Helen Carroll lived in the next house to the storehouse on the corner, and the No. 650 was on this next house, and not on the storehouse. Both she and her husband, Gus Carroll, and George Houston, lived in this house; also Mary Hutchison, George Hutchison, and Ulysses

Hutchison, the mother and two brothers of Helen Carroll, and all of these people were acquainted with the sendee. It further appears that the sendee had, about a month before the time in question, taken up her residence in Mobile, nearly a half a mile beyond No. 650, and had specially requested of Helen Carroll and her husband to permit her mail to be delivered at No. 650, and exacted a promise of Helen and her husband that they would transmit her mail to her residence. She had also informed Carroll and wife that her father was very ill, and that she was expecting, at any time, a telegram announcing his death, and had instructed that this telegram be sent to No. 650, and asked that, if it came, it be transmitted to her. As a matter of fact, several letters did come to No. 650, addressed to Mrs. Louis Franklin, and were caused by Helen Carroll to be immediately conveyed to her by the hand of one of Helen's brothers, or her husband. In view of these facts, it is incredible that Helen Carroll told the messenger boys she did not know Mrs. Louis Franklin, or that George Houston said anything of the kind. There is evidence in the record, therefore, from which it may be inferred that the messenger boys never in fact visited the house, No. 650, but probably inquired only at the corner. The mistake possibly occurred from the fact that the city directory gave the corner storehouse as No. 650, although it was not so marked—indeed, was not marked at all—while the next house to it, between which house and the store a vacant lot intervened, was really numbered 650.

We think, therefore, that neither of the messenger boys visited No. 650. If they had inquired at that house, we have no doubt they would have learned from its inmates that Mrs. Louis Frankin did not reside at that place, and was not there at the time, and that her home was half a mile further out, beyond the free delivery limits of the telegraph company.

They would probably have learned, also, that the sendee had made Helen Carroll and her husband, Gus Carroll, her agents to receive and forward the telegram. If they had been so informed, and such information seemed reasonable, they would have been justified in leaving the message. It is true the company had no intimation of any kind that such agency existed; therefore it would not have been incumbent upon the messengers to inquire for the agents. It was held in *Western Union Telegraph Co.* v. *Redinger* (Tex. Civ. App.), 66 S. W. 485, and we think correctly, that where such agency has been conferred it is the duty of the agent, when inquiry is made as to the whereabouts of the principal, to inquire of the telegraph messenger whether he has a message for the principal, and to inform him of the agency. The message could not have been left with any one at No. 650 without information of the agency. For example, a telegram cannot be delivered to the clerk of the hotel at which the sendee is living, unless the hotel clerk has been authorized by the sendee to receive it, or unless such is the known custom of business at the hotel. *Western Union Telegraph Co.* v. *Cobb*, 95 Tex., 333, 67 S. W. 87, 58 L. R. A., 698,

93 Am. St. Rep. 862. But, of course, where the sendee has made any one his agent, as, for example, the clerk of a hotel, to receive and forward his telegrams, it is the duty of the company to recognize such agency and make delivery accordingly. *Western Union Telegraph Co.* v. *Barefoot,* 97 Tex., 159, 76 S. W. 914, 64 L. R. A. 491.

The leading principle, of course, is that the delivery must be made personally to the sendee, if that can be effected by the exercise of reasonable effort. *Western Union Telegraph Co.* v. *Mitchell,* 91 Tex. 454, 44 S. W. 274, 40 L. R. A. 209, 211, 66 Am. St. Rep. 906. But, as stated, delivery might be made to an agent, under the circumstances already indicated (*Western Union Telegraph Co.* v. *Whitson,* 145 Ala., 426, 41 South. 405; *Lyles* v. *Western Union Telegraph Co.,* 84 S. C., 1, 65 S. E. 832, 137 Am. St. Rep. 829),. or should be delivered to one in whose care it is addressed (*Telegraph Co.* v. *McCaul,* 115 Tenn., 99, 90 S. W. 856).

It is possible, of course, that on inquiry at No. 650 the messenger might have encountered some resident of the building other than Helen Carroll and her husband, or her brothers, and from these might have learned only the fact that the sendee was not there, and the duty would then have existed only to make further inquiry elsewhere. It is possible, also, that, even if inquiry had been made of the Carrolls, or of the other persons who were acquainted with the agency, the message, although received, might not have been forwarded. This latter supposition, however, seems wholly improbable, because the custom had been to forward letters promptly, in accordance with the duty assumed by the acceptance of the agency.

It is true that such contingencies were involved as above indicated. But we think there is no doubt the plaintiff in error breached its duty when its messengers failed to apply at No. 650. It may be that, if inquiry had been so made, no information would have been elicited, except that the sendee was not at the address. On the other hand, the question asked might have developed information of the agency. Having failed in the primary duty of making inquiry at the address given, we think it does not lie in the mouth of the plaintiff in error to speculate on the contingencies that might have arisen if such inquiry had been made. Where we can see that, if inquiry had been made, it is probable there might have been a legal delivery effected, this is sufficient. From the evidence we are quite sure that, if Carroll and wife had been inquired of, they would have communicated their agency, and, on delivery of the telegram to them, would have promptly forwarded it to the sendee, and that she would have reached Memphis in time to have attended the funeral of her father.

We therefore think the judgment of the court of civil appeals must be affirmed.

BAKER WATKINS SUPPLY CO. *v.* FOWLKES.

(*Jackson.*   April Term, 1914.)

1. JUSTICES OF THE PEACE. Execution. Lien. Creation.

The purpose of Acts 1899, ch. 39, providing that whenever any
execution, issued by a justice of the peace, is levied on real
estate, the title to the real estate shall not be affected as
to third parties, unless the execution or the papers in the
case are filed in the circuit court within ten days after the
levy, is to give third parties notice of the lien of the execution,
and is for the protection of third parties. (*Post, p.* 667.)

Code cited and construed: Secs. 4808-4810 (S.); subsec. 8, sec.
5892 (S.); subsecs. 3, 6, sec. 5938 (S.).

Acts cited and construed: Acts 1899, ch. 39.

**2. JUSTICES OF THE PEACE. Execution. Validity. Loss of
summons.**

An execution issued by a justice of the peace was not rendered
invalid by the fact that at the date of its issuance the original
summons was lost, and no steps had then been taken to supply
it; Shannon's Code, sec. 4800, providing that, when the docket
book and the original papers are destroyed, the justice of the
peace may supply them, and issue execution as though they
had not been destroyed, not being applicable, since it outlines
the practice where all the papers and docket book are lost, and
not where the summons alone is lost. (*Post, pp.* 668-671.)

Code cited and construed: Sec. 4800 (S.); sec. 5701 (S.); subsec.
3, sec. 5938 (S.); subsec. 6, sec. 5938 (S.); sec. 5941-5946 (S.).

**3. EXECUTION. Filing transcript in superior court. Loss of
summons. Establishment and restoration.**

Under Shannon's Code, sec. 5701, providing that any record,
proceedings, or paper, filed in an action, either at law or equity,
if lost or mislaid, may be supplied, upon application, under

the orders of the court, where a cause had been transferred
from a justice of the peace to the circuit court after the levy
of an execution on land for the purpose of obtaining an order
of condemnation, the circuit court could make an order supplying the original summons, though it had never been on file in
that court, it having been lost before the transfer of the
cause, since the power vested in courts by the statute is not
limited to papers filed in the court which makes the order,
but applies to any paper "filed in an action." (*Post, pp.* 671-
675.)

Code cited and construed: Sec. 5701 (S.); secs. 4800, 5701 (S.).

Act cited and construed: Acts 1899, ch. 39.

Cases cited and approved: Crabtree v. Bank, 108 Tenn., 483;
Tyree v. Magness, 33 Tenn., 276; Elliott & Co. v. Jordan, 66
Tenn., 376; Childress v. Lewis, 61 Tenn., 12; Lane v. Jones,
42 Tenn., 318; Graves v. Keaton, 43 Tenn., 9; Faust v. Echols,
44 Tenn., 398; Glass v. Stovall, 29 Tenn., 453; Hollins v. Johnson, 40 Tenn., 346; Parker v. Swan, 20 Tenn., 81; Farquhar
v. Toney, 24 Tenn., 502; Stole v. Gardner, 81 Tenn., 135.

Cases cited and distinguished: Halliburton v. Jackson, 79 Tenn.,
471; Anderson v. Talbot, 48 Tenn., 410.

FROM DYER.

Appeal from the Circuit Court of Dyer Coun-
ty to the Court of Civil Appeals and by *certiorari* from
the Court of Civil Appeals to the Supreme Court.—
Jos. E. Jones, Judge.

Ashley & Campbell, for plaintiff.

Draper & Rice, for defendant.

Mr. Justice Buchanan delivered the opinion of the
Court.

The supply company procured a judgment before a justice of the peace against Fowlkes, and caused execution to be issued on the judgment and levied on land owned by Fowlkes. The date of the judgment was January 1, 1908. The execution was issued, levied on the land, and filed in the office of the clerk of the circuit court with the return of the levying officer on April 15, 1912. During the June term of the circuit court for 1913, and on the 30th day of that month, plaintiff in execution moved the circuit court to be permitted to supply the original summons, together with the indorsements thereon, for the purpose of obtaining an order of condemnation. This motion the court disallowed, and the plaintiff excepted. Whereupon the defendant in execution moved the court to quash the execution and levy thereof in this cause, and to dismiss the proceedings, which motion the court allowed, and accordingly adjudged, from which judgment, plaintiff in execution prosecuted its appeal to the court of civil appeals, where by a divided court, the majority opinion being by Mr. Justice Moore, the judgment of the circuit court was reversed, and the cause remanded. It is now before us on petition for *certiorari* of defendant in execution. His assignments of error raise two questions:

(1) Was the circuit court in error in disallowing the motion to supply by proof the lost summons and the returns thereon?

(2) Was the trial court in error in sustaining the motion of the execution debtor, and in quashing the execution, and dismissing the proceeding?

Since the two questions may very well have been framed as one, we will consider them so. Section 4808 of Shannon's Code provides:

"Where an execution issued by a justice of the peace is levied on real estate, it shall be the duty of the justice to whom the same is returned to return the execution, together with the judgment and the papers in the cause, to the next circuit court of his county for condemnation."

See, also, subsections 3 and 6, section 5938, Shannon's Code.

Section 4809, Shannon's Code, provides:

"The circuit court, upon the return thus made, may condemn the land, and order the same, or so much thereof as it may see proper, to be sold by the sheriff of the county, in satisfaction of the judgment and costs."

The next section (4810, Shannon's Code) provides:

"If the circuit court condemn the land to be sold, the clerk shall enter on the minutes the warrant, attachment, or other leading process, with the officer's return thereon, the prosecution and other bonds, where the condition has not been discharged, affidavits for attachment or other process, the judgment of the justice, the execution levied with the officer's return, and the judgment of the court."

The above legislation was supplemented by chapter 39, Acts of 1899, which, so far as material here, reads as follows:

"Section 1. That hereafter, whenever any execution, issued by a justice of the peace, is levied on real estate, and ten days from the date of the levy has expired, the title to the real estate shall not be affected as to third parties until said execution or the papers in the cause are filed in the circuit court of the county in which the land lies.

"Section 2. That the officer making said levy shall, within ten days thereafter, return the execution to the circuit court, where said cause will be at once docketed, and he will return the fact of the return of such execution to the circuit court, to the justice of the peace issuing the execution, whereupon the justice shall file the remaining papers in said cause in the circuit court, as now required by law."

It is manifest that the policy underlying the last-quoted act was the protection of third parties; for, to preserve the lien as against them, the first section of the act requires filing in the circuit court either of the execution or of the remaining papers in the cause. Subsection 8 of section 5892, Shannon's Code, makes it the duty of the clerk to record at full length on the minutes of his court the papers returned into court by a justice of the peace, for the purpose of having a condemnation of land levied on by execution from such justice, and also the order of sale; this, of course, only after order of sale has been made. The second section of chapter 39, Acts 1899, supra, provides for an immediate docketing of the cause when the levying officer under the terms of that act has returned the execution into the circuit court, the purpose of all of which is to give third parties notice of the lien of the execution.

The transcript fails to disclose that the rights of third parties are involved in the present case; but, even if they were, it is clear that the execution was returned into the circuit court on the same day it was issued and levied. The execution debtor insists that, when the court sustained his motion, no lien was in existence by reason of the levy of the execution on the land, because, as he says, the summons was lost before the execution was issued by the justice of the peace, and no valid execution could be issued until the lost summons was supplied, and that it should have been supplied by a compliance with section 4800, Shannon's Code, before the issuance of the execution. That section does provide that:

"When the docket book and original papers belonging to the office of a justice of the peace are destroyed, and said justice shall make oath to that effect, it shall be lawful for said justice, or his successor in office (upon the plaintiff, his agent, attorney, or returning officer filing with said justice, or his successor in office, an affidavit setting forth the name of the plaintiff or plaintiffs, defendant or defendants, the date and amount of his, her, or their judgment as near as may be, and that the same has not been paid), to issue execution as though the original papers and docket book had not been destroyed; and the same.shall be as good and valid, and have the same force and effect, as other executions issued by justices of the peace.''

But the section just quoted does not support the insistence of the judgment debtor in the case at bar, because it is not one where the docket book and original papers are destroyed. The docket book, with its record of the judgment, is still in the custody of the justice of the peace by whom the judgment was rendered. The original summons, the indorsements on it, and the copy of the account attached to it alone are lost. Section 4800, Shannon's Code, seems to be a special one, outlining the practice where all the papers and the docket book have been destroyed, and it does not apply in the present case. Section 5701, Shannon's Code, reads:

''Any record, proceeding, or paper filed in an action, either at law or equity, if lost or mislaid unintentionally, or fraudulently made away with, may be supplied, upon application, under the orders of the court, by the best evidence the nature of the case will admit of.''

The summons in this case was on the files of the justice of the peace, and under subsection 3 of section 5938, Shannon's Code, it was his duty to retain, preserve, and file away in order, and properly marked for easy reference, all the papers in civil cases before him, unless returned or transmitted in pursuance of law, to the circuit court upon the appeal or otherwise; and under subsection 6 of said section 5938 it was his duty to return the summons and all the other papers pertaining to the case to the circuit court, on the second day of the term next after the levy. It affirmatively appears that the loss of this summons was not due to the negligence of the plaintiff in execution or its counsel, but wholly to the failure of the justice of the peace, whose duty it was to keep it until levy was made on the land, and then to return it into the circuit court as stated.

By section 5941, Shannon's Code, it is provided:

"Every justice of the peace shall keep, in a well bound book properly ruled for that purpose, a docket of all judgments rendered by him, showing in whose favor and against whom each judgment is rendered, the names of the parties in full, and the date and amount of the judgment."

Section 5942 provides for the keeping by him of an execution docket, and that section and section 5943 prescribe such entries as shall be made therein, while by section 5944 it is provided that:

"A substantial compliance with these requirements will be sufficient to render the proceedings and entries valid for all purposes, so far as the parties litigant are concerned, and all persons claiming under them."

Yet section 5945 makes it a misdemeanor for any justice not to keep the docket and make the entries required, and upon conviction he may be removed from office and subjected to a fine of $50 for each omission, to be recovered by any one who sues therefor. And by section 5946 he is also made liable in damages to any person injured for failing to keep his papers or dockets.

The sections referred to above are as numbered in Shannon's Code.

A certified copy of the judgment in this case, as it appears on the docket book of the justice of the peace, was read in evidence on the trial of the motion in this cause. There was also read an affidavit of the justice of the peace who issued the summons, to which he attached as Exhibit A a true copy, as he states in his affidavit, of the original summons, which was in proper form, and the indorsements on this copy of the summons show service on the defendant and the date of same, the date when the case was set for trial, the date and amount of the judgment, and that it was for the plaintiff and against the defendant. The certified copy of the judgment from the docket book does not show the date of the judgment, but does show the correct style of the cause and the amount of the judgment, and that it was rendered for plaintiff and against the defendant by name.

We do not think the validity of the execution was destroyed by the mere fact that at the date of its issuance the summons was lost and that no steps had then been taken to supply it. The plaintiff in execution, so far as this record shows, may have been ignorant of the loss of the summons when it ordered issuance of the execution. The validity of the execution in the respect here questioned depended only upon whether the summons was in proper form and was personally

served on the defendant, and not on the physical whereabouts of the paper evidencing these vital facts. It
is true that the summons was the leading process, but
its loss from the files did not affect its validity nor that
of the execution. There must, of course, have been a
valid service of the summons, a valid judgment, a valid
execution and levy on real estate of the defendant, in
order that a valid lien should exist. We think the
validity of all these appears from the transcript, unless, as is next insisted for the execution debtor, the
circuit court was without jurisdiction to make an order
supplying the lost summons after hearing the evidence
to which we have referred. The argument on this
point is that the lost summons was never filed in the
circuit court and was not lost from its files, and therefore that court was without jurisdiction to order it to
be supplied. The power conferred by section 5701,
Shannon's Code, is very broad, and vests in courts of
law and equity the power to supply lost papers, etc.,
and that power is not limited by the terms of the statute to papers filed in the court which makes the order,
if the paper was "filed in an action," it falls within
the terms of that section. Now the paper here in question was "filed in an action," and that action, by operation of law, was removed from the court in which the
paper was filed to the circuit court, and along with the
action passed the power of cognizance, the power to
condemn and pass judgment on the rights of the parties, and as a necessary incident of the power to
adjudge there must exist the power and the duty to see

the evidence of the right to condemn, to see the papers on file; but one of them was lost. It was not on the files of the circuit court, had never been there; but it was filed in that action, the same action, while it pended before the justice of the peace. When the levying officer returned the execution into the circuit court, and the cause was there docketed as the second section of chapter 39, Acts of 1899, required, the transfer of jurisdiction was complete. *Crabtree* v. *Bank*, 108 Tenn. (24 Pickle), 483, 67 S. W. 797, and we think it beyond dispute that the circuit court had full jurisdiction, under section 5701, Shannon's Code, to make the order. supplying the lost summons, to the end that it might be recorded on the minutes as required by law. The case of *Halliburton* v. *Jackson*, 79 Tenn. (11 Lea), 471, is not in conflict with our view. There the original summons and the note on which the action was based were lost, and what purported to be copies of those papers were certified up to the circuit court, and they, with the execution and return of the levying officer, were made the basis for the judgment of condemnation. This court held, and correctly so, we think, that this was neither compliance with our statute, section 4800 Shannon's Code, which was section 3070a, Code 1858, nor with section 5701, Shannon's Code which was section 3907, Code 1858, and that the facts stated should be under oath. The court did not in that case, however, as there was nothing to call for it, note the distinction which we have noted here

between a case where all written evidence of the judgment—that is, docket book and all the papers—is destroyed, and where, in order to have execution, the
proceeding before the justice of the peace must be,
under Shannon's Code, section 4800, and a case, on
the other hand, such as this, where certainly under
our Acts 1899, ch. 39, the return of the execution into
the circuit court transfers to that court full jurisdiction over the action and rights of the parties to it. In
general accord with one phase or another of the views
we have expressed are the following cases: *Tyree* v.
Magness, 1 Sneed (33 Tenn.), 276; *Elliott & Co.* v.
Jordan, 7 Baxt. (66 Tenn.), 376; *Childress* v. *Lewis,* 2
Baxt. (61 Tenn.), 12; *Lane* v. *Jones,* 2 Cold. (42
Tenn.), 318; *Graves* v. *Keaton,* 3 Cold. (43 Tenn.), 9;
Faust v. *Echols,* 4 Cold. (44 Tenn.), 398; *Glass* v. *Stov-
all,* 10 Humph. (29 Tenn.), 451; *Hollins* v. *Johnson,* 3
Head (40 Tenn.), 346; *Parker* v. *Swan,* 1 Humph. (20
Tenn.), 81, 34 Am. Dec. 619; *Farquhar* v. *Toney,* 5
Humph. (24 Tenn.), 502; *Stole* v. *Gardner,* 13 Lea (81
Tenn.), 135, 49 Am. Rep. 660.

We do not think under the facts of this case that
the action of the circuit judge can be sustained by application of the principles announced in *Anderson* v.
Talbot, 1 Heisk. (48 Tenn.), 410.

The transcript shows, as stated, a copy of the summons, and that copy recites that a copy of the account
on which the suit was based was attached to the summons as Exhibit A. We think this copy of the account
should have been proved, as well as the copy of the

summons. And we think it clear that the trial judge
was in error in disallowing the motion of plaintiff in
execution. He should have required proof to be made
of the copy of the account which was attached to the
summons, and, upon that being made, the evidence
was sufficient to have warranted an order of condemnation. The above being true, he was, of course, clearly
in error in granting the motion of defendant in execution.

Modified as above indicated, there is no error in the
judgment of the court of civil appeals. Wherefore
let the writ of *certiorari* be granted, and the judgment
of the court of civil appeals be modified as above, and,
as modified, be affirmed, and the cause remanded, and
with the *procedendo* let a copy of this opinion go down,
in lieu of that of the majority of the court of civil appeals.

CITY LUMBER Co. v. BARNHILL *et al.*

(*Jackson.* April Term, 1914.)

1. **HUSBAND AND WIFE. Wife's Separate Estate. Liability to charge for benefits.**

Real property not shown to be the separate property of a married woman cannot be charged as such, even for benefits accruing to her interest. (*Post, pp.* 677, 678.)

Case cited and distinguished: Shacklett v. Polk, 51 Tenn., 104.

2. **HUSBAND AND WIFE. Evidence as to ownership. Presumption.**

There is no presumption that a married woman's property is her separate estate rather than her general estate, but the presumption is rather to the contrary. (*Post, pp.* 677, 678.)

Case cited and distinguished: Shacklett v. Polk, 51 Tenn., 104.

3. **HUSBAND AND WIFE. Wife's separate estate. Lien.**

Under the express provisions of Shannon's Code, secs. 3532, 3533, a furnisher's lien on the real estate of a married woman, both her separate and general estate, cannot be established when there is no contract evidenced by a writing signed by her, and, where the one furnishing the goods for which the lien is sought to be established knew that the right and title to the realty was in her, he has no right to remove the goods. (*Post, pp.* 678, 679.)

Codes cited and construed: Secs. 3532, 3533 (S.).

Cases cited and approved: Cage v. Lawrence (Ch. App.) 57 S. W. 192; Baker v. Stone (Ch. App.) 58 S. W. 761.

Appeal from Chancery Court of Madison County. J. W. Ross, Chancellor.

D. W. HERRING and W. T. ROGERS, for plaintiff.

BOND & BOND and C. E. PIGFORD, for defendant Barnhill.

MR. JUSTICE WILLIAMS delivered the opinion of the Court.

This case is before the court on a petition to rehear. Petitioner, City Lumber Company, urges that the real estate of Mrs. Barnhill, a *feme covert,* should be subjected to liability as her separate estate under the doctrine of the case of *Shacklett* v. *Polk,* 4 Heisk. 104, 113, to the effect that the separate estate of a married woman may be held liable for debts created for its benefit and preservation, with or without an express undertaking on her part to bind it. It is sufficient to reply to this contention that the City Lumber Company, as complainant, did not proceed on an allegation that the real estate sought to be affected was the separate estate of Mrs. Barnhill, or on any proof to that effect. The bill of complaint merely states that she bought the property and took title in her own name with the consent and approval of her husband, and that it is immaterial to complainant company whether it is her separate or general estate. Without a showing that this property was the separate estate of the married woman, we are unable to see how it may be charged as

such, even for benefits accruing to her holding. There
is no presumption that a married woman's property
is her separate estate rather than her general estate.
The presumption would seem to be to the contrary—
that the property was her general estate. Enc. Ev.
823. The deed to Mrs. Barnhill, for the property was
not introduced in evidence to show the nature of the
estate vested in her, and her answer makes no admission respecting the same. The bill was filed for the
purpose of enforcing a furnishers' lien under the statute, and not to charge the property as a separate estate
benefited.

The statute specifically governs the matter of lien
or no lien on the property of a married woman,
whether separate or general and the stipulation for a
lien in behalf of a furnisher is made to depend upon
the wife, whose land is sought to be charged, entering
into a contract signed by her. Code (Shan.) section
3532, provides that the lien "shall apply to and embrace within its provisions the lands, both separate
and general estate, of *femes covert,* when the contract
is made with the wife whose land is sought to be
charged with the lien, and evidenced by a writing
signed by her." It clearly appears from the proof that
there was no contract entered into evidenced by a writing signed by Mrs. Barnhill. The effort to fix a furnishers' lien therefore fails by force of the terms of
the statute. *Cage* v. *Lawrence* (Ch. App.) 57 S. W.
192; *Baker* v. *Stone* (Ch. App.) 58 S. W. 761-763.

A further contention of complainant lumber company was that it had a right to remove the materials furnished the. married woman.   Code (Shan.) section 3533, again in this instance names the conditions. for removal of such materials, and one of these conditions is ignorance on the part of the furnisher of the married woman's right or claim to the realty.   The bill of complaint of the lumber company sets forth knowledge on its part of the fact that the right and title to the land in question was in Mrs. Barnhill.   The right to remove the materials furnished therefore fails by reason of the statute's plain provision. *Baker* v. *Stone,* supra.

The petition for a rehearing must be disallowed.

NEIL, C. J., incompetent in this case.

WILLIAMS V. BIRMINGHAM & N. W. RY. Co. *et al.*

(*Jackson.* April Term, 1914.)

1. **RAILROADS. Liens for labor. Suit to enforce. Bill. Description. Definiteness.**

A bill to enforce a lien for railroad construction work must, in the absence of an attachment, describe the property on which it is sought to enforce the lien with sufficient definiteness to identify it and segregate it. (*Post, p.* 684.)

Act cited and construed: Acts 1891, ch. 98.

Case cited and distinguished: Luttrell v. Railroad, 119 Tenn., 492.

2. **RAILROADS. Liens for Labor. Suit to enforce. Bill. Sufficiency.**

A bill to enforce a lien on a railroad for construction work, which alleges that defendant railroad company owned and operated a line of railway from a designated point through enumerated counties, that codefendant, the principal contractor, contracted with the railway company for the construction of its line of road, and that complainant performed work described, sufficiently identifies and locates the line of railroad on which the lien is claimed, as required by Acts 1891, ch. 98, secs. 2, 3. (*Post, p.* 684.)

Act cited and construed: Acts 1891, ch. 98.

Case cited and distinguished: Luttrell v. Railroad, 119 Tenn., 492.

3. **STATUTES. Construction. Rules of construction.**

The rule for the construction of statutes to which all other rules must yield is that the intention of the Legislature must prevail. (*Post, pp.* 685-690.)

Acts cited and construed: Acts 1883, ch. 220; Acts 1891, ch. 98.

Williams v. Railroad Co.

Code cited and construed: Sec. 399 (S.).

Cases cited and distinguished: Barnes v. Thompson, 32 Tenn., 314.

Cases cited and approved: Campbellville Lumber Co. v. Hubbert, 112 Fed. 718; Union Bank v. Laird, 15 U. S., 390; Brown v. Hamlett, 76 Tenn., 735; Gold v. Fite, 61 Tenn., 248; Maxey v. Powers, 117 Tenn., 103; Alley v. Lanier, 41 Tenn., 541; Kay v. Smith, 57 Tenn., 42; Steger v. Arctic Refrigerator Co., 89 Tenn., 453; Ragon v. Howard, 97 Tenn., 341.

4. STATUTES. Construction. Legislative Intent.

The court, in seeking to ascertain the intent of the Legislature in adopting a statute, must look to the whole statute, and give to it such a construction as will effectuate the legislative purpose. (*Post, pp.* 685-690.)

5. RAILROADS. Mechanics' liens. Enforcement. Venue.

Acts 1883, ch. 220, as amended by Acts 1891, ch. 98, giving to subcontractors and laborers who perform work in the construction of a railroad a lien thereon, which "may be enforced by suit . . . in the circuit or chancery court of the county or district where the work . . . was done," does not limit the venue of suits to enforce liens, and does not prohibit suits in the county where the principal office of a railroad is situated and in which a material part of its line is located, though the work was done elsewhere. (*Post, pp.* 685-690.)

6. LIENS. Statutes. Construction.

Lien statutes must be liberally construed, to carry out the legislative purpose, and to secure and protect those entitled to a lien. (*Post, pp.* 685-690.)

7. STATUTES. Construction. Meaning of words. "May."

The word "may" in a statute will not be construed to mean "shall," where such a construction will tend to defeat the object of the statute, though it will be so construed, where such a construction is necessary to effectuate the purpose of the act. (*Post, pp.* 685-690.)

8. RAILROADS. Foreclosure of liens. Parties.

Where a contractor under a subcontractor from the principal
contractor for the construction of a railroad brought suit to
enforce a lien, and alleged an indebtedness from the principal
contractor to the subcontractor, and averred that the state of
accounts between them on the one hand, and complainant and
the subcontractor on the other, was open, the principal contractor was at least a proper party. (*Post*, *p.* 690.)

FROM MADISON.

Error to the Chancery Court of Madison County.—
J. W. Ross, Chancellor.

T. W. Pope, for plaintiff.

R. F. Spragins, for defendant.

Mr. Justice Lansden delivered the opinion of the
Court.

The original bill was filed by the complainant, Williams, against the Birmingham & Northwestern Railway Company as owner, the Jackson Construction
Company, a Tennessee corporation, as principal contractor, and Mrs. Susie E. Wright, administratrix of J.
W. Wright, Jr., deceased, as subcontractor, for the purpose of enforcing a claimed lien upon the line of railway of the defendant railway company for approximately $2,000 claimed to be due for work and labor
done in the construction of the line of railway belong-

ing to the defendant railway company. The chancellor sustained a demurrer to the bill, from which the complainant has appealed and assigned errors. The defendants the railway company and the construction company have filed the record for writs of error to review those parts of the decree of the chancellor in which he overruled certain other grounds of demurrer assigned to the bill. There were fourteen grounds of demurrer in the court below, only four of which were sustained by the chancellor, and this opinion will be confined to discussion of the questions presented by those grounds.

The bill charged that the defendant railway company "is a railway corporation, with its home office at Jackson, Tennessee, owning and operating a line of railway from Jackson, Tennessee, through the counties of Madison, Crockett and Dyer, which railway company owns its rights of way, tracks, ties, rails tanks, switches, bridges, tunnels, depots, engines, equipments, and franchises"; that the Jackson Construction Company is a Tennessee corporation, with its principal place of business in Jackson, Tennessee, and entered into a contract with the railway company as principal contractor for the construction of its line of railroad; that J. W. Wright, Jr., now deceased, and the intestate of Mrs. Susie E. Wright, entered into a contract with the construction company for the construction and building of the entire line of railway aforesaid; and that the complainant was subcontractor under Wright, in which capacity he did certain work set out in the bill, and for which Wright is indebted to him in the sum of $2,701.81.

The demurrer raised the question that the bill failed to sufficiently describe the line of railroad upon which the lien is claimed, and, there being no attachment of the property, the lien must fail.

It is not insisted that an attachment is necessary to secure the lien, and could not be under the authority of *Luttrell* v. *Railroad*, 119 Tenn. 492, 105 S. W. 565, 123 Am. St. Rep. 737; but it is said that in the absence of an attachment, under sound rules of pleading, the bill must describe the property upon which it is sought to fix the lien with sufficient definiteness to identify it and segregate it as the property upon which the lien is claimed. This is unquestionably a sound principle. So the question for determination is whether the description is sufficient. The bill was manifestly modeled after the description contained in *Luttrell* v. *Railroad*, supra. In that case it was said:

"The bill is framed in strict conformity with the provisions of sections 2 and 3, chapter 98, of the Acts of 1891. It describes the lines of railroad upon which the lien is sought as leading from Jellico, through the counties of Campbell, Anderson, and Knox, to Knoxville."

The description herein is somewhat more specific than that just quoted, and which the court considered to be in strict conformity with the act of 1891. It is entirely clear that any person reasonably acquainted in the community could identify and locate the line of railroad upon which the lien is claimed from the description contained in the bill. The bill further shows that the railroad company is the owner of its tracks, ties, etc. Hence this assignment is sustained.

It is next said that the chancery court of Madison county is without jurisdiction to entertain the bill, and declare and enforce the lien which it seeks, for the reason that the bill shows that the work done out of which the lien claim arises was performed in Dyer county, and the bill was not filed either in the county or the district or chancery division in which the work was done. A proper determination of this question makes it necessary to consider chapter 220, Acts of 1883, and chapter 98, Acts of 1891, amendatory thereof. The first act gave a lien to persons contracting with railroads for work and labor done and material furnished in the construction or repairing of the railroad. Section 2 provided that the lien created by the act "may be enforced by a suit against the railroad company in the circuit court of the county or district where the work or some part thereof was done or material of some part thereof was delivered."

Section 3 of the act, while not giving a lien to subcontractors upon the railroad property, provided for a garnishment proceeding in favor of subcontractors and others against the principal contractor in such way as to fix a lien upon funds due the principal contractor from the railroad company in favor of subcontractors and the others. It was provided that this claim "may be enforced against the railroad company

as garnishee, and the principal contractor as debtor
in the circuit court, or before any justice of the peace
of the county having jurisdiction of the amount
claimed''; and section 4 of the act gave a like remedy
in favor of laborers, material men, and others employed by subcontractors against the principal contractor, and provided that this remedy ''may be enforced against the principal contractor as garnishee
and the subcontractor as debtor in the circuit court or
before any justice of the peace of the county having jurisdiction of the amount.'' Section 3 of this statute
was amended by chapter 98, Acts of 1891, so as to place
subcontractors and others mentioned in section 3 of the
act of 1883 on the same basis with respect to their liens
as principal contractors. It was provided, however,
that notice shall be given to the railroad company within 90 days after the work and labor done, or the materials are furnished or services rendered. It is then
provided in section 2 as follows:

''The liens provided for in this act may be enforced
by suit brought against such railroad company in the
circuit or chancery court of the county or district
where the work or material or any part thereof was
done or furnished or any part of said services was rendered.''

The question made is that the foregoing section is
exclusive of all other remedies, and the lien claimant,
in order to secure his lien, must bring his suit against
the railroad company in the circuit or chancery court
of the county, or district, where the work or material

was done or furnished or the services rendered. As
previously stated, the work out of which the present
claim arises was done in Dyer county, and Dyer and
Madison counties are not in the same chancery division. The suit was brought, however, in the county in
which the principal office of the railroad company is
situated and in which a part of its line of railway is
located. Personal service was had on the defendant.

The argument made here to support the ruling of the
learned chancellor is based chiefly upon *Barnes* v.
Thompson, 2 Swan, 314, in which it was held that the
mechanic's lien must be enforced by attachment. The
language of the act of 1846 (chapter 118), under consideration in that case, is that "the lien herein given
may be enforced by attachment, either at law or in
equity." The court held that the word "may" should
be construed as meaning "shall," and that the requirement of the statute was imperative that attachment
should issue and be levied upon the property upon
which the lien was claimed. It should be observed,
however, that the court stated that before the passage
of this act doubts were entertained, at the bar and on
the bench, both as to the proper form and mode of proceeding to be resorted to for the enforcement of this
lien. "These doubts," said the court, "were thrown
out in the case of *Foust* v. *Wilson*, 3 Humph. 33. . . .
We think this section was intended to clear up all
doubts of the remedy."

In addition to expressing the opinion that the act
under consideraton was passed for the express pur-

pose of definitely fixing the practice in such cases, the court said that the attachment was necessary for the safety of other creditors and the officer in whose hands final process may come for execution.

We are cited to many rules of construction found in standard authorities, all to the effect that when a new right is given by statute, and a specific remedy provided, or a new power and also the means of executing it are therein granted, the power can be executed and the right vindicated in no other way than that prescribed by the act. Sutherland on Statutory Construction, section 399; *Campbellville Lumber Co.* v. *Hubbert*, 112 Fed., 718, 50 C. C. A. 442; *Union Bank* v. *Laird*, 15 U. S., 390, 4 L. Ed. 269. These authorities are eminent in their respectability, and the rule of construction stated is undoubtedly sound. However, the one fundamental rule to which all others must yield is that the intention of the lawmaking power must prevail, and in order to ascertain the legislative intent the whole instrument must be looked to, and a construction given it as a whole which will effectuate the purpose of the Legislature. *Brown* v. *Hamlett*, 8 Lea, 735; *Gold* v. *Fite*, 2 Baxt., 248; *Maxey* v. *Powers*, 117 Tenn., 403, 101 S. W. 181.

This court has long since asserted that it was the intention of the Legislature, in passing this and other similar lien statutes, to secure to a worthy class of citizens the benefit of their labor, and accordingly it has announced that the construction to be given to those statutes by it is a liberal one, to carry out the legislative purpose, and to secure and protect those entitled to the lien. *Barnes v. Thompson,* supra; *Alley v. Lanier,* 1 Cold., 541; *Kay v. Smith,* 10 Heisk., 42; *Steger v. Arctic Refrigerator Co.,* 89 Tenn. 453, 14 S. W. 1087, 11 L. R. A. 580; *Ragon v. Howard,* 97 Tenn. 341, 37 S. W. 136.

It was said in the last case cited that it is the policy of our law "to protect and enforce these liens of mechanics and furnishers, and not to allow them to be defeated by any technical niceties of construction."

In other words, the word "may" will not be construed to mean "shall," where such a construction would tend to defeat the objects and purposes of the legislation, although "may" will be construed to mean "shall," if such a construction is necessary to uphold and effectuate the purpose of the act. No reason is suggested by counsel, and none occurs to us, why the Legislature should forbid that a suit of this character should be brought in a county where the principal office of the railroad company is situated and in which a material part of its line of railway is located, although such county may not be the county in which the work and labor was done, or in the chancery district of such county. The more reasonable construction is that the Legislature intended to confer an additional remedy in favor of the lien claimant by authorizing suit to be brought in any county in the district where the work or some part thereof was done. It certainly was not intended to take from the chancery court the jurisdiction which it has had from time immemorial to en-

129 Tenn. 44

force liens upon property where it has jurisdiction both of the subject-matter and of the person. At least, such a construction would not be given the statute unless it appeared to be necessary in order to effectuate its ends, and certainly it will not be done when the construction will tend to defeat its main purposes.

It is next said that the Jackson Construction Company was not a necessary or proper party to this proceeding. The chancellor so held, and dismissed the bill. In this we think there was error. While the complainant contracted with Wright, a subcontractor under the construction company, the bill shows that there is a claimed indebtedness from the construction company to Wright, and that the state of accounts between the principal contractor and the subcontractor upon the one hand, and the complainant and the subcontractor upon the other, are open and unadjudicated. While the principal contractor in such case is perhaps not a necessary party, we think he is a proper party. If the principal contractor should confess by plea or otherwise to no interest in the controversy between his subcontractor and complainant and the railroad company, he would be entitled to be dismissed with his costs; but, from what appears upon the face of the bill, he is a proper party and should not be dismissed upon demurrer.

The result is that the decree of the chancellor is reversed, and the case remanded for further proceedings at the cost of the appellees. Other questions made upon the writ of error were disposed of orally.

HAROWITZ *v.* CONCORDIA FIRE INS. CO. *

(*Jackson.*   April Term, 1914.)

1. INSURANCE.   Adjustment of loss.   Appraisal.

An insurer was not entitled to demand an appraisement, to determine the loss under a policy providing for such an appraisement
in case of disagreement, where it made no objections to the
proofs of loss submitted, or any effort to agree on the amount
thereof, but its whole attitude was a denial of all liability.
(*Post, pp.* 693-699.)

Case cited and distinguished: Hickerson & Co. v. Insurance Co.,
96 Tenn., 198.

2. INSURANCE.   Adjustment of Loss.   Appraisal.

While provisions in an insurance policy for an appraisement are
valid, and may be made a condition precedent to bringing suit,
they cannot oust the courts of their jurisdiction as to the
insured's legal liability; and where an insurer's attitude was a
denial of all liability, the court's jurisdiction was not ousted
by a demand for an appraisal.   (*Post, pp.* 699, 701.)

Case cited and distinguished: Hickerson & Co. v. Insurance Co.,
96 Tenn., 198.

3. INSURANCE.   Adjustment of Loss.   Appraisal.

An insurer's demand for an appraisement of the loss was a concession of its liability for some amount.   (*Post, pp.* 701-703.)

Case cited and distinguished: Hickerson & Co. v. Insurance Co.,
96 Tenn., 198.

Cases cited and approved: Grand Rapids Fire Ins. Co. v. Finn,
50 L. R. A., 555; Grady v. Home Fire & Marine Ins. Co., 4 L.
R. A., 291; Graham v. German American Ins. Co., 15 L. R. A.,
1060.

---

*The question of arbitration as condition precedent to action on in-
surance policy is treated in a note in 15 L. R. A. (N. S.), 1055.

4. INSURANCE. Actions on Policies. Penalties.

Under Acts 1901, ch. 141, authorizing the court in its discretion to impose a penalty upon an insurer, if its refusal to pay a loss was not in good faith, the chancellor was within his judicial discretion in refusing to assess the penalty, where the evidence disclosed that the fireman and others discovered gasoline or coal oil on the goods, justifying a suspicion that the fire was of dishonest origin, though that defense was not made. (*Post*, *pp*. 703, 704.)

Acts cited and construed: Acts 1901, ch. 141.

FROM SHELBY.

Appeal from the Chancery Court of Shelby County. —Hon. F. H. HEISKELL, Chancellor.

J. H. MALONE and H. H. LITTY, for plaintiff.

R. LEE BARTELS, for defendant.

MR. JUSTICE BUCHANAN delivered the opinion of the Court.

The bill prayed for a decree for the full amount of an insurance policy covering the stock of goods in a tailor shop, also for interest and the statutory penalty of twenty-five per cent. of the face of the policy. The decree granted was for the full amount of the policy, $2,000, and interest, $155. Recovery of the penalty was denied. Both parties appealed, and each have assigned errors here.

The company's complaint is that a decree for any amount was erroneous, while Harowitz insists that, in addition to the other amounts, he was also entitled to recover the penalty. The answer of the company admitted issuance of the policy and that a fire had occurred in the shop of assured, but denied total loss of the value of the goods. It admitted that the company had received proofs of loss, and made no complaint of informality or insufficiency of the same, but averred that the damage consisted solely of water damage to the woolens and other materials. It then set up what we take to be the real defense relied on, to wit, that the insurer had demanded an appraisal of the goods, and that by reason of default of assured no appraisal had occurred, and that, under the terms of the contract of insurance and facts of the case subsequent to the fire, appraisal of the goods and determination thereby of the sound value and loss was in law a condition precedent to the right of assured to recover upon the contract. The answer denied liability for the penalty, and averred that conditions existed on the premises of the assured after the fire such as justified the conviction that the fire was of incendiary origin; but the answer did not charge the fire to have been set by assured, or to have been caused by his negligence or procurement. In conclusion, the answer states:

"And now, having fully answered, it prays to be dismissed, with costs."

The policy contains a clause as follows:

"No suit or action on this policy for the recovery
of any claim shall be sustainable in any court of law
or equity, unless commenced within twelve months
next after the fire."

The fire occurred August 1, 1912. It is manifest
that if the defense made by the answer should be successful, and this suit should be dismissed, and a new
suit be instituted, the beginning of the new suit would
be more than twelve months next after the fire, as the
date of the fire was August 1, 1912; and therefore it
is clear that the defense made by the answer amounts
in substance to a denial of all liability by the company. In fact, the averment in the answer that the
damage to the goods consisted solely of water damage to the woolens and other materials amounts in
substance to a denial of all liability under the policy,
since under its terms the company was only liable for
loss and damage caused by fire.

It has been held by this court that:

"Upon the happening of a fire loss, the insured is
required to give notice and furnish a detailed statement of his loss. When this is received by the company, it is incumbent on the company to examine the
same, and, if not agreed to, specific obections must be
pointed out by the company, and an honest effort must
then be made to adjust the differences. A mere general objection to the proofs, without pointing out in
detail the items excepted to, will not be sufficient; but
the objection must be so specific, with detail of items,
as to enable the assured to see upon what points dif-

ferences exist, and a counter statement, if necessary, should be furnished, showing the contention of the companies in such way that the difference, if practicable, may be adjusted and settled. If this should fail after an honest effort is made, an appraisal may be demanded by either party, and only in such event." *Hickerson & Co.* v. *Insurance Companies,* 96 Tenn., 198 33 S. W. 1042, 32 L. R. A. 172.

The conduct of the company in the present case does not measure up to the standard laid down for it in the quotation last above set out. What was done on each side in respect of the demand for an appraisal which was made is to be gathered from the testimony of two witnesses, one of whom testified on behalf of the insured, and one of whom testified on behalf of the insurer. The witness who testified on this subject for the insured was Mr. H. H. Litty, attorney for the insured. It appears from his evidence that he was employed by the insured about September 1, 1912, to act for assured in the adjustment of this loss, and that he immediately called upon the local agent for the insurer, and was by that agent referred to Mr. Hart, adjuster for the insurance company. Litty called on Hart, and was advised by the latter to make proof of loss and send it to the company. This Litty did, and mailed the proofs of loss to the home office of the company by registered letter on September 7, 1912. No reply was made by the company to Litty acknowledging receipt of the proofs of loss, but in due season Litty received through the post office the registry, return receipt, showing delivery of the proofs of loss to the company on September 9, 1912. Some time afterward Litty and Hart met on the street, and the latter requested Litty to call at his (Hart's) office. This Litty did, whereupon Hart demanded having an agreement entered into submitting the matter to appraisers, to which Litty says he agreed. Whereupon he says Hart named as an appraiser for the company Mose Plough, and Litty named Ed. Rapp. Hart immediately objected to Rapp on the ground that Rapp was biased, basing such claim upon the fact that Rapp had examined all of the goods damaged by fire, and had made this examination at the request of Litty, and had also made an estimate for Litty of the damage caused by fire to some of the goods. Litty says that he selected Rapp, because Rapp was regarded as an expert. He further says that he had called on Rapp and had submitted to him a copy of the oath required of appraisers, and that Rapp was willing to take the oath, and that in view of these matters he refused to withdraw the name of Rapp, and thereupon he stated that Hart refused to enter into an appraisement with Rapp acting for Harowitz. Litty complains that the conduct of Hart was overbearing, dictatorial, and insulting to such an extent that Litty was led to believe that Hart's demand for an appraisement was not in good faith. Litty furthermore says that, when Hart named Mose Plough as one of the appraisers, he (Litty) did not object, although he had always understood that Plough had some interest in the insurance company's affairs, and frequently acted for them as an auctioneer in selling salvage.

Mr. Hart, the witness for the insurer, in his evidence admits that he objected to Rapp as an appraiser for Harowitz, and gives as his reason that Rapp had been working with Harowitz, and had made an estimate *ex parte* as to what he (Rapp) considered the damage to the goods was by fire, and that he (Hart) considered Rapp was incompetent to act as an appraiser under the oath demanded. Hart further testifies that after the first interview between himself and Litty, where the difference between them developed as to the competency of Rapp as an appraiser, he had another interview with Litty, in which he suggested that Litty select some other man, but that Litty never agreed to suggest any person other than Rapp. Hart denies in his evidence the statement of Litty in respect of his (Hart's) overbearing, dictatorial, and insulting conduct, and states in substance that he was not only willing, but anxious to have the matter submitted to appraisement, and that he so advised Mr. Litty, and requested Litty to get some one else to act in place of Rapp.

It was further held in *Hickerson & Co.* v. *Insurance Companies,* supra:

"That in the selection of appraisers it is not contemplated that either party shall select a person with a view to sustain his own views or further his own interest, but the appraisers are to act in a *quasi* judicial capacity, and as a court selected by the parties, free from all partiality and bias in favor of either party, and so as to do equal justice between them. This tribunal, selected to act instead of a court and in place of a court, must be like a court, impartial and not partisan; and if these provisions are not carried out in this spirit, and for this purpose, neither party is precluded from going into the courts to reach his just deserts, notwithstanding the provisions.''

The word ''provisions'' in the quotation last above refers to provisions for appraisement in policies of insurance. The provisions for appraisement in the policy in the present suit are substantially the same as were those quoted in the opinion in *Hickerson & Co. v. Insurance Companies,* 96 Tenn., 195, 196, 33 S. W. 1041, 32 L. R. A. 172. The provisions for appraisement in the present case contained in the policy in suit are as follows:

''. . . . The loss or damage shall be ascertained, . . . and said ascertainment or estimate shall be made by the insured and this company, or, if they differ, then by appraisers, as hereinafter provided.''

''The amount of loss or damage having been thus determined, the sum for which this company is liable shall be payable sixty days after due notice, ascertainment, estimate, and satisfactory proof of the loss have been received by this company in accordance with the terms of this policy.''

''In the event of disagreement as to the amount of loss, the same shall, as above provided, be ascertained by two competent and disinterested appraisers, the assured and this company each selecting one, and the two so chosen shall select an umpire. . . . The award in writing of any two shall determine the amount of the loss.''

''And the loss shall not become payable until sixty days after the notice, ascertainment, estimate, and satisfactory proof of the loss herein required have been received by this company, including an award by appraisers, when appraisal has been required.''

''No suit or action on this policy shall be sustainable for the recovery of any claim in any court of law or equity, until after full compliance by the assured with all of the foregoing requirements.''

There appears in the transcript on behalf of the assured the deposition of Ed. Rapp, who was suggested by Mr. Litty as one of the appraisers on behalf of the assured. His evidence is intelligent, and he is seemingly a fair and unbiased witness. It may be that he was unduly biased in favor of the insured; but, if so, the fact certainly does not appear upon an examination of his evidence.

Upon the facts, it is clear that the conduct of the insurer, from the time of the happening of the fire down to and including the recitals in its answer filed in this cause, amounts practically to a denial of all liability under the policy.

The fire occurred on August 1, 1912. A month from that date elapsed before the insured employed Mr. Litty to represent him in the adjustment of the loss.

During that month it is clear that the goods were at all times open to the inspection of the insurer, and it had full opportunity to ascertain the extent of the loss and damage. It is in evidence that on the day after the fire representatives of the insured were in the business house where the fire occurred, making a full examination of the stock of goods and of the premises in which the fire occurred, and of the origin of the fire. It is clear from the evidence that the insurance company suspected the origin of the fire to have been incendiary, and we have no doubt from this evidence that it suspected the fire to have been a dishonest one in its origin, so far as the insured and his son were concerned.

This view of the matter is borne out by the fact that although the insurer, through its adjuster, Hart, demanded an appraisement of the goods, it made no specific objections to the proofs of loss, and pointed out no detail or item wherein the same was incorrect, and furnished to the insured no counter statement of the proofs of loss, showing the contention of the insurer in respect of any infirmity in the proofs of loss, or any overestimate thereby of the sound value and damage to the goods. Without doing this, we are of the opinion that, under *Hickerson & Co.* v. *Insurance Companies,* supra, the insured was entirely beyond its rights when it demanded an appraisement under the terms of this policy. Provisions for appraisement in a policy of insurance providing a speedy and reasonable method of estimating and ascertaining the sound value and damage are valid, and such provisions may be made a condition precedent to the beginning of a suit on a policy; but such provisions are never permitted to oust the courts of their jurisdiction as to the legal liability of the insurer. When the insurer denies liability *in toto* upon the policy, it is a question for the courts. The conduct of the insurer in the present case does not disclose any point of difference between himself and the insured in respect of sound value and damage to the goods. Its attitude, on the contrary, is one disputing any liability whatsoever. We have seen how it treated the proofs of loss when they were submitted to it by the insured, we have seen how these proofs of loss were treated in the answer, and now, when we come to examine the proof taken by it, we find the testimony of the five witnesses which it introduced devoted wholly to matters tending to exculpate it from all liability uner the policy; no one of the five witnesses testifying to any fact materially contradicting the evidence on behalf of the insured as to the amount of the sound value and loss by the insured as the result of the fire.

In *Hickerson & Co.* v. *Insurance Companies,* supra it is said that the insurer cannot demand an appraisal and arbitration of the amount of the loss, while at the same time it denies all liability under its policy, and a demand for appraisal by the insurer is a waiver of other defenses going to the question of liability. The evidence for the insured shows loss resulting from fire in this case to have been a considerable amount more than the face of the policy, and the evidence on its behalf in the above respect is practically undisputed by

any evidence introduced on behalf of the insurer. The
attitude of the insurer was inconsistent. Its demand
for arbitration was a concession of its liability for some
amount (*Hickerson & Co.* v. *Insurance Companies,*
supra, and *Insurance Co.* v. *Morton, Scott, Robertson
Co.,* 108 Tenn., 390, 67 S. W. 816) ; And the next step
in order was for the insured and the insurer under the
first clause of the quotation from the policy, supra, to
ascertain and agree upon the loss or damage. The insurer evidently made no effort to ascertain and agree
upon the loss or damage. It makes no contest of the
amount thereof by its proof. It was in no attitude to
demand an appraisal until it had made an effort to
agree on the sound value and damage. If it had, prior
to its demand for an appraisal, made an effort to comply on its part with the first clause copied from the policy supra, and then found itself unable to agree with
the insured on the loss and damage, it would have been
in position to call on the assured to comply with the
other requirements quoted supra from the policy.

From what has been said, it is apparent that the
question of who was in fault in respect of the failure of
the parties to agree on the appraiser proposed by the
insured is not reached. They did not agree, and this
suit resulted, and we hold that the defense interposed
is not good (1) on the ground that the insurer never entitled itself to demand an appraisal by making an effort to agree with insured on the sound value of and
damage to the goods; and (2) on the ground that the
attitude of the insurer throughout its defense to this

suit has been that of denying all liability, thus raising an issue of which no contract between the parties could oust the courts of jurisdiction.

Each of these grounds are announced in *Hickerson & Co.* v. *Insuarnce Companies,* supra. That case has been extensively cited and approved by courts of last resort in other states, as will appear by examination of Volume, 4, Extra Annotations, L. R. A. 820. This case is cited also in the footnotes to *Grand Rapids Fire Ins. Co.* v. *Finn,* 50 L. R. A. 555; *Grady* v. *Home Fire & Marine Ins. Co.,* 4 L. R. A. (N. S.) 291; *Graham* v. *German American Ins. Co.,* 15 L. R. A. (N. S.) 1056. Examination of the cases cited will show that the grounds on which we place our decisions are well sustained by authority.

We think there is no merit in any assignment of error made by the insurer in this case. Nor do we think there is any merit in the assignment of error made by the insured. The statute invoked by him is chapter 141 of the Acts of 1901. It authorizes the penalty referred to, provided that it shall be made to appear to the court or jury trying the case that the refusal to pay the loss was not in good faith, and provided further that the imposition of the liability shall be within the discretion of the court or jury trying the case, and be measured by the additional expense, loss, and injury thus entailed.

We think the chancellor was well within his judicial discretion in refusing a decree for the penalty in this cause upon the ground that the evidence on behalf of the insured clearly discloses that when the firemen entered the building after the discovery of the fire, and extinguished the fire, they and other persons who visited the building later discovered evidence that, in some way not explained on the record, bolts of goods in the tailor shop, inclosed in glass cases, were dampened and smelled strongly of gasoline or coal oil, clearly justifying a suspicion that the fire was of dishonest origin. While this is true, the evidence would not sustain a defense based on that ground, and no such defense was made, yet we think there was sufficient ground for the denial of the penalty.

It results from the above views that the decree of the chancellor is affirmed, with costs.

STATE *et al. v.* UNION RY. Co.

(*Jackson.*　April Term, 1914.)

1. COURTS. Judgment. Stare Decisis. Res Judicata.

A decision that railway company is, in view of its charter and
its work, a commercial and not a terminal railway is conclusive as to rights based thereon, whether under the rule of
res judicata or *stare decisis*, which rights will be protected
as against a subsequent demand involving the same question.
(*Post, pp.* 707-711.)

Cases cited and distinguished:　Collier v. Union Railway Co.,
113 Tenn., 96; State ex rel. Wellford v. Union Railway Co.,
113 Tenn., 96.

Case cited and approved:　Wilkins v. Railroad, 110 Tenn., 422.

2. RAILROADS. Privilege taxes. "Railroad terminal corporation."

A railway company which leases from other railway companies
their terminal facilities, and which contracts to do their terminal business, and to provide adequate terminal facilities, and
take possession of trains entering receiving tracks, and switch
and deliver cars therein to their respective destinations within
the switching district, including the delivery of cars to connecting lines, and to render all switching services required for
the prompt handling of cars for loading, unloading, or repairs,
and to set apart exclusively for the business of the other companies terminal facilities, with the right of exclusive management and control of the terminal facilities, etc., contracts for
the performance of duties falling within the functions of a
railroad terminal corporation within Shannon's Code, secs. 2430,
2431, providing for the organization of railway terminal companies, and it is liable to privilege taxes imposed on railroad
terminal corporations; a railroad terminal corporation being
an instrumentality which assists railroad transportation com-
129 Tenn. 45

panies in the transfer of traffic between different lines, and in the collection and distribution of traffic. (*Post, pp.* 711-728.)

Case cited and distinguished: United States v. Terminal R. R. Association of St. Louis, 224 U. S. 383.

Cases cited and approved: Dean v. St. Paul Union Depot Co., 41 Minn., 360; Brady v. Chicago Great Western Railway Co., 114 Fed., 100; Floody v. Great Northern Railway Co., 102 Minn., 81; Belt Railway Co. of Chicago v. U. S., 168 Fed., 542; Union Depot & Railway Co. v. Londoner, 50 Colo., 22; Hunt v. N. Y., N. H. & Hartford Ry. Co., 212 Mass., 102; Memphis & Little Rock R. R. Co. v. State of Tennessee, 77 Tenn., 218.

FROM SHELBY.

Appeal from the Chancery Court of Shelby County. —JULIAN C. WILSON, Special Chancellor.

J. W. CANADA and PRATHER McDONALD, for appellant.

BARTON & BARTON and D. B. NEWSOM, for the State.

MR CHIEF JUSTICE NEIL delivered the opinion of the Court.

This bill was filed on the 28th of September, 1911, to recover of the defendant, as a railroad terminal corporation, the privilege taxes fixed by the Legislature on business of that kind for the years 1905 to 1911, inclusive. The chancellor rendered a decree in favor of the State for a total of taxes and penalties, $5,462.50, and in favor of the county for $4,750 taxes, and $712.50

penalty, and for the costs of the cause. From this decree, the defendant has appealed and assigned errors.

It is insisted in behalf of the defendant that it was chartered, not as a railroad terminal company, but as a commercial railway, and such is the fact. It is further insisted that this court, in the consolidated cases of *Collier* v. *Union Railway Co.* and *State ex rel. Wellford* v. *Union Railway Co.*, 113 Tenn., 96, 83 S. W., 155, considered the business it was doing in connection with the terms of the regular form of charter prescribed for commercial railways under which the defendant was chartered and organized, and held that the work it was engaged in fell within the terms of the charter of such commercial railway. It is therefore urged that it is not guilty of exercising privileges not conferred by its charter, and conferred only by the charter of railroad terminal corporations.

State ex rel. Wellford v. *Union Railway Co.* was a *quo warranto* proceeding under which it was insisted that the Union Railway Company had no lawful right to exercise the functions it was exercising under the charter of a commercial railway company, and it was sought to forfeit the charter because of these *ultra vires* acts. *Collier* v. *Union Railway Co.* was a case in which the complainant asked an injunction against the railway company's condemnation of certain of the complainant's lands for right of way; the ground of objection being that its business was such that it had no right to condemn lands for the purposes of a commercial railway company. Both cases resulted in an affirmation of the decree of the trial court in favor of the railway company.

The road, as described in the opinion referred to, was a belt line, beginning and ending at the same point in the city of Memphis, running around the city in an irregular circle or loop, throwing out here and there spurs and feed lines for the purpose of connecting with the various railroads entering the city of Memphis, and also with the numerous industries that are located · in that city.

It was stated in the opinion that the bulk of the business of the road would consist in the transfer of loaded and empty cars from one railroad to another, and from the various industries to the several lines of road centering the city of Memphis and back again; but at the same time, by its charter, it was obligated to do a general railroad business, both as to freight and passengers. The court said:

"In the present case it is shown by the principal officers of the road that it is the purpose of the company to switch cars from one road to another, to receive freight on the line of its road, and give bills of lading over its own and other roads to any part of the world—in other words, to perform all of the functions of an ordinary road. We think, therefore, that it is clearly established both by the charter and parol evidence that the road is intended to subserve a public use, to confer a public benefit, to meet a public necessity; in short, to do any and everything that is required of an ordinary public commercial railroad."

Again the court said:

"The fact that its principal and most important business is the transfer of loaded and empty cars from one point to another does not make it any the less a commercial railroad under the provisions of the general law. The fact that a railroad running through a coal section does most of its business in the hauling of coal does not make it any the less a commercial road such as is contemplated by the general statutes. The fact that passengers may rarely, if ever, pass over the line does not deprive it of its character as a railroad. The fact that it may run in a direction or through localities where passengers do not desire to go does not deprive it of its *status* as a railroad. The fact that its main business is freight business, and a business in bulk, does not make it the less a public use."

The evidence in the present case shows that defendant has failed in actual conduct to answer, in some respects, the description given of its anticipated activities. It does not perform any of the functions of an ordinary commercial railway, except in the matter of conveying freight from one industry to another situated on its line or lines. It does not transfer cars in the sense that commercial railroads do when they accept cars from a connecting line, and deliver on their own line, and return to the company from which they were received. It does no passenger business, nor does it issue any bills of lading in its freight business, but only orders to its trainmen showing where cars are to be taken up

or delivered. It does not participate in a division of
through rates with the railway companies it serves,
but exacts a fixed charge prescribed by ordinances of
the city; and its dealings are wholly with the railroads,
and are not at all with the shippers, except in conveying freight from one industry in the city to another.
But the court held in the cases referred to, to which the
State was a party, that athough the bulk of its business
was to consist "in the transfer of loaded and empty cars
from one railroad to another, and from the various industries to the several lines of road centering in the
city of Memphis and back again," it was nevertheless a
commercial railroad, because by its charter it was obligated to do a general railroad business both as to
freight and passengers, and that its charter rights
were not subject to forfeiture because of the nature of
the bulk of its business above referred to, and
that it might condemn property as a commercial railway. Whether that decision be sound
or not, it is bootless to inquire with a view
to the settlement of the present controversy.
Vested rights of a very important nature are
based on it, and are entitled to protection. Therefore,
whether we view the case from the standpoint of *res
adjudicata,* specially pleaded by the defendant, or on
the broader ground of the necessity of standing by decisions in respect of rights based on them, although
the decisions may have been originally erroneous (a
subject discussed at length in *Wilkins* v. *Railroad,* 110
Tenn., 422, 452-461, 75 S. W., 1026), so much of the bill

must be dismissed as is rested on the fact that the defendant transacts the bulk of its business in the manner already stated.

We are of the opinion, however, that a different result must be held to follow under a contract which the Union Railway Company entered into with the Iron Mountain Railroad Company of Memphis and the St. Louis, Iron Mountain & Southern Railway Company on October 1, 1909.

Under that contract the Union Railway Company leased from the two railroads mentioned their terminal facilities, consisting of sundry tracks in the city of Memphis, also a roundhouse, repair shops, a turntable, and freight and passenger depots. In return for the lease the Union Railway Company, in addition to keeping down certain fixed charges on the property, contracted to do the terminal business of the second named company, and also of an associated company, the St. Louis Southwestern Railroad Company. It agreed that it would provide and maintain a connection of its tracks with those of the Kansas City & Memphis Railway & Bridge Company, the bridge of which company had to be used by the St. Louis, Iron Mountain & Southern Railway Company to get into Memphis from the Arkansas side; that it would provide adequate terminal tracks, depots, or other facilities in the city of Memphis, and would perform all services that from time to time should be required during the full term of the contract to promptly and satisfactorily receive and forward the passenger and freight trains of the said rail-

way company, and of the St. Louis Southwestern Railroad Company handled by the first-mentioned company; that upon the delivery of the trains of the said
St. Louis, Iron Mountain & Southern Railway Company, called for brevity's sake in the contract the
Iron Mountain Company, within the city of Memphis
upon the tracks of the said Union Railway Company,
designated by it for receiving said trains, the latter
would promptly take possession thereof and switch
and deliver the cars therein to their respective destinations within the Memphis switching district, including the delivery of cars destined to connecting lines;
that it would promptly receive from connecting lines
cars destined for forwarding *via* the Iron Mountain
Company, or by the St. Louis Southwestern Railway
Company, and would classify and assemble said cars
into trains with such cars as might be made ready for
forwarding upon the tracks of the said Union Railway
Company, and those leased or operated by it; that the
cars should be assembled into trains in such manner
as the Iron Mountain Company should from time to
time direct; that when so assembled the trains should
be forwarded to a connection with the tracks of the
Kansas City & Memphis Railway & Bridge Company
with the locomotives and train crews of the Iron Mountain Company at such time and in such manner as the
Iron Mountain Company should direct; that it would
render any and all switching services required for the
prompt handling of cars to be loaded, unloaded, or repaired, received from or for the Irom Mountain Com-

pany as aforesaid; that it would maintain and operate the passenger depot facilities used at the time the contract was entered into by the Iron Mountain Company and the St. Louis Southwestern Railway Company until such time as these companies should for any cause desire to discontinue the use of the said passenger depot facilities; that the Union Railway Company would furnish all employees required in or about said passenger depot, except the ticket agent, both of the St. Louis Southwestern Railway Company, and of the Iron Mountain Company, assuming full and complete liability for the acts, neglect, and defaults of employees furnished as aforesaid; that it would maintain the freight depots and tracks of the Iron Mountain Railroad Company of Memphis, called for short in the contract the Memphis Company, occupied and used at the time the contract was entered into by the Iron Mountain Company and by the St. Louis Southwestern Railway Company, and would from time to time during the term of the agreement extend and improve said facilities to such extent as might be required to promptly and satisfactorily handle the freight business of the Iron Mountain Company and of the St. Louis Southwestern Railway Company that it would employ a joint agent and sufficient force of joint employees to conduct the business of the parties to the contract at the said freight depots, and to satisfactorily handle the freight business of the Iron Mountain Company, to perform all station work, including the receipt, checking, weighing, billing, loading, transferring, unloading, de-

livery of, and collection of charges upon all freight
of the Iron Mountain Company; that such joint agent
and other employees should at all times be persons satisfactory to the Iron Mountain Company; that, if such
joint agent or other joint employees were not satisfactory to the Iron Mountain Company, he or they
should, upon written request, be removed, and other
persons acceptable to the Iron Mountain Company be
engaged in their stead by the Union Company; that
such joint agent and all other joint employees should,
in respect of the business done for each company, "be
subject to the rules, regulations, control, and requirements of each of the parties hereto," the same as if
employed solely by such party; that the Iron Mountain Company should furnish to the said joint agent
sufficient of its own printed forms and stationery with
which to transact its business, and should be reim-
bursed monthly by the Union Railway Company for
the cost thereof; that such joint agent and other employees should at all times transact the business of the
parties to the contract impartially, showing or giving
no preference to either party as against the other; that
the said joint agent and all other joint employees, so
far as the custody of any moneys and revenues might
be concerned, should be considered the sole and separate agent and employees of the company for which he
or they should receive or handle such moneys and revenue, and that neither party should be liable to the other party to the contract through the handling of
moneys of the other party by such joint agent or other

joint employees; that, in case of default, theft, or loss of money through the negligence of such joint agent or other joint employee, the amount of cash on hand at the time of such defalcation, theft, or loss should, on investigation being made to determine the amount be apportioned between the parties to the contract on the basis of the amount due each company, such amount to be determined by the audit of the parties of the accounts of such joint agent and other joint employees; that the Union Railway Company should assume full and complete liability for the acts, neglects, or defaults of such joint agent and other joint employees in respect of the freight business of both parties to the contract, that is, of the Iron Mountain Company, and of the St. Louis Southwestern Railway Company, except as to the loss of money; that the Union Railway Company should carry fire insurance in such amounts as the Iron Mountain Company should from time to time direct upon freight while in the possession of said Union Railway Company, received for or from the Iron Mountain Company, such insurance being placed with insurance companies approved by the Iron Mountain Company, and covering freight loaded in cars or wherever located upon property owned, leased, or operated by the Union Railway Company; that it would promptly remit to the treasurer of the Iron Mountain Company all moneys received by it from the collection of Iron Mountain storage charges, car demurrage charges, and from whatsoever source received for account of revenue earned by or apportionable to the

Iron Mountain Company; that all records and accounts of the Union Railway Company affecting the business of the Iron Mountain Company to be done under the contract should be kept as directed by the Iron Mountain Company, and subject to inspection by the officers of the Iron Mountain Company at all times.

The contract further required that the Union Railway Company should provide and maintain facilities equal to those used at the making of the contract by the Iron Mountain Company for cleaning and storing Iron Mountain locomotives, including those of the St. Louis Southwestern Railway Company when received with their trains by the Union Railway Company; that it should make running repairs to locomotives, equip them with supplies, and deliver them, attached to trains ready for forwarding, to the employees of the Iron Mountain Company, or to those of the St. Louis Southwestern Railway Company, as the case might be, and would also make running repairs to other locomotives of the Iron Mountain Company when requested by that company to do so; that it would store, clean, and furnish supplies to passenger coaches and equipment of the Iron Mountain Company and the St. Louis Southwestern Railway Company; that it would carefully inspect the trains received from the Iron Mountain Company and the St. Louis Southwestern Railway Company, and would, when ready for forwarding, deliver the cars therein to said companies in the same condition of repair as when received, or properly carded under the rules of the Master Car Builders' Association,

for defects or damages sustained while in the possession of the Union Railway Company; that cars received from the Iron Mountain Company requiring repairs preparatory to loading, or to make them safe for
forwarding, should be so repaired by the Union Railway Company; that cars destined to connections should
be delivered in the same condition of repair as received
by the said Union Railway Company, or if such cars
when received should require repairs under Master
Car Builders' Association rules, or local rules effective at Memphis, before connections could be required
to receive them, such repairs should be promptly made
by the Union Railway Company; that the said latter
company would carefully inspect cars from connecting
lines destined for forwarding *via* the Iron Mountain
Company, and would receive or reject them under
Master Car Builders' Association rules, or local rules
in effect at Memphis; that such cars as it should be required to receive under said rules which were unsafe to
be forwarded should be transferred or repaired by the
said Union Railway Company; that the repairs of cars
made by the latter company which were chargeable under the rules of the Master Car Builders' Association
to the owners of the cars should be made at the expense of the owners, and the Union Railway Company
should collect such charges from the owners; that
proper bills for repairs chargeable to the Iron Mountain Company should be presented to that company for
payment.

It was further agreed that the Union Railway Company should set apart exclusively for the business of the Iron Mountain Company, and of the St. Louis Southwestern Railway Company, as directed by the Iron Mountain Company, all of the lands, tracks, buildings, and terminal facilities of the Memphis Company in the city of Memphis (the Memphis Company as stated, being the Iron Mountain Railroad Company of Memphis), except such lands, buildings, tracks, or portions of them as the Union Railway Company might desire to use in receiving cars from connecting lines for forwarding, and for, or in connection with, the handling of traffic, originating upon, or destined for delivery upon, the tracks of the Union Railway Company, or upon industrial tracks connecting therewith.

In consideration of these obligations so entered into on the part of the Union Railway Company and others specified in the contract, but not mentioned in this opinion, the Iron Mountain Company agreed that upon execution of the contract it would surrender the use and operation of the said terminal facilities.

It should be stated that the Iron Mountain Railway Company of Memphis, called the Memphis Company, as stated, owned the terminal facilities, but, under an arrangement between that company and the Iron Mountain Company, the latter had the right to operate these terminals, and had sublet certain passenger and freight depot facilities of the Memphis Company to the said St. Louis Southwestern Railway Company, and had agreed to transport its freight cars between

Memphis and Fair Oaks, Ark., and perform the necessary switching services at Memphis. The passenger
trains of the St. Louis Southwestern Railway Company
are also handled between Memphis and Fair Oaks over
the Iron Mountain Company's tracks by St. Louis
Southwestern Railway Company's locomotives and
crews. These two companies had no tracks of their
own in the city of Memphis, or in the State of Tennessee. Their lines terminated in Arkansas, but connected with the tracks of the bridge company across
the Mississippi river, and these with the tracks of the
Memphis Company. These two companies, it thus
appears, were wholly dependent for their terminal operations on the trackage and terminal facilities of the
Memphis Company, which, as stated, were under the
control of the Iron Mountain Company.

It was agreed that the Iron Mountain Company
would, during the full term of the contract, deliver to
the Union Railway Company all of its freight trains
destined to the city of Memphis upon the tracks of
the Union Railway Company designated by it for receiving such trains, and would, with its motive power,
train crews, and enginemen, and at its sole expense of
operation, transport said trains over tracks owned,
leased, or operated by the Union Railway Company to
such point within the city of Memphis; that it would,
during the full term of the contract promptly receive
all of its freight trains originating at Memphis destined to its line from the Union Railway Company at
such points within the city of Memphis as the latter

might from time to time designate, and would transport the same, with its motive power, train crews, and enginemen, at its sole expense of operation over the tracks owned, leased or operated by the Union Railway Company to a connection with the tracks of the bridge company within the city of Memphis, provided that the expense to the Iron Mountain Company of transporting such trains from the points assembled to a connection with the tracks of the bridge company should not exceed the expense heretofore incurred by the Iron Mountain Company in transporting said trains between Calhoun avenue and the said connection; that it would, during the full term of the contract, or until it should have given reasonabe notice of its desire to otherwise arrange, deliver to, and receive from the Union Railway Company its passenger trains and those of the St. Louis Southwestern Railway Company at the point where the passenger station was located at the time of the contract.

It was further provided that the Union Railway Company should have exclusive management and control of the property of the Memphis Company during the life of the contract. The contract also contained this provision:

"In delivering its trains to the Union Railway Company as herein provided, notwithstanding that the enginemen and trainmen are paid by the Iron Mountain Company, said enginemen and trainmen shall, while on its tracks, be considered the employees of the Union Railway Company, and subject to its rules, regulations, and directions. If said enginemen and trainmen shall refuse or fail to obey instructions given by proper officers of the Union Railway Company, or disregard its rules, regulations, or directions, they shall be disciplined by the Union Railway Company, and a proper officer of the Iron Mountain Company shall be duly notified thereof.

"Said Union Railway Company shall defend and save harmless said Iron Mountain Company and said Memphis Company from all claims and demands, suits, and causes of action for damages on account of injuries to or death of persons, loss of and damage to property caused by the operation of engines, trains, and cars of the Iron Mountain Company, and the equipment of other companies delivered to said Union Railway Company by said Iron Mountain Company, and said Union Railway Company shall also pay said Iron Mountain Company all damages done to its engines, trains, and cars, and to the equipment of other companies delivered by the Iron Mountain Company to the Union Railway Company."

It was further provided that the Iron Mountain Company should direct the time and manner of the loading, moving, and disposition of all cars handled by the Union Railway Company for account of the Iron Mountain Company, in the same manner as if said cars were upon the rails of the Iron Mountain Company.

We are of the opinion that nearly all of the duties thus assumed by the Union Railway Company are such as fall within any definition of the functions of a terminal company, and that many of them are such as do not pertain to the duties of a commercial railway. Some of them certainly go far beyond the very comprehensive construction given to the charter of the Union Railway Company in the cases of *State ex rel. Wellford* v. *Union Railway Co.*, and *Collier* v. *Union Railway Co.*, supra.

In the case of *United States* v. *Terminal R. R. Association of St. Louis*, 224 U. S., 383, 402, 32 Sup. Ct., 507, 512, 56 L. Ed., 810, 816, 817, we find a definition of terminal companies as distinguished from railroad transportation companies.

Speaking through Mr. Justice Lurton, the court said:

"We are not unmindful of the essential difference between terminal systems properly so described and railroad transportation companies. The first are instrumentalities which assist the latter in the transfer of traffic between different lines, and in the collection and distribution of traffic. They are a modern evolution in the doing of railroad business, and are of the greatest public utility."

Referring to a litigation in Missouri that has been instituted for the purpose of dissolving a combination between two terminal companies, the court further said:

"For the purpose of enforcing this Missouri prohibition the State instituted a proceeding to dissolve the combination of the properties of the Merchants'

Bridge Terminal Railroad Company with the Terminal Railroad Association of St. Louis, upon the ground that the railroads operated by those companies were parallel and competing lines of railroad. Relief was denied. The Missouri court held that the merger of mere railway terminals used to facilitate the public convenience by the transfer of cars from one line of railway to another, and instrumentalities for the distribution or gathering of traffic, freight or passenger, among scattered industries, or to different business centers of a great city, were not properly railroad companies within the reasonable meaning of the statutes forbidding combinations between competing or parallel lines of railroad. Referring to the legitimate use of terminal companies, the Missouri court said:

" 'A more effectual means of keeping competition up to the highest point between parallel or competing lines could not be devised. The destruction of the system would result in compelling the shipper to employ the railroad with which he has switching connection, or else cart his product to a distant part of the city, at a cost possibly as great as the railroad tariff.

" 'St. Louis is a city of great magnitude in the extent of its area, its population, and its manufacturing and other business. A very large number of trunk line railroads converge in this city. In the brief of one of the well informed counsel in this case it is said that St. Louis is one of the largest railroad centers in the world. Suppose it were required of every railroad company to effect its entrance to the city as best it could and establish its own terminal facilities; we would have a large number of passenger stations, freight depots, and switching yards scattered all over the vast area and innumerable vehicles employed in hauling passengers and freight to and from those stations and depots. Or suppose it became necessary, in the exigency of commerce, that all incoming trains should reach a common focus, but every railroad company provide its own track; then not only would the expense of obtaining the necessary rights of way be so enormous as to amount to the exclusion of all but a few of the strongest roads, but, if it could be accomplished, the city would be cut to pieces with the many lines of railroad intersecting it in every direction, and thus the greatest agency of commerce would become the greatest burden.' [*State* v. *Terminal R. R. Ass'n*] 182 Mo. 284, 299, 81 S. W., 395.

"Among the cases in which the public utility of such companies has been recognized are *Bridwell* v. *Gate City Terminal Co.*, 127 Ga., 520, 56 S. E., 624, 10 L. R. A. (N. S.) 909; *Indianapolis Union R. Co.* v. *Cooper*, 6 Ind. App., 202, 33 N. E., 219; *State ex rel. Little* v. *Martin*, 51 Kan., 462, 33 Pac., 9; *Worcester* v. *Norwich & W. R. Co.*, 109 Mass., 103; *Fort Street Union Depot Co.* v. *Morton*, 83 Mich., 265, 47 N. W., 228; *State* v. *St. Paul Union Depot Co.*, 42 Minn., 142, 43 N. W., 840, 6 L. R. A., 234; *Ryan* v. *Louisville & N. Terminal Co.*, 102 Tenn., 124, 50 S. W., 744, 45 L. R. A., 303."

The court was considering in *United States* v. *Terminal Railroad Association of St. Louis* the question whether a combination of the several railroad terminal companies in St. Louis was a violation of the Sherman anti-trust law; but the observations made in the course of the opinion upon the nature and character of railway terminal companies which we have quoted are very useful as showing the views of the highest court of the land upon this important subject. Other cases which are in strict accord as to the nature and character of these companies as they are described in the opinions of the courts are as follows: *Dean* v. *St. Paul Union Depot Co.,* 41 Minn., 360, 43 N. W., 54, 5 L. R. A., 442, 16 Am. St. Rep., 703; *Brady* v. *Chicago Great Western Railway Co.* 114 Fed., 100, 52 C. C. A., 48, 57 L. R. A., 712, 717, 718; *Floody* v. *Great Northern Railway Co.,* 102 Minn., 81, 112 N. W., 875, 1081, 13 L. R. A. (N. S.), 1196; *Belt Railway Co. of Chicago* v. *United States of America,* 168 Fed., 542, 93 C. C. A., 666, 22 L. R. A. (N. S.), 582; *Union Depot & Railway Co.* v. *Londoner,* 50 Colo., 22, 114 Pac., 316, 33 L. R. A. (N. S.) 433;*Hunt* v. *New York, New Haven & Hartford Railway Co.,* 212 Mass., 102, 98 N. E., 787, 40 L. R. A. (N. S.), 778, and notes.

Such companies have not only the right of eminent domain, as laid down in our own case of *Ryan* v. *Louisville & N. Terminal Co.,* supra, but can also be compelled by *mandamus* to observe an order of the railroad commission to admit another railroad to its privileges pursuant to the order of such commission prescribing terms. 26 Cyc. 375, and notes.

The fact that commercial railway companies necessarily, under through routings, deliver the cars of other railroad companies on their own terminals to the destinations of such cars thereon, which duty is likewise imposed by the charter of such companies in this State, should not be confounded with the more complicated terminal duties of railway terminal companies which act as go-betweens or intermediaries between the numerous railroads with which they are in physical contact.

We have in this State a form of charter for railway terminal companies, passed by the Legislature in the year 1893. Its terms are meager but are sufficiently broad and general to cover the duties which companies of this character are designed to serve in modern business.

That charter provides:

"Said corporation shall have the power to acquire, in this or any other State or States, and at such place or places as shall be found expedient, such real estate as may be necessary on which to construct, operate, and maintain passenger stations, comprising passenger depots, office buildings, sheds and storage yards and freight stations, comprising freight depots, warehouses, offices and freight yards, roundhouses and machine shops; also main and side tracks, switches and cross-overs, turnouts, and other terminal railroad facilities, appurtenances and accommodations suitable in size, location, and manner of construction, to perform promptly and efficiently the work of receiving, delivering and transferring all passenger and freight traffic of railroad companies, with which it may enter into contracts for the use of its terminal facilities at such place or places. Said corporation shall have the power, by purchase, lease, or assignment of lease, to acquire and hold, and to lease to others, such real estate as may be necessary for the above-mentioned purpose of its incorporation; and it may also acquire such real estate by condemnation in pursuance of the general law authorizing the condemnation of private property for works of internal improvement, as set forth in sections 1844-1867, inclusive.''   Shannon's Code, section 2430.

The next section provides:

''Whenever it may be necessary, in order to enable said corporation to acquire and construct proper railroad terminal facilities in any town or city, or to connect such facilities with the tracks of any railroad company with whom said corporation may have contracted to furnish such facilities, said corporation, with the consent of the proper authorities of such town or city, shall have the right to lay and operate a track or tracks across or along or over or under such of the streets or alleys of such town or city as may be necessary for that purpose, and said corporation may also, with such consent, construct such passenger or freight depots or stations across or along, over or under, any such street or alley when it shall be necessary in order to furnish proper railroad facilities in said town or city. But no street or alley of any town or city shall be obstructed or interfered with until the consent of the proper authorities of said town or city shall have been first obtained.''

It is perceived from the description we have given by quotations from our statutes, and from the decisions of courts, there can be no doubt that under the contract which the Union Railway Company entered into with the Iron Mountain Company and other companies in that interest, in the year 1909, it is doing the business of a terminal railway company, and as such it is liable for the privilege taxes assessed against such companies by the State and Shelby county for the years 1909, 1910, and 1911. It has been held that, where a commercial railway company superadds to duties required of it by its charter other forms of business, it must pay the privilege tax therefor. It was so held in the case of *Memphis & Little Rock Railroad Co.* v. *State of Tennessee*, 9 Lea (77 Tenn.), 218, 42 Am. Rep., 673, in which case it appeared that the railway company had added to its ordinary business that of an express company.

The result is that the decree of the chancellor, in so far as it held the defendant liable for privilege taxes prior to the year 1909, must be reversed but, as to the taxes for the subsequent years, it is affirmed.

The costs of this proceeding will be divided in the following proportions: One-fourth to be paid by the State of Tennessee, one-fourth by Shelby county, and one-half by the defendant.

INDEX.

ABATEMENT AND REVIVAL.

Death of party. Revival. Necessary parties. "Leasehold."
Under Shannon's Code, sec. 511, "leaseholds" are interests in land descending to the heirs at law and hence where a lessee died pending an action of unlawful detainer by the lessor, the heirs at law of the lessee are necessary parties upon the revival. *Matthews* v. *Crofford*, 541.

, ACTIONS—RIGHT AND CAUSE.

1. *Master and servant. Actions for wrongful discharge. Nature and form.*
   Where a contract of employment for one year at an annual salary of $1500, but payable in monthly installments of $125, was breached by the employer, the remedy of the employee was an action for damages for the breach, and not for salary for the period after the discharge, since readiness of the employee to perform after discharge is not equivalent to performance, and such a contract is to be treated on breach as an entire and individual one, for the breach of which only one action will lie. *Menihan* v. *Hopkins*, 24.

2. *Receivers. Foreign receivers. Permission to sue.*
   While a receiver, at least an ordinary chancery receiver, has no legal right to sue in a state other than that of his appointment, the privilege of doing so will be accorded, as a matter of comity; the suit being neither inimical to the interest of local creditors, or of anyone who has acquired rights under a local statute, nor in contravention of the policy of the forum. *Hardee* v. *Wilson*, 511.

3. *Landlord and tenant. Nonpayment of rent. Forfeiture.*
   Where a tenant, against whom judgment for possession because of nonpayment of an installment rent, was rendered in unlawful detainer proceedings, begun in justice court, removed the proceedings to the circuit court, giving the *supersedeas* bond for the value of the rent of the premises during the litigation required by Shannon's Code, sec. 5111, it was unnecessary to institute successive actions to enforce the forfeiture for non-

ACTS CITED AND CONSTRUED.

ACTION—RIGHT AND CAUSE—Continued.

payment of each installment of rent as it fell due, for the single *supersedeas* bond covered the whole contract. *Matthews v. Crofford*, 541.

4. *Malicious prosecution. Element of suit. Termination of original case.*

In order to maintain a suit for malicious prosecution, plaintiff must allege and prove that the original prosecution has terminated in his favor. *Scheibler v. Steinburg*, 614.

5. *Malicious prosecution. Termination of original proceeding. Nolle prosequi.*

The entry of a *nolle prosequi* without procurement of the defendant is such a termination of the criminal prosecution in defendant's favor as to sustain a suit by him for malicious prosecution, though the suit for malicious prosecution is brought on the day following entry of the *nolle prosequi*, while the court had power to set the *nolle prosequi* aside, since the court, in an action for malicious prosecution, could look no further than the final judgment to determine whether the prosecution had terminated in favor of the defendant therein. *Ib.*

ACTS CITED AND CONSTRUED.

1901, ch. 141, sec. 1. Insurance. Fire insurance. Nonpayment of premiums. Penalties. Demand for payment. *Insurance Co. v. Kirkpatrick*, 55.

1901, ch. 141, sec. 1. Insurance. Fire insurance. Payment of loss. Demand. *Ib.*

1901, ch. 141, sec. 1. Insurance. Fire insurance. Nonpayment of loss. Penalties. *Ib.*

1901, ch. 141, sec. 1. Insurance. Penal statute. Strict construction. *Ib.*

1901, ch. 141, sec. 1. Insurance. Fire insurance. Nonpayment of loss. Penalty. *Ib.*

1899, ch. 94, sec. 120. Principal and surety. Discharge of surety. Reservation of rights against surety. Statutory provision. *Dies v. Bank*, 89.

1905, ch. 31. Replevin. Judgment. *Keelin v. Graves*, 103.

1913, ch. 1, sec. 5. Commerce. Interstate commerce. State regulations. Validity. *Palmer v. Express Co.*, 116.

1913, ch. 1, sec. 9. Commerce. Interstate commerce. State regulations. Validity. *Ib.*

1913, ch. 1. Statutes. Title. Constitutional provisions. *Ib.*

1913, ch. 1. Statutes. Title. Constitutional provisions. *Ib.*

ACTS CITED AND CONSTRUED.

ACTS CITED AND CONSTRUED—Continued.

1897, ch. 10, secs. 15, 17. Carriers. Freight. Common-law duties. Discrimination. *Lumber Co. v. Railroad*, 163.

1871, ch. 54, secs. 1, 9. Corporations and organization. Statutes. *State, ex rel., v. Vanberbilt University*, 279.

1871, ch. 54. Corporations. Incorporators. Conferences. *Ib.*

1871, ch. 54. Colleges and universities. Incorporation. Charter. *Ib.*

1857-58, ch. 32. Colleges and universities. Governing boards. Officers. Visitation. Supervision. *Ib.*

1895, ch. 6. Statutes. Subjects and titles. Statute relating to corporations. *Ib.*

1895, ch. 6. Colleges and universities. Officers and governing boards. Statutes. "Patron." *Ib.*

1895, ch. 6. Colleges and universities. Officers and governing boards. Statutes. *Ib.*

1829, ch. 23, 1871, ch. 56. Rape. Assault with intent to rape. Female under age of consent. Statutory provisions. *State, ex rel., v. Rimmer*, 383.

1871, ch. 56, 1893, ch. 129. Rape. Statutory rape. Repeal. *State, ex rel., v. Rimmer*, 383.

1891, ch. 22. Costs. In criminal prosecutions. Liability of State. *Woolen v. State, ex rel., Portis*, 455.

1891, ch. 123. Costs. In criminal prosecutions. Liability of State. *Ib.*

1911, ch. 29. Appeal and error. Review. Amount of damages. *Grant v. Railroad*, 398.

1875, ch. 83, 1891, ch. 123. Constitutional law. Costs. Jury. Escape of prisoners. Working out costs of recapture. Due process of law. *Strong v. State*, 472.

1881, ch. 58, 1883, ch. 105, 1907, ch. 602. Taxation. Exemptions. "Educational institution." Property used for educational purposes. *Ward Seminary v. City Council*, 412.

1907, ch. 82. Supersedeas. Jurisdiction. Supreme Court. *Walker v. Lemma*, 444.

1913, ch. 2. Intoxicating liquors. Nuisance. Injunction. Violation. Erroneous injunction. *State v. Ragghianti*, 560.

1897, ch. 78. Master and servant. Wages. Liens and preferences. Enforcement. *Drug Co. v. Stone*, 608.

1913 (2d Ex. Sess.), ch. 1. Criminal law. Appeal and error. Review. Harmless error. Sentence. *State v. Green*, 619.

1899, ch. 39. Justices of the peace. Execution. Lien. Creation. *Supply Co. v. Fowlkes*, 663.

1891, ch. 98, secs. 2, 3. Railroads. Liens for labor. Suit to enforce. Bill. Sufficiency. *Williams v. Railroad Co.*, 680.

AGENCY—ALLEGATIONS.

AGENCY.

1. *Principal and agent. Unauthorized execution of note by agent. Liability of principal.*

Where an agent, with authority to make sales and collect the price, but without authority to borrow money, was a defaulter, and then borrowed money and executed a note therefor in his principal's name, and remitted out of the loan a sum less than the amount of the defalcation, the principal, receiving the remittance as one on sales, was not liable on the note, under the equitable doctrine that, where a principal obtains the benefit of a loan procured by his agent without authority, he ratifies the same and makes himself liable to the lender. *Calhoun* v. *Realty Co.,* 651.

2. *Telegraphs and telephones. Messages. Delivery agent.*

A telegram cannot be delivered to any one but the addressee, unless he has appointed an agent to receive it, or there is a custom warranting delivery to another. *Telegraph Co.* v. *Franklin,* 656.

3. *Telegraphs and telephones. Nondelivery of messages. Actions. Defenses.*

Where the addressee of a death message had an agent who was to bring it to her from the place of address, and the telegraph company's messenger failed to make inquiry or to offer the message for delivery at the place of address, the company cannot escape liability for nondelivery on the theory that the addressee's agent might not have performed her duty, or might not have been at the place of address when the inquiries were made. *Ib.*

ALLEGATIONS.

1. *Pleading. Allegation of time. Pleading and proof.*

Not only may plaintiff allege that the personal injury for which she sues was inflicted "on or about" a certain day, but, being unable to do so, she may not be required to allege the date with greater particularity, and may recover on her testimony that the accident occurred in the month alleged, and to the best of her recollection on the day alleged. *May* v. *Railroad,* 521.

2. *Nuisance. Injunction. Violation. Erroneous injunction.*

That a bill for an injunction against the maintenance of a nuisance brought in the name of the State did not allege that the State sustained any special injuries by reason of the nuisance was immaterial in a proceeding to punish a violation

ANIMALS—APPEAL AND ERROR.

ALLEGATIONS—Continued.

of the injunction as a contempt even if such an allegation was necessary. *State* v. *Ragghianti*, 560.

3. *Injunction. Violations. Proceedings to punish. Petition for attachment.*

Where defendant answered a petition for an attachment for contempt in violating an injunction by alleging various matters of excuse and avoidance, he could not attack the petition on appeal on account of its general averments and lack of specific allegations. *Ib.*

ANIMALS.

1. *Injuries to persons. Liability.*

The owner of premises who permits another to harbor thereon dogs which the owner knows are vicious, is liable for injuries inflicted by the dogs upon another. *Missio* v. *Williams*, 504.

2. *Injuries to persons. Liability. Knowledge of vicious character.*

The owner or keeper of a domestic animal is not liable for injuries inflicted by the animal, unless he has knowledge of its vicious habits; but, where he has such knowledge his liability is not limited to negligence in the custody of the animal, but he is bound to keep the animal from doing mischief. *Ib.*

3. *Personal injuries. Liability. Knowledge of vicious character.*

Knowledge by the owner or keeper of a dog that it is vicious is sufficient to render him liable for injuries inflicted by the dog, without a showing that it had ever before bitten any person. *Ib.*

APPEAL AND ERROR.

1. *Master and servant. Injuries to servant. Request to charge.*

Where plaintiff was injured by the breaking of a defective ladder, and defendant claimed that the ladder was a simple tool the defective character of which was a risk that plaintiff assumed, it was error to refuse requests submitting the doctrine of simple tools. *Roofing & Mfg. Co.* v. *Black*, 30.

2. *Review. Question reviewable.*

Only those matters assigned in the motion for new trial can be reviewed on appeal. *Matthews* v. *Crofford*, 541.

3. *Harmless error. Admission of evidence.*

Where, in an action on a fire policy, there was no evidence that insured had knowingly made a false statement of the

APPRAISEMENT—ARBITRATION.

APPEAL AND ERROR—Continued.

value of the property destroyed, except in so far as the proof related to his supposed knowledge of another machine of substantially the kind destroyed by fire, but there was no evidence that he had any such knowledge at the time of making the proof, the error in permitting complainant to testify that insurer did not, up to the filing of its crossbill, state to him that a knowingly false proof of loss had been made to defraud insurer, was not prejudicial to insurer, and must be disregarded, as required by Acts 1911, ch. 32. *Compress Co.* v. *Insurance Co.*, 586.

4. *Criminal law. Trial. Assessment of punishment.*
Const., art. 6, sec. 14, providing that no fine shall be laid in excess of $50 unless assessed by the jury, requires the assessment by the jury of the fine for an offense finable in excess of $50 at discretion, if it merits more than that amount, and it was error for the court to assess the fine for transporting intoxicating liquor in violation of Acts 1913 (2d Ex. Sess.), ch. 1, imposing a fine of $100 to $500 therefor. *State* v. *Greene*, 619.

5. *Review. Harmless error. Sentence.*
Error in the court's assessing the fine for transporting intoxicating liquor in violation of Acts 1913 (2d Ex. Sess.), ch. 1, imposing a fine of $100 to $500 therefor, instead of submitting its amount to the jury, as required by Const. art. 6, sec. 14, was harmless, where the fine was made $100, as it could not be made less. *Ib.*

APPRAISEMENT.

1. *Insurance. Adjustment of loss. Appraisal.*
An insurer was not entitled to demand an appraisement, to determine the loss under a policy providing for such an appraisement in case of disagreement, where it made no objections to the proofs of loss submitted, or any effort to agree on the amount thereof, but its whole attitude was a denial of all liability. *Harowitz* v. *Fire Ins. Co.*, 691.

2. *Insurance. Adjustment of Loss. Appraisal.*
An insurer's demand for an appraisement of the loss was a concession of its liability for some amount. *Ib.*

ARBITRATION.

Appeal and error. Harmless error. Instructions.
Where, in an action a fire policy stipulating that it should be void if insured concealed any material fact, or in case of any

ATTACHMENT.

ARBITRATION—Continued.

fraud touching any matter relating to the insurance before
or after a loss, it appeared that insurer agreed to arbitration,
but subsequently withdrew therefrom, whereupon insured
brought the action on the policy, the refusal to charge that
insurer could withdraw from the arbitration whenever it saw
fit to do so without giving any reason therefor, which withdrawal did not prejudice its rights under the policy either to
contest the amount of the loss or to question the good faith
of insured in making proof of loss, was not prejudicial to the
insurer, where it was allowed to introduce such evidence as
it had on the question of the good faith of insured in making
proof of loss and submitting the issue to the jury. *Compress
Co.* v. *Insurance Co.*, 586.

ATTACHMENT.

1. *Necessary parties. Attachment of mortgaged property.*

A creditor attaching the property of a nonresident debtor under
Shannon's Code, sec. 5211, must, where the legal title is in a
mortgagee, make the mortgagee a party defendant; for otherwise the mortgagee may assert his rights and cut off the
attachment by foreclosure, and the property, if sold under the
attachment, will not bring a fair price. *King* v. *Patterson*, 1.

2. *Proceeding. Amendment.*

Where numerous creditors of a nonresident debtor were striving for priority by attachments on his property, complainants,
who did not join as a party the mortgagee of land which
they attached, are not entitled to permission to amend their
bill so as to correct the defect; defendants having already
acquired valid attachment liens thereon, having made the
mortgagee a party. *Ib.*

3. *Grounds. Nonresidence.*

One may be a temporary nonresident of the state, so as to
authorize an attachment, though his domicile is still in the
State. *Keelin* v. *Graves*, 103.

4. *Grounds. Nonresidence.*

In an action to replevy goods, attached by defendant on the
ground that plaintiff was a nonresident, the court instructed
that the plaintiff went to North Carolina to engage in business, with no definite idea as to when he would return, to
make that state his residence, or if, after he got there, he
determined to make it his residence, and actually resided
there when the attachment was levied, he would be a non-

AUTOMOBILES.

ATTACHMENT—Continued.

resident, though he might not have carried his family with
him, but if he went on a visit, with the intention of returning
when his visit was out, he would not be a nonresident, and
that if plaintiff left Tennessee with the intention of obtaining employment, and did so without any definite idea of returning to that state, and found such employment, he was
thereafter a nonresident. *Held* that, while the instruction
did not refer to domicile and involved only the idea of nonresidence, it was substantially correct on the question of
change of domicible. *Keelin* v. *Graves*, 103.

5. *Master and servant. Wages. Liens and preferences. Enforcement.*
A petition for the establishment of the preferred lien for employees' wages given by Acts 1897, ch, 78, as amended by
Acts 1905, ch. 414, was properly denied where it merely described the property, which was in the hands of a receiver
appointed by the court, as the drug business at the corner
of C. and M. avenues in M., particularly as there were prior
liens on part of the property, as it should have described the
property specifically, with a statement of the nature of the
lien, or an attachment should have been issued and levied.
Drug Co. v. *Stone*, 608.

6. *Railroads. Liens for labor. Suit to enforce. Bill. Description. Definiteness.*
A bill to enforce a lien for railroad construction work must,
in the absence of an attachment, describe the property on
which it is sought to enforce the lien with sufficient definiteness to identify it and segregate it. *Williams* v. *Railroad Co.*,
680.

AUTOMOBILES.

1. *Master and servant. Negligence of chauffeur. Joint liability.*
Where a brother and sister jointly own an automobile, each
paying one-half of all expenses, including the wages of the
chauffeur jointly employed, and with an equal right to the
use of the machine, with the exception that the brother had
a preference in being taken to and from work, the sister is
liable for injuries sustained in a collision with a buggy while
the chauffeur, alone in the machine, was racing with another
machine on his way to take the brother home from work.
Goodman v. *Wilson*, 464.

BAIL—BILLS AND NOTES.

AUTOMOBILES—Continued.

2. *Negligence. Dangerous instrumentalities.*

An automobile is not such a dangerous machine as would require it to be put in the category with the locomotive, dangerous animals, explosives, and the like, so as to render the owner liable from its use. *Ib.*

BAIL.

Liability of surety.

Sureties upon a bail bond conditioned that accused should not depart without leave of court are not liable where, after conviction and sentence which provided for incarceration in the county jail pending the coming of proper authorities to carry accused to the penitentiary, and sheriff improperly allowed accused to go without custody for a few days, and he escaped, for, the sureties having delivered accused into the custody of the court, there was no further liability on the recognizance. *Suggs* v *.State*, 498.

BILLS AND NOTES.

1. *Principal and surety. Discharge of surety. Taking additional surety. Note of principal debtor.*

The sureties on a note, which expressly stipulated that they should not be discharged by an extension of time granted to the principal, are not released by the acceptance by the payee of an additional note from the principal debtor payable at a later date, not as a renewal of the former note, but as an additional evidence of the debt. *Dies* v. *Bank*, 89.

2. *Discharge of surety. Reservation of rights against surety. Statutory provision.*

The Negotiable Instruments Act (Acts 1899, ch. 94, sec. 120, subsection 6), providing that a surety is not discharged by the taking of a renewal note from the principal extending the time of payment, where the extension is given under an express reservation of the right of recovery against the surety, applies where the original note is retained in possession by the payee, and the right of action thereon against the surety is thereby reserved. *Ib.*

3. *Novation. Burden of proof.*

The burden of proving novation of a note by a later note is upon him who asserts it. *Ib.*

BILLS AND NOTES.

BILLS AND NOTES—Continued.

4. *Payment. New note. Presumption. Express agreement.*
Where a new note is given to represent the original consideration and the old note is retained, while it is presumed that
the old note is extinguished by the later one, an express agreement by the parties as to the payment or nonpayment of the
old note will control. *Dies* v. *Bank*, 89.

5. *Collateral securities. Notes representing the same debt.*
Two notes representing the same debt may be outstanding at
the same time, the one as collateral to the other, and either
the original or the renewal note may be held as collateral to
the other. *Ib.*

6. *Collateral security. Notes of same maker.*
While the maker of a note, which was signed by two others as
securities, cannot pledge the note as collateral for a note
executed by himself alone and evidencing the same debt,
since that note is a liability of his and not an asset which
may be a subject of pledge, that rule does not prevent the
payee of the secured note from holding it as collateral for the
second note. *Ib.*

7. *Judgment. Separate notes for same debt. Collateral satisfaction.*
In such a case the creditor can make but a single proof against
the debtor and have but one satisfaction. *Ib.*

8. *Collateral security. Notes of the same maker. Different debts.*
The fact that the subsequent note included other indebtedness,
or a new one in addition to that represented by the old note,
does not affect the rule. *Ib.*

9. *Principal and surety. Discharge. Note held as collateral. Part
payment of principal note.*
Where the payee of a note, signed by a principal and two
sureties, accepted another note from the principal representing the same and additional indebtedness, under the express
agreement that the old note was to be retained as collateral
for the new, the proceeds of property mortgaged as security
for the new note, which were applied to the payment of the
debt represented thereby, released *pro tanto* the sureties on
the old note. *Ib.*

10. *Sales. Conditional sales. Recovery of property. Right to sue.*
Where reservation of title to property conditionally sold was
contained in the contract, and not in the notes for the unpaid
price, the seller, though having indorsed the notes, was still

BONDS—CARNAL KNOWLEDGE.

BILLS AND NOTES—Continued.

entitled to enforce the condition and recover the property in replevin; he being interested as indorser in securing satisfaction of the notes to the holder out of the proceeds of the sale. *Automobile Co.* v. *Bicknell*, 493.

11. *Principal and agent. Unauthorized execution of note by agent. Liability of principal.*

Where an agent, with authority to make sales and collect the price, but without authority to borrow money, was a defaulter, and then borrowed money and executed a note therefor in his principal's name, and remitted out of the loan a sum less than the amount of the defalcation, the principal, receiving the remittance as one on sales, was not liable on the note, under the equitable doctrine that, where a principal obtains the benefit of a loan procured by his agent acting without authority, he ratifies the same and makes himself liable to the lender. *Calhoun* v. *Realty Co.*, 651.

BONDS.

1. *Insurance. Employers' liability insurance. Question for jury.*

In an action by a bank against a guaranty company upon a fidelity bond indemnifying it against loss due to the fraud or dishonesty of its cashier, *held*, a question for the jury whether the bank had in good faith made reasonable examinations of the books and accounts of the cashier as required by the contract with the guaranty company. *Hunter* v. *Guaranty Co.*, 572.

2. *Insurance. Employers' indemnity insurance. Contracts. Construction.*

A fidelity bond indemnifying an employer against loss due to the dishonesty of an employee is to be construed as an insurance contract and, in cases of doubt, against the insurer. *Ib.*

3. *Insurance. Employers' indemnity insurance. Contracts. Construction.*

Words and phrases in an employers' fidelity bond are to be construed according to their context. *Ib.*

CARNAL KNOWLEDGE.

See Rape.

CARRIERS—CHARTERS.

CARRIERS.

1. *Freight. Facilities for shipment. Discrimination.*
Since railroad companies are organized primarily for the public interest and convenience, a railroad company cannot arbitrarily prevent the use by a shipper of the instrumentalities of other roads beyond its own lines which it has acquired the right to use. *Lumber Co. v. Railroad,* 163.

2. *Freight. Discrimination against shippers.*
It is the common law duty of a railroad company to serve the public without discrimination in service or charges. *Ib.*

CERTIORARI.

See SUPREME COURT.

CHANCERY COURTS.

Colleges and universities. Incorporation. Charter.
Under the general incorporation act (Acts 1871, ch. 54), requiring that the petition to the chancery court set forth the objects of the corporation, it was proper for the court, upon petition for incorporation "for the purpose of soliciting subscriptions and donations for the erection and maintenance of an institution of learning of the highest order, . . . together with the rights, powers, and privileges which, by law, may belong to literary institutions chartered by the laws of the State," to inquire into its objects and to include in the decree or charter the amplified and particular terms found in the resolutions of a denominational convention constituting the plan upon which the institution was to be incorporated and built. *State, ex rel., v. Vanderbilt University,* 279.

CHARTERS.

1. *Corporations. Incorporation by chancery court. Ministerial act.*
The chancery court, in granting a decree or charter under Acts 1871, ch. 54, though acting according to judicial forms, acted ministerally, and could not depart in substance from the petition. *State, ex rel., v. Vanderbilt University,* 279.

2. *Incorporators. Choice of successors.*
Where neither the general incorporation act nor the charter itself provided how successors to the individual incorporators should be chosen, such right in the case of a corporation

CHARITIES—CHURCH POLITY.

CHARTERS—Continued.

aggregate, by necessary implication, vested in the persons so
incorporated. *Ib.*

3. *Colleges and universities. Incorporation.*

Under the general incorporation act (Acts 1871, ch. 54), requiring that the petition to the chancery court set forth the objects of the corporation, it was proper for the court, upon
petition for incorporation "for the purpose of soliciting subscriptions and donations for the erection and maintenance
of an institution of learning of the highest order, . . .
together with the rights, powers, and privileges which, by
law, may belong to literary institutions chartered by the laws
of the State," to inquire into its objects and to include in
the decree or charter the amplified and particular terms
found in the resolutions of a denominational convention constituting the plan upon which the institution was to be incorporated and built. *Ib.*

4. *Colleges and universities. Incorporation. Amendment of
charter.*

Resolutions of a denominational convention looking to the establishment and incorporation of a denominational university
and stating the number and character of the schools, its
name, location, and board of trustees, and providing for general supervision by the bishops of that denomination, included
in a charter incorporating the designated individual trustees,
were not eliminated by an amendment empowering it to
change its name and to increase or diminish the members
of the board of trust, and passing to the university under its
new name all rights, franchises, etc., originally conferred,
but were rather confirmed by the amendment. *Ib.*

CHARITIES.

Administration. Visitation.

At common law visitorial power was a property right belonging
to the first donor and founder of a charity, arising by implication from the gift, and which might be vested by him in his
appointee. *State, ex rel., v. Vanderbilt University, 279.*

CHURCH POLITY.

1. *Colleges and universities. Governing boards and officers.*

The action of the board of trust of a denominational university
in adopting resolutions accepting a report of a commission
appointed by a general conference to inquire into the rela-

CHURCH POLITY.

CHURCH POLITY—Continued.

tions of the university to the denomination, recognizing the ownership of the church in the university and welcoming any supervision by the college of bishops, so as to insure observance of the charter, etc., was not an acceptance of the commission's conclusion that since 1898 the general conference, as assignee of the annual conferences is the sole member of the corporation, that the university was founded by the annual conferences, and not by an individual donor, and that the college of bishops had no other rights or powers than that of common-law visitation. *State, ex rel.,* v. *Vanderbilt University,* 279.

2. *Colleges and universities. Incorporation. Amendment of charter.*

Resolutions of a denominational convention looking to the establishment and incorporation of a denominational university and stating the number of and character of the schools, its name, location, and board of trustees, and providing for general supervision by the bishops of that denomination, included in a charter incorporating the designated individual trustees, were not eliminated by an amendment empowering it to change its name and to increase or diminish the members of the board of trust, and passing to the university under its new name all rights, franchises, etc., originally conferred, but were rather confirmed by the amendment. *Ib.*

3. *Colleges and universities. Organization. Foundation.*

A convention of a religious denomination composed of delegates from participating conferences, without power to bind such conferences by its action, framed "articles of foundation" for a university for such denomination, named the board of trust to procure an act of incorporation, and authorized and enjoined such board, when incorporated, to seek and find a founder who would supply the necessary funds, and which prescribed $500,000 as the minimum amount upon which it could be founded, in pursuance of which efforts to raise the needed amount were only partially successful, including a comparatively small amount given to secure a location. An individual donor gave it the amount necessary for foundation and afterwards gave the full endowment. *Held* that, in so far as the donor's conditions of his gift were valid, he, and not the individual incorporators, or the conferences they represented, was the founder and original patron of the university upon the plans outlined by the convention. *Ib.*

CHURCH POLITY.

CHURCH POLITY—Continued.

4. *Colleges and universities. Organization. Incorporators as trustees.*

Persons chosen by a convention of a religious denomination as a board of trustees to incorporate a denominational university and to administer it according to a plan formulated by the convention, who were incorporated by charter including such plan in full and describing the individual incorporators as representatives of the several conferences from which they came, were, under the charter and the law, trustees of the property for the purposes of the corporation, with all the lawful conditions imposed by the donor of the fund by means of which the university was established; the charter itself constituting a declaration of trust. *Ib.*

5. *Colleges and universities. Incorporation. Governing boards and officers.*

The convention of a religious denomination, composed of delegates without authority to bind their conferences, adopted resolutions looking to the establishment of a denominational university to be called the "Central University of the Methodist Episcopal Church, South," consisting of different schools, and to the raising of a minimum amount as a foundation, and appointed a board of trust to obtain a charter which should provide for a fair representation in its management to any patronizing conference, and that the board of trust should make all by-laws necessary to carry out such resolutions. After incorporation the board first allowed each conference four members, which number was subsequently reduced to one, and changed their election from nomination by the conferences and confirmation and election by the board to nomination by the board and confirmation by the conferences, and afterwards admitted members not representing or confirmed by the conferences, and finally terminated relations with the conferences by mutual consent, and substituted therefor the general conference of the whole denomination, which was to confirm members elected by the board. *Held* that, under such resolutions and by-laws and their practical construction, the relation between the board and the conferences, and afterwards between it and the general conference, was not one of ownership by the conferences, but of cooperation and representation in its management, and that such relation was a trust relation, which neither party could ignore or violate. *Ib.*

CODE CITED AND CONSTRUED.

CHURCH POLITY—Continued.

6. *Colleges and universities. Powers. By-laws.*
A denominational university, incorporated for educational purposes and the management of property by officers and trustees, had the implied power to pass by-laws and to enter into agreements relating to the appointment and election of members of its board of trustees. *State ex rel. v. Vanderbilt University*, 279.

7. *Colleges and universities. Governing boards. Officers. Visitation. Supervision.*
Under a charter of a denominational university founded by an individual donor, including a resolution of a previous convention to the effect that the bishops of the Methodist Episcopal Church, South, be and be requested to act as a board of supervision of the university or any of its departments and jointly with the board of trust to elect officers and professors and prescribe the course of study and plan of government, etc., but without appointing the bishops to anything, the college of bishops was not vested with the common-law right of visitation over the corporation; the power of "supervision" not being equivalent to or necessarily including that of visitation. *Ib.*

8. *Colleges and universities. Right of visitation. Estoppel.*
In such case the college of bishops, who had assumed and exercised uncertain and occasional rights and privileges, and a part of whose number had at one time been elected to active membership in the board of trust, and who for nearly forty years after the charter was granted and they had declined all official relations to the corporation had asserted no common-law right of visitation, were estopped from asserting such right. *Ib.*

9. *Colleges and universities. Claim of parties. Renunciation.*
If the general conference should voluntarily renounce the right to confirm persons elected to the board of trust, or cease to co-operate with the university, its right to membership in the board of trust and in its management, the board could act independently of the conference in the election of members of the board. *Ib.*

CODE CITED AND CONSTRUED.

§ 5211 (S.). Attachment. Necessary parties. Attachment of mortgaged property. *King* v. *Patterson*, 1.

§ 6137 (S.). Equity. Pleading. Multifariousness. *Ib.*

§ 5144 (S.). Replevin. Judgment. *Keelin* v. *Graves*, 103.

COLLEGES AND UNIVERSITIES.

CODE CITED AND CONSTRUED—Continued.

§§ 1470-1473 (M. & V. 1858). · Corporations. Incorporation and organization. Statutes. *State, ex rel., v. Vanberbilt University,* 279.

§ 2520 (S.). Colleges and Universities. Officers and governing boards. Statutes. *Ib.*

§ 3798 (S.). Homestead. Conveyance. Joint deed. *Mitchell* v. *Denny,* 366.

§§ 6451, 6459, 6471 (S.). Rape. Assault with intent to rape. Female under age of consent. Statutory provisions. *State, ex rel.,* v. *Rimmer,* 383.

§ 6458 (S.). Rape. Statutory rape. Repeal. *Ib.*

§ 7423 (S.). Constitutional law. Costs. Jury. Escape of prisoners. Working out costs of recapture. Due process of law. *Strong* v. *State,* 472.

§§ 5072, 5078, 5088 (S.). Guardian and ward. Ward's real estate. Sale. Purchase by witness. Statutes. *Arbuckle* v. *Arbuckle,* 485.

§ 5088 (S.). Guardian and ward. Ward's realty. Purchase by witness. Statutes. *Ib.*

§§ 2199-2200 (S.). Taxation. Exemptions. "Educational instruction." Property used for educational purposes. *Ward Seminary* v. *City Council,* 412.

§ 6106 (S.). Receivers, Foreign receivers. Permission to sue. *Hardee* v. *Wilson,* 511.

§§ 4702, 5111 (S.). Appeal and error. Review. Question reviewable. *Matthews* v. *Crofford,* 541.

§ 5090 (S.). Landlord and tenant. Forfeiture. Nonpayment of rent. Re-entry. What constitutes. *Ib.*

§ 5111 (S.). Landlord and tenant. Nonpayment of rent. Forfeiture. *Ib.*

§ 63 (S.). Appeal and error. Review. Questions presented. *Ib.*

§ 1574 (S.). Railroads. Statutory requirements. Approaching city or town. *Railroad* v. *Griffin,* 558.

§ 5919 (S.). Intoxicating liquors. Injunction. Violation. Extent of punishment. *State* v. *Ragghianti,* 560.

§ 4800 (S.). Justices of the peace. Execution. Validity. Loss of summons. *Supply Co.* v. *Fowlkes,* 663.

§ 5701 (S.). Execution. Filing transcript in superior court. Loss of summons. Establishment and restoration. *Ib.*

COLLEGES AND UNIVERSITIES.

1. *Governing boards and officers.*

The action of the board of trust of a denominational university in adopting resolutions accepting a report of a commission

COLLEGES AND UNIVERSITIES.

COLLEGE AND UNIVERSITIES—Continued.

    appointed by a general conference to inquire into the relations
of the university to the denomination, recognizing the ownership of the church in the university and welcoming any
supervision by the college of bishops, so as to insure observance of the charter, etc., was not an acceptance of the commission's conclusion that since 1898 the general conference,
as assignee of the annual conferences is the sole member
of the corporation, that the university was founded by the
annual conferences, and not by an individual donor, and
that the college of bishops had no other rights or powers
than that of common-law visitation. *State, ex rel.*, v. *Vanderbilt University*, 279.

2. *Officers and governing boards. Statutes.*
    Acts 1895, ch. 6, entitled "An act for the benefit of incorporated
educational institutions," by section 2 provided that whenever
any such institution shall be maintained and patronized by
any religious denomination, the representative governing body
of such denomination shall have power to elect its board of
directors or trustees to fill vacancies therein, and, with the
consent of such board, to change the number of members
thereof, did not apply to a denominational university chartered under the general incorporation act (Acts 1871, ch. 54),
providing by section 9 that the chancery court might incorporate institutions of learning with the powers and privileges prescribed by Code 1858, sec. 1471, *et seq.*, which authorized members of a corporation to fix the number of
trustees, subsequently required by Shannon's Code, sec. 2520
to be not less than five nor more than thirty-three, all of
whose incorporators chose to act as trustees, but dealt only
with the election of directors or trustees, and not with members of the corporation, and applied rather to educational
institutions organized under Acts 1875, ch. 142, sec. 2, or
similar acts, and under the patronage of some religious
denomination. *Ib.*

3. *Officers and governing boards. Tenure.*
    Under the inherent power of the board of trust of an incor-
porated denominational university to fill vacancies in its own
body, new members elected and installed by it were entitled
to their seats on the board *ad interim* until such time as
they should be rejected by the general conference, or its
general board of education, acting for it and under its
authority, in pursuance of an agreement between the board

CONSTITUTION CITED—CONSTITUTIONAL LAW.

COLLEGE AND UNIVERSITIES—Continued.

of trust and the general conference whereby the board was to appoint and the general conference to confirm the trustees. *Ib.*

CONSTITUTION CITED AND CONSTRUED.

§ 5. Commerce. Interstate commerce. State regulations. Validity. *Palmer* v. *Express Co.*, 116.

§ 18, art. 3. Constitutional Law. Judicial power. Validity of enactment. *Webb* v. *Carter*, 182.

§ 21, art. 2. Statutes. Enactment. Vote of legislature. *Ib.*

§ 18, art. 3. Statutes. Enactment. Journal of house of representatives. Entry of vote. *Ib.*

§ 18, art. 3. Statutes. Enactment. Disapproval by governor. Re-Enactment. Order of Procedure. *Ib.*

§ 17, art. 2. Statutes. Subjects and titles. Statute relating to corporations. *State, ex rel.,* v. *Vanderbilt University*, 279.

§ 11, art. 11. Homestead. Conveyance. Joint deed. *Mitchell* v. *Denny*, 366.

§ 28, art. 2. Taxation. Exemption. "Educational institution." Property used for educational purposes. *Ward Seminary* v. *City Council*, 412.

§ 17, art. 2. Master and servant. Wages. Liens and preferences. Enforcement. *Drug Co.* v. *Stone*, 608.

§ 14, art. 6. Criminal law. Trial. Assessment of punishment. *State* v. *Green*, 619.

CONSTITUTION OF UNITED STATES.

§ 8, art. 1. Constitutional Law. Costs. Jury. Escape of prisoners. Working out costs of recapture. Due process of law. *Strong* v. *State*, 472.

CONSTITUTIONAL LAW.

1. *Validity of statutes. Right to raise questions.*
   A party having no interest in provisions of a statute cannot require the court to determine the constitutionality of such provision. *Palmer* v. *Express Co.*, 116.

2. *Statutes. Title. Constitutional provisions. Construction.*
   The purpose of Const. art. 2, sec. 17, providing that no bill shall embrace more than one subject, which shall be expressed in the title is to prevent omnibus legislation; but particulars leading directly or indirectly to the furtherance of the pur-

CONSTITUTIONAL LAW.

CONSTITUTIONAL LAW—Continued.

pose appearing in the title may be embodied in the body
of the act. *Palmer* v. *Express Co.*, 116.

3. *Statutes. Validity.*

Where one construction of a statute will make it void, and
another will render it valid, the latter will be adopted,
though the former at first view is the more natural interpretation of the words used. *Ib.*

4. *Judicial power. Validity of enactment.*

The constitutionality of the passage of an enrolled bill or act
of the legislature may be inquired into by the courts, though
the enrolled bill is an act of a co-ordinate branch of the
State government. *Webb* v. *Carter*, 182.

5. *Statutes. Enactment. Journal of house of representatives.
Entry of vote.*

Const. art. 3, sec. 18, requiring the votes of both houses upon
reconsideration of a bill after its disapproval by the governor
to be determined by "ayes" and "noes" and the names of all
members voting for or against the bill entered upon the
journals of their respective houses, is mandatory, so that the
"aye" and "no" vote must be entered upon the legislative
journals. *Ib.*

6. *Statutes. Enactment. Disapproval by governor. Re-Enactment. Order of procedure.*

Const. art. 3, sec. 18, provides if the governor refuse to sign a
bill he "shall" return it with his objections to the house in
which it originated, and said house "shall" cause said objections to be entered upon its journal and proceed to reconsider
the bill, and, if "after such reconsideration a majority of all
the members elected to that house shall agree to pass the
bill notwithstanding the objections, it shall be sent with said
objections to the other house by which it shall be likewise
considered." *Held,* that the provision as to the order in which
a bill must be reconsidered by the legislative houses is
mandatory, so that a bill originating in the house of representatives was not validly passed over the governor's veto,
where it was reconsidered and passed by the house, acting
without a quorum, and was then sent to the senate, which
also passed it over the veto, and subsequently, in an attempt
to cure the defect in the action of the house, the house passed
it again with a quorum present, but did not thereafter send
it to the senate for its action. *Ib.*

CONTRACTS AND CONTRACTORS.

CONSTITUTIONAL LAW—Continued.

7. *Statutes. Subjects and titles. Statute relating to corporations.*
Acts 1895, ch. 6, entitled "An act for the benefit of incorporated educational institutions," by section 1 empowering such institutions to acquire and hold property, and by section 2 providing that any religious denomination maintaining or patronizing such institution should have certain powers in the election of directors and trustees, in filling vacancies, and in increasing' or diminishing the number of members thereof and authorizing the consolidation of two or more such institutions, did not violate Const., art. 2, sec. 17, providing that no bill shall embrace more than one subject, to be expressed in the title; such title being general enough to include all the provisions of the act, within the rule that generality of title is not objectionable, so long as it is not made to cover legislation incongruous in itself, or which may not be considered as having a necessary or proper connection with the subject expressed. *State, ex rel., v. Vanderbilt University,* 279.

8. *Costs. Jury. Escape of prisoners. Working out costs of recapture. Due process of law.*
Workhouse Act (Shannon's Code sec. 7423), providing that a prisoner, who escapes, when recaptured shall be made to work out the costs of the same, in addition to the other costs in the case, and making no provision for hearing and without fixing what is a reasonable amount for recapture, is unconstitutional as denying the right to trial by jury and due process of law guaranteed by Const. art. 1, sec. 8. *Strong v. State,* 472.

9. *Intoxicating liquors. Constitutionality of acts. Abatement and injunction.*
Acts 2d Ex. Sess. 1913, ch. 2, making the conducting, maintaining, carrying on, or engaging in the sale of intoxicating liquors, and all buildings, fixtures, etc., used for such purpose, public nuisances, subject to abatement thereunder, and authorizing injunctions restraining the continuance of such nuisances and closing the building or place where it is conducted, is constitutional. *State v. Ragghianti,* 560.

CONTRACTS AND CONTRACTORS.

1. *Carriers. Freight. Point of delivery.*
It is implied in a contract for the shipment of logs that they shall be delivered at a point enabling the shipper to receive

CONTEMPT.

CONTRACTS AND CONTRACTORS—Continued.

without delay or inconvenience. *Lumber Co. v. Railroad*, 163.

2. *Contracts. Construction. Practical interpretation.*

The practical interpretation of a contract by the parties thereto is entitled to great, if not to controlling, influence. *State, ex rel., v. Vanderbilt University*, 279.

3. *Sales. Conditional Sales. Collateral security.*

Where a seller under a conditional sale contract subsequently takes security, personal or collateral, he does not thereby divest himself of his retained title or authority to retake the goods for the buyer's failure to pay the price. *Automobile Co. v. Bicknell*, 493.

4. *Railroads. Foreclosure of liens. Parties.*

Where a contractor under a subcontractor from the principal contractor for the construction of a railroad brought suit to enforce a lien, and alleged an indebtedness from the principal contractor to the subcontractor, and averred that the state of accounts between them on the one hand, and complainant and the subcontractor on the other, was open, the principal contractor was at least a proper party. *Williams v. Railroad Co.*, 680.

CONTEMPT.

1. *Intoxicating liquors. Nuisance. Injunction. Violation. Erroneous injunction.*

Assuming that under Acts 2d Ex. Sess. 1913, ch. 2, sec. 4, relative to injunctions against nuisances consisting of the conducting, maintaining, or engaging in the sale of intoxicating liquors, a temporary injunction should not have been issued without notice to the defendant, an injunction issued without notice was merely erroneous, as a matter of procedure, and was not void or in excess of jurisdiction, and a violation thereof was punishable as a contempt. *State v. Ragghianti*, 560.

2. *Nuisance. Injunction. Violation. Erroneous injunction.*

That a bill for an injunction against the maintenance of a nuisance brought in the name of the State did not allege that the State sustained any special injuries by reason of the nuisance was immaterial in a proceeding to punish a violation of the injunction as a contempt even if such an allegation was necessary. *Ib.*

CONVERSION.

CONTEMPT—Continued.

3. *Intoxicating liquors. Nuisance. Injunction. Violations. Proceedings to punish. Petition for attachment.*

Where, upon a bill alleging that defendant was engaged in the sale of intoxicating liquors, a temporary injunction was issued enjoining defendant from further engaging in the sale of liquors, from moving or disturbing his stock of liquors and bar fixtures, or from entering the barroom of his building and interfering therewith, a petition for an attachment for contempt, charging that he had continued the sale of intoxicating liquors in willful disobedience of the injunction, showed a violation of the injunction; it not being pretended that defendant supposed himself to be charged with selling liquors at any place other than his barroom. *Ib.*

4. *Injunction. Violations. Proceedings to punish. Petition for attachment.*

Where defendant answered a petition for an attachment for contempt in violating an injunction by alleging various matters of excuse and avoidance, he could not attack the petition on appeal on account of its general averments and lack of specific allegations. *Ib.*

5. *Intoxicating liquors. Nuisance. Injunction. Violation. Extent of punishment.*

Shannon's Code, sec. 5919, providing that, where not otherwise specially provided, the circuit court, chancery, and Supreme Court are limited to a fine of $50 and imprisonment for not exceeding ten days in punishing contempts, does not apply to violations of injunctions issued under Acts 2d Ex. Sess. 1913, ch. 2, relative to enjoining the business of selling intoxicating liquors, as that act provides that any person violating any injunction shall be imprisoned not less than thirty days nor more than six months and be fined not exceeding $50. *Ib.*

CONVERSION.

Trover and conversion. Conversion by carrier.

The sale of logs shipped by a railroad company for demurrage when the freight charges due had been paid, so that no demurrage was chargeable, was a conversion of the logs by the company. *Lumber Co. v. Railroad, 163.*

CORPORATIONS.

CORPORATIONS.

1. *False pretenses. Prosecution. Sufficiency of evidence.*
In a prosecution for obtaining money from a national bank by
false pretenses, evidence *held* to sustain a finding that the
bank was at least a *de facto* corporation. *Bond* v. *State*, 75.

2. *Ownership of property. Proof of ownership.*
It is sufficient to sustain a conviction for obtaining money by
false pretenses from a corporation that the proof showed a
de facto corporation. *Ib.*

3. *Possession of property. Sufficiency.*
The possession, by persons assuming without authority to be a
bank, of money left with them by depositors, would give them
such a title as would support a prosecution for obtaining
money by false pretenses, in fraudulently obtaining the money
from them. *Ib.*

4. *Incorporation and organization. Statutes.*
Acts 1871, ch. 54, secs. 1, 9, passed in pursuance of Const. 1870,
forbidding charters by special act, providing by section 1
that persons desiring to be incorporated shall file a petition
in the chancery court of the county in which the largest
number of them reside, setting forth the purposes of the
corporation, prescribing publication of the petition, and directing an *ex parte* hearing thereof, and a decree or charter
enumerating such usual powers of corporations as might be
necessary to carry out the corporate objects, and by section
9 providing that the court may incorporate educational,
religious, and charitable institutions with powers and privileges as prescribed in Code 1858, secs. 1470-1473, was a general act covering the whole subject and superseding the
Code provisions, except so far as they were adopted thereby,
and as to institutions of learning expressly gave the same
powers as enjoyed by like corporations under the Code.
State, ex rel., v. *Vanderbilt University*, 279.

5. *Incorporators. Conferences.*
Acts 1871, ch. 54, requiring incorporators to file a petition in
the chancery court, which, after publication and *ex parte.*
hearing, shall by decree or charter enumerate the usual
powers of corporations necessary to carry out the corporate
objects, and which extends the power of the court to incorporations of institutions of learning, etc., contemplated the incorporation of actual persons and not of corporations or
voluntary associations, so that conferences composed of delegates from the several churches within their limits were not

CORPORATIONS.

CORPORATIONS—Continued.

competent to associate with each other for incorporation, or without express statutory authority to act as members of a corporation, nor were the delegates to such conferences competent to act as incorporations. *Ib.*

6. *Colleges and universities. Incorporations and organizations. Ratification.*

Where the action of a religious convention did not intend to incorporate any but individuals composing the board of trust thereby appointed, and where a by-law adopted in furtherance of the convention's action, declared that the charter should leave "the perpetuity of the board in its own power," and requested the several co-operating conferences to nominate four members for election thereto, which by-law was certified, together with the charter obtained by such trustees, to the conferences, their ratification of such action, even if they understood that they thereby became incorporators, could not change the legal effect of the charter, which made the trustees the incorporators. *Ib.*

7. *Colleges and universities. Petition for incorporations. Incorporators.*

The petition to the chancery court for incorporation is the basis and measure of the charter, and while the court may grant less, it may not grant more, than is sought by the petition; and hence the petition for a charter for a denominational university, filed by the designated board of trustees as individuals and not as representatives, made them and no others the incorporators, with the right of perpetual succession; the fact that they were described in the charter as representatives of certain annual conferences being immaterial. *Ib.*

8. *Charter. Incorporators. Choice of successors.*

Where neither the general incorporation act nor the charter itself provided how successors to the individual incorporators should be chosen, such right in the case of a corporation aggregate, by necessary implication, vested in the persons so incorporated. *Ib.*

9. *By-Laws. Requisites and effect.*

The by-laws of a corporation must be consistent with the spirit and terms of its charter, and while in force they become as much a part of the law of the corporation as though they had been made a part of the charter; and a by-law of a non-

CORPORATIONS—Continued.

> stock-holding corporation entering into a declaration of trust between the corporation and its beneficiaries, could not be repealed, so as to deprive the parties of the rights thereunder. *State ex rel.* v. *Vanderbilt University,* 279.

10. *Statutes. Subjects and titles. Statute relating to corporations.*
> Acts 1895, ch. 6, entitled "An act for the benefit of incorporated educational institutions," by section 1 empowering such institutions to acquire and hold property, and by section 2 providing that any religious denomination maintaining or patronizing such institution should have certain powers in the election of directors and trustees, in filling vacancies, and in increasing or diminishing the number of members thereof and authorizing the consolidation of two or more such institutions, did not violate Const., art. 2, sec. 17, providing that no bill shall embrace more than one subject, to be expressed in the title; such title being general enough to include all the provisions of the act, within the rule that generality of title is not objectionable, so long as it is not made to cover legislation incongruous in itself, or which may not be considered as having a necessary or proper connection with the subject expressed. *Ib.*

COURT COSTS.

1. *In criminal prosecutions. Liability of state.*
> Under Shannon's Code, secs. 7606, 7619-7622, declaring that costs shall include the safe-keeping of accused before and after conviction, and providing that costs in felony cases shall be paid by the State, the State is liable for costs for confining in the county jail one convicted of a felony; the commutation of the sentence not changing the grade of the offense. *Woolen* v. *State, ex rel. Portis,* 455.

2. *In criminal prosecutions. Liability of State.*
> Acts 1891, ch. 123, sec. 11, providing that the State shall pay for the board of State prisoners, covers safe-keeping in a workhouse before and after conviction, on commutation from penitentiary confinement. *Ib.*

CRIMES AND PUNISHMENTS.

Rape. Assault with intent to rape. Female under age of consent. Statutory provisions.
> In view of the history of the legislation which makes a distinction between carnal knowledge of a female forcibly and

CRIMINAL LAW.

CRIMES AND PUNISHMENTS—Continued.

against her will, which is rape, and carnal knowledge of a female under the age of consent, where the character of the act is not affected by the consent of the female, Shannon's Code, sec. 6459, making any person who assaults a female with intent, forcibly and against her will, to have carnal knowledge of her, punishable by imprisonment for not less than ten years nor more than twenty-one years, applies only to assaults upon females over the age of consent, while Shannon's Code, sec. 6471, imposing a different punishment upon one who assaults another with intent to commit any felony, etc., where the punishment is not otherwise prescribed, applies to assaults with intent to have carnal knowledge to a female under the age of consent. *State, ex rel.,* v. *Rimmer,* 383.

CRIMINAL LAW.

1. *Admission of evidence. Insanity.*

Accused was charged with having obtained money in November, 1908, by false pretenses, and pleaded insanity as a defense. In November, 1909, a lunacy inquisition was held, and it was adjudged that accused was of unsound mind, and that he had been so since the spring of 1908; and on May 12, 1910, he was put to trial on his plea of present insanity, and the jury returned a verdict that he was then insane and incapable of defending the charge against him. *Held,* that the lunacy proceedings and the verdict on the plea of present insanity were admissible in evidence. *Bond* v. *State,* 75.

2. *Evidence. Other offenses.*

In a prosecution for placing in the yard of a negro, a note telling him that he was given twenty days to leave the State, or he would otherwise be killed, evidence of other outrages against the negroes in that vicinity, and of the fact that the trial of accused upon a charge of shooting into the prosecutor's house was interrupted by force, was inadmissible as showing the intent of the threats; the note being unequivocal, and there being no showing of a general scheme on the part of accused to intimidate the negroes of that community. *Parrish* v. *State,* 273.

3. *Appeal. Review. Harmless error.*

In a prosecution for placing in the yard of a negro a communication warning him to leave the country, or that he would be killed, the admission of evidence of other outrages committed upon negroes in that vicinity, and of the trial

DAMAGES.

CRIMINAL LAW—Continued.

    of accused for shooting into the prosecutor's house, was prejudicial, where the evidence tending to show accused's guilt was nicely balanced. *Parrish* v. *State*, 273.

DAMAGES.

1. *Master and servant. Actions for wrongful discharge. Other employment as ground for reduction of damages.*

    Where plaintiff was employed by defendant as its salesman for one year, and was wrongfully discharged before that time, defendant could, in an action for the wrongful discharge, set off in mitigation of damages any compensation received by plaintiff under other employment during the unexpired period. *Menihan* v. *Hopkins*, 24.

2. *Death. Action for death.*

    Under Shannon's Code, secs. 4025-4028, authorizing an action for death by wrongful act, and the recovery of the damages suffered by the beneficiaries for the loss of decedent and such damages as decedent could have recovered had he survived, a widow, suing for the death of her husband by wrongful act, may recover, not only the damages she has sustained as the result of her husband's death, but such damages as he might have recovered had he survived. *Railroad* v. *Carter*, 459.

3. *Actions for death. Punitive damages.*

    In an action under Shannon's Code, secs. 4025-4028, for death by wrongful act, exemplary damages are recoverable. *Ib.*

4. *Actions for death. Excessive damages.*

    Where the declaration, in an action for death by wrongful act, demanded exemplary damages, and the court found that decedent was shot by an employee of defendant, acting as a special officer, while attempting to arrest decedent for the misdemeanor of stealing a ride on a train of defendant, a judgment for $2,000 would not be disturbed as excessive, for punitive damages were recoverable. *Ib.*

5. *Excessive damages. Reduction.*

    The power of the trial court to suggest a remittitur, in a case of tort involving unliquidated damages, may be exercised where the verdict is merely excessive, and is not limited to cases where passion, prejudice, or caprice on the part of the jury appears. *Grant* v. *Railroad*, 398.

DANGEROUS INSTRUMENTALITIES—DEEDS.

DAMAGES—Continued.

6. *Excessive damages. Reduction.*
Though a verdict is so excessive as to indicate that it was influenced by passion, prejudice, or caprice, it may be cured, and will stand, if a remittitur is accepted by plaintiff, and the verdict reduced to a reasonable amount. *Ib.*

7. *Excessive damages. Reduction.*
The trial judge, in an action for personal injuries, who saw plaintiff and heard her injuries described, might infer passion, prejudice, or caprice on the part of the jury from an excessive verdict alone. *Ib.*

DANGEROUS INSTRUMENTALITIES.

Negligence. Automobile.
An automobile is not such a dangerous machine as would require it to be put in the category with the locomotive, dangerous animals, explosives, and the like, so as to render the owner liable from its use. *Goodman* v. *Wilson*, 464.

DE FACTO CORPORATIONS.
See CORPORATIONS.

DEEDS.

1. *Homestead. Conveyance. Joint deed.*
Under Const., art. 11, sec. 11, providing that the homestead property shall not be alienated without the joint consent of husband and wife, and Shannon's Code, sec. 3798, containing substantially the same provision, homestead property can only be conveyed by the joint deed of husband and wife, whether the homestead be vested or a mere floating right. *Mitchell* v. *Denny*, 366.

2. *Logs and logging. Deed of standing timber. Defeasance. Time for removal.*
A deed of standing timber, with provision that the grantee is to be allowed five years, but no longer, to cut and remove it, passes a title to the timber, subject to defeasance as to such of it as is not removed within the time specified; the grantee's title terminating as to timber not then removed. *Bond* v. *Ungerecht*, 631.

3. *Logs and logging. Deed of standing timber. "Removal."*
Within a deed of standing timber, allowing five years to cut and remove it, cutting and sawing into saw logs does not constitute a removal. *Ib.*

DISCRETION OF COURTS.

Insurance. Actions on policies. Penalties.

Under Acts 1901, ch. 141, authorizing the court in its discretion to impose a penalty upon an insurer, if its refusal to pay a loss was not in good faith, the chancellor was within his judicial discretion in refusing to assess the penalty, where the evidence disclosed that the fireman and others discovered gasoline or coal oil on the goods, justifying a suspicion that the fire was of dishonest origin, though that defense was not made. *Harowitz* v. *Fire Ins. Co.*, 691.

DOMICILE.

"Change of domicile."

Every one has a legal domicile, which is not changed until a new one is acquired, and to work a "change of domicile" he must have removed to another State to make his home there; a mere removal for business purposes, though long continued, not changing his domicile, if he intends to return to this State upon the completion of his business, though a mere floating purpose to return to the state at some indefinite time will not destroy the presumption that his change of residence changed his domicile (citing Words and Phrases, vol. 3, title "Domicile;" see, also, Words and Phrases, vol. 2, pp. 1053, 1054). *Keelin* v. *Graves*, 103.

EASEMENTS.

1. *Selection of way. Selection by owner.*

   Where a way by necessity, such as a way over private grounds to a burial ground, has not been selected, the owner of the servient estate has a prior right to select the way, provided it be reasonable; but the route is to be determined by the reasonable convenience of both parties, and not by the sole interest of either. *McMillian* v. *McKee*, 39.

2. *Way by necessity.*

   A way by necessity passes by the presumed intention of the grantor, and hence should ordinarily be over such a route as the grantor would reasonably select. *Ib.*

EDUCATIONAL INSTITUTIONS.

Taxation. Exemptions. Property used for educational purposes.

Const. art. 2, sec. 28, provides that all property shall be taxed, but the Legislature may except such as may be held and used for purely religious, charitable, scientific, literary, and

EMPLOYER AND EMPLOYEE—ENTRY—RIGHT OF.

EDUCATIONAL INSTITUTIONS—Continued.

educational purposes, etc. Acts 1907, c. 602, sec. 2, subsec. 2, exempts all property belonging to any educational institution when used exclusively for educational purposes, or is unimproved or yields no income, but that all property belonging to such institution used in secular business shall be taxed on its whole or partial value in production as the same may be used in competition with secular business. *Held* that the words "educational institution" should be construed to mean school, seminary, college, or educational establishment, not necessarily a chartered institution, so as to limit the exemption to educational corporations, and that under such act all property, whether owned by a corporation or a private individual, used exclusively for educational purposes, without reference to whether a profit was made therefrom or not, was exempt from taxation, but vacant real property, used for no purpose connected with the institution and property belonging to the institution, on which stores were erected and rented for business purposes, was subject to taxation. *Ward Seminary* v. *City Council*, 412.

EMPLOYER AND EMPLOYEE.

1. *Master and Servant. Liability for injuries. Burden of proof.*
Where a scaffold, which an employer was bound to keep safe by the exercise of reasonable care, was not defective when constructed, but collapsed because of the negligence of a workman in dislodging a brace, thus permitting a board set on edge to turn flat and break, the burden was on an employee, suing for injuries, to overcome the presumption of due care on the part of the employer by proof that he had notice of the defective condition, or in the exercise of ordinary care should have known thereof. *Griffin & Son* v. *Parker*, 466.

2. *Master and servant. Liability for injuries. Burden of proof.*
No presumption of negligence could arise from an employer's failure to discover a defect in a scaffold within an hour and a half after it became defective by the displacement of a brace. *Ib.*

ENTRY—RIGHT OF.

Landlord and tenant. Forfeiture. Nonpayment of rent. Re-entry. What constitutes.
In view of Shannon's Code, sec. 5090, declaring that no person shall enter upon any lands and detain or hold the same, but

EQUITY—EVIDENCE.

ENTRY—RIGHT OF—Continued.

where entry is given by law, then only in a peaceable manner, the action of unlawful detainer is a substitute for an entry by a landlord to forfeit a lease for nonpayment of rent; the institution of the action having the same effect as an entry. *Matthews* v. *Crofford*, 541.

EQUITY.

1. *Pleading. Multifariousness.*
Under Shannon's Code, sec. 6137, providing that the uniting in one bill of several matters of equity, distinct and unconnected, against one defendant is not multifariousness, the joining in one bill of attachment suits by numerous unsecured creditors does not render the bill multifarious. *King* v. *Patterson*, 1.

2. *Pleading. Multifariousness.*
Where a bill by numerous attaching creditors also sought equitable relief, defendants must, under the direct provisions of Shannon's Code, sec. 6135, raise the objection of multifariousness by motion to dismiss or demurrer, or it will be waived. *Ib.*

ESTOPPEL.

1. *Persons estopped. Municipal corporations.*
The doctrine of estoppel due to laches and acquiescence is applicable, in certain cases, to a county, as a *quasi* municipal corporation. *Putnam County* v. *Smith County*, 394.

2. *Counties. Boundaries. Estoppel by conduct.*
A county which acquiesces for twenty years, the common law period of prescription, in the detachment of a part of its territory, so as to reduce its territory to less than 500 square miles in area, contrary to Const. 1870, art. 10, sec. 4, will be estopped by laches from maintaining a suit to recover the detached territory. *Ib.*

EVIDENCE.

1. *Criminal law. Admission of evidence. Insanity.*
Accused was charged with having obtained money in November, 1908, by false pretenses, and pleaded insanity as a defense. In November, 1909, a lunacy inquisition was held, and it was adjudged that accused was of unsound mind, and that he had been so since the spring of 1908; and on May

EVIDENCE.

EVIDENCE—Continued.

12, 1910, he was put to trial on his plea of present insanity, and the jury returned a verdict that he was then insane and incapable of defending the charge against him. *Held*, that the lunacy proceedings and the verdict on the plea of present insanity were admissible in evidence. *Bond* v. *State*, 75.

2. *Criminal law. Evidence of insanity.*
Evidence of insanity after the commission of the offense charged is competent to enable the jury to determine the state of accused's mind at the time the offense was committed. *Ib.*

3. *False pretenses. Prosecution. Sufficiency of evidence.*
In a prosecution for obtaining money from a national bank by false pretenses, evidence *held* to sustain a finding that the bank was at least a *de facto* corporation. *Ib.*

4. *False pretenses. Ownership of property. Proof of ownership.*
It is sufficient to sustain a conviction for obtaining money by false pretenses from a corporation that the proof showed a *de facto* corporation. *Ib.*

5. *Novation. Burden of proof.*
The burden of proving novation of a note by a later note is upon him who asserts it. *Dies* v. *Bank*, 89.

6. *Criminal law. Other offenses.*
In a prosecution for placing in the yard of a negro, a note telling him that he was given twenty days to leave the State, or he would otherwise be killed, evidence of other outrages against the negroes in that vicinity, and of the fact that the trial of accused upon a charge of shooting into the prosecutor's house was interrupted by force, was inadmissible as showing the intent of the threats; the note being unequivocal, and there being no showing of a general scheme on the part of accused to intimidate the negroes of that community. *Parrish* v. *State*, 273.

7. *Criminal law. Appeal. Review. Harmless error.*
In a prosecution for placing in the yard of a negro a communication warning him to leave the country, or that he would be killed, the admission of evidence of other outrages committed upon negroes in that vicinity, and of the trial of accused for shooting into the prosecutor's house, was prejudicial, where the evidence tending to show accused's guilt was nicely balanced. *Ib.*

EVIDENCE.

EVIDENCE—Continued.

8. *Master and servant. Liability for injuries. Burden of proof.*
   Where a scaffold, which an employer was bound to keep safe
   by the exercise of reasonable care, was not defective when
   constructed, but collapsed because of the negligence of a
   workman in dislodging a brace, thus permitting a board set
   on edge to turn flat and break, the burden was on an
   employee, suing for injuries, to overcome the presumption
   of due care on the part of the employer by proof that he
   had notice of the defective condition, or in the exercise of
   ordinary care should have known thereof. *Griffin & Son* v.
   Parker, 466.

9. *Subject of expert testimony. Matter directly in issue.*
   In an action by a mill company for damages from the burning of its storehouse and the stock therein, on the theory
   that lightning struck the telephone line of the defendant
   about three-quarters of a mile from the storehouse, and
   that the current of electricity followed the wire into the
   building in which a telephone was installed, causing the
   ignition, and alleging defendant's negligence in failing to
   have ground connections and appliances near the point of the
   wire's entrance into the building to arrest such a current,
   in which the defendant claimed that the building was directly struck by lightning without the intervention of its
   wire as a conductor, the answer of plaintiff's expert that,
   assuming that the hypothesized facts were true, the fire was
   probably due to the lightning discharged from the wire, was
   inadmissible as an opinion on the ultimate fact to be determined, invading the province of the jury. *Tel. & Tel. Co.* v.
   Mill Co., 374.

10. *Subject of expert testimony. Negligence.*
    Though there are exceptions, an expert witness may not give
    an opinion as to what is imprudent or negligent, by way of
    exception to the general rule that experts may not testify
    in the form of an opinion as to an ultimate fact to be de-
    termined by the jury. *Ib.*

11. *Subject of expert testimony. Cause and effect.*
    Where the cause of an existing condition of injury is in dis-
    pute, and where the jury must determine which of the
    causes urged by the respective parties is the right one, an
    expert opinion is generally admissible to the effect that a
    certain cause could or might produce the condition. *Ib.*

EXECUTION.

EVIDENCE—Continued.

12. *Guardian and ward. Ward's realty. Purchase by witness.*
    A witness having purchased certain undivided interests in land agreed with the guardian of a minor owning a one-sixth interest to purchase the same for $500. In proceedings to confirm the sale, the witness was subpoenaed by the guardian and testified that he was familiar with the property, that he owned five-sixths thereof, that he and the minor's guardian, who was an intelligent woman, had contracted for a sale of the minor's interest to a witness for $500, and, though he had paid $1,000 for an undivided one-third interest in the property and $650 for an undivided one-sixth interest, he thought the price he proposed to pay was fair. *Held*, that such testimony did not bar the witness from purchasing or authorize an avoidance of the sale under Shannon's Code, sec. 5088, declaring that no witness shall purchase at a guardian's sale, or at any time within five years after the removal of the existing disabilities, etc. *Arbuckle v. Arbuckle*, 485.

13. *Appeal and error. Harmless error. Admission of evidence.*
    Where, in an action on a fire policy, there was no evidence that insured had knowingly made a false statement of the value of the property destroyed, except in so far as the proof related to his supposed knowledge of another machine of substantially the kind destroyed by fire, but there was no evidence that he had any such knowledge at the time of making the proof, the error in permitting complainant to testify that insurer did not, up to the filing of its cross-bill, state to him that a knowingly false proof of loss had been made to defraud insurer, was not prejudicial to insurer, and must be disregarded, as required by Acts 1911, ch. 32. *Compress Co. v. Insurance Co.*, 586.

14. *Telegraphs and telephones. Nondelivery of message. Actions. Sufficiency.*
    In an action for damages for nondelivery of a death message, evidence *held* insufficient to show that defendant's messengers made inquiries at the address given in the message. *Telegraph Co. v. Franklin*, 656.

EXECUTION.

Justices of the peace. Validity. Loss of summons.
    An execution issued by a justice of the peace was not rendered invalid by the fact that at the date of its issuance the

EXEMPTIONS—FELLOW SERVANTS.

EXECUTION—Continued.

original summons was lost, and no steps had then been taken to supply it; Shannon's Code, sec. 4800, providing that, when the docket book and the original papers are destroyed, the justice of the peace may supply them, and issue execution as though they had not been destroyed, not being applicable, since it outlines the practice where all the papers and docket book are lost, and not where the summons alone is lost. *Supply Co.* v. *Fowlkes*, 663.

EXEMPTIONS.

1. *Persons entitled to benefit.*
The exemption laws, both as to personalty and realty, are exclusively for the benefit of citizens of the State having a domicile herein. *Keelin* v. *Graves*, 103.

2. *Nonresidence.*
The exempt property of one whose domicile is in Tennessee, though he may be personally absent from the State for a considerable time on business, is free from attachment or execution for debt, even though he be absent long enough to authorize an attachment in lieu of personal service as to other kinds of property. *Ib.*

3. *Domicile. "Change of domicile."*
Every one has a legal domicile, which is not changed until a new one is acquired, and to work a "change of domicile" he must have removed to another State to make his home there; a mere removal for business purposes, though long continued, not changing his domicile, if he intends to return to this State upon the completion of his business, though a mere floating purpose to return to the state at some indefinite time will not destroy the presumption that his change of residence changed his domicile (citing Words and Phrases, vol. 3, title "Domicile;" see, also, Words and Phrases, vol. 2, pp. 1053, 1054). *Ib.*

FELLOW SERVANTS.

Master and servant. Liability for injuries. Unsafe scaffolds.
While the rule that an employer must use reasonable diligence to furnish a safe place and safe instrumentalities for the work to be done is subject to the exception that where he supplies ample material of good quality and competent labor for the construction of a scaffold, which he is not required

FINES AND IMPRISONMENT—FORFEITURE.

FELLOW SERVANTS—Continued.

to furnish in a completed state, and which the employees within the scope of their employment are themselves required to construct, he is not liable for the negligence of a ployer must either furnish the scaffold complete for use, or leave the employees unembarrassed in selecting the material from that furnished, and where the selection is intrusted to a foreman, he is deemed a vice principal. *Griffin & Son* v. *Parker*, 466.

FINES AND IMPRISONMENT.

1. *Intoxicating liquors. Nuisance. Injunction. Violation. Extent of punishment.*
   Shannon's Code, sec. 5919, providing that, where not otherwise specially provided, the circuit court, chancery, and Supreme Court are limited to a fine of $50 and imprisonment for not exceeding ten days in punishing contempts, does not apply to violations of injuctions issued under Acts 2d Ex. Sess. 1913, ch. 2, relative to enjoining the business of selling intoxicating liquors, as that act provides that any person violating any injunction shall be imprisoned not less than thirty days nor more than six months and be fined not exceeding $50. *State* v. *Ragghianti*, 560.

2. *Criminal law. Trial. Assessment of punishment.*
   Const., art. 6, sec. 14, providing that no fine shall be laid in excess of $50 unless assessed by the jury, requires the assessment by the jury of the fine for an offense finable in excess of $50 at discretion, if it merits more than that amount, and it was error for the court to assess the fine for transporting intoxicating liquor in violation of Acts 1913 (2d Ex. Sess.), ch. 1, imposing a fine of $100 to $500 therefor. *State* v. *Greene*, 619.

FORFEITURE.

1. *Landlord and tenant. Rent. Nonpayment.*
   The necessity of demand, which is a condition precedent to the forfeiture of a lease for nonpayment of rent, may be waived by agreement in the lease. *Matthews* v. *Crofford*, 541.

2. *Landlord and tenant. Nonpayment of rent. Re-entry.*
   Before a landlord can declare a lease forfeited for nonpayment of rent, re-entry must be effected. *Ib.*

FORFEITURE—Continued.

3. *Landlord and tenant. Nonpayment of rent.*
Where a lessor declared a forfeiture of a lease for the non-payment of an installment of rent, and instituted an action of unlawful detainer to recover possession, the lessee cannot, by a tender of the accrued rent, avoid the forfeiture. *Matthews* v. *Crofford*, 541.

FRAUD.

Insurance. Fire insurance. Appraisement.
If an arbitration of the amount of loss fails because of fraud or intermeddling by insured, he cannot sue on the policy; and, if it fails by the fraud, etc., of the company, insured may abandon the arbitration and sue on the policy. *Insurance Co.* v. *Kirkpatrick*, 55.

GAMBLING AND GAMBLING DEVICES.

1. *Gaming. Offenses. Slot machine.*
A slot machine inscribed "5 Cents" "Insert and receive a package of Liberty Bell Gum Fruit," at the top of which was an indicator showing the player each time he played and before he played what he would receive on each play and which always indicated either the word "Gum" on one of the even numbers from 2 to 20, so that, when it showed the word "Gum," the player received a package of gum on putting five cents into the slot, and if it showed a number, he received a corresponding number of checks worth five cents in trade at the place where the machine was located, was a gambling device, the use of which was an offense, since the lure and chance of gain induced players to continue, although without ultimate loss to the owner of the machine; it not being essential that there should be the chance of loss to the players as well as of extraordinary or greatly disproportionate gain. *State* v. *McTeer*, 535.

GUARDIAN AND WARD.

1. *Ward's real estate. Sale. Purchase by witness. Statutes.*
Shannon's Code, sec. 5078, provides that on an application for sale of a ward's real estate the pleading shall set forth fully the age and condition of the ward, what other property, if any, he owns, and the reason why a sale was sought. Section 5088 declares that no guardian, next friend, or witness in such cause shall purchase at such sale, or afterwards until five

HOMESTEAD.

GUARDIAN AND WARD—Continued.

years from removal of existing disabilities, and, if he does so, the sale shall be void. *Held*, that only such witnesses are deprived of the right to purchase as resort to their testimony as an artifice to bring about a sale of the infant's property in order that they may purchase, and hence a purchaser within the prohibition must testify to facts which would reflect in some material degree on the jurisdictional facts included in section 5078, and this testimony must have influenced the court's judgment in the decision of those questions. *Arbuckle* v. *Arbuckle*, 485.

2. *Ward's realty. Purchase by witness.*

A witness having purchased certain undivided interests in land agreed with the guardian of a minor owning a one-sixth interest to purchase the same for $500. In proceedings to confirm the sale, the witness was subpœnæd by the guardian and testified that he was familiar with the property, that he owned five-sixths thereof, that he and the minor's guardian, who was an intelligent woman, had contracted for a sale of the minor's interest to a witness for $500, and, though he had paid $1,000 for an undivided one-third interest in the property and $650 for an undivided one-sixth interest, he thought the price he proposed to pay was fair. *Held*, that such testimony did not bar the witness from purchasing or authorize an avoidance of the sale under Shannon's Code, sec. 5088, declaring that no witness shall purchase at a guardian's sale, or at any time within five years after the removal of the existing disabilities, etc. *Ib.*

HOMESTEAD.

1. *Conveyance between spouses.*

A conveyance by a husband to his wife of an undivided one-third interest of land owned by him when he was married, and in which he had a homestead right after marriage, did not destroy the wife's right of homestead in the entire tract. *Mitchell* v. *Denny*, 366.

2. *Land subject.*

A homestead does not attach to undivided interests in land. *Ib.*

3. *Floating right of homestead.*

If the value of land owned by the husband at his marriage exceeded $1,000, the wife's homestead right therein was a mere floating right; but if its value did not exceed that

HOMESTEAD—Continued.

sum, she had a vested right of homestead therein. *Mitchell v. Denny*, 366.

4. *Conveyance. Joint deed.*

Under Const., art. 11, sec. 11, providing that the homestead property shall not be alienated without the joint consent of husband and wife, and Shannon's Code, sec. 3798, containing substantially the same provision, homestead property can only be conveyed by the joint deed of husband and wife, whether the homestead be vested or a mere floating right. *Ib.*

HUSBAND AND WIFE.

1. *Homestead. Conveyance between spouses.*

A conveyance by a husband to his wife of an undivided one-third interest of land owned by him when he was married, and in which he had a homestead right after marriage, did not destroy the wife's right of homestead in the entire tract. *Mitchell* v. *Denny*, 366.

2. *Homestead. Floating right of homestead.*

If the value of land owned by the husband at his marriage exceeded $1,000, the wife's homestead right therein was a mere floating right; but if its value did not exceed that sum, she had a vested right of homestead therein. *Ib.*

3. *Liability of wife. Torts.*

A married woman who permitted, during her husband's absence, another to keep vicious dogs on her premises is liable for the injuries inflicted by them, since she is liable for her own personal torts not committed in the presence or under the supposed influence of her husband. *Missio* v. *Williams*, 504.

4. *Liability of husband. Torts of wife.*

Where a married woman, during her husband's absence, permitted vicious dogs to be kept upon the premises, the husband is liable jointly with her for the injuries inflicted by the dogs upon another. *Ib.*

INDICTMENT AND JUDGMENT.

Indictment and information. Aider by verdict. Description of offense.

The uncertainty of an indictment charging the unlawful transportation of intoxicating liquors "from one point or county in this State to Tipton county" was made certain by proof that the initial point was in Shelby county, and was cured by the verdict of conviction. *State* v. *Greene*, 619.

INJUNCTIONS.

INJUNCTIONS.

1. *Railroads. Freight. Performance of duties. Remedy.*
Injunction is the proper remedy to compel a railroad company to deliver to a shipper on a spur track the freight shipped to it, where it appears that the discontinuance of switching services to the shipper would be destructive of its business; the legal remedy being inadequate. *Lumber Co. v. Railroad,* 163.

2. *Railroads. Freight. Remedy of shipper.*
In a suit to compel a railroad company to switch cars shipped to complainant on its industrial siding, the injunction issued was properly framed so as to require the company to receive and deliver to complainant on its spur track all freight, etc., according to complainant's reasonable needs and consistent with the company's duties to other shippers it was required to serve. *Ib.*

3. *Intoxicating liquors. Nuisance. Violation. Erroneous injunction.*
Assuming that under Acts 2d Ex. Sess. 1913, ch. 2, sec. 4, relative to injunctions against nuisances consisting of the conducting, maintaining, or engaging in the sale of intoxicating liquors, a temporary injunction should not have been issued without notice to the defendant, an injunction issued without notice was merely erroneous, as a matter of procedure, and was not void or in excess of jurisdiction, and a violation thereof was punishable as a contempt. *State v. Ragghianti,* 560.

4. *Intoxicating Liquors. Nuisance. Abatement and injunction. Bill. Sufficiency.*
Acts 2d Ex. Sess. 1913, ch. 2, authorizing injunctions restraining the continuance of a nuisance consisting of the carrying on of the sale of intoxicating liquors on a bill filed by citizens and freeholders or by the attorney-general or district attorney, changes with respect to the nuisances to which it relates, the rule that parties seeking to enjoin a nuisance must show special injury. *Ib.*

5. *Intoxicating liquors. Nuisance. Violations. Proceedings to punish. Petition for attachment.*
Where, upon a bill alleging that defendant was engaged in the sale of intoxicating liquors, a temporary injunction was issued enjoining defendant from further engaging in the sale of liquors, from moving or disturbing his stock of liquors

INJUNCTIONS—Continued.

and bar fixtures, or from entering the barroom of his building and interfering therewith, a petition for an attachment for contempt, charging that he had continued the sale of intoxicating liquors in willful disobedience of the injunction, showed a violation of the injunction; it is not being pretended that defendant supposed himself to be charged with selling liquors at any place other than his barroom. *State* v. *Ragghianti*, 560.

6. *Intoxicating liquors. Nuisance. Violation. Extent of punishment.*

Shannon's Code, sec. 5919, providing that, where not otherwise specially provided, the circuit court, chancery, and Supreme Court are limited to a fine of $50 and imprisonment for not exceeding ten days in punishing contempts, does not apply to violations of injunctions issued under Acts 2d Ex. Sess. 1913, ch. 2, relative to enjoining the business of selling intoxicating liquors, as that act provides that any person violating any injunction shall be imprisoned not less than thirty days nor more than six months and be fined not exceeding $50. *Ib.*

INSANITY.

Criminal law. Responsibility.

Under the plea of insanity the question for determination is, whether accused had capacity and sufficient reason to enable him to distinguish between right and wrong as to the particular act, and a knowledge and consciousness that the act was wrong and criminal. *Bond* v. *State*, 75.

INSTRUCTIONS.

1. *Master and servant. Injuries to servant. Request to charge.*

Where plaintiff was injured by the breaking of a defective ladder, and defendant claimed that the ladder was a simple tool the defective character of which was a risk that plaintiff assumed, it was error to refuse requests submitting the doctrine of simple tools. *Roofing & Mfg. Co.* v. *Black*, 30.

2. *Attachment. Grounds. Nonresidence.*

In an action to replevy goods, attached by defendant on the ground that plaintiff was a nonresident, the court instructed that the plaintiff went to North Carolina to engage in business, with no definite idea as to when he would return, to make that state his residence, or if, after he got there, he determined to make it his residence, and actually resided

INSURANCE.

INSTRUCTIONS—Continued.

there when the attachment was levied, he would be a nonresident, though he might not have carried his family with him, but if he went on a visit, with the intention of returning when his visit was out, he would not be a nonresident, and that if plaintiff left Tennessee with the intention of obtaining employment, and did so without any definite idea of returning to that state, and found such employment, he was thereafter a nonresident. *Held* that, while the instruction did not refer to domicile and .involved only the idea of nonresidence, it was substantially correct on the question of change of domicile. *Keelin* v. *Graves*, 103.

3. *Appeal and error. Harmless error.*

Where, in an action a fire policy stipulating that it should be void if insured concealed any material fact, or in case of any fraud touching any matter relating to the insurance before or after a loss, it appeared that insurer agreed to arbitration, but subsequently withdrew therefrom, whereupon insured brought the action on the policy, the refusal to charge that insurer could withdraw from the arbitration whenever it saw fit to do so without giving any reason therefor, which withdrawal did not prejudice its rights under the policy either to contest the amount of the loss or to question the good faith of insured in making proof of loss, was not prejudicial to the insurer, where it was allowed to introduce such evidence as it had on the question of the good faith of insured in making proof of loss and submitting the issue to the jury. *Compress Co.* v. *Insurance Co.*, 586.

4. *Trial. Laying stress on evidence.*

A requested instruction, which lays stress on a special item of evidence, is properly refused. *Ib.*

5. *Trial. Assumption of fact.*

A requested instruction, which assumes a fact not shown by the evidence, is properly refused. *Ib.*

6. *Appeal and error. Harmless error. Erroneous rulings.*

In an action on a fire policy against an insurer which had confessed liability, an issue whether insured furnished fraudulent proof of loss was immaterial, and rulings on the issue were not prejudicial. *Ib.*

INSURANCE.

1. *Fire insurance. Waiver of forfeiture.*

Forfeiture of a fire policy by the sale by insured of the damaged property, when the policy gave the company the option of

INSURANCE.

INSURANCE—Continued.

taking the part of the articles saved from the fire at the appraised value, was waived by the company by thereafter demanding an arbitration and appraisement of the loss; such demand being equivalent to an admission of liability on the policy. *Insurance Co.* v. *Kirkpatrick*, 55.

2. *Fire insurance. Admission of liability.*

A demand by a fire insurance company for an appraisement and arbitration pursuant to the policy is equivalent to an admission of liability thereon. *Ib.*

3. *Fire insurance. Arbitration of loss. Refusal to arbitrate. Effect.*

If insured fails to comply with a demand by the company for arbitration of the loss pursuant to an arbitration clause, he cannot sue thereon, and such refusal, if unreasonably persisted in, forfeits the policy, and, if the company refuses such a demand, insured may sue on the policy at once. *Ib.*

4. *Fire insurance. Appraisement. Fraud.*

If an arbitration of the amount of loss fails because of fraud or intermeddling by insured, he cannot sue on the policy; and, if it fails by the fraud, etc., of the company, insured may abandon the arbitration and sue on the policy. *Ib.*

5. *Fire insurance. Arbitration of loss. Reappraisement.*

If the parties have appointed appraisers to determine the loss pursuant to an arbitration clause in a fire policy, and the appraisement has failed without fault of either party, insured cannot be required to select another arbitrator. *Ib.*

6. *Fire insurance. Arbitration.*

Upon the filing of a bill by a fire insurance company to set aside an award of arbitrators, the court acquired jurisdiction of the controversy, and could set aside the award and enforce the policies under a cross-bill praying for their enforcement, without the selection of new arbitrators. *Ib.*

7. *Fire insurance. Award of arbitrators. Actions to set aside. Cross-bill.*

In a suit by fire companies to set aside an award of arbitrators, defendant could file a cross-bill to enforce the award, or, in the alternative to enforce the policies, if the award was set aside. *Ib.*

8. *Fire insurance. Nonpayment of premiums. Penalties. Demand for payment.*

Under Acts 1901, ch. 141, sec. 1, providing that insurance companies who refuse to pay the loss within 60 days after

INSURANCE.

INSURANCE—Continued.

demand by the policy holder shall be liable to pay the holder, in addition to the loss, a sum not exceeding 25 per cent, on the liability for said loss, if such refusal to pay is not in good faith, a formal demand for payment must be made by the insurer after maturity of the policy, and, if the company fails to pay within 60 days thereafter, insured may sue on the policy or award and recover the penalty, if the refusal was not in good faith. *Ib.*

9. *Fire insurance. Payment of loss. Demand.*
   If no demand is made for arbitration of the loss under a fire policy, it matures, for the purpose of authorizing a formal demand for payment in order to fix the penalty pursuant to Acts 1901, ch. 141, sec. 1, at the expiration of the number of days fixed in the policy for maturing; but, if the policy provides for payment a certain number of days after the filing of an award, the date of maturity would be governed by the number of days so fixed. *Ib.*

10. *Fire insurance. Nonpayment of loss. Penalties.*
    If an award of arbitrators as to the amount of loss under, a fire policy was defective, and the company sued to set the award aside, no penalty could be imposed under Acts 1901, ch. 141, sec. 1, imposing a penalty on the company for a bad-faith refusal to pay the loss within 60 days after demand; the time for making a formal demand for payment not having arrived. *Ib.*

11. *Penal statute. Strict construction.*
    Acts 1901, ch. 141, sec. 1, imposing a penalty on insurance companies refusing in bad faith to pay the loss within 60 days after demand is made, is penal, and must be strictly construed. *Ib.*

12. *Fire insurance. Nonpayment of loss. Penalty.*
    Under Acts 1901, ch. 141, sec. 1, providing that, upon the refusal of an insurance company to pay the loss within 60 days after demand, it shall be liable to pay a certain sum as a penalty, if the refusal was not in good faith, the failure to pay the loss within 60 days after demand would place the burden on the company of showing that such failure or refusal was in good faith. *Ib.*

13. *Employer's liability policy. Loss. Necessity of payments.*
    An employer's liability policy provided that no action would lie thereon unless brought in the name of assured for loss actually sustained and paid in money by the assured in satis-

INSURANCE.

·INSURANCE—Continued.

faction of a judgment after trial. *Held*, that payment by and loss to the insured were conditions precedent to a recovery on the policy, and hence, where the insured transferred a claim under the policy to an injured employee, and after judgment .against it recovered by the employee brought suit for his benefit on the policy without having paid the judgment, insured could not recover. *Lumber Co. v. Insurance Co.*, 477.

14. *Employers' indemnity insurance. Contracts.. Construction.*
A "continuation certificate" made by the president of a bank to a guaranty company in contemplation of the renewal of a fidelity bond, indemnifying it against losses due to the fraud or dishonesty of its cashier, certified that the books of the cashier "were examined from time to time in the regular course of business and found correct in every respect, all moneys or property in his control or custody being accounted for with proper securities and funds on hand to balance his accounts, and he is not now in default." *Held*, that the certificate was not a warranty of the correctness of such accounts, but merely that examinations were made as represented, and no errors or falsifications were discovered; the phrase "and he is not now in default," not being a substantive and distinct warranty, independent of the preceding language, but only expressing the result of the examinations. *Hunter v. Guaranty Co.*, 572.

15. *Employers' indemnity insurance. Contracts. Construction.*
A fidelity bond indemnifying an employer against loss due to the dishonesty of an employee is to be construed as an insurance contract and, in cases of doubt, against the insurer. *Ib.*

16. *Employers' indemnity insurance. Contracts. Construction.*
Words and phrases in an employers' fidelity bond are to be construed according to their context. *Ib.*

17. *Policy. Construction. Warranties.*
Warranties by the insured are not favored by construction. *Ib.*

18. *Appeal and error. Harmless error. Submission of unnecessary issues.*
Where, in an action on a fire policy, the issue was the amount of the loss, the action of the court in submitting the issue of insurer's good faith in refusing to pay the loss was not prejudicial to insurer, especially as the question of good

INSURANCE.

INSURANCE—Continued.

faith was found in favor of the defendant. *Compress Co.* v. *Insurance Co.*, 586.

19. *Fire insurance. Confession of liability.*

An insurer, agreeing to an arbitration to ascertain the amount of a loss, thereby confesses its liability on the policy, and it cannot escape from the admission by subsequently violating the arbitration agreement, or by withdrawing from the arbitration. *Ib.*

20. *Fire insurance. Loss. Liability.*

Where insurer refused to replace machinery destroyed by fire with another plant, which could then have been obtained cheap, or to furnish the money to buy it, it could not insist that the loss by the fire should be measured by the cost of the plant it refused to buy. *Compress Co.* v. *Insurance Co.*, 586.

21. *Fire insurance. Total loss. "Cash value."*

Where there was a total loss of property covered by a fire policy, and the property included a machine which insured purchased for $11,500 at a sacrifice sale, and which was as good as new at the time of the loss, and the machine was insured for $15,000, and insurer failed to settle by procuring an equally good machine for $15,000 several months after the fire, and there was no evidence that the latter machine could have been procured at that price at any earlier or later date, or any other machine of the kind for that price, insured could recover the actual cash value of the property destroyed; "cash value" meaning what it would cost to reproduce it in the same condition as before the fire. *Ib.*

22. *Adjustment of loss. Appraisal.*

An insurer was not entitled to demand an appraisement, to determine the loss under a policy providing for such an appraisement in case of disagreement, where it made no objections to the proofs of loss submitted, or any effort to agree on the amount thereof, but its whole attitude was a denial of all liability. *Harowitz* v. *Fire Ins. Co.*, 691.

23. *Adjustment of loss. Appraisal.*

While provisions in an insurance policy for an appraisement are valid, and may be made a condition precedent to bringing suit, they cannot oust the courts of their jurisdiction as to the insured's legal liability; and where an insurer's attitude was a denial of all liability, the court's jurisdiction was not ousted by a demand for an appraisal. *Ib.*

INTOXICATING LIQUOR.

INTOXICATING LIQUOR.

1. *Commerce. Interstate commerce. Congressional regulations. Effect.*

The Interstate Commerce Act (Act Feb. 4, 1887, ch. 104, 24 Stat. 379 [U. S. Comp. St. 1901, p. 3154]), which applies to all corporations engaged in the transportation of property, and which declares that the term "transportation" shall include cars, facilities of shipment, etc., and the Wilson Act (Act Aug. 8, 1890, ch. 728, 26 Stat. 313 [U. S. Comp. St. 1901, p. 3177]), subjecting intoxicating liquors transported into the State to the State laws on arrival, and Crim. Code U. S. (Act March 4, 1909, ch. 321, 35 Stat. 1136 [U. S. Comp. St. Supp. 1911, pp. 1661, 1662]) secs. 238, 239, prohibiting a carrier from delivering liquor to any person except the consignee, and prohibiting carriers from collecting the price, or carrying C. O. D. shipments of liquor, etc., regulate interstate commerce in intoxicating liquors, and exclude all State action on the subject, and Acts 1913, 2d Extra Sess., ch. 1, sec. 5, forbidding the delivery of an interstate shipment of liquor to any person other than the consignee, and section 8, applying to interstate shipments, and section 9, subsec. 5, prohibiting an interstate carrier from delivering intoxicating liquors, unless the consignee presents a statement setting forth enumerated facts, are void, because they conflict with the federal statutes on the subject. *Palmer v. Express Co.*, 116.

2. *Commerce. Interstate commerce. Congressional regulations. Effect.*

The Webb-Kenyon Act (Act March 1, 1913, ch. 90, 37 Stat. 699), prohibiting the transportation from one State into another of liquor for sale in violation of any law of the State where received, does not apply to a liquor shipment for the personal use of the consignee and his family. *Ib.*

3. *Commerce. Interstate commerce. State regulations.*

Acts 1913, 2d Extra Sess., ch. 1, sec. 3, requiring carriers of interstate shipments of liquor to file with the county court clerk of the county in which the liquor is delivered a statement giving the name and address of the consignee, the place of delivery, the kind and amount of liquor delivered, though imposing a new duty on interstate carriers of liquor, does not impose a direct burden on interstate commerce, and is not in conflict with the interstate commerce clause of the federal constitution, or with the federal statute making it unlawful for any carrier to disclose any information which may be

INTERSTATE COMMERCE.

INTOXICATING LIQUOR—Continued.

used to the prejudice of a shipper or consignee, but not preventing the giving of such information to any officer of any State in the exercise of his powers. *Ib.*

4. *Constitutionality of acts. Abatement and injunction.*

Acts 2d Ex. Sess. 1913, ch 2, making the conducting, maintaining, carrying on, or engaging in the sale of intoxicating liquors, and all buildings, fixtures, etc., used for such purpose, public nuisances, subject to abatement thereunder, and authorizing injunctions restraining the continuance of such nuisances and closing the building or place where it is conducted, is constitutional. *State* v. *Ragghianti,* 560.

5. *Criminal law. Appeal and error. Review. Harmless error. Sentence.*

Error in the court's assessing the fine for transporting intoxicating liquor in violation of Acts 1913 (2d Ex. Sess.), ch. 1, imposing a fine of $100 to $500 therefor, instead of submitting its amount to the jury, as required by Const. art. 6, sec. 14, was harmless, where the fine was made $100, as it could not be made less. *State* v. *Greene,* 619.

INTERSTATE COMMERCE.

1. *Commerce. State regulations. Validity.*

Acts 1913, 2d Extra Sess., ch. 1, sec. 5, forbidding any interstate carrier of intoxicating liquor to deliver liquor to the consignee unless the latter delivers a statement giving his name and address, and stating the use for which the liquor was ordered, directly interferes with interstate commerce as imposing a condition precedent, on the exercise by the carrier of the right to make delivery of an interstate shipment, and on the right of the consignee to receive delivery, and cannot be sustained as an exercise of the police power, or as authorized by the Wilson Act, which subjects liquor to State regulation, but which does not apply before actual delivery to the consignee. *Palmer* v. *Express Co.,* 116.

2. *Commerce. State regulations. Validity.*

Acts 1913, 2d Extra Sess., ch. 1, sec. 9, subsec. 2, declaring that nothing in the act prohibiting the carrying into the State of intoxicating liquor shall make it unlawful for one to order, and have shipped and delivered to him from without the State, for his own use, intoxicating liquor in quantities not exceeding one gallon, operates as a regulation of interstate commerce so as to restrict deliveries to one gallon at a time

INTERSTATE COMMERCE.

INTERSTATE COMMERCE—Continued.
   where liquors are intended for the personal use of the consignee, and is invalid. *Palmer* v. *Express Co.*, 116.

3. *Commerce. Congressional regulations. Effect.*
   The Interstate Commerce Act (Act Feb. 4, 1887, ch. 104, 24
   Stat. 379 [U. S. Comp. St. 1901, p. 3154]), which applies to
   all corporations engaged in the transportation of property,
   and which declares that the term "transportation" shall
   include cars, facilities of shipment, etc., and the Wilson Act
   (Act Aug. 8, 1890, ch. 728, 26 Stat. 313 [U. S. Comp. St. 1901,
   p. 3177]), subjecting intoxicating liquors transported into
   the State to the State laws on arrival, and Crim. Code U. S.
   (Acts March 4, 1909, ch. 321, 35 Stat. 1136 [U. S. Comp. St.
   Supp. 1911, pp. 1661, 1662]) secs. 238, 239, prohibiting a carrier from delivering liquor to any person except the consignee,
   and prohibiting carriers from collecting the price, or carrying
   C. O. D. shipments of liquor, etc., regulate interstate commerce in intoxicating liquors, and exclude all State action
   on the subject, and Acts 1913, 2d Extra Sess., ch. 1, sec. 5,
   forbidding the delivery of an interstate shipment of liquor
   to any person other than the consignee, and section 8, applying to interstate shipments, and section 9, subsec. 5, prohibiting an interstate carrier from delivering intoxicating
   liquors, unless the consignee presents a statement setting
   forth enumerated facts, are void, because they conflict with
   the federal statutes on the subject. *Ib.*

4. *Commerce. Congressional regulations. Effect.*
   The Webb-Kenyon Act (Acts March 1, 1913, ch. 90, 37 Stat.
   699), prohibiting the transportation from one State into
   another of liquor for sale in violation of any law of the
   State where received, does not apply to a liquor shipment
   for the personal use of the consignee and his family. *Ib.*

5. *Commerce. State regulations.*
   Acts 1913, 2d Extra Sess., ch. 1, sec. 3, requiring carriers of
   interstate shipments of liquor to file with the county court
   clerk of the county in which the liquor is delivered a statement giving the name and address of the consignee, the place
   of delivery, the kind and amount of liquor delivered, though
   imposing a new duty on interstate carriers of liquor, does
   not impose a direct burden on interstate commerce, and is
   not in conflict with the interstate commerce clause of the
   federal constitution, or with the federal statute making it
   unlawful for any carrier to disclose any information which

JUDGMENTS AND DECREES.

INTERSTATE COMMERCE—Continued.

may be used to the prejudice of a shipper or consignee, but
not preventing the giving of such information to any officer
of any State in the exercise of his powers. *Ib.*

JUDGMENTS AND DECREES.

1. *Replevin.*
Under Shannon's Code, sec. 5144, requiring the judgment in
replevin to provide for the return of the goods to the defendant, or, on failure to do so, that defendant recover their value,
with interest and damages for their detention, and Acts
1905, ch. 31, prescribing substantially the same form of
judgment in actions before a justice, in an ordinary action
of replevin originally brought before a justice, it was error
to render a money judgment for defendant on the bond,
in absence of evidence as to the value of the property.
Keelin v. *Graves,* 103.

2. *Damages. Excessive damages. Reduction.*
Though a verdict is so excessive as to indicate that it was
influenced by passion, prejudice, or caprice, it may be cured,
and will stand, if a remittitur is accepted by plaintiffs, and
the verdict reduced to a reasonable amount. *Grant* v. *Railroad,* 398.

3. *Landlord and tenant. Surrender. Effect.*
While a surrender of demised premises, duly accepted, relieves
the lessee, from any liability for rent subsequently accruing,
yet where a lessee, who defaulted in payment and against
whom the lessor had brought an action of unlawful detainer,
retained possession pending a removal of the case to the
circuit court, by giving the bond required by Shannon's
Code, sec. 5111, a surrender pending the litigation did not
relieve the lessee and her surety from liability on the bond,
consequently, while it was unnecessary for the court to render
judgment awarding the lessor possession, yet under section
4702, providing that judgment should be molded to suit facts,
the judgment should recite the facts, including the surrender,
and declare the lessor entitled to possession and assess damages on the bond. *Matthews* v. *Crofford,* 541.

4. *Appeal and error. Review. Questions presented.*
Where the circuit court to which an action of unlawful detainer
was appealed by the lessee, rendered judgment on the lessee's
supersedeas bond, but failed to render judgment for possession against the heirs of the lessee, the action having been

JURISDICTION.

JUDGMENTS AND DECREES—Continued.

revived in the name of the heirs and administrator, of the
lessee who died before judgment, the court of civil appeals
may, upon appeal by the surety alone, reform the judgment
and render judgment against the heirs. *Matthews* v. *Crofford*,
541.

5. *Courts. Stare decisis. Res judicata.*
A decision that railway company is, in view of its charter and
its work, a commercial and not a terminal railway is conclusive as to rights based thereon, whether under the rule
of *res judicata* or *stare decisis*, which rights will be protected
as against a subsequent demand involving the same question.
State v. *Union Ry. Co.*, 705.

JURISDICTION.

1. *Insurance. Fire insurance. Arbitration.*
Upon the filing of a bill by a fire insurance company to set
aside an award of arbitrators, the court acquired jurisdiction
of the controversy, and could set aside the award and enforce
the policies under a cross-bill praying for their enforcement,
without the selection of new arbitrators. *Insurance Co.* v.
Kirkpatrick, 55.

2. *Commerce. Interstate commerce. State regulation.*
While the State courts cannot directly interfere with interstate
transportation, by regulating its conveniences or charges,
they may control intrastate transportation, and the fact that
a railroad company carries interstate freight, would not
deprive the State courts of jurisdiction to compel it to switch
cars for a shipper on an industrial siding. *Lumber Co.* v.
Railroad, 163.

3. *Supersedeas. Supreme Court.*
Under Acts 1907, ch. 82, sec. 8, providing for the review by the
supreme court upon *certiorari* of the cases appealed to the
court of civil appeals, the supreme court can take jurisdiction of such cases only through that writ, and then only
after final decree or judgment in the court of civil appeals,
and it has no jurisdiction to issue a writ of *supersedeas*
suspending or discharging a *supersedeas* granted by the court
of civil appeals. *Walker* v. *Lemma*, 444.

4. *Insurance. Adjustment of loss. Appraisal.*
While provisions in an insurance policy for an appraisement
are valid, and may be made a condition precedent to bringing
suit, they cannot oust the courts of their jurisdiction as to

LACHES—LEGISLATIVE QUORUM.

JURISDICTION—Continued.

the insured's legal liability; and where an insurer's attitude was a denial of all liability, the court's jurisdiction was not ousted by a demand for an appraisement. *Harowitz* v. *Fire Ins. Co.*, 691.

LACHES.

Counties. Boundaries. Estoppel by conduct.

A county which acquiesces for twenty years, the common law period of prescription, in the detachment of a part of its territory, so as to reduce its territory to less than 500 square miles in area, contrary to Const. 1870, art. 10, sec. 4, will be estopped by laches from maintaining a suit to recover the detached territory. *Putnam County* v. *Smith County*, 394.

LANDLORD AND TENANT.

1. *Rent. Forfeiture.*

   In order to forfeit a lease for nonpayment of rent, the landlord must demand it on the day, due before sunset, and at the most public place on the land. *Matthews* v. *Crofford*, 541.

2. *Nonpayment of rent. Forfeiture. Re-entry.*

   Before a landlord can declare a lease forfeited for nonpayment of rent, re-entry must be effected. *Ib.*

LEGISLATIVE INTENT.

1. *Statutes. Construction. Rules of construction.*

   The rule for the construction of statutes to which all other rules must yield is that the intention of the legislature must prevail. *Williams* v. *Railroad Co.*, 680.

2. *Statutes. Construction.*

   The court, in seeking to ascertain the intent of the Legislature in adopting a statute, must look to the whole statute, and give to it such a construction as will effectuate the legislative purpose. *Ib.*

LEGISLATIVE QUORUM.

1. *Statutes. Enactment.*

   In determining whether a quorum was present when a bill was considered by the house of representatives, the court may look to the journal of the house. *Webb* v. *Carter*, 182

LIABILITY.

LEGISLATIVE QUORUM—Continued.

2. *States. Legislature. Journals. Enactment.*

House Bill No. 759, subsequently purported to have been enacted as Pub. Laws 1913, ch. 37, was reconsidered by the house of representatives on April 3, 1913, after being disapproved by the governor. The journal of the house on that day showed that 52 representatives were present and voted, "Aye," in favor of passing the bill notwithstanding the governor's objections, and that 4 representatives present voted, "No," and 2 representatives answered, "Present, but not voting;" and further showed that when the names of 35 other representatives were called the speaker answered, "Not voting." A representative who voted, "No," offered an explanation of his vote which is not set out in the journal, which shows, however, that when the explanation was being read another member made the point of order that the question of "no quorum" could only be determined by a roll call, whereupon the speaker ruled that the explanation was out of order. *Held,* that the journal, when read in the light of all permissible presumptions in its favor, showed that there was no quorum of 66 members present when the bill was attempted to be passed; presumptively showing that the 35 members answered for by the speaker were not present. *Webb* v. *Carter,* 182.

LIABILITY.

1. *Master and servant. Injuries to servant. Defective ladder. Simple tool. Assumed risk.*

Where plaintiff was injured by the breaking of a section of a ladder used to reach the roof of a house, such ladder as so used was a simple tool, the defective character of which was a risk which the servant ordinarily was required to assume as incident to his employment. *Roofing & Mfg. Co.* v. *Black,* 30.

2. *Master and servant. Injuries to servant. Defective ladder. Master's knowledge of defect. Effect.*

Where defendant's superintendent had been notified of a defect in a ladder, by the subsequent breaking of which plaintiff was injured, but notwithstanding such notification the superintendent insisted that the ladder was safe, defendant would be liable for plaintiff's injury while using the ladder without notice of the defect, which was not of such a nature as to be discoverable by observation which would naturally accompany its use. *Ib.*

LIABILITY.

LIABILITY—Continued.

3. *Insurance. Fire insurance. Admission of liability.*
   A demand by a fire insurance company for an appraisement and arbitration pursuant to the policy is equivalent to an admission of liability thereon. *Insurance Co. v. Kirkpatrick,* 55.

4. *Master and servant. Liability for injuries. Unsafe scaffolds.*
   While the rule that an employer must use reasonable diligence to furnish a safe place and safe instrumentalities for the work to be done is subject to the exception that where he supplies ample material of good quality and competent labor for the construction of a scaffold, which he is not required to furnish in a completed state, and which the employees within the scope of their employment are themselves required to construct, he is not liable for the negligence of a fellow servant in the construction of the scaffold, the employer must either furnish the scaffold complete for use, or leave the employees unembarrassed in selecting the material from that furnished, and where the selection is intrusted to a foreman, he is deemed a vice principal. *Griffin & Son v. Parker,* 466.

5. *Nuisance. Persons liable. Landowners.*
   An owner of real property is not responsible for a nuisance erected thereon without his knowledge, actual or constructive, and generally it must have been created by his authority. *Grant v. Railroad,* 398.

6. *Master and servant. Independent contractors. Nuisance.*
   Where a railroad company employed an independent contractor to construct an underpass beneath its tracks 100 or more feet from the street, and the contractor placed a portable forge near the street on the railroad company's land, though not directed by the railroad company, which did not know thereof, to do so, and though the forge might have been, and ordinarily would have been, located near the work, the contractor alone, and not the railroad company, was liable for the damages resulting from a horse becoming frightened at such forge. *Ib.*

7. *Master and servant. Negligence of chauffeur. Joint liability.*
   Where a brother and sister jointly own an automobile, each paying one-half of all expenses, including the wages of the chauffeur jointly employed, and with an equal right to the use of the machine, with the exception that the brother had a preference in being taken to and from work, the sister is

LIABILITY—Continued.

liable for injuries sustained in a collision with a buggy while the chauffeur, alone in the machine, was racing with another machine on his way to take the brother home from work. *Goodman* v. *Wilson*, 464.

8. *Master and Servant. Negligence of chauffeur. Liability of master.*

The mere fact that a driver of an automobile was defendant's servant will not make defendant liable, unless it is further shown that at the time of the accident the driver was in the master's business, and acting within the scope of his employment. *Ib.*

9. *Insurance. Employer's liability policy. Loss. Necessity of payments.*

An employer's liability policy provided that no action would lie thereon unless brought in the name of assured for loss actually sustained and paid in money by the assured in satisfaction of a judgment after trial. *Held*, that payment by and loss to the insured were conditions precedent to a recovery on the policy, and hence, where the insured transferred a claim under the policy to an injured employee, and after judgment against it recovered by the employee brought suit for his benefit on the policy without having paid the judgment, insured could not recover. *Lumber Co.* v. *Insurance Co.*, 477.

10. *Bail. Liability of surety.*

Sureties upon a bail bond conditioned that accused should not depart without leave of court are not liable where, after conviction and sentence which provided for incarceration in the county jail pending the coming of proper authorities to carry accused to the penitentiary, and sheriff improperly allowed accused to got without custody for a few days, and he escaped, for, the sureties having delivered accused into the custody of the court, there was no further liability on the recognizance. *Suggs* v. *State*, 498.

11. *Animals. Injuries to persons.*

The owner of premises who permits another to harbor thereon dogs which the owner knows are vicious, is liable for injuries inflicted by the dogs upon another. *Missio* v. *Williams*, 504.

12. *Animals. Injuries to persons. Knowledge of vicious character.*

The owner or keeper of a domestic animal is not liable for injuries inflicted by the animal, unless she has knowledge of its vicious habits; but, where he has such knowledge his

LIABILITY.

LIABILITY—Continued.

liability is not limited to negligence in the custody of the animal, but he is bound to keep the animal from doing mischief. *Ib.*

13. *Animals. Personal injuries. Knowledge of vicious character.*
Knowledge by the owner or keeper of a dog that it is vicious is sufficient to render him liable for injuries inflicted by the dog, without a showing that it had ever before bitten any person. *Ib.*

14. *Animals. Injuries to persons. Wild animals.*
Owners or keepers of animals which are naturally vicious are liable for the acts of such animals, even though no notice of their vicious propensities is shown. *Ib.*

15. *Husband and wife. Liability of wife. Torts.*
A married woman who permitted, during her husband's absence, another to keep vicious dogs on her premises is liable for the injuries inflicted by them, since she is liable for her own personal torts not committed in the presence or under the supposed influence of her husband. *Ib.*

16. *Husband and wife. Liability of wife. Negligence of husband.*
A married woman is not liable for torts committed through the negligence of her husband under the rule *respondeat superior*, since she is not liable *ex contractu*. *Ib.*

17. *Insurance. Fire insurance. Confession of liability.*
An insurer, agreeing to an arbitration to ascertain the amount of a loss, thereby confesses its liability on the policy, and it cannot escape from the admission by subsequently violating the arbitration agreement, or by withdrawing from the arbitration. *Compress Co.* v. *Insurance Co.*, 586.

18. *Telegraphs and telephones. Nondelivery of messages. Actions. Defenses.*
Where the addressee of a death message had an agent who was to bring it to her from the place of address, and the telegraph company's messenger failed to make inquiry or to offer the message for delivery at the place of address, the company cannot escape liability for nondelivery on the theory that the addressee's agent might not have performed her duty, or might not have been at the place of address when the inquiries were made. *Telegraph Co.* v. *Franklin*, 656.

An insurer's demand for an appraisement of the loss was a concession of its liability for some amount. *Harowitz* v. *Fire Ins. Co.*, 691.

LIENS.

1. *Justices of the peace. Execution. Creation.*

   The purpose of Acts 1899, ch. 39, providing that whenever any execution, issued by a justice of the peace, is levied on real estate, the title to the real estate shall not be affected as to third parties, unless the execution or the papers in the case are filed in the circuit court within ten days after the levy, is to give third parties notice of the lien of the execution, and is for the protection of third paries. *Supply Co.* v. *Fowlkes*, 663.

2. *Husband and wife. Wife's separate estate.*

   Under the express provisions of Shannon's Code, secs. 3532, 3533, a furnisher's lien on the real estate of a married woman, both her separate and general estate, cannot be established when there is no contract evidenced by a writing signed by her, and, where the one furnishing the goods for which the lien is sought to be established knew that the right and title to the realty was in her, he has no right to remove the goods. *Lumber Co.* v. *Barnhill*, 676.

3. *Railroads. Liens for labor. Suit to enforce. Bill. Description. Definiteness.*

   A bill to enforce a lien for railroad construction work must, in the absence of an attachment, describe the property on which it is sought to enforce the lien with sufficient definiteness to identify it and segregate it. *Williams* v. *Railroad Co.*, 680.

4. *Railroads. Liens for labor. Suit to enforce. Bill. Sufficiency.*

   A bill to enforce a lien on a railroad for construction work, which alleges that defendant railroad company owned and operated a line of railway from a designated point through enumerated counties, that codefendant, the principal contractor, contracted with the railway company for the construction of its line of road, and that complainant performed work described, sufficiently identifies and locates the line of railroad on which the lien is claimed, as required by Acts 1891, ch. 98, secs. 2, 3. *Ib.*

5. *Railroads. Mechanic's liens. Enforcement. Venue.*

   Acts 1883, ch. 220, as amended by Acts 1891, ch. 98, giving to subcontractors and laborers who perform work in the construction of a railroad a lien thereon, which "may be enforced by suit . . . in the circuit or chancery court of the county or district where the work . . . was done," does not limit the venue of suits to enforce liens, and does

MARRIED WOMEN—MASTER AND SERVANT.

LIENS—Continued.

not prohibit suits in the county where the principal office
of a railroad is situated and in which a material part of
its line is located, though the work was done elsewhere.
Ib.

6. *Statutes. Construction.*
Lien statutes must be liberally construed, to carry out the
legislative purpose, and to secure and protect those entitled
to a lien. *Ib.*

MARRIED WOMAN.

1. *Husband and wife. Wife's separate estate. Liability to charge
for benefits.*
Real property not shown to be the separate property of a
married woman cannot be charged as such, even for benefits
accruing to her interest. *Lumber Co. v. Barnhill, 676.*

2. *Husband and wife. Evidence as to ownership. Presumption.*
There is no presumption that a married woman's property is
her separate estate rather than that her general estate,
but the presumption is rather to the contrary. *Ib.*

3. *Husband and wife. Wife's separate estate. Lien.*
Under the express provisions of Shannon's Code, secs. 3532, 3533,
a furnisher's lien on the real estate of a married woman, both
her separate and general estate, cannot be established when
there is no contract evidenced by a writing signed by her,
and, where the one furnishing the goods for which the lien
is sought to be established knew that the right and title
to the realty was in her, he has no right to remove the
goods. *Ib.*

MASTER AND SERVANT.

1. *Actions for wrongful discharge. Nature and form.*
Where a contract of employment for one year at an annual
salary of $1500, but payable in monthly installments of $125,
was breached by the employer, the remedy of the employee
was an action for damages for the breach, and not for
salary for the period after the discharge, since readiness
of the employee to perform after discharge is not equivalent
to performance, and such a contract is to be treated on breach
as an entire and indivisible one, for the breach of which
only one action will lie. *Menihan v. Hopkins, 24.*

MASTER AND SERVANT.

MASTER AND SERVANT—Continued.

2. *Judgment. Merger and bar. Contract of employment. Recovery for breach.*

Where a servant is wrongfully discharged before the expiration of his contract of employment, any recovery in a suit by him for services for a part of such unexpired period before the period has expired becomes *res adjudicata*, barring a subsequent action for services during a subsequent portion of the period. *Menihan* v. *Hopkins*, 24.

3. *Actions for wrongful discharge. Other employment as ground for reduction of damages.*

Where plaintiff was employed by defendant as its salesman for one year, and was wrongfully discharged before that time, defendant could, in an action for the wrongful discharge, set off in mitigation of damages any compensation received by plaintiff under other employment during the unexpired period. *Ib.*

4. *Injuries to servant. Defective ladder. Simple tool. Assumed risk.*

Where plaintiff was injured by the breaking of a section of a ladder used to reach the roof of a house, such ladder as so used was a simple tool, the defective character of which was a risk which the servant ordinarily was required to assume as incident to his employment. *Roofing & Mfg. Co.* v. *Black*, 30.

5. *Injuries to servant. Defective ladder. Master's knowledge of defect. Effect.*

Where defendant's superintendent had been notified of a defect in a ladder, by the subsequent breaking of which plaintiff was injured, but notwithstanding such notification the superintendent insisted that the ladder was safe, defendant would be liable for plaintiff's injury while using the ladder without notice of the defect, which was not of such nature as to be discoverable by observation which would naturally accompany its use. *Ib.*

6. *Injuries to servant. Tools. Duty to furnish. Inspection.*

Although the master is not required to inspect simple tools, previously furnished to the employee, to discover defects of which the employee using such implements should be aware, and although generally no inspection of a simple tool may be necessary at the time it is delivered to an employee, yet if the master furnishes such a tool, with a dangerous defect of which he has actual knowledge, he is negligent. *Ib.*

MULTIFARIOUSNESS.

MASTER AND SERVANT—Continued.

7. *Injuries to servant. Descending ladder. Contributory negligence.*

A servant, who was injured by the breaking of a defective ladder, was not negligent as a matter of law because he descended the ladder with his back to the ladder, instead of backwards, which would have been more safe, under the rule that where an employee has two methods of doing his work, one of which is safe and the other dangerous, he is negligent if he adopts the dangerous method and is injured. *Ib.*

8. *Respondent superior. Nature of doctrine.*

The doctrine of *respondeat superior* applies only when the relation of master and servant is shown to exist between the wrongdoer and the person shown to be charged with the injury resulting from the wrong, and in respect of the very transaction out of which the injury arose. *Goodman v. Wilson,* 464.

9. *Negligence of chauffeur. Liability of master.*

The mere fact that a driver of an automobile was defendant's servant will not make defendant liable, unless it is further shown that at the time of the accident the driver was in the master's business, and acting within the scope of his employment. *Ib.*

10. *Wages. Liens and preferences. Enforcement.*

A petition for the establishment of the preferred lien for employees' wages given by Acts 1897, ch. 78, as amended by Acts 1905, ch. 414, was properly denied where it merely described the property, which was in the hands of a receiver appointed by the court, as the drug business at the corner of C. and M. avenues in M., particularly as there were prior liens on part of the property, as it should have described the property specifically, with a statement of the nature of the lien, or an attachment should have been issued and levied. *Drug Co. v. Stone,* 608.

MULTIFARIOUSNESS.

1. *Equity. Pleading.*

Under Shannon's Code, sec. 6137, providing that the uniting in one bill of several matters of equity, distinct and unconnected, against one defendant is not multifariousness, the joining in one bill of attachment suits by numerous unsecured cred-

MUNICIPAL CORPORATIONS—NEGLIGENCE.

MULTIFARIOUSNESS—Continued.

itors does not render the bill multifarious. *King* v. *Patterson*, 1.

2. *Equity. Pleading.*

Where a bill by numerous attaching creditors also sought equitable relief, defendants must, under the direct provisions of Shannon's Code, sec. 6135, raise the objection of multifariousness by motion to dismiss or demurrer, or it will be waived. *Ib.*

MUNICIPAL CORPORATIONS.

Estoppel. Persons estopped.

The doctrine of estoppel due to laches and acquiescence is applicable, in certain cases, to a county, as a *quasi* municipal corporation. *Putnam County* v. *Smith County*, 394.

NEGLIGENCE.

1. *Master and servant. Injuries to servant. Descending ladder. Contributory negligence.*

A servant, who was injured by the breaking of a defective ladder, was not negligent as a matter of law because he descended the ladder with his back to the ladder, instead of backwards, which would have been more safe, under the rule that where an employee has two methods of doing his work, one of which is safe and the other dangerous, he is negligent if he adopts the dangerous method and is injured. *Roofing & Mfg. Co.* v. *Black*, 30.

2. *Contributory negligence. Questions for court or jury.*

Questions of negligence and contributory negligence are ordinarily for the jury, though the facts are undisputed, if intelligent minds may draw different conclusions as to whether, under the circumstances conceded, plaintiff's conduct has been that of an ordinarily prudent man. *Ib.*

3. *Carriers. Injuries to person on track. Contributory negligence.*

The railroad was not liable to the plaintiff under the common law, for the plaintiff had no legal right to suppose that the company would receive him as a passenger at the point where the train first stopped, and his action in walking down to meet the train, without taking any care or precaution, was gross contributory negligence. *King* v. *Railroad*, 44.

4. *Master and servant. Liability for injuries. Burden of proof.*

No presumption of negligence could arise from an employer's failure to discover a defect in a scaffold within an hour and

NEGLIGENCE—Continued.

a half after it became defective by the displacement of a brace. *Griffin & Son* v. *Parker*, 466.

NEGOTIABLE INSTRUMENTS ACT.

Principal and surety. Discharge of surety. Reservation of rights against surety. Statutory provision.

The Negotiable Instruments Act (Acts 1899, ch. 94, sec. 120, subsection 6), providing that a surety is not discharged by the taking of a renewal note from the principal extending the time of payment, where the extension is given under an express reservation of the right of recourse against the surety, applies where the original note is retained in possession by the payee, and the right of action thereon against the surety is thereby reserved. *Dies* v. *Bank*, 89.

NOLLE PROSEQUI.

1. *Criminal law.*

A *"nolle prosequi"* is a formal declaration of record by the prosecuting officer that he will no further prosecute the case either as to some of the counts of the indictment or as to some of the defendants, or all together. *Scheibler* v. *Steinburg*, 614.

2. *Malicious prosecution. Termination of original proceeding.*

The entry of a *nolle prosequi* without procurement of the defendant is such a termination of the criminal prosecution in defendant's favor as to sustain a suit by him for malicious prosecution, though the suit for malicious prosecution is brought on the day following entry of the *nolle prosequi*, while the court had power to set the *nolle prosequi* aside, since the court, in an action for malicious prosecution, could look no further than the final judgment to determine whether the prosecution had terminated in favor of the defendant therein. *Ib.*

NOTICE.

1. *Railroads. Persons liable. Landowners.*

Where parties, who had contracted with a railroad company to construct an underpass beneath its tracks 100 or more feet from the street, about 6 o'clock in the morning placed a portable forge, which made much, noise and emitted a good deal of smoke, at a point near the street, and an accident, resulting from a horse becoming frightened, occurred about

NUISANCE—PARTIES TO ACTION.

NOTICE—Continued.

four hours later, before the railroad company or any person
connected with it had any knowledge of such location, the
lapse of time was insufficient to charge it with constructive
notice. *Grant* v. *Railroad*, 398.

2. *Animals. Injuries to persons. Liability. Wild animals.*
. Owners or keepers of animals which are naturally vicious are
liable for the acts of such animals, even though no notice of
their vicious propensities is shown. *Missio* v. *Williams*, 504.

NUISANCE.

1. *Persons liable. Landowners.*
An owner of real property is not responsible for a nuisance
erected thereon without his knowledge, actual or constructive,
and generally it must have been created by his authority.
Grant v. *Railroad*, 398.

2. *Intoxicating liquors. Abatement and injunction. Bill. Sufficiency.*
Acts 2d Ex. Sess. 1913, ch. 2, authorizing injunctions restraining the continuance of a nuisance consisting of the carrying
on of the sale of intoxicating liquors on a bill filed by citizens and free-holders or by the attorney-general or district
attorney, changes with respect to the nuisances to which
it relates, the rule that parties seeking to enjoin a nuisance
must show special injury. *State* v. *Regghianti*, 560.

PARTIES TO ACTIONS.

1. *Attachment. Necessary parties. Attachment of mortgaged
property.*
A creditor attaching the property of a nonresident debtor under
Shannon's Code, sec. 5211, must, where the legal title is in a
mortgagee, make the mortgagee a party defendant; for
otherwise the mortgagee may assert his rights and cut off
the attachment by foreclosure, and the property, if sold under
the attachment, will not bring a fair price. *King* v. *Patterson*, 1.

2. *Motion to quash. Nonjoinder of parties. Waiver.*
Defendants and complainants filed separate bills for attachments
on the property of a nonresident debtor. After consolidation of the suits, defendants moved to quash complainants'
attachments, and excepted to the report of the master fixing
priority. *Held* that, as defendants were not parties until the

PENALTIES—PLEADING AND PRACTICE.

PARTIES TO ACTION—Continued.

consolidation of the suits, their right to object to the failure of complainants to join the mortgagee of the debtor's property, who was the holder of the legal title, as a party defendant had not been waived, and might be raised by the objections made. *Ib.*

3. *Abatement and revival. Death of party. Revival. Necessary parties. "Leasehold."*

Under Shannon's Code, sec. 511, "leaseholds" are interests in land descending to the heirs at law and hence where a lessee died pending an action of unlawful detainer by the lessor, the heirs at law of the lessee are necessary parties upon the revival. *Matthews* v. *Crofford*, 541.

4. *Railroads. Foreclosure of liens. Parties.*

Where a contractor under a subcontractor from the principal contractor for the construction of a railroad brought suit to enforce a lien, and alleged an indebtedness from the principal contractor to the subcontractor, and averred that the state of accounts between them on the one hand, and complainant and the subcontractor on the other, was open, the principal contractor was at least a proper party. *Williams* v. *Railroad, Co.*, 680.

PENALTIES.

Insurance. Actions on policies.

Under Acts 1901, ch. 141, authorizing the court in its discretion to impose a penalty upon an insurer, if its refusal to pay a loss was not in good faith, the chancellor was within his judicial discretion in refusing to assess the penalty, where the evidence disclosed that the fireman and others discovered gasoline or coal oil on the goods, justifying a suspicion that the fire was of dishonest origin, though that defense was not made. *Harowitz* v. *Fire Ins. Co.*, 691.

PLEADING AND PRACTICE.

1. *Attachment. Proceeding. Amendment.*

Where numerous creditors of a nonresident debtor were striving for priority by attachments on his property, complainants, who did not join as a party the mortgagee of land which they attached, are not entitled to permission to amend their bill so as to correct the defect; defendants having already acquired valid attachment liens thereon, having made the mortgagee a party. *King* v. *Patterson*, 1.

PLEADING AND PRACTICE.

PLEADING AND PRACTICE—Continued.

2. *Motion to quash. Nonjoinder of parties. Waiver.*
   Defendants and complainants filed separate bills for attachments on the property of a nonresident debtor. After consolidation of the suits, defendants moved to quash complainants' attachments, and excepted to the report of the master fixing priority. *Held* that, as defendants were not parties until the consolidation of the suits, their right to object to the failure of complainants to join the mortgagee of the debtor's property, who was the holder of the legal title, as a party defendant had not been waived, and might be raised by the objections made. *King* v. *Patterson,* 1.

3. *Actions. Defenses. Mode of raising.*
   Where numerous attachment suits were consolidated, motions to quash complainants' attachments and exceptions to the report of the master fixing the priorities of the parties are the proper methods of raising the question whether complainants' attachments were void for failure to join the holder of the legal title of the property attached. *Ib.*

4. *Marshaling assets and securities. Right to marshaling.*
   Where numerous creditors who had no liens upon the property of their debtor all sought to acquire liens by attachments, some of which were not duly perfected for want of necessary parties, there can be no marshaling of assets between the successful and unsuccessful creditors; for the doctrine of marshaling arises only where one creditor has a lien upon two funds or two parcels of land, and another having a lien upon only one of them, in which the first creditor will, in equity, be required to seek satisfaction first out of that fund or property upon which the second creditor has no lien. *Ib.*

5. *Railroads. Freight. Performance of duties. Remedy.*
   Injunction is the proper remedy to compel a railroad company to deliver to a shipper on a spur track the freight shipped to it, where it appears that the discontinuance of switching services to the shipper would be destructive of its business; the legal remedy being inadequate. *Lumber Co.* v. *Railroad,* 163.

6. *Railroads. Freight. Remedy of shipper. Injunction.*
   In a suit to compel a railroad company to switch cars shipped to complainant on its industrial siding, the injunction issued was properly framed so as to require the company to receive and deliver to complainant on its spur track all freight, etc.,

POWERS OF COURTS.

PLEADING AND PRACTICE—Continued.

according to complainant's reasonable needs and consistent with the company's duties to other shippers it was required to serve. *Ib.*

7. *Pleading. Allegation of time. Pleading and proof.*

Not only may plaintiff allege that the personal injury for which she sues was inflicted "on or about" a certain day, but, being unable to do so, she may not be required to allege the date with greater particularity, and may recover on her testimony that the accident occurred in the month alleged, and to the best of her recollection on the day alleged. *May v. Railroad,* 521.

8. *Justices of the peace. Execution. Validity. Loss of summons.*

An execution issued by a justice of the peace was not rendered invalid by the fact that at the date of its issuance the original summons was lost, and no steps had then been taken to supply it; Shannon's Code, sec. 4800, providing that, when the docket book and the original papers are destroyed, the justice of the peace may supply them, and issue execution as though they had not been destroyed, not being applicable, since it outlines the practice where all the papers and docket book are lost, and not where the summons alone is lost. *Supply Co. v. Fowlkes,* 663.

POWERS OF COURTS.

1. *Statutes. Enactment. Legislative quorum.*

In determining whether a quorum was present when a bill was considered by the house of representatives, the court may look to the journal of the house. *Webb v. Carter,* 182.

2. *Damages. Excessive damages. Reduction.*

The power of the trial court to suggest a remittitur, in a case of tort involving unliquidated damages, may be exercised where the verdict is merely excessive, and is not limited to cases where passion, prejudice, or caprice on the part of the jury appears. *Grant v. Railroad,* 398.

3. *Execution. Filing transcript in superior court. Loss of summons. Establishment and restoration.*

Under Shannon's Code, sec. 5701, providing that any record, proceedings, or paper, filed in an action, either at law or equity, if lost or mislaid, may be supplied, upon application, under the orders of the court, where a cause had been transferred from a justice of the peace to the circuit court after the levy of an execution on land for the purpose of

POWERS OF STATE—POSSESSION.

POWERS OF COURTS—Continued.

obtaining an order of condemnation, the circuit court could
make an order supplying the original summons, though it had
never been on file in that court, it having been lost before
the transfer of the cause, since the power vested in courts
by the statute is not limited to papers filed in the court
which makes the order, but applies to any paper "filed in an
action." *Supply Co.* v. *Fowlkes*, 663.

POWERS OF STATES.

1. *Commerce. Interstate commerce. State regulations. Validity.*
Acts 1913, 2d Extra Sess., ch. 1, sec. 5, forbidding any interstate
carrier of intoxicating liquor to deliver liquor to the consignee
unless the latter delivers a statement giving his name and
address, and stating the use for which the liquor was ordered,
directly interferes with interstate commerce as imposing a
condition precedent, on the exercise by the carrier of the
right to make delivery of an interstate shipment, and on
the right of the consignee to receive delivery, and cannot be
sustained as an exercise of the police power, or as authorized
by the Wilson Act, which subjects liquor to State regulation,
but which does not apply before actual delivery to the consignee. *Palmer* v. *Express Co.*, 116.

2. *Commerce. Interstate commerce. State regulation.*
While the State courts cannot directly interfere with interstate
transportation, by regulating its conveniences or charges, they
may control intrastate transportation, and the fact that a
railroad company carries interstate freight, would not deprive the State courts of jurisdiction to compel it to switch
cars for a shipper on an industrial siding. *Lumber Co.* v.
Railroad, 163.

POSSESSION.

Landlord and tenant. Nonpayment of rent. Forfeiture.
Where a lessor declared a forfeiture of a lease for the nonpayment of an installment of rent, and instituted an action
of unlawful detainer to recover possession, the lessee cannot,
by a tender of the accrued rent, avoid the forfeiture. *Matthews* v. *Crofford*, 541.

PRACTICE AND PROCEDURE.

Insurance. Fire insurance. Award of arbitrators. Actions to set aside. Cross-bill.

In a suit by fire companies to set aside an award of arbitrators, defendant could file a cross-bill to enforce the award, or, in the alternative, to enforce the policies, if the award was set aside. *Insurance Co.* v. *Kirkpatrick*, 55.

PROPERTY RIGHTS.

Charities. Administration. Visitation.

At common law visitorial power was a property right belonging to the first donor and founder of a charity, arising by implication from the gift, and which might be vested by him in his appointee. *State, ex rel.*, v. *Vanderbilt University*, 279.

QUESTION FOR JURY.

1. *Evidence. Subjects of expert testimony. Matter directly in issue.*

In an action by a mill company for damages from the burning of its storehouse and the stock therein, on the theory that lightning struck the telephone line of the. defendant about three-quarters of a mile from the storehouse, and that the current of electricity followed the wire into the building in which a telephone was installed, causing the ignition, and alleging defendant's negligence in failing to have ground connections and appliances near the point of the wire's entrance into the building to arrest such a current, in which the defendant claimed that the building was directly struck by lightning without the intervention of its wire as a conductor, the answer of plaintiff's expert that, assuming that the hypothesized fact were true, the fire was probably due to the lightning discharged from the wire, was inadmissible as an opinion on the ultimate fact to be determined, invading the province of the jury. *Tel. & Tel. Co.* v. *Mill Co.*, 374.

2. *Evidence. Subject of expert testimony. Negligence.*

Though there are exceptions, an expert witness may not give an opinion as to what is imprudent or negligent, by way of exception to the general rule that experts may not testify in the form of an opinion as to an ultimate fact to be determined by the jury. *Ib.*

3. *Evidence. Subjects of expert testimony. Cause and effect.*

Where the cause of an existing condition or injury is in dispute, and where the jury must determine which of the causes

RAILROADS.

QUESTION FOR JURY—Continued.

    urged by the respective parties is the right one, an expert opinion is generally admissible to the effect that a certain cause could or might produce the condition. *Tel. & Tel. Co. v. Mill Co.*, 374.

4. *Insurance. Employers' liability insurance.*

    In an action by a bank against a guaranty company upon a fidelity bond indemnifying it against loss due to the fraud or dishonesty of its cashier, *held*, a question for the jury whether the bank had in good faith made reasonable examinations of the books and accounts of the cashier as required by the contract with the guaranty company. *Hunter v. Guaranty Co.*, 572.

RAILROADS.

1. *Carriers. Accidents to persons on track. Statutory lookout and warning.*

    Plaintiff and his companion, desiring to board a train in the nighttime at a flag station, signaled it to stop. By reason of the fact that the signal was not given in time, the train ran about 100 yards beyond the station before it stopped. Plaintiff started down the track toward the train, but was struck by it as it was backing to the station at the rate of 3 or 4 miles an hour. The train had the usual rear lights, and the light inside the coach shown out through the glass of the rear door; but plaintiff testified that he did not see that the train was in motion until it struck him. *Held* that, in such a case, Shannon's Code, secs. 1574-1576, requiring certain lookouts on, and warnings to be given by, moving trains, does not apply, since the movement of the train in this case was a switching in its depot grounds, to which the statutes are not applicable. *King v. Railroad*, 44.

2. *Carriers. Injuries to person on track. Contributory negligence.*

    The railroad was not liable to the plaintiff under the common law, for the plaintiff had no legal right to suppose that the company would receive him as a passenger at the point where the train first stopped, and his action in walking down to meet the train, without taking any care or precaution, was gross contributory negligence. *Ib.*

3. *Carriers. Accidents to persons on track. Statutory lookout and warning.*

    Plaintiff and his companion, desiring to board a train in the nighttime at a flag station, signaled it to stop. By reason of the fact that the signal was not given in time, the train ran

RAILROADS.

RAILROADS—Continued.

about 100 yards beyond the station before it stopped. Plaintiff started down the track toward the train, but was struck by it as it was backing to the station at the rate of 3 or 4 miles an hour. The train had the usual rear lights, and the light inside the coach shown out through the glass of the rear door; but plaintiff testified that he did not see that the train was in motion until it struck him. *Held* that, in such a case, Shannon's Code, secs. 1574-1576, requiring certain lookouts on, and warnings to be given by, moving trains, does not apply, since the movement of the train in this case was a switching in its depot grounds, to which the statutes are not applicable. *Ib.*

4. *Switching services. Right to discontinue.*

If a shipper denies his liability for demurrage, the railroad company cannot discontinue its switching services on account of the nonpayment of demurrage. *Lumber Co.* v. *Railroad,* 163.

5. *Carriers. Freight. Demurrage.*

If a railroad company knew that a shipper would not accept logs in cars placed on a certain track, before the cars were delivered there, the shipper could not be charged with demurrage for not receiving the cars at that point. *Ib.*

6. *Trover and conversion. Conversion by carrier.*

The sale of logs shipped by a railroad company for demurrage when the freight charges due had been paid, so that no demurrage was chargeable, was a conversion of the logs by the company. *Ib.*

7. *Carriers. Freight. Facilities for shipment. Discrimination.*

Since railroad companies are organized primarily for the public interest and convenience, a railroad company cannot arbitrarily prevent the use by a shipper of the instrumentalities of other roads beyond its own lines which it has acquired the right to use. *Ib.*

8. *Carriers. Freight. Discrimination against shippers.*

It is the common law duty of a railroad company to serve the public without discrimination in service or charges. *Lumber Co.* v. *Railroad,* 163.

9. *Persons liable. Landowners.*

Where parties, who had contracted with a railroad company to construct an underpass beneath its tracks 100 or more feet from the street, about 6 o'clock in the morning placed a porta-

RAILROADS.

RAILROADS—Continued.

ble forge, which made much noise and emitted a good deal
of smoke, at a point near the street, and an accident, resulting from a horse becoming frightened, occurred about four
hours later, before the railroad company or any person connected with it had any knowledge of such location, the lapse
of time was insufficient to charge it with constructive notice.
Grant v. *Railroad*, 398.

10. *Master and servant. Independent contractors. . Nuisance.*
Where a railroad company employed an independent contractor
to construct an underpass beneath its tracks 100 or more feet
from the street, and the contractor placed a portable forge
near the street on the railroad company's land, though not
directed by the railroad company, which did not know thereof,
to do so, and though the forge might have been, and ordinarily
would have been, located near the work, the contractor alone,
and not the railroad company, was liable for the damages
resulting from a horse becoming frightened at such forge.
Ib.

11. *Statutory requirements. Approaching city or town.*
Shannon's Code, sec. 1574, subsec. 8, providing that, in approaching a city or town, the bell or whistle of a train shall be
sounded when at a distance of one mile, and then at short
intervals till it reaches the depot or station, and also on leaving a town or city, etc., applies to through trains which do
not stop at a town or city as well as to local trains that do
stop. *Matthews* v. *Crofford*, 541.

12. *Liens for labor. Suit to enforce. Bill. Sufficiency.*
A bill to enforce a lien on a railroad for construction work,
which alleges that defendant railroad company owned and
operated a line of railway from a designated point through
enumerated counties, that codefendant, the principal contractor, contracted with the railway company for the construction of its line of road, and that complainant performed work
described, sufficiently identifies and locates the line of railroad on which the lien is claimed, as required by Acts 1891,
ch. 98, secs. 2, 3. *Williams* v. *Railroad Co.*, 680.

13. *Mechanics' liens. Enforcement. Venue.*
Acts 1883, ch. 220, as amended by Acts 1891, ch. 98, giving to
subcontractors and laborers who perform work in the construction of a railroad a lien thereon, which "may be enforced by suit . . . in the circuit or chancery court of
the county or district where the work . . . was done,"

RAPE.

RAILROADS—Continued.

does not limit the venue of suits to enforce liens, and does not prohibit suits in the county where the principal office of a railroad is situated and in which a material part of its line is located, though the work was done elsewhere. *Ib.*

14. *Privilege taxes. "Railroad terminal corporation."*
A railway company which leases from other railway companies their terminal facilities, and which contracts to do their terminal business, and to provide adequate terminal facilities, and take possession of trains entering receiving tracks, and switch and deliver cars therein to their respective destinations within the switching district, including the delivery of cars to connecting lines, and to render all switching services required for the prompt handling of cars for loading, unloading, or repairs, and to set apart exclusively for the business of the other companies terminal facilities, with the right of exclusive management and control of the terminal facilities, etc., contracts for the performance of duties falling within the functions of a railroad terminal corporation within Shannon's Code, secs. 2430, 2431, providing for the organization of railway terminal companies, and it is liable to privilege taxes imposed on railroad terminal corporations; a railroad terminal corporation being an instrumentality which assists railroad transportation companies in the transfer of traffic between different lines, and in the collection and distribution of traffic. *State* v. *Union Ry. Co.*, 705.

RAPE.

Assault with intent to rape. Female under age of consent. Statutory provisions.
In view of the history of the legislation which makes a distinction between carnal knowledge of a female forcibly and against her will, which is rape, and carnal knowledge of a female under the age of consent, where the character of the act is not affected by the consent of the female, Shannon's Code, sec. 6459, making any person who assaults a female with intent, forcibly and against her will, to have carnal knowledge of her, punishable by imprisonment for not less than ten years, nor more than twenty-one years, applies only to assaults upon females over the age of consent, while Shannon's Code, sec. 6471, imposing a different punishment upon one who assaults another with intent to commit any felony,

RAPE—Continued.

>etc., where the punishment is not otherwise prescribed, applies to assaults with intent to have carnal knowledge to a female under the age of consent. *State, ex rel.*, v. *Rimmer*, 383.

RATIFICATION.

Principal and agent. Unauthorized execution of note by agent. Liability of principal.

>Where an agent, with authority to make sales and collect the price, but without authority to borrow money, was a defaulter, and then borrowed money and executed a note therefor in his principal's name, and remitted out of the loan a sum less than the amount of the defalcation, the principal, receiving the remittance as one on sales, was not liable on the note, under the equitable doctrine that, where a principal obtains the benefit of a loan procured by his agent acting without authority, he ratifies the same and makes himself liable to the lender. *Calhoun* v. *Realty Co.*, 651.

RECEIVERS.

Foreign receivers. Permission to sue.

>While a receiver, at least an ordinary chancery receiver, has no legal right to sue in a state other than that of his appointment, the privilege of doing so will be accorded, as a matter of comity; the suit being neither inimical to the interest of local creditors, or of anyone who has acquired rights under a local statute, nor in contravention of the policy of the forum. *Hardee* v. *Wilson*, 511.

RES ADJUDICATA.

Judgment. Merger and bar. Contract of employment. Recovery for breach.

>Where a servant is wrongfully discharged before the expiration of his contract of employment, any recovery in a suit by him for services for a part of such unexpired period before the period has expired becomes *res adjudicata*, barring a subsequent action for services during a subseqent portion of the period. *Menihan* v. *Hopkins*, 24.

RES JUDICATA.

Courts. Judgment. Stare decisis.

>A decision that railway company is, in view of its charter and its work, a commercial and not a terminal railway is con-

RESPONDEAT SUPERIOR—SCOPE OF EMPLOYMENT.

RES JUDICATA—Continued.

> clusive as to rights based thereon, whether under the rule of *res judicata* or *stare decisis*, which rights will be protected as against a subsequent demand involving the same question. *State* v. *Union Ry. Co.*, 705.

RESPONDEAT SUPERIOR.

1. *Master and servant. Nature of doctrine.*

   The doctrine of *respondeat superior* applies only when the relation of master and servant is shown to exist between the wrongdoer and the person shown to be charged with the injury resulting from the wrong, and in respect of the very transaction out of which the injury arose. *Goodman* v. *Wilson*, 464.

2. *Husband and wife. Liability of Wife. Negligence of husband.*

   A married woman is not liable for torts committed through the negligence of her husband under the rule *respondeat superior*, since she is not liable *ex contractu*. *Missio* v. *Williams*, 504.

REPLEVIN.

Judgment.

> Under Shannon's Code, sec. 5144, requiring the judgment in replevin to provide for the return of the goods to the defendant, or, on failure to do so, that defendant recover their value, with interest and damages for their detention, and Acts 1905, ch. 31, prescribing substantially the same form of judgment in actions before a justice, in an ordinary action of replevin originally brought before a justice, it was error to render a money judgment for defendant on the bond, in absence of evidence as to the value of the property. *Keelin* v. *Graves*, 103.

REVIVAL.

See ABATEMENT AND REVIVAL.

ROADS AND BRIDGES.

Easements. Jurisdiction. Selection of way.

> A court of equity has jurisdiction to locate a way by necessity. *McMillan* v. *McKee*, 39.

SCOPE OF EMPLOYMENT.

See FELLOW SERVANTS.

STARE DECISIS—STATUTES, STATUTORY CONSTRUCTION.

STARE DECISIS.

See RES JUDICATA.

STATUTE CITED AND CONSTRUED.

Carriers. Freight. Common-law duties. Discrimination.
Acts 1897, ch. 10, secs. 15, 17, prohibiting carriers from discriminating as to charges or services or from giving any unreasonable preferences, are merely declaratory of the common law. *Lumber Co.* v. *Railroad*, 163.

STATUTES AND STATUTORY CONSTRUCTION.

1. *Insurance. Penal statute. Strict construction.*
Acts 1901, ch. 141, sec. 1, imposing a penalty on insurance companies refusing in bad faith to pay the loss within 60 days after demand is made, is penal, and must be strictly construed. *Insurance Co.* v. *Kirkpatrick*, 55.

2. *Title. Constitutional provisions.*
Though the title of an act is double, in violation of Const. art. 2, sec. 17, the act will be upheld where only one of the subjects is embraced in its body. *Palmer* v. *Express Co.*, 116.

3. *Title. Constitutional provisions.*
Acts 1913, 2d Extra Sess., ch. 1, prohibiting the transportation into the State of intoxicating liquor except in the manner prescribed, is but a regulation, and not a prohibition, of transportation of intoxicating liquors, and is not broader than the title entitled "An act regulating the shipment and delivery of intoxicating liquor," etc. *Ib.*

4. *Colleges and universities. Officers and governing boards. "Patron."*
Acts 1895, ch. 6, by section 1 empowered educational institutions to acquire and hold property, and by section 2 provided that, whenever such institution was established and was being maintained and patronized, or, having been otherwise established, was being maintained and patronized by any religious denomination, the representative governing board of such denomination might, at its option, elect its board of directors or trustees, or fill vacancies therein, or change the number of members thereof. A denominational university, designated as the "Central University of the Methodist Episcopal Church, South," was incorporated on petition of the individual members of its board of trust, and an effort to raise by subscriptions from the conferences and churches

STATUTES AND STATUTORY CONSTRUCTION.

STATUTES AND STATUTORY CONSTRUCTION—Continued.

the required endowment of $500,000 resulted in subscriptions for about $100,000, from which about $15,000 was realized, devoted to an incidental "sustention fund" for students, and in contributions of about $50,000 for the purchase of its campus and erection of its buildings, and about $325,000 for specific endowments of chairs, lecture courses, and scholarships, nearly all of which were in the theological school, without to any extent relieving the general endowment from allowances to that department. Soon after its incorporation a wealthy layman, through the bishop, gave to the university $500,000, and an equal amount to complete its entire endowment, members of his family also giving another $1,-000,000, whereupon the name of the university by resolution was then changed to that of such donor. *Held*, that according to the dictionary definitions of "establish," "maintain," and "patronize," and of "patron" as an endower or a perficient founder, to establish, maintain, and patronize meant to found and support, he was its patron and founder, and that the denomination had not maintained and patronized the university, so as to entitle its general conference to elect the board of trust or fill vacancies therein. *State, ex rel.*, v. *Vanderbilt University*, 279.

5. *Colleges and universities. Officers and governing boards.*

Acts 1895, ch. 6, entitled "An act for the benefit of incorporated educational institutions," by section 2 provided that whenever any such institution shall be maintained and patronized by any religious denomination, the representative governing body of such denomination shall have power to elect its board of directors or trustees to fill vacancies therein, and, with the consent of such board, to change the number of members thereof, did not apply to a denominational university chartered under the general incorporation act (Acts 1871, ch. 54), providing by section 9 that the chancery court might incorporate institutions of learning with the powers and privileges prescribed by Code 1858, sec. 1471, *et seq.*, which authorized members of a corporation to fix the number of trustees, subsequently required by Shannon's Code, sec. 2520 to be not less than five nor more than thirty-three, all of whose incorporators chose to act as trustees, but dealt only with the election of directors or trustees, and not with members of the corporation, and applied rather to educational institutions organized under Acts 1875, ch. 142, sec. 2, or similar acts, and under the patronage of some religious denomination. *Ib.*

STATUTES AND STATUTORY CONSTRUCTION.

STATUTES AND STATUTORY CONSTRUCTION—Continued.

6. *Rape. Statutory rape. Repeal.*
   Code 1858, sec. 4614, later codified as Shannon's Code, sec. 6455, made punishable any person who should carnally know and abuse a female under the age of ten years. It was amended by Act 1871, ch. 56, as to the punishment, and again amended by Act 1879, ch: 63, so as to read that any person who should assault a female under the age of ten years with intent to carnally know her should be punishable as in the case of rape. Act 1893, ch. 129, amended section 4614 as amended in 1871 so as to change the age to twelve years, and re-enacted it as amended, but made no reference to the act of 1879, and did not incorporate its provisions. *Held*, that the amendment by the act of 1879, which was an addition to, and not a substitution for, section 4614, was repealed by the amending act of 1893. *State, ex rel., v. Rimmer*, 383.

7. *Railroads. Statutory requirements. Approaching city or town.*
   Shannon's Code, sec. 1574, subsec. 3, providing that, in approaching a city or town, the bell or whistle of a train shall be sounded when at a distance of one mile, and then at short intervals till it reaches the depot or station, and also on leaving a town or city, etc., applies to through trains which do not stop at a town or city as well as to local trains that do stop. *Railroad v. Griffin*, 558.

8. *Construction. Rules of construction.*
   The rule for the construction of statutes to which all other rules must yield is that the intention of the legislature must prevail. *Williams v. Railroad Co.*, 680.

9. *Construction. Legislative intent.*
   The court, in seeking to ascertain the intent of the Legislature in adopting a statute, must look to the whole statute, and give to it such a construction as will effectuate the legislative purpose. *Ib.*

10. *Liens. Construction.*
    Lien statutes must be liberally construed, to carry out the legislative purpose, and to secure and protect those entitled to a lien. *Ib.*

11. *Construction. Meaning of words. "May."*
    The word "may" in a statute will not be construed to mean "shall," where such a construction will tend to defeat the object of the statute, though it will be so construed, where such a construction is necessary to effectuate the purpose of the act. *Ib.*

SUPERSEDEAS—SURETY AND SURETYSHIP.

SUPERSEDEAS.

Landlord and tenant. Nonpayment of rent. Forfeiture.

Where a tenant, against whom judgment for possession because of nonpayment of an installment rent, was rendered in unlawful detainer proceedings, begun in justice court, removed the proceedings to the circuit court, giving the *supersedeas* bond for the value of the rent of the premises during the litigation required by Shannon's Code, sec. 5111, it was unnecessary to institute successive actions to enforce the forfeiture for nonpayment of each installment of rent as it fell due, for the single *supersedeas* bond covered the whole contract. *Matthews* v. *Crofford*, 541.

See SUPREME COURT.

SUPREME COURT.

1. *Appeal and error. Review. Amount of damages.*

Under Acts 1911, ch. 29, providing that, when the trial judge suggests a remittitur because of prejudice, partiality, or unaccountable caprice, plaintiff may accept the remittitur under protest, and appeal, the supreme court will not ordinarily interfere with the decision of the trial court, approved by the court of civil appeals, as to the amount of damages. *Grant* v. *Railroad*, 398.

2. *Supersedeas. Jurisdiction.*

Under Acts 1907, ch. 82, sec. 8, providing for the review by the supreme court upon *certiorari* of the cases appealed to the court of civil appeals, the supreme court can take jurisdiction of such cases only through that writ, and then only after final decree or judgment in the court of civil appeals, and it has no jurisdiction to issue a writ of *supersedeas* suspending or discharging a *supersedeas* granted by the court of civil appeals. *Walker* v. *Lemma*, 444.

SURETY AND SURETYSHIP.

1. *Principal and surety. Discharge of surety. Taking additional security. Note of principal debtor.*

The sureties on a note, which expressly stipulated that they should not be discharged by an extension of time granted to the principal, are not released by the acceptance by the payee of an additional note from the principal debtor payable at a later date, not as a renewal of the former note, but as an additional evidence of the debt. *Dies* v. *Bank*, 89.

TAXES AND TAXATION.

SURETY AND SURETYSHIP—Continued.

2. *Bills and notes. Collateral securities. Notes representing the same debt.*

Two notes representing the same debt may be outstanding at the same time, the one as collateral to the other, and either the original or the renewal note may be held as collateral to the other. *Dies* v. *Bank*, 89.

3. *Bills and notes. Collateral security. Notes of same maker.*

While the maker of a note, which was signed by two others as sureties, cannot pledge the note as collateral for a note executed by himself alone and evidencing the same debt, since that note is a liability of his and not an asset which may be a subject of a pledge, that rule does not prevent the payee of the secured note from holding it as collateral for the second note. *Ib.*

4. *Bills and notes. Collateral security. Notes of the same maker. Different debts.*

The fact that the subsequent note included other indebtedness, or a new one in addition to that represented by the old note, does not affect the rule. *Ib.*

5. *Principal and surety. Discharge. Note held as collateral. Part payment of principal note.*

Where the payee of a note, signed by a principal and two sureties, accepted another note from the principal representing the same and additional indebtedness, under the express agreement that the old note was to be retained as collateral for the new, the proceeds of property mortgaged as security for the new note, which were applied to the payment of the debt represented thereby, released *pro tanto* the sureties on the old note. *Ib.*

TAXES AND TAXATION.

1. *Counties. Division of territory.*

A county suing to recover territory which had been detached from it and added to another county by unconstitutional statutes was entitled to recover taxes collected by such other county, after the original bill was filed in the suit, on lands affected by the unconstitutional statutes. *Putnam County* v. *Smith County*, 394.

2. *Exemptions. "Educational institution." Property used for educational purposes.*

Const. art. 2, sec. 28, provides that all property shall be taxed, but the Legislature may except such as may be held and used

TAXES AND TAXATION.

TAXES AND TAXATION—Continued.

for purely religious, charitable, scientific, literary, and educational purposes, etc. Acts 1907, ch. 602, sec. 2, subsec. 2, exempts all property belonging to any educational institution when used exclusively for educational purposes, or is unimproved or yields no income, but that all property belonging to such institution used in secular business shall be taxed on its whole or partial value in production as the same may be used in competition with secular business. *Held*, that the words "educational institution" should be construed to mean school, seminary, college, or educational establishment, not necessarily a chartered institution, so as to limit the exemption to educational corporations, and that under such act all property, whether owned by a corporation or a private individual, used exclusively for educational purposes, without reference to whether a profit was made therefrom or not, was exempt from taxation, but vacant real property, used for no purpose connected with the institution and property belonging to the institution, on which stores were erected and rented for business purposes, was subject to taxation. *Ward Seminary* v. *City Council*, 412.

3. *Railroads. Privilege taxes. "Railroad terminal corporation."*
A railway company which leases from other railway companies their terminal facilities, and which contracts to do their terminal business, and to provide adequate terminal facilities, and takes possession of trains entering receiving tracks, and switch and deliver cars therein to their respective destinations within the switching district, including the delivery of cars to connecting lines, and to render all switching services required for the prompt handling of cars for loading, unloading, or repairs, and to set apart exclusively for the business of the other companies terminal facilities, with the right of exclusive management and control of the terminal facilities, etc., contracts for the performance of duties falling within the functions of a railroad terminal corporation within Shannon's Code, secs. 2430, 2431, providing for the organization of railway terminal companies, and it is liable to privilege taxes imposed on railroad terminal corporations; a railroad terminal corporation being an instrumentality which assists railroad transportation companies in the transfer of traffic between different lines, and in the collection and distribution of traffic. *State* v. *Union Ry. Co.*, 705.

TELEPHONE AND TELEGRAPH.

1. *Nondelivery of message. Actions. Evidence. Sufficiency.*
   In an action for damages for nondelivery of a death message, evidence *held* insufficient to show that defendant's messengers made inquiries at the address given in the message. *Telegraph Co.* v. *Franklin*, 656.

2. *Delivery of messages. Inquiries.*
   Where a telegraph message contained no intimation that the addressee had an agent to receive it at the place to which it was sent, the telegraph company's messenger need not make inquiries as to whether there is such an agent, but the agent should reveal himself in case of inquiry at the place of address. *Ib.*

3. *Delivery of messages. Duty of telegraph company.*
   A telegraph company should, if possible by a reasonable effort, deliver messages personally to the addressee. *Ib.*

TITLES.

1. *Sales. Conditional sales. Collateral security.*
   Where a seller under a conditional sale contract subsequently takes security, personal or collateral, he does not thereby divest himself of his retained title or authority to retake the goods for the buyer's failure to pay the price. *Automobile Co.* v. *Bicknell*, 493.

2. *Sales. Conditional sales. Recovery of property. Right to sue.*
   Where reservation of title to property conditionally sold was contained in the contract, and not in the notes for the unpaid price, the seller, though having indorsed the notes, was still entitled to enforce the condition and recover the property in replevin; he being interested as indorser in securing satisfaction of the notes to the holder out of the proceeds of the sale. *Ib.*

3. *Logs and logging. Deed of standing timber. Defeasance. Time for removal.*
   A deed of standing timber, with provision that the grantee is to be allowed five years, but no longer, to cut and remove it, passes a title to the timber, subject to defeasance as to such of it as is not removed within the time specified; the grantee's title terminating as to timber not then removed. *Bond* v. *Ungerecht*, 631.

TRUSTS AND TRUSTEES.

TITLES—Continued.

4. *Specific performance. Contract to convey land. Separate tracts. Partial failure of title.*

Where a vendor contracted to convey separate tracts of land, and thereafter discovered that because of a failure of title as to a tract which formed an insignificant portion of the whole he was unable to perform as agreed, and the tract as to which the title failed was immaterial to the purchaser's enjoyment of the rest, the vendor was entitled to enforce specific performance of the part as to which he was able to perform, allowing a proportionate rebate in the price for the deficiency. *Investment Co. v. Vernon*, 637.

5. *Justices of the peace. Execution. Lien. Creation.*

The purpose of Acts 1899, ch. 39, providing that whenever any execution, issued by a justice of the peace, is levied on real estate, the title to the real estate shall not be affected as to third parties, unless the execution or the papers in the case are filed in the circuit court within ten days after the levy, is to give third parties notice of the lien of the execution, and is for the protection of third parties. *Supply Co. v. Fowlkes*, 663.

TRUSTS AND TRUSTEES.

1. *Corporations. By-laws. Requisites and effect.*

The by-laws of a corporation must be consistent with the spirit and terms of its charter, and while in force they become as much a part of the law of the corporation as though they had been made a part of the charter; and a by-law of a nonstock-holding corporation entering into a declaration of trust between the corporation and its beneficiaries, could not be repealed, so as to deprive the parties of their rights thereunder. *State, ex rel., v. Vanderbilt University*, 279.

2. *Wills. Construction. "Survivors."*

Testator bequeathed certain real property to a trustee, to collect the rents and apply the net income to testator's children, and at the death of either of the children the child or children of the one so dying should receive the portion of the rents and profits that their father or mother enjoyed under the will, and should any of testator's children so specified die without child or children, then his or her portion should be paid to the "survivors" in equal portions and the children of such as may have died leaving issue. *Held*, that such clause was divisible into two parts, the first providing for the vesting of

UNLAWFUL DETAINER.

TRUSTS AND TRUSTEES—Continued.

the fee in each portion of testator's estate held by his trustee
for either of testator's children in the event of the death of
his children leaving a surviving child or children, in which
event such surviving grandchild or grandchildren took *per
stirpes* that part of the estate to the use of which the deceased
parent had been entitled for life, and the second part providing for the vestiture of the fee in each portion of the estate
so held in the event either of testator's children died without
child or children surviving, in which event the fee vested *per
stirpes;* the word "survivors" being used to mean, not only
testator's children who survived, but also children of such
children as had theretofore died leaving children surviving
them. *Lee v. Villines,* 625.

3. *Wills. Construction.*

Under such clause, on the death of either of testator's children,
the trust ceased as to the share of such children, and the absolute fee vested in the remaindermen. *Ib.*

UNLAWFUL DETAINER.

1. *Landlord and tenant. Surrender. Effect.*

While a surrender of demised premises, duly accepted, relieves
the lessee, from any liability for rent subsequently accruing,
yet where a lessee, who defaulted in payment and against
whom the lessor had brought an action of unlawful detainer,
retained possession pending a removal of the case to the circuit court, by giving the bond required by Shannon's Code,
sec. 5111, a surrender pending the litigation did not relieve
the lessee and her surety from liability on the bond, consequently, while it was unnecessary for the court to render
judgment awarding the lessor possession, yet under section
4702, providing that judgment should be molded to suit facts,
the judgment should recite the facts, including the surrender, and declare the lessor entitled to possession and assess
damages on the bond. *Matthews v. Crofford,* 541.

2. *Landlord and tenant. Forfeiture. Nonpayment of rent. Re-
entry. What constitutes.*

In view of Shannon's Code, sec. 5090, declaring that no person
shall enter upon any lands and detain or hold the same, but
where entry is given by law, then only in a peaceable manner, the action of unlawful detainer is a substitute for an
entry by a landlord to forfeit a lease for nonpayment of rent;
the institution of the action having the same effect as an
entry. *Ib.*

VENDOR AND VENDEE—WARRANTIES.

VENDOR AND VENDEE.

Specific performance. Contract to convey land. Separate tracts. Partial failure of title.

Where a vendor contracted to convey separate tracts of land, and thereafter discovered that because of a failure of title as to a tract which formed an insignificant portion of the whole he was unable to perform as agreed, and the tract as to which the title failed was immaterial to the purchaser's enjoyment of the rest, the vendor was entitled to enforce specific performance of the part as to which he was able to perform, allowing a proportionate rebate in the price for the deficiency. *Investment Co.* v. *Vernon,* 637.

VERDICTS.

1. *Appeal and error. Conclusiveness.*

   A verdict sustained by any evidence cannot be disturbed by the court on appeal. *Compress Co.* v. *Insurance Co.,* 586.

2. *Indictment and information. Aider by verdict. Description of offense.*

   The uncertainty of an indictment charging the unlawful transportation of intoxicating liquors "from one point or county in this State to Tipton county" was made certain by proof that the initial point was in Shelby county, and was cured by the verdict of conviction. *State* v. *Green,* 619.

WARRANTIES.

1. *Insurance. Employers' indemnity insurance. Contracts. Construction.*

   A "continuation certificate" made by the president of a bank to a guaranty company in contemplation of the renewal of a fidelity bond, indemnifying it against losses due to the fraud or dishonesty of its cashier, certified that the books of the cashier "were examined from time to time in the regular course of business and found correct in every respect, all moneys or property in his control or custody being accounted for with proper securities and funds on hand to balance his accounts, and he is not now in default." *Held,* that the certificate was not a warranty of the correctness of such accounts, but merely that examinations were made as represented, and no errors or falsifications were discovered; the phrase "and he is not now in default," not being a substantive and distinct warranty, independent of the preceding

WILLS.

WARRANTIES—Continued.

language, but only expressing the result of the examinations. *Hunter* v. *Guaranty Co.*, 572.

2. *Insurance. Policy. Construction.*
Warranties by the insured are not favored by construction. *Ib.*

WILLS.

1. *Construction. "Survivors."*
Testator bequeathed certain real property to a trustee, to collect the rents and apply the net income to testator's children, and at the death of either of the children the child or children of the one so dying should receive the portion of the rents and profits that their father or mother enjoyed under the will, and should any of testator's children so specified die without child or children, then his or her portion should be paid to the "survivors" in equal portions and the children of such as may have died leaving issue. *Held*, that such clause was divisible into two parts; the first providing for the vesting of the fee in each portion of testator's estate held by his trustee for either of testator's children in the event of the death of his children leaving a surviving child or children, in which event such surviving grandchild or grandchildren took *per stirpes* that part of the estate to the use of which the deceased parent had been entitled for life, and the second part providing for the vestiture of the fee in each portion of the estate so held in the event either of testator's children died without child or children surviving, in which event the fee vested *per stirpes;* the word "survivors" being used to mean, not only testator's children who survived, but also children of such children as had theretofore died leaving children surviving them. *Lee* v. *Villines*, 625.

2. *Construction.*
Under such clause, on the death of either of testator's children, the trust ceased as to the share of such children, and the absolute fee vested in the remaindermen. *Ib.*